THE BRITISH ABROAD

THE

GRAND TOUR

IN THE EIGHTEENTH CENTURY

JEREMY BLACK

The History Press

Pippa's Book

This book was first published in 1992 by Sutton Publishing Limited

This paperback edition first published in 2003
Reprinted 2004

Reprinted in 2009 by
The History Press
The Mill, Brimscombe Port,
Stroud, Gloucestershire, GL5 2QG
www.thehistorypress.co.uk

Reprinted 2011, 2013

British Library Cataloguing in Publication Data
A catalogue record for this book is available from the British Library.

ISBN 978 0 7509 3169 4

Typeset in 10/11pt Joanna MT.
Typesetting and origination by Sutton Publishing Limited.
Printed and bound in Great Britain by CMP (uk) Limited.

CONTENTS

PREFACE

T he Grand Tour involved essentially a trip to Paris and a tour of the principal Italian cities, namely Rome, Venice, Florence and Naples. Around this basis a variety of possible itineraries could be devised. Personal preference, fashion, convenience and the impact of external factors – war, political disorder and disease – were all of importance. Because travel arrangements were essentially personal, there was little rigidity in itineraries, other than the constraints produced by the climate, especially winter snow and summer heat. As a consequence it is not helpful to treat the Grand Tour as a rigid itinerary, and thus to neglect those who sought pleasure and interest, enjoyment and education outside Paris and Italy. It is rather the case that while certain repeated itineraries can be discerned, the list of regions and cities frequently visited has to be expanded to include the Low Countries, Hanover, Berlin, Dresden, Prague, Vienna, Munich and Geneva. A 'cultural' emphasis necessarily directs more attention to tourists who visited Florence or Venice, rather than Hanover or Berlin, but this introduces an artificial distinction that has little relevance in terms of the experiences of many tourists and neglects an important aspect of the tourism of the period. Although lengthy trips to the Continent can be distinguished readily from, for example, quick journeys to Paris or visits to Spa for reasons of health, it is very difficult to distinguish the 'standard' Grand Tour from the travels of many young men, not all of whom stayed abroad for so long or visited the same countries, but all of whom encountered the problems and experienced the joys of foreign travel.

This work seeks to devote due attention to tourism outside the parameters set by travel to Paris and Italy. The sources employed are another distinctive feature. The lack of a comprehensive listing of sources for the Grand Tour outside Italy[1] is unfortunate as it encourages resort to a small number of familiar sources. This is related to a more general neglect of manuscript source material. There are three categories of extant tourist writing: manuscript accounts, accounts published by contemporaries, and those published subsequently. The first and third categories are different from the second, there being a clear division between material that was intended for publication and that designed for personal recollection, family or friends. A lack of clarity has arisen from the habit of conflating these types of material and treating them indiscriminately as sources for the Grand Tour. Instead, published travel literature should be sharply differentiated from letters and journals never intended for publication. Artifice could, of course, play a role in the latter. A youth writing home to his parents might have many reasons to disguise his activities and gloss over his responses. Journals were shown to others, letters handed around by friends and relations. However, even if the written record was somewhat contrived, there was a major difference between writing for an intimate circle, and producing a work for a large anonymous market, in which the sole identifiable readers would be publishers and booksellers concerned about commercial appeal. The conventions expected by the market and the reviewers had to be respected.

Most of the well-known accounts of seventeenth- and eighteenth-century tourism fall into the category of travel literature. They vary in their methods, tone, and areas covered, but they share a concern for impact and style. It is not surprising that scholars have concentrated on these writings, some of which were by major literary figures, such as Addison. The views expressed are more accessible, through being printed, and the texts themselves are easier and more attractive to read than subsequently printed accounts that were never intended for publication. In addition, much of the work on tourism has been done by amateurs lacking the time or resources to search for manuscript sources, and by scholars of literature whose forte has generally lain elsewhere. It is not surprising that both groups have concentrated on readily accessible published material by prominent figures, without appreciating that such accounts should not be seen as typical of the writings and views of tourists, but rather as works of literature. Thus, Tobias Smollett's *Travels through France and Italy* (1766) rested in part on plagiarism, while many of the letters it contained, supposedly sent from France and Italy, were in fact written after his return to England. A similar point has recently been made in an edition of an hitherto unpublished set of travel letters about Ireland that have been described as 'immensely more insightful than the large number of derivative and stereotyped travelogues that rapidly became the norm once Ireland became a popular place for travel writers to visit.'[2]

Nearly half the front page of the *St James's Chronicle* of 10 May 1766 was devoted to an extract from Smollett's new work, preceded by an anonymous note, presumably by the printer-conductor of the paper, Henry Baldwin:

. . . In this Paris-loving age, we will venture to say, they will not be without their merit also, in keeping others at home; as after the very contemptible, but just character given in them of the French, no one who is not through necessity driven there, will wish to spend his money among them. . . .

Smollett, of course, did not stop the period from being a Paris-loving age. He had been a prominent journalist. Journalism not only provided a somewhat precarious income, it was also the only way in which men of humble social background could play a major role in the political world. Journalism sprang from, provided, and sustained a comprehensive and partisan world-view in which everything was related, all suffused with politics, political commitment and moral viewpoints. Thus travel literature could provide political statements or, at least, an ideological slant on what was reported and the way in which it was discussed. Writers were not neutral figures. Their works commonly sought to make specific as well as general points for a readership that was political and did not recognize any barriers to partisan viewpoints and political images. There was no more reason why travel literature should be immune from these influences than history or ecclesiastical writings, both of which were heavily politicized.

Such literature became less hostile towards the Continent from the 1740s, as former ideological prejudices seemed less relevant as Britain became politically and culturally more secure.[3] In the 1760s a second wave of anti-foreigner literature appeared in, for example, the works of Sharp and Smollett. It was, however, no longer defensive in character. Travel literature can still be seen to be at a remove from the experiences of ordinary tourists, not least because, in some cases, it is probable that it was written to be read as much as a form of fiction, as interesting works at times similar to picaresque novels, rather than as objective descriptions of the travels of individual tourists. Travel literature was not uniform. Smollett's tone was different from Moore's stately character. One of the most interesting features of later eighteenth-century travel literature is the way it generally moves from the supposedly objective to the frankly subjective in, for example, the writings of William Beckford. Travel snobbery characterized some of the professional travel writers, especially in the following century.[4]

Concentrating on manuscript accounts is not without its problems. Much tourist correspondence is poorly catalogued and scattered in general political or family correspondence and, in consequence, difficult to find. A lot of the surviving material is anonymous, some is illegible or provides isolated items of information concerning tourists about whom little else is known. As with the printed material, so with the unprinted; much is repetitive. Yet there is much of value, not least because of its spontaneity. Letters written on the spot and at the time are a more accurate guide to experience than the polished prose of calm recollection, however quotable or literary the latter might be. By ignoring the vast bulk of unprinted material and concentrating on a relatively small number of familiar texts, a somewhat narrow conception of eighteenth-century tourism has developed.

Travel literature has been used to a certain extent in this work since, employed carefully and with sufficient attention to the differences between particular texts, it can provide valuable perspectives. Published sources have also been employed extensively. The range of archival sources employed in *The British and the Grand Tour* (1985) has been extended considerably. Research for that work was carried out between 1978 and 1984, the book was written in 1984 and published in 1985. Since the book went out of print in 1987, it has been suggested on several occasions that it be reprinted, but I have preferred to write a different work. This addresses some of the omissions in the first book, but also incorporates much of the new material I have uncovered since 1984. Much of this has been found in archives I had already worked in, such as the British Library and the Leeds Archive Office, but, in addition, I have benefited from research in archives that were new to me. In Britain these have included the House of Lords Record Office, the National Library of Scotland, the Guildhall Library, London, the Petworth House Archives, Mount Stuart and county record offices in Carmarthen, Chester, Exeter and Worcester; abroad the Bibliothèque Nationale in Paris, New York Public Library, the John Carter Brown Library in Providence, the Huntington Library in San Marino, California, the Lewis Walpole Library in Farmington, and, most valuably, the Beinecke Library in New Haven.

The chronological span of this work reflects the impact of two periods of sustained conflict. Britain was at war with France for most of the years 1689 to 1713 and 1793 to 1815 and these conflicts influenced British tourism greatly. The 'Glorious Revolution' of 1688–9 led both to the outbreak of war with France and to the creation of a new ideological context within which relations with the Continent were discussed. While concentrating on the period 1713–93, this work also considers the years 1689–1712.

As far as possible, I have included frequent and lengthy quotations from the writings of eighteenty-century tourists, as it is by reading them, rather than contemporary travel accounts and the secondary literature, that one approaches most closely to their preoccupations, interests and atittudes.

While I was writing this book, my father had two strokes. It was with him that I first visited many of the cities mentioned in this work – Amsterdam, Munich, Paris, Rome, Vienna. I owe him much for this, as for much else. The book is dedicated to my daughter, in the hope that she also will one day visit these places, if not with me then with someone else who loves her.

Jeremy Black
June 2003

NOTES

1. R.S. Pine-Coffin, *Bibliography of British and American Travel in Italy to 1860* (Florence, 1974), supplement in *Bibliofilia* 83 (1981).
2. P.G. Adams, *Travellers and Travel Liars 1660–1800* (Berkeley, 1962), p. 90; J. Kelly (ed.), *The Letters of Lord Chief Baron Willes to the Earl of Warwick, 1757–1762* (Aberystwyth, 1990), ix; Adams, *Travel Literature and the Evolution of the Novel* (Lexington, Kentucky, 1983) is a comprehensive study of travel literature.
3. Black, 'Tourism and Cultural Challenge: The changing scene of the eighteenth century', in J. McVeagh (ed.), *English Literature and the Wider World, I. All Before Them* (1990), pp. 185–95; H.J. Müllenbrock, 'The Political Implications of the Grand Tour: Aspects of a Specifically English Contribution to the European Travel Literature of the Age of Enlightenment', *Trema* 9 (1984); L.J. Colley, 'The English Rococo', in M. Snodin (ed.), *Rococo. Art and Design in Hogarth's England* (1984), p. 17; G. Newman, *The Rise of English Nationalism. A Cultural History 1740–1830* (1987), p. 171.
4 B. Porter, '"Bureau and Barrack": Early Victorian Attitudes towards the Continent', *Victorian Studies* 27 (1984), p. 412.

ABBREVIATIONS

Add.	Additional manuscripts.
AE	Paris, Quai d'Orsay, Archives des Affaires Etrangères.
Andrews 1784	J. Andrews, *Letters to a Young Gentleman on his setting out for France.*
Andrews 1785	J. Andrews, *A Comparative View of the French and English Nations in their manners, politics and literature.*
AO	Archive Office.
Bennet	Travel Diary of William Bennet, Bod. MS. Eng. Misc. f. 54.
BL	London, British Library.
Bod.	Oxford, Bodleian Library.
Chewton	Chewton Mendip, Chewton House, papers of James, 1st Earl Waldegrave.
CP Ang.	Correspondance Politique Angleterre.
CRO	County Record Office.
Creed	Journal of Richard Creed, in private possession.
CUL	Cambridge, University Library.
Eg.	Egerton manuscripts.
Gardenstone	Lord Gardenstone, *Travelling Memorandums made in a tour upon the Continent of Europe in the years 1786, 1787 and 1788* (3 vols, London, 1791).
Garrick 1751	*The Diary of David Garrick being a record of his memorable trip to Paris in 1751* (New York, 1928).
Gateshead	Gateshead Public Library.
HL	San Marino, California, Huntington Library.
HMC	Reports of the Historical Manuscripts Commission.
HP	R.R. Sedgwick (ed.), *The History of Parliament. The House of Commons 1715–54* (2 vols, London, 1970).
HW	Farmington, Connecticut, Lewis Walpole Library, Hanbury Williams papers.
jnl	Journal.

L	Lucas papers.
Lo	Loudoun papers.
MS Cardiff	Mount Stuart, papers from Cardiff.
Maclaurin	Aberdeen, University Library, Maclaurin papers.
Munich	Munich Bayerisches Hauptstaatsarchiv, Abteilung II, London.
NLS	Edinburgh, National Library of Scotland.
Orrery	John, Earl of Cork and Orrey, *Letters from Italy, in the years 1754 and 1755* (1773).
PRO	London, Public Record Office, State Papers.
RA	Windsor Castle, Royal Archives.
RO	Record Office.
Russell	London, Bedford Estate Office, Russell Letters.
SP	Stuart papers.
SRO	Edinburgh, Scottish Record Office.
Stowe	Stowe manuscripts.
Swinton	Oxford, Wadham College, A 11.5, Swinton journal.
Thicknesse 1768	P. Thicknesse, *Useful Hints to those who make the tour of France.*
Thicknesse *Pais Bas*	P. Thicknesse, *A Year's Journey through the Pais Bas and the Austrian Netherlands* (1784).
Thicknesse 1786	1786 edition is fuller.
UL	University Library.
Wharton	Durham, University Library, Wharton papers.
WW	Sheffield, City Archives, Wentworth Woodhouse manuscripts.

Notes on Dates and Currency

Dates

In the eighteenth century, until the 1752 reform of the calendar, Britain conformed to Old Style, which was eleven days behind New Style, the Gregorian calendar used in most of the rest of Europe. In this work all Old Style dates are marked (os). The New Year is taken as starting on 1 January, not 25 March.

Currency

Prices are given in eighteenth-century – i.e. pre-decimalization – British units of currency: £1.00 = 20 shillings (s) = 240 pennies (d). Therefore 1s = 5 new pence. A guinea was 21s. The usual French units of account were sols/sous, livres and louis d'or. By modern standards exchange rates, particularly after the reform of the French currency in the mid-1720s, were remarkably constant. The following were usually quoted:

1 sol, sou	½d
1 livre	10d
1 louis d'or	£1

In Italy the sequin (zecchini) was worth 10s (i.e. 2 = £1).

ACKNOWLEDGEMENTS

I am grateful to a large number of archivists, colleagues, friends and owners of manuscripts, without whom it would have been impossible to carry out research on this topic. In the space available it is impossible to name more than a small number of those who have helped. I would like to thank Her Majesty the Queen for permission to work in the Royal Archives. The Duke of Beaufort, the Duke of Bedford, the Duke of Richmond, the Marquis of Bute, the Marquis of Salisbury, the Earl of Crawford, the Earl of Elgin, the Earl of Malmesbury, Earl Waldegrave, Lady Lucas, Richard Head and the Trustees of Wentworth Woodhouse Estates permitted the consultation of their collections of manuscripts. I am indebted to a large number of archivists, to those who superintend the archives mentioned in the selective lists of sources, and to many more. I owe a particular debt to Peter Barber, Roger Norris, David Pearson and Beth Rainey. All or part of the work was read by David Aldridge, Edward Chaney, Francis Haskell, Maurice Hutt, Colin Kidd, J.G. Links, John Lough, Peter McKay, Frank Salmon, John Stoye, David Sturdy, Henry Summerson and Shearer West and they made many helpful comments. John Lough, who has helped me greatly throughout my work on tourism, also kindly assisted with the proofs. Colin Jones, Grayson Ditchfield, Norman Hampson, Spencer Mawby, Mark Vickers and David Williams gave valuable assistance. Parts of this work were first presented in papers at Leeds and St Andrews Universities, the Institute of Historical Research, Peterhouse History Society, the Hull branch of the Historical Association, the Cirencester Archaeological and Historical Society, the New Jersey Institute of Technology and the University of Columbia, Missouri. I am grateful for the comments I received.

A large number of friends aided the course of research, especially by providing invaluable hospitality. I would particularly like to mention Peter Bassett, Richard Berman, John Blair, Peter Cull, Jonathan Dent, Robert Gildea, Michelle Hampson, Dan and Stella Hollis, Peter Spear, Philip Winston, Paul Zealander and my sister Vivienne Aldis. This book owes much to archival research supported by the British Academy and the Staff Travel and Research Fund, Durham University. Particular thanks are due to those who helped on my research trips to America in 1988, 1990 and 1991: to the Beinecke Library, the most impressive synthesis of deep scholarship and the spirit of modernity I have encountered, and its superb staff, especially Steve Parks, Bob Babcock and Lori Missura; the staff of the Lewis Walpole Library, particularly Marie Devine and Anna Malicka; and the friendship of Paul Binski, Marilyn Morris and Katherine Reese. I owe much to the help and forbearance of Rosemary Aspinwall, Wendy Duery and Janet Forster.

In writing a book about travel, my thoughts naturally turn to those I have travelled with. Memories of times together hold strong across the years and I thank those who have given love and friendship.

INTRODUCTION

'Without their assistance, how should we be able to dress ourselves, or our victuals?', exclaimed Mrs Clack of the French in Samuel Foote's satirical play *A Trip to Calais* (1776). The fictional Mrs Clack was no oracle – she was amazed at how well the French spoke French – but her attitude captured one of the essential features of eighteenth-century tourism, its relationship to the greater tension between cosmopolitanism and xenophobia. This tension was personified in the characters in Foote's play, which made fun of Frenchified British travellers. The Francophile Luke Lappelle complained 'there's a roughness, a *bourgoisy* about our barbarians, that is not at all to my taste', while the more robust Gregory Gingham exlaimed 'victuals! soup, that tasted as if wrung from a dish-clout, and rags stewed in vinegar, are all the victuals I have seen', leading Lappelle to the rejoinder, 'Ah! poor Gingham has a true English stomach; nothing will do but substantials; he has no taste for *ragoutes, intermeats,* and *rottis.*'

More seriously, travel and discussion about travel were both a focus for and an aspect of the relationship between cosmopolitanism and xenophobia. As such, it was far from novel, but the debate over British tourism in the eighteenth century was in some respects new because, after the succession of the Hanoverians in 1714, it was freed to a considerable extent from the religious and political context of the previous two centuries. The Reformation had not only shattered the cohesion that had bound monarchs and social élites uneasily together across Europe; it had also divided dynasties and what might, at the risk of some anachronism, be termed states and nations from each other. The combination of domestic and international rivalries created a marked degree of paranoia in the political culture of Europe. Dissident minorities were made more dangerous by their links to foreign rulers and paranoia was justified by the conspiracies of the period. In an atmosphere of plot and assassination, insurrection and invasion, in a world fed by lurid black propaganda about the intentions and activities of members of the other confession, it was difficult to interpret cultural links in a non-political fashion.

The Catholic, autocratic and Francophile tendencies of the Stuart court were seen as evidence of political inclinations and designs. Cultural preferences were testaments of loyalty. This attitude did not dissuade many from travelling and, as ever, travel as an aspect of cultural preference did not totally accord with other indications about the views of individuals. Nevertheless, this context ensured that tourism in the seventeenth century[1] was different in kind from that of the mid-eighteenth, when Jacobitism had been crushed and Britain appeared less threatened, at home by Catholicism and autocracy, abroad by Spain or France, though the *Daily Advertiser* could still warn on 23 October 1747 that 'journeys of devotion and trips to the waters of Spa or Aix, have often served to cover political designs'. This change can be defined and dated in a number of different ways but it helped to ensure that the eighteenth century, the age of the so-called Grand Tour, was recognizably new as far as British tourism was concerned.

A further shift arose from what has been seen as the consumer revolution of the eighteenth century. The expansion of foreign tourism was but part not only of a general growth in tourism that was particularly marked in Britain, but also of a more widespread consumerism that was general throughout both the social élite and the middling orders. The facets of this consumer revolution were numerous. There was an increase in the consumption of necessaries, such as foodstuffs, but more obviously of non-essentials such as luxury furniture.[2] An information revolution was one aspect of this development, with a massive growth in the production of books, newspapers and other printed material. The output of existing forms expanded greatly, while new forms, such as magazines and daily newspapers, were founded.[3] The information revolution encouraged the development of different genres of literature, including travel accounts. Authors, such as Tobias Smollett, and publisher-booksellers produced such literature because they knew there was a market for it among those with the money to buy and the leisure to read. An important stimulant to the growth in foreign travel in the eighteenth century was the increased appearance of travel accounts. At times travel literature provided an opportunity for autobiography and literary amateurism, not least in the readable context of an heroic or mock-heroic journey. Yet, apparently objective accounts were consulted by actual travellers and cannot therefore be seen as completely distinct from tourism. Richard Lassel's *Voyage of Italy* (1670) was given as an authority sixty years later by a Catholic writer seeking to refute the notion that the Pope profited from prostitution in Rome. In 1730 Joseph Atwell cited Joseph Addison and Misson on Vesuvius. William Lee mentioned reading Addison on Venice, an anonymous tourist of 1754–5 read Thomas Nugent on Fréjus, Addison and Misson on Florence. Addison's Whiggish *Remarks on Several Parts of Italy* (1706) had gone through ten editions by 1773 and were referred to by many tourists, for example Andrew Mitchell in 1734. Thomas Brand and his charge read Addison at breakfast in Geneva in 1781. In her *Observations and Reflections made in the course of a Journey through France, Italy, and Germany* (1789), Mrs Thrale/Piozzi (1741–1821) cited Addison, Brydone, Burney, Chesterfield, Cork and Orrery, Hamilton, Howell and Moore. In 1791 Richard Dreyer mentioned Ireland's recently-published tour. Randle Wilbraham referred in 1793 to pursuing from Vienna 'Coxe's route by Cracow to Warsaw'. Some tourists also benefited from manuscript notes by their counterparts, Samuel Rogers having some by John Mitford. Nevertheless, the sheer volume of the published accounts and the extent to which they have been accepted as objective have helped to complicate, if not confuse, assessment of foreign tourism in this period. John, 3rd Earl of Bute, was unhappy with what he found in travel books, many of the subjects 'useless or improper', which he blamed on the fact that 'writing is become a trade'. He noted that writers drew heavily on other works.[4]

British domestic travel and tourism boomed in the eighteenth century. As roads were improved, not least by the turnpike trusts, journey times shortened dramatically and became more predictable. More frequent coach services appeared on major routes and facilities, such as coaching inns, increased. Maps and other information for domestic travel appeared in greater quantities, charting the widespread improvement. The great stress on health and sociability ensured the triumph of the spa. Numerous watering places were founded or expanded in the eighteenth century, mostly inland, though towards the end of the century coastal resorts developed under royal patronage, Weymouth benefiting from the visits of George III, as Brighton was to benefit from the residence of the Prince Regent.[5] Such resorts had become popular even without royal support. The *Salisbury Journal* of 22 July 1754 listed eighteen 'persons of distinction' who had arrived at Lymington 'to drink the sea water and take the diversion of the place', while the issue of 2 September 1754 named a further thirteen. In addition, the development of the leisure facilities of many towns made them attractive places to visit.

Domestic tourism, however, was neither unlimited nor without its problems. Scotland, Ireland and Wales received relatively few tourists, and played a smaller role in tourism than Bath, Buxton or Tunbridge Wells. The attitude of royalty was indicative of a wider lack of interest within the élite. In the eighteenth century no monarch visited Scotland, Ireland or Wales, or, for that matter, the north of England, or most of the Midlands. Those who did visit Scotland, Ireland or Wales were struck by the lack of facilities. This was not only true of such distant destinations. Lady Anson was not the only visitor to a major spa, in her case Buxton in 1751,[6] who was bored and dissatisfied.

It would, however, be misleading to suggest that those who could afford it preferred to tour abroad, leaving their less fortunate compatriots to make do with a trip to the local spa. The lists of those who visited Bath or Tunbridge Wells, the fashionableness of the seasons there, would scarcely suggest such a conclusion. In the season, Bath was almost a counterpoint of the royal court, a court which itself lacked the glamour and social centrality of most of its continental counterparts. There were clearly aspects of social differentiation in British tourism. The visitor to Bath might have time and money; his counterpart in Venice assuredly did. And yet, the situation was more complex. Having gone abroad once, most, although by no means all, British tourists did not cross the Channel again. Thus, the tourist proceeded as it were from Venice to Bath, from the surprises of foreign travel to the relative predictabilities of domestic tourism. The latter was not confined to the spas: visiting literary shrines, country houses, picturesque ruins and the natural landscape all became fashionable.[7]

Tourism on the Continent was more adventurous. In the summer of 1784 Charles Sloane toured in the Alps:

> partly over the tops of some of the great snowy Alps themselves, and partly among vallies which afforded the most wonderful scenes by much I ever saw in my life. The mountains of Wales, [Scottish] Highlands etc. are a joke to them. I was obliged to lead my horse great part of the way for fear of falling over the high precipices. This climbing was fatiguing, but amply recompensed by what I saw.[8]

Tourism was also more varied than is sometimes suggested by the phrase the 'Grand Tour', with its implications of set purposes achieved by a distinct itinerary. Aside from the fact that Britain and France were at war, whether declared or not, in 1689–97, 1702–13, 1743–8, 1756–63, 1778–83 and from 1793, which, at the very least, complicated any itinerary of France and Italy, British tourists were individuals seeking different objectives and following different routes. The young man keen on a future military career who attended Prussian manoeuvres in Silesia or his counterpart who studied the glaciers of the Alps is as worthy of attention as his counterpart admiring the contents of the Uffizi. Any consideration of the routes tourists followed indicates that a stress on variety is justified.

NOTES

1. First-rate works include J. Stoye, *English Travellers Abroad 1604–1667* (1952; revised edn New Haven, 1989); E. Chaney, *The Grand Tour and the Great Rebellion. Richard Lassels and 'The Voyage of Italy' in the seventeenth century* (Geneva, 1985). Also note Stoye, 'The Grand Tour in the Seventeenth Century', *Journal of Anglo-Italian Studies* I (1991).

2. N. McKendrick, J. Brewer and J.H. Plumb, *The Birth of a Consumer Society* (1982).
3. J. Black, *The English Press in the Eighteenth Century* (1987).
4. Beinecke, Osborn Shelves c 366 1 p. 95; Atwell to Lady Sarah Cowper, 13 May 1730, Hertford CRO D/EP F234; Beinecke, Lee papers Box 3, 26 April 1753, Osborn Shelves c 200 pp. 68, 99, f.c 11 p. 43, Osborn Files 33, 159; BL Add. 58319 f. 7; Brand to sister Susan, 16 Jan. CUL Add. Mss. 8670/10; Chester CRO DBW/N/Bundle 4 no. 4; Bute, CUL Add. Mss. 8826.
5. R. Gard (ed.), *The Observant Traveller: Diaries of Travel in England, Wales and Scotland in the Country Record Offices of England and Wales* (1989); R.P. Evans, 'Thomas Pennant (1726–1798): the father of Cambrian tourists', *Welsh History Review*, 13 (1987), pp. 395–417. P. Hembry, *The English Spa 1560–1815. A Social History* (1990).
6. Stafford CRO D 615/P (s) 1/1/40 A–B.
7. E. Moir, *The Discovery of Britain: The English Tourists 1540 to 1840* (London, 1964); J.M. Stochholm, *Garrick's Folly: The Shakespeare Jubilee of 1769* (1964); M. Andrews, *The Search for the Picturesque: Landscape Aesthetics and Tourism in Britain, 1760–1800* (Aldershot, 1989); I. Ousby, *The Englishman's England. Taste, travel and the rise of tourism* (Cambridge, 1990); P. Borsay, 'Gentry Papers: A Key Source for Urban Cultural History', *Archives* 19 (1991), pp. 377–9.
8. London, House of Lords Record Office, CAD/4/3.

1

NUMBERS

The eighteenth century witnessed a substantial increase in the number of British men and women travelling abroad for pleasure. In addition, the widespread conviction that large numbers were travelling helped to widen the perception of the social and cultural importance of the Grand Tour. Britain was not alone in this development: an increase in tourism was general across much of Europe, and larger numbers than hitherto of French and Germans, Poles and Russians travelled for pleasure. The French envoy in London reported the arrival of 'beaucoup de français' in July 1772, 'leurs voyages n'ayant eu pour objet que leur curiosité'. It was generally agreed, however, by this date, that the Grand Tour was dominated by British tourists, and the fact of tourism by other nationalities rarely played a part in the debate within Britian over the merits of tourism. It is impossible to provide accurate figures for the number of tourists as passes were not compulsory and there were no reliable figures for Channel crossings. Neither the British nor the French government kept accurate records of travellers between their countries. Of 350 travellers to France between 1660 and 1715 mentioned in letters, diaries and journals, only eleven acquired passes. Passes are, therefore, a poor guide to tourism, not least because a single pass could be issued for a group.

The rise in numbers was commented on by British diplomats, called upon to provide hospitality, introductions and other assistance, and by the tourists themselves. In 1725 the envoy in Florence, Francis Colman, complained 'I have hardly had one hour to myself this week by reason of the concourse of English gentlemen that are here at present, of whom there have been above twenty'. That summer Francis Head wrote from the fashionable Ardennes watering-place of Spa, 'Three quarters of the strangers here at present consist of the English and I believe there may be near an hundred of our nation who are most of 'em here for their health.'[1]

The largest numbers were attracted by Paris and Italy. When in 1728 Horatio Walpole, the envoy in Paris and, no less crucially, brother of the first minister, Sir Robert Walpole, gave a splendid feast to celebrate the king's birthday, the company included 'fifty Lords and Gentlemen of the British nation'. Four years later his successor, James 1st Earl Waldegrave, noted, 'the town swarms with English. I had near upon a dozen newcomers dined with me yesterday, and shall have near as many more today.'[2]

Many of these tourists would have pressed on to Italy. Joseph Atwell, bearleader of 2nd Earl Cowper, and later Rector of Exeter College Oxford, found 'no less than thirteen' in Florence in June 1730 and wrote 'the swarms of them have been so great in Italy this year, that we have met with them in almost every place.' William, 3rd Earl of Essex (1697–1743), wrote of Bologna in 1733, 'the finest opera that ever was heard, and vast deal of company, there was 32 English.' The following year Richard Pococke (1704–65) noted forty English in Rome, while in 1737 Arthur Villettes, the Secretary at Turin, commented on 'a great number of English in this town' and listed twelve travellers. In December 1739 Frederick Frankland MP (c. 1694–1768), who, having separated from his recently married second wife, was making a rapid tour to Italy, wrote from Florence, 'From the cold weather and number of English in this place I have sometimes almost fancied myself in England. It is reckoned we shall be about eighty at Rome.'

These figures put what was seen as a great expansion in the number of tourists into context. Diplomats emphasized their numbers because they had to spend time and money on them, but the numbers who travelled in the first half of the century, although large by seventeenth-century standards, barely hinted at the numbers who were to travel in the second half. In addition, many tourist centres often had few if any British visitors. In August 1740 Lord Deskford found only two other British visitors in Venice, Lady Mary Wortley Montagu and the Hon. James Stuart Mackenzie.[3]

The European conflicts of 1739–48 led to war between Britain and both Spain (1739–48) and France (fighting 1743–8) and to hostilities across much of the Continent. They did not stop British tourism, but the number of tourists was limited. After the war there was a marked revival, 'cargoes of English almost every day entering into Paris'. In one morning in Paris in 1751 the celebrated actor David Garrick 'made twenty visits of English gentlemen'. Frederick, Lord North (1732–92), later First Lord of the Treasury, observed 'There are about 40 travellers of our nation now in Rome reckoning females.' On the other hand, Robert Keith, the envoy in Vienna, who wrote in August 1750 'there is at present a good number of our countrymen here', named only five. George II's visit to Hanover that year attracted 'a great many English', apparently seven and 'some others', according to Edward Digby (1730–57) who also went there, but the following September there were only eight at Leipzig.[4]

The early 1750s witnessed a return to the level of tourism in the 1730s. William, 2nd Earl of Albermarle, noted in January 1751 that he had seen 'about 300 [British] people of fashion' since he arrived at

Paris as ambassador on 25 July 1749. This level was not to be passed decisively until the Peace of Paris of 1763 ended the Seven Years' War. The press then signalled the departure overseas of many tourists. On 25 January 1763, for example, the London Chronicle reported that Francis, 3rd Duke of Bridgewater (1736–1803) Francis, Marquis of Tavistock (1739–67) and John, 2nd Earl of Upper Ossory (1745–1818), had set off for France the previous day. Ossory had recently left Cambridge. That May, Thomas Robinson wrote from Paris, 'The English flock over daily, and the citizens seem to want to come a pleasuring here instead of an airing to Brighthelmstone' (later Brighton), a comment on the extent to which foreign tourism was now possible for and attractive to those not in the social élite. The St James's Chronicle of 23 August 1763 claimed that 7,400 French passports had been signed already that year and that this would lead to the loss of 'an immense sum'. Thereafter the level remained high, albeit falling when Anglo-French hostilities commenced over the American rebellion in 1778 and spread to encompass Spain (1779) and the United Provinces (1780). Figures in the letters from Horace Mann, envoy in Florence, to his friend Horace Walpole, youngest son of Sir Robert Walpole, are instructive. On 21 July 1744 he noted twelve tourists, on 20 August 1751 about thirty-five, 'a larger flight of woodcocks this year than has been seen for many past', on 28 January 1752 'the crowds of unmeaning young men who pass by', on 11 August 1752 thirty-four or thirty-five, on 18 October 1768, possibly a bit late in the season, at least thirty-seven, and on 19 December 1772 Mann wrote that the English colony 'which a few weeks ago was near sixty is now reduced to about a dozen'.

There was a marked upsurge after the Treaty of Versailles (1783) ended the war, and this continued to be the case until the French successes in the early stages of the French Revolutionary War (which began in 1792), made Italy, the Low Countries and the Rhineland as apparently unsafe as the French Revolution had already made France. In March 1784 the 3rd Duke of Dorset, ambassador in Paris, noted 'English crowd in upon us here every day'. John Brooke suggested that the height of the Grand Tour's popularity was in the 1730s and 1740s, that twenty years later it was by no means as fashionable and that the majority of the MPs who made the tour were the eldest sons of peers or landed families, rather than younger sons or those without considerable wealth. His assessment, however, can be queried. All indications suggest that tourism became more commonplace, and, if many tourists did not take the full Grand Tour, it is possible to suggest that a rigid definition of its itinerary is misguided.

Large numbers continued to visit France and Italy and tourists were very conscious of the presence of their compatriots. In 1775 Robert Wharton (1751–1808) found 'upwards of thirty' English at Dijon and

Geneva 'brimfull of English who live truly a l'Angloise have Horse Races and all their Appendages'. In 1784 Joseph Cradock (1742–1826) found Paris so full of British tourists that he had little opportunity to practise his French. William Bennet (1746–1820), Fellow of Emmanuel College Cambridge and later Bishop of Cloyne, who had already accompanied the Earl of Westmorland to France in 1777, near the end of his second tour took the road from Abbeville to Montreuil in October 1785, writing, 'I have met crowds of English carriages on it. Nothing surprises foreigners so much as the numbers of our countrymen that travel. The Swiss in particular often asked me how it happened, and said our country must be very unhealthy that everyone was so eager to get out of it.'[5]

Numbers varied greatly by season and year. This was especially true of Italy, where seasonal variations in the weather were of great importance for the convenience and safety of tourists. In addition, the blocking of Alpine passes by winter snows affected the rhythms of travel within Italy. Rome and Naples were considered undesirable during the summer because of heat and the risk of malaria, while in the depths of winter some tourists preferred the more clement temperatures of Naples to colder Rome. On 8 May 1792, at a time when the Grand Tour was at its climax but already being affected by the spreading international crisis, Lady Philippa Knight wrote from Rome, 'we have had a hundred and fifty English here this spring, but few of them are left.' In February 1794 Thomas Brand estimated the number of English tourists in Naples as about 130, 'a most numerous band'.[6]

Several regions saw a distinct expansion in the number of British tourists in the late eighteenth century. The Riviera became somewhat popular in the 1780s as a winter resort, though numbers varied. Nice, then a possession of the King of Sardinia, ruler of Savoy-Piedmont, was the town visited most frequently. Numerous British tourists were there in the winter of 1784–5, but in December 1789 Nathanial Green, the Consul, observed, 'There are but few English, about twenty individuals.' This may have been a consequence of the troubles in France. There was a marked increase in the numbers visiting Switzerland. Geneva had always been popular for educational reasons and because it was close to the Mt Cenis route into Italy, but in the latter half of the century tourism in Switzerland developed. In 1770 one British traveller noted 'there were a good many English at Geneva'; in 1785 another wrote from Lausanne, 'I suppose the English colony consists of about 80.' Long-term British residents have to be taken into account in such figures, for another feature of the growing British impact on the Continent was the number of individuals who chose to settle abroad, not for financial, political or religious reasons, but simply because they preferred to do so.[7]

As tourism became less the prerogative of the wealthy, increasing numbers of not so affluent tourists travelled. This was part of a more general expansion of leisure activities by the British, most obviously in Britain, which led to the growth of the numbers visiting spas and other sites. Less affluent British tourists preferred a shorter and less expensive alternative to the classic option of Paris and Italy. Italy presented problems because any tour there would entail a considerable amount of time and thus cost; and there were additional costs to travelling in Italy itself, such as those arising from the relative absence of public transport. A quicker and less expensive option was provided by a tour to Paris and the Low Countries, both of which witnessed a considerable expansion in British tourism after 1763. The journals of British tourists in both areas frequently noted the presence of compatriots.

Another area that saw a marked expansion in British tourism was east-central Europe, centring on the courts of Berlin, Dresden and Vienna, and the routes to and between them. In 1769 Robert Murray Keith, envoy to the Saxon court at Dresden, complained, 'I have within this month, had an inundation of English, who have nearly eaten me out of house and home. The nine and twentieth left me a week ago.' Five years later, transferred to Vienna, he grumbled, 'here come half a score of Etonians', and seeing a chess-playing automaton at Pressburg (Bratislava), Keith noted the presence of another sixteen British travellers. In November 1782 he had '15 or 16 countrymen', the following January 'a dozen John Bulls to dine with me', and in February 1783 Keith wrote of his 'English colony of sixteen or seventeen'. In 1785 he wrote, 'I am to have a prodigious colony of John Bulls this winter: Lords Wycombe, Ancram, Guildford, Glasgow, Dungannon, etc. etc., and commoners by the scores.' Keith added that in twelve years he had presented four hundred 'young gentlemen at the Imperial Court', the same figure that he gave Lady Elizabeth Craven (1750–1828), who reported in December 1785, 'there are so many Englishmen here, that, when I am at Sir Robert Keith's, I am half tempted to fancy myself in England.' Brand found 'but two or three English' in Vienna in June 1792,[8] but by then Austria was at war with France and tourism was being disrupted by war and revolution. The earlier increase in the number of tourists visiting Vienna may have been in part a function of the presence of the Keiths themselves, with letters of introduction, like chain letters, increasing exponentially. Keith reported to the Foreign Secretary, the Marquis of Carmarthen, in January 1788 that in the twelve years he had been in Vienna (in fact he had arrived in November 1772), he had given hospitality to over five hundred British visitors.[9] The numbers visiting Berlin also rose, the British envoy writing, albeit in May 1791 at a time of heightened interest because of a royal visitor, 'I am teased, amidst all my occupations, with the Duke of York and above thirty English.'[10]

Numbers therefore varied greatly, and though British tourists could be sure of the company of compatriots in Paris and the major Italian cities, this was not the case elsewhere. By modern or even nineteenth-century standards there were very few tourists, but contemporaries had no doubt that they were witnessing a significant change. Brand wrote from Lausanne in 1783, 'I mean to be at Rome Decr. the 1st. There is such a shoal of English upon the road thither that "the like was never known"!'[11]

NOTES

1. AE CP Ang. 500 f. 69; D.J. Sturdy, 'English Travellers in France, 1660–1715' (unpublished PhD, Dublin, 1969) pp. 78–9; Colman to Charles Delafaye, Under-Secretary in the Southern Department, 29 June 1725, PRO 98/25; Head to William Wake, Archbishop of Canterbury, 5 Aug. 1725, Christ Church Oxford, Wake Mss.
2. [A. Boyer], *The Political State of Great Britain* (1728) p. 457; PRO 78/201 f. 188.
3. Atwell to Lady Sarah Cowper, 23 June 1730, Hertford CRO D/EP F234; Essex to Bowen, 30 June 1733, Pococke to his mother, 4 Feb. 1734, BL Add. 60387, 22978; Villettes to John Couraud, Under-Secretary in Northern Department, 4 Sept. 1737, PRO 92/41; Leeds Archive Office, Newby Hall Mss. 2825 no. 77; Deskford to Ludovick Grant, 10 Aug. 1740, SRO GD 248/48/1/4.
4. William Wood to Charles Hotham, 30 July 1750, Hull UL DDHo/4/4; *The Diary of David Garrick being a record of his memorable trip to Paris in 1751* (New York, 1928) p. 26; North to John Hallam, 21 Feb. 1753, BL Add. 61980; HW 51 f. 102, 134, 54 f. 13.
5. Albemarle to Newcastle, 13 Jan. 1751, BL Add. 32724 f. 18; Robinson to Lord Grantham, 15 May 1763, Leeds AO Vyner Mss. 6032 no. 12296; Dorset, BL Eg. 3499 f. 15; L. Namier and J. Brooke (eds), *The History of Parliament. The House of Commons 1754–90* (3 vols, 1964) I, 113; Wharton to his mother, 18 July, Wharton to Dr Baker, 26 Aug. 1775, Durham, Wharton; Cradock, *Literary and Miscellaneous Memoirs* (1826) II, 162; Bod. Ms. Eng. Misc. f. 54 f. 196; L. Stainton, *Hayward's List – British visitors to Rome 1753–1775*, Walpole Society 49 (1983).
6. E.F. Elliott-Drake (ed.), *Lady Knight's Letters from France and Italy 1776–1795* (1905); Brand to Wharton, 1 Feb. 1794, Wharton.
7. Green to Sir Robert Murray Keith, envoy in Vienna, 14 Dec. 1789, BL Add. 35541.
8. Farmington, Hanbury Williams vol. 51 f. 102; Mrs G. Smith (ed.), *Correspondence of Sir Robert Murray Keith* (2 vols, 1849), I, 123, 469, II, 180; HL HM 18940 pp. 229, 233, 238; Craven, *Memoirs of the Margravine of Anspach* (2 vols, 1826) I, 135, 151; Brand to Wharton, 30 June 1792, Durham, Wharton.
9. PRO Foreign Office, 7/15 f. 37.
10. Ewart to James Bland Burges, Bod. Bland Burges papers vol. 34 f. 149.
11. Brand to Wharton, 25 Sept. 1783, Durham, Wharton.

2

ROUTES AND DESTINATIONS

CROSSING THE CHANNEL

The first stage in any tour was the journey to the British coast. Short or lengthy, a quick trip from London across the Kent countryside or a lengthy journey through the shires, it was at least familiar, posing no problems in terms of language, currency or regulations. Most tourists went to Dover in order to cross to Calais, the shortest route to the Continent and that used by the packet boat which carried the royal mail and could take paying passengers. In addition, private arrangements were made with captains of boats. The terrors of a Channel crossing in poorly stabilized ships encouraged British tourists, most of whom had never been to sea before, to plump for the shortest crossing. The St James's Chronicle of 20 May 1769 commented on the increased popularity of the Dieppe route, but observed 'however much this may suit the trading people, Calais will always be the port for our gentry, who had rather go thirty leagues more post by land than cross twenty leagues of water instead of seven'.

Although the Calais route remained the favourite, there were other sailings to France. It was common to sail from Dover to Boulogne. Henry Temple, 2nd Viscount Palmerston MP (1739–1802), did so in late December 1762; 'We were detained a little at Dover by a contrary wind which hindered our vessel from getting out of the harbour, and were forced at last to take up with a vessel less commodious than what we had first pitched on as being easier got out.' He then had 'a very good passage' to Boulogne. After 1763 an increasing number of tourists chose crossings further west. Sailing from Brighton or Southampton to Le Havre, Dieppe or Cherbourg became more common. The journey from Dieppe to Paris was much shorter than from Calais or Boulogne, 104 miles against 170 from Calais. In August 1768 the young John Harford (1754–1815), then on holiday at Weymouth with his parents and brothers, went with his father, brothers and six others to Cherbourg. They hired a boat with an intention to land at Guernsey, and from thence to go to Normandy; but the wind being contrary, could not reach the first place, and were obliged to steer directly for Cherbourg. We had a very rough sea and several squalls, with contrary winds; but after a passage of twenty eight hours we arrived there, which I thought the longest I had ever known, being very sea-sick, and did not eat, nor drink anything, except two apples, in all that time, till a little before we arrived, I grew better and ate a piece of bread and cheese . . . when I came on shore, I could hardly stand, everything seemed to turn round owing to the motion of the ship.

The passengers had to transfer to a rowing-boat to land. On the return this proved very difficult, 'the wind was so high and the tide so rough that we could scarce get on board . . . I was sick almost as soon as I got into the ship which rolled prodigiously from one side to the other which was much worse than when we sailed . . . I was not so sick in our voyage back as going for I could eat and drink.' The passage back took thirty-five hours. Nineteen years later, the lawyer, John Mitford (1748–1830), later 1st Lord Redesdale and Lord Chancellor of Ireland, took a Brighton–Dieppe crossing en route to Paris via Rouen, while in 1788 Sir Charles Blagden (1748–1820), Secretary of the Royal Society, travelled to Paris via Cherbourg, sailing from Brighton.[1]

At times of Anglo-French tension, tourists would take crossings further east. The most common were Dover to Ostend, in the Austrian Netherlands, and Harwich to Helvoetsluys, a packet-boat route. The Dutch port was the destination for those who intended to tour the United Provinces and possibly to go on to Germany (the Holy Roman Empire) and Italy. A traveller on that route in August 1695, when England and France were at war, sailed under the convoy of two Dutch warships, and had an unpleasant trip: 'fell to rain and blew hard, which made every passenger very sick'. The boat struck a Dutch ship on the way over, though fortunately it received no real damage. In order to land, the passengers were obliged to transfer to a smaller vessel, a fishing boat, always a trying, and sometimes hazardous, task. The passage was clearly a very difficult one, as he noted, 'my son Richard still continued very ill to that degree as made me almost repent of bringing him over'.

In May 1699 this anonymous traveller set out to repeat the journey. Thanks to contrary winds, the packet was delayed at Harwich for a fortnight:

our diversions were bowling, cards and walking about the town . . . On Wednesday the 24th we sailed for Holland, though the wind was still high and contrary as could be, having 4 mails with us and much company on board and on Thursday the 25th at 2 in the afternoon we landed at the Brill in Holland, being all in good health. During our stay at Harwich we put 4 times to sea in the packet boat but the wind being easterly and high we returned 3 times back to Harwich and carried out the first time 12 hours the 2nd time 36 hours and the 3rd time about 24 hours, for the most part of these hours we lay at anchor at Owsley Bay and Orfordness and the sea being high made me very sick. Mr. Fisher and Mr. Blunt were not at all indisposed.[2]

Making the same crossing in July 1791, Richard Dreyer was affected not by contrary winds but by calms.[3] Very few tourists sailed directly to the Baltic or Mediterranean, although the usual way to get to Portugal was to sail to Lisbon. In the absence of passenger ships to the Baltic and the Mediterranean, it was necessary to rely on a warship, a merchantman or a privately hired ship, such as the yacht in which Charles, 5th Lord Baltimore, cruised round the Baltic in 1739.

The three principal difficulties connected with a crossing were adverse winds or a calm, seasickness and problems of disembarkation. Total dependence on the wind led to irritating delays. In February 1767 James, 2nd Earl of Fife (1729–1809) complained from Calais, 'Here have I been three days, tired to death, detained with contrary winds now going aboard at eleven o'clock at night, but likely to be drove back again.'[4]

Too much wind could be as troublesome as too little. In March 1730 Charles Thompson was driven down the Channel by a strong easterly wind so that he landed at Dieppe instead of Calais. Five years later the Duchess of Norfolk was nearly drowned in a storm when crossing from Calais to Dover. Lady Craven made the same passage in a gale with her terrified mother Elizabeth, Countess of Berkeley, and a sister who fainted. In November 1789 Brand crossed from Harwich to Helvoetsluys:

The wind was boisterous and changeable and the sea very high. We were obliged to lay to during 10 hours of the night under storm-sails for fear of approaching too near the coast of Holland. My poor young man [Lord Bruce] all this while bringing to his recollection in much too lively colours every picture of shipwrecks and marine distress that he had ever seen . . . though I was neither frightened nor sick I was bitter sorry. We were 30 hours at sea.[5]

Seasickness was a major drawback to a Channel crossing, not least to the comparatively short ones. The boats responded to the movements of the waves by pitching and rolling in a manner with which the tourists were unfamiliar. Laconic entries in journals testified to the misery of many crossings. Having had to wait two days for the packet at Calais in 1699, during which he was not allowed to visit the citadel, one tourist was 'very sick' in his six-hour crossing to Dover.[6] Fine crossings were no safeguard, as the Duchess of Queensberry discovered in 1734. Despite 'a most excellent passage' to Calais in February 1775, Wharton was 'sea sick most part of the way. It is the most disagreeable sickness imaginable.' A young Londoner recorded in March 1789 'About 11 o'clock in the morning we sailed from Dover and were the whole time very sick. Arrived at Calais at 3 o'clock in the afternoon.'[7]

Not all were sick. 'Poor Mrs. [Elizabeth] Carter' was a 'good deal' sick on the Dover–Calais crossing in 1763, though her companions, Mrs Elizabeth Montagu (1720–1800) 'was not in the least sick . . . Mr [Edward] Montagu and Dr. Douglas eat cold ham all the way. My Lord Bath was in gay spirits.'[8]

Sickness was not the only problem. Many found their crossing an arduous experience. In late 1719 one traveller, returning from the Low Countries, was apparently 'three weeks in a most terrible tempest', in which he was driven to the Norwegian coast. Fife spent 'two terrible days at sea' in the Channel in 1766. Spark Molesworth had to rest at Calais in 1739 after 'the great fatigue of the sea'. Terror gripped the Duchess of Bedford in 1732, when Wriothesley, the 3rd Duke (1708–32), planned a trip to Lisbon and Naples. She complained to her grandmother Sarah, Dowager Duchess of Marlborough, 'I have the greatest dread imaginable of it; going by sea I know would kill me, the least retching in the world gives me a pain in my side, and breast, and to be so sick as almost everybody is at sea, I should never go through.'[9]

Having crossed the Channel, it was often difficult to land. Contrary winds, calms or low tides, ensured that the packet or other ship often could not get into Calais, and then it was necessary for the passengers to transfer to an exposed rowing boat, bobbing alongside. This was hazardous. William Cole, while changing boats in a rough sea in the dark off Dover, was injured in 1765. The frightened tourist was also subject to extortion. Sacheverell Stevens's boat was prevented by the tide from anchoring in Boulogne harbour in 1738 and he found the demands of the French sailors excessive. Having paid heavily for the rowing boat, the often drenched tourist was frequently landed some distance from his inn. Lady Mary Coke was drenched in 1764 and could be landed no nearer than four miles from Calais.[10] Then the irritation of passing customs, a new experience for most tourists, had to be faced. Harford recorded of Cherbourg in 1768 'immediately on our landing, some officers came to us, and as we passed the guard they just put their hands to Mr. Elton's pockets.' The return journey could lead to problems with the English customs. After passing customs tourists had to arrange accommodation. Fortunately, there were a number of good inns in Calais, most prominently, Dessien's.[11] John Judd, the son of a London merchant, who visited Paris and the Low Countries in 1770, not his first trip to the Continent, had a poor crossing, but a more satisfactory reception at Calais. He had embarked on the packet at Dover at 11 p.m., and reached Calais next morning:

> . . . at six in the morning many passengers went ashore with the mail, but I was detained by seasickness on board till about one o'clock in the afternoon, when the tide served for the packet to run into the harbour. After the usual ceremony of giving my name to the Governor I proceeded to Monsr. Grandsires at the Silver Lyon where I ordered dinner at four o'clock till which time we had our hands full of business, the first thing to be done was to get our passe-avant then to the custom house to see our baggage searched, corded and plumbed. At the time we had transacted this business dinner was on the table and after a regale with an excellent fricassee de poulet and drinking a cheerful glass of champagne . . .

Judd went to obtain a carriage.[12] In his Calais hotel the tourist could recuperate for the next stage of his journey and begin to notice differences between Britain and France. One commented in 1775, 'the difference of dress, dialect, manners and persons struck us exceedingly'. Though Edmund Dewes, the servant of a tourist, wrote in 1776, 'the oddity of the people don't appear so strange now, as it did the first time', he was still, on this second journey, struck by the clothes of the French and felt that the people were 'not a bit cleaner'.[13]

In September 1785 Edward Nares (1762–1841), later Regius Professor of Modern History at Oxford, arrived at Calais with his brother:

> nothing could exceed my astonishment to be awakened out of my first sleep, by three armed men at my bedside, enquiring in the French tongue, who I was, whence I came, whither I was going, and what my business might be in France. They were officers of the Police . . . The short sleep I had taken had been just sufficient to obliterate all traces of my journey, and all recollection of my sudden change of abode; so that I thought I was still at my fathers, and the appearances around me, seemed totally inexplicable – what account I gave of myself I know not, but their behaviour was civil, though their figures were so alarming, and I was soon rid of their company. This was not the first surprize I had been in – The moment we disembarked on the pier head at Calais, we seemed to be in a New World – nothing could be greater than the contrast between the English and the French shores. And we looked back with amazement at Dover Castle, scarcely capable

of persuading ourselves that England could really be at so small a distance . . . Monks were to be seen in all the streets, in the habits of their order, with their feet bare or in sandals . . . The carriages, carts, horses and even dogs were different, so that the scene altogether was particularly striking . . . my brother . . . declared . . . that considering all things, particularly its near neighbourhood to England, he was very much more struck with the differences of manners, persons, customs, etc. etc. than upon his first interview with the American Indians. I do not mean to insinuate that the comparison was altogether in favour of England; It would be illiberal, and unjust to say so; yet we certainly felt a strong preference towards our native country, and in some things could not but consider it as having a manifest advantage.[14]

Mitford first travelled to the Continent in 1776. This, like the travels of many other MPs, is not recorded in the *History of Parliament*, and makes its low estimate of the number who travelled[15] suspect. Arriving in Calais in July, he wrote:

To a traveller leaving his own country for the first time every object is new: the most minute circumstances therefore often strike his attention, while possibly what may be more worthy of it remains unobserved . . . The town of Calais is much handsomer than Dover; but alas! that the distance of one and twenty miles across the sea should make such a difference in the women. The fair sex at Dover are not the beauties of England, but the women of Calais are not entitled to the appellation of fair: they are browner and much uglier than the men.

Going on to Montreuil, he found the women ugly, coarse and big limbed.[16]

To Paris

Most tourists set off first for Paris, generally seen as the most important sight not only in France, but in Europe. A few tourists did not wish to visit the city, and some, who did so, did not enjoy the experience. Robert Trevor (1706–83), later 1st Viscount Hampden, left Paris in 1729 'without the least regret, being heartily tired of it', as did Lord Grosvenor. Lord Boyle disliked the Parisians. In 1770 Prince Charles of Sweden was much struck by the multifaceted appeal and vitality of Paris, but also shocked by its depravity.[17]

Nevertheless, whatever the complaints, large numbers of travellers visited the city. The journey from Calais was short, along reasonably good roads with inns that were prepared for tourists if only to charge them too much. Most took the post-route through Boulogne, Abbeville, Amiens and Chantilly. Hurrying along, most only commented on Chantilly and the treasures of the abbey of St Denis.

The countryside attracted little attention. Richard Creed, who accompanied John Cecil, 5th Earl of Exeter, to France and Italy in 1699, noted that wolves were a serious problem near Abbeville, a significant observation as it is too easy to forget that in much of Europe agriculture still represented a bitter struggle between men and wild animals: 'It is a fine country here without enclosures, many pretty little woods in which there are many wolves; so that the shepherds are forced to have little huts built on wheels by the sheep fold where they lie all night with guns to shoot the wolves.' Lieutenant-Colonel George Carpenter MP (c. 1695–1749), later 2nd Lord Carpenter, noted in 1717 that wolves caused a lot of trouble between Roye and Senlis.

In 1771 the Reverend Norton Nicholls (1750–1811) found the country between Calais and Paris 'chiefly open corn land like Cambridgeshire or Huntingdonshire'.[18] Not everyone found the countryside uninteresting. In 1763 Thomas Robinson (1738–86), already an MP and later an ambassador and Foreign Secretary, wrote of the journey from Clermont to Paris, that it was 'varied and in some part romantic. There is perhaps too great a sameness in the causeway and roads planted one tree each side, but it is amended for by the greatness of the plan upon which they are directly struck, from the extremities to the capital.'[19]

George Seymour, Viscount Beauchamp (1725–44), reached Paris in October 1742 after 'an extreme pleasant journey, only a few accidents of our chaise, which delayed us longer than we intended'. The postilion's carelessness had led to their nearly overturning at Abbeville, though a good supper there was some compensation, while their carriage broke down at the entrance to Amiens. Beauchamp was very impressed by the cathedral at Amiens, though he confessed his 'concern to see so fine a place given up to the use of idolators'. After a breakdown at Chantilly, Beauchamp visited the Prince of Condé's seat there, liking the park but complaining about the garden, 'full of minced pie borders and little squirts of water'.[20]

An anonymous account of about the same period offered one of the fullest descriptions of the journey to Paris. The tourist first visited the famous cloth factory set up at Abbeville in 1675 by the Dutchman Van Robais, with governmental encouragement: 'in some of the apartments you see the looms which weave the cloth, in others the people who card the wool, in another part the dye house and in short everything laid out with the utmost convenience'. After visiting a château at Picquigny, the tourist came to Amiens:

a very old built town, without anything in it that I could learn worth
the curiosity of a stranger, except the great old church, which I think
would not tempt one who had been in Flanders . . . The country about
Amiens is extremely pretty and one shall see few open country as this
is, that please the eye better . . . Clermont where I saw a fine house
and gardens which were laid out by the Marechal Berwick . . . the
next morning on my setting out found the country entirely changed
from bare chalk hills to a fine soil full of vineyards and I travelled from
Clermont to Lingueville all upon a fine causeway with vineyards and
fruit trees dispersed about the cornfields. This you may be sure was
pleasing to one who had never seen anything of that kind before: a
little after I was past Lingueville the scene changed upon me again and
I found myself in a barren sandy soil and a whole country laid open
for to make a forest for the Duke of Bourbon in which the plantations
dispersed up and down make a pretty effect as well as shelter the game.
This forest brings you to one of the beautifullest gardens in the world,
I need not tell you that I mean Chantilly; what do you think of a canal
2 miles long bordered by a rising ground on each side covered with
woods which are finely disposed in ridings and walks? Yet I would not
have you think that this scene though very charming comes up to the
scene about the canal in Studley Park. . . .[21]

There are many descriptions of Chantilly. The most interesting is that
of Judd. He had been delayed a night at Boulogne by the lack of post
horses and then came via Abbeville, where he condemned as 'ridiculous
superstition' the execution four years earlier of the Chevalier de la Barre for
allegedly mutilating a crucifix, and Amiens, which pleased him, 'it being a
place of great antiquity and agreeably situated on the river Somme'.
On 18 July 1770 Judd reached the Prince de Condé's château:

Here nature has left but little room for art to make an addition to
its beauties; in short it is quite a paradise. The Duke of Bourbon the
Prince's eldest son . . . was married yesterday, to a daughter of the Duke
of Orleans, and this day the Prince gives on that occasion an elegant
entertainment and hunt in the woods, sure nothing could be more
fortunate than our arriving at Chantilly to partake of this amusement
so new to an English gentleman whilst we were at breakfast we were
serenaded by bands of music in the street; about half after ten all the
company that intended going to the woods with the Prince drew
up in the park before the palace, and the following was the order of
procession.
1st   A pack of hounds led by the Prince's domesticks in rich
       liveries.

2ly   A band of music consisting of thirty performers on horseback.

3ly   Near a hundred of the Princes servants in superb liveries on horseback leading a great number of the fine hunters.

4ly   One hundred and fifty gentlemen on horseback, two, and two, with cockades, and swords drawn.

5ly   The Prince of Conti and Duke of Bourbon were drawn by six beautiful horses in an open carriage of droll construction on the front was carved two horses upon which were seated some gentlemen and ladies that accompanied the Prince.

6ly   Came two open carriages full of ladies, these with silk curtains of the same colour, drawn by sets of horses. The procession closed with many of the Princes servants in livery with colours, drums, and fifes etc.

In this manner the cavalcade proceeded into the woods of Chantilly about two miles and a half from the Palace; where there were three large tents for their reception.

The dinner was served up in high taste, and in one of the tents was an elegant dessert. The gentlemen on horseback with swords drawn formed a circle round them and whilst the Prince was at his repast sat with their hats off. The band of music being inclosed in the circle and playing alternately with the drums and fifes we were highly delighted with the sight of this august ceremony having the honour to be in the same tent with the Prince, who is a man of a sprightly turn with a keen and penetrating eye. Whilst the Prince was at dinner a little insect crept down the neck of Madm. de L—— who sat at his right hand, he immediately arose and politely offered to assist her which occasioned a good deal of mirth, the Lady refused his offer and blushed – this was a circumstance I could not but notice, it being so foreign to the charactistic of a French Lady to blush at such a piece of galant officiousness.[22]

After Chantilly tourists visited the abbey of St Denis, where many saw their first relics, as well as the royal tombs and treasure,[23] before pressing on to Paris.

PARIS

Paris was the single most impressive sight seen by British tourists,[24] the leading goal for the majority of them. It offered more than any other city. If it did not have the antiquities of Rome, the art of Florence, or an opera house to compare with that of Naples; it did have a royal court nearby at Versailles, an enormous range of cultural and social activities that tourists could participate in, an active artistic life, and a large number of splendid sights. This was aside from its crucial closeness to Britain. Furthermore, the climate was acceptable all year long, unlike, for example, Rome and Naples, and there were activities for the tourist throughout the year. This was because of the vitality of the city. Tourists to Paris were not dependent for their amusement on the royal court as, to a considerable extent, they were in Vienna, Madrid, Berlin, Dresden and the smaller German courts, as well as, even more clearly, in St Petersburg, Copenhagen, Stockholm and Warsaw. As a consequence, the departure from one of these cities of the ruler, for hunting, military reviews or other purposes, could lead to a serious curtailment of tourist activities, as could any ill-health or death in the royal family. A trip to Versailles to watch the king take part in the public rituals of the court, especially eating, going to mass and hunting, was a major part of the tourist itinerary in Paris, but the court played a smaller role in this itinerary than in the comparable ones for all other capitals of monarchies, with the papal capital being a special case.

Close to London, Paris could be reached from Dover in three days, though the journey usually took longer. It had a range of accommodation greater than that of any other tourist centre, as well as food that was plentiful and commonly of high quality. French was the foreign language that most British tourists were conversant with, and the city was well used to dealing with tourists. The Parisian luxury trades, especially tailoring, were a particular attraction to many tourists.

Sights included the Louvre and Tuileries, the Luxembourg, the Duke of Orléans' Palais Royal, the *hôtels* (town houses) of the prominent, public buildings, especially the Invalides and the Observatory, squares, such as the Place des Victoires, luxury factories, such as the Gobelins tapestry works and the Sèvres porcelain factory, and churches, such as Notre Dame, the Val de Grâce and St Sulpice. Humbler sights, such as open-air shows, were also appealing. In 1764 Thomas Greene and the painter George Romney viewed the outside of the Louvre, 'and were well entertained there by a mountebank and his monkey. We could not but admire the sagacity and drollery of the animal and at the same time could not forbear concluding that it had much more the appearance of the human species than many strutting Frenchmen that we had seen.' Any list of sights could be greatly extended to take note of the particular interests of individual tourists. William Drummond who had often been to Paris, returned there on 3 November 1787, towards the end of a lengthy tour: 'I found here, as usual, more health, happiness and spirits, than I have done anywhere since I left England. The climate agrees with me and I like the place, the manners, and customs of Paris, and I have some valuable friends here.' Drummond's principal interest was visiting hospitals. He was unimpressed by what he saw at the Hôtel-Dieu:

. . . there are still in some wards four sick in a bed . . . It is almost impossible any sick person can recover in the Hôtel de Dieu. The insane people in this hospital are taken proper care of. They put them into cold water baths, and let cold water fall on their heads, in the worst conditions of their insanity. The keepers told me that they were always worst at the New and Full Moon. If it were possible to be merry when seeing and contemplating the most pitiable and afflicting condition of human nature, I should always laugh to ecstasy when in a French mad house. The insanity of French people, differs as much from the insanity of English people as their sober and common habits differ. Laughing, singing, a desire to please, with a thousand little tours of expression, and flashes of levity, with the politest manners, reign in a French Bedlam. I heard many soft and pleasing discourse, this day, from two or three French mad women, than I ever heard in my life: – And as for repartee, and strength of abrupt thought, I never heard the best company excel a man, who was a cook in some family before his misfortune, and who played off another madman, that was bound down in the same bed with him this morning.[25]

As well as the sights in Paris itself, there were also those that could be reached in a day trip. Versailles was pre-eminent, but other frequently visited places included St Germain-en-Laye, St Cloud, St Denis, Marly and Sceaux.

Individual sights were very striking, but tourists tended to be more impressed by the overall impact of the city. One was asked in 1738, 'Do you still retain a laudable partiality for the streets of London, or like a great many of our good countrymen who are immediately struck with a new face of things, do you begin to fancy there is nothing but what is most hideous in the country where God and nature designed to plant them?'[26]

About the same time, a tourist wrote:

The first thing that must strike a strangers eye is the beautiful appearance that the bridges and quays make: for here the houses are built at a distance from the river and you see the two quays for a quarter of a mile together . . . covered on one side by two of the kings palaces and the Tuileries Gardens and on the other by a range of very fine hotels . . . and truly it is in the article of their hôtels which they principally excel us; the magnificence of their apartments, the lighting of them and the furniture is what you don't see in England.[27]

In 1763 Thomas Robinson reported his first impressions:

The approach from St. Denis is very grand, and the town itself by degrees grows upon one, as the greatest city in the world, the height of the houses, the numberless shops, though not showy and the various appearance of numerous inhabitants in so many different shapes is very striking. What can one say of the scenery from the bridge [Pont Neuf], the Louvre, the Quatre Nation College, the Tuileries etc. which all contribute to the composition of the richest piece of perspective imaginable.[28]

This was a period when new developments were making Paris more magnificent. Work began on the Place Louis XV (now Place de la Concorde) in 1755 and continued until 1775. The Concorde bridge was opened in 1790. In 1758 work began on the church that was to become the Panthéon, and in 1764 on the Madeleine. Aside from the sights, Paris was fascinating because of the range of activities it could cater for. William, Viscount Pulteney (c. 1731–63) claimed in 1749, 'Paris is certainly the centre of all gaiety and pleasure.' John Mitford wrote in 1777, 'Paris is always gay. In the winter it has only the gaieties of a town. In summer it has some of those of the country. Operas, plays, balls, and entertainments of various kinds, are perpetual resources for the idle.'

Interests, hobbies and vices could all be pursued in an attractive setting. The activities of British visitors varied greatly. George James Cholmondeley ran a gaming table; Hans Stanley studied international law; Evelyn, 2nd Duke of Kingston (1711–73) returned to London in 1736 with the wife of a Parisian civil servant. Tourists were helped by the relative tolerance of their activities and by the presence of a large sophisticated social world that was ready to receive them. There was both Anglomania and Anglophobia in France, and British tourists definitely benefited from the former. Ready access to the circles they sought is repeatedly an impressive feature of tourists' correspondence and journals. It was not surprising that Paris was popular, not only with men, but also with women. In February 1786 John, 3rd Duke of Dorset, the affable cricket-loving British envoy, noted, 'We have always numbers of English and many ladies which is uncommon at this time of year.' The following month he added, 'We have a great number of English as usual particularly women.'[29]

THE REST OF FRANCE

Many British tourists saw little of France aside from Paris, the road to it from Calais and the routes from it to Italy. Relatively few toured provincial France and those who travelled through it tended to do so for a specific reason: to attend the academy at Lunéville, go for medical treatment at Montpellier, as Henry de Grey did in 1717, travel between Paris and Germany or, like Arthur Young, to travel for reasons of scholarly enquiry. Financial problems, as well as poor health, drove some to France. Commenting on heavy expenditure in the recent general election, the *Edinburgh Evening Courant* of 3 April 1784 claimed, 'The south of France will be found as necessary to decayed purses as to decayed constitutions.' War forced some to visit France. In December 1778 Major John Bowater of the Marines, who had been captured crossing the Atlantic, found about thirty other officers at Pontivy in central Brittany. Sent there on their word of honour, they were not imprisoned. Bowater wrote of the town:

> if it did not incessantly rain would not be a disagreable town. I have been treated with great politeness. We are limited to six miles round the town and the Duke of Rohan who has the manors and great property hereabouts has given leave to all the British officers to shoot, hunt, and fish. The town is very ill built but the country is beautiful and plenty of everything. We have two courses and a dessert with claret and white wine for half a crown, a card assembly every night and sometimes dancing.[30]

Such an involuntary and circumscribed stay can scarcely be seen as tourism, although, as ever, it is worth noting the response of British visitors. In this case, it is clear that Brittany, which had very few tourists, was clearly not without something to offer. Other ranks tended, however, to have a difficult time as prisoners of war.

The Loire valley was fairly popular in the first half of the century, as it had been throughout the seventeenth century. At Angers, Blois and Tours young travellers could learn French and acquire expertise in some of the attributes of gentility, such as dancing, fencing and riding, without, it was hoped, being exposed to the vices of the metropolis. Such skills could also be acquired at Besançon, where Richard Lyttleton studied in the academy in 1737, Protestant Geneva, and Lunéville, where the academy (as in Turin) possessed the advantage of the proximity of a court, in this case the ducal court of Lorraine. The Loire academies were, however, especially valued because of the purity of the French spoken in the area. Simon, 2nd Viscount Harcourt (1714–77), subsequently 1st Earl Harcourt and envoy to Paris, and Edward Mellish, both in the Loire valley in the early 1730s, noted the presence of other British visitors. James, 3rd Earl of Berkeley (1680–1736), and his wife Louisa visited Viscount Bolingbroke at his seat at Chanteloup near Amboise in 1735. Alexander Lord Balgonie (1749–1820), later 9th Earl of Leven, stayed at Tours in 1774.[31]

The Loire, however, was not visited by large numbers of tourists and by the second half of the century its relative popularity had fallen sharply. Thomas Prowse (1707–67), MP for Somerset, spent months in 1763 in

Tours for his health. His wife Elizabeth advised Sir Charles Kemys Tynte that a friend of his who proposed going there

> will find the situation of Tours and the country about it very delightful, but I fear he may be disappointed of the company and amusements he may expect . . . we found the people very poor, much prejudiced against the English, and more so against heretics. I think there are 200 priests in the town, but only one of them made an acquaintance with us, a sensible worthy man . . . There are very few people of any fashion or fortune . . . I believe the language is better spoken at Tours than in any other part of France. The climate is moderate and agreable to an English constitution. Provisions are very reasonable.

Charles Mellish MP, who went to France in 1777, as a result of financial difficulties, found several English families in Orléans. Captain William Townshend went to Tours in 1783 to improve his French, but, as Joseph Cradock noted, 'Blois, though particularly interesting, is not, even now, much frequented by the English; indeed it lies out of the general route.'[32] Possibly the gentle beauty of the Loire did not appeal to a generation increasingly concerned with mountains and the raw beauty of nature, happier to attempt Mt Blanc than to follow the precepts of their predecessors. Probably the towns of the valley suffered from the fact that, in tourist terms, they led nowhere. Dijon, Chalon-sur-Saône and Avignon did not appeal to eighteenth-century tastes more than Angers, Blois and Tours; that they were visited most often reflected the popularity of Italy and the unpopularity of Spain and south-western France.

Travelling in provincial France was made less attractive by the poor state of some of the roads. The 7th Earl of Leven noticed this when he left the St Omer–Lille road in 1749 and Elizabeth, Lady Craven complained of bad cross-country roads in Touraine in 1785.[33] And yet, a number of tourists did travel through provincial France. They can be divided into two categories, which roughly correspond to travel east and west of a line from Le Havre to Paris and then on to Nevers, Roanne and Montpellier. The former were essentially tourists whose travels represented a diversion from the more customary itineraries linking the Channel ports, Paris and Italy, although there were tourists who travelled with specific goals in this area, for example, Lunéville. On the other hand, those tourists who visited western France were very obviously leaving the usual itinerary, and were instead fashioning one based on a tour of proyinicial France.

In the eastern half of France tourists were most likely to visit French Flanders, as part of an itinerary based on Paris and the Low Countries, or as a detour from the Calais–Paris route. Rees Thomas wrote to his father from Lille in June 1787:

We arrived here this morning about 9 o'clock. It was our full intention to have reached this place . . . last night, but an unforeseen accident of our chaise breaking down twice detained us a full hour on the road, which misfortune obliged us to take up our night's abode at Armentieres, a wretched inn in a wretched place . . . If it had not been for Mr. Rhys Davies, we should have most probably continued on the road all night: for with his dumb shows and signs and his skill in wheelery, he made the carpenters understand their own business which they absolutely did not before – I never saw such profound ignorance in my life . . . The French are very particular and scrupulous in their religious ceremonies. In every place there are many crosses with our Saviour: the blood is represented as running from his left side.[34]

Eastern France was crossed by those travelling between Paris and Germany. In September 1753 William Lee (c. 1726–78) visited Strasbourg, and managed to meet the leading celebrities:

. . . dined today with the Governor of Strasbourg to whom I was recommended by the French minister at the court of Wurttemberg, and have been this afternoon to make a visit to Mr. Voltaire whom I found with a body emaciated and weakened with ill health, his mind strong and penetrating; and a French vivacity that seemed to give little time to reflect upon his deplorable condition. I endeavoured to sift his thoughts of the King of Prussia[35] whom he has had many opportunities of knowing to the bottom, but he always changed the conversation and seemed to dislike it. He commended our constitution and the English nation, the only nation where the least shadow of liberty remains in Europe, wondered at our interposing so strenuously in the affairs of the Continent where we could be no gainers and may be great losers. The last war[36] he said we entered into par grandeur d'ame et generosité, the Dutch were forced into it par un coup de pied, the Queen of Hungary par recipite and the French par étourderie. I quote his words more for the singularity than the justness of his observation. I invited him much to come to England and told him the reputation his works had gained in that country. He was pleased with having the approbation of so judicious a nation and was pleased to say he should be glad to breathe the air of liberty and leave his bones in a free country . . . I propose staying only two days longer at Strasbourg the town is soon seen and nothing else can engage a travellers curiosity.[37]

Trips in south-eastern France could be taken as part of the route to or from Italy, or as a detour from it. Many tourists visited Aix-en-Provence,

Montpellier and Nimes; Norton Nicholls, for example, seeing all three in early 1773 on his return from Italy.

Tourists who visited western France tended to do so as part of an itinerary that did not not include Italy. In 1737 John Mucklow visited Paris, Dijon, Geneva, Lyons, Avignon, Aix, Marseilles, Toulouse, Bordeaux, Poitiers, Blois and Paris again. He wrote of his journey from Bordeaux to Barbézieux, ' . . . mostly over barren heaths or low shrubby forests . . . The towns and villages we passed through in this part of the country were miserable and houses much out of repair, very few glass windows in them and the streets ill paved and dirty.'[38]

Eight years earlier, an anonymous tourist who had spent three months at the academy at Angers, travelled thence to Bordeaux. He was clearly interested in the country he was travelling across. At Saumur he noted:

> The duty upon salt is one of the greatest burdens the country complains of, for its price is exorbitant, and the number of officers employed in collecting it eats up the most part of the revenue. Most families are obliged to take such a quantity . . .

Soon after leaving Saumur, 'the horse in the shafts of my chaise fell directly upon his head in an unlucky hole'. Unexpectedly, its neck was not broken, but the traveller 'took horse' instead to Montreuil where he found the wine at the inn 'wretchedly bad'. Crossing the 'fine open corn country' of Poitou and visiting châteaux and castles, the tourist reached Poitiers, where he could not find the Roman antiquities mentioned in his guidebook. Bad roads delayed his journey to Niort and at Mauzé 'my chaise stuck fast in a hole . . . but we got it out by the help of 4 oxen'. At La Rochelle he

> had great difficulty to find horses for my carriage to Rochefort, for everything is farmed[39] in this country so that no man dare let out his horses (unless it be across the country) without a liberty from the Bureau de Messager who would not give me horses unless it were to go all the road to Bordeaux which left me to the mercy of those fellows who let out horses and who knew very well how to take an advantage of strangers, for they must pay something to the Bureau to have a liberty to assist travellers upon the road. How far such treatment is contrary to the rules of hospitality strangers are best judges . . . one thing which I have observed all over the country, it is that the women do all the business, for if one has to do with a merchant or a tradesman, the husband is but a cypher for the wife does all and commonly talks a great deal and is wretchedly covetous, especially when she speaks *en conscience*. There is another thing very remarkable

in France it is that they send all their children to be nursed in the country . . . and they never see their faces till they are fit to be sent to school, which gave occasion to a French gentleman to say that perhaps he was only the son *d'un gentilhomme paisan*, for poverty may engage a poor nurse (when the child she suckles dies) to put her own son in the place of a marquis.

Travelling by 'wretchedly bad' roads via Saintes, he finally reached Bordeaux after being imposed upon considerably in crossing the Garonne.[40] The Jacobite Viscount Quarendon (1718–72), later 3rd Earl of Lichfield and Chancellor of Oxford University, whose Grand Tour is not mentioned in the *History of Parliament*, kept a journal of his travels from 1738 to 1740. These included Italy and the Low Countries, but in the summer of 1739 he travelled through western and southern France. Quarendon disliked Jesuits and ridiculed relics. He could be sharply critical: of Poitiers, he wrote, 'the town vies with Angers for deformity'; of Niort, 'an exceeding ugly town containing nothing worth notice'. Dockyards were a particular passion and Quarendon commonly noted the sources of water supply. In Toulouse he recorded:

the in a certain time after burial. With these they have filled a great vault among whom they show a lady called La Belle Paul as having been the greateCordeliers have in the aisle of their church a kind of earth which dries the bodies to a kind of mummyst beauty that town had produced. The present figure might serve as a good lesson to the beauties of the present age; the different postures of these various sorts of people make a serious and striking reflection in the breast of any person unused to such sights.

Quarendon was sufficiently curious to seek explanation for the mummification; he attributed it to the high lime content of the soil. Like many British tourists, Quarendon would have liked to see dark and narrow medieval streets replaced by the wide vistas of classical piazzas. Towns with narrow streets, such as Montpellier or Avignon, were thus condemned, while the broad streets of Marseilles met with approbation.[41]

A younger and less illustrious tourist, John Harford, visited Cherbourg in August 1768. Ten years earlier, during the Seven Years War, the fortification and harbour works had been destroyed by the British. Arriving at his inn:

Our landlord conducted us upstairs into a chamber, (for the French innes have no Parlours, nor Dining Rooms, but all Bedchambers) Where they laid the cloth for supper, put for each of us a four prong silver fork, a silver spoon, and a small glass tumbler, which held about a quarter of a pint, but no knives; for it is the custom in France for every Frenchman to carry a knife in his pocket, with which they eat their meat: We told them we had got no knives and we must have some, they could only raise amongst the whole family a few old rusty ones (for they never clean them) and then they serv'd up supper, which consisted of soups boil'd and roast fowls, without any sauce, and so overdone that you might tear them to pieces. We asked for some melted butter and they brought up a silver porringer full, turned to clear oil, which we could not eat. At supper we drank what they call Vin de Campagne, out of the small glasses, the same as we do cyder in England, for they have no beer: the price was 16 sols or abt. 7½ per bottle and after supper we had frontiniac and burgundy but could not get any champagne, which we wanted, they have stone stairs at their inns, which is not very common in England. The next morning Tuesday 23rd August (my giddiness was intirely gone off) we went to breakfast, but were obliged to eat dry bread with our coffee and tea, the butter being so excessive bad that none of us could touch it: they have no fresh butter that is so good as our worst salt, tho' their milk is sweet, (their cheese is also very bad) and their bread is very light. After breakfast my father, my brother, Mr. Perne and self went to the Great Church to hear Mass performed and it happened to be a very remarkable day being appointed solemnly to pray the Queen of France's soul out of Purgatory. In the middle isle near ye entrance into the choir was a coffin covered with black cloth placed on stools. After they had said their prayers with seeming great devotion and remained silent a great while, I suppose at their private prayers, a little bell was rung, immediately all the congregation kneeled down, and the Priest went up the middle isle of the Church and went on his knees before the coffin, and Mr. Perne (that was with us) went up with him, the Priest took hold of his coat and made him also kneel. He made a motion for us to do the same, but being near the Door chose rather to stand there and see it: which we did: and saw the whole ceremony very well. . . . After we had been at mass went by the seaside . . . The women in Normandy wear no hats but great long cloaks, and slippers instead of shoes and many of the common, men, boys and girls wear wooden shoes, but are all very fond of dressing and powdering their hair. After we had viewed the piers etc went to the custom house for our Portmanteaux and trunks. The commissary came downstairs in his morning gown, and asked if any of us could talk French, my father answered in the affirmative, that there were several of us could. He then asked him whence we came and where we were bound. He told him, we came from Bristol to Weymouth, and from thence to

Cherbourg on a party of pleasure and were bound for Guernsey. He then desired the keys of our Portmanteaux and trunks which we gave to one of his officers, who just opened them, lockt them again and returned us the keys, but he asked very particularly whether we had any tobacco. . . . we had a little dispute with one of the inferior priests owing to a dog which Captain Read brought with him from Weymouth. When we went into the chapel the dog went in with us and ran up the steps to the altar (when he came down we took hold of him and try'd a handkerchief round his collar, in Roman Catholick Countrys they dont suffer dogs to go into their churches) and the Priest said the dog's life was forfeited but when Mr. Du Veil told him we did not know it, he said very little more, he then asked if we were Roman Catholicks, Captain Read answered with a sneer of contempt, we are Catholicks Apostolick, upon which he said if we had a mind to save our souls and not go to the Devil, we must turn Roman Catholicks, my father desired to speak with two English nuns that were there, He said one was sick and the other was too young we then asked to see some of the French nuns, he said they were going to dinner and seemed determined we should not see any of them.

Harford's trip was a short cross-channel visit, a product of the growing appeal of foreign travel and the greater variety of means of satisfying it. Other tourists were wider-ranging. John Jervis (1735–1823), later 1st Earl of St Vincent and First Lord of the Admiralty, went on a circular tour from Paris to Toulouse and back via Bordeaux. Thomas, 8th Earl of Kinnoull, spent 'three months making the tour of the southern parts of France' in 1773.[42] Balgonie visited Brittany in 1774 and Brand Toulouse in 1783. The Cradocks went on a round trip from Paris to Marseilles, Toulouse and Bordeaux in 1785. Tourists penetrated even to the Pyrenees and Auvergne. Toulouse and Montpellier drew many British tourists. The appeal of provincial France was, however, limited. In his tour, Jervis did not visit Italy. Few would have copied his decision to visit Bordeaux and Toulouse instead.

FROM PARIS TO THE ALPS

From Paris to Italy the route was clear to Lyons. Most travellers went to Chalon-sur-Saône, either by the Lyons diligence or in other vehicles. At Chalon they would usually embark on the *diligence par eau* for a two-day trip down the Saône to Lyons. Most found this a very pleasant trip. Mitchell observed, 'this way of travelling is expeditious and would not be disagreeable if one was sure to find good company: The charming prospects along the banks of the river are very entertaining.' Going as far as Mâcon, whence he was to take a coach to Geneva, Robert Wharton found pleasant company on the boat, 'we talked and chatted till the cool of the evening when we went on deck above the chamber and enjoyed the prospect. The river . . . sides covered with rich pastures abounding in cattle. At a distance are seen the mountains of Bresse and Bugey.' At the end of November 1772 Jervis took the boat to Lyons:

> a very convenient passage boat and must be a very agreeable way of travelling in a more favourable season, being attended with no fatigue and affording a delightful prospect of the country on the borders of the river. This boat stops to dine and lie at different places in its course. They have the bad habit of rewarding their coachman and boatmen before they arrive at their place of destination whereby the passengers are entirely neglected and left a prey to a crowd of canaille under the name of porters, many of them sharpers and all imposters – which we had full demonstration of on our arrival at Lyons – the boat being constantly filled with these people, who but for the friendly interposition of a French gentleman, would have fleeced us handsomely – This mode of travelling, so apparently commodious to weakly people, has one great inconvenience, the want of a necessary, which indeed may be supplied by a portable close stool.

Most tourists hurried through Lyons, but it was generally thought agreeable, and had many attractions. In 1765 Sir William Farrington found 'the situation wonderfully romantick, tis a most beautiful and noble city'. He visited the factory making gold and silver wire with his servant who found it 'a most surprising sight. I drawed some myself.' William Bennet, however, was less impressed twenty years later: 'its inferior streets are disgraced with that dirt and shabby appearance, so disgusting to strangers even in Paris itself.'[43]

After Lyons the problem of the Alps had to be confronted. It was necessary to cross them or circumvent them by sea; a coastal route on land was not practicable. It was possible to go on land from Marseilles and Toulon to the Sardinian border, in order to reach Nice and Monaco, but there was an absence of good roads in the Sardinian county of Nice. An anonymous tourist crossed the Var between Antibes and Nice in 1754 'but not without taking guides with us, who were always ready to wade through, find out the best fords for your chair and support it, if there should be occasion: the sands move frequently, which makes the bottom extremely dangerous.' In 1776–7 another anonymous tourist noted:

> These torrent-courses are the roads, and, in some parts, the only roads of the country. . . . A road has been formed from Nice over Montalban

to Villafrance, just practicable for a carriage, but so steep and so rough
that it is scarcely safe; and a carriage is very seldom seen on it. . . .
The road to Monaco is practicable only for mules, asses, or mountain
horses; and in some parts is scarcely safe with any of them.

This road was so bad that he got off his mule and went on by foot. Lady
Craven wrote from Antibes, the frontier-town, in 1785, 'Most part of the
road from Hyères to this place is very mountainous and narrow.'[44] East
of Monaco the Ligurian mountains fell sheer to the sea, the corniche
road on the Riviera was not opened until Napoleon's time, and it was not
practicable to go by land to Genoa via Oneglia, Finale and Savona. It was
possible to cross the Alps from Nice to Turin through the Col (pass) of
Tende, though a traveller in the mid-1770s found

the road is utterly impracticable for a carriage, and scarcely to be
found, travelled by an ordinary horse; mules are chiefly used on it; and
tender ladies and infirm men have no succedaneum but a sedan chair.
It is three days journey over the mountains to the plains of Piedmont
for a mule, and five for a sedan chair. The narrow rugged path which
is called the road, is conducted up the courses of different torrents.

A carriage road was then being built to Turin. It was to be opened
the following decade: the first complete opening of an alpine pass to
wheeled traffic. The writer, concerned more with the convenience of
tourists than the interests of Victor Amadeus III, regretted that the road
was not being built from Nice to Genoa. Samuel Boddington, however,
used the route in 1789.[45]

BY BOAT TO ITALY

Tourists had to choose between the Alps and the Mediterranean. Neither
was an attractive prospect. By sea there was the risk of storms and
shipwreck, and the lesser risk of Barbary pirates, which Lady Craven was
warned of in 1785, as well as the major inconvenience of contrary winds
or being becalmed, and the minor one of the quality of accommodation
available. The boats used, the feluccas, were small, vulnerable to storms
and dependent on the wind. In 1723 John Molesworth, envoy in Turin,
wrote, 'No mariners in the world are so cowardly as the Italians in
general, but especially the Genoese; so that upon the least appearance
of a rough sea, they run into the first creek when their feluccas are
sometimes wind-bound for a month.' He also commented on the impact
of storms on the feluccas. Andrew Mitchell (1708–71), later an MP and

envoy in Berlin, had a troublesome passage from Genoa eleven years later: 'I was detained some weeks longer at Genoa than I intended, and that by bad weather, for if it blows the least or if there is anything of a sea, the feluccas won't go out. I hired a felucca with 3 men from Genoa to Antibes for 3 pistols and a half.' On 1 November he sailed from Genoa to Savona. The next contrary wind obliged Mitchell to put into Loana and have the felucca hauled onshore as there was no harbour. 'I was detained here a whole day by the laziness of the Italian sailors who chose rather to lie in the port and take their chance for a wind afterwards than to put to sea in fair weather. If there is the least swell in the sea they will by no means venture out.' Later in the trip, he was delayed for another two days by adverse winds and indolent sailors.

The situation did not improve in the second half of the century. Lady Knight sailed from Marseilles to Civitavecchia in 1778: 'our voyage was somewhat tedious, as we were, after seven weeks waiting for a wind, thirty days on our passage, putting into different ports'. Indeed, the continued problems of sea travel contrasted with the gradual improvement in overland journeys during the century. Tourists could cope with discomfort. It was the uncertainty that storms, contrary winds and calms brought to timetables that was the crucial problem. Though there was quite a lot to do in Genoa, tourists generally did not wish to wait for any length of time in Marseilles, though several such as the Cradocks spent the winter there, or in Antibes, Livorno (Leghorn) or Civitavecchia, and some of the fishing settlements on the Ligurian coast were very uninviting. It would, however, be misleading to suggest that travelling by boat was always an unhappy experience. There were definite visual attractions. Francis Head was very impressed by the beauty of the Ligurian coast, and the approach to Genoa was generally regarded as very attractive. In addition, the trip could be quick, offered an alternative to passes closed by snow and enabled the tourist who wanted to head south in Italy a great deal, for he or she could sail direct to Lerici, Livorno or Civitavecchia.[46]

ACROSS THE ALPS

The majority of tourists preferred to cross the Alps. This was less hazardous and unpredictable than the maritime route, though it was even more affected by seasonal factors. The most common route into Italy was from Lyons to the Franco-Savoyard frontier at Pont-de-Beauvoisin. Most tourists then saw mountains for the first time. In 1765 Sir William Farrington found the sight of the mountains along the road 'very extraordinary'; his servant thought the Alps 'prodigious odd and

..omantick, I saw a great rock appear above a great white cloud it had the oddest appearance I ever saw anything in my life'.[47] Crossing the frontier back from Italy in 1777, John Mitford noted 'a quick change . . . in the manners of the people. The plain bluntness of the Savoyard is ill supplied by the affected politeness of the lower rank of people among the French'.[48] Such a remark was characteristic of many tourists. They placed excessive weight on their supposed ability to discern national characteristics.

From Pont-de-Beauvoisin, tourists set off across the Duchy of Savoy, which was then part not of France but of Savoy-Piedmont (a state referred to after 1720 as the Kingdom of Sardinia), over the Mt Cenis pass to Susa, their crossing of the Alps; and thence to Turin, the chief town of Piedmont and the capital of the Kingdom of Sardinia. As the pass was not suitable for wheeled vehicles, it was necessary to dismantle carriages near the foot of the pass. These were then carried over the pass on mules, while the tourists were carried in a type of sedan chair by porters. The means of transportation did not change during the period, as the route did not become a carriage road until the following century. Crossing in 1734, Richard Pococke was 'carried down in a chair without legs, with poles to the sides, carried by two men'. He was delighted by the 'speed of the crossing' and observed 'it is nothing at all'. Thomas Pelham noted in early 1777, 'crossing Mont Ceni is certainly a great undertaking in point of conveying the carriages etc, but as to our own persons there is neither danger nor inconvenience; it was so hard a frost that when we came to the top of the mountain we left our chairs and descended in sledges which though very trying to the *nerves* was not unpleasant. It was the clearest day imaginable and our view beyond all description.' Thomas Brand crossed in October 1783:

We passed Mt. Cenis after bad weather and it was covered with snow six or eight inches deep but even in that state we could not help shrugging our shoulders and shaking our heads at the extravagant exaggerations of danger which most travellers indulge themselves in in describing that famous passage. It was indeed a little cold in going up but once on the plain the air was temperate enough and at the descent it was mild beyond expectation. We rode up upon mules and were carried down by porters: you sit in a kind of chair carried on poles like a sedan with a piece of wood or a cord to press your feet against and a little elbow to rest your arms on. In this manner with your legs and thighs in a straight horizontal position and in the plane of the poles the porters whisk you with incredible strength and celerity down a steep stony road with sharp angles at each turn. Perhaps for the first five or six minutes I was under some fright but the firmness of their steps soon set me at ease and the beautiful cascades that present themselves on every side and the majesty of the hoary mountains that surrounded me furnished me with sufficient matter of admiration and astonishment. The porters are fond of conversing with you.[49]

Tourists' experience of crossing the Alps varied. If Sir Carnaby Haggerston 'had a very pleasant passage of Mount Senis' in 1719, Henry Ellison junior 'passed the Alps without danger and almost without difficulty' in early 1764, and Brand had 'a most delicious passage of the Mt Cenis' in 1790, George Lyttleton did not enjoy his crossing of the Alps in terrible weather in November 1729. Heavy snow, a sharp cold, high wind, a thick mist and slippery precipices all combined to make him very frightened.[50]

SWITZERLAND

The Swiss cantons were very much off the usual tourist route, but interest in them increased during the century. This owed much to a greater interest in mountains. Walter Chetwynd (1710–86), a Fellow of King's College, Cambridge, was one of the earliest visitors to the valley of the Chamouni, which he visited with some companions in 1740.[51] William, 4th Earl of Rochford, envoy in Turin, spent a fortnight in the Savoy Alps in 1751, visiting glaciers and collecting mineral samples. An anonymous traveller from Basle to Solothurn in 1758 wrote of the 'romantic views' of the 'high mountains . . . We saw many plantations of pumpkins, which the common people feed on much, boiling them in broth.'[52] The following year Thomas Robinson (1738–86), later 2nd Lord Grantham and Foreign Secretary, found the journey along Lake Geneva from Geneva to Lausanne 'the pleasantest that can be imagined, the country on both sides of the lake being exceedingly fine'. He was impressed by Switzerland: 'I saw a great deal of very beautiful country, and reformed my ideas of it, which were rather unfavourable.'[53] Edward Tucker wrote from Lausanne in May 1760 that Switzerland was

a country, where most people, especially strangers are troubled with disorders at this season of the year occasioned by the prodigious and quick alterations of the weather from cold to hot – this country which two months since, seemed one vast plain of snow surrounded by mountains of almost incredible height, is now perhaps one of the finest amphitheatres in the world covered everywhere by trees and divided by some of the finest pieces of water in the universe.[54]

In 1763 George Keate's poem *The Alps* was published. In 1770 the 2nd Viscount Palmerston spent six weeks visiting the Swiss Alps, guided by Horace-Bénédict de Saussure, a professor at Geneva who was a distinguished botanist, geologist and mountaineer, and accompanied by the painter William Pars.[55] The following year Norton Nicholls crossed Switzerland on his way from Paris to Milan. He travelled via Berne and Zurich, writing from the latter on 17 September:

> Here I have all sorts of recommendations; and have passed three days of seeing cabinets of natural history, and with the learned people of the place such as they are; – principally with Mr. Gesner [Salomon Gessner] the poet, author of the death of Abel of which you have read the translation, he is a man of genius and amiable; – I pass everywhere like current coin as the friend of poor Mr. [Thomas] Gray, his respected name procures me more civilities than I deserve . . . It is a passport through all Europe.

He had been to 'the Glacieres', a sight of increasing interest in the second half of the century, reflecting greater concern with natural phenomena, and was also enchanted with Zurich, offering a response to the sublime: 'The situation of this place is delightful. My window, commands the beautiful lake, whose banks gradually rising are adorned with vineyards, with trees, with scattered houses and churches, and villages all white; – behind mountains rise, range upon range, the last mixing their eternal snow with the clouds.' The response from England was somewhat different. Nicholls was greatly dependent on his uncles, yet one responded with concern to the financial implications of Nicholls' new ambitions. 'Travelling, no doubt, is very entertaining and instructive; and almost a necessary accomplishment for persons of rank and adequate fortunes' he accepted, but he was concerned about 'the certain and great expence' of his nephew's plans.

Nicholls meanwhile was pressing on in Swizerland. At Zurich he met two other British tourists, Messrs Drake and Maxwell:

> we passed the lake of Zurich together, which for its size is as beautiful as that of Geneva the same sloping banks covered with vines intermixed with groves; with white villages, and churches, and overlooked by mountains covered with eternal snow and emulating in size and horror those of Savoy. The lake was calm and smooth as glass, the sun bright and not the least chill of autumn we did not arrive at our inn till the moon had drawn her line of trembling splendour cross the lake.

Nicholls' prose was recognizably different from that of tourists earlier in the century. The three companions passed on to a pilgrimage church 'in a frightful solitude'. He thought the treasury magnificent and was impressed by the devotion of pilgrims, where earlier in the century tourists emphasized their credulity:

> a proof of the force with which that religion acts on the minds of men, as well as the long journeys undertaken by starving families who often I believe perish by famine on the road, by women and children; the lake was scattered over with boats of them singing their litanies as they passed. From hence we divided I towards Glaris they . . . to Berne . . . I went to Glaris capital of a democratical canton shut up among dreadful mountains. I had a letter to the Landaman or principal magistrate who told me all that could be told of his government in a few hours. You may judge whether luxury has much to do here when I tell you that a bailiff or governor of a district kept the inn at which I lodged madame his lady cooked my supper and served it afterwards, and all the family kept me company to do me honour though we did not understand a syllable of each others language.

From Glaris, Nicholls pressed on to Chiavenna, travelling part of the way through 'a most astonishing country of rocks', with a member of the Salis family, the most influential clan in the Grisons. He found the climate 'quite changed', vines and forests of ripe chestnuts, and purchased some stoneware pots which he thought hitherto unknown in England and free from the problems of contamination presented by copper utensils. The set cost half a guinea, though including transport to England the price was 4 guineas. On 2 October Nicholls wrote to his mother from Chiavenna:

> Today I am going into the Valtelline said to be a paradise with the Governor of that country Count de Salis – He was brought up at Eton. I shall stay with him two or three days and be at Milan about the 10th – everything is prepared for me there a lodging taken (not as for an Englishman but at the same price an Italian would pay) by the civility of a gentleman here. I have letters [of recommendation] more than I want.

His next letter described his journey through the Valtelline and across Lake Como:

> the first part of our journey was along the valley in which Chiavenna stands, part meadow, part spoiled by the ravages of the Liro which rushes along it, enclosed between very high mountains, till it opens to the lake which is called here the lake of Chiavenna but is part of the great lake of Como, we made a little voyage of 2 or three hours

and landed just at the mouth of the Adda where the Valtelline spread itself into a considerable plain: this part of the lake is horrid without much beauty, frightful naked rocks, cut into precipices, and cleft asunder as if they were prepared for destruction from one side, the other is less savage, covered with forests of chestnut, intermixed with a few vineyards and only covered with rock . . . I stayed with Count de Salis at Sondrio (the place of the Governor's residence) . . . From thence I travelled hither in company with some Italian gentlemen to whom he had recommended me – 30 miles at least of the way was by water on the Lake of Como . . . The banks soon lose their savage aspect, the rocks are no longer so threatening but mountains equally high, covered partly with chestnuts, the towns that adjoin to the very brink of the water are better built than those in Switzerland ennobled by palaces, and climbing the sides of the hills; – white churches everywhere, even on the summits – after 3 or 4 hours olive trees in abundance mix their pale sickly green with the lively tints of the chestnuts and walnuts, escaliers of lemons adorn the coast, the trees are large and the fruit fine, but they stand under frames ready to be covered in the winter. At Tremezzo about ½ the voyage the lake opens into a magnificent theatre, the mountains are covered as usual with chestnuts, olives, and walnuts but mixed with vineyards, the whole coast on either side is spread out with palaces and villas belonging to the great families of Milan.[56]

In 1775 Lord Herbert toured Switzerland with his bearleader William Coxe (1747–1828). In 1779 Coxe published the letters he had written then in his *Sketches of the Natural, Civil and Political State of Swisserland*. After further tours in 1779, 1785 and 1787, Coxe published an expanded version, *Travels in Switzerland* (1789). In 1783 Lord Stopford travelled from Lausanne to Vienna via Neuchâtel. On his first night he stayed in 'a small inn, tolerable beds and supper, only a mouse tried hard in the night to eat its way through to us'. En route for Berne, on his second night he stayed at 'Anet a small place, but tolerable accommodations [i.e. accommodation and food]; a band of music that happened to be there, afforded some entertainment.' He found 'very level and good roads from Berne to Zurich, and everywhere the roads were in good order, which the fine weather contributed much to'.[57] The following year William Farrington toured Switzerland, ending in Lausanne, 'a pleasant town in summer but notwithstanding all kinds of amusements one meets with there, we were heartily tired of it before winter was over'.[58] Geneva, which was outside the Swiss confederation, was much frequented by British visitors. Many went there to be educated, Geneva offering the French language without the pitfalls of Catholicism.

ITALY

Piedmont

Turin was the first major Italian city reached after crossing the Cenis. Some tourists rushed through on the way to other Italian towns, but many lingered. Augustus, 3rd Duke of Grafton (1735–1811) spent six weeks there in 1761. The Reverend Patrick St Clair hoped that Ashe Windham's son, on the Grand Tour in 1738, would 'stay a fortnight at least at the King of Sardinia's court, which is now the politest in Europe'. The rulers were patrons of the academy, a kind of finishing school, which attracted a fair number of British youths: there were seven there in September 1737. Frederick, 5th Earl of Berkeley was there in the early 1760s. Many British tourists liked Turin, its rectilinear street plan, and the spectacular new buildings erected under Victor Amadeus II. In 1779 Wraxall found it 'a very elegant, well built, pleasant city'. The court was regarded as pro-British. On the other hand, some found the amusements of Turin limited, Philip, 2nd Earl Stanhope writing in 1733 of 'so mournful a place as Turin'.[59] Robert Lowth (1710–87), bearleader of Lords George and Frederick Cavendish and later Bishop of London, complained in 1750 that there was little there, but that summer the marriage of the king's grandson to a Spanish infanta drew lots of British guests.[60]

From Turin there were several routes for tourists going into Italy: to Milan, Parma and Genoa. There was no set course for the Italian section of the Grand Tour. Tourists were influenced by their point of arrival and of expected departure; the season of the year, which was important because of summer heat and the onset of malaria near Rome; the inclinations, if any, of their travelling companions; their desire to meet friends; and their wish to attend specific events: the opera in Reggio, Bologna and Milan, the Carnival in Naples and Venice, and religious, especially Easter, ceremonies in Rome. In 1740 Frederick Frankland MP wanted to see the forthcoming papal coronation in Rome and the liquefaction of the blood of St Januarius at Naples, but his nephew warned him 'that he must not think of quitting Rome till the heats are over, if he stays there till they begin'. 'Everybody is going to Venice for the [Feast of the] Ascension', noted Sir John Fleming Leicester in Rome in 1786.[61]

Actual itineraries often differed from what had been planned. Spending longer in one place left less time for others, and tourists often found cities they were visiting more or less interesting than they had anticipated. Much depended on how long the tourist had to spend in what Wharton termed 'the land of ancient virtue and modern virtu (otherwise called taste)'. Francis Head observed that Italy was 'like a fine mistress which is always the more agreeable on a larger acquaintance'. The purposes of travel to Italy varied. Charles Thompson presented in print the respectable reasons:

> . . . being impatiently desirous of viewing a country so famous in history, which once gave laws to the world; which is at present the great school of music and painting, contains the noblest productions of statuary and architecture, and abounds with cabinets of rarities, and collections of all kinds of antiquities.[62]

A somewhat different aspect was presented by a tourist who reflected, 'I don't doubt but a great many of our gentlemen-travellers have reason enough to be cross on account of some modish distemper the Italian ladies may have bestowed on them with the rest of their favours'.[63]

Italy was a country for the pursuit of virtu but also one where it was very easy not to be virtuous, 'a country that affords such ample matter for your entertainment', as Metcalfe Robinson noted in 1705.[64] For whatever reason, many would have agreed with Dr Johnson, who remarked in 1776 that 'A man who has not been in Italy is always conscious of an inferiority from his not having seen what it is expected a man should see. The grand object of travelling is to see the shores of the Mediterranean.'

Northern Italy

The three major sights in northern Italy were Genoa, Milan and Venice. Travelling in northern Italy was not without its problems. In September 1776 John Mitford found the roads bad between Turin and Novara because the rivers were often changing course, so that 'the traveller is continually dashing through water, or dancing in a ferry boat', and he wrote of Novi:

> This spot of junction of the Sardinian and Genoese dominions is often dangerous to the benighted traveller. The neighbouring mountains afford a shelter for robbers, and the difference of government renders the police of these borders very inefficient for the purposes of extirpating these banditti. Possibly a traveller may never reach this place of danger; for about two miles from Tortona the road necessarily passes the Scrivia . . . This rapid stream is very uncertain in its motions. Sometimes merely a swift rivulet, it is passed without difficulty. At other times a vast torrent, no one dares attempt to stem it. These changes are so sudden that the unwary often fall a sacrifice to this treacherous stream, which, appearing shallow, invites the inexperienced to venture the ford, and then overwhelms them with its flood of waters or sinks them in its quicksands.[65]

Once safe at Genoa, the tourist encountered a town very different to Turin: no royal court to serve as a focus for activities, but numerous artistic treasures in aristocratic palaces to which access was readily granted. Lord John Pelham Clinton (1755–81) noted, 'I have been to see some of the beautiful palaces of this place, which infinitely exceed the ideas I had formed of them; I have just taste enough to admire a good picture, when it is pointed out to me, but not judgement enough to find it out by myself.'[66] There were criticisms too. One tourist in late 1729 was surprised by the liberties of married women and their male companions, the *cicisbei*, which he felt set a bad example for British women tourists, while another who was there in 1778 and described the government and history of Genoa in his diary, observed 'The police is ill regulated at Genoa and murderers are frequently left to escape with impunity.'[67]

It was normal to sail from Genoa to the Tuscan ports of Lerici or Livorno (Leghorn). Travelling overland along the coast could be very difficult. Metcalfe Robinson did so in 1705 because his companion disliked the sea. He found the journey 'very bad and unpleasant' as far as Massa, but the Duchy of Massa, between the republics of Genoa and Lucca, 'the fruitfullest and pleasantest I ever saw. It is generally corn, all covered with olives, walnuts, orange trees and other fruits, those that bear none of their own, have vines engrafted on them so that it is a perfect garden.'[68]

Most tourists to Milan came east from Turin or west from Venice. Entering the Milanese from the west in 1776, John Mitford discerned readily

the change of government. The Sardinian monarch, supporting with difficulty a large military establishment, and a numerous royal family, draws from the hands of the peasant every farthing which the ingenuity of the farmers of the revenue can find means to extort. The imperial family, supporting their state with less difficulty, do not bear so hard upon the inhabitants of the Milanese. A traveller soon perceives a labour bestowed upon the cultivation of the lands, a neatness in the various habitations, and a comfortableness in the appearance of the peasants which he does not meet with in Piedmont.[69]

Milan was not noted for artistic treasures to rank with Genoa, Florence, Rome or Venice, but most tourists found it pleasant. Milanese society was welcoming, especially during the administration of the Anglophile Count Firmian, and there was a good opera. La Scala was opened in 1778 with a new opera by Salieri.

From Milan there were two major routes further into Italy. Tourists could go east, via Brescia, Verona, Vicenza and Padua, to Venice, or south-east, via Piacenza, Parma, Reggio and Modena to Bologna, whence they could continue to Pesaro and the Adriatic coast, or turn south across the Apennines to Florence. Venice and Florence were the major attractions, but many of the cities of Lombardy, the Veneto and, in particular, Emilia-Romagna offered much to see. Parma and Modena were the capitals of duchies, Bologna a major centre of artistic treasures. The sale of the Modenese collection to Augustus III of Saxony-Poland was a grave disappointment. Robert Lowth wrote in 1750, 'It vexes my Patriot soul to think that this purchase was not made by our King; I look upon it as a great opportunity lost for the glory of England . . . you perceive I have made some progress in virtù.'[70]

Venice attracted with its treasures, pleasures and spectacles, most notably the carnival on the Feast of the Ascension of the marriage with the sea. There were usually quite a few British tourists there. Charles Wyndham (1710–63), later 2nd Earl of Egremont and a Secretary of State, found 'about thirty English in town' in January 1730.[71]

Some British tourists were quite critical not only of Venetian government and society, but also of its pleasures. One wrote of the opera in 1730, 'here the noble Venetians . . . are guilty of an abominable piece of rudeness, and inhumanity, to their fellow-subjects of an inferior rank; for they make no more bones of spitting and spawling out of their boxes, upon the folks that sit below in the pit, than if they spit upon so much dung or dirt'. Growing 'sick of the insipid diversions of the carnival', he preferred a trip to visit the Roman amphitheatre at Pola in Istria. Fifty-seven years later, Brand was not keen 'to return a second time to row through stinking canals in those coffin-like gondolas in the heats of that unwholesome climate'.[72]

Central Italy

The two foci of tourists in central Italy were Florence and Rome. They came to Florence from Bologna, and from the Tuscan coast via Lucca, Pisa and Livorno; to Rome from Florence and, less commonly, over the Apennines from Loreto via Foligno and Terni.

Florence stood for art, 'a most agreeable place abounding in every species of virtu that one can wish to see, sculpture, painting and the arts carrying to the greatest perfection', in the words of William Lee in 1752.[73] Sir Horace Mann, who represented British interests from 1738 until 1786, introduced tourists to the local social and cultural life. Arriving at the end of 1751, Colonel Henry Seymour Conway MP (1719–95), later a Secretary of State and Commander-in-Chief, was, for example, given hospitality by Mann and introduced by him to Giovanni Buonavita, the Keeper of the Uffizi, with whom he was to take a 'course' on antiquities. Lord John Pelham Clinton was disappointed by the paintings in the Uffizi, but the statues

> infinitely exceeded my expectations, especially the Venus, which is certainly finer, than any idea it is possible to have without seeing her; in my opinion a person, who has no great knowledge of virtu, may judge of sculpture with more exactness, than he can of painting, as the faults or the beauties are more striking.[74]

Evenings could be passed at the opera, when open,[75] but Florence was not without its drawbacks, one tourist complaining in 1778:

> If it were not for the resources of the Gallery and the advantages of having so good an Italian Master as the Abbé Peloti [Antonio Pellori] Florence would be really insupportable, but with these one might pass a couple of months here with profit and pleasure. There is not a single house that receives strangers.[76]

The relative appeal of Florence faded as the century proceeded, not least because of growing determination to visit Naples and its environs on the part of the tourists to Italy.

Rome

Rome was the goal of many tourists, the furthest point of numerous tours, both reality and symbol of what was desirable about foreign travel. William Vyse spent the winter of 1769–70 in Rome not Naples, noting that he found 'such a fund of entertainment from the many objects of curiosity at Rome'. Metcalfe Robinson wrote thence to his father in 1705 from what he called.

> the famousest place in the world and the first motive that induced me to become a traveller: for indeed ever since I knew the name of Rome, and much more as I got an insight into its greatness and the stupendous effects of it in buildings, aqueducts, ways, sculpture etc. which yet are to be admired in these glorious remains of antiquity; I found always my desire increase of having a better knowledge of them, than is to be found in descriptions, and rather to admire the things themselves.

In a culture dominated by the classics, Rome was the focus of interest, and British tourists responded accordingly. 'The town is perfectly filled with English', Sir John Fleming Leicester observed in Rome in 1786.[77]

Philip Francis had suggested in 1772 that 'to a man really curious in the polite arts, Rome alone must be an inexhaustible fund of entertainment',[78] while Charles Sloane, who visited the city in late 1784, thought, 'it is as impossible for a person to dash through it, as it is for him to fly. I stayed a full fortnight there, and only had time to get just such a general idea of the numberless wonders both of modern and ancient times, as to determine me to spend 2 or 3 months there before my return to England.' He indeed returned in 1789 for 'a regular and most interesting course of antiquities'.[79] The best-known course, provided by James Byres, lasted six weeks.

One of the attractions of Rome was that it was readily possible to find such education. Rome, like Paris, had the facilities a tourist could wish for, but, in addition, tourists were more important to the economy of the town.[80] They purchased paintings and antiquities, hired antiquarians and sought artistic advice, Thomas Pelham turning to Mengs in 1777. Mengs was a German. It was the artistic colony, of all nations, that made the marvels of Rome accessible to the tourist. Rome offered classical and Baroque art, sculpture, architecture and painting, and many tourists treated it as the cultural goal of their travels. A vast range was on offer, from the works of Bernini – 'all the affectation and flutter for which he is remarkable' commented Mitford, who thus testified to the decline of his reputation from the start of the century when Bernini had been rated with Michelangelo and the classics – to the classical sites that were being excavated in the second half of the century.[81]

Henry Carr arrived in the city in late 1739 and wrote to his brother-in-law:

for people who have any taste for antiquities, statuary, painting or music here is sufficient entertainment for almost every hour. As to the appearance of the town itself considering the very great number of palaces that are in it I believe that most people are disappointed, for setting aside the churches, fountains, pillars and obelisks which are of themselves a great ornament the rest does not answer one's expectation, the lower part of fine palaces being frequently let off and divided into little shops and greatness and meanness are so jumbled together (as we often see them in life in the same person) that the appearance they make upon the whole is but very indifferent, and even where the palaces are not so disguised, the contiguous houses being often ill built there is not any of them which strikes the eye at once like Grosvenor or St. James's Square, or several other squares and streets we have in London. The inside of their churches surpasses imagination, every age adding fresh ornament and no riches being spared to complete them.[82]

Naples

From Rome many tourists pressed on to Naples. There was 'a great concourse of English gentlemen' there in December 1749, ten in total,[83] a reminder of the, by modern standards, small numbers that created such an impression. Not everyone appreciated the city. Frederick, 2nd Viscount Bolingbroke (1734–87), wrote to his uncle in 1753:

> My stay at Naples was not very long, nor does it deserve ones attention above a fortnight or three weeks. The town is very ugly but finely situated. The natural curiosities of the place and some few inconsiderable remains of antiquity amused me for a few days; Being presented at court, and dining with some of the chief persons employed the rest of my time. I then quitted that city with as little regret I shall do every city in Italy.

The Neapolitans were not popular with all tourists, William Blackett writing in 1785, 'I never saw a rougher, more unpolished people both in countenance and manners in my life. They have a vulgarity and ignorance about them which is particularly disgusting.'[84] The responses of Norton Nicholls and of Thomas Pelham (1756–1826), later 2nd Earl of Chichester, were more positive. Nicholls wrote in July 1772 of a city where 'the nights are so delightful and the days so hot' that no one slept at night: 'I am become a greater friend of the moon than the sun.' Pelham described his activities in letters to his parents:

Naples May 3 1777

If you were as fond of a sea view as I am, I should say you could conceive nothing more beautiful than the one from my windows, from whence, I can see nothing but sea; a very different one from what we are accustomed to in the north with a climate that is at present in the most perfect state of temperature –

I arrived here on Thursday the 1st in two days from Rome; the generality of English perform this journey without stopping. However as I did not wish to lose any of the country, by travelling in the night; and being accustomed to bad inns, a Neapolitan inn was not so horrible to me as others: – the entrance into Naples is by no means equal to Genoa, and though the bay is certainly much larger at the former, I think the latter more beautiful. Mount Vesuvius is certainly a wonderful object, but I imagine that it is necessary to see it from the bay, in order to admire it as so fine a feature in the general view of Naples: the Court is at present at Portici, I dine today with the

Portuguese Minister when we shall settle the time of presentation – there are few English and they are going, excepting Mrs. Swinburne who waits Mr. Swinburne's and Sir Thomas Gascoyne's return from Sicily.

There is no opera nor any publick amusements. I shall therefore give up my time to Naples and its environs . . .

. . . it is a general complaint that the English do not mix with the people of the country, they are in; which in France or Germany I should grant to be a fault, but in Italy I believe to be rather a fortunate circumstance, for the Italians I have seen are either the most ignorant, or the most artful men that can be seen and from whose conversation you cannot gain any new idea or improvement. Italy is certainly worth the notice of every man of reading as the seat of so many interesting transactions but in every other respect, it is the worst country, that a young man can go to –

Naples May 13 1777

The Climate of this Place is delightful and as yet we suffer no inconvenience from the heat. I was, the other day, on the top of Vesuvius, highly delighted and astonished as you may easily imagine. The Volcano was very quiet no fire visible and little smoke; the different views of Naples, Pozzuoli, Baia, Capri etc. etc. are charming and in beauty and extent exceed any view I ever saw . . . Of all my letters from Spain that to the Portuguese Minister has been of most service to me. His civility has been very great indeed and I believe that I may say more than to the generality of English; he never goes to any assembly, without inviting me to go with him and has introduced me not only to all the people of the first fashion but likewise to many houses of the mezza nobleza, which as the Court is out of town is a great resource:

. . . The Princess Francavilla remembers you perfectly and made many enquiries after you.

Naples May 18 1777

. . . I am going tomorrow to Paestum with Sir James Long . . . it is not a very agreeable journey but as being the first Grecian settlement in Italy and the only remains of Grecian architecture it is a very interesting place. The more I see of Naples, the greater is my delight in it: and I rejoice exceedingly in not having been here during the Carnival: for this is by no means too hot a season and the country is infinitely more beautiful than it could have been in January: I do not see Vesuvius in its' greatest rage it is nevertheless a most wonderful object − . . . the great theatre is to be opened on St. Ferdinand's day (the 30th) and the 2nd of June there are to be reviews Comic Operas and Balls at the Palace at Portici for six or seven days; After these festinos I propose going to Rome and staying till the heats drive me out; . . .

Naples May 27 1777

. . . it is impossible to stir out of Naples without receiving the greatest pleasure from the delightful country and climate; I went the other day to the island of Capri with Mr. Swinburne, yesterday to Castel de Mari a most beautiful sea port with Lord Tylney, Sir James and Lady Long and a Dr. Drummond a most sensible and well informed man in every subject and particularly concerning this country: I shall however not stay longer than next week for fear of the heats at Rome coming on before I have finished. The great theatre opens this week and in the next the reviews and festinos at the palace will begin −

Naples June 3 1777

. . . my being still here and the reviews and camps and fêtes being deferred till Saturday my stay will prove much longer than I intended which I by no means regret as I think it is the most agreeable place I have ever been in. The great theatre is open and to my great disappointment the opera is very bad. There is one good singer and he is so excellent that he fills the house notwithstanding the wretchedness of his companions.

. . . foreigners of every denomination are violent Americans and unanimous in thinking us the greatest tyrants imaginable, for which I can not account unless from envy of our unbounded success during the last war, which successes have undoubtedly made many enemies to us in Europe.[85]

Nearby sights such as Baia, Cuma, the Grotta di Cocceio, Pozzuoli, the Solfatara and Vesuvius were one of the great attractions of Naples. At the Solfatara, a still active volcanic area, Lord William Mandeville (1700–39), later 2nd Duke of Manchester, discovered in 1719 that 'the crust of earth upon which one walks, is generally not above a foot thick, and wherever one pierces it, as I did in several places with my sword, there comes out a sulphurous vapour, hot enough to burn one's hands or feet, if in the way'.[86] The Greek remains at Paestum were profoundly influential for the formation of Neo-Classical taste.

British tourists were also attracted to Naples by the foundation of a royal court there after the Spanish conquest in 1734, and by the hospitality of Sir William Hamilton, envoy from 1764–1800. The region was made more interesting by the excavations at Herculaneum and Pompeii, which began in 1738 and 1748 respectively. The discoveries played a major role in the development of European taste, in part thanks to the relative inaccessibility of classical remains in Turkish-ruled Greece and Asia Minor. The German classicist Johann Winckelmann helped to popularize the finds. The response to the excavations varied. Joseph Spence wrote of Herculaneum, which he visited in 1741 when the excavations were still very new:

> I have walked two miles about the streets of it . . . one is obliged to creep almost all the way through narrow passages . . . with two or three smoking flambeaus before you; and I don't see anything really worth seeing, perhaps for half a mile together. It is a journey fitter for a mole, than a man . . . I had much greater pleasure in seeing the collection of pictures, which had been taken out of it.

On the other hand, Spence noted the appeal of the excavations, writing in 1752 of one tourist setting off for 'Naples and the underground town'.[87] Sloane visited the excavations in 1784–5 and wrote from Naples:

> This is also a wonderful place, or rather its' environs are so. The town itself except the great street of Toledo is beastly, but the Quay (on which I live in an excellent hotel with a noble view of the Bay) Mt. Vesuvius which is all red hot every night, Portici, Pausilippum, and the rest of the towns on the sea coasts, form one of the most wonderfully delightful scenes I ever saw. The carnival is now begun, and the town full of plays, masquerades, operas, pickpockets etc.[88]

Southern Italy and Sicily

Though the vast majority of tourists followed predictable routes and visited the same places, a few travelled to other areas: Iberia, Italy south of Naples, eastern Europe, the Balkans and the Baltic. The numbers visiting these areas increased during the century, though they never attained widespread appeal. Roads and facilities for travellers and tourists were generally very poor and sights were less fashionable and apparently fewer.

Italy south of Naples was the most visited of these regions. Many tourists anyway went to Naples, there were many classical sites in southern Italy and Sicily and it was possible to sail to all the major towns. Travel overland was far less easy. In 1772 Philip Francis planned to travel down the east coast of Italy, but he only got as far as Ancona: 'Our original intention was to have crossed the kingdom of Naples in order to avoid the Campania di Roma; but upon inquiry we found that the roads were impracticable, without posts or inns, and the people to the last degree brutal and barbarous. So we took the high road home.'[89]

Of the few that went further, most were interested in classical architecture and archaeology. St George Ashe visited Apulia in the late 1710s, with George Berkeley as his tutor. Berkeley, who was very impressed by the Baroque architecture of Lecce, which he attributed in part to the influence of classical Greek culture, went on to visit Sicily, including the 'Valley of the Temples' at Agrigento. John, Lord Burdenell (1735–70) went to Paestum and such remote sites as Taranto and Agrigento in the late 1750s. Sir William Young (1749–1815) visited Apulia and Calabria in 1772, Sir Richard Colt Hoare (1758–1838) visited classical sites on his second continental tour nearly twenty years later. In 1819 Hoare published *A Classical Tour through Italy and Sicily.*

Sicily could be reached by sea from Naples or Rome. Distance ensured that relatively few tourists visited the island, which had a semi-civilized reputation. Messina was the last city in western Europe to have an outbreak of the plague, in 1747. John, 4th Earl of Sandwich (1718– 92), toured the Mediterranean by sea in 1738–9, visiting Sicily, Greece, Turkey, Rhodes, Cyprus, Egypt and Malta.[90] William Dowdeswell and Sir William Gordon visited Sicily in the mid-1740s, on a trip that also took them to Greece. Sir William Stanhope MP (1702–72) went from Naples to Sicily in 1754. On his second trip to Italy, Richard Payne Knight (1750–1824) visited Sicily in 1777, while Charles Sloane toured the island and climbed Etna in 1785, reaching the crater at dawn, having walked eight miles over the snow.[91] Sir James Hall (1761–1832) was also in Sicily in 1785, though he was 'stormstay'd' a week in Stromboli on the way there. This probably did not bother him as he was very interested in geological questions, especially the formation of volcanoes, and, to that end, studied rocks in Scotland, the Alps, Italy and Sicily.[92] Henry, 10th Earl of Pembroke (1734–94), another visitor to Sicily in the mid-1780s, went on by sea to Gibraltar and Lisbon. Towards the end of an epic journey that had taken him from Vienna through the Balkans to Constantinople (Istanbul), and thence to Cyprus, Crete and Greece, John Hawkins in February 1788 underwent a month's quarantine at Messina on his way from Zante to Naples.[93] Brand accompanied Lord Bruce to the island four years later. Their voyage from Naples to Palermo in 'nearly a perfect calm' took three and a half days. From Palermo they took a trip to the classical remains at Segesta, before moving on towards Messina. Lord Bruce climbed Etna. Brand was unimpressed by the quality of Sicilian roads and of accommodation outside the cities: 'There is not a wheel in the whole country, the roads are mere paths for a single mule and the few huts scattered round are as bad as Hottentot kraals . . . we are sick of Sicilian roads and accommodation.' Brand wrote of the road to Segesta, 'it is rugged and precipice or mud'.[94] Soon after, Hoare visited the island and Malta.

Sardinia never enjoyed the vogue that Paoli's resistance to French occupation brought to Corsica, and it lacked important classical sites. Greater interest in southern Italy in the second half of the century produced a limited number of guidebooks and journals. The most important was Henry Swinburne's *Travels in the Two Sicilies in the Years 1777, 1778, 1779, and 1780*, a work published in 1783–5 that described Sicily and southern Italy. Swinburne (1743–1803), the fourth son of Sir John Swinburne of Capheaton Hall, Northumberland, was a Catholic educated in a monastic seminary in France, who was well-received in the courts of Paris and Vienna. Also author of *Travels through Spain in the Years 1775 and 1776* (1779), he played an important role in spreading information about travel in southern Europe. A different perspective was offered by Patrick Brydone, a bearleader, who in 1775 published his *Tour through Sicily and Malta*. The following year *A Voyage to Sicily and Malta* by John Dryden was published. This journey had been made by the poet's second son in 1700. In 1792 Brian Hill's *Observations and Remarks in a Journey through Sicily and Calabria in the Year 1791* appeared.

Despite this greater interest, most tourists still turned back at Naples. The variety of sights around the city provided tourists with lots to see and what was known of facilities for travellers further south provided little encouragement for tourism.

THE LOW COUNTRIES

If the majority of tourists who landed at Calais rushed south to Paris, a number travelled east. Some, such as Catherine, Duchess of Queensberry in 1734 and William Pulteney, 1st Earl of Bath (1684–1764) in 1763, travelled to Spa in the Ardennes, the most popular continental watering place for British tourists. There were nearly a hundred 'English gentlemen and ladies there' in August 1732.[95] The route to Spa was a good one, along excellent roads through Brussels to Liège, although from Liège the road deteriorated. It was possible to continue from Spa into Germany (the Holy Roman Empire), travelling through Aix-la-Chapelle (Aachen) to Cologne. Another route from the Channel ports ran through Lille, Rheims and Laon to Lorraine, where Nancy and the academy at Lunéville attracted tourists. Some tourists went no further,[96] but others passed on to Strasbourg and thence into Germany, or to Switzerland. From Calais, Ostend and Helvoetsluys, it was possible to tour the Low Countries and then enter Germany, to travel either up the Rhine towards Munich, Innsbruck and Italy, or eastwards across Westphalia, first to Hanover, and then to all or some of Berlin, Leipzig and Dresden, before travelling on through Prague and Vienna to Italy.

The Low Countries were a thoroughfare, but for many tourists they were also a goal in themselves. After Paris and Italy, they offered the third most important group of places visited by British tourists. Although the Low Countries might appear as a minor detour from the Grand Tour, they were very important to many tourists, not least those whose travels were restricted to the area, generally with the important addition of Paris. An extensive literature dealt with travel in the Low Countries.

Austrian Netherlands

The two states in the Low Countries formed a ready contrast and tourists frequently noted the differences between the Protestant United Provinces and the Catholic Austrian Netherlands. Public religiosity was especially noticeable in the latter and it struck Matthew Arnot in 1742:

> About a mile before you arrive at Brussels, on the right hand of the way, are placed the statues of the 12 apostles, at about 120 yards distance from each other. They are placed in a kind of house, grated with iron. But what the apostles have to do on the high road, I own myself at a loss to tell. The Roman Catholics cram every hole and corner with saints, whom the ignorant people worship with much devotion.

Another tourist, visiting Antwerp in 1758, remarked on the 'saints and crucifixes at the corner of almost every street'.[97] Arnot was impressed by Brussels:

> Both nature and art seem here to conspire for making this place all that can be agreeable and desirable by man. The situation is extremely pleasant, upon the gentle declivity of a hill, watered by the Sinne, and other rivers, and springs. The buildings, both public and private, are grand, and lofty; the streets, neat and regular, the company, genteel and polite, and, to all these, it stands in one of the most delightful countries the world affords.

Other tourists, such as Thomas Pelham, were also impressed by Brussels.[98] Although the Austrian Netherlands was largely a thoroughfare, most frequently between northern France and the United Provinces, that did not prevent tourists from receiving impressions. Randle Wilbraham crossed, en route to Aachen and Germany, in late 1793. Landing at Ostend, he travelled via Ghent to Brussels, 'after stopping in our way at Alost to see a famous picture in the Church'. He spent two days and three nights, on two of which he went to the theatre, in Brussels. Rain ensured that some of this was spent at the (indoor) tennis court, but Wilbraham also toured the convents and churches:

> that of St. Gudule attracted chiefly our notice. The outside makes indeed but an indifferent appearance, but within it is *vraiment superbe*; the aweful gloom occasioned by beautiful painted glass, the magnificence of the altar and of the Chapelle du Sacrament, together with the solemnity of their delightful church music (for the priests were at that time performing High Mass) had such an effect upon me that (for a few moments) I could have almost become a Roman Catholic.[99]

United Provinces

The United Provinces, in contrast, was a Protestant state.[100] Tourists spent most of their time in the province of Holland, generally travelling further afield only if they were on their way to or from another destination. Leyden was the university where most British students educated there studied. However, some tourists did tour more remote parts of the country. In 1717 Charles, 3rd Duke of Queensberry (1698–1778), wrote to John, 4th Marquis of Tweeddale (d. 1762):

> I hope the friendship we have contracted at Utrecht will remain as long as we live, and that your Lordship will do me the honour to reckon me among your friends . . . I am sorry you did not go as far as Rosendael, for you would have seen a very pretty place; for my part, I imagined myself transported into some enchanted castle, and it appeared the better for our having travelled over a very wild country thither, not having seen a man or a house all the way, which indulged my melancholy prodigiously. The prospect of Nimeguen diverted me pretty well.[101]

The scenery in Holland evoked different responses. Philip Yorke MP (1720–90), later 2nd Earl of Hardwicke, compared it in 1749 to the Isle of Ely, and wrote that the 'neatness and cleanliness in their towns, and even in the smallest villages strikes one extremely'.[102] On the other hand, three years later William, 4th Earl of Essex (1732–99) hoped

never to return this way again as I do not admire this country as much as most people do . . . I have not seen anything like a handsome prospect . . . The insolence of the common people in general is worse than ever I saw or heard of in my life. The Country would be much handsomer if with the verdure of the meadows there was some corn mixed with it . . . What are their gardens? Parterres and terrasses with regular walks surrounded with hedges cropped equally at bottom and top, all is art and nothing natural.[103]

On a different note, Arnot found Amsterdam 'very grand, but . . . the canals in summer time, stagnate, and stink abominably', while in 1758 those in The Hague were 'dirty and offensive', the sort of impression that a picture could not convey. Yet, Holland was more comfortable to tour than most of Europe and Brand was therefore happy to return to it in 1787:

> I am not so much dissatisfied with my return into Holland as I expected. It was my aversion when I saw it immediately after England but when one has made the vast round of France and Germany . . . it is really delightful to see what industry and perseverance will do to make a country rich and fertile and in the article of meat, drink and lodging we are infinite gainers. I have a bed here which I can sleep in diagonally . . . We are no longer starved upon liver and brains as in Italy or crammed with sour crout [sauerkraut] and stinking sausages as in Germany.[104]

There was much of interest to see in the major towns: artistic treasures, institutions, such as poor-houses and houses of correction, churches. The major civic buildings of Amsterdam had considerable grandeur. Amsterdam City Hall was the largest civic building in Europe when completed in about 1600. It was interesting to watch and listen to the religious services of a number of sects and faiths, and travelling between towns on the canals could be very pleasant. The United Provinces, however, lacked the thrill of Italy or Paris, the grandeur of the classics, the lure of the sun.

THE EMPIRE (GERMANY)

The number of British tourists who visited the Empire increased during the century. This owed much to the greater inherent interest and importance of Germany, as well as to greater adventurousness in routes to and from Italy. Culturally, Germany lacked the current and historical appeal of Italy, although its musical life was flourishing. Politically, the presence of several important courts provided a focus for tourists.

Accommodation and transport were worse than in France, but better than in eastern Europe. The role of courts in tourism in Germany, and the greater amount of time required if it was to be incorporated into an itinerary, ensured that there were fewer and, on average, more exalted tourists than in the Low Countries and Paris.

Hanover

The Electorate of Hanover had been visited by very few British tourists in the late seventeenth century. Its subsequent popularity owed everything to the accession of the Hanoverian dynasty to the British throne in 1714. Thereafter, British tourists visited the court at Hanover, though the rest of the Electorate was ignored, as was generally the case with tourism in Germany, concentrating as it did on major courts, with the sometime addition of Leipzig. George I and George II revisited Hanover frequently, though George III (1760–1820) never went there. It was the royal presence that encouraged British tourists eager for patronage or concerned to appear loyal. John Hervey (1696–1743), later Queen Caroline's confidante and Lord Privy Seal, was sent to Hanover in 1716 to ingratiate himself with Prince Frederick, the son of George, Prince of Wales (the future George II). Frederick had been left there as a pledge of the dynasty's continued loyalty to their native land. Hervey's father, the Earl of Bristol, wrote to him, 'when you see and are sure the foundation in Prince Frederick's favour . . . is laid as indelibly as you know I would have it . . . you may think of returning homewards'. The 1st Duke of Manchester hoped that his son, William, Lord Mandeville, would benefit from his stay by acquiring a knowledge of German that could be useful. George I's visit to Hanover in 1716 was matched by that of the sons of the Dukes of Bolton, Kent and St Albans, and by John Clavering (1698–1762), who complained of his reception there.[105] Edward Finch's (c. 1697–1771) search for preferment led him from an Italian trip to Hanover in 1723, while the Marquis of Carnarvon (1708–71), later 2nd Duke of Chandos, visited it on his way home in 1727 in order to solicit the post of Lord of the Bedchamber to Prince Frederick, an apparent prelude to future influence. He succeeded in his goal. Lord Strathnaver (1708–1750) was told to do the same by his grandfather. Charles Fane (after 1708–66) was advised by his father in 1727, that 'it would be both pleasant and proper to go to Hanover to pay his court to the Prince of Wales', a course of action decried by Sarah, Duchess of Marlborough, a noted critic of the Hanoverians.[106] The 4th Earl of Essex 'found a great many English' in Hanover in 1752, the year of George II's penultimate visit.[107] In 1785 Sir Grey Cooper sought to turn the presence in Hanover of the Duke of York, a son of George III, to some advantage. He decided that his son should return from Vienna to London via Berlin,

Hanover, Brussels and Ostend, and he wrote to Sir Robert Murray Keith, the envoy in Vienna, 'If you will honour him with a letter to his Royal Highness the Duke or to General Grenville, his reception at Hanover will repay him for his deviation from his road, and perhaps may procure him the distinction of being the bearer of any letters which his Royal Highness may at the time of his arrival have occasion to convey to London.'[108]

The reception of British tourists at Hanover was not always good. Lords Nassau Powlett and Burford complained of their treatment in 1716, Lord Gage was denied access to the court in 1723, and George II was very rude to noble tourists in 1750. Lord Nuneham found the court far from entertaining.[109] And yet other tourists praised their reception, Nicholas Clagett, Richard Pococke, John Baring and Sacheverell Stevens finding courtesy and hospitality.[110]

No British monarch visited Hanover after 1755, and the need for noble tourists to visit the town diminished. The number of tourists, however, remained high. This reflected the increased popularity of Germany for British tourists in the second half of the century, both as an end in its own and en route to and from Italy. Tourists who followed, or hoped to follow, a military career wanted to visit Berlin, Magdeburg or Silesia, the locations of the Prussian military reviews. In 1787 Captain John Barker, having attended reviews at Berlin, Potsdam and Magdeburg, visited Brunswick and Hanover on his way back to Britain. Lord Westcote's son met Colonel Charles Gordon in Silesia in 1787 while visiting the battlefield of Leuthen, and returned home via Hanover. Sir James Murray attended the Austrian reviews, and the Hon. Charles Stuart (1753–1801), an MP and half-pay lieutenant-colonel, those of Prussia and Austria.[111]

Saxony

Hanover also benefited from the growing popularity of Dresden and Vienna. In the first half of the century few British tourists visited Saxony. Charles Cottrell was in Dresden in June 1741, but his route was a highly unusual one for the first half of the century. He sailed to St Petersburg and then travelled by land to Königsberg (Kaliningrad), Dresden, Pressburg (Bratislava), Vienna, Munich, Basle and the United Provinces.[112] In 1751–2 Lord North (1732–92), the future 'Prime Minister', and his step-brother, William, 2nd Earl of Dartmouth (1731–1801), later Secretary of State for the Colonies, attended lectures at Leipzig. Dartmouth liked Leipzig, though he did not approve of all the social customs:

> This is a week of diversion . . . we dined one day in a tent with a large company of gentlemen and ladies, for the most part neither young nor handsome; as very few of them could talk anything but German, it

was disagreeable enough. There were no dishes set upon the table, they were all carved without and sent round one by one, so that we were 3 hours at dinner, though we had not above half a dozen dishes: in the meantime bumper glasses came round to loyal healths, but everybody filled as they pleased, and there were none that seemed inclined to drink to excess. When these were over a long German sentence came round for toast, which I did not in the least understand, but as soon as the first gentleman had drank it, to my great surprise, he got up, went round the table and kissed all the ladies. I happened to sit next so had no time to deliberate, but was obliged to follow his example; not without some reluctance; the weather was hot, and it was sad clammy work. The novelty of the thing surprised me, and the indecency of it shocked me; however agreeable it might prove in particular cases, I never wish to see the custom prevail in England.

George Yonge also studied in Leipzig, though he found the town dull. In early 1752 North and Dartmouth visited Dresden:

We spent a fortnight in a sort of little London, in a continual hurry of amusements; as they have no public diversions any part of the year except during the carnival, which begins upon twelfth-day and ends upon Shrove-Tuesday, they make all the use of that time that is possible and crowd diversions, upon the back of another, every day of the week, Sunday not excepted . . . We danced a great deal, and have been at 3 balls of a night. I did not expect to see English country dances so well danced, out of England; but I find they are universally esteemed and practiced in all the courts of Europe.[113]

Dartmouth and North travelled on to Vienna and Rome. In the second half of the century an increasing number of tourists visited Saxony, and, in particular, Dresden. The beautification of the city and the purchase of the bulk of the Duke of Modena's collection of Italian paintings attracted tourists. Dresden was less forbidding than Berlin and more cosmopolitan then either Berlin or Hanover. Brand was very impressed by the paintings in 1787, though less so by the entertainments:

. . . a beautiful town with a magnificent bridge over the Elbe with sentinels who make you go on one side and come back on the other, a restraint that Englishmen are very refractory about. I must own I never had so violent a desire to walk up and down the same side of a bridge in my life . . . we expected to have found much amusement and gaiety at Dresden but we had not a single invitation anywhere and there was not so much as a theatre.

Five years later he found Dresden 'full of English boys',[114] while the British envoy a month earlier noted the presence of nine tourists.

Berlin

Berlin was visited by relatively few British tourists prior to the reign of Frederick II 'the Great' (1740–86). John, Marquis of Carnarvon (1703–27), went there in 1723, but his Grand Tour was a long one beginning in 1721, and his preference for transalpine, rather than Italian, travels was unusual. Richard Bentley (1708–82) and his wife visited Brunswick, Gotha and Berlin in the winter of 1735–6. Berlin became more interesting during Frederick's reign, and in the interwar years of 1748–56, and then again after 1763 the number of British tourists rose. Robert Lowth went there in 1748: 'This is a very large and a very fine town: the palace is truly magnificent, the public buildings in general are handsome and in good taste; the streets spacious and well-built, especially the new town . . . you would wonder how ever they are supplied with provisions, if you were to see the country round about, which is a deep sand.'

Other visitors of this period included Thomas Steavens in 1748, and Lord North and the Earl of Dartmouth in 1752.[115] Berlin was a relatively short detour from Dresden, and a possible journey from Hanover, and the increasing popularity of those destinations encouraged trips there. The energetic traveller, Nathaniel Wraxall (1751–1831), found Berlin and Potsdam unattractive in 1777:

> The diversions of Berlin are mean. A very indifferent French Comedy and a German one with a weekly ball and concert in winter form all they have, except in the carnival during the King's stay, when His Majesty has operas and ridottos at his own expence . . . I saw few beautiful women – very few; but they are polite, easy, and well bred. I think it a magnificent, but not an agreeable city . . . To a soldier the first city in the world, to an individual deficient in those spectacles and amusements common in capitals, and consequently, after the charm of novelty has ceased, dull and unpleasant . . . Notwithstanding these superb palaces and gardens, with everything which art and expense have united to effect about Potsdam, the environs are destitute of any beauty or charm . . . There is a kind of gloomy grandeur and sombre magnificence which strikes, but does not pleasingly affect the mind – no marks of plenty, population, agriculture, or rural happiness are seen.[116]

Randle Wilbraham found the court more lively and welcoming in 1794 and left 'delighted with the civilities we had met with'. He set off for Dresden and Vienna: 'Our route lay through a flattish sandy country covered in a great measure with forests of fir, the blackness of which, contrasted with the snow which lay upon the ground, had a very fine effect, in one of the clearest moonlight nights I ever remember, during the whole of which we travelled.'[117]

William Lee, who visited Vienna, Dresden, Berlin, Hanover, Kassel, Frankfurt, Mannheim and Stuttgart in 1753, wrote on his departure from Germany:

> I have now finished my tour in Germany which I am very glad to have made but should not choose to begin it again. I have seen many things to admire some that have excited my displeasure, others contempt. The Germans in general are a good natured people, hospitable and generous, lovers of pomp and magnificence. I would not look for French vivacity, Italian cunning or English good sense amongst them. Take them as you find them and a traveller may pass his time very well amongst them. I speak of the German nation in general.[118]

Bohemia

The route from Saxony to Vienna went through Bohemia, initially through the hazardous Elbe gorge. Outside Prague accommodation was poor, as William Bentinck wrote to his mother in early 1727:

> This is the best country in the world to use one's self to hardness. Indeed in the towns one meets with pretty good houses now and then, but in all the villages, one must lie upon straw, very often stinking, because there is no fresh to be had, and when with a great deal ado, you have got one truss, if you ask for a second, they stare at you, like mad, being not used to so much magnificence. Add to that bugs and fleas, and the vermin that grows in the straw, and it will make a very pretty bed, but I have one suit of cloaths, which is condemned to serve me upon the road, which is already dirty as it can be and in that I lie down and sleep as comfortably as in a bed. In the beginning I did not like it a bit, but now, I do not mind it.[119]

Bohemian roads were not particularly good, though, as in most of Europe, they improved during the century. Most tourists spent very little time in Prague, though those that did pass a few days there tended to like the city. Randle Wilbraham, however, was unimpressed in early 1794: 'a large and dirty town, the streets are narrow, the houses high and ugly. The churches, which in most Roman Catholic cities are the chief objects of attention, are highly magnificent.'[120]

Vienna

In the Habsburg capital, on the other hand, tourists tended to stay for more than a few days. In the seventeenth century Vienna had not been an especially impressive town. Prague had competed with it as an imperial centre at the beginning of the century, the Austrian Habsburgs had been less powerful than their Spanish cousins, and Vienna had been a frontier town, actually besieged by the Turks in 1683. The years 1683 to 1720 had, however, witnessed a revolution in the fortunes of the Austrian Habsburgs. The Turkish siege of 1683 had been smashed, and subsequent victories in the conflict that lasted until 1699 and in the subsequent Austro-Turkish war of 1716–18 had given the Habsburgs modern Hungary and much of modern Romania, Croatia and Serbia, including Belgrade. The War of the Spanish Succession, in which the Austrians fought the French in 1701–14, had left them with the Duchies of Milan and Mantua (modern Lombardy), the Spanish, now Austrian Netherlands (Belgium and Luxemburg), the kingdom of Naples and the island of Sardinia. Success in conflict with Spain (1717–20) left Austria the dominant power in Italy, and able to exchange unprofitable Sardinia for the more important island of Sicily.

Political and military success were matched by ambitious building and the Vienna of Charles VI (1711–40) took on an imperial appearance with dramatic buildings such as the Karlskirche and the Upper Belvedere. An obvious foil to Louis XIV's France, Austria had also emerged as a great power and an active partner of Britain, jointly fighting France in 1689–97, 1702–13 and 1743–8, and Spain in 1718–20 and 1741–8. British tourists were generally assured of a good welcome. Opinions of the city and its society, however, varied greatly. Robert, 4th Earl of Sunderland, informed his grandmother, Sarah Marlborough, in 1722, 'Though this place is not usually the most agreeable in the world to strangers, yet for my part I can't complain of it, for everybody has showed me a vast deal of civility here.' In 1735 the 2nd Duke of Grafton was not sure that his son, Lord Euston, would benefit from a visit to Vienna: 'it is just come into mind that Vienna and what our young man will see there will not be a great addition to his education'. Thomas Robinson, who had been envoy there since 1730, observed in 1741: 'Society here is most dull and inanimate. Few men are to be found, and though one resolves to pass time well, it all amounts at last to eating and drinking, cheering the mere animal which is true Austrian life.'[121] Brand wrote in 1792, 'I wish I were away from Vienna. Here are but two or three English . . . and they are of a bad sort. They are of the two idea sort. The bottle is one.'[122] The etiquette and ceremony of the court and of Viennese society were attacked by travellers. In 1786 Keith informed the

Marquis of Lansdowne that his son, John, Earl Wycombe (1765–1809), later 2nd Marquis, and Wycombe's companion, Major Green, had not enjoyed their stay: 'I am afraid that from the stiffness of Austrian manners and the cold uninteresting style of conversation which prevails here, their stay at Vienna has, in point of amusement as well as of instruction, fallen short of their expectation, as well as of my wishes.'[123] Eight years later, Randle Wilbraham found the British envoy more welcoming than the Austrian aristocracy:

> . . . have been able to procure billets for public balls amongst the principal noblesse where the company is very select and where you become acquainted very pleasant. Sir Morton Eden has been extremely civil to us. We have dined twice with him . . . We have been introduced to several of the foreign ambassadors . . . the Germans themselves do the honours of Vienna to strangers as ill as the English do at London than which nothing can be worse excepting in some few instances. In short there is scarcely any private society to be met with for though there are men of immense fortunes as the Princes Esterhazy, Liechtenstein and Schwarztenberg . . . yet scarcely any of it is spent in keeping house, but most part in their stables . . . without even promoting gaiety at their own houses, which in their fathers time used to be open to foreigners and where, as now in Russia, a single invitation gave you the entree wherever you were disposed to go. Now however the age of hospitality is past and the town is divided into colonies, *à la Angloise* into which it would be extremely difficult to get introductions and which be only pleasant after one had become very intimate and that must be a work of longer time than travellers can allow for.[124]

Others praised the city. The 4th Earl of Essex enjoyed the carnival in early 1752, going to masquerades twice weekly, as did Harry Digby, who also went to the theatre and had his portrait painted.[125] Lady Craven visited it in December 1785 and was delighted by the affability of Viennese women and the range of food available: large crawfish, delicious pheasants, artichokes and asparagus. Though the number of British tourists to Vienna increased during the century, it never approached the figure for Paris. Vienna involved a longer and more expensive journey, while its court society did not attract non-aristocratic travellers. Lord Torrington, envoy in Brussels, claimed in 1786 that 'the English who go to Vienna, are a very different and superior class of people to those who come to Brussels, fewer in number and more respectable personages'.[126] The private papers of several of the envoys in Vienna, Waldegrave (1728–30), Robinson (1730–48) and Keith (1772–92), underline the increase in the number of tourists. In 1788 Lord Townshend could refer to 'the Vienna Club' in London, a group of friends who had enjoyed Keith's hospitality. Interest in Austria was increased by Joseph II's policies, and the improved facilities for travellers, especially roads which owed something to Charles VI's sponsorship of the Trieste Company, encouraged more tourists to travel to or from Italy via Vienna. To a certain extent the German alternative, the route to Italy that did not go through France, became less a matter of the Rhineland, Frankfurt, Munich and Innsbruck, and more one of Hanover, Dresden and Vienna. The shift received royal approval, George III telling the Earl and Countess of Courtown in 1783, 'You cannot do better than send your son to Vienna.' The son, Lord Stopford, had a hectic social time there. His bearleader Samuel Pohl sent reports home:

November 2 His Lordship took a ride with Sir James Hall, and Mr. Stratton *secretaire d'ambassade d'Angleterre*; returned at one, Mylord dressed and went with Sir Robert Keith to dinner at Prince Coloredo, came back at five, drinked tea, went to the play, and then to assemblys.
November 3 dined at home, from the traiteur, and went to the Italian Opera.
November 4 Lord Stopford rose early, went to breakfast with Sir James Hall and Mr. Stratton, from thence to the grand hunt with the Emperor at Hamersdorf; they came back by two; had not hunted above an hour, when they killed the stag. Lord Stopford dined with Sir James, came home to dress, went to the Comedie, and then to the Venetian Ambassadeur to supper, came home a little after 12.[127]

BALKANS

Hardship faced those who travelled beyond a line of Berlin, Dresden, Prague, Vienna and Trieste. The Balkans attracted very few British tourists in the first half of the century, and men such as Sir Francis Dashwood and Henry, 3rd Earl of Radnor, both of whom were in Vienna in October 1730, could be described as intrepid travellers, as much as tourists. Dashwood had travelled from Constantinople to Warsaw in 1729, while in 1730 Radnor went from Vienna to Constantinople. The Austrian war minister Prince Eugene, companion of arms to the Duke of Marlborough during the War of the Spanish Succession, gave Radnor letters to the governors of the Austrian garrison towns of Buda and Belgrade, and Radnor proceeded by boat to Belgrade, mooring in the middle of the river each night in order to prevent an attack by brigands. One night, a waterman was mistaken for a brigand by Radnor's companion, Mr

Green, while the latter was on watch, and shot. This led to a two-day delay at Buda while the matter was adjusted. Having left Vienna on 25 October, Radnor reached Belgrade on 10 November and Constantinople on 19 December 1730. The journey so tired him that he had to spend five days in bed, and thereafter, according to the British envoy, he saw very little before he sailed for Smyrna in February 1731. Sailing on via Malta, Radnor reached Leghorn on 12 April, John Swinton there recording:

> His Lordship says that all the way from Belgrade to Constantinople he met with but very indifferent treatment amongst the Turks who inhabited that track of land, who are mortal enemies to the Christians (which I suppose may in some measure be owing to the ravages of the Germans in the late war) so that they extorted from him extravagant and immense sums of money, and yet treated him with the greatest insolence, and accommodated his lordship with nothing scarce proper for him. His lordship says that in his opinion Constantinople is larger than London, but withall a concourse of all nations, and so filthy and dirty that in that respect it exceeds all the cities he ever saw.[128]

Travelling to the Aegean by sea, as Viscount Charlemont did from Leghorn in 1749, offered a far more attractive route, though cost and other difficulties closed the option to most tourists. In 1741–2 John Manners, Marquis of Granby (1721–70), extended the European tour he had taken after leaving Cambridge to include Greece and the Aegean. Accompanied by his former Eton tutor, John Ewer, who he had already presented to a richly-endowed rectory and who was to become Bishop of Bangor, Granby made much of the Aegean tour in a large Turkish boat called a volique. He explored Greece ancient and modern, the classical accounts of Strabo and Pliny as present as the Greek dancing that Granby enjoyed. While in the Aegean, Granby, who was to be a hero of the Seven Years War and to become Commander-in-Chief, was elected MP for Grantham.

An increasing number of travellers visited the Balkans in the second half of the century, in part thanks to the Austro-Turkish peace of 1739–87. Some were on their way back from India, as was Lord William Murray in 1787. Two years earlier Sir Robert Ainslie, ambassador at Constantinople, wrote to Keith to introduce three officers on their way back from India, who had come overland from Basra to Aleppo and then sailed via Smyrna. Ainslie sent Keith letters of introduction on the same day for a civilian returning from India and for a member of the Turkey Company. Later in the year he sent one for Willey Reveley, an artist who had accompanied Sir Richard Worsley Bt. on his travels.[129] An indefatigable traveller, Worsley (1751–1805) visited Iberia, Asia Minor, Greece and Russia in the 1780s, meeting two other similar travellers, Lady

Craven (1750–1828) and Charles Sloane, later 1st Earl Cadogan of the second creation, in Constantinople in 1785. In February 1785 Worsley had left Rome for Athens. From there he toured Greece and visited Rhodes, Cairo and Constantinople. In 1786 he travelled to Troy and the Crimea. By the time of his return to Rome in April 1787 he had accumulated a large collection of statues, reliefs and gems.

Separated because her husband had found her in bed with the French ambassador in 1773, Lady Craven found it convenient to spend much time out of Britain, as did a number of other women with controversial pasts, such as Margaret Rolle, the wife of the 2nd Earl of Orford, Elizabeth Chudleigh, Dowager-Duchess of Kingston (1720–88) after her bigamy was proved in the House of Lords in 1776, Lady Ligonier after her adultery was exposed in 1771, and, later, the Prince Regent's wife Caroline. Chudleigh, who died in Paris, travelled independently in Germany, before her marriage to the 2nd Duke of Kingston, getting badly drunk at the marriage of Frederick the Great's heir in 1765. Lady Craven made an impressive journey in 1785–6 from Vienna through Cracow, Warsaw, St Petersburg, Moscow and the Crimea to Constantinople, a trip greeted with inaccurate scandalous tales of her actions in Athens and smutty sneers in such papers as the *World* of 3 January 1787. From there she toured the Aegean before returning to Vienna via Varna, Bucharest and Transylvania. She benefited greatly from her connections, not least through obtaining the assistance of British diplomats, and in 1789 published her *Journey through the Crimea to Constantinople*, but by then war had blocked the route. Russia and Turkey were at war from 1787 to 1792, Austria and Turkey from 1788 to 1791. At Ansbach, Lady Craven met the Margrave. They lived together until her husband's death in 1791 allowed her to marry him. The Margrave sold his principality to the King of Prussia in 1792 and they moved to England. He died in 1806, his widow at Naples in 1828.

Sloane visited Hungary, Poland, Egypt, Cyprus and Greece, leaving an account of his lengthy travels in a series of letters to his brother. His journey from Vienna to Constantinople in the summer of 1785 took six weeks and 'though I far prefer our manners and customs to those of the people of this country, yet the sudden change could not fail of being interesting on account of its novelty. The country between Belgrade and this affords nothing very interesting on account either of its beauty or fertility, but Hungary and its gold and silver mines are hardly to be paralleled.'[130]

Very few British tourists visited the kingdom of Hungary, which then included Croatia, Slovakia and Translyvania. The majority who made the journey did so as an excursion from Vienna. This was true of Lord Granard in 1778 and Earl Wycombe in 1786. Wycombe set off to visit

Belgrade, since 1739 a Turkish fortress again, but found the journey more than he had bargained for. He wrote to Keith from Peterwardein (Novi Sad) of:

> . . . a very fatiguing journey of four and a half days from Pest, through a very fertile country which is at present as disagreeable as incessant rain and bad communications are capable of rendering it. The roads are so much worse than we expected, and the distances from place to place so much greater than we understood they were, that our scheme of seeing Belgrade is likely to cost us more time than we originally intended to bestow upon it . . . Wherever we have been we have met with the most hospitable and gracious reception imaginable.

Four days later, Wycombe's travelling companion, Major Green, wrote from Semlin that they were unable to cross the River Sava because of very contrary winds.[131] Wycombe's illegitimate half-brother Petty, who travelled with his wife and daughter, was more adventurous, crossing the Carpathians from Transylvania to Bucharest in 1784,[132] though the footloose Wycombe was himself to add the newly-independent United States to his list of travels.

The Hungarian mines attracted visitors. Randle Wilbraham saw them in 1794

> to great advantage having brought letters from Vienna to the director who showed us every process from the first digging the materials out of the mine to the purifying and coining the gold. We went down one to the depth of above 600 feet to see a water machine consisting of 3 wheels the diameters of which are 36 feet, the erection of this you will easily conceive to have been a stupendous undertaking, upon considering that such a distance underground the solid rock has been excavated to receive it. After staying a week amongst the mines we departed highly delighted with what we had seen.

Later in the year he travelled from Vienna to Constantinople, via Buda and Temesvar, but he was obliged to leave the usual route via Belgrade there:

> Servia being infested by robbers and a little infected by the plague, travellers were obliged to follow a different route to proceed east to Hermanstadt [Sibiu] in Transylvania and from thence by Bucharest to Turkey. We accordingly set out . . . the country changed and became much pleasanter on account of the inequality of ground and the appearance of woods which sight we had not enjoyed for a long time. One evening late we passed through a very thick forest where for the

first time in my life I saw glowworms flying about in great numbers which had a very curious and pretty effect. After travelling 3 or 4 days we arrived at Hermanstadt where we were obliged to make a little stop on account of passports, being there near the frontier of the Emperor's dominions. From hence we passed through the defiles of the Wallachian mountains which are beyond description beautiful, and made us ample amends for the ugliness of the country we had travelled through to arrive at them.[133]

The Revd Robert Stockdale, who travelled from Vienna to Constantinople via Belgrade and Edirne (Adrianople) that summer, noted on 16 July, 'we passed the first impalement we had seen but it was very old, and did not strike one with those feelings of horror which a more recent execution produces . . . [more like] . . . an old gibbet in England'. John Hawkins (c. 1758–1841), a Cornish gentleman interested in mineralogy, pressed on from the Hungarian mines to Constantinople, though his journey was not an easy one, as he reported to Keith:

> stayed several days at Semlin and have been more than usually delayed by the badness of the roads and the severity of the season . . . I was detained four days at Belgrade until the roads became passable and with difficulty reached Nissa [Nish] in seven days. Instead of accompanying the mail, I took with me an extra janissary . . . the new commander of Semlin to whom you favoured me with an official letter of recommendation, with much outward civility possesses neither the manners of a gentleman nor even understanding or activity enough to be of the least service to any traveller.[134]

At Constantinople Hawkins joined forces with the botanist Dr John Sibthorp and a Captain Imrie of the army based in Gibraltar. They toured the Greek islands, including Cyprus, and the coasts of Greece and Asia Minor, Sibthorp finding new species and Hawkins boasting 'few men have made a more complete tour of Greece'.[135] Hawkins wrote a number of essays on his travels in the region. Sibthorp, Sherardian Professor of Botany at Oxford, had studied at Montpellier. In 1784 he set off on a botanical expedition to Greece. After receiving a doctoral degree at Göttingen, Sibthorp travelled via Vienna, Trieste, Venice, Bologna, Florence and Rome to Naples. He sailed thence in May 1786 for Crete where he spent much of the summer. Sibthorp then travelled extensively in the region, though a land journey through Greece was rendered impossible in 1787 by insurrection and the outbreak of plague. He nevertheless managed to visit Delphi, Mount Athos and Corinth before returning to England at the end of 1787. In March 1794 Sibthorp set off for Greece again. At Constantinople he was joined by Hawkins, who had come from Crete. They travelled widely in Greece and the Aegean, climbing Olympus, visiting the site of Sparta and being delayed at Mount Athos by nearby pirates. In the spring of 1795 Sibthorp visited the Ionian islands and the nearby coast, before returning home a sick man. On his travels he had collected three thousand species.

The route through Budapest, Belgrade, Nish, Sofia and Adrianople (Edirne) was the usual one between Vienna and Constantinople. Very few British travellers took any other route. Tourists did not cross from the Adriatic to the Aegean: Albania, Macedonia and mainland Greece were visited by very few, though Greece was becoming more popular by the 1780s, and in the following decade signs of Hellenism and Philhellenism, sympathy for Greece ancient and modern, became more frequent. The Romanian principalities of the Turkish empire, Wallachia and Moldavia, were largely unknown and Ainslie was worried by Lady Craven's decision to return through the Carpathians in 1786: 'Lady Craven and Colonel Vernon by the advice of their friends departed . . . by the way of the Black Sea, in a Greek boat for Varna, from whence they intend to proceed, through Moldavia and Wallachia, to Transylvania in their way to Vienna. I hope they will meet with no considerable inconvenience in this new route, which I should not have recommended.'[136]

This route was to be cut the following year by the outbreak of Russo-Turkish hostilities. In eastern Europe the effect of war on travel was more striking than in western Europe, for tourists could not rely on their passports being respected. The irregular forces in eastern Europe, Cossacks, hussars and Tatars, were particularly feared. The Russo-Turkish war of 1768–74 witnessed major conflict in the Danube basin, including the Russian capture of Bucharest, and serious naval conflict in Greek waters. This dissuaded all but the most hardy traveller. In addition, the unsettled nature of the Russo-Turkish border prevented the early development of the Moscow–Constantinople route that was to be used by Lady Craven. This route only appeared reliable after the Russian annexation of the Crimea in 1783. After the Russo-Turkish war of 1787–92, the route seemed possible again, Wilbraham writing in 1794: 'The communication between that country and the south of Russia is very easy and ships continually pass to and fro.'[137]

TURKISH EMPIRE

Difficulties of access restricted tourism both to the Ottoman (Turkish) and Russian empires. In the first half of the century travellers were so rare that their return to Britain merited a mention in the British press; such as that of William Lethieullier who returned in 1723 from the Ottoman Empire with a mummy.[138] He bequeathed it to the British Museum in 1756 with the rest of his collection of Egyptian antiquities. While Constantinople and the European part of the empire was visited by an increasing number of tourists, few visited the Asiatic or African parts. The coast of Asia Minor, Cyprus and Alexandria could all be visited by sea, though they involved longer sea journeys than those in the Aegean. Few ventured inland, while the coast of North Africa west of Alexandria was not welcoming. Privateers based on Algiers and Tripoli were a threat to shipping. In May 1786 Sloane wrote to his brother from Alexandria:

> . . . have had a delightful journey up and down two different branches of the Nile. I went up to Grand Cairo by Damietta, and came down here by Rozetta . . . even to this day everything of consequence still remaining goes under the name of Joseph's . . . I find a rational as well as interesting amusement in surveying the scenes of those actions I had before read of, and comparing the one with the other . . . the barbarians who now inhabit the country continue as they have done for ages to destroy everything of antiquity remaining.

He then returned to Constantinople 'after a delightful tour through Greece, Egypt, and Asia Minor', though his plans for visiting the Levant were curtailed by the plague raging there.[139]

North Africa was rather a sphere for exploration than tourism, although the distinction is not always an easy one. Thomas Shaw (1694–1751), chaplain to the English factory (mercantile community) at Algiers (1720–33), made tours to Egypt, Sinai and Cyprus (1721), Palestine (1722), Tunis and the ruins of Carthage (1727), and, on a number of occasions to 'the interior of Barbary', North Africa, west of Egypt. His *Travels or Observations relating to several parts of Barbary and the Levant* (Oxford, 1738) includes much information on the natural history of the area. Shaw became Principal of St Edmund Hall and Regius Professor of Greek in Oxford. Shaw's book was known by James Bruce (1730–94) who, after the death of his wife in 1754, visited first Iberia and then Italy, where he made the first accurate drawings of the ruins of Paestum, before becoming Consul at Algiers (1763–5). He then spent over a year on an archaeological tour of North Africa, sketching the Roman remains, was shipwrecked on the shore of North Africa and plundered by Arabs, visited the Roman remains at Palmyra and Baalbec, and then travelled via Egypt and the Red Sea to Abyssinia (Ethiopia), whose capital at Gondar he reached in 1770. After becoming fully involved in the murderous internecine politics of the kingdom and visiting his goal, the source of the Blue Nile, Bruce left Gondar in December 1771 and, after a very difficult overland journey through forests and deserts and detention at the hands of the natives for five months, reached Egypt the following November. The barren wastes of the Nubian Desert were far removed from the bright salons of Paris, but Bruce's travels testify, in a marked fashion, to an important element in the tourism of the period – curiosity. The source of the Nile was an unusual goal but tourists wanted to see famed sites, ancient and modern, the ruins of Rome and the splendours of Versailles.

RUSSIA

The route to Russia was far from easy. The overland journey was arduous, as well as being 'stupid' and 'uninteresting'.[140] Edward Finch, who made the journey in 1740 in order to take up his posting as envoy in St Petersburg, wrote from Königsberg (Kaliningrad), 'Courland, at all times a desert country . . . everything necessary for the subsistence of myself and servants must be carried with me, since I am assured that it will be impossible even to find bread and salt in any place nor in many so much as water . . . there is no such thing as posting, so that I am reduced to make use of the same horses . . . from hence to Riga.'[141]

Richard Woodward, however, who travelled overland from St Petersburg to Berlin with Richard Combe in May 1756, reported to the British envoy, 'From Narva the roads and weather were good beyond expectation, the accommodations appeared to us to great advantage, and the journey, though slow, was by your Excellency's care in providing for us so convenient, that it made some amends at least for our wretched expedition through Finland.'

William Willes had taken the same route four years earlier:

After a stay of 8 months at Petersburg I set out from thence about the middle of January with a Russian merchant, and we came upon a sledge as far as Konigsberg; but after having slid over several hundred miles in the most easy and expeditious manner possible we were obliged to take off the sledge from under our coach, and jolt through the rest of our journey upon wheels, the snow not favouring us any farther. Our stages were from Konigsberg to Dantzick, and from thence to Berlin, Dresden and Hanover, and so on to England. In my expedition I had an opportunity of seeing the Russian, Saxon, and Prussian courts, but the former for grandeur and magnificence has (I think) by far the preeminence.[142]

Most tourists preferred to travel by sea to St Petersburg, which Peter I (the Great) had made the capital of Russia. This was the method used by Sir Francis Dashwood in 1733, Lord Baltimore in 1739 and

Charles Cottrell in 1740. A Baltic trip was not, however, without its hazards. John, 20th Earl of Crawford, who sailed to St Petersburg in the late 1730s, recorded the dangers of fog, storm, rocks and bad navigation. Jervis, who went there in 1774, was unimpressed with Baltic seamanship. The journey could be unpleasant. Reginald Pole Carew (1753–1835), later a long-serving MP, wrote from St Petersburg in March 1781 about his passage from Stockholm, 'I was so ill provided with the clothing necessary for this latitude that I was a little pinched by the frost, though I put on my whole wardrobe at once, that is two pair of breeches, two pair of worsted stockings and fur boots upon them, two pair of gloves, two coats, two waistcoats, a greatcoat and a cloak over all and yet I sat shivering.' Most who visited St Petersburg, including Dashwood, Baltimore and Jervis, saw nothing more of Russia.[143] Distances were vast, the next most interesting town, Moscow, was a long way away in a direction in which further travel was not practicable until the Crimean route to Constantinople was opened up. The roads, including the main one to Moscow, were poor and the spring thaw made many impassable. Sledge travel delighted some, such as Lady Craven, but it could only be used during the winter. Yet St Petersburg was different and therefore interesting. Russian customs were certainly unusual, from the practice of the Orthodox church to the bathing which shocked Jervis: 'went to see the baths, which represented such a monstrous scene of beastly women and indecent men mixed together naked as our first parents without the least appearance of shame as to shock our feelings.' William Morton Pitt (1754–1836), later a long-serving MP, visited Russia in 1778. He was arrested in a suburb of Moscow when he came to the aid of his footman who had intervened to help some peasants being beaten up by policemen. Pitt was kept overnight in 'the heat, the smell, the lice, the filth' of a dungeon which he had to share with thieves and deserters.[144]

Most British travellers to Russia went for reasons of employment, busying themselves in trade or in the service of the Romanov dynasty, especially its naval service. An increasing number, however, went as tourists, like Edward Finch's friend Richard Meggot, 'whose curiosity brought him to see this country.'[145]

SCANDINAVIA

The Scandinavian lands saw few tourists. Scandinavia was divided between two ruling houses, that of Denmark, which also ruled Norway, and its Vasa rivals of Sweden, who also ruled Finland. There were, therefore, only two capitals to visit, while as yet there was no real interest in

Nordic scenery or sports. The trip of William Benson at the beginning of the century probably owed much to the fact that his father was a prominent iron merchant and Sweden was Britain's principal source of iron. Lord Clinton visited Copenhagen in the summer of 1727 and having crossed to Sweden journeyed by land to Stockholm where he spent a week. Lord Bruce visited Denmark, Sweden and Russia in the early 1750s, while Lord and Lady Effingham and Lord Howard toured Copenhagen, Stockholm and St Petersburg in 1769.[146] William Morton Pitt spent seven months in Sweden in 1778 taking notes on such matters as the state of agriculture. He also visited Denmark, Finland and Russia. Putting himself forward as an envoy to Stockholm in 1788, he wrote 'I believe no Englishman ever gave so much of his travels to Sweden as I did, or perhaps gave so much of his thoughts to the consideration of the state of that country – I was there seven months, travelled over the greatest part of the kingdom, examined even into the detail of each manufacture, I knew almost every person of any degree of eminence in the country, I was particularly countenanced by the King . . . I did know something of the language.' In 1786 Sir Henry Liddell Bt (1749–91), Matthew Consett and Stoney Bowes sailed from the Tyne on a three-month tour of Sweden, Swedish Lapland, Finland and Denmark, undertaken as a result of a wager by Liddell that he could go to Lapland and return with two reindeer and two Lapp women. He returned with a Lapland sledge, two reindeer (that perished the following winter) and two women, Sigree and Anea, who remained for some time at Ravensworth Castle, where they were considered as great curiosities, before being sent home at Liddell's expense. An interesting journal of the trip written by Consett and with plates by Thomas Bewick was published in 1789.[147] Norway was visited by very few. Poyntz went on a 'northern expedition' to Norway and Sweden in 1761. An astronomical expedition set off for the North Cape to view the transit of Venus in 1769; George Norman travelled in Norway and Russia in 1784.[148] Iceland was exciting tourist interest by the end of the century. John Stanley (1766–1850) went there in 1789, stopping en route at the Faroes. Stanley knew a reasonable amount about Iceland's natural curiosities before he set off and his learned party included the physicist and later astronomer Mark Beaufoy (1764–1827), who in 1787 had been the second person, and first Englishman, to reach the summit of Mont Blanc.[149] Aside from Copenhagen, Denmark received few tourists. Most called at Copenhagen en route to or from the Baltic by sea.

POLAND

Poland was another area that was not popular with tourists. For the British it did not have the cultural resonances or educational facilities of Italy, the Empire and the Low Countries, and was not on the route to any popular destination. During the period 1697–1763, when two successive Electors of Saxony were elected kings of Poland, Poland's court was for much of the time at Dresden. In 1772, 1793 and 1795 the country was partitioned, so that Poland became a geographical expression and a national aspiration rather than a political reality. Facilities for travellers, particularly accommodation, were poor. The diplomat George Woodward claimed in 1729, 'There is not an inn in Poland, that I have yet seen fit to lodge a dog. I'll only compare them to the worst in Westphalia and leave you to judge of them.' In 1785 Petty commented on southern Poland, then Austrian-ruled:

> the wretched inns kept by more wretched Jews, render travelling through this rich country very disagreeable and for several nights we had no other beds than straw laid on the damp floors of the nasty habitations . . . I never saw a finer or richer country than Galicia . . . yet after all the poor miserable cottager almost starves on sour bread and water, even the cabarets on the road, afford nothing to eat, and few of them even beer. The iron hand of oppression seems to reign throughout. Nor is there any encouragement for an inn to be well supplied, as the Poles always carry their own provisions with them, and their beds.

Petty added that his wife and daughters were well, despite 'their difficulties of often going on foot where the badness of the way rendered it dangerous to stay in the carriage and the troops of vermin among these blest abodes of the sons of Israel'.[150] Lady Craven on the other hand left a more positive account later that year. She had Polish friends, was impressed by King Stanislaus Poniatowski and found the journey 'not so very formidable as it is represented'.[151]

Wraxall had been depressed by the Polish countryside, and wrote in 1778:

> Warsaw appears to me to be the most singular and extraordinary capital in Europe. It bears little or no resemblance to any other which I have seen. Instead of those regular streets, that assemblage of citizens and persons of middle life who constitute the bulk of the inhabitants in large cities, Warsaw presents only opulence and misery, magnificence and poverty to the view. Palaces and sheds, hotels and

wretched cottages scarce habitable, intermixed with gardens, open places scarce levelled, and vast interstices unbuilt and unoccupied – such is Warsaw! It seems . . . a picture of the Republic itself, intermediate classes of people common in all other kingdoms, but almost unknown in Poland. In the midst of Warsaw one may suppose oneself in some scattered and half ruined village.

Wraxall found Cracow similarly unimpressive: 'There are no scavengers, or people employed, as in most European cities, to clean the streets. Consequently the dirt and the smells are extremely noisome and inconvenient. The old spouts, now almost disused in England and France, which project into the street, are common.'[152]

Sloane had to spend a long time at Cracow waiting for an eye operation. Poland might have been interesting to contemporaries as an increasingly enlightened country of considerable political importance, but few British tourists went there other than inveterate travellers such as Craven, Petty, Sloane and Wraxall.

SPAIN

Spain was another major European country that received few British tourists. Travel there caused surprise, as Charles, 2nd Duke of Richmond (1701–50), discovered in 1728. Viscount Townshend, Secretary of State for the Northern Department, could not 'well conceive what curiosity should lead his Grace so much out of the usual road of travellers'. Lord Tyrawley, envoy in Lisbon, wrote to Richmond, 'Point du point I think Spain and Portugal excite ones curiosity more than any other countries, as being the least known, and quite out of the Old John Trott beaten, pack horse road of all travellers, and will make you as famous to later posterity as Dampier, Sir John Mandeville, Hacklyut or Fernand Mendez Pinto',[153] all famed travellers. When Theophilus, 9th Earl of Huntingdon (1696–1746), died, the *Gentleman's Magazine* noted 'some part of his younger years he gave to Italy and France, and at last finished his travels with a tour, which few of our nobility, of late years, have had the courage to make, through Spain'. The *Worcester Journal* recorded his inscription, 'He visited France, Italy, and even Spain.' His successor visited Spain in 1752. The number of British travellers to Spain increased later in the century, the envoy William Eden writing in September 1788 that he had presented five or six that day to the royal family, including the peripatetic Earl of Wycombe. An Irish civil servant wintered at Valencia in 1783–4. Thomas Hardy wrote from Malaga in 1786 that poor health had led him 'to elope from one of our northern winters and to seek for summer on the shores of the Mediterranean . . . The climate of this southern coast is certainly the finest in Europe and I am surprised that it is never thought of for the invalids who are sent to shiver in the South of France or in Lisbon.'[154] Travel literature devoted to Spain was published, Swinburne's book appearing in 1779 and Townsend's in 1791.

Spain was not regarded as the most interesting country to visit. Madrid lacked the cosmopolitan, accessible culture of Paris and its society was perceived as dull and reclusive. Language was also a barrier, though most Spanish aristocrats spoke French, that language and Italian being widely used at court, and the Jacobite diaspora ensured that there were many prominent English-speakers. William Vyse was entertained at Valencia in 1769 by an English merchant. Outside Madrid there appeared to be little to see. There was no vogue for the beach, the mountains lacked the splendour and glamour of the Alps, the Roman antiquities were less well known than those of Italy and there was little interest in the Moorish remains. The diplomat William Stanhope wrote from Madrid in July 1718, 'Lord Essex has been with me ten days, which I daresay is long enough to make him repent his expedition.' Stanhope's successor Benjamin Keene described Spain as 'the dullest country in Europe'.[155]

Travellers to and in Spain encountered major difficulties. The journey there by land was very long, involved a passage of the Pyrenees and suffered from poor facilities for travellers. Stanhope complained from Bayonne in 1729 that it was impossible to travel fast in Spain, without going post on horseback, and that if mules were employed the traveller had to use the same set for a hundred leagues.[156]

The alternative approach was by sea, usually to Lisbon, and thence into Spain. Thomas Pelham chose this route in 1775, the Earl of Pembroke in 1786. Pembroke disliked travelling in Spain, a view shared by Arthur Young, who went through Catalonia the following July. Young complained both of 'natural and miserable roads' and of the accommodation, and he was often forced to walk. Sir John Fleming Leicester, who travelled from Perpignan to Barcelona in 1784, found the inns 'wretched' and the journey very slow, but 'extremely fine'.[157]

Two interesting accounts of Spain were left by an anonymous tourist in 1754, who travelled up the east coast from Valencia, and by Thomas Pelham in 1775–6. The traveller in 1754 was thoroughly bitten by mosquitoes and fleas and suffered from shocking roads. At Barcelona, however, he found satisfactory provisions, including 'admirable English beer of 2 or 3 different sorts, good Cheshire cheese'. He went to the opera twice and to a bullfight and visited a Spanish warship.[158]

Pelham stayed for many months in Madrid, where he benefited from the hospitality of the ambassador, Lord Grantham, who had himself toured in France and Italy in 1763. From Madrid, Pelham went on a trip to Andalusia and thence to France, via Granada, Alicante, Valencia and Barcelona. This was a most unusual tour, which he described in letters to his parents. He decided to 'see the south of Spain, which is not only a very interesting tour from its having been the scene of so many transactions in the Roman History and consequently retaining many curious antiquities but likewise as being the most fruitful and commercial part of modern Spain'.

It was necessary to prepare carefully for the journey:

> My bed is repairing, and a boiler is making that may hang under my chaise to boil my dinner, for there are as many precautions to be taken for travelling in this country as if I were going into Arabia: my journey from Lisbon has taught me all the *desagremens* and how many of them are only imaginary ones for after two or three days travelling you fancy your boiled chicken or rabbit better than all the . . . ragouts from a French kitchen.

Setting off for Cordoba in late September 1776, Pelham took a lot of food and a Spanish edition of *Don Quixote*:

> . . . the inns we stop at being the same as those in which he met with so many adventures: the room I am writing in is worthy of one of his castles no window, a hole in the wall that admits light in the day and is stopped up with a board at night, an indifferent door, a large pillar in the middle of the room that supports the roof, and round which we and our servants are to lay down our armour and set up our beds, and the walls naked except where some pedlar has left a few shabby prints.

Pelham found Andalusia 'most delightful', but was delayed at Cadiz by heavy rainfall which swelled the rivers. The same cause held him up at Lorca, while he was unimpressed by the quality of the roads near Gibraltar and Cartagena. Pelham's phlegmatic character enabled him to bear the difficulties of Spanish travel:

> . . . it is really beyond all description but I make it a rule to go into a Pasada without asking any questions, have no wants, and as little intercourse with my landlord as possible who is never satisfied, with what you give him and will cheat whenever he has an opportunity: we buy our own provisions and that for our beasts all which excepting game are as dear and by no means as good as in England. After all this I can assure you with great truth that I never felt the least annoy or uneasiness, for the want of conveniences in the inns makes one more

active in providing them for oneself, and when found they give double pleasure for their rarity: I would never recommend a Spanish journey to a lady, but it is by no means a bad beginning for a young traveller.[159]

PORTUGAL

British tourists in Portugal went by sea, though the trip across the Bay of Biscay was not always a comfortable one.[160] Many who went there were enthusiastic travellers: Radnor and Richmond in 1729, Pembroke in 1786. Those going to the Mediterranean by sea usually called at Lisbon, Swinton leaving a good account in his journal of his visit in 1730.[161] Travel accounts were published, William Dalrymple's *Travels through Spain and Portugal in 1774* appearing that year. Some British travellers to Portugal, such as the young Garrick, went to acquire commercial experience. Thomas Benson MP for Barnstaple fled there in 1753 after his fraud was discovered. An increasing number travelled to Lisbon for reasons of health. The air and climate were regarded as among the best in Europe, Lady Craven noting that they made her hair grow very long and extremely thick. The Cambridge antiquarian, the Reverend William Cole (1714–82) went to Lisbon for his health in 1737, and visited Mafra and Cintra.[162] Many, however, found death rather than recovery: Henry Fielding in 1754, Lady Tavistock, of consumption, in 1768, Patrick Moran on his passage from Bristol in 1769,[163] William Montagu MP in 1774 and Lord John Pelham Clinton in 1781.

There was very little travel in Portugal outside Lisbon, except for those going to Madrid who tended to follow the main road,[164] although Creed went to Oporto in 1700. He found the roads 'very rough' and complained, 'The worst dog kennel in England is a palace in comparison to the best inn I saw on this road. No bed in any inn. The inns generally have two rooms; one for the passengers and the other for the mules . . . everybody carry all their provisions with them.'[165] A traveller from Lisbon to Badajoz in 1729 wrote, 'I never underwent more hardship in travelling.'[166] Facilities for travellers outside Lisbon were poorly developed. In 1760 John, 7th Earl of Strathmore and his Cambridge contemporary Thomas Pitt, 1st Lord Camelford (1737–93) travelled around Lisbon before journeying on to Madrid. Plagued with poor health, Pitt chose to begin his foreign travels at Lisbon, the obvious point of departure for a tour of Iberia and the Mediterranean at a time when much of the Continent was rendered problematic by the Seven Years War. Pitt was to travel on from Madrid via Granada, Barcelona and Genoa to Florence, where he received the news of his father's death. His aunt Anne was very unhappy about the idea of his travelling in Iberia: 'what disturbs me the most is the dreadful journey he is taking in the hottest part of the year, in the hottest part of the hottest country in Europe, after his experience in Lisbon where I find he was ill again of the complaint he had almost got the better of . . . it makes me sick to think of all he is exposing himself to, as I really think his journey must be a greater fatigue and a greater danger than a campaign.' Charles Lyttelton wrote that he should 'not be at all at ease about him till I hear he had turned his back on the Pyrenean mountains'.[167]

CONCLUSIONS

There were few British travellers to Iberia, the Balkans, the Baltic and eastern Europe, and many of them could not accurately be described as tourists. Fashion and convenience restricted most tourists to several well-worn routes, where the whims and wishes of those who travelled for pleasure were appreciated. Across much of Europe roads were poor and accommodation for travellers minimal. Thomas Pelham had to stay in a private house between Cadiz and Gibraltar. Plentiful and good-quality food, and bankers and merchants who had correspondents in London could not be found throughout Europe. Language was also a problem over much of the Continent. The French known by most British tourists was not very useful in eastern Europe, especially in the first half of the century, as the lingua franca was then German.

Aside from these negative factors, there were reasons encouraging travel to France and Italy. They were fashionable, exciting, and fairly pleasant to visit. The ardours of travel were generally limited to the crossings of the Channel and the Alps. It was not necessary to be well-connected to enjoy a visit to either. This contrasted markedly with the position elsewhere. Thomas Pelham's trip round Spain was dependent on the support of Grantham. Keith played a crucial role for many travellers in eastern Europe. These connections could not be so easily utilized by those outside the social élite. That most chose to follow similar routes, however, did not mean necessarily that their responses to travel and to the experience of continental culture and society were identical.

NOTES

1. Beinecke, Osborn Gift 29.221; Bristol, Record Office, 28048 J1/1 pp. 9–10, 49–50; Beinecke, Osborn Shelves c 114; Gloucester CRO D 2002 F1.
2. Beinecke, Osborn Shelves b 155.
3. Beinecke, Osborn Shelves f c 11 pp. 18–19; Leake journal, Hertford CRO 84595 pp. 1–2; J. Aikin, 'Journal of a visit to the Low Countries', in L. Aikin, *Memoir of John Aikin* (1823) I, 67.

4. A. and H. Taylor (eds), *Lord Fife and his Factor* (1925) p. 39; Arbuthnot to Keith, 15 May 1787, BL Add. 35538; A. Young, *Travels during the years 1787, 1788, and 1789* (2nd edn, 2 vols, 1794) I, 88, 116.

5. *The Travels of the late Charles Thompson* (Reading, 1744) p. 2; *London Journal* 30 Aug. (os) 1735; Craven, *Memoirs* I, 20; Brand to Wharton, 24 Nov. 1789, Durham, Wharton.

6. Beinecke, Osborn Shelves b 155.

7. Queensberry to Mrs Herbert, 4 Aug. 1734, BL Add. 22626; Wharton to mother, 18 Feb., Wharton to Miss Raine, 26 Feb. 1775, Durham, Wharton; Beinecke, Osborn Shelves c 393.

8. R. Blunt (ed.), *Mrs Montagu 'Queen of the Blues'* (2 vols, 1923) I, 47.

9. *Fife* p. 28; *Original Weekly Journal* 9 Jan. (os) 1720; Molesworth to Gregor, 24 Mar. 1739, BL Add. 61830; BL Add. 61449 f. 120.

10. Stevens, *Miscellaneous Remarks made on the spot in a late seven years tour through France, Italy, Germany and Holland* (no date), p. 3.

11. Harford, p. 10; Pelham to Thomas Pelham of Stanmer (no date), Trevor to Thomas Trevor, 24 May 1729, BL Add. 33085 f. 41, 61684; Orrery I, 43, 48.

12. Beinecke, Osborn Shelves f c 97 p. 4.

13. SRO GD 26/VI/233 p. 3; Bod. Ms. Eng. misc. d. 213 p. 9.

14. Nares autobiography, Merton College Oxford, E. 2, 42, pp. 90–2.

15. L. Namier and J. Brooke (eds), *The History of Parliament. The House of Commons 1754–1790* (1964) I, 113.

16. Gloucester CRO D 2002 F1 pp. 1, 7–8, 12.

17. Trevor to Thomas Trevor, 24 May 1729, BL Add. 61684; Orrery I, 43, 48; G. von Proschwitz (ed.), *Gustave III par ses lettres* (Stockholm, 1986) pp. 90–1.

18. Bod. Ms. Douce 67 p. 36; Beinecke, Osborn Shelves c 467 I, 114.

19. Leeds, Vyner Mss. 6032 no. 12297.

20. Alnwick Castle, papers of the Duke of Northumberland, letters vol. 113.

21. Beinecke, Osborn Files 3.422.

22. Beinecke, Osborn Shelves f c 97 pp. 7–8, 10–12. There are many other manuscript accounts of visits to Chantilly including BL Add. 61684 f. 80, 32689 f. 379–80; Chelmsford CRO D/DMy 15M50/1302; HW 75 f. 24–5; Preston CRO DDF 14–15.

23. Beinecke, Osborn Files 3.422.

24. A.F. Woodhouse, 'English Travellers in Paris, 1660–1789: A Study of their Diaries' (unpublished PhD, Stanford, 1976) is very good, though far from comprehensive.

25. Preston CRO DDGr F/3 f, 16–17; Beinecke, Osborn Shelves c 331.

26. Beinecke, Osborn Shelves c 456 2/67.

27. Beinecke, Osborn Files 3.422.

28. Leeds, Vyner 6032 No. 12297.

29. Hull UL DDHo 4/3, 4 Sept. 1749; Gloucester CRO D 2002 F1 p. 94; F. Acomb, *Anglophobia in France 1763–1789: An Essay in the History of Constitutionalism and Nationalism* (Durham, North Carolina, 1950); J. Grieder, *Anglomania in France 1740–1789. Fact, Fiction and Political Discourse* (Geneva, 1985); Beinecke, Osborn Files, Dorset.

30. M. Balderston and D. Syrett (eds), *The Lost War. Letters from British Officers during the American Revolution* (New York, 1975) p. 180.

31. Knight to Essex, 6 Aug. 1735, BL Add. 27734; W. Fraser, *The Melvilles Earls of Melville and the Leslies Earls of Leven* (Edinburgh, 1890) II, 278; Aberdeen UL 2727/1/235–7.

32. Taunton CRO DD/5/WH/B55; Nottingham UL NeC 4227; Matlock CRO 239 M/O 528; Cradock, *Memoirs* p. 165.

33. Fraser, *Melvilles* I, 326; E. Craven, *A Journey through the Crimea to Constantinople* (Dublin, 1789) p. 14.

34. Beinecke, Osborn Gift 37.444.

35. Frederick II (the Great).

36. War of the Austrian Succession, 1740–8.

37. Beinecke, Lee papers, Box 3.

38. Beinecke, Osborn Shelves c 319.

39. Rented out from the government.

40. Matlock CRO D2375 M/76/186.

41. Oxford CRO Quarendon papers.

42. Bristol RO 28048/J1/1; HL PU 783.

43. Mitchell, BL Add. 58314 f. 50; Wharton to Thomas Lloyd, 14 Aug. 1775, Durham, Wharton; Jervis, BL Add. 31192 f. 17–18; Stevens pp. 69–70; Thompson I, 46; Farrington, Preston CRO DDF 14 f 4, 15; Bennet, Bod. Ms. Eng. Misc. f. 54 f. 133.

44. Beinecke, Osborn Shelves c 200 pp. 71–2; BL Add. 12130 f. 113, 125–6, 130; Craven, *Journey* p. 76.

45. BL Add. 12130 f. 122–3; Guildhall Library, London, Ms. 10823/5b.

46. Molesworth to Carteret, 10 Feb., Molesworth to Robert Walpole, 18 Aug. 1723, PRO 92/31; Mitchell, BL Add. 58319 f. 61–7; E. Elliott-Drake (ed.), *Lady Knight's Letters from France and Italy 1776–1795* (1905) p. 47; Craven, *Journey* pp. 77–8; Francis Head-Wake Correspondence, Christ Church Oxford, Wake papers vol. 264 p. 9; Stevens, pp. 82–91; Paris, Bibliothèque Nationale, naf. 23678 f. 5.

47. Preston CRO DDF 14 f 6, 15.

48. Mitford, Gloucester CRO D 2002 F1 p. 93.

49. BL Add. 22978 f. 90; Thomas to Lord Pelham, 5 Feb. 1777, BL Add. 33127; Brand to Wharton, 24 Oct. 1783, Durham, Wharton; William Windham, 'Journey through France and Italy', Wigan RO D/DZ.

50. Haggerston to mother, 9 April 1719, Northumberland CRO Haggerston; Gateshead RO, Ellison Mss. A12; Brand to Wharton, 27 Oct. 1790, Durham, Wharton; M. Wyndham, *Chronicles of the Eighteenth Century* (1924) I, 27.

51. H.E. Chetwynd-Stapylton, *The Chetwynds of Ingestre* (1892) p. 173.

52. Beinecke, Osborn Shelves c 469 pp. 43, 45.

53. Leeds AO Vyner 6032 Nos 12299, 12320.

54. Bod. Ms. Don. b 23 f. 89.

55. P. Barber (ed.), *Switzerland* (1991) pp. 54–6.

56. Beinecke, Osborn Shelves c 467 I Nos. 120, 122–4.

57. Beinecke, Osborn Files uncatalogued.

58. Preston CRO DDF 16.

59. W. Anson (ed.), *Autobiography . . . of . . . Duke of Grafton* (1898) p. 17; St Clair

to Windham, 26 Oct. (os) 1738, Norfolk CRO WKC 6/24 401X; Arthur Villettes, envoy in Turin, to Couraud, 4 Sept. 1737, PRO 92/41; BL Add. 35517 f. 68; Stanhope to Earl of Essex, 6 Jan. 1733, BL Add. 27732.

60. Bod. Ms. DD Dashwood (Bucks) B 11/7/14a; PRO 92/89 f. 293.
61. Leeds AO NH 2826 No. 49; Chester CRO DLT/C9/22; Brand to Wharton, June 1784, 6 Dec. 1790, Durham, Wharton.
62. Wharton to Brand, 19 June 1775, Durham, Wharton; Head to Wake, 21 Nov. 1724, Christ Church, Wake Mss. vol. 264; Thompson I, 67.
63. Beinecke, Osborn Shelves c 366 I p. 91.
64. Leeds AO Vyner 6005.
65. J. Boswell, *Life of Johnson*, ed. by R.W. Chapman (Oxford, 1980), p. 742; Gloucester CRO D2002 F1.
66. Nottingham UL NeC. 2401.
67. Beinecke, Osborn Shelves c 366 I pp. 20–1, c 332.
68. Leeds AO Vyner 6005.
69. Gloucester CRO D 2002 F1.
70. Bod. Ms. DD Dashwood (Bucks) B11/7/14a.
71. Petworth Archives Ms. 6320.
72. Beinecke, Osborn Shelves c 366 I pp. 332–3, 337; Brand to sister, 14 April 1787, CUL Add. Mss. 8670/21.
73. Beinecke, Lee papers Box, 3, 15 Oct.
74. Nottingham UL NeC 2397.
75. Beinecke, Osborn Shelves c 332 24, 27, 30 Sept. 1778.
76. Beinecke, Osborn Shelves c 332, 3 Oct.
77. Vyse to Harris, 6 Feb. 1770, Winchester CRO, Malmesbury papers, vol. 169; Metcalfe to Sir William Robinson, 15 Dec. 1705, Leeds AO Vyner Mss. 6005; Chester CRO DLT/C9/19. For the large number of British tourists there in the early 1750s, Beinecke, Osborn Shelves c 455 64/66.
78. BL Add. 40759 f. 30.
79. House of Lords RO CAD/4/4, 23.
80. H. Gross, *Rome in the Age of Enlightenment* (Cambridge, 1990) p. 94.
81. BL Add. 33127 f. 216; Gloucester CRO D 2002 F1 p. 87.
82. Gateshead, Public Library, Ellison Mss. A 28 No. 63. Mitford made a similar point about the palaces: Gloucester CRO D 2002 F1.
83. PRO 93/12 f. 75.
84. BL Add. 34196 f. 157; William to Edward Blackett, 8 Jan. 1785, Newcastle, Northumberland CRO ZBL 239.
85. Beinecke, Osborn Shelves c 467 II, No. 28; BL Add. 33127 f. 234–54.
86. Huntingdon CRO DD M36/20 f. 20.
87. Beinecke, Osborn Shelves c 455 64/66, 21/66.
88. House of Lords RO CAD/4/4.
89. Francis, BL Add. 40759 f. 11.
90. E. Chaney, 'Architectural Taste and the Grand Tour: George Berkeley's Evolving Canon', *Journal of Anglo-Italian Studies* (1991) pp. 86–90; Sandwich's journal is in the National Maritime Museum, London, Sandwich papers F/50. It was published by John Cooke, *A Voyage performed by the late Earl of Sandwich round the Mediterranean* (1799).

91. House of Lords RO CAD/4/6.
92. Brand to Wharton, 13 July 1785, Durham, Wharton.
93. Hawkins to Keith, 26 Feb. 1788, BL Add. 35540.
94. Brand to Wharton, 3, 22 April 1792, Durham, Wharton; Black, 'Sicily in 1792: The account of a British traveller', *Archivio Storico per la Sicilia Orientale*, 80 (1984), pp. 273–8; Chaney, 'British and American Travellers in Sicily', in A. Macadam (ed.), *Blue Guide Sicily* (1988).
95. James Dayrolle, Resident at The Hague, to Tilson, 9 Aug. 1732, PRO 84/319.
96. BL Add. 60522, 61684 f. 85.
97. Beinecke, Osborn Shelves c 49 p. 39, c 469 p. 97.
98. Beinecke, Osborn Shelves c 49 p. 40; BL Add. 33127 f. 393.
99. Cheshire CRO DBW/N/Bundle 4, Packet A No. 4.
100. H.L.A. Dunthorne, 'British travellers in eighteenth-century Holland', *British Journal for Eighteenth-Century Studies* 5 (1982) pp. 77–84.
101. Edinburgh, National Library of Scotland, Ms. 14421 f. 3.
102. Bedford CRO L30/9/113/19.
103. HW 67 f. 158.
104. Beinecke, Osborn Shelves c 49 p. 21, c 469 p. 68; Brand to sister, 22 Oct. 1787, CUL Add. 8670/26.
105. R. Halsband, *Lord Hervey* (Oxford, 1973) p. 30; Manchester to the Hanoverian minister, Friedrich Wilhelm von Görtz, 9 Nov. (os) 1718, Darmstadt, Staatsarchiv F23/44/7; Clavering letters to Lady Cowper, Herts. CRO D/EP F196.
106. Captain Fish, bearleader to Marlborough's grandsons, to Duchess, 30 Oct., Marlborough to Fish, 24 Oct. (os) 1727, BL Add. 61444.
107. HW 67 f. 155.
108. Cooper to Keith, 17 Mar. 1785, BL Add. 35534.
109. Clavering to Cowper, 9 Oct. 1716, Herts. CRO D/EP F196; Stephen Poyntz to Delafaye, 25 Sept. 1723, PRO 43/5; HP II, 534; *Harcourt Papers* III, 74.
110. Baring to Keith, 4 Aug. 1788, BL Add. 35541; Stevens p. 382.
111. Murray to Keith, 29 Mar., Barker to Keith, 9 June, Gordon to Keith, 8 Sept. 1787, Stuart to Hawkesbury, 31 Dec. 1786, BL Add. 35538–9, 38221.
112. J. Vinogradoff, 'Russian Missions to London, 1711–1789', *Oxford Slavonic Papers* 15 (1982), p. 72.
113. Dartmouth to Edward Stillingfleet, 13 Aug. 1751, 9 Mar. 1752, BL Add. 62114 K; HW 52 f. 13, 15, 132, 181, 214–17.
114. Brand to Wharton, 10 Sept. 1787, 11 Sept. 1792, Durham, Wharton; BL Add. 34444 f. 70.
115. James Scott, envoy in Berlin, to Delafaye, 2 Oct. 1723, Guy Dickens, envoy in Berlin, to George Tilson, 7 Jan. 1736, PRO 90/105, 41; Bod. Ms DD Dashwood B11/7/13a; HW 67 f. 174.
116. Beinecke, Osborn Shelves c 23 pp. 3, 7.
117. Chester CRO DBW/N/Bundle E, Packet A No. 6.
118. William Lee to his father, 7 Sept. 1753, Beinecke, Osborn, Lee papers Box 3.
119. Bentinck to Countess of Portland, 18 Jan. 1727, BL Eg. 1711.

120. Chester CRO DBW/N/Bundle E, Packet A No. 7.
121. Sunderland to Marlborough, 5 May 1722, Grafton to Essex, 2 May (os) 1735, BL Add. 61444, 27733; Robinson to Weston, 20 May 1741, PRO 80/145.
122. Brand to Wharton, 30 June 1792, Durham, Wharton.
123. Keith to Lansdowne, 25 Mar. 1786, BL Add. 35536.
124. Chester CRO DBW/N/Bundle E. Packet A.
125. HW 54 f. 256, 19, 134–49, 198–203.
126. Torrington to Keith, 3 Mar. 1786, BL Add. 35536.
127. Townshend to Keith, 2 May 1788, Duke of Montagu to Keith, 6 Sept. 1783, BL Add. 35540, 35529; Beinecke, Osborn Files uncatalogued. Aside from Keith's papers in the British Library, there is also a valuable volume of letters from him to his cousin Frances Murray in the British Library, HM 18940 and other letters from him among the papers of the Earl of Crawford deposited in the NLS: Acc. 9769, 72/2/1–96.
128. Robinson to Tilson, 25 Oct. 1730, Kinnoull to Newcastle, 5 Jan., 5 Feb. 1731, PRO 80/69, 97/26; Radnor to Robinson, 11 Nov. 1730, BL Add. 23780.
129. W.E. Manners, *Some Account of the ... Life of ... Marquis of Granby* (1899) pp. 9–10; HW 64 f. 120; Ainslie to Keith, 17 Sept. 1787, 1 Sept., 8 Nov., 3 Dec. 1785, BL Add. 35539, 35535.
130. Lady Craven to the Marquis of Carmarthen, Foreign Secretary, 25 Dec. 1786, BL Add. 27915 f. 16; House of Lords Record Office, CAD/4/7.
131. Wycombe to Keith, 12 April, Green to Keith 16 April 1786, General Conway to Keith, 25 Aug. 1785, BL Add. 35536, 35540.
132. BL Add. 35532 f. 194–5.
133. Chester CRO DBW/N/Bundle E, Packet A.
134. Stockdale ex. inf. Peter McKay; Hawkins to Keith, 21 Feb. 1787, BL Add. 35538; Ainslie to Marquis of Carmarthen, 10 Feb. 1787, PRO FO 78/8.
135. Ainslie to Carmarthen, 25 Aug. 1786, PRO FO 78/7; Ainslie to Keith, 24 July 1787, Hawkins to Keith, 26 Feb. 1788, BL Add. 35538, 35540.
136. Ainslie to Carmarthen, 10 July 1786, PRO FO 78/7.
137. Chester CRO DBW/N/Bundle E, Packet A/11.
138. *Whitehall Evening Post* 20 April (os) 1723.
139. House of Lords RO CAD/4/10, 11.
140. Chester CRO DBW/N/Bundle E, Packet A/11.
141. Finch to Harrington, 9 May (os) 1740, PRO 41/2.
142. HW 64 f. 146; Willes to his brother, Francis, 7 Oct. 1752, Trowbridge, Wiltshire CRO 161/124.
143. *Memoirs ... Lindesay* pp. 117–18; Pole Carew to Addington, 9/21 Mar. 1781, Exeter CRO 152 M/C 1781 F16.
144. BL Add. 31192 f. 98; Pitt, 11 June 1778, Winchester CRO, Malmesbury papers, vol. 163.
145. Finch to Harrington, 5 Sept. 1741, PRO 91/92; *Evening Advertiser* 6 April 1754.
146. Robert Jackson, Minister Resident in Stockholm, to Lord Townshend, 7, 14 June 1727, PRO 95/49; HMC *Rawdon Hastings* III, 105; *St James's Chronicle* 8 April, 13 May 1769.
147. Winchester, Malmesbury, vol. 163; Newcastle, Northumberland CRO ZRI 52/25; M.A. Richardson, *The Borderers's Table Book ...* (Newcastle, 1846) I,

305; *Monthly Chronicle of North-Country Lore and Legend* (Newcastle, 1887) pp. 14–15.

148. Walter Titley, envoy in Copenhagen, to Edward Weston, Farmington, Connecticut, Weston papers vol. 21; *St James's Chronicle* 16 May 1769; Norman's letters to his step-mother, Maidstone KAO U310, C3.

149. Chester CRO DSA 513–15; A. Wawn, 'John Thomas Stanley and Iceland: The Sense and Sensibility of an Eighteenth-Century Explorer', *Scandinavian Studies* 53 (1981). Stanley's account has been edited by J.F. West, *The Journals of the Stanley Expedition to the Faroe Islands and Iceland in 1789* (3 vols, Tórshavn, 1970–76). For Sir Joseph Banks's 1772 visit to Iceland, R. Rauschenberg, 'The Journals of Sir Joseph Banks's Voyage . . . to Iceland . . .', *Proceedings of the American Philosophical Society*, 117 (1973), pp. 186–226.

150. Woodward to Tilson, 28 May 1729, PRO 88/35; Petty to Keith, 1 Aug. 1785, BL Add. 35535.

151. Craven to Keith, 27 Dec. 1785, BL Add. 35535.

152. Beinecke, Osborn Shelves c 24 pp. 44–6, 22.

153. Townshend to Earl of Chesterfield, 17 Sept. (os), Keene, envoy in Spain, to Delafaye, 13 Dec. 1728, PRO 84/302, 94/99; Earl of March, *A Duke and his Friends* (1911) I, 171.

154. *Gentleman's Magazine* Dec. 1746; *Worcester Journal* 14 Sept. (os) 1749; HMC *Rawdon Hastings* III, 77–80; HL HA 8016; Eden to Sheffield, 8 Sept. 1788, BL Add. 61980; Robert Liston, envoy in Madrid, to Mountstuart, 2 Jan. 1784, BL Add. 36806 f. 59; NLS Ms. 5544 f. 49; M.F. Bacigalupo, 'An Ambiguous Image: English Travel Accounts of Spain, 1750–1787', *Dieciocho* 1 (1978).

155. Vyse to Harris, 10 June 1769, Winchester CRO, Malmesbury, vol. 169; Stanhope to Earl of Stair, 18 July 1718, Kent AO Stanhope papers U1590 0145/24; Keene to Waldegrave, 20 July 1733, Chewton.

156. Stanhope to Horatio Walpole and Stephen Poyntz, 30 Sept., Stanhope to Keene, 12 Oct. 1729, BL Add. 32763.

157. Lord Herbert, *Pembroke Papers* (1939–50) II, 315; Young, *Travels* (2nd ed.) I, 33–43; Chester CRO DLT/C9/6.

158. Beinecke, Osborn Shelves c 200.

159. BL Add. 33126 f. 316, 404, 33127 f. 67, 74, 96.

160. Craven, *Memoirs* I, 398.

161. Black, 'Portugal in 1730, by John Swinton', *British Historical Society of Portugal. Annual Report and Review* 13 (1986), pp. 65–87.

162. Craven, *Memoirs* I, 378; BL Add. 5845.

163. *St James's Chronicle*, 1 April 1769.

164. Black, 'Portugal in 1775. The Letters of Thomas Pelham', and 'Portugal in 1760: the Journal of a British Tourist', *British Historical Society of Portugal. Annual Report and Review* 14 (1987), pp. 49–55, 15 (1988), pp. 91–112.

165. Black, 'Portugal on the eve of the Methuen Treaties. Richard Creed's Journal of 1700', *British Historical Society of Portugal. Annual Report and Review* 14 (1987), pp. 43–8.

166. *Political State of Great Britain* (1729) p. 177.

167. HL MO 4109, 1252.

3

COST AND FINANCE

Eating, lodging, and chair hire are cheap enough here still, but as there is no manufacture in the country, and that everything must be imported that is necessary for cloaths, the carriage, duties, exchange and merchants advantage makes them very extravagant.

Humphrey Fish, bearleader of Charles Stanhope,
Lunéville, 1726[1]

In our *English* House at Rotterdam, for two wild ducks and two bottles of wine, we paid ten shillings *English Money*: and the Ducks (as we were credibly inform'd) cost but sixpence a piece, and the bottles of wine ninepence a bottle. This was a *Dutch Bill*.

Zachary Grey[2]

Cost was one of the principal planks of the attack on tourism, and it was possibly the major topic of the printed attack, particularly in the latter half of the century when Jacobitism had largely ceased to be an issue and the sense of threat posed by Catholicism had receded. The printed assault was constant: 'We expend more on travels than all Europe does besides . . . since Queen Anne's Peace, the Nation has thrown away near a Million of Species in foreign chaise-hire for our young quality . . . The meanest citizen would condemn a trade which carried out yearly upwards of 80,000 L. sterl. for outlandish commodities of real prejudice . . . all this national expense . . .'[3] On seeing a paragraph in the public papers, relating to the French prohibiting the English from travelling in France without passports, a gentleman declared, 'That it was too good news to be true; for he was much afraid the French would not, at their own cost, furnish a remedy to the most expensive of our national follies, which we passively suffer to run to an extravagant degree; nor hinder us from carrying them our cash, at a time when money is so scarce, and Provisions so dear in their country.'[4]

Newspapers produced estimates of expenditure by British tourists; one such in 1786 claimed that over a million pounds was annually spent in Paris by British tourists.[5] However, no official statistics were kept and in assessing the cost of tourism it is best to consider particular accounts, rather than general statements. Finance and cost were issues that played a major role in the correspondence of most tourists. Either they were young and dependent on relatives in Britain to arrange their finances and authorize their expenditure, as was the case with travellers such as William Drake, Thomas Pelham and Robert Carteret, or, as with Viscount Perceval, they were adult and concerned to arrange their financial affairs with British correspondents. Tourist correspondence and journals provide a mass of information but it is often fragmentary. Though many tourists kept accounts at some stage, few kept complete sets of accounts for their whole trip or, rather, only a relatively small number of such sets have survived.

FINANCE

Cash (that has been lodged in Sir Robt: Harris's hands for our use by Sir John Goodrick above ten weeks) had, either by miscarriage of letters, or the negligence of Sir Robt: Harris's office, not yet come to hand: by which circumstance, we are at present very low in pocket. Unknown as we are at Venice, I cannot hope to obtain cash there for a bill of mine drawn upon Messrs. Hoar [sic] and Co. for fifty pounds (my Banker in London) therefore request that you will have the goodness to procure me credit there to receive cash for a bill upon Hoar for that amount.

Major Gardner, 1787[6]

There were several methods of financing a foreign trip. An uncommon practice was to take British money. This was current in some towns in north-west Europe such as Rotterdam. In 1786 when Gardenstone changed his money at the leading Calais hotel, Dessein's, he was advised to keep his crowns and half crowns 'as they have a profitable currency in all parts of France'.[7] Thicknesse was ready to advise tourists to bring British cash with them.[8] Carrying British money any further than Calais was unusual, however. Furthermore, most tourists, probably unwilling to risk robbery, did not travel with large quantities of any currency. Insurance for Paris might be simple, but few seem to have considered it for further afield. Most tourists relied on paper instruments of credit. The most common arrangement was for a tourist to have an agreement by which he could draw on the foreign correspondents of his London banker for a certain sum. These correspondents were usually bankers themselves, though some were merchants. The tourist could also arrange to extend the geographical range of his borrowing by seeking credit from the correspondents of these correspondents. This system worked fairly well, reflecting the fact that most tourists spent much of their time in a small number of major towns.

James Compton drew on a Mr Knight in Venice in 1708. Ten years later the Northumberland tourist, Sir Carnaby Haggerston, profited from the connections of his Newcastle banker, Nicholas Fenwick. He drew £50 on him at Marseilles, £100 on his Leghorn correspondent, Mr Jackson, and had a £200 credit at Rome arranged for him by Fenwick's Italian correspondents. The same summer Perceval took up money at Calais and Bruges on the credit of the banker, Sir Alexander Cairns. Eight years later Perceval, planning a trip to the Low Countries, wrote from Paris to ask a London merchant to arrange credit at Antwerp and either The Hague or Delft. In 1728 Edward Carteret sent advice to J.C. Wetstein, Lord Dysart's bearleader: 'Mr. Boeheme tells me that the Freres Aubert will give you credit anywhere in Italy, and when you leave Italy he will give you fresh credit in Germany.' Two years later Edward Mellish received money at Blois through the banker Alexander at Paris, paying £5 commission for drawing upon his, Mellish's, uncle, the London merchant John Gore, for £200. When Mellish planned to go on a tour of provincial France he received a letter of credit on a Lyons banker from Alexander, and a connection of his uncle's, the leading Paris financier Samuel Bernard, provided him with letters of credit for Lille and Antwerp. Pococke relied on the London banker Hoare: 'I desire the favour of you to order Mr. Hoare to send me a bill of £15 on Langres and bill of £15 on Cambray, if he thinks it more proper he may only let me know where I may receive the money in these two cities.' In 1749 Joseph Yorke, the British envoy in Paris, complained that tourists were given credit upon the Pretender, 'James III's' banker. The 2nd Earl of Fife relied on another important London banking house, Drummonds.

During the century the techniques and connections of these houses improved and they were able to offer a more comprehensive service to tourists. Alexander was instructed in 1736: 'This will be delivered you by the Right Honble. Earl of Salisbury who I desire you will furnish with what sums of money he shall require of you during his stay in your kingdom, taking his bills upon Matthew Lamb Esq., which shall be allowed you in account.' Hoares acted as bankers for William Drake, Thomas Pelham and Robert Wharton. Wharton's uncle, Thomas Lloyd, like John Gore and Perceval's cousin, Daniel Dering, had financial connections and arranged matters with the banker. In 1775 Wharton sought approval for an Italian trip and asked, if it was granted, for £100 more 'which you will desire Mr. Hoare to send me a letter of credit for on some banker at Lyons or Marseilles where I shall change my letters for others on the Italian banks.' At Livorno he exchanged his French money for Italian zecchines with Monsr Berte and obtained bills on the latter's correspondents. Hoare's network served Pelham well on his Iberian trip: he was able to draw money at Madrid, Malaga, Lisbon and Cadiz. Planning his visit to Italy, Pelham asked his father for letters of credit from Hoare to his correspondents at Turin, Rome and Naples, 'in case of accidents, a letter to a banker at any great town would gain me credit at smaller ones, where I might have no letter.' Hoare instructed his correspondents at Lyons, Turin, Milan, Rome and Naples to supply him with up to £200 each and Pelham took advantage of the facility. Drake was less satisfied with Hoare's correspondents. In November 1768 he wrote to his father:

> My letter of credit from Mr. Hoare is upon the Tassins at Paris, who could give no other than on their correspondent at Lyons, Mr. Auriol; from whom I received one upon Mr. Debernardy at Turin, and from him another upon ye Marquis Belloni at Rome, if these several bankers are to have each their profit upon the money I take up at Rome, as may possibly be the case, will it not be better to have a letter from Mr .Hoare immediately on his correspondent there?

Two months later Drake's bearleader, Dr Thomas Townson, noted that the intermediary bankers were each charging 1 per cent commission. He complained bitterly of all Tassins' conduct:

> We never took up more money at a time or oftener than was necessary; and I was amazed to find the Tassins had drawn the whole sum, for which Mr. Hoare gave credit, out of your hands at one stroke: I believe no other bankers with whom English Gentlemen are concerned abroad, treat them in this manner; and in particular I believe you will find the Panchauds, who are Mr. Maxwells bankers, have not used him thus. At Paris they gave him more livres than Mr. Drake received, for £100 sterling; and furnished him with letters of credit separately upon the bankers in the several towns thro' which we were to pass, so that he cou'd draw upon the Paris banker in any of them without reference to a middle man.

Tourists frequently encountered problems, but bankers also faced difficulties, James and Thomas Coutts, for example, writing to the Countess of Bute in 1768 that, 'Sir John Lambert of Paris has drawn on us for £185 10sh and writes us it is by order of Mr. Charles being for Mr.

Frederick Stuart's expenses', but that they had not been informed of this by Mr Charles.[9]

The principal alternative to an arrangement with the correspondents of a particular banker was to take bills of exchange that could be exchanged by any banker. A major problem with this method was that many European merchants and bankers were hesitant about paying money to someone they knew nothing about whose bill might subsequently prove to be worthless. This problem affected some British tourists in 1721. Running short of money at Bruges they 'apply'd to some Irish merchants to change our Bill but they were so little acquainted with things of that nature that they told us they should not know one if they saw it'. At Ghent they found they did not have enough money to take them to Brussels but they were fortunate in meeting 'an English Gentleman Captain of an Ostend East India man who with the loss of 25s gave us money for the 30 £ bill and which was yet more strange without anybody to vouch for us that the bill was good a circumstance severall before us have been at a loss in and for that reason wanted the money'.

To wait until confirmation could be received that a bill had been honoured was a time-consuming affair.[10] In the second half of the century several London bankers, such as Sir Robert Harris, offered bills accepted by a large number of foreign bankers. These were a very attractive proposition financially. William Blackett wrote to his father from Naples in 1785: 'with a letter of credit the bankers all over Italy and Germany take two per cent commission. If you have Morlands or Harris's bills you pay no commission at all . . .'[11]

In difficult circumstances tourists could usually obtain money. It was possible to borrow from British envoys. Frank Hale borrowed £590 from Keith in 1778; Sidney Clive borrowed money several years later. Large or small sums could be borrowed from other tourists or from fellow-countrymen resident abroad. Lord Findlater lent Norton Nicholls 10 guineas at Naples and £30 at Venice in 1772. This was also a useful method for obtaining and disposing of small change. Thomas Pelham took all Lord Dalrymple's Neapolitan money from him in Rome. Wharton drew on the guide, James Byres, in Rome, while Byres arranged £50 credit for Nicholls. It was also possible to obtain money from well-intentioned local people. Francis's companion, Godfrey, did so in Lyons, 'having no letters of credit, borrows a hundred Louis dors of a good natured man'.[12]

Whatever the method employed, tourists usually complained about the commissions charged by bankers for dealing with bills of exchange and other financial devices, and the rates of exchange offered by them. Bankers were largely unregulated and free to charge and offer what they chose. Many were British, such as Sir Thomas Foley in Paris and

Thomas Jenkins in Rome. They could be of considerable use to tourists, in particular in arranging accommodation and introductions. Jenkins's windows were used by tourists keen to get a good view of Roman processions. Peter Beckford recommended prospective tourists to Sicily to ask their banker to arrange accommodation. In many eyes these possibilities scarcely compensated for the commission that they charged. Henry Nassau, Viscount Boston, who visited Paris in 1716, forgot to allow for the cost of changing money and ended up with less money than he had anticipated. Francis complained of the exchange rate offered by the mint at Nancy: 'Mr. G. changed 20 guineas for Louis d'ors at the mint, with a loss of 15 sous upon each. In other places a guinea is worth more than a Louis d'or and confessedly weighs more.' Norton Nicholls had problems with the Milanese banker Leonardi in 1771 who, 'endeavoured to practise a little dirty deceit on me of which an English banker would have been ashamed, it was to make a payment in zecchinis rating each beyond their value . . . if he should happen however to be Mr. Hoare's correspondent it will be better to say nothing about it, because he will not have it in his power to impose on me, the banker's profit is fixed, and it is always easy to inform myself of the value of the current coin'. Wharton complained about the rates offered by the bankers Sir John Lambert and Messrs Minet and Fectors. Thicknesse condemned the rate offered by Paris bankers, Dessein, and the bankers of Perpignan.[13]

Aside from the rate offered by bankers, another problem was to ensure that it was possible to obtain their services. If a tourist relied upon particular letters of credit from a London banker then a change of route or the non-arrival of these letters could create difficulties. Daniel Dering faced problems in Hanover in 1723: 'Mr. Schrader has not had any letter of credit which I assure you is a great disagreableness, for what we brought with us is much the greatest part spent.' John Clavering was worried in The Hague in 1717: 'I have no credit here upon any creature, and don't know who I shall draw upon in case of necessity.' Henry Nassau's London banker could not give him letters of credit on Dresden or Vienna in 1732 as he had no correspondents there. Henry obtained a credit on Vienna from his Rome banker, but at Munich he found it difficult to obtain money. Bankers could also go bankrupt.[14]

Bankers apart, difficulties could be encountered from variable exchange rates, a shortage of coins and the wide variety of currencies. James Hay complained in 1708 that the wide variety of Italian currencies made it difficult to do his accounts. Sacheverell Stevens wrote of his journey from Donauwörth to Nuremberg, 'we passed this day thro' four different Princes dominions, which made it very troublesome, on account of the exchange of money, the coin of each state being likewise different'. John Richard noted at Hanover: 'Nothing is more troublesome to a traveller than the passing through different principalities in Germany, as there is continual objection to the money you have, nothing is generally current but ducats, but as they are weighed at every post you are continually losing. The Jews intermeddle in this business, and, as usual, are great usurers.' Walker's experience in Italy was similar: 'We find the exchange of money a troublesome business amongst these little states, they succeed one another so fast; for we have travelled the length of the Dukedom of Parma this day; and we came through part of the Pope's dominions, and the whole Dukedom of Modena yesterday . . . I can reckon ten potentates to whom we have been subjects in the course of two months.'[15]

The financial problems of France in the 1710s and 1720s, particularly during the Regency, were linked closely to problems with the currency that only ceased with the reforms of 1726. These difficulties affected tourists. In 1720 Joseph Burnet, finding Paris too crowded and expensive, resolved to tour southern France. However, he could get no further than Orleans, 'for want of current spetie [sic] in the country and the country people would not take Bank-bills . . . obliged me to return to Paris'. The same year another tourist found an unwillingness 'to receive strangers for fear of Billets de Bancq which officers force upon 'em'. Perceval complained of the effects of attempts to reform the currency and claimed that they had led several tourists to abandon plans for visiting Paris.[16] Poor coinages also caused problems. Joseph Cradock was told in 1786 that it was best not to take 'the depreciated gold coin of France' into the United Provinces. Martyn noted that Genoese money would not be taken in any other state and advised tourists to Italy 'not to have more of the current coin of any state, than you are likely to dispose of before you quit it', with the exception of the sequins of Rome, Florence and Venice, on which there was the least loss elsewhere. Sir Richard Hoare 'found great difficulty in getting sequins at Turin, and Milan' and thought it best to take sufficient French louis d'or to reach Florence, where sequins were not scarce. Bennet complained of heavy silver coins wearing out his pockets.[17] The French Revolution brought financial chaos. A Paris report in the *St James's Chronicle* of 17 January 1792 warned, 'Though Englishmen gain above forty per cent by the exchange, still they run the greatest risk from the numberless false assignats that are abroad. Let those who visit France take particular care, or instead of returning home with considerable profit, they will find that they exchanged solid English paper, or gold, for forged paper money.'

How far financial problems affected the plans of tourists is unclear. In 1785 it definitely affected the plans of John and Judith Rolle and William Bennet for their trip through southern France, Bennet noting, 'It is my wish to have gone down the Garonne to Bordeaux . . . but having hastily parted with Sir Robert Herries's notes, and having established no credit in the southern provinces, we were forced to hasten to Paris for a fresh supply of money.'[18] Probably potential problems with finance were but one of the factors dissuading tourists from travelling outside the usual range of tourist activity. Within this range, particularly in France, Italy and the Low Countries, financial facilities were well-developed and Horace Walpole visiting Paris in 1765 found that even small British bankbills were accepted.[19] Further afield the situation was not so good, but it steadily improved during the century, and throughout most of Europe the far-flung nature of British commerce ensured that the connections of British banking were seldom too distant. In the last resort, well-connected tourists, who constituted the majority of those who went far afield could rely on the same sort of assistance that ensured them introductions at court, invitations to attend military manoeuvres and assistance in the event of legal difficulties. In 1778 Keith's bankers, Drummonds, wrote to inform him that the Earl of Bessborough wished him to procure credits for his son, Lord Duncannon, to the amount of £1,000 for his bills upon Drummonds. A man like Duncannon was rarely forced to rely on his own devices.[20]

COST

. . . when our bill was produced were struck dumb with the impudent charge of £7 9s for a day and two nights. It is the misfortune indeed of all who travel in Switzerland to experience these impositions, which are made every day without a blush. The only way to prevent it is to make a bargain beforehand what to pay for beds, what for eating etc. This we have done in every place but the present, and we have sadly experienced the neglect of it. As a proof of the difference it makes I who arrived first, and made a bargain paid only 2s 6d for my room. Mr. Rolle whose apartment was hardly better, was charged 10s 6d for his. There is no redress, and we were forced to submit to the injury, which was attended indeed with no small degree of insult. Rolle could only revenge himself by swearing heartily at the man in English, who did not understand a word he said.

Bennet, Lucerne, 1785[21]

The cost structure of an eighteenth-century tour was very different to that of a modern one, if only because it generally lasted for much longer. Allowances were often expressed in terms of so much per month or even year, and tourists, when they arrived at major towns where they intended to stay for a while, such as Paris, Rome and Naples, tended to strike a bargain for a period of weeks or months for their accommodation and often for their food. There was, therefore, a clear difference in price often between, on the one hand, accommodation and food over a long period and, on the other, for only a night or for a short period. This was related to another clear difference, namely between prices agreed in advance, often by bargaining, and those which had not been. The latter were often substantially higher. Tourists who were travelling had less opportunity to strike bargains for a number of nights. Arriving late in small settlements they were often obliged to pay whatever was demanded. At times outrage led tourists to push on and travel by night, as William Drake did at Gaeta in 1769, but this was rarely comfortable or possible outside Italy in the summer, where it was common for those who wished to speed through the malaria-infested Roman Campagna. Guidebooks advised tourists on the need to bargain on arrival at inns and those who tried generally found bargaining effective. An anonymous tourist, probably Colonel James Riddell, noted in his journal at Novalese, near the Mt Cenis pass: 'We have agreed with our Landlady at this place for 3½ livres a head for our dinner, wood or firing and wine, one livre a head for our coffee night and morning. The beds to be included. For the same fare yesterday we paid 23 livres owing to not having agreed.'[22] Charging bills in French livres was not uncommon in areas near France.

Travelling at speed, or in areas where there was little choice of accommodation, meant that tourists' costs rose. Areas that were popular and where demand exceeded supply by a large amount, became more expensive. This was true of the approaches to Mt Blanc in the 1780s and of Naples in the winters of the early 1790s.[23] It was reckoned generally that tourists who spent most of that time in one or two large towns, even expensive towns such as Paris, would spend less than those who were constantly travelling. Edward Carteret suggested that this was a factor in Lord Dysart's expenses in 1728, 'frequent journeys from place to place, which I believe must be more expensive than to reside sometime in a place'. Thomas Pelham and James Hay complained of the same effect.[24] The distribution of costs varied by tourist. However much many tourists might follow the same route, see the same sights, and often stay in the same hotels, eighteenth-century tourists were not on a package holiday. No two tourists did exactly the same thing. In particular they stayed for differing lengths of time in the same places. They had to make their own arrangements and, in both accommodation and food, provision was very varied. There was no standardized hotel accommodation. The only sphere in which governmental regulation brought some degree of uniformity in pricing was transport. Most posting systems were governmental, essentially provided for couriers and others on government business, and the price of posting was fixed. However, as many tourists discovered, these prices bore little relation to what they were expected to pay, and disputes often arose over the cost of posting. France had a very bad dispute in the Papal States in 1772.[25]

In so far as comparisons can be made, it could be suggested that as a proportion of their total expenditure eighteenth-century tourists probably spent less on food and accommodation and more on transport than their modern counterparts. Many purchased carriages, and though these were normally bought at the Channel ports on the understanding that they could be resold on return, the arrangement usually proved to be less attractive in practice than in theory. There were complaints about costs in every area. They were particularly marked in the case of Paris[26] and the United Provinces,[27] while there were comparatively few complaints about provincial France (particularly southern parts) and Germany.[28] In Italy there were many complaints about the cost of posting. In 1787 Walker claimed, 'Travelling in Italy is full dearer than in England, without a quarter the comfort, dispatch, or attendance. Our beds are, on an average, 2s 6d or 3s English, each per night; and nothing but a mattrass laid on a full bag of straw, coarse sheets, and no posts or curtains, dinners 5s and 6s a head, and travelling full 1s per mile. At Milan our charge was so extravagant, we resolved to leave the place as soon as possible . . .'[29]

Walker's comparison with British costs is interesting, because it is so unusual. Most British tourists had never toured for pleasure for any length of time within the British Isles. Aside from the Irish, Welsh and Scots, comparatively few had visited any part of the British Isles other than that portion of England that divided their county town or seat from the 'great wen', London. These British trips were comparatively short, and consequently difficult to compare with travel in Europe. Comparisons between Britain and the Continent were a common feature of tourist journals and correspondence, particularly between London and Paris, but also comparisons between most other facets of life, ranging from streetlighting and the length of women's petticoats to window casements, respect for old age, gardens, orphanages, churches and the width of the streets.[30] In contrast, however, few comparisons were made between travelling in Britain and Europe. After the exactions of the inns on the Dover road not many tourists could have stated honestly that high prices and overcharging were a foreign monopoly. Gardenstone compared French and British travelling costs to the benefit of the former.

There is no shortage of information about the cost of food and meals in Europe. Prices could be cut either by purchasing food in the markets or by making an agreement with a *traiteur* to supply meals on a daily basis at a set price. A *traiteur* cooked and provided the food, and the tourist went or sent a servant to collect it. A tourist who paid four louis d'or per week for a suite in the Hôtel de Moscovie in Paris 'settled with a traiteur for our dinner at 5 livres each and our supper, when we have any, 5 livres'. The Dowager Countess of Salisbury, widow of the 4th Earl, stayed in Paris in 1699 and 1702 during a lengthy continental tour. She had quite a large establishment and many of her bills have been preserved in the Cecil Papers at Hatfield. A sample bill, in livres and sols, from an undated bundle, 'Weekly expenses at Paris,' includes the following items:

	livres	sols		livres	sols
butcher	23	–	herbs and onions	1	12
fowls	18	6	10½ lb sugar	7	8
bread and flour	11	17	fruit	9	11
2 tongues	1	4	vinegar	1	4
2 lb bacon	1	4	oil	1	12
milk and cream	7	19	salads	3	4
11 lb butter	5	10	beans	–	6
fish	1	1	peas	2	5
artichokes	–	16	oranges	–	6
melons	6	–			

Perceval noted Paris market prices in British currency in 1725:

Hare	7sh	Beef	8d a pound
Partridge	2sh	Mutton	5½d a pound
Pigeon	1sh	a sole 8 inches long	2sh 9d
		egg	1d

James, 6th Earl of Salisbury, travelled through France and Italy in 1730–34. His accounts were kept by his bearleader Dr Samuel Haynes, who received the valuable rectory of Hatfield from the Earl in 1737. The accounts only noted the individual items of food when they were luxuries, three ortolans for 6 livres in June 1730, coffee and tea for 2 livres 18 at Blois in September 1730 and oysters for 7 livres in March 1730. 'Diet for a month' at Angers in 1731 came to 190 livres though it is not clear whether servants, and, if so, how many, were included. A tourist who stayed a fortnight at Aachen in June 1720 recorded: 'at Florintin the Dragon D'Or a good house but at some distance from the fountain. Things are there tolerably cheap. Dinner 3 shillings and 2 at supper. Burgundy and Champagne 2 shillings a bottle. Moselle 3 shillings.'

Very good veal cost about 2d a pound at Quesnoy in northern France in April 1721. Richard Pococke did not leave accounts but he included details of particular meals in his letters to his mother. At San Marino he 'demanded what I was to pay over night before I eat – they told me a penny my bed, I might have a pennyworth of soup, 1d meat and salad, to which at supper they added a 1d fricassee, and 1d cheese, and a large quart of wine 1d more; I had the best vermicelli soup I ever eat, all served very well, I paid 4d in the morning'. At Bologna he noted: 'the common price of wine on the road was 1d a quart and once I had it for ½ and good enough some of it; at Tolentino 4 pd. of cherries for ½, and the common price everywhere is a half penny a pd the best sorts; we pay here 1s 6d for dinner each, eat very well, five dishes and a dessert by ourselves, 6d each for beds'. A good dinner at Gravelines early the following decade cost 17d a head, while Martyn claimed that for four Venetian livres (about 20d) a good dinner could be had in Venice. When eating in their lodgings in Naples, Francis and his friend Godfrey paid three carlins each for breakfast, and, including wine, ten each for dinner and five for supper (57½ carlins then being worth a guinea). A guinea was considered too much to pay for 'some boiled perch and three bottles of Rhenish' in the Dutch village of Broek.

In Paris in 1750 the Reverend John Nixon noted, 'A traiteur provided our dinner at 3 livre a head for which he gave us a soup and bouille, an entre, quelque chose rotie and a dessert or fruit.' Twenty-five years later Robert Wharton regularly took a set-price dinner, generally agreed to be the best value. He had a good dinner and a pint of burgundy for two livres and left two sols for the waiter. William Blackett, visiting Lausanne in 1784, where he found 'quite a little colony of English, complained that 'provisions are exactly doubled within this few years . . . we cannot dine under six livres French a head, and for that a moderate dinner'. He wrote that if he stayed he proposed to hire a cook in order to save money. The following year Bennet was pleased to strike a bargain of three livres per head for supper at an inn on the Geneva-Lyons road and was scandalized by the minimum cost of five shillings for supper at Altdorf in Switzerland. In 1786 Gardenstone found French charges 'below the common rates in England'. In Boulogne he paid five livres for two bottles of very good burgundy, four livres for dinner for two and three for his lodgings. At Abbeville he dined very well, with a bottle of good burgundy, for six livres, and at Félixcourt he supped and stayed overnight at the post-house, 'and fared well for seven livres'. In Paris he 'settled terms with a reputable traiteur, at the rate of five livres, when alone, and six livres a head, when I have company – I am very well served and so plentifully that the fragments are always sufficient for the use of my servants'. The following year Mitford found that dinner cost two to three livres, coffee six sous, supper one livre ten sous and breakfast eighteen sous a head at Dieppe, while at Brussels 'breakfast for two persons, tea, and admirable rolls and butter' cost about 8½d a head and 'dinner for two

– consisting of two courses, four dishes in each, and a dessert, all very good' 2s 9d a head. A very good Bordeaux cost Mitford 3s 4d a bottle, an extremely good Moselle 2s 6d.

Foreigners could not be sure that they paid the same as the locals. Francis and Walker complained of being charged more in Spa and Rome respectively; and Arthur Young, when he bought three large peaches for a penny in Barcelona, was told that he 'gave too much, and paid like a foreigner'. Young left some detailed accounts of the cost of meals,[31] but his comments reveal what was only to be expected, namely that prices varied greatly, and that whereas some establishments aroused a sense of outrage, others were seen as being good value. There is no guide to the size of the portions: how ample was a good dessert? How much did a large eighteenth-century roast fowl weigh? Similar problems affect any discussion of the costs of accommodation. A 'large' or 'comfortable' room is difficult to compare with other such rooms, and rooms were far from standard in size or furnishings. Furthermore, there is often very little information available about accommodation for other members of a party: the bearleader and the servants. Best value was given usually if a guest ate where he stayed and many tourist costs are, therefore, expressed as board and lodging.

Lord Harold wrote from Paris in 1717 to his father, the Duke of Kent, in order to blame his costs on the visit of Peter the Great: 'I need not inform Your Grace how very dear and expensive a place I find Paris to be. I have not been able to get any lodgings that are tolerable under two hundred and fifty livres a month and a coach under three hundred the price of them being increased since the Czar's coming.'

Perceval visited Paris in 1725 with his wife and two children. He paid 400 livres a month rent 'and a 100 more for the use of the kitchen, table linen and stables for 9 horses'. He subsequently moved to new lodgings – three apartments, two coach-houses and stables for nine horses for 450 livres a month. Five years later the 6th Earl of Salisbury paid six livres for supper and lodging at the Tapis Vert in Montauban, though it is not clear how many servants were accommodated. Martyn claimed that in Venice, 'which however is not the cheapest place in Italy to live in', a stranger might rent a good room for 5–10d a day 'or he may provide himself with a genteel aparement and dinner for 4–4 sh 7d a day'. In 1734, Pococke stayed at 'Kennets a very good English publick house, but more like a lodging', in Venice for 1s 6d a night, half the price of his dinner. At Milan he stayed in 'an excellent Inn' for 2s. Samuel Smith stayed at the Hôtel des Trois Villes in Paris in 1752 and 'agreed for 2 chambers one within another at a Louis per week'. The 2nd Earl of Fife found accommodation very expensive in Spa in 1765, 'no less than 16 shillings a day'. Francis and Godfrey together paid 15 carlins (about 5s) a day for lodgings in

Naples in 1772, less than the daily hire of their carriage (16 carlins) and less than they each paid for dinner (20 carlins). At the Hôtel de l'Impératrice in Paris three guineas a week were charged for 'an elegant dining-room, with two bed chambers on the first floor, and a bed chamber in the entresol, with an apartment for the servant'. This was considered expensive but there were compensations: magnificent furniture, a good situation, the ready availability of carriages for hire and the charms of 'Mademoiselle Brunett'. Lord Balgonie's lodgings in Orleans in 1772 were considered 'rather dear, but the object here is to have a house near to where you dine and sup, and mine is only across a square. I give a guinea a week, and for this I have a very good room without a bed, a nice little room to sleep in, Mr. Marshal [companion] has above an excellent bedchamber where he will sit often, and a clever place for Edward [servant].'

In Paris, Robert Wharton lodged first at the Hôtel de Luxembourg for half a guinea per week. He then moved to lodgings costing '9 Louis a month, but then they were in the dearest place in Paris. I could have lodged well in several other places further from the spectacles and walks for 2 Louis.' In the Hôtel d'Angleterre in Turin in 1782 two bedchambers 'one good, the other bad without a fire place' cost 7 shillings a night. The following year Lord Stopford took 'very complete apartments' in Vienna 'at 14 ducats per month, which is about seven guineas'. William Blackett was very impressed by the low cost of accommodation in Lausanne in 1784. He looked round a house which was 'well furnished, four or five very good rooms which look to the lake, a pretty garden and terrace covered with vines from whence is a fine view of the lake and the mountains in Savoy, all for five Louis a month'. On the other hand, Sir John Fleming Leicester (1762–1827), later an MP and important art patron, thought the ten guineas he paid for the rent of a wonderful house there for a fortnight that year very expensive. In 1785, Bennet and the Rolles paid 7s 6d per day for their small but convenient lodgings at Spa. They thought this reasonable for a dining room and four bedrooms on the second floor. In 1766, a very good double-bedded room in Lyons cost 2s 6d a day.[32]

There is plenty of information available concerning transport costs. They were a well-covered item, in both journals and guidebooks. In 1720, a tourist crossed in a yacht to Calais for three guineas. In 1722, Colin Maclaurin missed the packet at Dover and some seamen offered to carry him to Calais 'in an open boat of six oars for thirty shillings'. He noted that a sloop could be hired for the passage for 3½ guineas. Figures printed in 1772 suggested that it should cost three gentlemen and one servant £8 on the Harwich–Helvoetsluys packet and £4 9s on the Calais–Dover packet. However, for the actual trip discussed in the book the expenses proved greater: 'This expence was occasioned by the time of the tide and roughness of the weather, which prevented the vessel coming into the harbour: Boats therefore came off to us, and took advantage of our sickness and impatience, by extorting two guineas for putting eight of us on shore at the distance of half a mile.' Four years later John Mitford spent five guineas on his passage in the packet, one for his carriage, one to the captain and a half to the men.

Regulated public transport was available on the rivers and canals of the United Provinces and on the Saône, Rhône and Canal du Midi in France. Tourists travelled in a boat on the Meuse from Liège to Huy in 1720 and 1721. The boats were towed and the charge was a shilling per person. Tourists who wanted to travel independently had to negotiate terms themselves. In Lyons in 1776 a tourist 'embarked myself, servant, and cabriolet in a *bateau de poste* navigated by two men. I agreed to pay four Louis and six francs, for the voyage down the Rhône to Avignon stopping when and where I pleased, or proceeding all night if I chose it.' Tourists on the Rhine and Danube and in the Baltic and Mediterranean made their own bargains. Transport was cheaper by sea than land, but not if a boat had to be hired. Bennet paid a shilling to be carried from Altdorf to Lucerne in a merchantman. The best service was available in the United Provinces, where Ann Radcliffe noted that the price in 1794, including tax, was 1d per mile and a trifle more to sit on the roof of the cabin.[33]

Land travel was very expensive. A major cause of expense was accidents, which were very frequent.[34] Even if none occurred it was still necessary to bear the costs either of bringing a carriage from Britain or of hiring or purchasing one on the Continent, which meant, in most cases, Calais. The Dowager Countess of Salisbury paid 260 livres for a month's hire of a coach and two horses in Lyons in 1699. In 1721, a post-chaise and five horses cost 200 livres at Nancy; in 1772, a carriage about £25 at Milan; in 1777, a cabriolet and an English coach-horse seventeen guineas at Calais. Maclaurin noted that it cost two guineas to hire a coach with four horses and two postillions from Calais to St Omer. In 1729 a tourist noted, 'I took 4 chaise and 2 saddle horses and 2 postillions from Saumur to Poitiers at 30 livres a day, which amounted (the 4 days I kept them and 2 days they took to return to Saumur) to 180 livres.' At Rochefort he made 'a bargain with a fellow to carry me (with 2 horses for my chaise and 2 saddle horses) for 130 livres to Cavignac . . . to take 4 days'. Such bargains were necessary if the post-roads were not followed. Drake hired a coach for the Calais–Paris trip in 1768 and paid six louis d'or. The cost was similar in the opposite direction. Lord Leven paid three guineas at Lille in 1749 for the use of a chaise to Paris. Leven was delighted by the absence of turnpike charges in France, but appalled by the cost of transport:

The multitudes of English in this country has made travelling as dear as in England, the expence of horses for one chaise by the king's ordinance comes to four shillings English every six miles, which is as much as we pay in England for both chaise and horses, except where they have close postchaises; for these we pay one shilling per mile . . . The guides [postillions], for I cannot call them boys, as they are generally old fellows, I have met with are allowed only threepence English per post, yet our countrymen have debauched them to such a degree that they grumble if they don't get double, and their post is generally but six miles.[35]

Posting charges varied by the number of people in, wheels on, and horses before a carriage. It was less expensive to use public transport though this was not available over much of Europe. In the 1770s it cost 55 livres (£2 5s) for a place on the Lille–Paris diligence. The price included provisions and lodging on the way. On the Paris–Lyons diligence in 1739 'the fare for each passenger is 100 livres, and everything found you upon the road, or 70 livres without'.[36] The diligence system did not extend into Italy. Tourists seeking to travel between Lyons and Turin agreed often with a *voiturier* to take them and their carriage between the two cities for a price that included accommodation, food and posting. The Dowager Countess of Salisbury used such a service in 1699 and Walker paid thirteen louis d'or for travelling in the opposite direction in 1787. Sir Richard Hoare paid more in 1785 as he had a larger party, and he went on to pay for the *cambiatura*, a payment which ensured free posting in Piedmont:

We paid the voiturier from Lyons to Turin for taking our two postchaises with four horses to each, a bidet [small horse] for my servant all our baggage etc. over Mount Cenis, and for our eating and lodging, forty six Louis d'ors, and we gave the drivers six Louis. They undertook the job somewhat cheaper, as they belonged to Turin, and had brought some gentlemen from thence to Lyons. From Turin you most procure the Cambiatura, which takes you near to Milan, viz to Buffalora: they made us pay in Octr. 1785 21 livres for 8 chaise and one small saddle horse, besides the postillions.[37]

In areas where there was no posting system it was necessary to make specific arrangements in order to travel. These could be expensive, as Thomas Pelham found with his mule-hire in Iberia, but they could also be reasonable: John Richard went on a thirteen-day coach journey from St Petersburg to Moscow: 'I engaged with a carrier for twelve roubles, which is about two pounds sterling, to drive me with three horses.'[38] In some areas it was more a problem of availability than money: shortage of horses were by no means unknown.

A separate transport cost prevailed within larger cities where it was usual to hire a carriage and this could be expensive. Perceval hired a carriage and two horses for 13 shillings a day in Paris in 1725. Nixon noted in Paris in 1750, 'We hired a valet at 30s and a Coach at 13 livre a day while in town, and 18 livre when we made excursions into the country.' Francis and Godfrey hired a carriage and a coachman for 18 carlins (about 7s) a day in Naples in 1772. Half-a-guinea a day, and a shilling for the coachman, was one charge in Paris in the early 1770s.[39]

Food, accommodation and transport were the principal costs met by tourists. In addition there was a rich miscellany of expense. A major one was clothes, on which tourists tended to spend a lot of money. One reason for this was that, as they were abroad for a long time, they needed often to replace items of clothing. Compton had to replace his British shirts in the United Provinces. More significant was the social environment that many tourists frequented. To move freely in society a gentleman was expected to dress well, and being a tourist did not alter this situation, although strangers were freed from some of the restrictions of European society: Joshua Pickersgill noted that strangers at the Turin carnival balls in 1761 were allowed to dance with whomsoever they wished, while the local citizens were not permitted to dance with noble women.[40] To appear in court society was expensive. Lord Nuneham bought new clothes for the celebrations in Hanover for the anniversary of George II's accession.

Tourists in Paris tended to spend a lot on clothes, in large part because French fashions for men were quite different from those of Britain. On arrival in Paris, tourists had to get new clothes and they were beset often by tailors. Robert Wharton bought new silk stockings and a pair of shoes for himself in Paris in 1775, and was pleased at the low costs charged for washing clothes; Charles Spencer apologized to his grandmother, Sarah, Duchess of Marlborough, for buying fine clothes in Paris in 1723; George Lyttelton complained of the cost of clothes in 1728 and 1729. In Lorraine in 1728 he found that dress was a major item in his expenditure. Attending the court at Lunéville obliged him to wear fine clothes, and he found that all entertainments necessitated gambling. In Paris the following year he complained of the cost of clothes, coach hire, gambling, fencing and dancing lessons, and could only assure his father that improvement abroad was impossible without expenditure. His brother Richard, sent to the academy at Besançon in 1737, was soon in debt as a result of clothing purchases and gambling. The accounts of Sir John Swinburne on his 1749–51 trip to France give some indication of the cost of clothes: 48 livres for a laced hat and feather bought at

Lille, 216 for a waistcoat of rich Lyons stuff, 84 for six pairs of worked ruffles, 1,367 for 'my Taylor's bill', 299 for a lined crimson velvet coat and breeches, 848 for the embroidering of 'a sute of cloaths in Gold' – all paid in Paris between 20 December 1749 and 17 May 1750. At Aix-en-Provence in early 1751 he paid a tailor's bill of 45 livres, and bills for 'cloth, lace etc.' for making into clothes of 591 livres. In Toulouse he spent 135 livres on clothes for his servant John; and 34 on a plain hat and feather; later that year in Paris he paid 210 for embroidering 'a suit of cloaths'; 60 for a laced hat and feather; and 719 for his tailor's bill. In France in the early 1730s the 6th Earl of Salisbury purchased several pairs of shoes and gloves, as well as some hats. Items in his accounts included silk cloth and stockings, gold and silver lace, and tailor's bills.[41]

It was not very expensive to attend the theatre or musical entertainments. In the 1730s a place in the 'Concert spirituel . . . the finest musick at Paris' cost three livres, and in the Opéra the most expensive seats were just over seven livres. In 1775 Wharton paid four livres to go to the Opéra in Paris and six to go to the Comédie. It helped, as so often with prices, if one paid oneself. William Drake was overcharged at the Siena theatre in 1769 because he entrusted his purchase to his guide.[42] Guides were a source of expense – it was usual to hire them in large cities, just as it was common to hire an extra servant (often the two were the same man). They were notorious for attempting to defraud tourists. As they were paid little, they sought to earn money by taking a commission from hotels, tailors, etc. whose services they secured for their temporary master.[43] Hiring teachers could also be an expense. Perceval paid 100 livres a month for a French master in 1725, and forty livres for sixteen lessons from a drawing master.[44] Charles, later 2nd Viscount, Fane paid his bearleader, Chais, £100 per annum, and gave him his keep and a servant in all large towns, a cost of over £200.[45]

Presents, either for oneself or for others, could of course be a major item of expense. Visiting Rome in 1726, Edward Southwell junior 'spent 150 £ on 5 marble tables, 2 landscapes of ruins, a little suite of brass medals, more for use than show, 50 £ worth of prints of modern and antique Rome and of the chief paintings, 2 or 3 fans, 2 or 3 cameo's etc.' Lord Nuneham sent melon and broccoli seeds home from Florence in 1756. The Dowager Countess of Salisbury paid 120 livres for a 'silver minute pendulum watch' in 1702. Perceval spent a lot of money in the Low Countries in 1718 buying lace for others. Richard Grenville bought his uncle four Italian paintings, costing £103 19s 2d in the early 1730s. Norton Nicholls found that for the time he was in Rome in 1772 James Byres cost fifteen guineas as a guide, while he could get a half-length portrait by Batoni for twenty.[46] Not all were drawn in 'to make some expences more than I should have done' by women, as Henry Pelham was at Caen in 1775; nor did many spend what was probably over £600 on a sumptuous ball for 250 people, as Lord Duncannon did at Lausanne in 1785; but all had to spend, as Robert Wharton did, money on cosmetics at the barber – shaving soap, lavender water, powders, and tincture for the teeth – and on washing clothes.[47]

Tips were a constant drain. Tipping was widespread, whether to the sailors on the Channel packets or to the servants of houses that were open to visit, such as the Palais Royal in Paris. Thomas Brand complained of the cost at the Saxon fortress of Königstein: 'It cost us a great deal of money at the different places we were taken to in making the round of the fortress – for the *fat* woman who shewed us the great Tun . . . for the perpendicular Engineer who shewed us the Arsenal . . . but I was really shocked when the *Parson* made a very servile bow for a florin for looking into his Church.'[48]

CONCLUSIONS

> . . . certainly neither Mr. Drake nor Mr. Maxwell has shown the least disposition to extravagance, or, as far as I can judge, been guilty of any; but the very expences of travelling have been very great, and not the less so for our following the track of so many English as are now abroad.

> Dr Townson, Florence, 1769[49]

The total costs of individual tourists were high by the standards of the annual costs of an artisan household, but, given the length of time they stayed abroad, the need to make independent arrangements and the distances many of them covered, they were not as high as might have been imagined, judging simply by press comment. Ashe Windham, who travelled in Europe in the 1690s, received an annual allowance of £600. In 1717–20 Charles Compton had £250 in his first year abroad, and £200 thereafter, though he received an extra £50 in Rome. Viscount Boston spent about £566 over a twelve-month period in 1715–16. Sir Carnaby Haggerston, his expenses increased by gambling losses, signed bills for £400 in a six-month period in Italy in 1718. Eight years later Charles Spencer rebutted complaints about his expenditure: 'it would be impossible for me to travel in any court of Europe with the least honour with £500 sterling a year'. His brother, Robert, 4th Earl of Sunderland, died in Paris in 1729 having drawn for all of the £1,000 credit he had there, and owing £300. From February 1730 to October 1732, the 6th Earl of Salisbury received £3,313 from his bankers. Robert Carteret aroused parental criticism, spending over £1,850 in 1740–1. Sir John

Swinburne spent £1,271 on his European trip from November 1749 to October 1751. An anonymous tourist who reached Helvoetsluys on 6 June 1758 had by 12 September spent £170 12d. This included £4 for Hanoverian, Austrian and Prussian passes. A coach for four days in the United Provinces then cost 10 shillings.

In 1760 John Tucker informed his nephew Edward that his annual allowance of £300 while abroad was 'full sufficient for any private gentleman to live there [Lausanne] with credit and reputation'. The 2nd Earl of Fife spent over £1,700 in a few weeks in Paris in the winter of 1766–7 but he was accompanied by his wife, 'liv'd in the first company in Paris', and spent a lot on clothes and on china, furniture, tapestry and damasks for his London house. William Drake received £1,039 from his bankers between October 1768 and August 1769. The future 7th Earl of Salisbury was allowed £130 per month while abroad in 1770 and was given an additional sum of £400 because of the cost of staying in Paris. Five years later a tourist with more modest tastes wrote from Paris. 'I think one might live very comfortably from £300 a year or with a little management for £250.' The accounts of Lord Stopford's bearleader Samuel Pohl, for 1 June to 15 October 1783, during which period Stopford was at Lausanne, totalled 3,083 Swiss livres 16 shillings (192 guineas 14s 9d in British money).

Post for letters	24	4
Sundries	53	17
Perfumery	35	14
Washing	56	16
Washing for silk stockings	28	18
Cambric for cravats and handkerchiefs	101	6
The merchant Mad. Pachaud	367	16
The merchant Mad. Bailey	26	1
taylor	175	11
shoemaker	76	10
hairdresser	78	10
travelling expences	91	3
horse hire	82	12
books and library	30	3
ices and lemonade	8	13
carriage for sundries to London and back	25	4
pair of pistols	64	–
doctors, tooth operator and apothecarys	222	5
fortifications master	101	14
German master	92	–
arithmetic master	48	–

philosophy and history master	85	13
dancing master	8	–
12 pair silk stockings	66	–
goldsmiths	51	11
seamstress	10	8
carriage repairs and furnishing out	35	1
chaise standing and furnishing out	13	10
Cerjats servants	240	–
To Lord Stopford for 20 weeks	320	–
To Pohl for 20 weeks	320	–
for lodgings	42	10

On the thirteen-day journey to Vienna that began on 16 October, they spent a further 38 louis and one penny.

In 1785 William Bennet did the accounts of the Rolles's trip:

> . . . He has performed it for about £550, which is less than £150 per month the sum generally allowed by persons who travel with an equipage. For this sum he has made what is called the little tour, and it is the best route imaginable for anyone who does not mean to visit Italy. He has seen Flanders both French and Austrian to great advantage: the courts of the three Ecclesiastical Electors, and all the part of Germany that borders upon the Rhine. Switzerland he is perfectly well acquainted with, having been on all the principal lakes, and over every one of the cantons except Appenzel and Unterwalden. Savoy he has visited enough to know the nature of it, and to admire the wonders of Mt. Blanc: and entering France by way of Lyons . . . he turned at Toulouse to penetrate through the centre of this kingdom.

They had arrived at Calais on 20 June 1785 and sailed thence on 30 October 1785. James Burges's total costs for his trip to Paris and the Loire in 1771, in his second long vacation from Oxford, 'from leaving London to my return to it, amounted to no more than £89 1s 7d including every charge'. The range of expenditure was great. In 1754 and 1755 Francis, 10th Earl of Huntingdon, spent £5,700. In contrast, the Scottish architect Robert Mylne (1734–1811), who was abroad from 1754 to 1759 studying architecture for four years in Rome before touring Italy, including Sicily, and returning home via Switzerland and the United Provinces, spent £30 per annum.[50]

It is impossible to state accurately the total cost to the nation of foreign travel. Lord North wrote from Rome in 1753 that in the recent Holy Year British tourists had drawn over £70,000 from one banker alone. Sixteen years later a London newspaper reported, 'A Gentleman who lately came from Calais assures us, that there are near 200 French remises to be sold there belonging to the English nobility and gentry, who leave them there at the end of their travels. This proves the vast sums of money left in France. Whether the English bring home anything deserving this expence, is a question that needs no answer.' In an undated fragment in his correspondence, presumably sent from France, William Blackett wrote, 'some time ago upon some occasion an inquiry was made how much money was spent in this country by strangers and it was computed at a million and a half sterling'. In 1785 Bennet noted, 'If the calculation of the English who are settled or are travelling abroad as said to be delivered to Mr. Pitt, can be depended upon, they amount to 40,000 and if each man spends only £100 per ann: drain each year £4,000,000 hard money from the nation.'[51]

It is clear that a lot of money was spent abroad, and this was not only seen as an issue in Britain. In April 1781, the Emperor, Joseph II, ruler of Austria, issued a decree forbidding young men under twenty-eight to travel abroad because they enriched other countries unnecessarily. It is unclear, however, whether the contemporary critics' accusations of extravagance were justified. Several travellers were convinced that their compatriots were extravagant. Bennet blamed the prevalence of beggars in Switzerland on tourism: 'This has arisen from the extravagance of the English, many of whom have thrown their money away in this country without either thought or use.' Captain John Barker complained from Brunswick in 1787: 'By the impositions through this part of Germany one perceives it to be the track of the English . . . I did not take that to be the character of the Germans; but it is our own countrymen have taught them.'[52]

On the other hand a mass of correspondence testifies to the efforts made to limit expenditure by parents, tutors and tourists. Those who were extravagant, such as Lord Dysart in 1728, were reprimanded severely. Others – Compton, Drake and Pelham among them – were constantly aware of parental supervision, and driven to defend their expenditure. Compton's tutor wrote in 1708, 'there's no avoiding spending what honour and necessity will have, and some allowance must be given to conveniency'. Thomas Pelham defended spending more than had been agreed: 'I flatter myself I am free from extravagance and that my expences are either necessary or such as fashion has made indispensable: I consider economy as much as possible and believe that in travelling, the continual change of place renders a fixed income very impolitick.'[53]

Norton Nicholls wrote to his mother from Naples in 1772 to blame his expenditure on his companion, the Earl of Findlater, a useful reminder of the social differences between tourists:

I assure you in spite of what I spend I am economical and spend not above ½ as much as the people with whom I live . . . I find at present the great inconvenience of living with a Lord . . . because I suffer for the impositions he undergoes; he is used to be preyed on by his servants, by the inn keepers, by all the world as we keep house together part of this falls on me, I scold eternally, and have changed some things for the better, but in general I find a considerable difference between living so and by myself.

He later wrote, 'there are but two methods of travelling, one being admitted everywhere as a gentleman and spending with the exactest economy a great deal, the other living at coffee-houses and spending little'.

Costs were put up by factors largely outside tourists' control. Though by modern standards it was modest, there was a certain amount of inflation in eighteenth-century Europe. Throughout the century there were complaints of increased costs in Paris. 'Everything is very dear to what it has been', complained Edward Southwell in 1723, noting a consequence of the financial chaos arising from the collapse of John Law's schemes for the fiscal regeneration of France. Forty years later Smollett wrote, 'Living at Paris, to the best of my recollection, is very near twice as dear as it was fifteen years ago.' In 1777 Thicknesse complained that over a decade most Parisian prices had risen by a third and many by 200 per cent. Judging from itemized expenditure figures these claims were overstatements, but no doubt it was difficult for tourists whose fathers had travelled, such as William Drake, to persuade them that the prices they remembered were no longer appropriate. Mitford recorded in 1787 that at Brussels supper cost 6d a head and 'lodging for four days for 2 viz 2 good bedchambers, and a sitting room at a distance . . . less than 2s 6d. These same things at Paris cost at least six times as much taking all the articles together.' He also commented on a rise in the price of a carriage in Paris from twelve livres a day on his last visit in 1776–7 to fifteen.[54]

There were other reasons for higher charges. It was claimed in 1786 that anti-British feeling in the United Provinces was leading to 'exorbitant charges'. Increased tourist demand, such as that which crowded Neapolitan hotels in the early 1790s, probably played a greater role than tourist extravagance in pushing prices up. Francis Head reported from Rome in 1725 that the price of antique coins had risen as a result of foreign demand, and that in Rome, because it was Holy Week, 'everything is excessively dear . . . lodgings, coaches are raised to more than double . . . what was vast numbers of all nations are at present here'.[55] It was not only the British who travelled for pleasure. Another reason advanced for high costs was the attempt to impose upon strangers – George Carpenter complained of it in the Austrian Netherlands in 1717, and Thomas Pelham in Spain in 1776. The same point was made about Britain. Crossing from Brighton to Dieppe in August 1788, John

Villiers met a Frenchman who had just toured England: 'He found an ample theme for abuse in the expences of the roads; the impositions of the inns; and the long retinue that were constantly gaping for reward on leaving them.'[56]

How far costs influenced the decisions of tourists to visit particular areas or only to spend a certain amount of time in them is unclear. Lady Craven found Russia very cheap, but there was no rush of tourists there. Arthur Young pointed out, in 1787, that 'the comparative dearness and cheapness of different countries is a subject of considerable importance, but difficult to analize . . . What we meet with in France, is a cheap *mode of living*.' It was not that living abroad was expensive – one guidebook claimed that the author had only spent £150 in eighteen months abroad – but that the 'mode of living' preferred by tourists was expensive. When Boswell planned a European tour in 1764 he wrote: 'I would by no means be extravagant; I would only travel genteelly.' This aspiration was shared by most tourists and it inevitably involved expense. This expense invited emulation, aroused criticism and defined for many the nature of tourism: 'it is a general conceived notion in England, that it is necessary to have a considerable fortune to make the tour of France', claimed the guidebook cited above.[57] Tourism was a luxury because most tourists spent in accord with their social status and their lifestyle at home. However, it was possible for men of medium incomes, such as Walker and Wharton, to travel and after the Peace of Paris (1763) such men travelled in increasing numbers. The nature of tourism was altering before the Revolutionary Wars.

Costs clearly led some tourists to change their plans. John Pelham wrote to a relative from Nancy, 'I have heard such an account of Paris that I am quite out of conceat of going there. Everything is insufferable dear . . . I had much rather fall down the Rhine into Holland.' Beaumont Hotham was to write to his son Charles in 1749: 'I am sensible Paris is not the place to learn economy in.' In 1734, George Stanhope turned down the suggestion of a trip from Paris into southern France on the grounds that he 'thought it too expensive'. Gibbon's shortage of money complicated his Italian tour.[58] Most tourists did not, however, alter their plans for financial reasons. Those who travelled were on the whole those who could afford to travel, and their 'mode of living' as tourists matched their situation.

NOTES

1. Fish to Sarah Marlborough, 11 Nov. 1726, BL Add. 61444.
2. Journal of Dr Grey, BL Add. 5957, f. 58; J.E. Smith, *A Sketch of a Tour on the Continent in the years 1786 and 1787* (3 vols, 1793), I, 44.

3. *Mist's Weekly Journal*, 8 July (os) 1727.
4. *The Gazetteer and New Daily Advertiser*, 20 Aug. 1770; *The Nonsense of Common-Sense*, 3 Jan. (os) 1738;*Westminster Journal* 29 May 1773, 27 Aug. 1774.
5. *Daily Universal Register*, 5 Oct. 1786.
6. Gardner to Keith, 14 Sept. 1787, BL Add. 35539.
7. Gardenstone, I, 11; BL Stowe 790, f. 163; *Tour of Holland* (1772), p. 237.
8. Thicknesse, 1768, p. 182.
9. James Hay, Compton's tutor, to George Compton, 5 Feb. 1708, BL Add. 38507; Fenwick to Lady Haggerston, 8 April (os) 1718, Northumberland CRO, Haggerston papers; Perceval to Daniel Dering, 17 June (os) 1718, Perceval to Clark, 16 April (os) 1726, Carteret to Wetstein, 27 June (os) 1728, BL Add. 47028, 47031, 32415; Mellish to father, 7 Dec. 1730, 25 April, 2 May 1731, Nottingham UL Mellish; Pococke to mother, 13 June 1734, BL Add. 22798; Windsor Castle, Royal Archives, Cumberland Papers 43/208; Hatfield, *Index of Cecil Papers*, IX, 57; Wharton to Lloyd, 20 May, 23 Oct. 1775, Durham, Wharton; Pelham to Lord Pelham, 18 Dec. 1775, 25 July, 24 Aug., 22 Oct., 29 Nov. 1776, 2 Aug. 1777, Lord to Thomas Pelham, 18 Sept. 1776, BL Add. 33126–7; Drake to father, 25 Nov. 1768, Townson to William Drake senior, 28 Jan. 1769, Aylesbury, D/DR/8/24, 3/4; Mount Stuart 2/34.
10. Anon., BL Stowe, 790, f. 75–6; *The Gentleman's Guide in his Tour through France by an Officer* ... (7th edn, 1783), p. 8.
11. Blackett to Sir Edward Blackett, 4 Jan. 1785, Northumberland CRO ZBL 188/289.
12. Drummonds to Keith, 19 May 1778, Sidney Clive senior to Keith, 18 Nov. 1785, BL Add. 35514, 35535; Beinecke, Osborn Shelves c 467 11 Nos 28, 43, 48; Chester CRO DBW/N/Bundle E, Packet A; Pelham to Lord Pelham, 28 June 1777, Francis, 20 Nov. 1772, BL Add. 33127, 40759; Wharton to Thomas Lloyd, 18 April 1776, Durham, Wharton.
13. Barbara Countess of Jersey to Countess of Grantham, 5 May 1716, Herts. D/E Na F8; Beinecke, Osborn Shelves c 467 vol. 1 No. 124; Wharton to Thomas Lloyd, 18 June 1775, Wharton jnl, Feb. 1775, Durham, Wharton; Thicknesse, 1768, pp. 180–3, 1777, I, pp. 10–11, 117, 1786, pp. 8–9.
14. Dering to Perceval, 25 Aug. 1723, BL Add. 47030; Clavering to Lady Cowper, 13 Mar. 1717, Henry Nassau to Count William Maurice of Nassau, 17 May 23 June 1732, Herts. D/EP F196, D/E Na F57.
15. Hay to George Compton, 20 May 1708, BL Sloane 405; anon., BL Add. 60522; Perceval to Daniel Dering, 4 Dec. 1725, 12 Feb. 1726, BL Add. 47031.
17. Cradock, p. 252; Martyn, vii–viii; Hoare, CUL Add. Mss. 3545, f. 1; Bennet, 11 July 1785.
18. Bennet, 21 Sept., 29 Oct. 1785.
19. *Walpole–Cole correspondence*, I, 98.
20. Drummonds to Keith, 17 July 1778, Captain Sebright to Keith, 1 June 1787, BL Add. 35514, 35538.
21. Bennet, 31 Aug. 1785.
22. *The Gentleman's Guide ... by an Officer* (7th edn, 1783), p. 10; Riddell(?) jnl, 20 Nov. 1770, Northumberland CRO ZRW 62; Drake to father, 10 April 1769, Aylesbury, D/Dr/8/2.

23. Brand to Wharton, 23 Nov. 1793, Durham, Wharton.

24. Carteret to Wetstein, 27 June (os) 1728, Hay to Compton, 1 Sept. 1707, BL Add. 32415, 38507.

25. Francis, BL Add. 40759, f. 18, cf. f. 2.

26. Spark Molesworth to Hugh Gregor, 24 March 1739, BL Add. 61830; Fife, 21 Dec. 1765; 6th Earl of Salisbury to Lady Brown, 27 May 1770, Hatfield, *Index* XI, 80; Edward Finch to Earl of Nottingham, 19 Nov. 1725; Leics. CRO Finch Mss. DG/7/4952.

27. Shaw, 1709, pp. 9, 27; Grey jnl, BL Add. 5957, f. 55; Bennet, 7 July 1785.

28. In 1720 Glenorchy complained about the costs of Hanover and Lord Molesworth about those of Augsburg.

29. Walker, p. 381.

30. Shaw, 1709, p. 27; anon. jnl, BL Add. 12130, f. 11–12; Crewe jnl, BL Add. 37926, f. 25, 54, 60, 81; Leven, p. 329; Mrs Montagu, I, 111; Jervis, BL Add. 31192, f. 11; Wharton to Thomas Lloyd, 4 April 1775, Wharton to Mrs Wharton, 26 Feb., 19 Mar., 9 April 1775, Brand to Wharton, 14 Aug. 1792, Durham, Wharton; *Tour of Holland*, p. 137; Andrews, 1784, pp. 11, 338, 393–4, 500; Carpenter, p. 48.

31. Anon., Bod. Ms. Eng. Misc. e 250, f. 14; Hatfield, *Index*, X, 180; Perceval to Daniel Dering, 31 Aug. 1725, BL Add. 47030; Hatfield Accounts, 132/23; anon., BL Add. 60522, Stowe 790 f. 43; Pococke, BL Add. 22978, f. 77, 78, 82, 87; John Ratcliff, CUL Add. Mss. 4216, f. 3; Martyn, xx; Francis, BL Add. 40759, f. 13; *Tour of Holland*, p. 71; Nixon, BL Add. 39225 f. 93; Wharton to mother, 26 Feb. 1775, Wharton jnl, Durham, Wharton; Blackett to father, 2 June 1784, Northumberland CRO ZBL 188/239, Bennet, 15 Sept., 28 Aug. 1785; Gardenstone, I, 12, 19; Mitford, Gloucester CRO D 2002 F1; Francis, f. 2; Walker, p. 324; Young, I, 24, 41, 58, 70, 78, 90, 98, 101–2, 150–2.

32. Bedford CRO L 30/8/33/30; Perceval to Daniel Dering, 26 Aug., 20 Oct. 1725, BL Add. 47030; Hatfield, Accounts, 89/1; Martyn, xx; Pococke, BL Add. 22978, f. 82, 87; Smith jnl, CUL Add. Mss. 7621; Fife, p. 16; Francis, BL Add. 40759, f. 13; *Tour of Holland*, pp. 131–2; W. Fraser, *The Melvilles* . . . I, 354; Wharton to mother, 26 Feb., Wharton to W. Baker, 29 April 1775, Durham, Wharton; Beinecke, Osborn Shelves c 289, Osborn Files, uncatalogued; Blackett to father, 2 June 1784, Northumberland CRO ZBL 188/239; Chester CRO DLT/C9/3; Bennet, 8 July 1785; Dewes jnl, Bod. Mss. Eng. Misc. d. 213, p. 150; Gardenstone, I, 18–19; Walker, p. 145; Young, I, 96, 104.

33. Anon., BL Add. 60522; Aberdeen, Maclaurin, f. 196–7; *Tour of Holland*, pp. 253, 251; Gloucester CRO D 2002 F1; anon., BL Add. 60522, Stowe 790, f. 130, Add. 12130, f. 50; Bennet, 29 Aug. 1785; Radcliffe, p. 17.

34. *Tour of Holland*, p. 248.

35. Hatfield, Accounts, 168/1; anon., BL Add. 60522; Beinecke, Osborn Shelves c 467 II No. 3; Thicknesse, 1777, I, 17; Aberdeen, Maclaurin, f. 198; Matlock CRO D 2375 M/76/186; Drake to father, Aylesbury, D/DR/8/2/2; *Tour of Holland*, p. 209; W. Fraser, *The Melvilles* . . . I, 327; Smollett, p. 41; Accounts of Sir John Swinburne, 4th, Bt., Northumberland CRO ZSW 456, 13 Nov. 1749, 16 May 1750. For complaints about costs between Trieste and Venice, *Public Advertiser* 5 May 1792.

36. *Tour of Holland*, p. 246; Wharton to mother, 12 Mar. 1775, Durham, Wharton; Stevens, p. 67; anon., BL Add. 60522.

37. Walker, p. 391; Hoare, CUL Add. Mss. 3545, f. I.

38. Richard, p. 47.

39. Perceval to Daniel Dering, 31 Aug. 1725, BL Add. 47030; Nixon, BL Add. 39225 f. 93; Francis, BL Add. 40759, f. 13; *Tour of Holland*, p. 132; Smollett, p. 43; anon., BL Add. 60522; Fish to Duchess of Marlborough, 12 Oct. 1727, BL Add. 61444.

40. Pickersgill to sister, April [1761], Aylesbury CRO, Saunders deposit.

41. Wharton to mother, 5 Mar. 1775, Durham, Wharton; Spencer to Duchess, 27 Oct. (os) 1723, Molesworth bills, BL Add. 61444, 61830; Swinburne, Northumberland CRO ZSW 456; Hatfield, Accounts, 89/1, 132/23; Fife, pp. 21, 39; Fish to Duchess of Marlborough, 11 Nov. 1726, BL Add. 61444.

42. Mitchell, BL Add. 58314, f. 24–30; Wharton; Windham, p. 4.

43. Bennet, 30 June 1785.

44. Perceval to Daniel Dering, 20 Oct. 1725, BL Add. 47031.

45. Fish to Sarah Marlborough, 30 Oct. 1727, BL Add. 61444.

46. Southwell to Perceval, 9 April 1726, Perceval to Daniel Dering, 1 July (os) 1718; BL Add. 47031, 47028; L.M. Wiggin, *The Faction of Cousins* (New Haven, 1958), p. 4; Nuneham to Lady Elizabeth Harcourt, undated, Aylesbury CRO D/LE E2/20; Beinecke, Osborn Shelves c 467 II No. 15.

47. Henry to Thomas Pelham, 21 Feb. 1775, Livingston to Keith, 14 Sept. 1785, BL Add. 33126, 35535.

48. Brand to Wharton, 10 Sept. 1787.

49. Aylesbury CRO D/DR/8/3/3.

50. R.W. Ketton-Cremer, *Country Neighbourhood* (1951), p. 24; P. McKay, 'The Grand Tour of the Hon. Charles Compton', *Northamptonshire Past and Present*, 7 (1986), pp. 246–7; H. de la Harp, Boston's tutor, to Earl of Grantham, 24 June 1716, Herts. D/E Na F8; John Thornton, Haggerston's tutor, to Francis Anderton, 18 Sept. 1718, Northumberland CRO ZH6 VIII; Spencer to Duchess of Marlborough, 29 April 1726, Sunderland to Spencer, 20 Sept, 1729, BL Add. 61444, 61667; Hatfield, Accounts, 132/33; Lord Carteret to Wetstein, 7 April (os), 16 June (os), 22 Sept. (os) 1741, BL Add. 32416; Beinecke, Osborn Shelves c 469 pp. 23–9; Bod. Ms. Don. b 23 f. 86; Fife, p. 39; Aylesbury CRO D/DR/8/4/2; Hatfield, *Index*, XI, 82, 88; Wharton to Brand, 17 Mar. 1775; Beinecke, Osborn Files, uncatalogued. This collection incudes Stopford's accounts for his year at Lausanne from June 1782; Bennet, Bod. Ms. Eng. Misc. f. 54 f. 198–9; 'Memoirs of my own life', Bod., Bland Burges deposit, vol. 75, f. 105; *Pembroke Papers* I, 29; D. Stroud, *George Dance* (London, 1971), p. 62.

51. North to Hallam, 21 Feb. 1753, BL Add. 61980; *St. James's Chronicle*, 23 May 1769; Blackett, Northumberland CRO NBL 188/239; Bennet, Bod. Ms. Eng. Misc. f. 54 f. 196; M. Postlethwayt, *Great Britain's True System* (1757), p. 290; Stevens, p. 275; Delafaye to Waldegrave, 30 Nov. (os) 1732, Chewton.

52. Bennet, 6 Sept. 1785; Barker to Keith, 9 June 1787, BL Add. 35538; *Tour of Holland*, p. 248; Andrews, 1784, p. 23; *Gentleman's Guide ... by an Officer*, p. 3.

53. Hay to George Compton, 28 Nov. 1708, Thomas Pelham to Lord Pelham, 8 Feb., 2 Aug. (quote) 1777, BL Add. 47030, 33127; William Drake to father, 25

Feb. 1778, Aylesbury CRO D/Dr/8/27; Beinecke, Osborn Shelves c 467 II, No. 19, 26.

54. J. Gerard to Duke of Kent, 18 Jan. 1715, Bedford CRO Lucas 30/8/28/1; Southwell to Perceval, 27 Sept. 1723, BL Add. 47030; Smollett, p. 44; Thicknesse, 1777, II, 152; Mitford, Gloucester CRO D 2002 FI.

55. *Daily Universal Register*, 22 July 1786; Head, 21 Mar. 1725, Christ Church, Oxford, Head-Wake correspondence.

56. Carpenter, pp. 32–3; Thomas to Lord Pelham, 16 Nov. 1776, BL Add. 33127; Villiers, *A Tour through part of France* (1789), pp. 3–5.

57. Young, I, 20; *Gentleman's Guide ... by an Officer*, p. 2; Pottle (ed.), *Boswell in Holland*, p. 222.

58. Pelham to Thomas Pelham of Stammer, BL Add. 33085, f. 41; Hull UL DD Ho 4/3; Stanhope to Earl Stanhope, KAO Chevening Mss. U1590 C708/2.

4

TRANSPORT

ROADS

The bulk of tourist travel was by road, and a major difference between eighteenth-century and modern comment on European travel was the stress in the former on road conditions. A wealth of information about these can be found in tourist accounts and in those of other travellers, such as diplomats. A reiterated theme was the dependence of road conditions on the weather.

German Roads

> . . . bad weather and impracticable roads from hence to Dresden, keep us at present . . . I would not travel the road from hence to Frankfurt for all the coronations in Europe.

> John Sturrock, Kassel, 1740[1]

British tourists had a poor opinion of German roads and this doubtless played a role in influencing their preference for Paris and Italy, although the more fashionable sights of the latter were more important. The road system of much of Europe in the eighteenth century was essentially still that laid down by the Romans. Germany lacked the basis of Roman roads that was still important in Italy, and the coordinated governmental activity that had made such a difference to French roads over the previous century. The existence of numerous independent territories within the Holy Roman Empire played a part in the relatively poor road system there, but roads were also indifferent within individual territories, such as Bavaria. Sacheverell Stevens was unimpressed, despite the fact that he followed some major routes. From Innsbruck to Munich: 'some heavy rains having lately fallen, we found the roads excessively bad, there being no sort of pavement as in France and Italy.' Between Munich and Augsburg, George, Viscount Parker (c. 1697–1764), later 2nd Earl of

Macclesfield, had found the roads so narrow in 1719 that he had been obliged to change his coach, while Stevens found the roads 'very bad', and on the way from Donauwörth to Nuremberg he recorded, 'we passed two posts through such exceeding bad roads, that we were obliged to walk almost half the way'. Between Kassel and Hanover, 'the roads were very bad, occasioned by some late rains'. There were 'bad roads' between Hamburg and Lübeck. A tourist who set off in June 1751 on a twenty-mile journey to Duderstadt, east of Göttingen, to see the ceremony of the nuns taking the veil, recorded:

> . . . the worst roads I have yet seen in Germany. The carriage broke into pieces before we got to the end of our journey, fairly separating the fore part of the chaise, from the hind, leaving us miserable and ridiculous spectators in the middle of the highway, whilst the postilion drove away with the coach box, and fore wheels. Mr. Hubert was fast asleep, when this happened, and I was reading Peregrine Pickle's verses on Lady Vane, but we were both obliged to change our easy situation for that of a hard trotting chaise horse, with miserable saddles so bad, that we were ashamed to ride into the town, therefore alighted at the gate, and walked to the inn.[2]

The following year, David, 7th Viscount Stormont (1727–96), was delayed on his journey from Leipzig to Hanover by 'the badness of the roads, which the late rains have made almost impracticable'. That September, William, 4th Earl of Essex (1732–99), went from Hanover 'to Utrecht as fast as possible night and day and think I never was so tired of a journey for would you imagine that going the post with six horses we were . . . four days and as many nights'. Bad roads deterred Essex from visiting Düsseldorf to see the picture collection. Colonel Charles Rainsford, who, as equerry, accompanied George III's brother, William, 5th Duke of Gloucester (1743–1805), on his 1769–71 trip to Denmark, Germany and Italy, commented on the new turnpike roads being made near Hanover, 'in the manner of a causeway, and wide enough to march in division and cost about £1,000 an English mile – These roads are very much wanted; the present ones being extremely bad, especially upon the least rain, that we had now a full opportunity of knowing.' Nathaniel Wraxall travelled from Dresden to Vienna in 1777 'through very bad roads'. George Ogilvie, who went from Hamburg to the United Provinces in January 1779, was unimpressed by the quality of the roads, but they were made more passable by a pretty severe frost. Frosts were very helpful in otherwise boggy areas and gave wheels a firm surface. In December 1785 Matthew Jenour found that a hard frost 'made the roads exceeding good' on his trip from Vienna to Paris via Munich. That spring Dawkins had found the road between Vienna and Prague, the major route in the Habsburg dominions, 'in general extremely bad . . . so much so, that we once held a consultation about returning'. Following the same route in the summer of 1787, Brand noted 'the roads are good'. Travelling from Lausanne to Vienna, via Ulm and Munich, in October 1783, James, Lord Stopford (1765–1835) was twice delayed in Austria by a shortage of post-horses, but the journey was a good one, 'the roads we found everywhere in good order and horses ready, the dry and fine weather made us push forwards, and have completed that journey in thirteen days'. He lost a few pounds of weight during that period.

Other travellers were less satisfied by the German roads and this affected their itineraries. Robert Arbuthnot noted, 'The roads from Mainz to Cologne are so bad that we were advised to take a boat and sail down the Rhine.' Sir John Macpherson, 'found the roads so bad in Germany, that I directed my course to Italy'. In 1719 George, Viscount Parker described one of the flying bridges which were found at a number of places including Nijmegen, Cologne, Koblenz and Mainz:

> It is made of two large lighters joined together, and covered with boards; each one of them has a mast, which are likewise fastened to one another by a beam, upon which rests a rope of a prodigious length, which is fastened at a great distance up the river; there is likewise a rudder, and by dextrously managing it the stream carries the machine to either side of the river. The space on the top is large enough to hold several coaches together with horsemen, and is railed in all round, but where the coaches come in and go out: and there a chain is put up during the passage for fear of accidents.

Parker, however, found the roads from Bonn to Mainz 'very bad, and in some places dangerous. The way for the most part mountainous; and in some places you go along upon the side of a mountain with a precipice just by you of about thirty or forty yards depth at the bottom of which runs the Rhine, and this continues sometimes for three or four hours together.'[3]

A vivid account of a journey from Dresden to Prague in November 1748 was provided by Thomas Steavens, who wrote to Sir Charles Hanbury Williams, the British envoy in Dresden:

> You were too moderate in your wit when you gave me a week for my journey from Dresden to Vienna . . . but, had you known the roads through which I was to pass, the dangers I was to risk, and the fatigue I was to suffer, you would have given me two months at least, and I believe in my conscience I shall take one . . . I reached Aussig . . .

seven miles in fourteen hours. Though I was shook to a jelly, and half
dead I called for horses at Aussig, and determined to go on directly,
but the postmaster could not answer for any accident. Upon this I
stayed at Aussig till next morning, and before I had been half a mile
out of the town, was fully convinced of the postmaster's veracity. I
travelled all this post upon a ridge of high mountains that goes down
perpendicular to the Elbe, and where there was often hardly room for
the chaise to pass, one wheel sometimes would slip into a great hole
and almost overturn the chaise, which made me funk my soul out and
curse my evil genius for having left the plain even roads of England,
for the rocky roads, and horrible precipices of Bohemia . . . the next
night I came to a place called Wellbern, where I was obliged again, by
the badness of the roads, to stay all night . . . I found the roads grow
worse and worse every post, and nothing but a chaise like mine could
have brought me through them; I mean a chaise of such a length, and
that has so great a distance between the a'fore, and 'hind wheels, and,
if you come to Prague in your coach, you will be overturned ten, if
in your vis a vis twenty times . . . with whatever force of reason Mr.
Evans may argue against six horses, four of the best in Europe would
not have drawn me out of the bogs, and up the hills I passed, and
about a mile from Aussig the chaise run back with the horses upon the
steepest and narrowest hill imaginable.

Fortunately, Prague brought a very comfortable hotel, a very good dinner
and a good production of the opera *Artaxerxes*. Having 'ordered two geese
and a ham to be dressed for me to carry away', Steavens set off for Vienna.
He found the roads much better, Viennese food very good, 'admirable
sower groat', and was delighted by Austrian hospitality. There was also
plenty to do: 'at night there is a German comedy with an intermezzo
between the acts, and an Italian opera, one night serious, another buffa'.
Early 1749 brought very different adventures for Steavens – half an hour
with Rosa 'in a beastly alehouse' and a visit to the Esterhazy palace near
Sopron: 'Nothing can exceed the pleasure and happyness of this place,
every man does exactly the thing he likes best, and nothing but that. There
is an ease and a profusion that are enough to make a cynic turn admirer of
the good things of this world. People eat, drink, and sleep, as they please,
and when they please . . . servants without number.'

Taking the same journey to Vienna in 1752, William, 2nd Earl of
Dartmouth (1731–1801), also encountered problems: 'I am surprised
our old coach performed the business so well, we broke one axle-tree
indeed before we came to Aussig, which kept us at that agreeable city a
whole day; but I defy any coach to stand the bangs and shocks it receives
in passing the mountains upon the edge of Bohemia.'⁴

The comments of tourists on German roads were supported by those of the diplomats, both British and foreign, and by those of other travellers. The theme that emerged repeatedly was the dependence of the road system on the weather: bad in snow, rain or thaw, better in frost. The impact of the weather was often more important than the state of the original road. Many road surfaces were largely unimproved, so that the nature of the soil, for example the sandy soil between Emden and Hamburg, very much affected ease of movement. The most comprehensive guide to Germany published in the 1730s claimed, 'The roads here are not much better than what nature has made them.'[5]

Italian Roads

We have paid the usual tribute to Venetian roads that of broken carriages and broken *commandments*. A *curse* on all Republics say I.

Brand, after journey from Innsbruck via Bergamo to Milan, 1792[6]

The Italian road system was better than that of Germany and tourist complaints about the major routes – Turin–Genoa, Milan–Parma–Bologna, Turin–Alessandria–Parma – were limited. The road system was best in Lombardy and Piedmont, both territories with reasonably effective government. Further south there was a deterioration in quality both of the major and of the minor roads, a factor that reflected terrain, the relative poverty of these areas and the limited effectiveness of their governments, although some efforts were made to improve roads near Naples after the Bourbons acquired the kingdom in 1734, and this helped tourists between Rome and Naples.

The Apennine chain posed a problem for tourists. There were few passable routes across it and these could be blocked by winter snows. These snows kept Norton Nicholls in Milan in the winter of 1771–2. Those hoping to visit Tuscany could avoid the Ligurian mountains east of Genoa by sailing direct to Leghorn (Livorno) or Lerici from Genoa or Marseilles. From nothern Italy the usual crossing of the Apennines was the road from Bologna to Florence, though in the 1780s the routes from Modena to Pistoia and Lucca were improved. A frequently used route, the major alternative to that from Bologna, was from Ancona via Loreto, Foligno, Spoleto and Terni. This served tourists travelling to or from Venice. In 1734 Jeremiah Milles (1714–84), later Dean of Exeter and President of the Society of Antiquaries, found this road 'disagreeable, along the sides of hills, and in some places dangerous'.

Opinions of the Apennine roads varied. Francis Head was very unimpressed by the Bologna–Florence road in 1723, and Sacheverell

Stevens thought that the best way to travel it was 'in a litter', as the mountainous road was bad for wheeled carriages. On the other hand, John, 5th Earl of Orrery (1701–62), praised the road.[7] The Tuscan roads were not as good as those in Lombardy. Travelling from Siena to Rome in 1741, Lady Henrietta Pomfret complained of a 'rough and dismal journey . . . obliged to get out and walk several times for fear of breaking our necks'. Stevens had noted of the same road two years earlier that rain and snow affected its quality, and the weather was a factor throughout Italy. In 1732 Andrew Mitchell commented on the Ferrara–Bologna road which ran over poorly drained clay, 'very bad when it has rained . . . if one days raining in summer was enough to spoil the roads, what must they be in the winter?' An anonymous tourist, entering the Papal States from Tuscany in 1778, 'soon began to find that everything changed for the worse, for though they forced us to take six horses at Centeno we waited an hour and a half at the bottom of a hill without being able to get up. Two oxen which happened to be passing by were harnessed to the chaise but had no effect until a little pony was sent for from Acquapendente which drew the carriage up the hill.'[8]

A major problem affecting road travel in Italy was the need to cross rivers, many of which flooded during the spring thaw and the autumn rains. Furthermore, there were very few bridges. As was the case in most of Europe, rivers were usually crossed by ferries which were difficult to operate if the river was in spate. Pococke found the system working well on his way from Milan to Turin in 1734: 'before we came to Novara we passed over the Tessino, very rapid . . . a horse drew the boat half a mile up the river, then being carried down in crossing a horse drew us up again to the landing place . . . a boat goes down 12 miles an hour without rowing'. Mitchell was less fortunate crossing the Trebia near Piacenza, 'by reason of a very small quantity of rain that had fallen the day before'. The river had a very wide channel and followed a varying course. There was no bridge, as was the case with most of the rivers that flowed from the Apennines to the Lombard plain. Mitchell also observed that many Apennine roads followed river beds and often could not be used. The overflowing of the rain-swollen Tiber affected Henry, 9th Earl of Lincoln (1720–94), on his journey from Florence to Rome in late 1740. An anonymous traveller from Florence to Bologna in 1755 had to turn back because rain swelled a stream; another from Turin to Vercelli in late November 1782, wrote: 'The road very good as is generally the case in his Sardinian Majesty's dominions; but two or three large rivers to pass which if flooded may give delay, or what is worse than delay its general companion danger.' In December 1785 Lady Craven found that the ferryman was unwilling to cross the Trevisa because of storms. Eighteen months later Robert, Viscount Belgrave (1767–1845), later 1st Marquis of Westminster, travelled from

Trieste to Venice: 'The weather was so bad that we were obliged to give up all thoughts of going by sea, so continued our journey on a road, which was tolerably good, except where the rivers Tagliamento and Prava had overflowed their banks, and almost deluged the neighbouring country, which delayed us considerably.' Flooding on the Milan–Turin road led to detours as far as Lake Maggiore. There were improvements, Mitford travelling from Campomorone to Genoa in 1776 along a new road that was protected from the Polavera, but they were limited.[9]

Few tourists travelled on roads in southern Italy aside from the road between Rome and Naples, and most found this route of a reasonable standard. A tourist who went from Naples to see the triumphal arch of Trajan in Benevento in 1779 commented: 'the road is for a great part of the way exceedingly bad, and in many places scarcely passable for a carriage'. Seven years later, Sir William Hamilton, the envoy in Naples, reported on the 'want of communication from one province to another' in the kingdom of Naples: 'in winter the roads are impassable, and scarcely passable in summer, even on horseback; in most of the provinces in this kingdom, and in Sicily, except in the City of Palermo, wheeled carriages are unknown'.[10]

There were complaints about roads in northern Italy. Stevens thought the Bologna–Ferrara road 'generally very bad'; 'a journey in miserable roads and bad weather from Venice' to Milan took Nicholls nine days in November 1772; Lady Craven thought it too easy to fall off the causeway on that from Cento to Ferrara. A tourist left Milan for Piacenza, generally a good road, on 3 December 1782, 'with three horses and bribery to take so few, but found the road so deep, that we made a virtue of necessity the 3rd post, and acquiesced to taking 4 horses which the Postmaster insisted on'.[11] In general, however, tourists praised the quality of northern Italian roads. Pococke was unhappy about the road west from Brescia, but noted that it was rare for him to be thus dissatisfied. Mitchell described the road from Voghera to Tortona as 'excellent'. Walker was very impressed by the roads from Ferrara to Bologna, Rimini to Fano, Siena to Florence and Bologna to Milan. He claimed that the road near Reggio was 'as good as our best turnpikes'. Swinton observed that the roads 'almost all over Italy' were good. Thompson praised that from Modena to Bologna. There were complaints, but no one was put off a trip to Italy by the state of the Italian roads.[12]

French Roads

The only French roads that most British tourists saw were those from Calais to Paris and thence towards Italy. The former was a fairly good one, Jervis noting in 1772, 'the road from Calais to Montreuil is not extraordinary, but from the latter to Amiens for the most part extremely good, being paved and trees on either hand'. Henry, 2nd Viscount Palmerston, observed in December 1762, 'It has froze excessively hard ever since we left London but I think it rather mends the French roads which upon the whole we found good.' Thomas Brand, however, recorded of his arrival in Paris in February 1786, 'arrived here . . . through bad roads and indifferent weather'.[13] The route from Paris to Lyons was generally a good one, but Spark Molesworth complained from there of 'a very fatiguing journey from Paris of 6 days and a half, the weather being all the way very bad, and the roads I believe in this country were never so bad, for where they could be bad they were so indeed'. The alternatives to the road to Châlons and then the boat down the Saône to Lyons was a road via Montargis, Nevers, Moulins and Roanne. Mitchell was not too pleased with 'the first 20 posts from Lyons' on this road, though Walker who took it in October 1787 found it acceptable. Between Lyons and Roanne he had to have a yoke of oxen added to the three carriage horses in order for the carriage to be dragged up a mountainous sector of the road. Towards Paris he noted, 'the roads improve, are very wide, level, hard'.[14] From Lyons to Marseilles it was usual to go to Avignon by river and thence by road via Aix. Mitchell thought these roads 'very good', but Robert Wharton was less happy about the journey: 'Were I to wish the greatest evil I could imagine to the worst of my enemies, it should be may he come from Avignon to Marseilles in bad weather and in a French voiture. Never did I suffer so much from any journey of 300 miles as I have in these 60. Never did I see such vile roads, and that too between two of the most considerable towns of France.'[15]

Roads in the rest of France varied. The importance of ferries, for rivers such as the Garonne and the Dordogne,[16] ensured that heavy rainfall created difficulties. Visiting Bordeaux in 1737, John Mucklow took ferries over the Garonne, Lot and Dordogne, and noted: 'we ferried over the Garonne just where the Tarn runs into it. The passage is long and when the water is high very troublesome.'[17] There was less flooding, however, than in Italy. The roads in northern France, especially in areas of heavy clay, tended to be more affected by rain than those in the south. In July 1734 Pococke was able to travel ninety miles from Thil through Vitry and Châlons-sur-Marne to Rheims in one day, thanks to the 'goodness of the road like a gravel walk, broad and lately made'. The following day, though, he went to Laon 'half of the way bad and the other very bad', and thence 'by indifferent roads . . . to Lafiere in Picardy'. In September 1738 Sacheverell Stevens travelled along the mostly paved Abbeville–Beauvais road: 'as it happened to rain very hard this day, it rendered the unpaved part like a quagmire, and made it excessively bad travelling'. Richard Hopkins went from Nantes to Port Louis, near Lorient, in 1749, suffering 'two days journey the most disagreable I had ever been, from the badness of the mountainous roads'. He wanted to press on, 'but it was impracticable, the roads of Bretagny those I had gone almost impassable, and we were well assured that to Brest, it was impossible to go with our chaise'. Charles Sloane found the roads from Spa to Nancy 'very bad in some places' in September 1783.[18]

The roads in Languedoc were generally highly praised. Mitchell was unimpressed by those near the Pont du Gard, but thought the Nîmes–Montpellier road 'excellent' and observed 'the roads in Languedoc are generally good and kept in repair', while Arthur Young wrote of the 'incredible number of splendid bridges, and many superb causeways' in Languedoc. Young was also very impressed by the Orleans–Limoges and Limoges–Brive roads, but the axletree of Brand's carriage broke near Montauban in 1783. Two years later Anna Cradock found the road from Saintes to Rochefort good and new, like, she claimed, most French ones. Lady Craven warned of another hazard when advising travellers not to go from Blois to Tours by night as the road was unfenced and it was easy to fall into the Loire or into low-lying meadows. The fact that the entire Orleans–Paris road was paved impressed an anonymous tourist of 1776–7 who added, 'The wide strait roads of France are convenient and magnificent, but they fatigue the travellers eye.'[19]

Very few tourists visited areas of France where the roads were poor, such as the Massif Central and the Jura, and those who did travel in provincial France found the roads in general reasonable, especially in good weather. The road system improved during the century, Mucklow travelling on new roads near Senlis and Paris in 1737,[20] but it was already in existence between the major centres at the beginning of the century. In the first half of the century the system was good enough for travellers to consider a stay at such provincial French academies as Angers, Besançon and Lunéville. Lunéville was in Lorraine, an independent duchy until 1766, but the roads there were of a similar standard to those in neighbouring areas of France. According to the dedication in the dedication copy of the first English edition of Augustin Calmet's *Dissertation upon the High-Roads of the Duchy of Lorraine* (1729), Henry, 3rd Duke of Beaufort (1707–45), had 'resided some time in Lorraine, travelled it over and over, and examined its high-roads, and other publick works with care and attention'.[21] Related facilities also improved. In 1724 appeared the first edition of Jean-Aymar Piganiol de la Force's *Nouveau Voyage de France. Avec un Itineraire, et des Cartes faites exprès, qui marquent exactement les routes qu'il faut suivre pour voyager dans toutes les Provinces de ce Rayaume. Ouvrage également utile aux François et aux Etrangers*. With fifteen folding maps, this was one of the best French road books. The routes that linked Paris to the Channel, Rouen, the Loire valley, Lyons and Strasbourg constituted what was, by eighteenth-century standards, a good road system. That most tourists did not visit more distant areas of France reflected not so much the quality of their roads, as a widespread lack of interest in these regions.

Roads: Other Countries, Conclusions

The roads in the United Provinces were well maintained, especially in the provinces of Holland and Utrecht. Tourists tended to comment rather on the Dutch canals, though Stevens described the Utrecht–Amsterdam road 'as one of the most agreeable roads in all Europe' and claimed that it was 'the same as if going through the finest walk or avenue in the best laid out garden'. The sandy nature of the soil did, however, make 'travelling go slowly on' in Holland, and John Judd complained in 1770 that 'the roads from Antwerp to the village of Moredyke are very disagreeable being chiefly a morass which obliged us to travel very slow.'[22]

Roads in the Austrian Netherlands (Belgium) were often badly affected by rain, but the major route, that from Antwerp to Brussels, was good, and the straight tree-lined roads delighted many British tourists. On the other hand, roads through the Ardennes were poor. At Mézières in 1767 John, 1st Earl Spencer (1734–83), and his wife, Georgiana (1737–1814)

had the mortification to find that we could not go to Namur by water [River Meuse] under three days or two at least with many inconveniences, so we were obliged to consent as we had no time to spare to go by land. They told us the road was not good but that we should do it with ease in less than 10 hours. However we did not arrive at Namur in much less than 16, after passing some dreadful roads indeed and a great part of them after it was pitch dark especially one hill in a very thick wood where we must have remained all night if we had not luckily found a cargo of wax candles which had been carried for the lanterns of the carriage and which we put together in little bundles and made very good torches of.

There could be problems even near the Channel. Returning to London in October 1763, Ladies Westmorland and Primrose gave

a melancholy account of the many disastrous perils they went through. Stuck fast in a bog on some heath, and then forced to walk above a mile in the dark to get to some dismal hovel . . . the day after like to have been lost on the sea sands, but Lady Westmorland with some threats and some entreaties, got the man to go back again to Nieuport after having been out above eight hours, striving to get to Dunkirk. At Nieuport they were forced to stay all the next day, to endeavour to get fresh horses, and then they got with much difficulty to Dunkirk; they stayed at Calais nine days for a wind, and afterwards were nine hours getting over the sea, being both of them all the while most extremely sick.[23]

Alpine journeys posed particular problems. Charles Hotham (1693–1738) reached Turin in 1711, 'after a very tedious journey of eight days through the Alps. The fifth day we got to the foot of the highest mountain called St. Bernard; we were six hours getting to the top of it; we found the snow so deep, it being in most places the depth of four horses, and no track made that we were once or twice upon the point of going back; but at last with the help of some men with shovels who made the way before us we got through.' Edward Tucker wrote from Lausanne to his aunt in 1760:

the roads in some parts so deep that I was obliged to have four oxen to draw out the chaise and horses and to set out at four o'clock in the morning and not get to the end of that day's journey till seven at night though it is but seven leagues. These bad roads lie between Genoa and Turin from whence to this place you have nothing but one continued chain of mountains, in crossing one of the highest of them called Mount Sine, my mule was buried in the snow three times, so I was obliged to throw myself off in doing which I had the misfortune to lose my much valued repeating watch . . . The prospects on this mountain are if I may be allowed the expression dreadfully pleasing, for though I saw nothing but snow for three days in succession, yet the different shapes of the cragged precipices with the narrow road and just room for a mule to pass . . . mixed with cataracts and waterfalls from a stupendous height, here and there a town whose inhabitants see nothing but snow eight months in the year, render it awful and at the same time agreeable . . . I came down the mountain of Sine which I was eight hours crossing in 9 minutes though the descent is more than three miles, which is faster than any race horse in England can go on the finest plain . . . you are placed on a sledge . . . a man sits at the head between your legs and with his feet guides it and though it goes with almost inexpressible velocity and the precipices on each side are tremendous, his dexterity by daily practice makes all kind of fear unnecessary.[24]

The passage to and from north-eastern Italy was far easier, Henry Oxenden finding that his journey from Venice to Vienna over the Tarvisio through Styria in early 1749 was on 'excessive good roads'. Sambrooke Freeman found the approach to the Brenner less easy, writing, 'Chiusa a very bad pass, over a rock the chaise drawn over by the soldiers of the Venetian garrison there'.[25]

The roads in Iberia, the Balkans, Poland and Russia were generally bad.

In 1785 Lady Craven found the unending forest view between Warsaw and St Petersburg very boring and no carriage track in Wallachia. Sir John Sinclair MP (1754–1835), who, after the death of his first wife, travelled extensively in northern and eastern Europe in 1786, meeting Catherine the Great, Joseph II, Gustavus III of Sweden and Stanislaus Poniatowski, King of Poland, described the route from Kiev to Warsaw on 'the most terrible of all journeys'.[26] Having travelled from Cracow to Warsaw in June 1778, Wraxall wrote, 'the roads are such as nature left them, and must in winter be exceedingly bad. In many parts they are however constructed with fir trees laid across, close to each other, as is common in Russia. I was obliged to have six horses, and frequently eight, during all the journey. The Polish horses are small and weak, yet the postilions contrive to drive at a good rate.'[27] In these areas there might be individual prestige roads, and there were attempts to improve important routes, but there was no road system. The intrepid tourists who visited these areas, however, were not put off by the roads, while the vast majority of tourists who never visited them had many reasons for not doing so besides the quality of the roads.

The vulnerability of coaches, the relative frequency with which they broke down, and the limited comfort of passengers on poor road surfaces, made the state of the roads of considerable importance. Tourists appear on the whole though to have borne the situation phlegmatically. The major effect of the nature of the roads was to encourage further the tendency for tourists to travel along a relatively limited number of routes.

Some tourists compared British and European road conditions. Walker commented on the absence of turnpike charges in France, as did an anonymous account that, however, drew attention to the *corvée*, forced peasant labour, that kept the roads in repair. Arthur Young thought French ferryboats better as it was possible to drive into and out of ferries, rather than forcing the horses to leap in, as in Britain. The final word can perhaps be left to the writer who claimed in 1738: 'There is no country, whose roads have more engaged the care of the Legislature, and upon which more expences have been bestowed, than the English; and perhaps there are few so bad.'[28]

CANAL, RIVER AND SEA

. . . embarked on board a Roman trading vessel bound to Ancona . . . passed the night in a hogsty (which the captain called his cabin) on a mattress, in the utmost misery. The vessel full of goods and stinking passengers. Calms or contrary winds all night . . . continuance of misery. Godfrey eating, Francis spewing!.

Journal of Philip Francis, 1772[29]

Waterborne travel by tourists in Europe was largely restricted to France and the canal networks of the Low Countries. The Low Countries was the area in Europe with the most highly developed system of water communications, and the most extensive system of public water transport, and outside it tourists tended to travel by road. Canal and river transport in Europe suffered from major disadvantages. A slow and inflexible means of communication, it was interrupted often by drought, flood or ice, and it was difficult to travel on many rivers against the direction of the current. Few rivers had been canalized and many suffered from rocks, shoals or shallows.

Outside the Low Countries tourists tended to use only a limited number of rivers and canals. They were rarely used in Iberia or eastern Europe. The standard tourist routes in Germany ensured that the rivers were rarely used, with the exception of the Rhine. It was usual to approach Vienna from Prague, Munich or Venice and not down the Danube from Regensburg. In northern Germany tourists travelled between Dresden, Leipzig, Berlin and Hanover, and from Hanover to the United Provinces. The Oder, Elbe and Weser led towards the Baltic and North Sea, and were not tourist routes. In Italy the river that was used most frequently was the Brenta from Padua to Venice. In France the principal routes used by tourists were the Saône from Chalon to Lyons, the Rhône thence to Avignon and the Canal du Midi from Béziers to Toulouse. Tourists generally praised their riverine trips in France. One, who arranged to travel from Lyons to Avignon in a *bateau de poste* for 4 louis and 6 francs (between £4 and £5), stopping when and where he pleased, noted: 'These boats are flat bottomed and of very rude construction, the materials being always sold for plank and firewood on their arrival at Avignon. My cabriolet served me for a cabin: The wheels being taken off were laid flat at the bottom of the boat, and the body of the carriage being set upon them, was thus kept above the bilge water, which came in so plentifully as to require frequent bailing.' Impressed by the beauty of Viviers from the river, he discovered one of the limitations of river travel:

> On such occasions the rapidity of the stream so convenient for the traveller who merely wishes for his journey's end, is a mortifying obstacle to those who would contemplate at leisure the beauties of the scenery they pass. It being such, in many parts, that there is no stopping those awkward machines, the *bateaux de poste*, without reaching the shore, and that cannot be done but by the utmost exertions of the boatmen with their clumsy oars for a considerable time together, during which the boat unavoidably drives a considerable way down the stream; and in some places rocks and shoals make it dangerous to quit a particular part of the channel.

In 1784 Sir John Fleming Leicester found 'the country the whole way delightful – hills covered with vineyards and bespeckled with chateaus were our constant companions.' Samuel Boddington and his friends paid 9 louis and 12 livres' duty in July 1789 for the journey from Lyons to Avignon on a boat

neither handsome nor commodious . . . committed ourselves and our carriage to the care of three men in a boat about 60 feet long . . . We went generally at the rate of 6 miles an hour sometimes considerably faster without the assistance of a sail and in general without using the oars which served principally to keep the boat in the best current . . . After we left the villas and fertile environs of Lyons the scenery on the Rhone was exceedingly mountainous and afforded us a most wonderful variety of beautiful and picturesque views, sometimes one side of the river was a rich plain covered with corn and meadows the opposite side perhaps a mountain with vineyards to the very top and here and there a small village appearing under the brow of some stately rock. At other times we seemed to be upon a large lake entirely surrounded with barren rocks which came down to the waters edge. This was frequently the case for the current of the river was so winding that we could seldom discover which way we were to proceed not a trace of anything human around us except an old ruined castle at the summit of some apparently inaccessible rock. We had many of these views in the evening of the first day. The total silence around us and the moon only affording sufficient light to trace the grand [word obscured] of the surrounding objects gave a solemnity to the scene which was very uncommon. We felt less inconvenience from the heat than we expected. The glass was generally about 85 in the shade and 105 in the sun but we had a constant breeze the whole way which was so pleasant that we did not at all regret the delay we suffered on account of its being against us.

Bennet had been less fortunate on this journey four years earlier. The boat ran aground on a sandbank, was too crowded, and returned to Lyons in the face of a storm.[30] Jervis, who lacked Boddington's romantic sensibility, took the post-boat to Toulouse on the Canal du Midi, 'which sets out every day backwards and forwards between Béziers and Toulouse and is three days and a half on the passage stopping to dine and to lie, is a very convenient, though slow conveyance, and the entertainment in the auberge very tolerable, good beds most of the way, the changing boats when there are double, or more locks appear tedious, on account of shifting the baggage'.[31]

Where facilities existed for tourists, as on the Saône, Rhône, Brenta and Rhine, river transport was pleasant. Stevens took the *burcello*, which was drawn by two horses, from Padua to Venice. William Lee took the journey in 1753: 'the number of the country houses and the beauty of the country on each side of the river made our little voyage very agreeable. When I came in sight of this great city I never was more surprised in my life. At a distance the whole town appears to be built in the sea.'[32] On the Rhine boats, 'one travels at the rate of four or five miles for a penny; their accommodation by day is good enough, and in the evening they commonly put into a town, where passengers sleep in the inn. When there are floods, or contrary winds, the passage is somewhat tedious; but sailing down the river, or having the wind, they sail at the rate of five or six miles an hour, and it is extremely delightful.' In 1785 Captain William Gordon found the trip 'very pleasant only a little tedious and cold', but two years later William, Earl of Ancram (1763–1824), and Robert Arbuthnot were delayed sailing from Mainz to Koblenz: 'There was a very high wind all day, with frequent hail showers. Once or twice I thought the boat would have overset.' William Lee noted in his accounts, 'From Frankfurt we went by water to Arnhem. As the boat was bad and lodgings worse it is better to go post to Amsterdam.' In 1788 it cost ten louis d'or for two boats from Mainz to Cologne, one with three apartments and a kitchen, the other for two carriages.[33]

In the Low Countries the canal system was best developed around Ghent and Bruges in the Flemish part of the Austrian Netherlands, and in the provinces of Holland, Utrecht, Friesland and Groningen in the United Provinces. Few British tourists visited Friesland or Groningen, but the canal system was used fully in the other areas. Tourists were able to rely on an efficient system of public transport, on boats designed to carry passengers rather than freight. The horse-drawn barges (*trechschuits*) of the Low Countries were inexpensive and relatively comfortable. In 1742 there were hourly services from Rotterdam to Delft and Amsterdam to Haarlem, and two-hourly services between The Hague and Leyden, the journey taking three hours, and between Leyden and Haarlem. The provision of a kind of first-class compartment added to the comfort. Meals could be taken on many of the barges, and the service was frequent, once-hourly in the summer for most of the Holland routes. The boats were punctual and reasonably quick, journey times in 1786 being three hours for The Hague–Leyden, four for Leyden–Haarlem, two for Haarlem–Amsterdam and eight for Amsterdam–Utrecht. In 1773 it cost James Essex 15d to travel from Nieuport to Bruges in the best apartment, with the same price for a large dinner. The prices were the same for the Bruges–Ghent stage.[34]

Not everybody, however, appreciated the Dutch boats. In 1763 James Boswell complained that they were sluggish and tedious. If the best apartment was not available and the top was lashed by rain it was necessary to share a generally smoky and crowded compartment. Travelling from Bruges to Ghent in 1717, Carpenter noted that 'the boat never went faster than a walk'.[35] Nevertheless, in general comments about canal travel were favourable. In 1742 Matthew Arnot took the twice-daily boat from Amsterdam to Utrecht, a thirty-five-mile journey that took seven hours: 'All the way between Amsterdam and this town, is delightful to travellers, for both sides of the river are mostly adorned with rows of gardens and gentlemens seats, which, in the spring time, afford a prospect mighty agreeable.'[36]

Canal journeys were certainly far better than those by sea. The Channel or North Sea crossing to the Continent was a rude introduction for most tourists to the problems of sea voyages. An anonymous tourist crossing from Dover to Calais in June 1775 was first delayed by wind, and, after he had sailed, 'the wind was very calm and not fair. We were once obliged to drop anchor for a quarter of an hour for want of it and were about eight hours and half making our passage. Extremely sick the whole time except two of the party who were not affected. It being low water, were obliged to land in a little boat.' Thereafter, tourist travel by sea can be divided into two categories: short hops usually designed to avoid difficult sections of land, and long voyages. In the first category the most common journeys were along the Mediterranean coast between Marseilles and Leghorn. Adverse winds and the limited facilities available for tourists in some of the small ports on the route frequently created problems. A tourist who in October 1754 hired a felucca and eight men at Nice to take himself, his companions, servants and a coach for 6 louis, wrote:

> . . . it is much better for those who go this way into Italy to come by land from Marseilles to Nice and there take a felucca . . . in the winter it is so bad a way of going that I would not advise anyone to go in one of those boats: not that there is any great danger at any time in them from the sea; the Genoese being so great cowards: but there is danger of being put on shore and being obliged to continue several days where you can neither get house to cover you, bed to lie on, or bread to eat. Then again they are in continual apprehensions from the Barbary corsairs . . . I would not advise any one to defer his passage by sea into Italy later than the middle of September.

A contrary wind so hindered his rowers that they had to put into Menton, Bordighera, where he stayed for four days, at first 'in a little fisherman's hut', and Savona, where the delay was three days. Bad weather subsequently delayed him a week at Genoa while ready to sail for Lerici. At Florence in 1725, Alan Brodrick found 'there remained nothing' left in Italy that he wanted to see 'but Genoa, Milan and Turin. My shortest way had been from Leghorn to Genoa by sea, but that way I could not go, having promised my aunt both before and since I left England, not to make any part of my journey by sea.' Mitford noted in 1776:

> From Genoa to Lerici travellers usually pass in a felucca to avoid the fatigue of a mountain journey along roads where mules only can keep their feet. These Mediterranean vessels are not formed for bad weather and they are manned by no very skilful mariners. Scarcely ever an oar's length from the shore they creep under the rocks, and trembling at every wind are always afraid to hoist a sail. If the wind is very fair, eight hours will carry the felucca from Genoa to Lerici. But if the wind is the least contrary, or if it is so high that these timorous seamen dare not trust a sail, twenty hours rowing will hardly suffice to double every projecting rock, and bring the bark to its destination. The beauty of the rocky coast, and the variety of its scenery afford some recompense for the tedious passage.[37]

Travelling to Venice was another cause of short voyages. In February 1721 Viscount Parker wrote from Venice to his father, the Earl of Macclesfield. 'The roads between this place and Ravenna being most extraordinarily bad, we determined to go to that place by water, and have been obliged to stay here longer than we intended by the bad weather.' Simon, 2nd Viscount Harcourt, sailed from Venice to Trieste in June 1734, en route for Vienna. Adam Inglis made the same journey in the opposite direction in 1786, 'a pleasant journey where we were obliged to remain three days the wind though fair being so high that we could not put to sea. We were two days on the passage which was rather disagreeable. By what we now hear of the new road by Clagenfurt we regret that we did not come by it as we shoud then have shunned the uncertainty of a sea passage.'[38]

The increased popularity of travel to Vienna and the improvements at the port of Trieste ensured that the Trieste–Venice run which had attracted few tourists early in the century was quite busy by the 1780s. Few sailed further south from Venice than Ravenna: the coast road to Ancona was good and the Adriatic coast was toured by very few. Facilities for tourists were scarce and there were no famous sites south of Ancona. The eastern shores of the Adriatic were largely under Venetian rule, but were an area of brigandage and piracy. The Roman antiquities on the Dalmatian coast were not on the tourist itinerary, and Robert Adam (1728–92), who went to Italy in 1754, chose to make a careful study of the ruins at Spalato (Split) because they had not been tackled hitherto. Returning to Britain in 1762, he published his *Ruins of the Palace of the Emperor Diocletian at Spalato in Dalmatia*. Frederick, 4th Earl of Bristol and Bishop of Derry

(1730–1803), travelled through Dalmatia with the Italian naturalist Fortis and investigated the subterranean rivers of Istria.

On the other hand, tourists sailed to both Sicily and Corsica. Such trips were not without their hazards. In May 1698 Robert Clayton planned to sail from Naples to Sicily:

We had hired for this voyage a felucca with 8 straight oars and the 15th at night we sent our provisions and other necessaries on board. The 16 in the morning we had a very clear sky, and a perfect calm; everything seemed to smile, and tempt us to the voyage, and promised a safe and quick passage to Messina. Accordingly about 9 in the morning we put to sea . . . we rowed directly over the Gulf for the isle of Capri, and when we were about 20 miles from Naples we felt a small breeze of wind, the sea began to swell, upon which our pilot steered directly to Massa a town near the point of the promontary and the nearest land we could make to. We had not rowed an hour but the sky grew cloudy and it blew very hard and the sea ran so high against us that we rather retired to Naples than advanced to Massa and at last our oars became useless, which obliged us to put up our sail and endeavour to gain Capri and so we beat for near an hour against the wind and sea both increasing still. Our vessel lay so much on one side that near a yard of the sail was continually under water whilst the sea ran over the other side of the boat and every wave seemed to threaten destruction. We were still 6 miles from Capri and found that we advanced but very little and that with great danger, and at last found no other security but to return before the wind to Naples . . . The weather continued still blustering and the season being somewhat advanced I believe I shall lay aside all other thoughts of pursuing this voyage.[39]

In 1785 Charles Sloane sailed from Sicily to Malta: 'We got over in 12 hours, and had a storm astern most of the way. I was dead sick, and had I not been so, should have been greatly alarmed for my safety, as we were in a boat with six rowers called a sparonara.'[40] In January 1760 Edward Tucker, who had come the previous year by sea from England to Genoa, nearly being captured by a French ship off Corsica, intended to spend only four or five days in Livorno, 'by the feluccas which (weather permitting) constantly pass and repass betwixt this and Leghorn every day – and for this month past have been in daily expectation of setting out for this place, but continual rain and hard gales of wind always rendered it impracticable for a felucca to put to sea till this I am now arrived in'.

Even if no storms were encountered, voyages could still be inconvenient. A tourist, who set off in September 1778 from Genoa for Livorno, recorded, 'not being sure of the wind the next morning and having passed a disagreeable uncomfortable night in the chaise which took up too much of the vessel that there was no room to stir two steps we turned up the Gulph of La Spezia and landed in Lerici'. On the other hand, in 1792 Brand and Lord Bruce

> had a most prosperous sail of four nights and three days and a half cross Hesperian seas from Naples to Palermo . . . it was nearly a perfect calm – indeed it was much fitter for the revels of Aphrodite and her maids of honour than for any mortal expedition . . . The Sicilian packets are the most convenient things you can imagine. Each passenger has his cabin. They have a good dining room and the captains of both of them have had an English marine education.[41]

In northern Europe there was little short-hop coastal movement by tourists, except in Dutch coastal and estuarine waters, where, as Joseph Shaw and Zachary Grey discovered, the effects of tide, wind and shoals could be very troublesome. Taking a boat from Zeeland to Antwerp, Grey ran aground. The boat floated off next tide, but sank as a result of being holed. Having struggled ashore, Grey had to walk fourteen miles to find lodgings.[42]

Long sea voyages were made by few tourists. In May 1739 the 5th Lord Baltimore sailed to the Baltic, travelling in his own yacht to St Petersburg and then Danzig, before going overland to Dresden, Berlin and Hamburg, which he reached in late September 1739. As he observed, his stay had been 'very short in most places'. Baltimore's trip aroused so much surprise that it was believed inaccurately that he had been entrusted with secret negotiations.[43] The same was also believed, again without cause, of the 2nd Duke of Richmond's trip to Madrid in 1728.[44] Though Lady Craven sailed from the Crimea to Constantinople in 1786, the Black Sea was not really on the tourist itinerary. It was safer and easier to sail across it than to journey around the shores, though Lady Craven was aware of the danger of drowning.[45]

Some tourists travelled round the Mediterranean by boat, but the absence of passenger services meant that it was necessary to rely on naval vessels as Swinton in 1731 and the Earl of Pembroke in the 1780s did, or on merchantmen, which usually lacked suitable accommodation or to arrange one's own transport, as did James, 4th Viscount Charlemont and John, 4th Earl of Sandwich (1718–92). Such a course required financial resources, while obtaining a passage in a warship was easiest for those with good connections. As a result, Mediterranean cruises were usually considered or enjoyed only by aristocratic travellers, such as Wriothesley, 3rd Duke of Bedford (1708–32), who planned a tour in 1732 to Lisbon, Naples and Turin. He died at Corunna. Hugh Percy, Lord

Warkworth (1742–1817), later 2nd Duke of Northumberland, went on a Mediterranean jaunt in January 1762, travelling with Henry Grenville, the recently-appointed ambassador to Constantinople. George Finch, 19th Earl of Winchelsea, followed about a decade later. Mediterranean travel, especially in the early decades of the century, was affected by the threat of attacks from the privateers of the Barbary states. Both Joseph Spence and Edward Wright mentioned this as a reason for not taking sea voyages. In 1749 Joshua Reynolds was given a passage to the Mediterranean on HMS *Centurion* which put in at Tetuan and Algiers in order to impress the privateers with British power.[46]

Charlemont (1728–99), who succeeded to his father's title in 1734, set out on his travels in 1746 and did not return to Dublin until 1755. He travelled both longer and further than most tourists. From The Hague, he crossed the Empire to Turin, where he attended meetings of the Royal Academy and resisted an attempt by David Hume to convert him to his sceptical philosophy. In April 1749 Charlemont sailed from Livorno in a captured French frigate he had chartered, a ship armed with cannon for defence. After visiting Sicily, where he joined forces with two Englishmen and the artist Richard Dalton sailing round Sicily, Charlemont sailed to Malta and then Constantinople. After visiting the islands of the eastern Aegean, he sailed south to Alexandria and travelled to Cairo; then, prevented by the weather from reaching Cyprus, he returned via the coast of southern Anatolia and the Cyclades to Athens. From there he proceeded to explore some of the major classical sites in the Peloponnese. Charlemont was the first modern traveller to describe the antiquities at Cnidos, and Dalton was the first to draw the sculptures of the mausoleum at Halicarnassus. The tour was not without its difficulties. The Aegean provided both the hazard of storms and the irritation of being becalmed. Turkish officials, as at Halicarnassus, were not always helpful.[47]

Lacking Charlemont's means, Charles Sloane found sailing across the eastern Mediterranean difficult in 1785, though he chose to sail in a particularly hazardous season. He wrote to his brother from Constantinople on 10 November: 'opportunities cannot be found to go from here to Alexandria, as you can step into the Reading Dilly and go to Chelsea', and again on 7 December, 'I have been detained here owing to the uncertainty of sea operations near double the time I intended to stay.'[48] Sea travel was perilous, novel to most tourists, unpredictable and fairly unpleasant. Most preferred to avoid it, other than for short hops, or for journeys for which there was no reasonable, comfortable alternative by land, such as that to Lisbon. Having crossed the Channel, tourists avoided if possible 'the mad, savage, tiger and leopard-like appearance and motions of the multitudinous sea'.[49]

VEHICLES

My travelling will be slow, as I go on horseback; having on account of
the reviews principally bought one at Dresden: I find it much the best
way of getting through this country for a man who has no carriage of
his own; and beyond all comparison the most agreeable.

Captain John Barker, Brunswick, 1792

I was not hurried with the alarming rapidity of Italian postillions nor
shut up in a close cramp carriage but mounted on a safe easy horse.

Thomas Brand, excursion to Lakes Como and Maggiore, 1793[50]

Tourists had two alternatives. They could take their own carriages to the
Continent or use vehicles that they found there. In the latter case they
could hire vehicles or use the transport available to the local inhabitants.
Many took their own carriages, particularly later in the century. Lord
Gardenstone found it perfectly satisfactory to travel round the Continent
in his own carriage in the late 1780s, and the taxation of British carriages
brought into France became an issue in the mid-1780s. The use of public
transport was widespread on the Lille–Paris and Paris–Lyons routes, and
in the Low Countries. Elsewhere, however, it was less common as there
were fewer facilities. The diligence, or public coach, from Lille to Paris
was described by many tourists. It was praised both because it was less
expensive than hiring a carriage, and because it provided an opportunity
to meet the French:

We . . . had no reason to regret having travelled in the diligence; as
by it we avoided the insolence of the postmasters and squabbles with
postilions; who, like the barren womb, are never satisfied, and say not,
it is enough. In respect to our company, we had much reason to be
pleased . . . Their behaviour was civil, and their conversation lively and
entertaining.

In his guidebook John Andrews praised the idea of always travelling

. . . in a public vehicle, where he might have a chance of conversing
with a diversity of characters . . .

Sacheverell Stevens praised the diligence he took from Paris to Lyons
in 1739, its speed, '300 miles, which it performs in four days', and cost,
'the fare for each passenger is 100 livres, and everything found for you

upon the road, or 70 livres without: this is the cheapest way, but not so expeditious and easy as a post chaise, but infinitely more diverting, occasioned by the odd assemblage of the passengers, such as monks, pilgrims, officers, courtezans etc.'[51] It is not clear how widely such printed sentiments were shared. Robert Wharton enjoyed his trip from Lille to Paris in 1775: 'the diligence from that place hither is only 3 Louis for which you are provided with supper the first night and dinner and supper the next days besides your journey'. Wharton defended travel by diligence as a 'way of seeing the French People as much as possible and being sure not to be imposed on'. Others did not relish the idea of spending several days in a confined space practising their schoolboy French with strangers. Thomas Greene and George Romney took a disagreeably-crowded diligence from Lille to Paris in 1764. Jervis, travelling from Paris to Chalon in 1773, found the diligence full, slow and noisy, and disliked being confined in it. He was also inconvenienced by the absence of a lavatory, unlike on the Flemish barges. Robert Ellison took the diligence from Lyons to Geneva in August 1781. The journey took two days. Arthur Young found that from Lille to Paris noisy and, though the Paris–Rouen diligence was inexpensive ('only half a guinea'), slow: travelling at three miles an hour it took two and a half days to cover ninety miles. This led one tourist to decide to ride post back to Paris and never to take a stage-coach again. He noted one principal disadvantage with taking public transport: the abrogation of tourist independence, 'the coachman as arbitrary as his monarch, and we the poor passengers were obliged to be as abject as his subjects'. The inflexibility of public transport was not much of a problem in the case of barges which usually travelled as fast as was possible and could not be expected to go on detours, but neither was the case with public transport on land.[52]

Some tourists took public transport elsewhere on the Continent. Aikin took the Ostend diligence from Bruges; an anonymous tourist of 1721 preferred 'the ordinary voitures' from Douai to Arras and thence to Lille, and the diligence from Courtrai to Ghent, but from Menin to Courtrai 'there was no passage but a wagonful of soldiers ladies, so we put our baggage in only and walked the pleasant road in about 3 hours'. For the sake of company Stevens took the stage-coach from Florence to Bologna.[53] Most tourists who did not take their own carriages, however, preferred to hire them on the Continent, often at Dessein's the leading inn at Calais. If brought back there at the end of the tour, a deposit could be reclaimed. William Drummond wrote on his return to Calais on 6 November 1787:

Thus finishes a tour of nearly four thousand miles on the Continent, in one carriage, which for strength and facility of movement, whether in pieces on the back of mules, or in transporting over rivers in boats, has exceeded my utmost expectation, and often raised my admiration. This matchless carriage, whose eulogium I could write with gratitude, was a cabriolet of two wheels, which we hired of Monsr. Dessin, for ten weeks, for ten louis d'ors: – and except the breaking of the under large leathers twice, it is now returned as sound as it went from his house.[54]

Alternatively, carriages could be hired for shorter stretches of a trip. Whatever the means employed, it was necessary to rely on the system of posting by which fresh horses could be obtained at the post-houses that were situated at regular intervals along major routes, or failing that, hire a set of horses for a specific journey. The quality of posting – the availability of horses, the cost and the speed with which the horses could be changed – varied greatly and was of major concern to tourists. Arriving at Basle from Mannheim in 1758, one tourist wrote: 'no post any further. Hired five horses for an ecu each for every day to Berne'. Twenty years later, a tourist 'set out from Lucca immediately after the Ball in order to be the first on the road, without which precaution we should have been stopped for want of horses, the number of carriages that were going that day to Florence'. The less fortunate Philip Francis was 'plagued and delayed' near Lyons in 1772 by another traveller taking all the post-horses before him.[55]

In Italy the price of posting varied by principality, being especially expensive in the Papal States. Brand, travelling from Milan to Florence in 1790, was dissuaded from the new road from Modena to Pistoia and Lucca in part because he was told 'that the posts were ill served and the accommodation very bad', but was not satisfied with his alternative choice:

> Nothing can exceed the ill behaviour both of men and horses at the posts between Bologna and Florence. *Sa Sainteté* has certainly some Jewish ideas of retaliation and thinks it but right that as he gives us one grand tremendous annual curse, he should receive thousands of daily maledictions from all those unfortunate heretics who travel through his patrimony and territories.[56]

Conversely, Swinton praised the posting system in Italy, the ease and speed of travelling, though he was extrapolating from his own experiences in Tuscany.[57]

There were complaints about posting in the Low Countries, the cost and delay of going from Utrecht to Breda, or the slow, rain-exposed journey on the heavy, sandy road from Ghent to Antwerp.[58] In the early years of the century there were gaps in the posting system in northern France, for example between Calais and St Omer, so that in 1722 'neither messengers nor travellers can get horses to go from the one place to the other, it being eight leagues, and no post established'. Nevertheless, the system worked reasonably well and tourist demand led to improvements during the century, especially from Dieppe to Paris. Tourists naturally compared travel in Britain and France. Lady Craven noted that the changing of horses was not as speedy in the latter, but Gardenstone commented in 1786: 'If the accommodations for travelling, in the articles of hired carriages, drivers, harness, are not yet so good here as in Britain, they are cheaper.' The following year Young travelled from Calais to Paris, observing 'that posting in France is much worse, and even, upon the whole, dearer than in England'. Unimpressed by the state of French stables, he also commented unfavourably on the difficulties of hiring carriages in provincial French towns, as compared to England.[59]

The situation was less favourable in southern France, Norton Nicholls complaining about the slowness of his Provençal travels in 1773.[60] There was sometimes a reliance upon mules, which could be an irritating form of transport. Travelling in a mule-drawn coach from Avignon to Aix, Robert Wharton was restricted to three miles an hour. En route from Cadenabbia on Lake Como to Porlezza on Lake Lugano in 1791, Brand and Lord Bruce 'for want of horses were obliged to mount asses and mules and for want of saddles, sacks of hay'. Walker stressed the advantages of the mules used to pull his coach between Viterbo and Siena in 1787:

> Our mules held out very well; they will travel for twelve hours together without a bait; but this we did not suffer. Their pace is but slow; but then it is all alike, uphill or down, rough and smooth . . . When we arrive at the post, the driver takes them into an open place, spreads a little straw; the mules then lay down, and begin to tumble over their backs, in a diverting manner, for several minutes. They then get up, shake themselves, and after a small feed, are as fresh as the hour they set out. It is an excellent animal, and so sure-footed, that I find myself much more at my ease than when horses are in the shafts.[61]

Despite their charms, mules were slow. Invaluable as they might be in mountainous regions and difficult terrain, their lack of speed was a problem for tourists in Mediterranean Europe, especially in Iberia, Italy south of Naples, inland Provence and the Massif Central.

Whatever the region, tourists faced several problems in common. Exposure to the elements made transport inconvenient and in some circumstances miserable. High winds and heavy rainfall were particular problems. Many tourists had quarrels over costs and delays with postilions, drivers and postmasters. Alexander, 7th Earl of Leven (c. 1699–1754), was dissatisfied by his visit to Paris in 1749 and especially disliked the trip from Lille to Paris:

> Oh! its miserable posting in this country, 5 or at most 6 miles an hour . . . They yoke 3 miserable beasts all in a breast, just as we do in harrows, and an old surly rascal as post boy, who will do nothing but what he pleases. One of them had the impudence this day to tell us, after we had given him sixpence to drink, that we paid like Frenchmen and not like Englishmen, and gave us names, upon which Sandie thrashed him.[62]

Some tourists found their drivers and postilions fraudulent, others simply troublesome, Lady Craven commenting, 'I might just as effectually argue with a horse as with a French postilion.' Lord John Pelham Clinton (1755–81) was glad when he reached Turin in 1776, 'as the voituriers had entirely exhausted my patience by their slow method of travelling'. En route from Geneva to Lyons in 1785, Bennet complained of 'the intolerable slow driving of the postilions . . . the want of horses at the two last houses. At St. Jean le Vieux in particular the postmaster appeared so desirous of making us sleep at the auberge that we determined not to sleep at all rather than submit to it. We accordingly set out on foot for the next post.'[63] Three years later William Smith MP encountered problems after dining at Cologne:

> We had not gone far on our way to Dusseldorf when we perceived our postilion to be a very obstinate fellow, who notwithstanding all the signs we could make, would not move beyond a foot's pace, till the gentlemen got out to walk, and then he endeavoured to ride away from them. We were near four hours going ten miles to Opladen; here the master of the inn used all his eloquence to make us pass the night, but finding it was all labour lost, he was near 40 minutes before he produced the horses with a postilion as slow as the last. Threats, entreaties, signs were as ineffectual as with the other. We still moved on, our accustomed funereal pace . . . between one and two the carriage stopped at the gates of Dusseldorf, having been nine hours coming 21 miles . . . We found, as we knew we should, the gates of the city shut, and had therefore the pleasure of sitting in the carriage till five o'clock when they were opened.[64]

Travelling from Paris to Dijon via Auxerre in July 1789, Samuel Boddington calculated that 214 miles took 31 hours, and complained: 'The shortness of the Posts with the dilatory disposition of the Post Boys in bringing out their horses and adjusting their curious tackle to the carriage consumes a great deal of time. If this was altered we should travel quite as expeditious if not more so than in England. They are seldom less than ¾ of an hour in changing horses.'[65] In Germany posting was fairly well organized on the major routes, but in eastern Europe tourists made do with the horses that they could find, most, such as Lady Craven, tending to take their own carriages. There were still problems, as Nathaniel Wraxall discovered near Cracow in 1778, 'our horses tired, and we remained from 11 o'clock at night till 3 in the morning next day before we could proceed. A peasant who accidentally passed us in a cart, at length extricated us, by lending us his horses.'[66]

British envoys could provide assistance, Hanbury Williams in 1750 getting Edward Digby a 'vis a vis: it is the easiest of all vehicles. I slept as well as in my bed . . . I was as fresh when I came here as if I was just got out of bed.'[67] Tourists in the United Provinces found that the quality of travel on land did not approach that on the Dutch canals. Thomas Brand left two vivid accounts of the journey taken by many British tourists from Helvoetsluys to Brill:

. . . we were equipped with a thing called a *coach* and a pair of horses without shafts with such machinery thereto belonging as you would suppose the very first inventor of carriages would not have used and the coach itself infinitely more ugly, clumsy and in every respect inconvenient than you can imagine. The basket of the blue fly is worth a 1000 such. But in this as in most other things they are at least a century behind us in England.

From Helvootsluis to the Brill there is still no other conveyance to be had than an open wagon which carries you and your baggage to the annoyance of one and the utter destruction of the other unless it is packed with the greatest care and address. Two of the most stupid looking animals of our species on this side the Cape of Caffres sat in the front and each drove his own pair of horses which every now and then dropped down in a muddy hole and were almost suffocated.[68]

Some tourists were happy to ride on horseback.[69] It is necessary, however, to put transport problems in perspective. Few cut short their trips because of such difficulties, and most accepted, albeit with grumbles, whatever they found. Bumpy roads and jolting vehicles were commonplace in Britain, as on the Continent. In 1730 Atwell wrote from Rome, 'yesterday morning they had two shocks of an earthquake here, but my Lord and I being upon the road we were too sensible of the shocks of our chaise to feel that of the Earth'.[70] William Lee observed in

June 1753, 'From Berlin I shall pass through Brunswick to Hanover. The roads they tell me are bad and the accommodations worse. I am very well accustomed to both these inconveniences and as I am in perfect health shall encounter them without much apprehension.'[71]

The principal difficulty affecting transport was the weather, and this was watched with great attention. As most tourists tended to follow those routes that were of great importance for domestic travel, they benefited from greater governmental concern with communications, a concern that was motivated by commercial and military interests, not tourism. Many regions did not benefit from this development, but, while travel for most tourists was a matter of moving as fast as possible from one major city to another, this was not too much of a problem, because it was the routes between these cities that improved most.

NOTES

1. Sturrock to Richard Neville Aldworth, 19 Dec. 1740, Essex CRO D/D By C1.
2. BL Stowe 750 f. 329; Stevens, pp. 369–73, 381; Beinecke, Osborn Shelves c 53 f. 65–6.
3. Beinecke, Osborn Shelves c 52 p. 8; HW 67 f. 158, 178, 169; BL Add. 23646 f. 29; *Montagu* II, 40; Aberdeen University Library, Ogilvie-Forbes of Boyndlie Mss., box 46, 24 Jan. 1779; Stopford, Beinecke, Osborn Files, uncatalogued; Jenour to Keith, 30 Dec. 1785, Dawkins to Keith, 27 Mar. 1785, Arbuthnot to Keith, 30 April 1787, Macpherson to Keith, 19 June 1790, BL Add. 35534–42; *Harcourt* III, 165; BL Stowe 750 f. 327–8.
4. HW 51 f. 189–9, 93–5, 207, 215–18, 67 f. 176.
5. Anon., *The Present State of Germany* (2 vols, 1738) II, 382.
6. Brand to Wharton, 5 Oct. 1792, Durham, Wharton.
7. Gloucester CRO D2663 Z8; Stevens pp. 324–5; Thompson I, 98–9; Cork and Orrery p. 71.
8. Pomfret 15, 16 Mar. 1741, Leics. CRO D67, Finch D5; Stevens p. 156; Mitchell, BL Add. 58316 f. 16; Anon., 19 Oct., Beinecke, Osborn Shelves c. 332.
9. BL Add. 22978 f. 89, 58319 f. 47–8, 51, Eg. 2234 f. 227; Beinecke, Osborn Shelves c 200 p. 147, c 289; Belgrave to Keith, 19 May 1787, BL Add. 35538; A. Walker, *Ideas suggested on the spot in a late excursion through Flanders, Germany, France, and Italy* (1790) pp. 381–3; Gloucester CRO D 2002 F1 p. 52.
10. Beinecke, Osborn Shelves c 332, 4 Feb.; Hamilton to Marquis of Carmarthen, Foreign Secretary, 20 Nov. 1786, PRO Foreign Office 70/3.
11. Stevens p. 331; Beinecke, Osborn Shelves c 467 II No. 48, c 289.
12. BL Add. 22978 f. 86, 58319 f. 48; Walker, pp. 186, 339, 341, 366, 369, 373; Swinton, 8 June 1731; Thompson I, 92.
13. BL Add. 31192 f. 3; Beinecke, Osborn Gift 29, 221; Brand to Wharton, 10 Feb. 1786, Durham, Wharton.
14. Molesworth to Gregor, 8 April 1739, BL Add. 61380; BL Add. 58319 f. 103; Walker pp. 422–3.

15. BL Add. 58319 f. 83–4; Wharton to Miss Mary Lloyd, 7 Oct. 1775, Durham, Wharton.
16. BL Add. 31192 f. 31; Young I, 18, 58, 62.
17. Beinecke, Osborn Shelves c 319.
18. Pococke, BL Add. 22978 f. 92; Hopkins to Pryse Campbell, 29 Aug. 1749, Carmarthen CRO Cawdor Muniments, Box 138; House of Lords RO CAD/4/2.
19. BL Add. 58419 f. 93, 97, 101, 12130 f. 188, 193; Young, I, 14–17, 54; Brand to Wharton, 12 Mar. 1783, Durham, Wharton; *La Vie Française à la Veille de la Révolution 1783–86, Journal inédit de Madame Cradock* (Paris, 1911), p. 227; Craven, Journey, p. 5.
20. Mucklow, Beinecke, Osborn Shelves c 319.
21. Maggs Brothers Ltd, *Catalogue* 1121, p. 25.
22. Stevens pp. 386–7; Beinecke, Osborn Shelves f c 52 p. 2, f c 97 p. 44.
23. Duchess of Queensberry to Mrs Herbert, 4 Aug. 1734, BL Add. 22626; Osborn Shelves f c 97 p. 41; Essex p. 55; BL Althorp F60; HL Mo 4440.
24. Hotham to father, Sir Charles, 25 Oct. 1711, Hull UL DDHo/13/4; Bod. Ms Don b 23 f. 85.
25. Huntingdon CRO DDM 49/7; Gloucester CRO D 1245 FF38 D9.
26. Craven, Journey, pp. 164–5, 386; HL Pulteney 1681.
27. Beinecke, Osborn Shelves c 24 pp. 42–4.
28. Walker p. 438; Anon., Tour of Holland (1772), p. 230; Young, I, 18; *Present State of Germany* II, 382.
29. BL Add. 40759 f. 10. They had embarked at Venice.
30. BL Add. 12130 f. 51, 61–2 (quotes), 31192 f. 17–18, 58313 f. 50; Chester CRO DLT/C9/5; Boddington, Guildhall Library, London, Ms. 10823/5B; Bennet, Bod. Ms. Eng. Misc. f. 54 f. 136; Wharton to Thomas Lloyd, 14 Aug. 1775, Durham, Wharton; Stevens, pp. 69–70; Craven, Journey, p. 37.
31. BL Add. 31192 f. 26–7.
32. Stevens p. 342; Lee, 26 April 1753, Beinecke, Lee Corresp. Box 3.
33. Present State of Germany II, 289; Gordon to Keith, 23 Mar. 1785, Arbuthnot to Keith, 30 April 1787, BL Add. 35534, 35538; Beinecke, Lee papers Box 3; Cambridge UL Mss. 7621.
34. Essex, pp. 10–11, 21–4; L. Aikin (ed.), Aikin I, 74; Cradock p. 265; Peckham, Tour of Holland (1772), p. 121; K.C. Balderston (ed.), The Collected Letters of Oliver Goldsmith (Cambridge, 1928), p. 24; J. Shaw, Letters to a Nobleman (1709), p. 43; Daily Universal Register, 28 Aug. 1786.
35. F.A. Pottle (ed.), Boswell in Holland 1763–1764 (1952), pp. 6, 11, 93; Tour of Holland (1772), p. 72; Bod. Ms. Douce 67 p. 12.
36. Beinecke, Osborn Shelves c 49 pp. 30–1.
37. Anon., SRO GD 26/6/233; Beinecke, Osborn Shelves c 200 pp. 72, 79–80, 83, 88–9; Guildford CRO Brodrick Mss. 1248/6. f. 302; Gloucester CRO D 2002 F1 pp. 86–7.
38. BL Stowe 750, Add. 22978 f. 84, Inglis to Keith, 4 Mar. 1786, BL Add. 35536.
39. Beinecke, Osborn Files 8.77.
40. House of Lords RO CAD/4/6.
41. Beinecke, Osborn Shelves c 332; Bod. Ms. Don. b 23 f. 74, 79; Brand to Wharton, 3 April 1792, Durham, Wharton.

42. Shaw, *Letters to a Nobleman*, p. 56; BL Add. 5957 f. 62–3.
43. Baltimore to Walter Titley, 20 June, 19 Sept. 1739, BL Eg. 2686; Guy Dickens to Lord Harrington, 15 Sept., Cyril Wych to Harrington, 29 Sept. 1739, PRO 82/60, 90/46; *Northampton Mercury* 8 Oct. (os), 5 Nov. (os) 1739.
44. Chesterfield to Townshend, 21 Sept. 1728, PRO 84/301.
45. Craven, *Journey*, p. 202.
46. BL Add. 61449 f. 120; Alnwick, Alnwick Castle Mss. 146; Leicester CRO Finch papers; Northcote, *Life of Sir Joshua Reynolds* (1819), pp. 28–30.
47. W.B. Stanford and E.J. Finopoulos (eds), *The travels of Lord Charlemont in Greece and Turkey 1749* (1984); BL Add. 32724 f. 232.
48. House of Lords RO CAD/4/8–9.
49. L. Temple [J. Armstrong], *A Short Ramble through some parts of France and Italy* (1771), pp. 4–5.
50. Barker to Keith, 9 June 1787, BL Add. 35538; Brand to Wharton, 24 Sept. 1793, Durham, Wharton.
51. *Tour of Holland* (1772), p. 131; Andrews, 1784, pp. 477–8; Stevens, pp. 66–7.
52. Wharton to Thomas Lloyd, 27 Feb., Wharton to Dr Baker, 12 Mar. 1775, Durham, Wharton; Greene, Preston CRO DDGr F/3 f. 14; BL Add. 31192 f. 16–17; Essex p. 22; Ellison, Gateshead, Public Library E1/3; Young I, 116; *Tour of Holland* (1772), pp. 201–5, 208; SRO GD 267/7/20.
53. Aiken I, 92; BL Stowe 790 f. 57, 60, 68, 67; Stevens, p. 324.
54. Beinecke, Osborn Shelves c 331.
55. Beinecke, Osborn Shelves c 469 p. 44, c 332; BL Add. 40759 f. 22. The mechanisms of the posting system are explained in C. Florange, *Etude sur les Messageries et les Postes* (Paris, 1925).
56. Brand to Wharton, 6 Dec. 1790, Durham, Wharton.
57. Swinton, 8 June (os) 1731; BL Add. 22978 f. 86.
58. *Tour of Holland* (1772), p. 85; Essex, p. 36.
59. Lord Polwarth to Charles Whitworth, 7 Sept. 1722, BL Add. 37839; Craven, *Journey*, p. 7; Gardenstone I, 15; Young I, 52.
60. Beinecke, Osborn Shelves c 467.
61. Wharton to Thomas Wharton, 4 Oct. 1775, Brand to Wharton, 21 July 1791, Durham, Wharton; Walker pp. 334–5; Thompson I, 54.
62. Fraser, *Melville* I, 326.
63. Craven, *Journey*, p. 11; Nottingham UL NeC 2407; Bennet f. 131.
64. Cambridge UL Mss. 7621.
65. Boddington, Guildhall Library, London, Ms. 10823/5B.
66. Beinecke, Osborn Shelves c 24 p. 14.
67. HW 51 f 134–5.
68. Brand to Wharton, 11 July 1779, 24 Nov. 1789, Durham, Wharton; *Aiken*, p. 68.
69. Pococke, 12 May 1734, BL Add. 22978; Fife, p. 23; Brand to Wharton, 9 Aug., 1 Sept. 1780, Durham, Wharton.
70. Atwell to Lady Sarah Cowper, 13 May 1730, Hertford D/EP F234.
71. Beinecke, Lee corresp. Box 3.

5

ACCOMMODATION

We are to sleep this night at a very good or rather fine house erected by Cosimo the First for the reception of strangers. I wish he had furnished it, for it is without windows and with very few doors, the furniture just enough to sit down to supper and lie down to sleep, for which our rough and dismal journey has prepared us.

Lady Pomfret, Radicofani (Tuscany), 15 March 1741

In the article of good eating, and drinking, France goes far beyond us; and we exceed them as much in the good accommodation of our inns. I hardly remember one place where some of us did not sleep in the same room in which we supped; – for it was generally furnished with two or three beds, and those beds almost as generally occupied with troops of bugs, and whole armies of fleas. The nightly excursions and attacks of those hopping and creeping gentry were a great annoyance to all the company except myself, who happily have not the honour of being to their taste.

Walter Stanhope, Paris-Berne, 1769[1]

An important factor encouraging tourists to spend as much time as possible in major towns and to rush from one to the next, was the nature of the accommodation available elsewhere. Small towns, villages and rural areas over most of the Continent could not offer acceptable accommodation for tourists accustomed in Britain since leaving school to a modicum of comfort. There was no network of inns or hotels to match the post-roads of Europe, and accommodation on any scale outside the major towns was only provided on a few of the major routes. The two-day boat trip from Chalon to Lyons was always broken at Mâcon where there was plenty of accommodation available, though some tourists disliked the town, describing it as old and ugly. Radicofani was a regular stop on the Rome–Siena route.

Tourists who wandered far from the usual routes could hardly have been surprised at the nature of their accommodation. It was bad in Spain: Thomas Pelham had a travelling bed made for his carriage. Arthur Young, during his brief trip to the Catalan Pyrenees in 1787, found hard beds, fleas, rats and mice, and was forced on at least two occasions to pass up unsatisfactory inns for the dubious pleasures of the private houses of a curé and a shopkeeper.[2] Wraxall observed in 1778: 'Between Cracow and Warsaw there is scarce a single house which can be termed an inn, or in which a decent bed can be procured.' Travelling from Moscow to the Crimea in 1786, Lady Craven was able to sleep in her coach which contained a travelling bed, though her excellent contacts were also of use: 'At Soumi I was indebted to Mr. Lanskoy and a brother of Prince Kourakin, who were both quartered there, for a lodging, as they obliged a Jew to give me up a new house which he was on the point of inhabiting.' Eight years later, in Slovakia Randle Wilbraham 'on account of the road detained one night in a public house consisting of only one room which was occupied by 11 human creatures besides dogs, cats and a pig. As however we had luckily had a great deal of exercise that day we slept very soundly upon some straw on the floor.' Later, en route for Constantinople, he was

> received into the home of a Wallachian boyar or nobleman, in whose absence his wife a very elegant and handsome woman did the honours with the utmost ease and politeness. She was dressed completely à la Grecque, which style is extremely becoming to a handsome woman with a fine figure, as that dress shows it off to great advantage. Here we slept upon a divan which is neither more nor less than a tailor's shopboard covered with cushions and which, in summer especially, is full as comfortable as a bed.[3]

The situation in much of Germany was poor. In 1748 Henry Legge complained of 'German extortion which at all the inns I have as yet frequented exceeds that of Holland'. Visiting a battlefield, a popular activity, two tourists spent a night in 1787 'on straw in the famous village of Leuthen' in Silesia. George Ogilvie found the accommodation in post-houses between Hamburg and Osnabrück unsatisfactory. At Leese he recorded, 'our beds stink abominably and half the panes of glass in the windows were broken, so that we were almost froze to death'. The post-house at Broompt was so dirty that he continued to Osnabrück, though it was January and he had to travel by moonlight.[4]

The position was little better outside the major towns in Italy, France, Germany and the Low Countries. Richard Pococke was dissatisfied with the inns on his descent from the Alps into Savoy in 1734. Andrew Mitchell found the inn at Ancona 'exceeding bad'. Stopping at Piperno on his way from Rome to Naples, Sacheverell Stevens observed 'the town affords but bad accommodations for travellers', and on the way from Florence to Bologna he spent a night at Scarparia where he 'found but very indifferent accommodations'. Leaving Florence on 29 December 1776 and arriving at Bologna on 2 January 1777, Mitford wrote:

> the road has few charms in a winter's journey . . . At all times this is a tedious journey, and in the winter it is dangerous from the vast quantities of snow collected in drifts among the mountains, and often raised by sudden gusts of wind and almost overwhelming the travellers. The unexpected delays these whirlwinds of snow occasion have produced many little inns upon the road, for a traveller is often arrested in his journey, and unable to proceed a mile one way or the other, and is therefore constrained to take the first shelter he can find. Miserable, however, is this shelter, for a cold uncomfortable house with paper windows is his usual defence from the storm.

Returning from an Italian excursion, Thomas Brand wrote, 'We met with some distresses from abundant vermin and from the indifferent accommodations of the *castles* of Piedmont.' At Cadenabbia on Lake Como in 1791, he 'found an inn clean as in England, a supper that would have done honour to a [diplomatic] residence, cook and people civil and *honest*. Did you think there existed such a place in Italy?' On his way from Siena to Viterbo, Walker stopped the night at Aqua Pendenta and complained of 'the bugs and fleas of this filthy town'.[5]

Fortunately the situation was very different in the major Italian towns. In these good accommodation was available and, in general, tourists were satisfied by the quality, though some, such as Walker in Milan, were angered by the cost. Pococke found 'a very good English public house' in Venice; Pomfret 'a very good inn' in Siena; Stevens was impressed by the accommodation in Naples. Difficulties could arise if it was impossible to get into the best inns, as happened to George, Viscount Nuneham (1736–1809), and Lord Bulkeley at Trieste in 1755 and 1785 respectively, but the wealthy British tourists in Italy rarely had problems in the major towns. The situation would probably have been different had the number of tourists approached Parisian figures, but until the end of the period Italy remained a largely exclusive area of tourism and most of the British tourists there were reasonably wealthy and did not share the concern with the cost of accommodation voiced by Walker or Nicholls. Nicholls indeed complained that aristocratic travellers had pushed up prices. An anonymous tourist complained about the three hotels in Turin in 1782, not least the absence of lavatories: 'all three seem on an equilibre as to inferiority, for *excellencies* they have none'.[6]

'In Germany . . . a man may travel many days and not find a bed to lie upon', claimed one British newspaper in 1722, and the situation there, outside the major towns, was generally regarded as fairly bleak. Travelling from Cologne to Lorraine in 1711, Sir Carnaby Haggerston was 'often content with straw to lie on'. Nine years later, John Molesworth complained from Augsburg of 'scurvy accommodation, but yet which I wonder at, as dear as at London or Paris'. Printed accounts were critical.[7] The bedding available was commented on by several travellers. Walker, like Wharton and the Scottish mathematician Colin Maclaurin, was amazed at the height of foreign beds, Walker claiming that Tyrolean beds were at an angle of 25 degrees, and the other two that they literally had to climb into bed.[8]

Tourists were, however, generally satisfied with the accommodation available in the major German towns, such as Vienna, Prague, Dresden, Munich, Hanover and Frankfurt. Viscount Palmerston stayed at Aix-la-Chapelle (Aachen) in 1766 'upon an odd footing. It is both an inn and boarding house. The people who keep it are genteeler than ordinary and have a good table at which the company who are in the house eat.' In the Hôtel d'Angleterre in Brunswick in 1770 William Philip Perrin found 'very commodious club rooms where German, French and English papers are taken in by subscription, as well as magazines . . . mercures etc.'. Lord Stopford's bearleader Samuel Pohl reported to his charge's father, the 2nd Earl of Courtown, from Vienna in November 1783, 'Mylord has two good rooms, and a small middle one: another for me, kitchen and other conveniencies, very complete apartments for a single gentleman.' Petty wrote from Prague in 1785, 'We are extremely well lodged in an handsome suite of apartments in a very good street, and everything comfortable about us.'[9]

In Switzerland most tourists only ever stayed in the larger towns, particularly Geneva and Lausanne. Here the accommodation was generally good. Walter Stanhope stayed with private families in Lausanne, but assured his mother that this was in order, and that he gained valuable introductions as a result, 'to take in boarders is not the least disgrace to the best families here'.[10] Equally there was concern if young men, abroad for their education, lodged in undesirable inns. Edward Mellish was forced to reassure his father and his uncle that it was the custom in France and the Low Countries to lodge in public houses when he stayed in Tours in 1730–1, 'being lately informed by an English gentleman who was some time at Tours that he was obliged to lodge and eat in a public house (as there were no private pensions for strangers).'[11] Accommodation in the Low Countries was generally satisfactory, though Sir James Porter complained that the post-house at Amersfoort was 'a most dirty, wretched hole'. Touring the Low Countries with an old friend in 1791, Richard Dreyer stayed in Rotterdam:

We are lodged at the Black Lion in the Wyn Straat, (where according to the custom of our countrymen abroad) they make you pay much dearer for accommodation than the natives. As we were but novices in the Dutch language, we did not think the extraordinary charge ill bestowed, for the satisfaction of opening our mouths in our own tongue, and of meeting some pleasant Englishmen at the Table d'Hote: the accommodations are good and Mrs. Coxon the landlady civil.

Travelling on to Delft, Dreyer found 'the Stadts Doele a most excellent inn, in the rooms of which are some fine old paintings. The entertainment is remarkably good and the civility of the mistress of the house (who speaks good French) rather resembled the attention of a friend, than the hired services of a landlady.'[12] Possibly tourists would have been less satisfied had they toured the landward provinces of the United Provinces, such as Groningen and Gelderland, or the south and east of the Austrian Netherlands, especially the Ardennes. George Tilson lumped part of the United Provinces in with Westphalia in his condemnation of 'the heaths, marshes, barns and dunghills of Overyssell and Westphalia'.[13]

There was a wide choice of accommodation available in Paris. 'They all generally lodge in the Fauxbourg S. Germain', noted the *Daily Post Boy* of 27 September 1731. It was possible to lodge with private individuals. Sir John Blair did so in 1787 in order to learn French. His bearleader, Arbuthnot wrote, 'I have within these few days removed to the house of a Mr. de Ville, a Secretaire du Roi, where we board. It is a situation attended with no other advantage, than its serving to forward Sir J. Blair in his knowledge of the French tongue, from his hearing no other language spoken at table.'[14] Most tourists stayed in hotels. The Hôtel de l'Impératrice in the Rue Jacob, a popular destination, was clearly comfortable: 'we have an elegant dining room, with two bed chambers on the first floor, and a bed chamber in the entresol, with an apartment for the servant, for three guineas per week. I confess the lodgings are dear, but the situation is good, and the furniture magnificent.'[15] Others were less satisfied. Jane Parminter stayed at the Hôtel de la Ville de Rome in 1785: 'a very dirty inn indeed, the staircase shaking, the maids bold and impertinent, the treatment sparing and the charge extravagant'. Lady Knight was pestered by bugs, a fate that also afflicted Jane Parminter at Chailly near Paris, and Elizabeth Montagu.[16]

There is a mass of comment available on the inns between Calais and Paris. This was the first experience of foreign accommodation for most tourists, and not all found it agreeable.[17] On the other hand, Smollett praised that at Montreuil and Amiens and Arthur Young the Hôtel de Bourbon at Cambrai. One visitor to Calais in 1775 found the beds twice as high as in England. Eight years earlier, en route from Paris to Spa with her husband, Countess Spencer found 'nothing but a very bad inn' in Soissons, and though the inn in Rheims was very good, it was also full, and a room was only obtained when two British tourists gave theirs up. Later they 'were forced to pass through Mézières where there was no inn to be got and lie at a miserable ale house in . . . Charleville'. Mitford encountered a different sort of problem at Senlis in 1787: 'a very tolerable inn, *au grand cerf*, which is remarkably clean. The postilions carry travellers *au grand-monarque*, because the *aubergiste* gives them a *piece de 24 sous*, which of course is squeezed again out of the traveller.'[18]

Young provided a lot of information about the state of accommodation available for travellers. He was pleased with Dunkirk (a view shared by James Essex), Pont l'Evêque and Nîmes, though at Bordeaux he was dissatisfied with one aspect of his hotel: 'The inns at this city are excellent; the Hotel d'Angleterre and the Prince of Asturias; at the latter we found every accommodation to be wished, but with an inconsistence that cannot be too much condemned: we had very elegant apartments, and were served on plate, yet the necessary house the same temple of abomination that is to be in a dirty village.' Near Limoges, Young stopped 'at an execrable auberge, called Maison Rouge, where we intended to sleep, but, on examination, found every appearance so forbidding, and so beggarly on account of a larder, that we passed on to Limoges'. In Pamiers the inn was terrible, though on the way from Bayonne to Bordeaux, 'everything at Aire seemed good and clean; and what is very uncommon, I had a parlour to eat my dinner in, and was attended by a neat well dressed girl'. Young was soaked as a result of a downpour, but 'the old landlady was in no haste to give me fire enough to be dried'. Young was very dissatisfied with the Breton inns:

> sleep at the *Lion d'Or* at Montauban, an abominable hole . . . This villainous hole, that calls itself the *Grand Maison*, is the best inn at a post town [Belleisle] on the great road to Brest, at which marshals of France, dukes, peers, countesses, and so forth, must now and then, by the accidents to which long journies are subject, have found themselves. What are we to think of a country that has made, in the eighteenth century, no better provision for its travellers.[19]

Provincial French inns failed to satisfy many tourists, especially on the score of cleanliness. There were many complaints about bugs, while Elizabeth Montagu stated that 'inns are so little frequented in France one often meets with damp beds'. Samuel Boddington wrote from Lyons in July 1789, 'I am now tolerably well reconciled to the accommodations of the French inns. I generally take off the thinnest matress and sleep upon the floor or rather stones. By this means and by the defence of my dress I have defended myself from bugs which are in great abundance. I last night was attacked by a new enemy fleas of an enormous size. They have used me most cruelly and they are such an active foe that there is no escaping from them.' He was 'most terribly maul'd by the fleas' in Lyons, despite staying at 'a very good inn'.[20]

Although French inns were subject to legal restraints, there was no effective control of hygiene or of the quality of food and bedding. Thus, in France tourists could find accommodation ranging from justifiably famous inns, such as the *Cheval Blanc* in Montpellier, to squalid boarding houses. Most inns fell between these two extremes.[21] Tourists accordingly found very varied accommodation. Arriving at Remoulins in 1785 after a journey on a very bad road from Avignon, Bennet noted, 'our courier had lost his way, and was not yet arrived. I was forced to enter and bargain, which I did at last with difficulty, the landlord drunk and the house full of people. We got however very tolerable beds and supper at three livres per head, and vin de pays at three pence per bottle.' Montpellier, on the other hand, offered only 'a very uncomfortable though the best inn'. Travelling north from Brive a fortnight later, Bennet complained that 'this road over the mountains' was marred by 'the badness of the accommodations and the want of horses'. The latter led to delays, but the former pushed him on. One night he found two post-houses full and did not find beds until 2 a.m.[22]

Faced with problems with accommodation, tourists could always carry camp-beds in their coaches. Sir Carnaby Haggerston, Thomas Pelham and Lady Craven all resorted to this inconvenient expedient. The nature of the accommodation was one of the factors that discouraged tourists from venturing off the beaten track. In addition, it encouraged them to move from city to city as fast as possible, for in the cities accommodation was generally of a better standard, less likely to be full, and there was more choice. Aside from inns and hotels, cities contained furnished accommodation, Mellish's 'private pensions', where tourists could settle for weeks, or indeed months or years. In 1780 Thomas Brand learnt the miseries of a trip in the country. Going from Geneva, where he was staying, to see the Perte du Rhône, a section of the river between Geneva and Lyons that ran underground, Brand endured

the miseries of bad weather, an open cabriolet . . . and a wretched inn. It was maigre day and as I was taken for a Curé or some limb of the church we found it difficult to get meat for our supper. The inn having but one fire place we were altogether a goodly company of men women children hogs and poultry . . . No sooner in bed than two numerous families, ancient inhabitants of the place, with that politeness so conspicuous in the French payd their respects to me. I am certain that not a *Puce* [flea] or a *Punaise* [bug] nelgected showing me how sensible they were of the honor we had done them. You'll guess that the first glimpse of the morning made me quit the luxury of my couch.[23]

On the other hand, tourists and their demands must have posed serious problems for many innkeepers. Arriving frequently at irregular hours, many tourists presented their demands vociferously and in terms that the innkeepers would sometimes have found difficult to understand. In addition, British accommodation was not necessarily any better. Lady Anson found Buxton 'purgatory . . . constant stinks all over the house, an absolute destruction of breakfast from the badness of butter . . .' and terrible noise.[24]

NOTES

1. Pomfret to Countess of Hertford, Leics. CRO D67 Finch D5; Stanhope to his mother, 11 July 1769, Bradford, Spencer Stanhope.
2. Pelham to Lord Pelham, 4 Nov. 1775, 12 Dec. 1776, BL Add. 33126–7; Young I, 31–4, 38; Carleton pp. 300, 326.
3. Beinecke, Osborn Shelves c 24 p. 42; Craven, *Journey*, 368, *Memoirs* I, 163; Chester CRO DBW/N/Bundle E, Packet A.
4. HW 51 f. 285; Gordon to Keith, 8 Sept. 1787, BL Add. 35539; Ogilvie, Aberdeen, 26 Jan. 1779.
5. BL Add. 22978 f. 90, 58320 f. 16; Stevens pp. 277, 325; Mitford, Gloucester CRO D 2002 F1 pp. 64–5; Brand to Wharton, 21 July 1791, Durham, Wharton; Walker p. 330.
6. Walker p. 381; BL Add. 22978 f. 82; Pomfret to Countess of Hertford, 13 Mar. 1741, Leic. CRO DG7 Finch D5; Stevens pp. 281–2; *Harcourt Papers* III, 161; Bulkeley to Keith, 12 Oct. 1785, BL Add. 35535; Beinecke, Osborn Shelves c 289.
7. *Weekly Journal, or Saturday's Post*, 15 Dec. (os) 1722; Haggerston to mother, 13 July 1711, Haggerston; Molesworth to Stanyan, 27 Nov. 1720, PRO 92/30; Pöllnitz, letters of 30 Aug., 10 Oct. 1729; Stevens pp. 372–84.
8. Walker, p. 92; Wharton to his mother, 18 Feb. 1775, Durham, Wharton; Maclaurin, Aberdeen UL Mss. 206 f. 202.
9. Beinecke, Osborn Gift 29.224; Matlock CRO 239 M F 15921; Beinecke, Osborn Files, uncatalogued; Petty to Keith, 15 Nov. 1785, BL Add. 35535.
10. Stanhope to mother, 25 Nov. 1769, Bradford, Spencer Stanhope.
11. Edward Mellish to John Gore, 17 Nov. 1730, Mellish to father, 22 Jan. 1731, Nottingham UL Mellish.
12. Beinecke, Osborn Shelves f c 11 pp. 38–9, 49; Essex p. 25; *Aikin* I, 43, 81; Cradock, pp. 255, 258.
13. Tilson to Delafaye, 29 June 1723, PRO 43/4.

14. BL Add. 35539 f. 242.
15. *Tour of Holland* (1772), pp. 131–2.
16. O.J. Reichel (ed.), 'Extracts from a Devonshire Lady's Notes of Travel in France in the Eighteenth Century', *Transactions of the Devonshire Association for the Advancement of Science, Literature and Art* (1902), pp. 268, 273; Knight, p. 6; Montagu, I, 320, 328.
17. Stevens, pp. 7–9; *Tour of Holland* (1772), p. 130; Smollett, pp. 42–3; Montagu, I, 315–16.
18. Smollett, p. 42; Young I, 87; SRO GD 26/VI/233 p. 4; BL Althorp F60; Gloucester D 2002 F1.
19. Essex p. 8; Young I, 88, 92, 49, 61–2, 14, 53, 58, 98.
20. Montagu II, 127; Guildhall Library, London, Ms. 10823/5B; Devonshire Lady pp. 273–4; BL Add. 31192 f. 19; Charles Stanhope to Essex, 18 Oct. 1732, BL Add. 27732.
21. Sturdy, 'English Travellers', pp. 66–7.
22. Bennet, Bod. Ms. Eng. Misc. f. 54 f. 149, 153, 165–6.
23. Brand to Wharton, 7 April 1780, Durham, Wharton.
24. Stafford CRO D615/P(S)/1/37B.

6

FOOD AND DRINK

Travelling independently and in relatively small numbers, tourists found that in much of Europe the facilities that existed for them were limited and often inadequate, a situation that further encouraged their tendency to concentrate on the major cities. Here they had an opportunity to participate in local social life, a process facilitated by their small numbers, the widespread use of letters of introduction, the universality of French as the language of diplomacy and civilized society and the belief that such socializing was an important aspect of the education that travel was believed to offer. Thus, rather than seeking special facilities, as Victorian tourists to rural regions of coastal or alpine Europe were to do, eighteenth-century tourists sought *entrées* into local society. Furthermore, the general absence of special arrangements for them encouraged tourists to participate in local life.

This can be shown by looking at the crucial topic of food. A number of factors combined to ensure that tourists who travelled widely, as those who followed the Grand Tour sought to do, ate what was available locally, for example mutton from the nearby Ardennes at Spa, and thus, in general, had a less predictable experience than their modern descendants. If eighteenth-century Europe was a continent of shortages of particular kinds of food, it was also one of variety of food. This variety was both geographical and seasonal, a result of the limited nature of refrigeration available. Cold cellars and the use of natural ice could provide a measure of refrigeration, but it was difficult to use these techniques for the long-distance transport of food. Similarly, smoking and salting could increase the range of food available in a specific place at any one time, but the primitive nature of transportation, both vehicles and routes, and the lack of adequate storage facilities created significant difficulties for preservation and ensured that distribution was very localized. When food was available all the year round it was worthy of comment, one tourist writing of Nice in 1754, 'they have peas here all year round; some of which we had and thought them vastly good'.

In general, it would be appropriate to discern two food regimes for tourists. The first was that of the rural areas through which they travelled, commonly characterized by a lack of variety, and often by a shortage of food. Breakfasting on the way from Geneva to Mt Blanc in 1787, Richard Garmston could only find some eggs for breakfast.[1] The concentration of many agrarian regions on grain monoculture created particular difficulties. The second was that of towns, particularly large towns, where quantity and variety were less of a problem for those who could pay. Towns were commonly surrounded by a zone of market gardens, whose productivity was enhanced by the use of night waste, and were thus centres of production. In addition, as centres of consumption, they were the markets for agricultural regions, and as centres of communication they were better supplied than other regions. Both food regimes were naturally affected by regular variations and irregular harvest and weather conditions such as the freezing of waterways.

Some British tourists clearly feared what they would encounter. In 1767 the bookseller Samuel Paterson commented on those who crossed the Channel:

> The English of all people are the most provident upon those occasions, from a natural dread of being starved, which many of them are seized with the moment they lose sight of their native land – so that in the packets between *Dover* and *Calais*, or *Ostend*, it is no unusual thing to find as many fowls tongues, pastry and liquours as would victual a ship for a month's voyage.

Samuel Pratt noted that those who travelled between Harwich and the Hook of Holland took their own food, the inns on both sides providing baskets. The food was often not finished and this was an accepted perk for the stewards. Crossing the sea without adequate provisions could be an ordeal. One tourist recorded a five-day passage from Hull to den Helder:

> I was forced to be content with bad beef and bread not of the best quality, our butter stunk so intolerably that I don't believe a dog would have eat it, and had I not accidentally taken a little sugar in my case, could not so much as drunk a dish of tea . . . the last day we were at sea was a day of fasting.[2]

William Bennet, who accompanied John Rolle MP to the Continent in 1785, wrote of the latter that his 'whole fear when he first landed was that he should be starved. At dinner he always asked if we knew where to get a supper, and at supper if we were sure of our breakfast, but being now pretty certain that a man may find something to eat in this country, he is extremely well reconciled to his tour, the fertility of French Flanders indeed is such that all idea of starving disappears at the sight of it.'[3]

Fear and experience led many tourists to take precautions. This was particularly important for those who chose to depart from the most frequented routes. In August 1725 Lord Egremont travelling in France wrote: 'we carry cold meat and wine every morning with us and make a second breakfast about one a clock' and again 'carry loaves of cold mutton from our inn'. In French Flanders in 1771 Eleanor Sutton, her sisters, mother and husband James (c. 1733–1801), an MP, 'dined in the carriages on cold tongue and chicken'. An anonymous tourist in the same region 'got some biscuits, wine and a large basket of strawberries to take into the carriage'. Travelling through the Ardennes in 1772, Philip Francis noted 'dined upon our own provisions'. Edmund Dewes, whose account is comparatively unusual as he was a servant, recorded in 1776 that information concerning the food available between Spa and Luxemburg led his master to take a leg of roast mutton which was eaten cold. Peter Beckford, who travelled a decade later, observed: 'some good wine, and a cold pie in the well of our carriage with the addition of a fresh egg, which is both clean and wholesome, will save you from a bad dinner, and the inconvenience of waiting for it'. In 1783 Lord Stopford took cold food with him on a night journey from Ulm to Augsburg. Joseph Townsend advised those who wished to travel in Spain that they required two servants:

His servants should be a Spaniard and a Swiss, of which, one should be sufficiently acquainted with the art of cooking, and with the superior art of providing for the journey, which implies a perfect knowledge of the country through which he is to pass, that he may secure a stock of wine, bread, and meat, in places where these excel, and such a stock as may be sufficient to carry him through the districts in which these are not to be obtained.

The baggage was to include 'a tablecloth, knives, forks, and spoons, with a copper vessel sufficiently capacious to boil his meat'. Crossing the prince-bishopric of Münster en route from Amsterdam to Bremen, one tourist found the inns bad, including one that was 'extraordinary':

It was one large room into which we drove with our waggon and horses, to the right hand stood 3 cows to left as many calfs and some hogs. Besides a standing for horses, at the end of the room opposite the door, was a large fire upon the ground with a pot and something for dinner; an old man and a little boy sat by the fire surrounded with smoke for there was no chimney. As we had been some time in a pretty sharp rain our great coats were very wet and we ourselves had no objections to taking part of the fire side to which the old don very courteously intreated us. After being thus decently placed in the parlour cowhouse stable hogsty and barn for this one room served for all those purposes, we enquired what we could have to eat and drink; but as nothing that we could eat was to be had, we applyed to our own provisions which consisted of a boiled tongue bread butter and cheese with which and a glass of good red wine we regaled ourselves.[4]

Travel in Spain took on the character of an expedition, as for Thomas Pelham in the 1770s. The situation was similar across much of Europe. Having travelled from Cracow to Warsaw in 1778, Wraxall noted 'The bread is execrable, black, and sour. We carried everything in the carriage except water, and even that is in general bad throughout all Poland, because there are few springs. The water is mostly stagnant, and consequently cannot be clean and wholesome.' Most tourists, however, neither wished to be burdened with equipment, nor employed vehicles that would make it possible. Instead of taking their own carriages, most tourists hired them or used public transport, such as the diligences in France, or boats in the Low Countries. Thus, taking supplies was usually a matter of a tourist purchasing food for lunch at his inn in the morning, rather than transporting cooking equipment. This left the tourist especially vulnerable if the food at his inn the following night was inadequate or unacceptable. This was a particular problem in rural areas. Sir William Lee wrote of the journey from Magdeburg to Berlin, 'little to eat but bad sour hard heavy rye bread, and salt butter'. Dewes found eggs and fish, but no meat, in an inn between Strasbourg and Basle. Travelling through southern Italy in 1772, William Young observed: 'eggs for breakfast, eggs for dinner, and eggs for supper, are the best fare one can in general meet with'. En route to Paris in March 1789, a young Londoner had 'soup and bouilly a roasted chicken and tarts' for dinner in Calais, but he supped that night in 'a poor ragged village . . . in a very smoky room upon fish and eggs', and the following day dined upon eggs; although on his last dinner before reaching Paris he 'dined at an inn which was kept by English people. Had eggs and bacon.'

On the other hand, some tourists praised what they found in rural areas. Crossing the Mount Cenis pass in 1776, John Mitford wrote:

. . . among these wild mountains are to be found good bread, good butter, and good milk; three good things not to be met with in many of the more frequented inns, in the rich plains of France; good fish, flesh, and fowl, and bon vin de Montmelian, much superior to the bon vin de Bourgogne of most of the French auberges.

Thomas Brand found 'exquisite' trout and milk of 'the finest flavour' in Switzerland in 1791.[5]

It would be misleading to suggest that difficulties were only encountered in rural areas. Lady Henrietta Pomfret supped badly in Ferrara in 1741, later writing 'considering it is Italy we have supped very well at Verona', though it is fair to note that she considered her dinner at Parma very good. Though the fruit and vegetables at Marseilles in 1754 were very plentiful, 'their butchers meat is excessive bad and they have neither good butter nor cheese . . . Their wine which is all red, like the wine in other parts of the south of France is too strong and fiery.' Lady Miller was unimpressed at Viterbo in 1771: 'our supper consisted of a soup, the chief ingredients of which were all sorts of livers and gizzards, collected from various birds, and I believe were of as various dates, sailing after each other in a muddy pool; very unlike the lake of Bolsena; broiled pigeons with oil, and a friture of livers, etc . . . You may be sure we are in no danger of a surfeit this night.'

In November 1776 Thomas Jones, arriving at the post-house in Modena, found that 'after fasting all day we could get nothing for supper but a few small fish fried in oil'. Eight years later Jane Parminter 'dined (or rather paid for a dinner) at St. Denis', and arriving at Chantilly in June 1787 Garmston could only get for supper 'an old fowl', some unpleasant asparagus and 'peas with a disagreeable sour sauce'. Breakfasting in Dieppe in August 1788 John Villiers found neither tongue nor ham and wrote 'the tea was bad, the sugar coarse, the butter intolerable'. Bennet complained about his journey through France in 1785:

> The accommodations of yesterday were as bad, and in point of eating worse, than any we have met with in the whole of our journey. We had been hurried from Morterolles literally without our breakfasts, ate a very scanty dinner of stale meat (which we could not get without difficulty) in our carriage, and had only one fowl and one duck for supper, though we paid a livre more than our usual allowance. Indeed the post house at Châteauroux is for imposition and bad attendance one of the worst in France, and nothing but the fear of not getting horses led us to it.[6]

Insufficient and bad food were not the only problems. Different cooking techniques and methods of preparation were also significant. Members of the social élite were familiar with foreign, though usually only French, cooking. In 1735 the Duke of Newcastle and Sir Henry Liddell MP (1708–84), later 1st Lord Ravensworth, who had been on the Grand Tour in about 1730, both hired Parisian cooks. Knowledge about and familiarity with foreign cooking took longer to spread more widely. The 4th Earl of Chesterfield's former cook, Vincent La Chapelle, published in 1744 *The Modern Cook* which included the *least expensive methods* of providing for private families in a very elegant manner. It was only in 1793 that there appeared *The French Family Cook: being a complete system of French Cookery. Adapted to the tables not only of the opulent, but of persons of moderate fortune and condition . . . The different modes of making all kinds of soups, ragouts, fricandeaus, creams, ratafias, compots, preserves etc. etc. as well as a great variety of cheap and elegant side dishes, calculated to grace a table at small expence.* Many tourists commented on differences, particularly the manner in which meat was prepared and the use of oil and garlic. George Carpenter complained in 1717 that 'all over Italy oil and garlic are put in every dish and are the chief ingredients'. An anonymous tourist noted in Frankfurt in 1743, 'Ordinarys here are good, though not much to the English taste, upon account of their boiling and roasting meat too much.' However, in 1775 Robert Wharton, travelling from Calais to Paris, found 'the victuals very eatable, not every dish full of onions as I expected'.[7] It was commonly argued that foreign food was excessively spiced, that sauces were too rich and meat poorly cooked or presented in inadequate quantities. Philip Thicknesse claimed of the Austrian Netherlands (modern Belgium) in the 1780s that 'though the tables of all orders of people are covered with a variety of dishes, which may catch the eye, or provoke the appetite, an Englishman whose stomach is not depraved, will soon wish to see a plain wholesome dish or two of meat à la mode d'Angleterre set before him'. The anonymous *Gentleman's Guide in his Tour through France by an Officer who lately travelled on a principle which he most sincerely recommends to his countrymen, viz., not to spend more money in the country of our natural enemy than is required to support with decency the character of an Englishman* informed its readers, 'The French certainly do not eat so great a quantity of solid meat as the English; nor do they dress it in the same manner; soup, fricassees, hashes, and ragouts, are preferred before whole joints, boiled or roasted; they choose to keep their meat so long before it is dressed, that it is so very tender; and stinks so frequently, that an unfrenchified Englishman is sure to be often disappointed at his meals.' Anne Scrope noted in Brussels in 1784, 'we live in the French style. There is nothing brought to the table but what is very tender.' In Paris in 1764 Thomas Greene 'saw with inexpressible pleasure what I had not seen for six weeks, a large piece of roasted beef'. In August 1789 Samuel Boddington and his friends reached Nice, recording, 'we are very comfortably lodged in the Hotel de York where we have had our palates gratified with good roast beef and have enjoyed ourselves in good beds without being molested by bugs – Mr. Morgan in particular has recruited himself here as the French ragouts have not suited him at all and he had been most terribly molested by the vermin.'[8]

Much could be attributed to the nature of foreign kitchens. Thicknesse claimed in 1768, 'nothing appears to me more absurd than our fondness for French dishes; because it is evident the want of coals is the cause of their cooks *dealing* so much with the stewpan. When I roast a large piece of beef it costs me near as much for firing as for the meat.' Peter Beckford was unimpressed by Italian meat: 'Butchers' meat is but indifferent; you must entirely forget, my good Sir, the Roast Beef of Old England, for they have neither jacks nor chimneys.' The view that British roast meat was best was not only held by the British. A Swedish scholar who visited England in 1748 recorded, 'The Englishmen understand almost better than any other people the art of properly roasting a joint, which also is not to be wondered at; because the art of cooking as practised by most Englishmen does not extend much beyond roast beef and plum pudding.'[9]

However, more than the absence of chimneys was involved. Ingredients on the Continent were often not to the taste of British travellers. Thicknesse wrote of Barcelona, 'nor could I find in this great city either oil, olives, or wine, that were tolerable. I paid a guinea a day at the *Fontain d'Or* for my table; yet everything was so dirty, that I always make my dinner from the dessert.' Specific dishes could be found abhorrent. Dewes' master like frogs. Dewes did not and when he unwittingly ate them fricasseed he decided to eat them no more. Dewes' journal is particularly valuable because, due to his status as a servant, he was especially conscious of the practical details of travel. He noted of one of his master's suppers, 'a roasted fowl stewed in a little iron pot with a great gob of grease on it, when put in, a dish of potatoes boiled in a frying pan with a collation of onions and lard'. On another occasion, when his master ordered roasted woodcock, he had to send it back twice as it was insufficiently cooked. Finally 'after half roasting and half broiling it, and three parts stewing it, they completely stewed it'. It came with 'some stewed spinach boiled'. Another servant, John Macdonald, shot the party's suppers as they travelled from Lisbon to Madrid. In Geneva in 1779, Brand was angry with the contents of his dinner, 'a very meagre soup almost all bread – that indifferent and cabbage; the bouilli and three dishes of vegetables, spinach or purslane, carrots, dandelion or chicory: a medley minced meat pudding and a dish of *game* viz. 2 thrushes, 3 starlings, a linnet and a water wagtail'. On the other hand, his health improved because he was 'drinking the light French wines instead of heavy soporific ale and strong inebriating port'. Near Antwerp Zachary Grey had 'cabbage salad made after the following manner. A cabbage very finely sliced, an apple or two minced, one large onion minced: mix all together, and eat them with pepper, vinegar and salt.'[10]

Presentation could be as unfamiliar as preparation. At Chantilly, Garmston 'had perch for dinner sent to table with the scales on and the guts in them: but the fish were good'. Another obvious difference arose from the conventions and regulations relating to Lent and Fridays. One tourist in France in 1721 during Lent complained, 'we were confined to what fish the country afforded, and could not on any account have a single egg, so bigotted are the people to the blind obedience of the injunctions of their Church.' Another found a supper of 'mackrel, cotelet and chickens, part good and part bad' at Arras, but at Breteuil dinner was 'a fried mackerel and an omelette, being maigre day again there was nothing else to be had'.

The timing of meals could also vary from the situation in Britain. Pratt commented on the early dinners of Westphalia, eaten at midday.[11] The degree to which tourists stressed differences varied. James, Lord Compton (1687–1754), writing from Amsterdam to his father, the 4th Earl of Northampton, in 1707, noted that the 'farther I go into the country, [the more] I find the English and Dutch differ very much as to their inclinations in meat and drink. However though in some places we fared hardly, yet in others we lived very well, and as our journey was most up the Rhine, so we seldom failed of very good Rhenish.' Lady Miller was willing to praise foreign food if better than British, as in the case of Piedmontese fennel, but she left her readers in no doubt of her delight when she found English dishes, as with the 'excellent British minced pies' she obtained in Florence. At Rome she wrote:

> Our table is served rather in the English style, at least there abounds three or four homely English dishes (thanks to some kind English predecessors who have taught them), such as bacon and cabbage, boiled mutton, bread-puddings, which after they have been boiled, are cut in pieces, fried and served with a wine sauce strongly spiced, etc. so don't think we are likely to starve here.

Evelyn, 2nd Duke of Kingston (1711–73), had Hampshire bacon, Cheshire and Gloucester cheese and beer sent over from England to France in 1727. Sixty years later, Mitford noted that if the bad roads from Dunkirk delayed a tourist until after the gates of Calais were shut, and he had to spend the night in the lower town, there was, nevertheless, an inn kept by Dessein's brother where 'the good lady of the house . . . has been taught to boil bacon and poach eggs à l'angloise'. Homely English dishes were, however, rarely in evidence, and those who published descriptions of their foreign travels found that culinary differences were an obvious topic for discussion. George Carleton wrote of finding in Madrid.

> such variety of delicious fruit, that I must confess I never saw any place comparable to it . . . their rabbits are not so good as ours in England; they have great plenty of partridges, which are larger and finer feathered than ours. They have but little beef in Spain, because there is no grass, but they have plenty of mutton, and exceeding good, because

their sheep feed only upon wild potherbs; their pork is delicious, their hogs feeding only upon chestnuts and acorns.

The anonymous Present State of Germany published in 1738 informed readers, 'What the Germans, and all other nations in Europe, are fondest of, is venison, bacon, wild and tame fowls, fish, tarts, custards, roots, salads, stewed and preserved fruits; most of which they have in greater plenty and perfection than we.' Twenty years later, a tourist had wild boar at Mannheim. Lady Miller clearly set out the unusual regional specialities that tourists could expect. Beckford informed his readers about the particular arrangement of Italian meals:

An Italian dinner usually consists of a soup, which never fails winter and summer; a piece of bouilli; a fry of some kind or other; a ragout; and the *roti*, which, whether it be a piece of meat, or a few small birds, is served up last. The soup is no better than broth, being the essence of the bouilli only, which, of course, is boiled to rags; and the roast meat being usually soaked in water before it is put to the fire, loses all its flavour . . . Raw ham, Bologna sausages, figs, and melons are eaten at the first course. Salt meat, unless it be hams and tongues, is totally unknown. No boiled leg of pork, and peas-pudding; no bubble and squeak; – vulgar dishes, it is true, but excellent notwithstanding: nor have they the *petits plats*, in which the French so much excel, to supply their places.[12]

Others wrote of the differences in individual dishes or unknown foods. Montpellier was 'supplied with little cream cheeses made of goats milk which when kept to a certain time are very good'. Tancred Robinson found that 'Italy abounds much with swines flesh; they are generally fat and black; in some places they are extremely fat, thanks to chestnuts etc'. In 1749 Thomas Barrett-Lennard had goats' milk in the Rhône valley and oranges fresh from the trees at Aix. In France in 1786 James Smith encountered at breakfast 'the Abricots du Pape. This fruit which has not yet been introduced in England, is about the size and colour of an Orleans plum, but downy. Its flavour approaches that of an apricot, though more spirited.' Travelling through Sicily in 1788, Thomas Watkins ate a 'cake of bread, whiter than any I have ever eaten' and wrote that the 'pigeons in this country are so much superior to any I have ever eaten, that they seem a different kind of bird. They are as large as grouse, as fat as ortolans, and so agreable to the taste, that if some of our English epicures were to feed upon them, they would probably eat themselves to death.' On the other hand, Pratt warned that German bread was dark and had a 'bitter and sour taste'.[13]

Tourists were thus fully aware, if they read the available travel literature, that they would encounter unfamiliar dishes and arrangements. The literature, though often disparaging and sometimes contemptuous concerning the situation abroad, rarely displayed, however, the robust xenophobia that characterized the treatment of foreigners and their food in, for example, British caricatures and on the British stage. In these popular genres foreign food was condemned simply for being foreign, while the food itself was both cause and consequence of the depravity and weakness of foreigners. In his 1753 play *The Englishman in Paris* the playwright and actor Samuel Foote, who had spent a considerable period in Paris and who was to die in Dover on his way to a health-induced rest in southern France, had Squire Buck say of an English barber resident in Paris, 'the rascal looks as if he had not had a piece of beef and pudding in his paunch these twenty years; I'll be hanged if the rogue has not been fed upon frogs ever since he came over'.[14]

Travel literature did not share this automatic sneer, the pantomime depiction of the foreigner and his life. Though Smollett was splenetic about the French, most other writers expressed a degree of prejudice that was very different from that of the stage and the caricature. It is of course difficult to sustain venom in multi-volume form, but although the particular conventions and problems of travel literature should not be ignored, it is appropriate to note that most writers presented an individual response that was not completely unsympathetic to continental circumstances, even if the common supposition was that British was best.

A similar conclusion could be advanced in the case of individual tourists who did not present their views through the prism of print. Dewes, though a servant, did not do too badly, even if his protein was often in the form of eggs. Dining near Geneva in an establishment with a filthy cook, he had 'no soup, all bread, after that a dish of stewed sliced turnips, and a dish of baked onions, and a pancake of eggs with three whole ones lay at top, very much resembling a cow dung with mushrooms sprung through it. After all this was plenty of fruit, such as grapes, peaches.' Later meals included 'supped upon mackaroni soup, stewed spinage, mashed eggs with a dessert of fruit', and a dinner of 'mackaroni soup, fryed kidney beanshells, an egg pancake, stewed turnips, a few eggs in the shell. Master had cold fowl roasted.'

Dewes' social superiors did better. One reiterated theme was the importance of fish at riverside stops. In 1714 James Hume noted, 'we dined at Pont L'Evesque in the best inn we have yet met with in this country, being Friday we had a fish dinner, viz thornbacks, flounders, and trouts, all extraordinary good in their kind and cheap enough . . . At St. Maturines our host carried us down to the River [the Loire] and brought up with a net several sorts of excellent fish, out of which we chose some for supper.' In 1769 Walter Stanhope wrote to his mother from Berne, 'This country is remarkable for the finest trouts in the world; we hardly ever see one at table less than four, or five pounds weight, and sometimes much larger . . . In the article of good eating, and drinking, France goes far beyond us.' Three years later Philip Francis wrote in Strasbourg, 'here we begin to live like ourselves – incomparable tench at dinner, and exquisite perch at supper, both from the Rhine. The master of the house . . . promises us wild boar, chevreuil, trout and carp in abundance.' In 1785 Lady Craven ate the most excellent crayfish and trout she had ever tasted in Marseilles.[15]

The references to fish serve to underline the importance of regional variations in the availability of food. The same was also obviously true of fruit and wine. Furthermore, seasonal factors were particularly important in the case of fruit and vegetables. Such differences are fairly obvious, but it was also the case that the availability and type of meat varied greatly. Standardized scientific breeding had not yet reduced the number of breeds and local traditions of preparation were strong. Thus observations such as Andrew Mitchell's at Spoleto: 'Be sure you eat mutton here', or Norton Nicholls's that Sorrento was famous for veal and butter, had considerable point to them. Visiting Genoa in early 1731, Swinton noted:

The pork and mutton are very good here, but not to be compared with the beef and veal, which is certainly the finest in the world. The beef is exceeding tender, most of the cattle being drove out of Piedmont to this place, and coming over many high and rugged mountains. The fatigue which they undergo is long and gradual, which is the reason the beef is so very sweet and tender at Genoa, though it is extremely tough and hard in Piedmont. The veal is very white, sweet, juicy, and of a very delicious flavour.

He also had broccoli for the first time, 'so tender and fine-tasting that no greens in England or elsewhere can come up to it'. Sir John Fleming Leicester, who was unimpressed by the milk in Nice in 1784, thought that Turin had 'the finest cream and the best butter in the world', which he attributed to its being surrounded by grassland. William Lee sent his father a Parmesan cheese from Milan and a liqueur from Venice to moisten it.[16] Distinctive dishes spread, though only to a certain extent; the rum baba being introduced to France from Poland by Stanislaus Leszczynski, while the croissant was brought there by Marie Antoinette's Viennese pastrycooks.

Local variety was also the case with drink, although it was easier to move beer, water, wine or spirits without significant loss of quality than most foodstuffs. Hume wrote in 1714 from 'Nantes, where there was no brandy to be got but what was worse than our English spirits; for their good old brandy they send abroad, but what is new and fiery they reserve for their own common use.' *The Gentleman's Guide* wrote of a famous Parisian tavern 'where all sorts of good wines may be had . . . The English are so accustomed to resort thither, that it will not be difficult for any stranger to find it out.'[17] The sparkling Champagne wine devised by Dom Pérignon in 1668 became fashionable under the Regency.

The technology for bottling and transporting liquids was relatively unsophisticated, and financial considerations only justified local distribution, except for expensive and well-known drinks, such as brandy, champagne, claret and port. As a result, tourists frequently encountered wines that were new to them, and were often delighted by the quality of what they drank. One traveller unsurprisingly praised the quality of Norman cider in 1729. Travelling up the Rhine in 1700 Grey Neville and his brother Henry visited Koblenz: 'here is admirable Moselle wine. We refreshed ourselves very well here . . . at Backarach [sic] we drunk admirable good wine.' Between Berne and Lausanne they 'began to drink most exquisite wines'. Rhenish wines were appreciated by other tourists. At Strasbourg Francis noted 'we drink good hock, and find it medicinal'. Adam Walker 'got excellent Rhenish wine' at Jülich, William Drummond the same at Bonn and Worms.[18] However, it was local Italian wines that generally proved of greatest interest. Near Etna, Watkins drank 'a flask of wine that was a perfect cordial', and of Syracuse he wrote 'the environs of the city produce thirteen kinds of excellent muscadine wines; all which we had before us every day at dinner'. Local Italian wines were praised by many tourists including Beckford, Carpenter, Garmston, Robert Gray, Sacheverell Stevens and Walker. Swinton found the ordinary wine in Genoa agreeable and thought it tasted like cider. It cost 2d a bottle.[19]

Tourists were not always appreciative, however, though Robert Poole's observations in Cambrai in 1741 are worth noting because they reveal the different responses of a group to the same drink: 'supper . . . was here furnished with beer for drink, which my companions liked well and commended; but it was by much too bitter for me to drink. We also had wine at 30 sol the bottle, but it was but very indifferent.' Travelling through Burgundy in 1752, William Lee complained that 'the wine which we expected to find in great perfection is not so good as I have often drunk in England'. Thomas Jones tried bottled beer in Parma in 1776 but found it 'very unpalatable stuff', while a year earlier Peter Wauchop wrote from Lille 'there's no beer drinkable and their wine both bad and dear'. An anonymous tourist in Turin in 1782 found 'the table wine (vin du pais) so bad, that we were obliged to buy some nice wine at 30 sols the bottle, which though not a pleasant wine we were obliged to be content with'. Sir John Fleming Leicester wrote from Lyons in 1784, 'wine of the country I cannot drink. It is like vinegar, Burgundy has been therefore my substitute, mixed with water, and has agreed perfectly.' Philip Thicknesse praised German and Hungarian wine, but was unhappy about that in the Austrian Netherlands:

> even the Bath road to London is not so dear as on the great roads in France, or Flanders, with this difference only, that the traveller thinks he drinks better wine; he certainly does drink weaker and perhaps wholesomer wine than English road port . . . to deal with the wine merchants of Brussels for wine, is, in general, giving your money for poison; they have a method of brewing several sorts of wine, and particularly what they call Burgundy, with pigeon's dung, and an artificial sweet wine, palatable enough, in which a quantity of brimstone is infused.

On the other hand, Lord Gardenstone, writing in the same period of France, noted 'the wine better, and cheaper; – good burgundy for the price of adulterated port in the English inns'.[20]

The poor quality of drinking water was commented on by many tourists, and was a particular problem in coastal areas, where it was often brackish. Few shared Lady Craven's fear of being poisoned by the waters of Tartary, but many experienced discomfort, usually in the form of diarrhoea, from drinking water in Europe. In 1737 Margaret, Viscountess Coningsby (c. 1709–61), wrote from Paris to reassure her sister on this head:

> I beg you'll be in no frights about the Seine water for we have it all passed through a sand fountain, which takes off the violent effects of it. However Riagett has felt a little of its operation but I believe it has rather been of service to her than otherwise; I seldom drink it without wine and if it should disagree with me I would drink Spa water.[21]

In short the principal theme is one of variety, variety of experience and of perception, James Hume finding this to be the case for successive meals in France in 1714. In face of the general tendency to treat the Grand Tour in terms of stereotypes, the overwhelming impression of the variety of food and drink available as well as the variety of responses to them is worth stressing. The expectation of tourists and of their friends and relations were far from uniform. When in 1746 George Oxenden wrote of his eldest son: 'if Italy don't spoil his chastity and Germany his sobriety I flatter myself he will preserve the character he sets out with of an honest worthy young man',[22] he was accepting the possibility of alternative developments. Alongside the polemic of cultural nationalism that could lead to the insubstantiality of French food being castigated for the benefit of British audiences, there is a strong impression from reading numerous tourist accounts that good food could be had abroad and that tourists were ready, indeed in some cases eager, to appreciate different traditions of cuisine. French recipes became increasingly complex, as quality rather than quantity was stressed. Food abroad did not have to be an unfortunate necessity. It could be enjoyable. Edward Mellish wrote in 1731 to his father from Tours about 'my good living at Blois, where with a good bottle of wine, a soup, a joint of mutton, and a fowl I used to regale myself with much pleasure'. Philip Francis in Strasbourg in July 1772 noted: 'very hot and nothing to do. No spectacle for the afternoon so we determine to eat a very good dinner, and be good company till supper.'[23] Menus often sound quite appealing: 'For dinner, nice soup and boulie, an excellent fricasee of beef and onion soup and part of a loin of veal and a dessert afterwards', being one French meal enjoyed by an anonymous tourist in 1786.[24] It is, however, worth noting the comment of George, Lord Lyttelton in 1762: 'our old fashioned English cakes will not please a French palate, let the stuff of which they are made be ever so good, no more than the excellence of their cookery will make their unsolid *kickshaws* satisfy our hungry stomachs'.

In addition, meals could be cheaper than in Britain. Pratt found that the set meal at his inn in The Hague was 20 pence 'for as good a dinner consisting of two excellent courses, (and a liberal dessert) . . . as you can have in any part of London, for half a crown a head'. In 1773 James Essex found at Dunkirk: 'our supper for four people at 15 pence a head . . . it consisted of two fowls boiled, a duck roasted, a very fine codling, a dish of artichokes and a fine salad, these were replaced by a dish of tarts, a plate of apricots, 2 plates of maccaroons with other confectionary'. On the boat between Bruges and Ghent, Essex had an excellent dinner 'served in as neat and elegant a manner as it could be in the best London tavern, and at far less expence being no more than fifteen pence each person without the extra charge of bread, beer etc., so commonly charged by the innkeepers in England'.[25] Other tourists were willing to comment on the good value of the meals they ate.[26] However some felt cheated,[27] and it was claimed that prices were raised for foreigners. Bennet wrote of France in 1785: 'wine ready to be taken out of the cellar at fifteen pence, becomes the finest brandy, and must not be touched under a crown . . . To prevent impositions in the article of eating, it will be best always to dine and sup at table d'hotes where you can. You are sure of being at a stated price.'[28]

Native travellers in Britain complained frequently about the quality, price or preparation of the food they received there, and it is unclear that the situation on the Continent was any worse, as opposed to being different. In 1780 Mary Montagu-Douglas-Scott reached Worksop:

> . . . a dirty inn;
> The meat was very tough and bad,
> and mother storm'd like any mad,
> But forced 'half pleased to be content',
> We munched our meat and on we went.[29]

As a postscript, it is worth printing an excellent account left by one of three tourists who spent most of August and early September 1699 in Paris:

As to our reports of the poverty of the French, it is true that the villages in the country are mean and the people as poor or poorer than the English, but on the contrary Paris and the other citys we saw are more populous than ours, their wine and bread finer than ours, they eat oftner than we do, and are more given to diversions and merriment than the English. Their butter, beer and cheese are not near so good as ours in England, and very little of them appears in their eating, as for their beef and veal, I think them not quite so good as the English, their veal especially is very bad, their rabbits, pullets and turkeys all very much short of ours. At the house where we ate in Paris our diet was regular, having every noon soup, afterwards a dish of boiled meat, mutton and beef with some other dishes either of broiled mutton, or a pie, or cold beef stuffed with bacon, and last of all a dessert. At night we always had roast beef, or mutton, or veal with a salad, and also roasted fowls tame or wild larded for the most part with bacon, or else fricasseed; after this we never failed of a dessert. This was always our custom the first 5 days in the week, the other 2 were fasting days and we never had any meat but always fish both noon and night, at noons on fasting days we had a soup of mutton made with herbs, then saltfish and besides that another sort of fish, with artichokes or cauliflowers and eggs fried; at night always saltfish and a salad with carp and eels stewed, and served up together, after these a dessert of fruit both at noons and nights as on flesh days; during this whole month we drank at our meals nothing but wine and water, a choppin of wine that is very near a pint being allowed to every person at each meal. Here we did not eat on plate though at other public houses we did, and is very familiar in Paris among the better sort of people, particularly the coffee houses seem to abound in it, and have most of their vessels in silver, the room hung with tapestry, and 5 or 6 large looking glasses in one room, their chocolate, coffee and tea are dear, the former is 10d, the other[s] 4d a dish, but the liquor is good, and the measure large, and served on a silver salvar with silver sugar dish and spoon, much spirits are drunk in their coffee houses, some biscuits or cakes being eaten with all sorts of liquors. Their taverns are not so good as ours, nor the attendance so good, but the wine rather better, though I believe the French do not drink so much as we do, they drink often at meals, but never drink afterwards as we do in England.[30]

NOTES

1. Beinecke, Osborn Shelves c 200 p. 72, c 331, 26 Aug. 1787; BL Add. 30271 f. 16.
2. R. Coriat [Paterson], *Another Traveller!* (2 vols, 1767) I, 28; Pratt, *Gleanings through Wales, Holland and Westphalia* (3 vols, 1795), II, 6; Beinecke, Osborn Shelves f c 52 p. 1.
3. Bod. Ms. Eng. Misc. f. 54, 22 June 1785.
4. Gloucester CRO D1571/F653; Bod. Ms. Eng. Misc. e 250 f. 3; BL 40759 f. 3; Bod. Ms. Eng. Misc. d 213 p. 53; Beckford, *Familiar Letters from Italy, to a friend in England* (2 vols, Salisbury, 1805) I, 17; Beinecke, Osborn Files, uncatalogued; Townsend, *A Journey through Spain* (3 vols, 1791) I, 1–2; Osborn Shelves f c 52 pp. 5–6; Gloucester CRO D2002 F1.
5. Beinecke, Osborn Shelves c 24 p. 42; CUL Ms 4377 p. 55; Bod. Ms. Eng. Misc. d 123 p. 75; A. Miller, *Letters from Italy* (3 vols, 1776) II, 89–90, 186–7, 210, 215; BL Stowe Ms. 791 p. 40; Beinecke, Osborn Shelves c 393; Brand to Wharton, 21 July 1791, Durham, Wharton.
6. Leicester, CRO D67, Finch D5 pp. 99, 118, 100; Osborn Shelves c 200 p. 50; Miller, *Letters* II, 189; Jones, *Memoirs of Thomas Jones* (1951), p. 49; O.J. Reichel (ed.), 'Extracts from a Devonshire Lady's Notes of Travel in France 1784', *Transactions of the Devonshire Association*, 34 (1902), p. 268; BL Add. 30271 f. 3; J.C. Villiers, *A Tour through part of France* (1789), pp. 10–11; Bod. Ms. Eng. Misc. f. 54 f. 169.
7. Bod. Ms. Douce 67 pp. 142–3; Anon. CUL Add. Mss. 8789; Wharton to his mother, 26 Feb. 1775, Durham, Wharton.
8. Thicknesse, *A Year's Journey through the Pais Bas, and Austrian Netherlands* (2nd ed., 1786), p. 177; *Gentleman's Guide* (7th ed., 1783), p. 193; Exeter CRO 1392 M/L18 84/3; Preston CRO DD Gr F/3 f. 35; Guildhall Library, London, Ms. 10823/5A.
9. Thicknesse, *Useful Hints to those who make the Tour of France* (1768), p. 176; Beckford, *Letters* II, 405; *Kalm's Account of his visit to England* (1892), p. 15.
10. Thicknesse, *A Year's Journey through France and Part of Spain* (2 vols, 1777) I, 162–3; Bod. Ms. Eng. Misc. d 213 pp. 138, 57, 154; J. Macdonald, *Memoirs of an Eighteenth Century Footman* (1790, reprinted 1985), p. 195; Brand to sister Susan, 10 Oct. 1779, CUL Add. Mss. 8670/8; BL Add. 5957 f. 63–4.
11. BL Add. 30271 f. 3, Stowe 790 f. 32; Bod. Ms. Eng. Misc. e 250 f. 4–5; Pratt, *Gleanings* III, 94.
12. BL Add. 38507 f. 5; Miller, *Letters* II, 72, 92, 189–90; HL Ellesmere Mss. 11031; Gloucester CRO D 2002 F1; Carleton, *A True and Genuine History of the last two Wars against France and Spain* (1742), p. 309; *Present State* II, 388; Beinecke, Osborn Shelves c 469 p. 40; Miller, *Letters* II, 66–7; Beckford, *Letters* I, 246–7.

13. Beinecke, Osborn Shelves c 200; Leeds AO NH 2911; Barrett-Lennard to Nicholas Hardinge, 30 July, Chelmsford, Essex CRO, D/DL C43/3/222; Smith, *A Sketch of a Tour on the Continent in the years 1786 and 1787* (3 vols, 1793) I, 72; Watkins, *Travels through Swisserland, Italy, Sicily, the Greek Islands, to Constantinople* (2 vols, 1792) II, 7, 56; Pratt, *Gleanings* III, 88.

14. *Englishman* I, i.

15. Bod. Ms. Eng. Misc. d 213 pp. 97–8, 143; BL Add. 29477 f. 16, 22; Bradford, Public Library, Spencer Stanhope papers, Stanhope to his mother, 11 July 1769; BL Add. 40759 f. 3–4; Craven, *A Journey through the Crimea to Constantinople* (Dublin, 1789), p. 44.

16. BL Add. 58320 f. 60; Beinecke, Osborn Shelves c 467 II No. 26; Swinton, 30 Jan., 4 Feb. 1731; Chester CRO DLT/CP/7, 23; Lee, 9 May 1753, Beinecke Lee Box 3.

17. BL Add. 29477; *Gentleman's Guide*, p. 231.

18. ? to Robinson, 21 Mar. 1729, Leeds, District Archives, Vyner Mss. 6018 13455; Reading, Berkshire CRO D/EN F18/1 pp. 47, 58; BL Add. 40759 f. 4; Walker, *Ideas Suggested on the Spot in a late Excursion* (1790), p. 45; Osborn Shelves c 331, 29 Aug., 2 Sept. 1787.

19. Watkins, *Travels* II, 7, 41; Beckford, *Letters* I, 52; Bod. Ms. Douce 67, p. 195; BL Add. 30271 f. 29; Gray, *Letters during the course of a Tour Through Germany, Switzerland and Italy* (1794), pp. 349, 453; Stevens, p. 363; Walker, *Ideas* p. 327.

20. Poole, *A Journey from London to France and Holland* (2nd ed., 2 vols, 1746–50) II, 11 Aug. 1741; Lee to his father, 9 Aug. 1752, Beinecke, Lee Box 3; Jones, *Memoirs*, p. 49; BL Add. 35509 f. 230; Anon., Beinecke, Osborn Shelves c 289; Chester CRO DLT/C9/4; Thicknesse, *Pais Bas*, pp. 6–7, 195–9; Gardenstone, *Travelling Memorandums made in a tour upon the Continent of Europe, in the years 1786, 1787 and 1788* (3 vols, 1791) I, 16.

21. HW 75 f. 19; Pococke, BL Add. 22978 f. 79; Crewe, BL Add. 37926 f. 32; Tracy and Dentand, Bod. Ms. Add. A 366 f. 52; Carpenter, Bod. Ms. Douce 67, p. 8; Muirhead, p. 1; Thomson, p. 146; Smollett, p. 22; Poole I, 40; Stevens, p. 22; Starke, pp. 92, 193, 203; *Harcourt* III, 6.

22. BL Add. 29477 f. 16, 20, 23822 f. 324.

23. NUL Mellish papers, 25 Jan. 1731; BL Add. 40759 f. 4.

24. Chichester, West Sussex CRO Add. Ms. 7236, 6 Nov. 1786; HL MO 1302.

25. Pratt, *Gleanings* II, 99; W. Fawcett (ed.), *Journal of a Tour through part of Flanders and France in August 1773* (Cambridge, 1888), pp. 8, 23, 66.

26. CUL Add. Ms. 4216 f. 3; Bod. Ms. Add. A 366 f. 6; Thicknesse, *France and Part of Spain* I, 58.

27. H. Peckham, *A Tour through Holland* (1772), p. 71.

28. Bod. Ms. Eng. Misc. f. 54 f. 203–4.

29. Montagu-Douglas-Scott to Lady Courtown, 13 July 1789, Beinecke, Osborn Files uncatalogued, prov. 80.6.33.

30. Beinecke, Osborn Shelves b 155.

7

WAR, DISPUTES, ACCIDENTS AND CRIME

WAR

The cloud which seems to threaten Italy, makes it a very improper place to reside in at present . . . Nobody can tell what may be the consequence of a general war in Italy; and how improper in every respect it may be for an English nobleman to be there at that time.

Duke of Newcastle to Earl of Lincoln, 1741[1]

International and civil wars affected British tourists to a varying extent. The circumstances in each conflict were different and much depended on the attitudes and position of the individual traveller. For Horace Walpole, son of the first minister, or the Earl of Lincoln, nephew and heir of the Duke of Newcastle, Secretary of State for the Southern Department, the situation was different to that for a tourist without powerful political connections. Both in Italy in early 1741 they were ordered home before they could be cut off by the Spanish forces which invaded Italy that year. Spain was then at war with Britain, partly over the matter of an ear removed without medical assistance in the Caribbean. Nevertheless, the war, which broadened into the War of the Austrian Succession that lasted until 1748, did not prevent other British tourists from visiting Italy. The relationship between war and tourism was a complex and ambivalent one.

Travel required permission – though the degree of stringency varied greatly. It was easy to leave Britain, though those holding posts and commissions were expected to stay in the country, especially in times of war and international crisis. In 1699 William III refused to allow William, 1st Duke of Devonshire (1641–1707), to travel to France because he was one of the Lords Justices, but the less important John, 5th Earl of Exeter (c. 1648–1700), was given permission. He died from a surfeit of fruit near Paris. Sir Richard Newdigate also went to France that year. In 1776 George III gave Richard Rigby, the Paymaster General, permission to make a flying visit to France. He returned convinced that it was 'a dunghill, not fit for a gentleman to live in'. On the Continent British tourists, in common with other travellers, were examined at many control points. Most towns were still walled with military posts at the gates at which travellers had to stop, identify themselves, declare the purpose of their travel and often where they were going to spend the night in town. Guards sometimes accompanied them to the hotel to check on the latter. When James Hume arrived in Dieppe in 1714 he was taken to see the governor, 'who examined us whence we came, what our profession was, and what business we had in France'.[2] Philip Francis was delayed leaving Paris in 1772 by the difficulty of obtaining a passport: 'impossible to get the passport in time to set out this evening, as I wished and intended. Everything in this country is calculated for check and control.'[3] The need for passports and for specific permission to enter a country varied within Europe. Some countries were very strict. On arrival in the Kingdom of Naples it was necessary to show a passport that had been obtained from the Neapolitan ambassador in Rome.[4] Difficulties were created over passports in the later years of the Walpole ministry, when Naples clearly supported the Jacobites. In eastern Europe passports were especially important. Petty wrote to Keith in 1785 of 'the passport which you was so good as to procure me when I went into Transylvania and which on several occasions I found *absolutely necessary*', and he asked for a new one.[5]

Europe was bisected by a plague *cordon sanitaire* and quarantine regulations were a variant on passport controls. Mediterranean tourists who had visited North Africa or the Turkish empire had to undergo lengthy quarantines. Thomas Glynn underwent one in Marseilles in 1784, and four years later John Hawkins had a thirty-day quarantine in Messina. Arriving at Ragusa (Dubrovnik) in 1791 from Venice on a boat he had hired, George Koehler, a German who had a commission in the royal artillery, encountered great difficulty in landing, because of fears that he had met ships at sea that were infected with plague:

> but on the sight of our passport as Englishmen we were received with the greatest attention, and from their never having seen an English passport before they supposed we must be persons of consequence to have one . . . gave us [as] a particular mark of favour and distinction, a letter to the Pasha of Bosnia . . . without whose protection no strangers can travel with safety in this country.

Koehler travelled on to Constantinople 'through several towns in which the plague was raging with violence, and slept always upon straw out in the open air and were more than a month without pulling off our clothes'.[6]

There was particular sensitivity about travellers visiting military posts, as one tourist discovered at Antibes in 1754: 'As Mr Clarke and I were walking upon the ramparts and looking at the batteries of guns pointed out over the sea, we were ordered by the sentinels to leave the place.' Mitford wrote of Valenciennes in 1787: 'Being a fortified town with a garrison, a traveller is exposed to the inconvenience of being under a necessity of showing his passport from Paris, and obtaining the order of the commandant for post horses before he can leave it.'[7] The need for passports increased in wartime, whether Britain was a combatant or not. They were generally readily granted.

Many travelled during the War of the Spanish Succession (1702–13), some perhaps, like James Compton, to view the war. Most tourists, such as Compton, specifically avoided France. Samuel Tufnell toured the United Provinces, Germany, Italy and Switzerland in 1703–5; Edward Montagu, Italy in 1708; David Papillon, Germany in 1709; Uvedale Price, France and Italy in 1709–12; and John Wallop, Italy and Germany in 1710. Having left Eton in 1704, the wealthy young baronet Sir Richard Grosvenor (1689–1732) spent the following three years in the Netherlands, Germany, Switzerland and Italy. Metcalfe Robinson, whose father was an MP, travelled to Italy in 1705, and British envoys helped him to obtain passes. At Geneva he found Theophilus, 9th Earl of Huntingdon (1696–1746), and George, 5th Earl of Winton. Sir Carnaby Haggerston's 1711 journey to a Lorraine school was affected by the war. At Antwerp he was advised to go via Cologne as the safest route, but at Cologne he was forced to renew his pass as Trier was in French hands. The previous year Sir John Anstruther (c. 1678–1753) obtained a British passport to go from Aachen to Paris. Several years earlier Joseph Shaw was warned not to travel late as he might be plundered by soldiers.[8] What is interesting, however, is that Shaw and Haggerston should have been travelling at all, especially the latter whose school lay very near to the zone of hostilities.

Aside from a brief war with Spain in 1718–20, Britain was not at war again until 1739, but international tension still affected tourists. In 1730 the threat of war in Italy delayed William Mildmay at Marseilles.[9] The War of the Polish Succession of 1733–5 involved major hostilities in Italy and the Rhineland. When war began in late 1733 several tourists who anticipated Britain's entry on behalf of Austria decided to return home via Germany rather than France. Two years later the views of Charles, 2nd Duke of Grafton, concerning the Grand Tour of his heir, George, Earl of Euston (1715–47), were guided by the war: 'considering the situation the country is in at present and the armies in the field without a preparation he cannot go there'.[10] Most tourists were not affected, however, by the conflict and the participants made no effort to limit British tourism, despite the widely held assumption that Britain would enter the war on the Austrian side. One London newspaper announced soon after the start of war that 'M. Chavigny [the French envoy] has acquainted the court, that the king of France hath sent orders to all his generals in Italy, to take care that none of the English noblemen and gentlemen, that are upon their travels, receive any molestation or injury whatever, but that they upon all occasions do pay them all the respect imaginable.' Tourists found no difficulty in obtaining passports and touring the field of conflict. In 1734 Walter Molesworth, his wife and son received an Austrian passport to go to Spa; Viscount Harcourt viewed the battle of Parma from the ramparts of the town; Sir Hugh Smithson and Sir Henry Liddell visited the French army near Mantua and Richard Pococke was allowed by the French to visit the castle in Milan where they were constructing new fortifications. Pococke returned home through France. Euston was received by Charles Emmanuel III of Savoy-Piedmont and discussed the war with him, while Henry Fox used his wartime stay in Turin as the basis for comments in a 1740 House of Commons debate on the augmentation of the army by the creation of new regiments. Andrew Mitchell was annoyed to find that as a result of the war the picture collections at Modena and Parma became inaccessible: the latter was moved to Genoa. He toured the battlefield of Parma with a French officer with whom he discussed the recent battle, and also discussed that of Guastalla with participants. Mitchell found many of the churches and monasteries in Parma full of wounded and 'cart loads of wounded and sick sent in everyday from the camp to the hospitals . . . miserable spectacle'. Nevertheless, bar the removal of the paintings, he suffered no inconvenience from the hostilities. Milles found the ducal apartments in Modena inaccessible in 1734, because the contents were packed up in case of French occupation. Tourism in France continued throughout the war though the Rhineland seems to have been avoided.[11]

Tourism did not cease during the next conflict in western Europe, that of the Austrian Succession, despite British participation. The legal situation was fairly complex. Britain was at war with Spain 1739–48, but war with France was not declared until the spring of 1744 even though Anglo-French hostilities in Germany had begun the previous year. War disrupted routes of communication, the seizure of horses harmed the posting system and travellers could be ill-used whatever their legal status. The Elbe causeway between Saxony and Bohemia was broken up in 1744 and the Earl of Holdernesse, a diplomat en route to Venice, was ill-used that autumn near Nuremberg by the hussars of Britain's Austrian ally. In 1739 Francis Hare, Bishop of Chichester, wrote to his son, then in Italy:

I had a letter from Mr. Spateman in which he says . . . if a war should break out, passports may protect you from public seizures of either your person or goods, yet private violence is always more busy in such times of commotions, and one travels with less safety, which no doubt is true, but I should hope with proper precautions there would be no great danger from thence. I have told him I believed you would govern your motions by what you saw other English gentlemen do.[12]

In general they did not panic. The press printed occasional atrocity stories about the fate of travellers, such as one in 1742 of a woman being raped on the Dutch crossing when her ship was captured by a Spanish privateer. There was also a press item at the beginning of the war that, 'The several British noblemen and gentlemen abroad on their travels have been wrote to by their relations and friends to come home.'[13] The reality was otherwise. Tourism continued. It was often best to leave the scene of conflict, Lady Mary Wortley Montagu leaving Chambéry in early 1742 because of the approach of Bourbon troops, but tourists in Italy in the early 1740s crossed between armies with little difficulty, and there could even be a somewhat facetious attitude towards the dangers posed by war.[14] The Channel crossings were generally safe in the early stages of the war, Spanish privateering not being much of a threat.[15] The situation changed with the outbreak of conflict in the Austrian Netherlands in 1744 and the subsequent French invasion. Ostend, the principal tourist port on that coast, fell to the French in August 1745, Brussels in 1746. In 1747 French forces invaded the United Provinces.

Nevertheless, tourism contined. Sacheverell Stevens in his trip down the Main had to go to the Austrian camp to obtain a passport from Marshal Traun, 'which he readily granted us'. He took a boat from Wertheim 'in order to avoid the trouble of passing thro' the army'. As Stevens also had a French passport, he

> passed in our boat down the river Main with little trouble, except that once a party of them (the French army being encamped on the side of a hill) descry'd us sailing down the Main, numbers of them came running to the river side, and forced us to come on shore to the commanding officer, to whom we produced our passport, notwithstanding which, with all their authority, they could not without great difficulty hinder the common soldiers from plundering us.[16]

The ending of conflict also brought disruption, Thomas Anson MP finding the route from Aachen to Paris in 1748 'full of troops and baggage returning' to his 'great inconvenience'. He complained about being forced to purchase passports for the journey.[17]

The Seven Years War (1756–63) had an effect on tourism. Deteriorating Anglo-French relations led to the end of the Italian tour of William, 17th Earl of Sutherland, and James Grant, both officers in the Royal Scots who were ordered to rejoin their regiment in Ireland in 1755. In the winter of 1755–6 the Earl of Orrery returned from Italy through Germany and the United Provinces, not France, because of the poor state of Anglo-French relations. The Prussian attack on Saxony in 1756 and the subsequent outbreak of hostilities on the Continent affected tourism in Germany. Richard Combe, who had travelled from St Petersburg via Riga and Berlin, wrote from Dresden that September: 'The Assembly at the Minister's, and all amusements were at an end, as soon as it was known that the Prussians were possessed of Leipzig . . . As we find it impracticable at present to pass through Bohemia, we shall go directly to Geneva, from whence after a short stay, we shall proceed to Rome.'[18] In 1759 Charles Selwin, a British banker at Paris, advised David Garrick against a return trip to Paris during the war. Passport conditions affected British tourists in France, though Lady Spencer was given a French passport for her intended trip to Spa and other passports were issued. The French envoy in the Palatinate was willing in 1758 to help an MP get a passport to enable him to take a Pyrenean cure for his severe gout. Sir Richard Lyttelton MP went abroad for his health, travelling through France in 1760. In February 1762, Elizabeth Montagu wrote to her sister-in-law, then at Rome, 'I am under some anxiety lest our rupture with Spain should occasion you an inconvenience.'[19]

Nevertheless, Italy was largely unaffected by conflict, and many still went on the Grand Tour. The British resident John Murray wrote from Venice in 1759: 'We are here in as perfect a state of tranquillity, as if there was a profound peace all over Europe.' The same year Murray's counterpart at Turin, James Stuart Mackenzie, reassured Sir John Rushout about the plans of the latter's son: 'As to public disturbances in this part of the world, he will run no risk of being incommoded by them in his travels through Italy, for there is not the most distant appearance of the present profound tranquillity of these countrys being disturbed.'[20]

Sir Wyndham Knatchbull-Wyndham toured in 1757–60 and spent a long time in Italy. James Ferguson and Sir Adam Fergusson were on the Grand Tour in 1757–8, and James Grant in 1758–60. Sir Humphrey Morice went to Italy for his health in 1760, returning for the autumn session of parliament in 1762. Francis Russell, Marquis of Tavistock, was abroad in 1761–2, mostly in Italy. While in Rome he met Augustus, 3rd Duke of Grafton (1735–1811), John, later 1st Lord, Crewe (1742–1829), Dr John Hinchliffe (1731–94), his tutor, later Master of Trinity and Bishop of Peterborough, 'Crauford, James and others'. Hinchliffe later married Crewe's sister, while Grafton became his patron after meeting him on the Continent and was responsible for his being appointed Chaplain in Ordinary to George III. Stuart Mackenzie's letters to his brother, the 3rd Earl of Bute, include references to many British tourists passing through Turin, and in March 1761 he reported that passports for travel via France could be obtained.[21] Edward Tucker noted the presence of seven or eight British tourists in Lausanne in March 1760, including the 3rd Duke of Roxburgh (1740–1804), who was taking a break from army winter quarters.[22] James Hutton noted eight British tourists in Geneva in December 1762.[23] Having left Oxford, William, Marquis of Titchfield (1738–1809), set off in December 1757 via Hamburg for Warsaw, where he stayed for over a year with the envoy, Viscount Stormont. In September 1759 Titchfield set off for Turin, to 'make the Tour of Italy', with Benjamin Langlois (1727–1802) as his bearleader. He was affected by the war, Langlois writing from Berlin in January 1760:

> We could get no passports from the French or Austrian Ministers at Warsaw, but when we left it were in hopes that the French would have been obliged to have repassed the Rhine and left us by that means a road open. But as they have been able to maintain themselves we cannot now continue our route without passports from the Duke de Broglie [French commander] which Lord Granby [British commander] to whom Lord Titchfield has wrote for this purpose, flatters us will be granted without any difficulty provided we come to the allied army.

Titchfield was successful, travelling through Germany to Italy, spending a year at Turin and then going to Florence, before setting off home in October 1761. His father, the 2nd Duke of Portland, had refused to grant the £3,000 per annum that Titchfield had sought, and would not exceed £2,500. Titchfield, the 3rd Duke, became the titular leader of the Whigs in 1782, and was First Lord of the Treasury in 1783 and 1807–9. Langlois became an MP and, eventually, a member of the Board of Trade.[24] Others travelled during the Seven Years War, including Robert Adam, Sir Brook Bridges (1733–91), Charles Compton, later 7th Earl of Northampton, the Earl of Moray, Thomas Robinson, the Earl of Stamford and Lord Warkworth.

Whereas most British tourists during the Seven Years War travelled in Italy, where conflict was small-scale, Grafton was able to visit France:

> Through the interest of the Marquis Du Quesne, a prisoner on his parole at Northampton, I obtained a passport, which for years past had been refused to every Englishman. We received quarters during our short stay at Paris. At the old and respectable Duke of Biron's I dined with a numerous set of officers; and his reception of me was flattering.

In Geneva Grafton met French aristocrats:

> We had the pleasure of meeting them frequently in different houses, for a foolish etiquette prevented us from visiting directly each other, while our countries were at war; but we were not prevented from interchanging every possible attention. With Voltaire there was not the same scruple.

In September 1762 Rachael, Dowager Duchess of Bridgewater wrote from Turin to her brother, the 4th Duke of Bedford, telling him that she had met George, 4th Duke of Marlborough (1739–1817), at Paris and Lyons, and added 'we are just setting out for Lyons where we have thoughts of passing the winter'.[25]

It was possible to travel through Germany. One tourist who did so in 1758, travelling from the United Provinces to Swizerland via Mannheim, purchased Hanoverian, Austrian and Prussian passes and was not molested by the French troops he encountered. The same year, Lord Mandeville obtained a passport from the French commander in Germany, enabling him to travel home from the Palatinate to London.[26]

Good social relations were not unknown during the War of American Independence. This was aided by the ambivalent attitude of many of the British élite to the war and by the fact that there were no hostilities on the Continent, with the exception of the Spanish siege of Gibraltar. Charles Drake Garrard recorded of his arrival in Calais in June 1778:

> In every respect except the necessary form of appearing before the commandant, we have experienced perfect freedom of action in our ramble about the town. We found the common people exceedingly civil, a civility which, I am afraid, our countrymen under similar circumstances would not have been inclined to have paid.'[27]

In 1778, Lady Knight left Toulouse, where she was staying, for Rome, 'for though I shall ever esteem the French I know, yet I could not have stayed contentedly in the country, it at war with England'. Two years later she observed, 'Travelling in time of war is not convenient.' Madame du Deffand, whose letters to Horace Walpole are an interesting source for British tourists in Paris, wrote to him in July 1778: 'Les Anglais qui sont en France y resteront tant qu'ils voudront, ceux qui n'y sont pas n'y viendront point parce qu'ils n'y voudront pas venir.' The British response to the war with France, which began in 1778, varied greatly, Brand writing from The Hague the following year: 'I am just come from dinner after laughing very heartily at a very absurd Frenchman and as absurd (or more so I think) Englishman who have been abusing each others country and gasconading most delightfully.' William Scott (1745–1836), later Lord Stowell, decided in August 1777 to go home from Strasbourg via the Rhineland and The Hague, because he thought 'Paris would be very disagreable to an Englishman', if, as seemed likely, war broke out. Keith, as a British envoy, could describe Bourbon celebrations in Vienna as 'poison to English lips', but he had to admit that the French envoy 'had my English colony at his balls even when the war was at the hottest'. Nevertheless, as with Henrietta Pomfret who in August 1738 had felt that she would have to leave Paris if there were Anglo-Bourbon hostilities, so in the later conflict many felt uncomfortable at the idea of visiting a state with which Britain was at war. Fortunately, the French were prepared to give passports. Seeking to return from Lausanne to London in 1779, Frank Hale decided to go down the Rhine to Brussels 'from whence I shall have a Pass to carry me to Calais'.[28] The same year the French envoy in Naples recommended that Thomas Pitt MP, who was convalescing there, be given a passport to return home via Paris. Lord North, the First Lord of the Treasury, was so little concerned about any danger to his travelling sons from the War of the Bavarian Succession (1778–9), in which Britain was neutral, that he suggested that they spend 1779 in Germany, writing to his father: 'the war there will be rather a scene of instruction than of inconvenience to a young English traveller'. It is clear from the correspondence of John, Viscount Mountstuart, envoy at Turin 1779–83, that many British tourists passed through the town during the War of American Independence. Robert Ellison had to travel to France via Ostend in 1781, but he was able to visit Paris and Lyons. In 1782 Ellison dined with the Resident of France at Geneva and went with him to an assembly. On the other hand, the war prevented Philip Yorke, later 3rd Earl of Hardwicke, from shipping home the artistic purchases he had made in Italy.[29]

The explosion in the number of tourists to France from 1782 when hostilities ceased (peace was not signed until 1783) would suggest that the war had restricted the numbers of those travelling. Tourists in the 1780s were not, however, to be free from the threat of war. In the Low Countries in 1784–5 they noted military preparations linked to an apparently imminent Austro-Dutch conflict. In 1785 war between Austria and Prussia was feared, Sir Grey Cooper wrote to Keith about his son's return route from Vienna via Berlin and Hanover: 'Perhaps from some intelligence I have received since I wrote my last letter, the route by Berlin will not be so proper at the time of his return: There are I fear appearances which portend a storm.'[30]

In 1787 a major European war appeared likely. Britain and Prussia supported the Orangist faction in the United Provinces while France backed the 'Patriots'. A Prussian invasion in September, supported by a

British naval demonstration, tipped the balance in favour of the Orangists. The threat of war affected tourists. Brand, then with Duncombe, wrote from Vienna in August: 'We are in great uncertainty about our motions. The disturbances in Holland and rebellion in Flanders have so far alarmed us as to make us hesitate whether to go our intended circuit by Dresden, Berlin and The Hague or straight to Paris.' The following month he wrote from Berlin: 'I know nothing of our future destination. If the Prince of Orange is victorious we may perhaps go to The Hague.' In the end he did so: 'the only marks of war which we saw were the destruction of a number of trees by the roadside to make batteries'. On the other hand, the travel plans of Lieutenant-Colonel Charles Gordon, then in Dresden, were 'entirely deranged'. Lord Charles Fitzroy, who had spent his time in Vienna playing cricket, riding in horse-races and brawling, returned through the United Provinces that autumn, but found no problems of note. At Turin, Walker, returning from Italy, was filled with foreboding by the prospect of war:

> Here are near a dozen English in our inn, the Albergo Reale, who have given us the first intimation that England is likely to be engaged in a war. This unhappy news will embitter the rest of our journey home! We have got from our ambassador here credentials, that 'we are good men, and true' – in case we should be molested on our passage through France.

Arthur Young was not allowed to visit France's major port, Brest, the following year.[31]

In the 1780s civil conflict became a major problem in various continental states. Geneva was followed by the Austrian Netherlands and United Provinces and then by France and the Prince-Bishopric of Liège. These civil disturbances were more serious for tourists than the wars earlier in the century. Then countries at war had been internally peaceful, and passports had been respected. Civil violence in the 1780s conjured up for many the fears of mob-rule and of the destruction of civil government. Furthermore, civil war, such as that in the Austrian Netherlands in 1787–90, disrupted communications and currencies. Towns were besieged, the roads full of threatening soldiers. British residents in Switzerland, such as Robert Ellison, were worried by the Genevan troubles of the early 1780s, but these appeared minor when compared with the civil war in the Austrian Netherlands.

The French Revolution was therefore not a new development as far as tourism was concerned and it did not lead to the immediate ending of tourism to France. Some, such as Dr John Moore, rushed to Paris filled with enthusiasm and interest. Paris and politics alone became an object for tourists, one rushing off to Paris and Versailles in October 1789 'for a very few days . . . The very extraordinary scenes which have arisen in France present an object of curiosity so irresistible.'[32] Others, such as Brand, found France a more inconvenient country to travel in: carriages were stopped by the National Guard and there was increasing antagonism towards foreigners. Arthur Young, who had been to hear a debate at the Estates General in June 1789, was in trouble in Alsace the following month for not having a revolutionary cockade, and he was further worried because he could not obtain a passport. That autumn Elizabeth Montagu urged her nephew Matthew not to visit France: 'I hope future opportunities will present themselves in which Mr. Wilberforce and you may indulge your benevolent intentions, and enjoy any scheme of pleasure, but to go into a country to partake of the horrors of a famine or mix in the confusion of civil war would be very unbecoming your prudence.' In December 1789 Robert Arbuthnot could still consider taking a pupil 'to Paris, where if we find things tolerably quiet, we shall remain some months'; but by May 1790 Lord Auckland, envoy at The Hague, could write: 'our countrymen are flocking much to this place, instead of going to Paris'.[33]

There was considerable ambivalence about the Revolution. Brand wrote in May 1791 about 'Sir Jemmy [Hall]'s trip to France. He wrote me a very long letter full of nonsense and mistaken zeal about the "mighty Revolution" which I answered immediately in two sheets labouring hard to correct certain republican and philosophical ideas which however I am afraid are incorrigible.' Brand's letters are a good source for the varied response of the British community in Italy to the Revolution.[34]

The French Revolutionary War broke out in 1792 with fighting in the Rhineland, the Austrian Netherlands and Savoy. Britain entered the conflict in early 1793. In one sense this war was not a new departure. Tourists had become accustomed in the 1780s to the problems posed by revolutionary governments and they still travelled widely in the 1790s. Tourism had been affected by the threat of conflict for years. Sir John Macpherson's travel plans in 1790 were affected not by the progress of the French Revolution, but by the prospect of war between Austria and Prussia.[35] In another sense the Revolutionary War was dramatically different. The bloodier acts of the Revolution aroused in most a sense of horror that meant that many not only did not wish to visit France but did not consider it safe. As French armies spread across the Continent, defeating Britain's allies, and new-modelling states, the Continent became an alien entity. Contacts were executed or forced to flee, British diplomatic representation withdrawn (from Paris and Brussels in 1792), artistic treasures were seized by the French and old activities such as visiting nunneries, attending academies, being presented at court, and watching the ceremonies of court and religious society, ceased. The French Revolutionary government had a different attitude to British tourists in wartime than that of its *ancien régime* predecessor. Much of the Continent became less accessible, less comprehensible, and hostile, and the old-fashioned Grand Tour was a victim of this change. Tourism continued, but it followed a different course.

DISPUTES

They look upon strangers as a prey, and squeeze from them what they can: this we found almost everywhere, but especially where we lodged this night; for we having anticipated our supper by an afternoon's repast, and our host thinking himself thereby baulked of some part of his expected profit, charged us no less than 10 sols for one candle.

James Hume, Brittany, 1714.[36]

Some English gentlemen went in a yacht to visit some of the English students there; among the company was a painter, who innocently making a drawing of some part of the town which was grotesque, they were all apprehended and detained some days till they could send to Paris and get their liberty.

Item about Caen, Gazetteer, 30 August 1770

As was to be expected, tourists were involved in many disputes, most involving money. Throughout much of Europe there were no set prices for accommodation and food, although there were usually set prices for transport charges: the cost of posting, bridge and ferry tolls, and barge charges. Guidebooks and published travel accounts frequently warned against fraud, and noted a variety of types. Pratt made the obvious point that it was easy to be defrauded if a tourist did not know the language. Stevens stressed the need to agree prices in advance. Northall wrote of young aristocrats being deceived by antiquarian guides in Rome into buying copies thinking they were original Raphaels, Titians and Michelangelos. Walker encountered difficulties with his postilions in the Austrian Netherlands and Italy and wrote of the Italians, 'As to the lower orders of men, they seem what we call blackguards, in the most savage sense of the word . . . ever on the watch to cheat or impose upon strangers.' Ever ready to complain, Thicknesse repeatedly warned against fraud: in Paris the postilions were bribed to take tourists to particular hotels and the town was not safe for young British tourists; in the

Austrian Netherlands 'it was impossible to trust anyone and it was not safe to play cards with the high and mighty'.[37]

The press fortified this impression of deceitful foreigners. In 1786 difficulties in the United Provinces were reported:

> the English who happen to be in the country, even on business or amusement, with difficulty escape insult from their supposed adherence to the Stadtholder. We found this temper very unpleasant in travelling; exorbitant charges were often made with wanton insolence, and we were obliged to submit in silence.[38]

The press did, however, also mention British tourists who caused a nuisance, often by drunken brawling. On Christmas night 1727 several blocked the passage to the Cordeliers' church in Paris and abused those who attempted to pass. The *General Evening Post* of 6 July 1786 carried a report from Vienna:

> that as three English gentlemen of distinction, in the military line, were driving a phaeton through one of the narrow streets of that metropolis, they were met by a Neustadt carrier, who refusing to make way for them, one of the gentlemen jumped out of the carriage, and, equally to the astonishment and entertainment of the multitude, attacked the driver with his fists; who, after a good thrashing lost several of his teeth by the blows. The offender and his two companions were immediately seized and carried before the tribunal of the Police, where the principal magistrate, after acquainting them in the most polite manner, that it was contrary to their laws to strike a blow in the streets of Vienna, condemned the noble bruiser to pay a fine of twelve ducats to the carrier, as a compensation for the injury he had sustained; which the Englishman readily complying with, the matter was dismissed to the satisfaction of all parties.

Some tourists brawled easily. John Lindsay, Earl of Crawford (1702–49), threw a French marquis who was rude to him into a pond at Versailles in 1723. The 2nd Duke of Kingston was involved in a lawsuit in 1729 as a result of killing his neighbour's pigeons. Lord Leven's son beat up a troublesome postilion at Lille. The future general, Sir John Moore, was taken to Paris in 1772, aged eleven, by his father, who was acting as bearleader to Douglas, 8th Duke of Hamilton (1756–99). The young Moore, on a walk in the Tuileries, disliked the French children's fashion of dressing like adults. He 'could only express his displeasure by gestures. Mutual offence was taken, and the parties proceeded to hostilities; but as French boys know nothing of boxing, they were thrown to the ground

AUGUSTUS, 3RD DUKE OF GRAFTON (1735–1811), 1st Lord of the Treasury, 1766–70 by Batoni, 1761
(Courtesy of the National Portrait Gallery)

A REGATTA ON THE GRAND CANAL by Antonio Canaletto, 1730s
(Bridgeman Art Library)

ANCIENT AQUEDUCTS, near the Capo Di Cino, Naples by William Pars c. 1781. Naples was becoming increasingly popular as a tourist attraction *(Birmingham Museums and Art Gallery/Bridgeman Art Library)*

THE GREAT CASCADE at Tivoli with Villa of Maecenas, by Prosper-Francois, Irene Barrigues (*Christie's Images, London/Bridgeman Art Library*)

TIVOLI: A VIEW OF THE VILLA OF MAENENAS, 1858 by Jonathan Skelton *(Birmingham Museums and Art Gallery/Bridgeman Art Library)*

THE LANDING OF SIR JOHN BULL AND HIS FAMILY AT BOULOGNE, 1792 (*Lewis Walpole Library*)

JOHN, 4TH EARL OF SANDWICH (1718–92) by Joseph Higmore, 1740.
Sandwich had recently returned from a lengthy tour of the
Mediterranean. Jeremy Twitcher, as he was to be known, was a
Secretary of State (1763–5) and first Lord of the Admiralty (1748–51,
1771–82) *(Courtesy of the National Portrait Gallery)*

A CARICATURE GROUP
IN FLORENCE, c. 1760
by Thomas Patch
(Royal Albert
Memorial Museum,
Exeter/Bridgeman
Art Library)

ITALIAN LANDSCAPE (Morning) by Richard Wilson, who was in Italy during 1750–6 (Yale Centre for British Art, Paul Mellon Collection, VSA/Bridgeman Art library)

LAKE ALBANO by
Richard Wilson
*(Private Collection/
Bridgeman Art
Library)*

AN ITALIAN VILLA by William Pars (*Victoria and Albert Museum, London/Bridgeman Art Library*)

one across the other.' Fifteen years later Brand referred to the British youth in Vienna, principally Charles Lennox (1764–1819), later 4th Duke of Richmond, and Lord Charles Fitzroy, 'disporting themselves in riding races and playing at cricket', adding 'the Rhine wine sometimes evaporates so strongly at their fingers ends that it knocks down every Austrian within its reach'.[39]

Tourists were rarely involved in political disputes, though the presence of Jacobite exiles could lead to problems, especially in periods of tension. In July 1714 Charles, 1st Duke of Richmond (1672–1722), was attacked on the Pont Neuf because he had offended a member of the Jacobite court at St Germain-en-Laye: 'Richard Hamilton . . . resented some disrespectful words spoken by his Grace against that court in an assemblée in his presence, who taking two or three friends with him to secure the footmen forced the duke out of his coach and after much threatening to beat him if he would not draw, he gave him two wounds'.[40]

Tourist conduct varied. Some might urinate on the Senate of Lucca from a balcony or excrete in Italian churches, but most behaved in an acceptable fashion. Townshend claimed that the reports of British conduct in Vienna were 'in general totally invented or aggravated'.[41] Disputes were not always the fault of tourists and many did what they could to avoid them. In 1741 Poole ran away to avoid having to kneel to the host in the street, as he feared he would otherwise be compelled to do so. Frances Crewe encountered the noisy disapproval of the pit when she went to see the burlesque play *Le Roi de Cocagne* in Paris because she hung her cloak over the front of the box, and wrote, 'I have since thought their etiquettes are cruel in the case of strangers who can never learn them but by such experiences as mine!' Thicknesse gave an account of a disturbance in Liège caused unintentionally by a short-sighted English lady tourist looking at the altar through an opera glass. William, Lord Kilmaurs (1748–68), the deaf heir of the 13th Earl of Glencairn, was involved in a duel in Marseilles in 1765 as a result of his talking loudly in the theatre.[42]

Not all tourists were careful. Charlemont went to see the whirling dervishes at Constantinople, knowing that it was not entirely safe to do so, and at Naples he was terrified that his presence as a heretic at the ceremony of the liquefaction of the blood of St Januarius might be detected: 'I never was in my life better pleased than when I found myself safely out of the church.' Most tourists, however, did not seek trouble and most of the disputes they became involved in related to difficulties over alleged frauds. In 1725 Francis Colman, envoy in Florence, had imprisoned a tailor and an attorney who had quarrelled with two tourists. Travelling from Rome to the Tuscan frontier in 1772, Philip Francis was 'cheated regularly at every post, in the very teeth of the tariff. There is no remedy, for if you refuse to pay, they take away the horses. At least we are clear of the Romans, and here I most devoutly pray that both they and their neighbours the Neapolitans may be everlastingly cursed. Sooner than live with such villains, I would renounce society.' Francis' views of the Italians were echoed by Robert Manners in 1779 – 'I think even in the very beggars I see falsity wrote on their countenances' – and Garmston:

> I do not approve of the people in the Venetian state, they impose upon strangers, more than any other people I ever met with, and you pay more for going, upon very bad roads, than in any other part of Italy, for the postilions and ostlers are never satisfied. The post horses are very indifferent, and the master of the post too proud to be spoken to, but he leaves all to the conduct of an impertinent staliere, who always takes part with the postilion.

In an attempt at extortion, Sir James Hall was falsely accused in Venice in 1784 of stealing a diamond when he visited the diamond polishers. He observed that Italy was the only country where rascals were not ashamed to have their rascality discovered.[43] An anonymous memorandum on touring in Italy recommended, 'everywhere in Italy agree for your bed, eating and everything else at the first coming to any places to avoid disputes'.[44]

Difficulties were not restricted to Italy. Disputes over posting, the availablity of horses and the speed or pay of the postilions, were common all over Europe. When James Smith Barry complained at Magdeburg in 1775 about being given totally inadequate horses and overcharged, he was threatened by the postilions with being left on the road. Disputes over the price of food and accommodation were frequent. Pratt complained that in Holland he was made to pay for a plate of shrimps and a glass of milk and Dutch gin four-and-a-half times what he had seen a Dutchman pay.[45] Arriving at Helvoetsluys from Harwich in July 1791, Richard Dreyer recorded:

> my spleen was soon moved by the imposition practised on us the moment we set our feet on land. Our trunks two in number were given to as many porters each driving a wheelbarrow, who instead of taking them directly to the commissaris (who is employed by the government to prevent impositions in the driver and at whose door you must be taken up) a distance of about 500 yards landed them at the sign of the Harwich packet, telling us (or at least the waiter who understood their tongue) that they would return and carry them the remainder of the way, when we had breakfasted: by which means, as they are paid by the job, and their pay regulated by the state they took us in for 16 stivers instead of 8.[46]

Wharton, travelling down the Rhône in 1775, was affected by a dispute between officers and the master of the boat, that led to them being put ashore at 'a wretched place where we could neither get victuals, drink, nor beds. At last we got a few eggs, and a loaf or two and some vile wine, and some laid down on the benches, others tried to sleep sitting . . .'. Bennet was involved in similar difficulties on the same journey a decade later.[47]

Many disputes reflected the absence of fixed prices, but, as some tourists such as Nicholls pointed out, the extravagant conduct of many British tourists made life difficult for their compatriots.[48] Faced with problems, tourists could have little hope of redress by local judicial institutions. Legal action was slow and expensive, and there were serious language difficulties. Many tourists encountered problems with customs officers. George Carpenter set off from Calais for Bruges in 1717 with the Duke of Gordon, but 'the customs house officers stopped us at the last gate of Calais: in order to impose upon us and we were forced to send to the Governor before they would let us out of the gate'. There were further difficulties at Dunkirk:

a little before we came to the gate we were stopped by some men belonging to the custom house, who carried us all to a little yard walled in, where they searched us after an excessive rude manner. They also used us ill. Some of them were pleased to say that they wished all the English at the bottom of the sea, and all this was upon pretence of our having not changed our money for their coin (which was impossible at Calais). They took from me ten guineas and my gold watch, and after having kept us two hours, turned us out to shift for ourselves. By this time the gates of the town were shut, so we were forced to lie that night in a little nasty house in the suburbs. The next day we sent to the Count de Rouville, Governor of the town, to complain of the insults we had received from the officers. All he did was to order our things to be restored to us and that the fellows should beg our pardon. He also invited us to dine with him the next day.[49]

The ability to appeal to British envoys, however, ensured that in the event of serious difficulties assistance could be obtained. In 1770 William Pulteney (1729–1805) wrote from Spa, where he was taking the waters with his wife and six servants he had brought from England, to the British envoy in Brussels:

I doubt not you will pardon the liberty which I take as a British subject and a member of Parliament, of applying to you in your public character to request that you will obtain for me and my family a passport that we may not be stopped and harrassed in the journey which I propose very soon to make through her Imperial Majesty's dominions on my way back to England. I understand that of late, several gentlemen and ladies have been stopped for hours, their trunks and portmanteaus searched, and they themselves treated with very little ceremony by certain officers of her majesty, in passing from this place to Brussels, under pretext of searching for unaccustomed or prohibited goods . . . If I can not obtain a passport, I propose to take another route and return home without entering her majesty's dominions for I do not choose to expose Mrs. Pulteney to the disagreeable situation of being rifled and insulted.[50]

Seventeen years later Mitford commented, 'In passing from the Emperor's dominions to those of the King of France, and in entering Lille, travellers are grossly plundered, as usual, to avoid the trouble of having their baggage pulled about.'[51]

Diplomats, such as Colman, Keith and Mann, complained often of the cost and time involved in entertaining tourists. They were expected to entertain them, present them at court, introduce them into local society, fulfil a number of miscellaneous requests and protect them from brushes with the law. Keith wrote in 1786 that his 'office (of *mentor general* to young English travellers) requires higher allowances for British ministers'.[52] Waldegrave was asked in 1733 to look after Sir John Shadwell, a relative of the wife of Under-Secretary Charles Delafaye, and ensure that medicines, chocolate and snuff for his use were not seized by the Boulogne customs. He also had to make lengthy representations on behalf of a Scottish visitor involved in a duel in the Loire valley. Well-connected tourists could be sure of letters of recommendation from ministers to envoys. Robert Carteret (1721–76), only son of Lord Carteret, one of the leaders of the opposition, obtained recommendatory letters to the envoys at Copenhagen, Dresden, St Petersburg and Vienna. Thicknesse recommended that tourists wait on British envoys in order to ensure protection, and noted the Earl of Rochford's defence of tourists in Paris, including one defrauded by sharpers. When Anthony Duncome MP went to France in 1737 he was recommended to Cardinal Fleury, the leading French minister, by Horatio Walpole, the brother of the first minister and a former envoy in Paris. The protection provided by the diplomatic service was an indication of the relatively small-scale nature of tourism and the role of personal connections in what was still essentially an aristocratic milieu.[53]

ACCIDENTS

> In turning upon one of the bridges this morning about a post from
> out inn, my friend Edward and I had the misfortune to be overturned,
> and if it had not been for the railing of the bridge the chaise might
> have gone complete into the river.
>
> Robson, Savoy Alps, 1787[54]

Carriages were very susceptible to accidents, especially given the poor
and often uneven nature of road surfaces. Many tourists were halted as
a result of such accidents, usually broken axletrees. Anne, Lady Exeter's
axletree broke near Loreto in 1699 and in 1727 William Bentinck's 'hind
axletree' broke and was badly mended. At Vercelli in 1772, Philip Francis
found 'the axle tree has again given way: a cursed plague and loss of
five hours'. Hale had a terrible journey from St Petersburg to Warsaw in
January 1779: 'losing our way, falling into rivers, breaking an axle-tree, a
spring, a wheel etc by which means I was upwards of three weeks upon
the road from Petersburg'. Brand found the roads so bad from Orleans to
Toulouse in 1783

> that at last our axletree broke near Montauban in a dark night when
> it rained as if it was a prelude to an universal deluge. Fortunately we
> were near a peasants house where we got shelter whilst we dispatched
> the postillion to Montauban to send us a carriage. In this cottage
> we saw a great deal of poverty but to make amends for it there was
> as much chearfulness. The Pere de Famille was a fine old hardfac'd
> fellow who could speak nothing but patois. His wife who had lived in
> Montauban spoke French such as it was. The daughter and sons spoke
> it still worse but I could understand their Provençal or Languedocian
> or whatever it is pretty well from its great affinity to the Italian. I never
> met anywhere with sincerer hospitality. It is almost worth while to
> break a wheel to experience it.

Nine years later his axletree broke on the way from Leghorn to Rome,
though fortunately 'it was within a mile of the only place in a whole
day's journey where it could have been well mended and we slept in an
excellent inn instead of the far fam'd and detested Radicofani'.[55]
Overturning was frequent and could be unpleasant. Shaw was
overturned near Leyden, though without hurt, 'through an excess of
complaisance in giving the way to a cart', Lady Craven twice en route
from St Petersburg to Moscow, noting that the postilions treated it as a
common occurrence, Frances Crewe between Amiens and Breteuil in

1786. She was unhurt but 'full of tremors ever since. For several stages after our accident I hardly could bear the appearance of a hill, or the sensation which the chaise gave me when inclined at all on one side.' The absence of a drag chain was the cause of the accident: when the heavy carriage went downhill the horses could not bear its weight. The following year Richard Garmston was nearly overturned passing another carriage on the Padua–Ferrara road which was too narrow for two to pass without great difficulty. In 1787 Brand, en route from Dresden to Berlin, was 'overturned upon the road so gently that not even the glass was broke', but in 1788 Payne had 'a complete overset of our coach between Zurich and Berne, which fractured all our glasses but spared our bones'.[56]

Wheels breaking were another problem. In 1770 William Philip Perrin 'broke a forewheel three miles from Magdeburg and waited the making new spokes (all of which were made 10 in number) at an adjacent village. This detained us from 8 am to 2 pm.' In 1792 Philip Francis 'lost a wheel which broke to pieces. Yet I paid a villain 3 louis for a carriage from Paris to Calais.' Two years later Conway's carriage wheels disintegrated in Upper Silesia and in 1786 Lady Craven had to stay four days in Hermanstadt to have a new set made.[57] En route from Paris to Lyons, Samuel Boddington encountered problems in July 1789:

. . . We went 15 or 20 miles to breakfast to Tournus intending to have reached Lyons that night but owing to the carelessness of and stupidity of a fellow who boxed our four wheels and in some measure owing to our own folly in trusting to his word rather than our own senses we were stopped in our career before we arrived at the next post. A violent squeaking and presently a furious smoke gave us the first intimation of our situation. We hallowed out with all our might to the Post boys but as we were then going down hill at a great rate on a stony road our exertions only served to make the temperature of our bodies bear the some affinity to that of the wheel. By the time we stopped our drivers there was too much mischief done for us to remedy on the road. We stationed ourselves in regular order with four half pint tin tumblers instead of buckets and threw water on the unfortunate member of our carriage with the utmost expedition and so far extinghished the smoke as to give us time to devise a method of taking off the wheel. Fortunately a man came by at that instant with a long pole by the assistance of which we hoisted the carriage upon a heap of stones. Off came the wheel but the wood in the inside burnt to a cinder and the iron box so fast fixed to the axle that all our efforts to move it were fruitless. There was nothing for us to do but to put on the wheel and proceed as cautiously as possible to the next town. To complete our ill luck we were now in the middle of one of the longest stages and the sun shining in his meridian splendour. For two hours and a half were our northern frames under the influence of his powerful beams. We got to St. Albin hot, dusty, and cross, and were set down to rest our weary limbs when Scheilds came with a grave face to inform us that the blacksmith had done his utmost and was now 'au desespoir'. We then sallied out and tried what could be done by force. We hammered a long time without effect but trusting that perseverance would produce something we continued our exertions. At last the box moved and repaid our labour, but so great had been the heat that the iron had absolutely been in a state of fusion. We had now nothing to do but wait with patience till the wheel was refitted. Mr. Morgan and myself attended the Blacksmith for the first time turned Coachmaker and by our skill and his labour we got out of our difficulties much better than we expected.[58]

Carriages were vulnerable to accidents. The leathers supporting Walker's carriage broke, and later, near Roanne, the broken road surface 'broke one of our spring stays . . . and we were obliged to walk back three miles, and to lose three hours in the mending it'.[59] Horses could also be a problem, difficult to control and prone to accidents or ill health. Stevens had to stay two days at Viterbo in 1739 because of lame horses. Reynolds' injuries, sustained when he and his horse fell 'down a precipice' in Minorca in 1749, caused his deafness in later life. In 1786 Frances Crewe was stopped on the way to Versailles, 'one of the horses tumbling down, and my maid and I being detained upon the bridge of Sèvres three quarters of an hour – both terrified to death, because we were on so narrow a part of it that every carriage which came by gave us a shock, as if it meant to tip us over into the Seine'. The following year on the way from Worms to Mannheim, one of Walker's horses fell down asleep and threw him among the feet of another horse. Not only horses fell asleep. En route from Bologna to Florence in July 1755, one tourist 'travelled all night by the light of the moon: 2 miles from the second post we were overturned by the postilion falling asleep'.[60]

For many coach accidents no details were given, but their number suggests that travel was more hazardous than has usually been realized. Anthony, Earl of Harold (1696–1723) was involved in a coach accident on the side of the Rhône in early 1716; Lord Leven's carriage broke down three miles from Paris in 1749 and that of Mary, Dowager Duchess of Ancaster near Florence in 1785. Lord Ancram was delayed for twelve hours in 1787 when his carriage broke down at St Tron in the Rhineland.[61]

Aside from vehicle breakdown, travellers faced a variety of hazards. Trunks could be lost,[62] litters break,[63] ships run aground and sink,[64] coaches become stuck in the snow,[65] crushed by falling customs barriers, as Cottrell nearly was in Riga in 1741, or almost fall in the river when postilions lost their way.[66] Wolves and other wild beasts could be a hazard. Horace Walpole lost his dog to wolves. The miscellaneous, yet frequent nature of accidents and mishaps is striking. It reflected a society where safety standards were perfunctory, technology limited, regulatory procedures absent in many spheres and the general rate of accidents high. Travellers fell down stairs,[67] had accidents with guns, leading to fatalities or injuries for themselves or others,[68] and ran the risk of being knocked over in Paris, where there was an absence of pavements.[69] Hume's horse was trapped on the bridge at Angers in 1714 when it was being repaired. The curtains of Cradock's carriage were forced open by the wind on the way from Amsterdam to Saardam in 1786, and his 'hat, with some other articles, were carried quite away'.[70]

Getting lost was a major hazard, especially for those who travelled by night or in the snow. Most roads were poorly marked, and this was a further disincentive to depart from established and major routes.[71] The weather was a particular hazard to tourists. Snow could make roads dangerous, rain make them difficult and thaw make them impassable. Storms prevented sea and lake travel, high winds river travel, and floods ferry passages. Travel was not easy, and it was rarely pleasant to spend days on end in coaches, another reason for the zeal with which tourists raced from town to town. Travel in Britain, however, was not trouble free. Coaches overturned and travellers were killed, horses fell because of bad roads and accidents were common. En route from London to Edinburgh, the American preacher Samuel Davies encountered difficulties in 1754 and noted, 'Providence, no doubt, has some important design in these alarming trials.'[72] Others were less phlegmatic, but for all tourists travel was a hazardous pastime.

CRIME

The people here are half starved, and are ready to devour you for money. Indeed they are all beggars. Wherever you stop to change horses they swarm about you like bees, I believe some of them would be wasps if they durst but they are generally cowards if spoken sharply to.

Richard Garmston, Spoleto, 1787[73]

Crime was a threat tourists had to face continually. A few were murdered, though this was rare. The most spectacular episode occurred in 1723 when four who had exchanged their money at Calais too publicly were robbed and murdered seven miles from the town. Reported extensively in the British press, the murders created a sensation. The Anglophile French foreign minister, Morville, who promised that he would do everything possible to preserve the safety of the roads, wrote to the chargé in London, 'Je ne suis point étonné que le menu peuple de Londres ait tenu les discours que vous marqués par rapport au meurtre commis aux environs de Calais, mais je n'aurois pas crû que des personnes de distinction, et des gens sensés eussent pû les adopter.' The murders continued to attract attention. A monumental cone was erected at the site of the murders and, when it was defaced in 1724, an engraving of the cone and its inscription was printed. The following year the press reported that 'Charles Evelyn and some other English gentlemen were lately robbed between Calais and Lyons by several highwaymen, and were afraid of being killed as the gentlemen near Calais were; but however, they had the good fortune to escape.'[74]

These murders created such a sensation because they were unusual. There are records of very few other tourists being murdered. In 1735 William Yates, 'a young gentleman who set out for his travels to Italy', was found killed near Ghent. The murder of four English gentlemen between Turin and Milan was reported without cause in London at the end of 1751.[75] Nevertheless, as it was usual for robbers to attack their victims, tourists had much to fear. They were warned in 1763 that foreign robbers tended to kill or wound. Some guidebooks recommended an iron fastener to secure hotel rooms at night. Boswell feared attack in the United Provinces and Craven in the Balkans. As Horace Walpole had his trunk stolen at Chantilly, William Cole determined not to go there. Henry Nassau and a friend were robbed in Venice; and in 1787 Adam Walker was attacked by highwaymen between Spa and Aachen, while James Walker was badly beaten and robbed when the Würzburg–Frankfurt diligence was attacked by ten highwaymen. In 1749, Lord Leven had a frightening trip from Calais to Paris: between St Omer and Béthune 'ruffians' abounded and Leven 'saw many that day who would have attacked us if they durst, but the gun frightened them . . . the appearance of being robbed took off some of the pleasure' of the trip. Stevens was threatened near Bolsena, an area in which military escorts were necessary in 1766, Jervis feared having his throat cut by the rowers on the boat he hired on the Rhône, Arthur Young feared attack at Montardier and Brand was robbed at Viterbo. Bennet was unhappy about travelling by night through the Black Forest in August 1785 and distrusted the slow postilion, 'the height of the chaussé, the awkward driving of four horses by loose broken reins, the loss of the prospects, and the fear of robbers, all concur to make it disagreeable'. William Drummond recorded his journey from Spa to Aachen in 1787:

. . . it was about ten o'clock at night, we were stopped by an highwayman armed with a gun and pistols. He pretended that he was a comis of one of the bureaus, and demanded to examine our baggage. I jumped out of the cabriolet, and seized him; but in jumping I much wounded my thigh with my sword. Messes. W. followed and we secured him, bound him, and carried him near Aix and then let him loose to avoid the delay of bringing him to justice.[76]

Tourists showed an understandable interest in the quality of the police, which was patchy in much of Europe.[77] The situation in both France and the Austrian Netherlands was praised, though Joseph Shaw warned of the dangers of Paris, 'there being nightly robberies and often murders committed', and witnessed a violent robbery from his window. Carpenter throught Paris dangerous in 1717: 'it is not safe to walk the streets after it is dark: there is seldom a night passes but somebody is found murdered. I was once persuaded by some company to go to see a criminal broke upon the wheel in this place, but had not resolution enough to stay it out.'[78]

The majority of tourists encountered no difficulties. James Essex was being over-optimistic when he claimed of the Austrian Netherlands, 'these roads are so safe in the day, that a child might travel with a purse of gold and not be robbed of it'. Travelling from Ghent to Brussels in 1717, Carpenter noted that robbers murdered their victims: 'there has been prodigious robbing hereabouts since the peace: there are near this road such a vast number of wheels, and gallows, and few without two or three carcasses at the least hanging on them'. He also saw the corpses of robbers displayed in a wood near Mons, and described torture methods.

Nevertheless, Wharton was well-satisfied with his experience of Paris in 1775: 'Nor are the people here such rogues as we imagine. I have twice left my knife at the Auberge, where however there are knives and forks laid at dinner, and it has been restored to me safe and sound, so that I do not think I shall be pillaged at least in this place.' Twelve years later Adam Walker thought 'it is a compliment . . . to Italy, that we neither were robbed, attempted to be robbed, or heard of a robbery, the time we travelled through it, and we travelled early and late'.[79] Mountainous regions were more frightening, especially near frontiers. Travelling from Lugano to Bellinzona in 1791, Bruce and Brand

crossed the famous Monti Cenera a place celebrated for ancient chestnut trees of wonderful beauty in whose hollows the proscribed villains of the Piedmontese, Milanese and Venetian states use to lurk to the great annoyance of unwary travellers. As we were a strong party and well armed I was under very little apprehension knowing the antipathy of your Italian to a pistol but the sight of frequent skulls some bleached with age and others too fresh enclosed in iron cages on the top of high posts stuck about the forest in terrorem convinced me it was necessary to keep a good look out.[80]

The hazards of travel can be exaggerated, but when ill health, crime and accidents are considered it is clear that tourists faced many dangers. It is important to place them in perspective. Coach accidents were frequent but usually not serious; most of those who died from illnesses were already poorly when they left Britain; a tourist was more likely to suffer from food-poisoning than a stiletto. Accidents were common in Britain, and some Continental states were better policed, especially France, as travellers such as Mildmay noted. It was nevertheless true that tourism entailed hazards that are too easily forgotten, and although these proved serious or fatal in only a few cases, that was scant consolation to travellers wondering whether they would be robbed, involved in a major accident or afflicted by a serious illness.

NOTES

1. Newcastle to Lincoln, 16 Mar. (os) 1741, BL Add. 33065.
2. AE CP Ang. 181 f. 176; James Vernon to William Blathwayt, 8 Sept. 1699, Beinecke, Osborn Shelves, Blathwayt Box 19; Nottingham UL NeC. 2813, 2827; Hume, 29 Mar. 1714, BL Add. 29477.
3. Francis, 9 Dec. 1772, BL Add. 40759.
4. Northall p. 177; Garmston, 1 Nov. 1787, BL Add. 30271.
5. Petty to Keith, 10 June 1785, BL Add. 35534.
6. Glynn to Keith, 11 July 1784, Hawkins to Keith, 26 Feb. 1788, BL Add. 35532, 35540; Bod. Bland Burges papers vol. 36 f. 95.
7. Beinecke, Osborn Shelves c 200 p. 71; Gloucester CRO D 2002 F1.
8. Duke of Manchester to Blathwayt, 6 Aug. 1700, Beinecke, Manchester Box; Metcalfe to Sir William Robinson, 30 Aug., 8 Oct. 1705, Leeds AO Vyner Mss. 6005; Haggerston to mother, 13 July 1711; Anstruther, Gloucester CRO D1299/F172; Shaw, *Letters* p. 7; Gloucester CRO D 421/F33.
9. Winchester CRO 15M50/1303.
10. 'The travels of three English gentlemen from Venice to Hamburg, being the grand tour of Germany in the year 1734', *Harleian Miscellany*, 4 (1745), p. 348; Grafton to Essex, 2 May (os) 1735, BL Add. 27733.
11. *Universal Spectator*, 29 Dec. (os) 1733; Count Philip Kinsky, Austrian envoy in London, to –, 13 May 1734, PRO SP 100/11; *St James's Evening Post* 28 Nov. (os) 1734; Pococke, BL Add. 22978 f. 87, 89, 80; Arthur Villettes, envoy in Turin, to Newcastle, 25 Dec. 1734, PRO SP 92/37; Cobbett, *Parliamentary History*, XI, 977; Mitchell, BL Add. 58319 f. 39–43; Milles, Gloucester CRO D 2663 Z8.
12. HMC *Hare* p. 250.
13. *Cirencester Flying Post* 9 Aug. (os) 1742; *Northampton Mercury* 16 July (os) 1739.
14. Sturrock to Aldworth, 19 Dec. 1740, Essex CRO D/D By C1.

15. HMC *Hare* p. 255.
16. Stevens pp. 376–8.
17. Bedford CRO L 30/3/4; BL Add. 15955 f. 108.
18. HW 64 f. 161–2.
19. Garrick 1751, p. 113; Bod. Ms. Don. b 23 f. 88; AE CP Ang. 444 f. 78; 329; Wachtendonck, Palatine foreign minister, to Haslang, envoy in London, 5 Sept. 1758, Munich 234; HL Mo. 1252; Joseph Yorke to Duke of Manchester, 26 July 1757, Huntingdon CRO DDM 49/7.
20. BL Add. 6830 f. 24; Stuart Mackenzie to Sir John Rushout, 14 April 1759, Worcester CRO 750: 66 BA 4221/26.
21. Stuart Mackenzie to Bute, 30 Jan., 22 Feb., 2 April, 18 June, 20 Sept. 1760, 14 Mar. 1761, MS Cardiff Public Library 4/5–17.
22. Bod. Ms. Don b 23 f. 88.
23. Hutton to Phelps, 3 Dec. 1762, Beinecke, Osborn Files, Hutton.
24. BL Add. 6861 f. 5; A.S. Turberville, *A History of Welbeck Abbey and its Owners* (1939), II, 381.
25. W. Anson (ed.), *Autobiography . . . Third Duke of Grafton* (1898), pp. 16–19; Bridgewater to Bedford, 18 Sept. 1762, Russell 45.
26. Beinecke, Osborn Shelves c 469 pp. 27, 42; Munich 234, 5 Sept.
27. Aylesbury CRO D/DR/8/10/1.
28. Knight pp. 47, 83; *Deffand–Walpole* V, 60; Brand to Wharton, 30 July 1779, Durham, Wharton; Scott, BL Add. 35512 f. 102; Keith to Lord North, 21 July, Hale to Keith, 27 April 1779, BL Add. 35517, 35516; HL HM 18940 p. 237.
29. Paris, Archives Nationales KK 1393, 21 Aug. 1779; Bod. Ms. North adds c 4 f. 188–9, BL Add. 33127 f. 391; Mountstuart, e.g. BL Add. 36801 f. 43, 112, 162, 204, 208; Ellison, Gateshead, Public Library E/E1, 3; Yorke, Belfast, Public Record Office of Northern Ireland, D 2433/D/5/21.
30. Cooper to Keith, 17 Mar. 1785, BL Add. 35534.
31. Brand to Wharton, 4 Aug., 10 Sept. 18 Oct. 1787, Durham, Wharton; Gordon to Keith, 12 Aug., Fitzroy to Keith, 14 Nov. 1787, BL Add. 35539; Walker p. 390; Young to Bronssonet, 22 Sept. 1788, Beinecke, Osborn uncatalogued.
32. Pigott to Burges, 8 Oct. 1789, Bod. Bland Burges 18.
33. Young I, 124–6, 159, 162; Arbuthnot to Keith, 28 Dec. 1789, Auckland to Keith, 7 May 1790, BL Add. 35541–2.
34. Brand to Wharton, 30 May 1791, 14 Dec. 1793, 26 Jan. 1793, 1 Feb. 1794, Durham, Wharton.
35. Macpherson to Keith, 19 June 1790, BL Add. 35542.
36. Hume, BL Add. 29477 f. 14.
37. Pratt II, 48–9; Walker pp. 9, 266–7, 203, 157, 307; Northall p. 127; Stevens p. 388; Thicknesse 1768, pp. 134–5, 160–2; Thicknesse Pais Bas, pp. 3–4, 49, 6.
38. *Daily Universal Register* 22 July 1786.
39. *Evening Journal* 26 Dec. (os) 1727; *London Evening Post* 21 May (os) 1730; Stephen Poyntz to Delafaye, 24 Mar. 1729, PRO SP 78/190 f. 321; J.C. Moore, *Life of Lieutenant General Sir John Moore* (1833) I, 5; Brand to Wharton, 4 Aug. 1787, Durham, Wharton.
40. Beinecke, Osborn Files 19. 252.
41. Townshend to Keith, 12 Mar, Bulkeley to Keith, 13 Mar. 1787, BL Add. 35538.

42. Poole I, 56; Crewe, BL Add. 37926 f. 95; Thicknesse *Pais Bas*, pp. 178–9; *St James's Chronicle* 2 May 1765.

43. Stanford and Finopoulos (eds), *Charlemont* pp. 224–6; Colman to Delafaye, 18 Aug. 1725, PRO SP 98/25; Francis, 22 Oct. 1772, Manners to Keith, 24 April 1779, Garmston, BL Add. 40759, 35516, 30271 f. 24; Hall to Wharton, June 1784, Durham, Wharton.

44. Beinecke, Osborn Shelves, Lee papers Box 3.

45. Barry, Winchester CRO, Malmesbury vol. 144; Craven, *Memoirs* I, 137; Pratt II, 96–9.

46. Beinecke, Osborn Shelves f c 11 pp. 22–3.

47. Wharton to mother, 2 Oct. 1775, Durham, Wharton.

48. Beinecke, Osborn Shelves c 467, II Nos 19, 27, 48.

49. Bod. Ms. Douce 67 pp. 3–5.

50. HL PL 1907.

51. Gloucester CRO D 2002 F1.

52. HL HM 18940 p. 359.

53. Delafaye to Waldegrave, 25 July (os) 1733, Chewton; Carteret, BL Add. 32693 f. 401–2; Thicknesse 1768, pp. 158–60; AE CP Ang. 395 f. 21.

54. Robson, 5 Aug. 1787, BL Add. 38837.

55. Creed; Bentinck to mother, 18 Jan. 1727, BL Eg. 1711; Hale to Keith, 28 Jan. 1779, BL Add. 35515; Brand to Wharton, 12 Mar. 1783, 13 Nov. 1792, Durham, Wharton.

56. Shaw, *Letters* p. 28; Craven, *Memoirs* I, 162; Crewe, BL Add. 37926 f. 120–2; Garmston, 18 Oct. 1787, BL Add. 30271; Brand to Wharton, 10 Sept. 1787, Durham, Wharton; Payne to Keith, 1 Nov. 1788, BL Add. 35541.

57. Matlock CRO 239 MF 15921; Francis, 10 Dec. 1772, BL Add. 40759; Conway to Keith, 11 Sept. 1774, *Keith ... Correspondence* II, 24.

58. Guildhall Library, London, Ms. 10823/5B.

59. Walker, pp. 96, 424.

60. Stevens p. 162; Northcote, *Reynolds* pp. 30–31; Crewe BL Add. 37926 f. 70; Walker pp. 71–2; Beinecke, Osborn Shelves c 200 p. 142.

61. Earl of Harold to Lord Henry Grey, no date, Bedford CRO L30/5; Leven p. 328; Davies to Keith, 30 Dec. 1785, Arbuthnot to Keith, 6 May 1787, BL Add. 35535, 35538.

62. Young I, 8.

63. Stevens p. 325.

64. Grey journal, BL Add. 5957 f. 62–3.

65. Giffard to Keith, 9 April 1785, BL Add. 35534.

66. Sutton to Townshend, 1 May 1727, PRO SP 81/22.

67. Essex p. 65.

68. *Loyal Observator* 31 Aug. (os) 1723; Moore p. 3.

69. Stevens pp. 63–4.

70. Cradock p. 269.

71. Shaw, *Letters* pp. 7–9; Stevens pp. 156–8.

72. G.W. Pilcher, *The Reverend Samuel Davies Abroad* (Urbana, 1967), p. 87; Cradock, *Memoirs* p. 17.

73. Garmston, 23 Oct. 1787, BL Add. 30271.

74. *Reading Mercury* 16 Sept. (os), *Post Boy*, 17 Sept. (os), *Flying Post* 17 Sept. (os), *Northampton Mercury* 23 Sept. (os) 1723; AE CP Ang. sup. 7 f. 94; *Applebee's Original Weekly Journal* 27 June (os) 1724; *Wye's Letter* 16 Sept. (os) 1725.

75. *General Evening Post* 29 May (os) 1735; PRO 92/60 f. 21.

76. *St James's Chronicle* 27 Sept. 1763; *Tour of Holland* p. 229; Pottle, *Boswell* pp. 230–54; *Cole–Walpole correspondence* I, 98; William Cole, *A Journal of my Journey to Paris in the year 1765* ed. by F.G. Stokes p. 328; Herts CRO D/E Na F57; Walker to Keith, 20 Nov. 1787, BL Add. 35539; Walker p. 38; Leven, pp. 326–7; Bod. Ms. Add. A 366 f. 51; Jervis, BL Add. 31192 f. 19–20; Young, I, 51; Brand to Wharton, 13 Nov. 1792, Durham, Wharton; Bennet, Bod. Ms. Eng. Misc. f. 54 f. 73; Beinecke, Osborn Shelves c 331, 27 Aug. 1787; Stevens p. 160; Mitchell, BL Add. 58314 f. 46; *Worcester Post-Man* 13 Dec. (os) 1723; *Present State of Germany* II, 366; Carleton pp. 271–2.

77. I.A. Cameron, *Crime and Repression in the Auvergne and the Guyenne, 1720–1790* (1982); J.R. Ruff, *Justice and Public Order in Old Regime France* (1984).

78. *Tour of Holland* pp. 229–30; Thicknesse *Pais Bas* p. 17; Shaw, *Letters* p. 119; Bod. Ms. Douce 67 p. 49.

79. Essex p. 38; Bod Ms. Douce 67 pp. 16–18, 24, 33; Wharton to mother, 5 Mar. 1775, Durham, Wharton; Walker p. 414.

80. Brand to Wharton, 21 July 1791, Durham, Wharton.

8

HEALTH AND DEATH

The second day after my arrival at this place the gnats stung my legs
so bad I was obliged to lie in bed a week and the bugs bit my face so
much in the night that I was swelled prodigiously, that I did not leave
my chamber for a fortnight, but by taking Physic and the use of the
vegito mineral water and the pomatum of goulard I got well.

Richard Garmston, Geneva, 1787[1]

TRAVEL FOR HEALTH

One of the most important motives for travel to Europe was helath,
although this was less true for the younger age group. The idea
of travelling for health became well-established in eighteenth-
century Britain as large numbers travelled to the developing spas such
as Bath, Buxton, Scarborough and Tunbridge Wells. To travel abroad for
health represented a fusion of two of the more important developments
in upper-class activities in this period: tourism and travelling for health. It
did not need to involve much time, for the leading Continental watering
place visited by British tourists, Spa, was a relatively easy journey from
London. Those who travelled for health did not share the same itinerary
as those on the classical Grand Tour. Italy (apart from the Bay of Naples),
Paris, Vienna and the United Provinces were replaced by the watering
places, principally Spa and Aachen, by Portugal and Montpellier and later
by the Provençal coast and Nice. In 1776 William Congreve, who had
found the Bath waters ineffective for the constant pain he was suffering
after the loss of a hand, received 'great relief' at Barèges in the Pyrenees
from French water treatments. Travel for health was restricted to Europe,
though John Macdonald, who visited St. Helena in 1773, praised its
virtues: 'St. Helena is a wholesome, pleasant place, and a fine keen
searching air. If noblemen and gentlemen of Great Britain and Ireland
would go to Madeira and St. Helena for their health, instead of going to
France and Portugal, they would be sure to reestablish their health.'[2]

In the early decades of the century most went to Spa and Aachen. Lady Glenorchy went in 1725; Sir Robert Sutton, his wife Lady Sunderland, and her sister following three years later; Colonel Pulteney went to Aachen in 1730; the Duchess of Newcastle to Spa in 1731; Walter Molesworth, his wife and son to Spa four years later. Sir James Porter, envoy in Brussels, remarked in 1764, 'Physicians when they do not know what to do send all to Spa and I see little effects on the return where the ill is inveterate. Those whose nerves are attacked through application at home recover by relaxing air and exercise does it.'³ Other areas were also visited. George Berkeley on his second European tour acted as companion and tutor to St George Ashe, the son of the Bishop of Clogher, who travelled for health and education. Ashe visited Italy, including Apulia, and in early 1718 Sicily, before dying in Brussels in 1721. In the mid-1720s Dr Josiah Hort, Bishop of Ferns, visited Montpellier and Marseilles, but doubted if his health was better as a result of 'his long and expensive journey'. In 1731, Dr King, the Master of the Charterhouse, went to Blois. Edward Mellish, who was there, was clearly impressed by King who, he wrote, 'is seventy years old, and is come here upon the account of his health, having been troubled with an asthma; however he has found so much benefit by this air, that he is become younger than any of us; and has a much better appetite for eating, and drinking'. Lord Berkeley went with his wife to the Loire in 1735 for his health, and stayed with Bolingbroke. The following year William Pulteney went to the United Provinces to take medical advice; and Sir William Wyndham went to France in 1737 for his health; two years later Spark Molesworth died at Naples, whither he had gone for his health; Erasmus Philipps MP survived a similar trip the same year; in 1741, John Bethel went to Italy for his asthma; in 1742, the Earl of Essex, accompanied by his wife, went to France to see if a change of air would lead to his cure, but the trip was unsuccessful.⁴

Despite this variety, the majority of health-seekers continued to go to Spa and Aachen (Spa being the more popular). Francis Head reported to Archbishop Wake, in August 1725, that nearly a hundred British travellers were at Spa for their health. In 1743 Cuthbert Ellison wrote to his brother Henry that, as he had received benefit 'by the last season at Spa', he should try another. Spa had many attractions. Being small it could be dominated by the tourists, and their money brought them great power. They could act as though they were in Britain. Spa's popularity, unlike that of Montpellier, remained strong throughout the century. In 1731 the Earl of Portmore and Lord James Cavendish visited it and Edward Mellish found a large company in July including the Duchess of Newcastle; 'Sr. Thomas Littleton Bart, his two sons, my Lady Jersey, Mr. Webb and his Lady, My Lord Marr [the prominent Jacobite] Sir Robert Long Bart; Mr.

Holbitch, Sr. James Folbin, Mr. Warburton, Captain Halked, Mr. Price and his Lady, Sir Alexander Macdonnal Bart. Mr. Forringal, . . .' The following August 'near 100 English gentlemen and ladies' were there. In 1734 it was visited by the Queensberrys, the following summer by Colonel Martin Bladen. When the Earl of Bath was ill in 1763, a journey to the Spa waters was prescribed for him, and thither he went with Dr Douglas, later Bishop of Salisbury, and Mrs Montagu, the 'Queen of the Blues'. In 1768 Henry Ellison went to Spa with the Ryders because of concern about the health of Mrs Ryder. The following year Lord and Lady Marchmont, Sir Charles Bunbury and Colonel and Lady Gore went in a group. Thus, travelling to Spa was often a matter not of solitary invalids, but of groups of travellers, not all of whom were ill. The invalid's need for the waters provided the excuse for a group trip that was further facilitated by its proximity to London, the good roads from the Channel to Liège, Spa's reputation for a good social life in the summer season, and the British love of travelling with and finding compatriots, that was commented on by many. Montpellier lacked these advantages, but, although there was some decline in the late eighteenth century, Montpellier continued, as in the second half the seventeenth century, to attract many tourists from Britain and other countries. Aside from a Mediterranean climate, Montpellier had a medical faculty, a theatre, and a reasonable social life, and the presence of compatriots encouraged other British tourists. It was only in the 1780s, when Spa was affected by the disturbances in the Austrian Netherlands and the Bishopric of Liège, that there was a discernible shift towards the distant sun of the Riviera. Nevertheless, the British envoy in The Hague writing to his Berlin counterpart in June 1791, was 'interrupted by a large arrival of our countrymen on their way to Spa'.[5]

The waters of Spa seem to have been fairly efficacious, though it is equally likely that regular hours, fresh air and the relative sobriety of Spa activities had a beneficial effect. Charles Sackville of Stoneland, who visited Spa in 1788, noted that he had been well ever since leaving England: 'I owe all this health that I am boasting of, almost entirely to change of air and change of scene, for I own that Spa is, this summer, one of the most stupid places I ever saw.' Mrs Ryder 'received benefit from the waters' and Henry Ellison was pleased by his trip there:

> As far as I can yet judge the society seems to be on an agreeable and easy footing arising from the concourse of people from all nations. The English are by much the most numerous, and among them we have . . . Lord Northington and Lord Clive. The former has already received benefit here, if I may judge from his countenance, and the latter has profited still more by having wintered in France [Languedoc] . . .

William, 4th Duke of Devonshire, however, died there in 1764, while Admiral Keppel found his trip to Spa useless. He took the waters, 'a series of torment', and recovered, but relapsed after leaving. Keppel subsequently spent the winter of 1785–6 in Naples, sailing there directly. In 1770 Andrew Stuart was told by his doctor that Spa water would be more effective 'than all other medicines', while Frances Pulteney received considerable benefit from her course.[6]

Travelling for health lost none of its popularity as the century advanced, though Naples and the south of France became increasingly popular. Weak in his feet and legs, Charles, 3rd Duke of Bolton (1685–1754), was told in 1751 'that a warmer climate and a clearer air such as the South of France would give . . . better health . . . and certainly prevent a return next winter'. He took the advice, writing that July:

> this villa I had the luck to get, I intend to stay at during the summer. It is prettily situated on the River Tarn, with good gardens and a great deal of shade half a league from Montauban . . . I had a very long journey from Paris hither, as I came but a little way in a day, found a great dearth of provisions, and an entire want of conveniences on the road, notwithstanding which, I am very much improved in my health, and perceive the heat of this climate agrees with me.

George, 3rd Earl of Albermarle (1724–72), wrote in 1770, 'I set out tomorrow for the South of France with great regret, but I am so pulled down with my late illness that I must go to pass my winter in a constant climate, so says Sir Clifton.' His brother, William Keppel (1727–82) went to Lisbon for his health in 1755. Lord Cornbury went abroad in 1748 to seek a better climate for the recovery of his health; the Graftons travelled for the Duchess's health in 1761; Lord and Lady Fife went to Spa in 1765 for Lady Fife's health. Patrick Moran died on the way to Lisbon in 1769; and William Montagu MP died in Lisbon itself in 1775; both had gone for their health. John Armstrong went to the Mediterranean for his health in the early 1770s; and the Gloucesters were there in 1771 for the health of the Duchess. William Dowdeswell MP was ordered abroad in 1774 and died in Nice the following February; Lord John Pelham Clinton MP had no better luck in Lisbon in 1781; nor Sir Thomas Wroughton in 1787 – he died in Maastricht – while Lord Heathfield died at Aachen in 1790 where he had gone for his health. Dining at Lord Holland's in Nice in February 1770 George, later 2nd Earl Spencer (1758–1834), noted, besides his host, the presence of eleven other British visitors, eight of them women, including the five members of the Finch family. Norton Nicholls found a little colony of British invalids in Aix-en-Provence in January 1773, Sir John Fleming Leicester another in Nice in December

1784. Philip Yorke went to Switzerland for health reasons; and Lady Craven was visited in Paris in the early 1780s by her sister-in-law, Lady Emily Berkeley, and the latter's mother, Lady Louisa Lennox, who were going to the south of France for Lady Emily's health, and by her brother the Earl of Berkeley who was going to Florence for his gout. In 1788 Philip Lloyd and his wife were both 'much advised to try the heat of an Italian summer' for their health.[7]

Travelling abroad for health remained the prerogative of a small group. Whereas it was possible for the 'middling orders' to take a 'mini-Grand Tour', a brief tour to Paris and possibly the Low Countries, such as that outlined in William Lucas's 1750 guidebook, *A Five Weeks Tour to Paris, Versailles, Marli*, it was not so easy to take a quick trip to a health resort, other than Spa. Furthermore, cures were generally lengthy: a prolonged course of taking the waters or a long period in the warm air of Portugal, the Riviera or Naples. Thus most who needed to travel for health went to British spas. This partly accounts for the customary picture of eighteenth-century British tourism: travel for health or for health-related purposes was usually within Britain, but travel for education and pleasure was generally abroad.

LOSS OF HEALTH

Thank God I keep my health, which is a great happiness in travelling.

Charles Cadogan[8]

Lanced the swelling in my throat myself with a penknife, and find great relief.

Philip Francis, Florence[9]

Ill health while travelling could be a serious problem. To fall ill in the major cities, as Henry Ellison did in Paris in 1765, at least ensured medical attention, a mixed blessing in this period, but in much of Europe it was difficult to obtain such attention. Sir Henry Liddell became 'exceedingly ill' in Savoy in 1733 and Shallett Turner had to ask the British envoy, the Earl of Essex to persuade the royal physician at Turin to send advice. Travellers who had accidents crossing the Cenis generally had to send to Turin for assistance.[10] When, in 1783, Sir James Graham became ill in Paris, his bearleader Brand was 'thankful that we had got no further and that we were not stopped in a village or country town where we could not have had proper advice or attendance'. Yet even in the towns the situation was far from perfect and British travellers had little confidence in the attention that they could expect. In Hamburg there was a hospital staffed by 'a Physician and Surgeon, with necessary medicines for poor strangers and travellers, that fall sick or lame'. Whatever the charitable provision for poor travellers, British tourists in Europe tended to rely on local doctors. This did not always have beneficial results. The death of the 4th Earl of Sunderland was blamed, albeit by a rival doctor, on bad medical advice. In 1785 the consul in Venice, John Strange, attributed his wife's death to the unparalleled 'Treachery and Malversation' of a local doctor: 'I ever must look upon [him] as her deliberate Murderer . . .' Six years later Brand, who had 'a vile scorbutic humour', wrote that he had 'no confidence in the medical people of this country if I should find it necessary to employ them'. There was a general preference for British doctors. When Frances Crewe was in Paris her mother became ill. She sent for Dr Lee,

> . . . an English physician, who had resided here since he left off practice, and is good enough to give assistance to people of our own country when they stand in need of it . . . a plain good sort of regular physician . . . But, had he been the lowest in our school he would have been worth fifty of the French practitioners who talk such old fashioned nonsense, even the best of them, about bleeding in the foot, a seventh day crisis, and a thousand other long exploded notions, as prove them to be very far behind us in this science. It is not likely indeed the case should be otherwise for the profession is treated in so humiliating a way that no Gentleman can enter into it . . . in general they are certainly bunglers.

Suffering from colic in 1767, Countess Spencer was unimpressed by the Parisian treatment:

> I have been forced to submit to the manners of the place and have been squirted with clysters almost incessantly which have at last relieved me a little. Madame de Guerchi is my physician and really does very well if she did not tell the whole circle of men, how often I have a motion and how many more lavements I am to take with a long dissertation on how much more convenient their squirts are than our method of doing the same thing.

However, a preference for British doctors was not always best. In February 1784, Brand wrote from Italy that Sir James Graham had had 'a very violent fever . . . His partiality to everything English made him consult a Physician [Metcalfe] whose skill I hold in sovereign contempt for I found he had no confidence in himself and would have prescribed anything that I proposed. He would have given him Madeira and roast veal when his pulse beat 120 in a minute. Lady Warren's maid died under his care.' Fortunately Metcalfe fell ill and Brand was able to persuade Graham to consult the well-regarded Neapolitan doctor, Cyrillo, who had studied in London, and who cured him. The following October Lord Bulkeley became ill with 'a bilious fever' because of the heat and fatigue of a journey from Vienna to Venice. At Trieste the British Consul recommended 'an excellent Physician'. Lady Granard found very good doctors at Linz in 1787. That year Sloane had an operation on his right eye at Cracow: 'The cornea of my eye was ulcerated all round, and formed a hard spot over it like a skin, which I was obliged to have cut through in 4 different places with a lancet.'[11]

Much of the ill health suffered was intestinal, due to bad water and poorly-prepared food. Shaw had the flux almost all the time he was in Paris; Lady Derby had the gripe at Munich in 1782; the Duke of Gloucester the flux in Tuscany in 1771; and Dawkins had a 24-yard tapeworm removed in Dresden in 1785.[12] Coughs and colds were another problem. Francis had a violently sore throat in Tuscany in 1772; Richard Garmston caught a bad cold twice in 1787. On the Paris–Lyons diligence 'it was exceeding hot in the day six passengers on the inside, I caught cold the first night by sleeping with the windows open'. At Naples he suffered as a result of watching an eruption of Vesuvius from his balcony for three hours. Despite a very bad cold, Lord Bruce wanted to go to The Hague fair in 1790.[13] Vesuvius had a more serious effect on Frederick, 4th Earl of Bristol and Bishop of Derry (1730–1803). Visiting the crater while the volcano was near erupting in 1766, he was seriously injured by a falling stone.

Malaria was a fear in the Campagna;[14] Lord Balgonie was nearly bitten by a scorpion which had crept into his bed at Padua in 1775; James Coutts died at Gibraltar in 1778, possibly of respiratory illness (he was travelling home from Turin, where his unstable mental condition had led to his being confined); Lord Wycombe had a very bad inflammation in Paris in 1787.[15] For most tourists there is, however, no indication of what they were suffering from. They were simply reported as ill, as Charles Dering was in Amiens in 1730, Mr Heneage in Venice in 1787, and Lord Downe, Lady Ann Wellesley and Miss Payne in Paris in 1786.

Illness clearly affected travel plans. The 2nd Earl Cowper fell seriously ill at Venice in early 1730 and his return home was strongly pressed by a British doctor, John Hollings, who was consulted by post. Hollings advised the taking of '40 grains of a viper in powder every morning and evening at any hour he likes best, either in two or three spoonfuls of chicken broth, or wine and water, whichever he pleases, asses milk twice daily and cassia pulp dissolved in a glass of warm barley water twice weekly'. Thanks probably to his youth, Cowper recovered. William Coxe had to cut short his Swiss trip in 1779 due to ill health, while Randle Wilbraham found that the measles disrupted a journey from Vienna to Warsaw in 1794.[16] The difficulties of being ill abroad underlined the degree of bravery shown by many on the Grand Tour. Despite their wealth and connections and the knowledge that they could rely on the British diplomatic service, tourists faced an alien and to some extent dangerous environment. This was more striking as it contrasted so sharply with their experience of life in Britain. Aside from the dangers presented by crime and the ever-present threat of vehicle accidents, tourists faced a situation in whch illnesses, that by modern standards would rank as holiday mishaps, could well be fatal. Limited medical knowledge could turn minor ailments into killers.

DEATH

A large number of British travellers died abroad. Many would have been travelling for their health and, in particular, a certain number died of tuberculosis in Naples or Portugal. Death is not usually seen as part of the Grand Tour but it was frequent. Tourists were often reminded of the risk of mortality. In 1787 Walker saw in Rome the gravestone of Mr James Six, a young fellow of Trinity, Cambridge, who had died in the city the previous December. Richard Garmston's passage along the dangerous Tolentino–Foligno road, where there was no barrier between the road and its neighbouring precipice, was not eased by the knowledge that several years earlier a British traveller had been killed and his carriage dashed to pieces by the carelessness of the driver. Readers of Philip Thicknesse's tour of the Austrian Netherlands could have taken little comfort from his mention of the recent loss of the Dover packet with all its passengers on the Margate–Ostend crossing.[17]

Most references to deaths give few if any details. It is impossible usually to ascertain whether the traveller was ill before leaving Britain, or whether he or she died as a result of an accident or an illness. Furthermore, most accounts, particularly the brief items printed in newspapers, do not distinguish between those who were travelling for pleasure, those who were travelling for health and those who were residing abroad. Sir Humphry Morice (c. 1723–85), who died at Naples, spent most of his last ten years in the city. Thus, it is difficult to suggest how many tourists died or how likely death was to end a Grand Tour. Possibly it is best simply to note the large number of deaths and suggest that this aspect of the Grand Tour, as much as the ill health that afflicted so many tourists, should not be forgotten when one sees the self-confident poses of aristocratic tourists in their portraits.

NOTES

1. BL Add. 30271, f. 12.
2. Stafford CRO D1057/M/F/29; Macdonald, *Memoirs of an Eighteenth-Century Footman*, p. 172.
3. L30/8/10/94–101; P. Kinsky to –, 13 May 1734, PRO 100/11; Chesterfield to Waldegrave, 23 July 1728, Chewton; *London Evening Post*, 17 Feb. (os) 1730, Ailesbury, *Memoirs* (2 vols, 1890), II, 504; BL Add. 57927 f. 317.
4. Bishop Downes of Meath to Bishop Nicolson of Derry, 18 Mar. (os) 1725, *Nicolson correspondence* (2 vols, cont. pag.), II, 599; Mellish to father, 12 Mar. 1731; HP, II, 343; Ossorio, Sardinian envoy in London, to the Sardinian foreign minister, 6 Nov. 1742, Turin, Archivio di Stato, LM Ing. 48; BL Add. 6861 f. 133.
5. Ellison, A19, No. 26; *Daily Post-Boy*, 21 Sept. (os) 1731; Mellish to father, 2 July 1731; Dayrolle to Tilson, 9 Aug. 1732, PRO 84/319; *Daily Gazetteer*, 30 Aug. (os) 1735; Matlock, Derbyshire CRO 239 M/O 759.
6. Sackville to Hotham, 7 July 1788, Hull UL DDHo/4/23; Ellison, A15, No. 24, 23; WW R1–1680; T.R. Keppel, *Life of Augustus Viscount Keppel* (1842) II, 416–17; HL PU 2000, 1908.
7. Bolton to Newcastle, 25 Mar. 21 July 1751, BL Add. 32724 f. 212, 459; WW R1–1313; Cornbury to George II, 6 June 1748, BL Add. 32715; Ellison, A8, No. 26; *St James's Chronicle* 1 April 1769; Cradock, *Memoirs*, p. 154; *Gentleman's Magazine* (1787), p. 838; BL Althorp F1; Beinecke, Osborn Shelves c 467 II No. 55; Chester CRO DLT/C9/8; Yorke to Keith, 12 May 1779, BL Add. 35516; Craven, *Memoirs*, I, 121–2; Lloyd to Jenkinson, 30 June 1788, BL Add. 38471 f. 199.
8. Cadogan to Sir Hans Sloane, 19 Mar. 1720, BL Add. 4045.
9. Francis, 1 Nov. 1772, BL Add. 40759.
10. Turner to Essex, 12 Sept. 1733, BL Add. 27732.
11. Brand to Wharton, 2 Feb. 1783, Durham, Wharton; anon., *Present State of Germany*, II, 416; Doctor De la Coste to –, 8 Oct. 1729, Strange to Keith, 15 Sept. 1785, BL Add. 61667, 35535; Brand to Wharton, 3 Jan. 1791, Durham, Wharton; Crewe, BL Add. 37926, f. 65, 76, Althorp F 60, 13 Aug. 1767; Brand to Wharton, 18 Feb. 1784, Durham, Wharton; Fortescue to Keith, 7 Oct., Bulkeley to Keith, 12 Oct. 1785, BL Add. 35535; Granard to Keith, 23 July 1787, BL Add. 35538; House of Lords RO CAD/4/12.
12. Shaw, *Letters*, p. 118; Wharton to Thomas Wharton, 21 Mar. 1775, Durham, Wharton; Jane Campbell to Keith, 12 June 1782, BL Add. 35525.
13. Garmston, BL Add. 30271, f. 8, 32; Brand to Wharton, 14 May, 4 June 1790, Durham, Wharton.
14. Sarah Marlborough to Fish, 15 May (os) 1727, BL Add. 61444.
15. Memorandum on Coutts, BL Add. 37848, f. 11–12; Robert Arbuthnot to Keith, 16 Nov. 1787, BL Add. 35539.
16. Hollings to Atwell, 23 Jan. (os) 1729/30, undated, Herts. D/EP F 55 f. 31–4; Coxe to Keith, 26 Sept. 1779, BL Add. 35517; Chester CRO DBW/N/Bundle E, Packet A.
17. Stevens, p. 130, 327; Walker, p. 310; Garmston, 23 Oct. 1787, BL Add. 30271; Thicknesse, *Pais Bas*, p. 13.

9

LOVE, SEX, GAMBLING AND DRINKING

I cannot omit setting down here an adventure that happened to Mr. [Thomas] Dixon at the Comte de Douglass assemblée: after he had played at cards some times with Madam de Polignac: a very handsome lady: she profered to set him at home in her coach: which he very willingly accepted of: this young gentleman (who was a man of pleasure) finding himself alone with a fine young lady: could not forbear putting his hand where some women would not let him: after he had pleased himself thus for some time and she had bore it with a great deal of patience: she told him (in a pleasant manner) that since he had been so very free with her: she could not forbear being familiar with him: upon which she handled his arms: and finding them not fit for present service: she beat him very heartily: he said all he could for himself: telling her that he had been upon hard duty for some time in the wars of venus: and if she would give him but one day to recruit on: he would behave himself like a man: she minded not his excuses but turned him out of the coach: and gave him this advice – 'Never to attack a young handsome lady as she was when his ammunition was spent'.

George Carpenter, Paris, 1717[1]

LOVE AND SEX

. . . afterwards to the Thuillerie Gardens and walked by moonlight, which would have been extremely agreeable, but for the interruption of too many of the votaries of Venus for the most part of the lowest class.

Jervis, 1772[2]

Travel abroad provided a major opportunity for sexual adventure. Tourists were generally young, healthy and wealthy and were poorly, if at all, supervised. Many enjoyed sexual relations while abroad, but to a great extent it was the well-behaved, such as Wharton, young prigs, such as Thomas Pelham, and scholars, such as Pococke, who wrote lengthy letters home to their relatives. There is very little personal correspondence, other than demands for money, from those whose conduct was castigated by their contemporaries. The vast majority of the journals that have been preserved relate to blameless or apparently blameless tourists. In his lengthy published account of his travels, John Breval (c. 1680–1738), who had gone abroad in 1720 as bearleader to George, Viscount Malpas, made no mention of the Milanese nun he had had a relationship with. Breval had earlier lost his Fellowship of Trinity College, Cambridge after assaulting his mistress' husband. The diary of Edmund Rolfe (1738–1817) made no mention of his relationship with Julia de Martino, with whom he had an affair at Lausanne during the winter of 1759–60, nor of the son she bore him. Philip Francis might speculate on whether he would prefer relations with the Venus de Medici, a source of erotic impulses for other tourists, or Titian's Venus, but such daydreaming was banished from the accounts of his more respectable contemporaries. There is evidence in quite a few cases that journals and correspondence have been tampered with subsequently, presumably by descendants, and this may have been widespread. Some of the obliterations in Charlemont's manuscript narrative are opposite passages describing matters of sexual interest. A letter of 1764 from the Marquis of Tavistock to the Earl of Upper Ossory included the sentence, 'I am amused at your account of Beauclerk but wish rather to see him gaming and setting up in England than engaged with so dangerous a woman as the Cornara', the phrase 'engaged with' being added in a different hand above another that has been obscured. Obliterations in a journal, possibly by Marmaduke William Constable-Maxwell, may have removed sexual references. A line in a letter of 1788 by Charles Sackville describing the social life in Spa was subsequently written over. Some obscure references in journals may be sexual. One anonymous tourist referred to being 'introduced to 2B' in July 1754, while, a year later, he 'took Lena'.[3]

The public attitude to sexual adventure abroad was generally unfavourable. Encapsulating the sense of threat that foreign travel aroused, it was heavily influenced by the prevalence of venereal disease, the ravages of which substantially defied contemporary medicine, and the consequences of which could be serious not only from the point of individual health, but also because it harmed the chances of securing heirs to an estate. In 1725 *Mist's Weekly Journal*, the leading Tory London newspaper, attacked the conduct of British tourists abroad. On 14 August (os) the paper printed a letter from 'Tibullus', who had been sent on his travels when seventeen 'and spent betwixt three or four years abroad, during which time I worshipped the merry deities, and only acquired the languages necessary for entertaining the fair'. On 18 September (os) it carried an account of British tourists in Paris who went drinking until 2 or 3 a.m. and 'then return home, unless they chance to stumble into a bordel by the way; a misfortune which has often happened . . . the whole account of their travels is generally no more than a journal of how many bottles they have drunk, and what loose amours they have had'. On 9 July (os) 1731, the *Daily Post-Boy* claimed that British gentleman-travellers spent all their time drinking and whoring; while on 7 August (os) 1731 'Civicus', in an anti-travel piece in the *London Journal*, stressed the sexual risks presented by women travelling: 'it is highly probable, that by means of our ladies travelling, some of our noble families may be honoured with a French dancing master's son for their heirs'. There was a clear sexual allusion in a newspaper comment of 1739: 'I look upon France as the hot-bed to our English youth, where they are immaturely ripened, and therefore soon become rotten and corrupt at home.' Another of 1788 reported that 'the English when at Paris, make Opera girls and actresses objects of idolatry'. A guidebook warned of the prevalence of venereal disease in the south of France, and of the expense that it entailed, adding:

> You will, no doubt, be frequently accosted in the streets, by fellows who are lookers-out to bawdy-houses; asking you, if you want a jolie fille; and happy are they when they can lay hold of an Englishman, as the girls say they bleed freely: the reward on those occasions, is to break your cane over their shoulders; for many unguarded foreigners have been seduced by those notorious villains, into places from whence they have never more made their appearance.[4]

Venereal disease was indeed a problem. In 1734 Lewis, 2nd Earl of Rockingham (*c.* 1714–45), was upset by claims that he had it; Charles Howard, Viscount Morpeth (1719–41), died of venereal disease contracted in Italy, precipitating a by-election in Yorkshire; and in 1754 Charles Hotham (1729–94) wrote from Naples, 'Sir James Gray carried me to the Princess Francavillas who my Lord Rockingham has still I fear some reason to remember. If she was no handsomer when he had to do with her than she is now, he in my opinion deserved what he got, the p-x, for his pains. Such a parcel of ugly women as is in this town, I think I never saw in any one place in my life.' The 2nd Marquis of Rockingham (1730–82) was later First Lord of the Treasury. Hotham, who was to be a MP and a Major General, noted that he had been spoilt at Siena where he had met a very beautiful woman. Henry Pelham Clinton, Earl of Lincoln, contracted venereal disease in Italy from Maria Lamberti, a dancer who supplemented her income by prostitution. Hotham's brother-in-law, John, 2nd Earl of Buckinghamshire, revealed, albeit in Britain, fears of contracting venereal diseases that may have been very widespread. A masturbatory reverie led him to a nightmare vision of the pox:

> In flannel were his limbs array'd
> With spittle smear'd and snot;
> Attended by a nurse-like shade
> That held a spitting pot.
> Feebly the specter took his stand,
> All withered, wan, and sick,
> Supporting, in a shrivled hand,
> His oozing shankered prick.
> Behold! thou faithless wretch, he cried,
> The fiend that's doomed by fate,
> The injured fair ones cruel wrongs
> Fully to vindicate.
> I am the Pox, the scourge of sin,
> You soon shall feel my smart,
> My baleful venom lurks within
> Your vile offending part.
> Fanny the deadly taint conveyed
> Through treacherous condum's crack . . .

A long series of distinguished tourists remembered their travels for years afterwards for reasons that bore little relation to the restrained portraits by Batoni that decorated their libraries. Joseph Shaw noted the preference of the gentry for French surgeons, 'having travelled into France, and brought home French vices and diseases, to the disgrace of the nation, they are glad to make use of those surgeons who best understand their distempers'.[5] An anonymous writer suggested that 'a great many of our gentlemen travellers have reason enough to be cross, on account of some modish distemper the Italian ladies may have bestowed on them with the rest of their favours'. Henry Harris wrote to Richard Evans in 1749: 'brag, as you please, you must have got, at Dresden, more poxes than languages'. The following year he expressed his conviction that Henry Fox's nephew, Henry Digby (1731–93), later 7th Lord Digby, was 'deep in foreign interests or cunts'. Digby indeed acquired a persistent affliction that was difficult to cure. In late 1750 his uncle wrote to Hanbury Williams about Hanover, which George II was then visiting, 'Digby's venereal affairs should call him there not prevent his going Calcraft having, in a box which he will find in Mr. Stone's hands, sent him an injection which he swears will cure his present disorder, and condoms, which if he pleases I am sure may prevent future ones'.

Fox referred later in the year to 'Digby's obstinate clap'.[6] British condoms, used largely to prevent men from contracting venereal disease, rather than to stop women becoming pregnant, were then regarded as sufficiently good for Louis XV to request a supply.[7] Thomas Steavens (c. 1728–59), would have been well advised to use them. In December 1751 Edward Digby, who had himself earlier in the year enjoyed the benefit of 'a very good pimp',[8] wrote:

> Steavens is in England and going back to Paris in a very little time to be salivated, and I verily believe he will have need enough of it before he gets there for he goes to all the bawdy houses he can find and fucks the first whore he meets bare reckons himself very happy if he can find one that tells him she is only clapped because owning so much he looks upon to be a mark of her sincerity and he has the best of such a bargain.[9]

On the other hand, Steavens' lengthy letter of the following July to Hanbury Williams from Angers makes it clear that he was a more complex figure. He described his visit to Italy, especially his response to a lover, 'the Ancilla':

> about half a mile from Leghorn I met the Ancilla who had heard of my being there . . . [meeting] began on mine [side] by an entire loss of sense and motion. As soon as I could move, I got into her chaise, and as soon as I could speak I began to reproach, though I had no sort of reason to be angry, but, though we were but half a mile from Leghorn, I had questioned, argued, reproached, quarrelled, and made everything up before we reached the gates of the town. We stayed there that night, and I promised to see her back to Florence . . . We lay the next night at Lucca and the night after at Florence, I was there three days, without once thinking of the Venus of Medicis; as for our parting, – if you can form to yourself all the wilderness of misery and grief, all the agonys, tremblings and torments that can enter into the heart of man, you will have an idea of my condition; I had never known till then what happiness and misery were, and I must take this opportunity of saying that, if all the foolish and all the malicious devils that infest this world were to tell me that the Ancilla did not love me at that time, I would not believe them. I know Italian nature well enough, but I know human nature too well to think that the latter can be so far disguised by the former. Vice may wear an appearance to virtue, there may be policy in that, but I have proofs of this girl's

sincerity and generosity too. I left Florence about three in the morning, when I came to Lucca began a letter to the Ancilla, but was too miserable to end it, sent on my baggage to Lerice, and returned to Florence. I stayed there two days more, and then set out again.

Steavens then left, to spend the summer at Paris, before returning home:

I was indiscreet enough to desire the enjoyment of Miss Sally Clerk, a young lady who sells oranges at Drury Lane Playbouse; and she cruel enough to consent to it, in short an unnatural flame on my side, and a still more unnatural one on hers had made such a bonfire of my body that I was obliged to apply to mercurialium custos virorum as soon as I reached Paris. Monsieur Fagel did my business in one sense to a miracle, for he perfectly cured me, no gleet, no obstructions, no remains whatever, but he was near doing my business in another sense by killing me in the cure. I intended going through a slight operation of this sort, as you had always advised me to do, and this was one reason for my returning to Paris that it might be the more secret . . . to be sound and to be well are two very different things. I know the golly hogs in England (for I prefer that reading to golly dogs) treat mercury as a trifle. They do not seem to be sensible of any of the effects of the god either in the head, or the body, as for the latter my stomache and nerves have been in a most terrible condition, but I am much better at present, and mend every day.

Recuperating at Angers and commenting on the works of Bolingbroke and Chesterfield, Steavens' thoughts returned to the Ancilla:

As I have said so much of the Ancilla to myself, I send you an ode on that subject, but I must give you a key to it, it shall be as short as possible. After I had left the Ancilla, we wrote constantly to one another, but, however pressing her letters might be, I always declined giving her any hopes of seeing me again, notwithstanding this, I was miserable beyond measure when I heard, about three months afterwards, that a Mr. Lethalier was excessively in love with her. She informed me herself of this, and desired to know whether she should let him visit her; her motive was want of money for, though she was strong in gowns, lace, snuffboxes etc. she had not much of the ready. My motive for not forbidding her Lethalier's company was the fear of laying myself under an obligation to return to her, thus was I divided between love and prudence. I wrote her however most violent letters for doing what I had tacitly consented to, that is letting Lethalier frequent her house. I reproached her with it when we met, but her behaviour at that time, as well as what I had learnt at Naples, from English who were come from Florence, and at Leghorn, where she had danced at the Carnival, convinced me that I was the amant du coeur, and the other merely an affair of convenience – this then is the subject of my ode which was made at Genoa.

Steavens included a poem of love and sexual jealousy.[10]

The language used by these writers is noteworthy – a clear contrast to Addisonian restraint and the discourse of politeness that has received so much scholarly attention. Any stress on this politeness[11] has to address the question as to how far it was deliberately inculcated in order to cope with a very different culture. A self-image of politeness must be understood as a cultural artefact, a socio-ideological aspiration designed to foster particular ends of moral improvement. Christian purpose and social order. Such a conclusion is also suggested by the contrast between the stress on sobriety and restraint and what is known about drinking levels in the period. Similarly the language of order in Restoration England, as represented for example in the works of Dryden, was in part a reaction against a strong sense of recent and current disorder.[12]

Paris was the great centre of sexual activity for British tourists: it was the city in which they tended to spend most time, access to local society was relatively easy, and there were numerous prostitutes. According to one London paper, it was 'a city the most noted for intrigues of any in Europe', and French women had a reputation for flexibility:

> It is observable, that the French allow their women all imaginable freedoms, and are seldom troubled with jealousy; nay, a Frenchman will almost suffer you to court his wife before his face, and is even angry if you do not admire her person: And, indeed, by the liberties I have often seen a married lady use, I have been at a loss to distinguish her husband from the rest of the company.

John, Lord Glenorchy wrote of the Danish court, 'the ladies are much in the French way extremely free'.[13]

The picture painted in Britain was one of British sexual conquests, albeit often for mercenary considerations, the press reporting:

> Our Gentry will make themselves as famous in making conquests among the French women, as their brave ancestors have been heretofore in subduing the French men . . . We hear from Paris, that one of the dancers at the opera, called La Salle, so remarkable for her chastity, as to have obtained the name of Vestal, has at last surrendered to a young English nobleman, who was introduced to her at an

assembly in woman's apparel, and so far insinuated himself into her favour, as to be permitted to take part of her bed.

A pamphlet Letter to a Celebrated Young Nobleman on his late Nuptials (1777) depicted the prior conduct of Sir Charles Maynard: 'those amiable days when you were drawn gently along the Boulevards at Paris, reclined in the arms of an Opera Dancer, who was supporting your pallid figure . . . The French . . . were in raptures at the sight of a young Nobleman who showed such fondness for a woman somewhat advanced in life.' Thicknesse stated:

> It is certain that men of large fortunes can in no city in the world indulge their passions in every respect more amply than in Paris; and that is the lure which decoys such numbers, and in particular Englishmen, to this city of love and folly; and occasion such immense sums to be drained from other countries, and lavished away in debauchery of every kind, in a town infinitely inferior to London. I verily believe Paris to be the theatre of more vice than any city in the world, drunkenness excepted.

He claimed that Parisian wives, including those who were religious, were generous with their sexual favours and was sardonic about the sexual adventures of British tourists, writing with reference to the gift of £1,000 by the son of an English duke 'to one little piece of readymade love . . . This is one instance, and I could give you a thousand, of the great influence of novelty, change of country, and of manners; for in London the same woman, and consequently the same charms, would not have produced a tythe of such liberality. But it was Paris, a Paris opera girl, and an Englishman at Paris, who is nobody without he cuts a figure.'[14]

There was a certain basis to these reports. The 20th Earl of Crawford had an intrigue with a French noblewoman 'of the greatest quality' in 1723. When Lord Clinton left Paris in 1725 he left 'behind him a fine lady'. Thomas, 2nd Viscount Weymouth (1710–51) caused diplomatic complications when he took his mistress, Mlle Petit Pas, back to Britain in 1732. She was one of the leading dancers at the Opéra and 'being of the French King's musick, and consequently a menial servant of His Majesty's she ought to be sent back'. Petit Pas returned to Paris in May 1733 'avec quarante mille livres, beaucoup de joie, et un petit milord dans le ventre'. In 1736 the 2nd Duke of Kingston brought his Parisian mistress, Madame de la Touche, back to Britain. Her husband, a royal official, wrote to Lord Hardwicke, the Lord Chancellor, to complain. Sixteen years later John Mackay wrote from Paris:

There is a mother and a daughter that embarrass me greatly, the latter I am fond of as you may imagine, and the other has a kind of friendship for me; you know I am somewhat conscientious, and would not choose to try both, though that seems to be the only chance I have for succeeding . . . Lord Huntingdon continues to talk of his going to Spain. Mlle Lany is 7 months gone with child, they are still fond of each other, which does not a little surprise me, considering how changeable his Lordship is; I believe a little vanity in being Papa contributes greatly to keep up the attachment.

In 1786 George, Viscount Malden, needed to marry for money because 'a certain Mlle Adeline . . . in Paris did him the honour of having spent [a] large sum of money . . .'. The same year Thomas, 7th Earl of Elgin (1766–1841), had an affair with a married woman in Paris and wrote her compromising letters, though he refused to run away with her. Elgin fled the city and, to his mother's relief, no scandal threatened his favour with his prudish patrons at the British court. The young handsome milord was clearly attractive to women. He wrote to his mother from Germany in 1787: 'I have only to show myself to excite tender passions. *Veni, vidi, vici.*' Given that these tourists would have had access to the numerous London prostitutes and to opportunities for relations with other women, it is reasonable to speculate as to whether Parisian women had any distinctive sexual characteristics and practices. It is possible that much of the appeal was the element of the different, if not exotic. Lord Dalrymple, brother of the British envoy, was not especially impressed by the women in 1715:

I have not been long enough here, to know, whether London or Paris is the most diverting town. The people here are more gay, the ladies less handsome, and much more painted, love galantry, more than pleasure, and coquetry more than solid love. This place is good for all those, that have more vanity than real lust . . . This is the most diverting time to be at Paris because of the Fair Saint Germain. All the ladies go their every night at six o'clock and stay till ten. All that time they stroll about from the fair to the play and rope dancing and the rest of the things to be seen there and I am sure if the people there have a mind to be happy there is no difficulty to lose themselves. It is impossible to take more freedom, than that place allows of, and men and women stroll about without ceremony and everybody are taken up with their own projects so much that they do not mind what other people are doing. I am sure were such opportunities at London there would be many happy lovers. My brother being here makes it easy for me to get into good company though I am not as yet in love with anybody nor are the ladies handsome. I believe I shall only make love as I used to do to some chambermaid. I have already had some adventures of that kind.

Forty years later Lord Nuneham confessed to his sister that he found French fashions alluring, certainly more so than their German counterparts that he was encountering at Hanover: 'I never could nor never shall bear anything but the French dress for ladies, and I am fonder of rouge well put on than ever . . . to me the finest pale face, the finest shape ill dressed is nothing.'[15]

Philip Francis observed: 'In England the commerce between the sexes is either passion or pleasure; in France it is gallantry, sentiment or intrigue; in Italy it is a dull insipid *business*.' Many tourists found their time in Italy far from dull. Italy was notorious for prostitution, especially Venice whose courtesans were reputed for their skill. Some tourists became heavily involved. Pococke wrote from Venice in June 1734, 'Mr. Wynn . . . has been 2 or 3 years at Venice, enchanted with a mistress'. Three years later the Earl of Radnor's dominance by a Venetian mistress attracted comment. One of the brothers of the 4th Earl of Chesterfield 'spent a great deal of money on a Venetian woman, whom he thought in love with him'. In 1763 the Marquis of Tavistock warned the Earl of Upper Ossory that 'Venice is the most calculated for luxurious idleness of any place I know and therefore very dangerous to you'.[16]

Venice was not the only cockpit of sexual adventure in Italy. Thomas, 2nd Lord Mansell (1720–44), was provided in 1739 with a list of Italian villas, palaces and churches to see. These were marked as the journey progressed, but he was also notorious for his whoring in Italy. Chesterfield wrote of his illegitimate son Philip Stanhope's time in Rome: 'The Princess Borghese was so kind as to put him a little upon his haunches, by putting him frequently upon her own. Nothing dresses a young fellow more than having been between such pillars, with an experienced mistress of that kind of manège.' Stanhope does not appear to have been alone. In 1760 the British envoy in Turin wrote of Boothby, 'He attached himself while here to a very clever woman, who was of great service to him; she brushed him up greatly.'[17] Stanhope's teacher, Agnese Colonna (1702–80), was indeed popular with British tourists. In December 1740 Horace Walpole wrote to Henry Fiennes-Clinton, 9th Earl of Lincoln (1720–94), then recently arrived in Rome:

I did not give you so strong an idea of the Princess Borghese, as you seem to have contracted. I did not imagine *she would even surpass what you could have the assurance to hope for*. I knew your merit, and thought on some occasions you would not want assurance; and her benevolence and penetration have been known. I only hope that the presence of the Prince did not confine her good nature to under the pharaoh table.[18]

Lincoln himself had a somewhat mixed Grand Tour from the emotional point of view. He fell in love with Lady Sophia Fermor, whom he met at Florence in late 1740,[19] and made himself unhappy on her account. On the other hand, he was also noted for his vigour as a lover. Walpole sought to lure him from Turin to Genoa by telling him there were 'millions of pretty women'.[20] Among Hanbury Williams' papers is an ode he wrote to Lincoln in February 1743:

> Oh! Lincoln Joy of Womankind
> To thee this humble Ode's design'd
> Let Cunt inspire the Song
> Gods! with what Powr's art thou indue'd
> Tiberius wasn't half so lewd
> Nor Hercules so strong
>
> 'Tis Fucking now my Pen employs
> And whilst I sing of Heav'nly Joys
> From Heav'n my Notes I'll bring
> And tho' the Lyrick Strain I chuse
> I'll open like the Mantuan muse
> Prick and the man I'll sing
>
> But you shall have no Flattery
> From such an honest Bard as me
> Dear Noble Vigorous youth
> For when I say that you fuck more
> Than ever Mortal did before
> You know it is but truth
>
> Four times each Night some amorous Fair
> He swives, throughout the circling year
> This Course of Joy pursuing
> Of Feats like these what Annals speak
> 'Tis eight and twenty times a week
> And, faith, that's glorious doing
>
> His Manner captivates the Fair
> His Tongue ev'n Vestals might ensnare
> His Prick that always stands

That never baulks him with Delays
It's willing Lord alone obeys
And all the Fair commands

Could Messalina fuck with you
Whom no one Man could e'er subdue
Tho' many a Roman try'd
She'd own your Vigour and your Charms
And melting dying in your arms
Cry out, I'm satisfy'd

Pursue Delight with loosn'd Reins
While youth is boiling in your Veins
And sparkling in your Face
With Whores be Lewd, with Whigs be hearty
And both in Fucking and in Party
Confess your Noble Race

To you and steady Pelham then
With Joy I'll dedicate my Pen
For both must be my Theme
Since both divided England share
You have the Love of ev'ry Fair
He ev'ry Man's Esteem.[21]

George Lyttelton set off for Italy in 1729 with a warning from his father against 'grapes, new wine, and pretty women'. The engagement of George's son Thomas (1744–79), later an MP, was broken off in late 1764 because he was 'detained by Circes and Syrens of the coast about Genoa'. He had been thoroughly warned by his father of the 'danger from Italian amours' as well as 'of the other danger', presumably homosexual encounters. His father thought religion the only safeguard 'against the circes of Italy', but as Thomas was not devout he feared that he had no protection 'against a handsome countenance'. Francis Whithed had an affair in Florence that resulted in a daughter to whom he eventually left £6,000. 'Known by all the young English' visiting Florence, 'La Rena', the wife of a wine merchant, came to England in 1757 with the Earl of Pembroke, assuming the bogus title of contessa on the way. Francis Russell MP, Marquis of Tavistock (1739–67), and his close friend Thomas Robinson MP (1738–86), later 2nd Lord Grantham, were both tempted by married Italian women. In April 1762 Tavistock wrote to Robinson from Bologna, 'I got your letter two days before I left Rome. I tried 2 or 3 times to see the Contesstabilessa but was always unfortunate, and as her husband is said to be very watchful at present, I was afraid to send it her by a note as I thought is might produce disgrazzias in the family.' That December he wrote again from Genoa:

> whether my constancy is as frail in Vertue as in Love, I cannot tell – at Turin I saw the D–s, who was very civil to me as well as her husband, yet in spite of her beauty, Vertue (not Virtue) conquered Love . . . As to the D. I lived a good deal in their house and found it very agreeable as his Grace is in great spirits and good humour, but I kept clear of all thoughts of Love. Indeed I hope to do the same all through Italy for if once that gets hold of me, I can no longer answer for myself. The Princess Gilles and I were very well together for our short acquaintance. She charged me with a 1000 humourous messages for Lord Charles Spencer [MP 1740–1820] through you on the subject of the Gabrieli. Tell him if ever he hopes again for her good graces to write to her and renounce the Gabrieli, who carries his picture round her arm and his heart on her neck.

Caterina Gabrielli was an opera singer whose favours were enjoyed by more than one tourist. In 1785 the British envoy in Turin had to intervene in the case of a 'silly young countryman of our's Mr. Fox Lane, a man of fashion and great fortune having, from an infatuated complaisance to the lady he was in love with, changed his religion, or rather for the first time adopted one, which unluckily for him, is the Roman Catholic . . . I cannot but look upon this step as an act of infatuation and childishness'. Horace Mann commented on how 'an English traveller frequently deranges the whole harmony of "cicisbeship"', by which a married Italian woman had a male companion who accompanied her to social gatherings, and was sometimes her lover. Thomas Pelham of Stanmer (1728–1805), later Lord Pelham and eventually 1st Earl of Chichester, had a long affair, in Florence in 1750, with a married woman, Countess Acciaioli, who then took another British lover. Her married friend Maria Serristori had a relationship with Rockingham in 1748–9. In June 1760 Mann had written to Horace Walpole about the 21-year-old George, Viscount Fordwich, later 3rd Earl Cowper, 'losing his whole time by acting the *cicisbeo* to the Marchesa [Corsi]'. 'Scorched by . . . burning eyes', Sir Richard Worsley (1751–1805), was in the summer of 1784 'totally attached to a very common Italian woman . . . a strange taste . . . for a man of any degree of delicacy'. He was separated from his adulterous wife.[22]

Foreign travel also provided an opportunity for people to live together unconstrained by the pressures of British life. Consequently there were many elopements to Europe. Lord Euston, heir to the 2nd Duke of Grafton, eloped to Italy in 1744 with a Miss Nevill 'of a very ancient family in Lincolnshire, with eleven thousand pounds for her fortune, and a celebrated beauty', giving her a promise of marriage that he never fulfilled. In December 1778 Amelia D'Arcy, Lady Carmarthen, ran away to the Continent with John Byron, the father of the poet, and married him when Lord Carmarthen obtained a divorce. In 1785 Keith's source of British gossip wrote to him, 'Mr. M: is I am told gone to France with Miss Johnson and left Lady Catherine to pray for his soul.'[23] Those who were trying to live down scandal could find it convenient to travel. Ostracized socially and criticized in the press for his elopement with Lady Sarah Bunbury, which had finished when she returned to the house of her brother, the 3rd Duke of Richmond, Lord William Gordon (1744–1823), who had already toured abroad in 1762–3, left England in 1770 vowing never to return. With a knapsack on his back and no company other than a very big dog he aimed to walk to Rome. By 1774 he was back in London and five years later he became an MP.

Lovers who did not elope still found it convenient to leave the country. Free from prying eyes, Henry Fox could live with his older protector, Mrs Strangeways Horner, in Europe in the early 1730s. In 1730 Viscount Harcourt met a former MP, Richard Cresswell, living with his mistress in a public fashion that would have been more difficult in Britain. Italy was a haven for wives who didn't get on with their husbands, irrespective of whether they had other relationships. Margaret Rolle, Countess of Orford, pleaded ill health to stay in Italy with her lover. Horace Mann wrote to Horace Walpole in September 1743: 'The reputation of our female travellers is very low.' Frederick, Lord Baltimore, who had been acquitted of rape in England in 1768, died in Naples in 1771 leaving 'a whole *seraglio* of white, black, etc to provide for'. Charles Grenville took his mistress Emma Hart with him to Naples in 1786 and passed her on to his uncle Sir William Hamilton. William, 6th Earl of Craven took his mistress on a trip to the Continent. Living with another's spouse was also easier abroad:

> The Florentine minister [William Wyndham] is parted in due form from his wife. She returned with Lord Wycombe to England. At present they halt at Bologna, in company with Lady Webster and Lord Holland. They talk and act as their convenience directs. I am told laws civil and divine, are not any guide to their words or actions. Lady Plymouth was there with her husband, at least he was in the same house. Mr. Amherst does all the leading honours to the lady . . . our present ladies out-Herod Herod, or to speak more modernly, live with more effrontery than even their teachers, the French ladies.

Henry Fox, 3rd Lord Holland (1773–1840), had visited Paris during his Oxford long vacation in 1791, being introduced to Lafayette and

Talleyrand. The following year he toured Denmark and Prussia, the British envoy in Berlin writing of

> Sir Godfrey and Lady Webster. They are I presume upon the brink of separation. She is a handsome woman but the most saucy insolent coquette I ever saw. I never yet met with such pretensions to fineness. In proportion as she insults her husband she makes her addresses to Lord Henry on whom she seems to have formed a plot. I know not whether His Lordship has the continence of Joseph, but she has perseverance as I understand that her departure for Vienna will be regulated by his.

In 1793 Holland went abroad again. Having visited Spain and Italy, he settled in Florence, whence he returned to England in 1796 with Lady Elizabeth Webster (1770–1845). They lived together, she had a son by Holland and in 1797 married him after her husband divorced her. Charles Wyndham's travelling companion Mr Campbell had an affair with Lady Ferrers in Paris in 1729. Lord John Pelham Clinton wrote from Geneva in 1776, 'Lord Allen passed through . . . he was very grave, [Archibald] the [9th] Duke of Hamilton took my Lady from him at Naples'. While it was possible to conduct an affair perhaps more openly than in London, local society on the Continent could be disapproving. Sir Brook Bridges withdrew completely from Florentine society while carrying on a torrid affair in 1760. In 1778 Ferdinand IV of Naples and his wife Maria Carolina refused to receive Nancy Parsons, Lady Maynard at court, because she had a past, including an earlier visit to Naples as a ducal mistress.[24]

Homosexuality was regarded in Britain as a foreign vice of Mediterranean origins, as indeed was sodomy. Homosexuality had long been particularly associated with Italy, was indeed sometimes called 'the Italian vice', and in some writings linked to Catholicism. Cresswell got into trouble for homosexual activity in Genoa in 1716. The British envoy Davenant informed his counterpart in Paris:

> I met with a very dirty piece of business upon my arrival here. The 4th instant Mr. Cresswell was arrested by an order of a Deputation of the Senate, which has the inspection in cases of sodomy, they call them here il *Magistrato dei Virtuosi*. He was immediately carried to the prison of the palace, with a young Genoese boy he had lately dressed up, and nobody is admitted to see him. He has been so public in his discourse and actions that they can fix on him the fact above 38 times, in his own house, the streets, in porches of churches and palaces, in short I never heard of so flagrant a delinquent, however I have some hopes

of stifling the process, in regard of the nation's honour, and of the circumstances of my being here at this time to make them a compliment from His Majesty. They have been encouraged to this proceeding, by my not permitting him to visit me, but it is my opinion they would have shown more respect to His Majesty and the nation, if they had traced out one of their people for an example of severity, without fixing it on an Englishman.

The following year in Paris, George Carpenter, 'could not help observing one thing that was entirely new to me, which was several boys that walked about in the evenings to be picked up, as women do about the playhouses in London. The whores seemed to be very angry at this filthy practice. I heard some of them say aloud that it had almost quite spoilt their trade.' Swinton was accosted by a pimp in Lisbon in 1730 who offered him men or women. Nine years later Swinton was involved in the celebrated Wadham sodomy scandal, when the Warden Robert Thistlethwayte was accused of sodomy with a college servant and with one of the undergraduates. Swinton, the latter's tutor, tried to suppress the accusations, and was, in turn, accused of sodomy. Thistlethwayte fled to Boulogne.

In the second half of the century a period of repression replaced the relative tolerance of the first half, when the laws were not enforced. As no such equivalent hardening of attitudes took place in France or Italy, it seemed apparent that travel abroad offered the best opportunities for practising homosexuality. William Beckford had a homosexual crush in Venice in 1780 and in 1785 left Britain for Switzerland as a result of a homosexual scandal. The British envoy stopped him from being introduced at court in Lisbon in 1787. Four years earlier, the Earl of Buckinghamshire, commenting on the nudity of bathers at Weymouth, observed, 'the exhibition of boys is far more numerous. Had Lord Tylney visited Weymouth he could never have deserted his native country.' John, 2nd Earl Tylney (1712–82), died at Naples where he had spent many years.[25]

The sexual activities of most tourists caused few problems. General Dalrymple could run after 'the filles de l'opéra' in Paris; Lord Pembroke could appear in Florence 'with a Brunette en homme'; and an Irish peer could live in Pisa with both his wife and an Italian comtessa as his mistress. The Earl of Essex remarked complacently in 1752 that his uncle had probably got a married woman pregnant in Vienna 'and now he has the charity to play at cards with her *tête à tête* every night'.[26] The activities of adults gave little concern. In addition, the *cicisbeo* system in Italy, by which Italian married women were escorted by a man other than their husband, provided opportunities for a relationship that was in accordance with local customs. In the spring of 1791 Brand took Charles, Lord Bruce (1773–1856), to Siena 'to see an old lady to whom Lord Ailesbury

[Thomas, 4th Earl, 1729–1814] was cavalier servente thirty nine years ago! . . . She gave us many anecdotes of Ld. A's Siena life which perhaps had better been concealed.' The lady urged Bruce to live like his father, 'the very reflexion' Brand had wished to avoid. There was less interest in a similar arrangement for British women. In 1752, the beautiful and newly-married Mary Gunning, Lady Coventry (1732–60) 'met with an affront from some prince or nobleman at Paris who proposed to lie with her', a proposition described in the British press as 'an insult of the grossest kind'.²⁷

Problems were created when impressionable young men fell in love. Venereal disease was bad, but so was a *mésalliance*. Tourists could fall in love with either female British tourists or with other women. This entailed the risk that the careful matrimonial economy of dowries and connections would be upset and represented a more serious threat to aristocratic prestige and parental supervision than other forms of tourist activity. Brand, who served as a bearleader for over a decade, found himself forced to consult the parents of his charges on several occasions. In 1783 his pupil fell for the elder Miss Berry in Boulogne; in 1793 in Rome, Lord Bruce fell for Henrietta Hill, a slightly older English tourist. The latter episode led to a marriage in Florence, but with the blessing of the Earl of Ailesbury. In 1767, on his second tour to the Continent, 2nd Viscount Palmerston met Frances Poole at Spa and, though she was poor and ten years older than him, he married her. In Italy in the early 1740s, Lincoln fell for Lady Sophia Fermor and became morose as a consequence of disappointed hopes.²⁸

Foreign women were also the targets for British hearts, leading to much heartache and helping to underline to British relatives the degree of volatility and social uncertainty that the Grand Tour could give rise to. At Besançon on his tour to France, Geneva and Lorraine in 1733–4, William Pitt the Elder fell in love with a local beauty, and wrote about her to his sister Anne as if he had considered marriage. Pitt regretted that her background was not an exalted one, 'c'est là le diable', and he soon wrote of the relationship as one of the 'flammes passagères', which had left no trace. Wharton met some very attractive French women in 1775, and had to reassure his relations about his intentions: 'You have no occasion to fear my being in danger of captivity from any French Beauties. I see nothing in them capable of touching an Englishman like his own countrywomen.' Randle Wilbraham wrote reassuringly from Vienna in 1794:

> The women are very beautiful but in avoiding that excessive freedom of manners and spirit of gallantry which so strongly characterised the last generation of Vienna Belles, they have run into the unpleasant

extreme of coldness and reserve. I have however met with some amongst them whom I find very agreeable. This account of the state of society will I trust calm your apprehensions with regard to the petits soupers and gaming parties which no longer subsist, however prevalent they may have been some years back.[29]

Forceful intervention was necessary in other cases. George, Viscount Parker's involvement with an Italian woman, and his failure to heed the instructions of his father, Lord Chancellor Macclesfield, led Macclesfield to mobilize the resources of British diplomacy to regain his son. The young James Stuart Mackenzie fell for the famous opera-dancer Barberini and arranged to marry her in Venice. This was prevented by Archibald, 3rd Duke of Argyll, who used his friend John, 3rd Earl of Hyndford, envoy in Berlin, to have Barberini brought to Berlin and Mackenzie banned from Prussia. She had earlier engaged the attention of Samuel Dashwood. John, 3rd Duke of Roxburgh (1740–1804), fell for Christiana Sophia Albertina, the eldest daughter of the Duke of Mecklenburg-Strelitz, while on his Continental tour in 1761. As, however, her younger sister Charlotte soon became engaged to George III, it was deemed politically necessary to break off the match. Roxburgh never married.[30]

It is not surprising that impressionable young men, poorly, if at all, supervised, sometimes fell for local women. Much desire was unconsummated. In 1787 the young William Drummond dined at the Poste at Montebauer between Bonn and Frankfurt:

> The man who keeps it, has a beautiful daughter, who attended us at dinner. A more elegant, innocent, graceful, and engaging creature I scarcely ever have met with in my travels. She charmed us so, that had we not been wiser than the companions of Ulysses, we should have remained there too long: we did leave it with regret, and shall not forget her.

Very few went as far as one of Sarah Marlborough's grandsons, William Godolphin, Marquis of Blandford, and married a local woman whom they had met abroad. Although Maris Catherine de Jong, whom he married in 1729, was daughter of the Burgomaster of Utrecht and brought him a dowry of £30,000, she was received coldly by most of his family. In 1783, however, George, 4th Lord Onslow, was very pleased with the choice of his son Edward who, at Clermont-Ferrand, had fallen in love 'with a charming girl of great fashion'. They married with parental approval. Some older tourists married on their travels. Charles, 1st Duke of Shrewsbury (1660–1718), married Adelhida, daughter of the Marquis Palleotti of Bologna in 1705, a match that was criticized by his English friends. In 1750 Rear-Admiral Charles Knowles, a widower, married Maria Magdalena Theresa, daughter of the Comte de Bouget at Aix-la-Chapelle.

Such unions were, however, unusual. Brief affairs or visits to brothels were more common, though it is impossible to assess the extent to which tourists took advantage of the possibilities. Prostitution was open and readily available, though some towns, such as Venice, were particularly notorious for it. A tourist, possibly Marmaduke William Constable-Maxwell, wrote of Marseilles in 1784: 'it is one of the most debauched towns in France. It is astonishing the quantity of whores. They are impudenter and bolder than in any other town.' Harcourt's tutor, Bowman, might write of 'the low vices of our countrymen in Italy', but some tourists were uninterested in or contemptuous of such activities. William Bentinck smugly informed his mother from Paris, 'All the young men here are *petit Maîtres*, and there is no conversing with them without falling into their way and being debauched with them, which I do not design to begin now for myself . . . whereas among people of a certain age, and character, there is all the good breeding and politeness, and sense and knowledge of the world that one can desire.' William Windham found French women unattractive and claimed that licentiousness was more gross and common in London than in Paris.[31] If one is to judge from correspondence and journals 'low vices' were of less interest than accommodation and food, paintings and statuary. However, contemporary printed criticism of tourism would suggest the contrary. There was no common response in the opportunities of travel, and there was no reason why there should have been one.

GAMBLING

The French only regard strangers according to the money they spend and figure they make with their equipages, and provided you game and play you will be well received in the best company at Paris; where one risques losing five ten or fifteen pounds sterling in two hours time, besides at games of hazard the French of the very best fashion, make no scruple of cheating you, for they will do it to one another, therefore I can . . . compare seeing (what is styled) the very best company of Paris to nothing else but a company of sharpers, and pickpokkits, and at all their great assemblys the conversation consists of cards, and trifles, which will by no means contribute to the improvement of young people and moreover every stranger that runs into this fashionable way of life, ought to have about two or three thousand pound a year to support this figure, which is not to be done by people of moderate circumstances.

Edward Mellish[32]

Gambling played a major role in polite society in eighteenth-century Europe. The British gambled a lot at home, to the despair of contemporary moralists, and it was not surprising that when they went abroad many gambled heavily. Gambling was an integral part of eighteenth-century life and people gambled on everything – political, social and economic news as well as sports such as horse-racing, boxing, billiards and cards. The same happened abroad. Charles James Fox won a bet with William, Marquis of Kildare (1749–1804) in Florence in 1767 on how many sheets of paper the latter had with him. Most tourists, however, gambled on cards, and this was the activity on which some lost heavily, and which earned the denunciation of commentators. Charles James Fox's elder brother Stephen (1745–74), who was sent abroad for the good of his health after leaving Eton in 1759, was criticized by his father in March 1761 for losing on cards in Geneva.[33]

Gambling was of great importance in France: 'An itch for gaming has infected the generality of French, and may be deemed one of the plagues of the nation: and yet one would think it impossible for people who seem naturally restless, and desirous of moving from place to place, to sit cutting and shuffling the cards for five or six hours together.'[34] Andrew Mitchell wrote:

It is a great misfortune for a stranger not to be able to play but yet a greater to love it. Without gaming one can't enter into that sort of company that usurps the name of *Beau Monde*, and no other qualification but that and money are requisite to recommend to the first company in France, for this reason several sharpers, whose characters obliged them to leave the country, are here well received and caressed only because they play and are rich.

He commented on the Parisian custom of gambling in respectable houses on the footing of an assembly, where the banker paid the lady of the house for the privilege of fleecing her guests: 'I knew several gentlemen drawn in unwarily to such company, which obliged them to leave the place sooner than they otherways would have done.'[35] In 1727 Sarah Marlborough instructed Humphrey Fish not to let her grandsons gamble in France. She noted the cost involved and added: 'I know, in France they will all be wonderful civil, in hopes of cheating you: and when they find people won't play, they grow very cool . . . it is better to be without such civilities.' Three years later Edward Mellish wrote to his uncle from Blois that he had been 'lately informed by an English Gentleman who was sometime at Tours . . . that if one expected to be well received by persons of the best fashion, one must be obliged to play deep and game sometimes which would have been very inconsistent with the money I proposed to have spent at Tours.' The following February he wrote to his father from Saumur, 'I avoid gaming as much as is possible, which is a most pernicious entertainment, and there is no country in the world free from it except England' – a surprising statement. Having arrived in Paris he reported that he would 'avoid all play as much as possible; tho it is very difficult even in the best companys to avoid it at Paris'. He added that it was necessary to gamble if one wished to see women of quality and the sons of the aristocracy. Richard Lyttelton, who was sent to the academy in Besançon in 1737, informed his father, 'Tis impossible to avoid play and keep any company.' He was soon in debt as a result.[36] The *Westminster Gazette* of 23 November 1776 carried an account of a British aristocrat deliberately losing at cards in Paris in order to gain the favours of a woman, but without success.

Some British tourists lost heavily. Robert, 4th Earl of Sunderland, who died in Paris in 1729, 'had lost a considerable sum at play at Versailles'. The previous year George Lyttelton, who claimed that Parisian society necessitated gambling, wrote to his father: 'I am weary of losing money at cards'. Harry Pelham, studying at the Caen academy, ran up a debt of 50 guineas as a result of gambling on backgammon games at Harcourt. The *Daily University Register* claimed that English tourists were defrauded regularly by Parisian card sharpers.[37]

Andrew Mitchell, Edward Mellish, Richard and George Lyttelton were correct in noting the pressures to gamble, but it is clear that some British tourists enjoyed gambling and that some of the sharps were British. George James Cholmondeley ran a public gaming table in Paris and a faro bank at Brooks Club. Edward Wortley Montagu and Theobald Taaffe, both then MPs, were arrested in Paris in 1751 accused of cheating a Jew at cards and robbing him when he refused to pay. Both were imprisoned. They were cleared in the first court hearing, but this favourable verdict was overturned by the *Parlement* of Paris and they were fined 300 livres each with costs. Taaffe, who acted as a faro banker, continued his Parisian activities. In 1755 he won a large sum of money from Sir John Bland MP, who committed suicide after being arrested (at Taaffe's instigation) because of the dishonouring of the bills he had given for the debt. Thus, France provided opportunities for both the professional gamester and for the simply enthusiastic gambler, such as those (including women) whom Lady Knight noticed in Toulouse in 1776–7.[38]

Paris was not the only centre of gambling. There was a lot of gambling in the Austrian Netherlands, and, in particular, in the nearby watering places of Spa and Aachen. Charles Sloane found 'all kinds of gambling' in Spa in 1783. Four years later, Walker noted the dominance of gambling and wrote that the town was becoming 'a den of thieves . . . I recognised more of my countrymen than that of any other nation'. Thicknesse warned against gambling in the Austrian Netherlands and of the particular need to avoid Spa and Aachen where he claimed a lot of British money was lost to sharps who congregated there specifically in order to defraud young British tourists.[39] The United Provinces were not noted as a centre for gambling, but John Stanhope managed to lose £450 there; Edward Coke gambled heavily in 1737; Oliver Goldsmith characterized the English on the Dutch passenger-barges as playing cards; and Boswell gambled.[40] In Italy many of the British tourists gambled on cards, though usually with each other. Alexander Cunningham reported them doing so in Venice in 1717; Charles Stanhope gambled heavily in the same city in 1732; the Duke of Gloucester 'played at cards with a few English Gentlemen' at the masked ball held in his honour in Leghorn in 1771; and both Thomas Brand and Lady Knight commented on British gamblers in Italy in the early 1790s. Tavistock wrote of his time in Turin in 1762: 'I played almost every night for want of something to do and generally lost about 10 or 20 pistoles but the last night but one I had an immense run of luck and won about 80 which brought me near exactly home. I should be sorry to be thought to game deep amongst such thieves as these are.'

Losses could be serious. The Jacobite Catholic baronet, Sir Carnaby Haggerston, who visited Italy in 1718, showed a great facility for losing money that made his frequent requests for more funds less acceptable. In 1717, he wrote from France to his mother's Jesuit counsellor, Francis Anderton, that he had lost nearly £200: 'what wonder that young people who stay so long without exercises and without change fall into some change of fortune desiring to try at game since he cannot in battles . . . I've taken a resolution never to playe more except to oblige companie and that only at small games.' His resolution was unsuccessful. The following September his Jesuit bearleader, John Thornton, informed Anderton that Haggerston had lost £150 lately, though he consoled himself by writing: 'He has indeed avoided all gaming for some time and I both hope and suppose he will fall no more into it finding the inconveniencys must necessarily attend it.'[41] Gambling could be disastrous and the frequent denunciations of the habit arouses no surprise. Gambling losses, like venereal disease, often left scars that never healed. They could wreck family fortunes and represented the threat posed by whim and passion to the attempt to safeguard order and stability in the fortunes of Georgian families. Tourism accentuated the risks in both cases.

DRINKING

> Strangers and especially the English are more in danger than the people
> of the country, only because they will drink foreign wines, which do
> not agree with the air of the country, and will not be moderate upon
> eating, but sup and sit up late.

William Bentinck, 1727[42]

Many British tourists drank heavily. Alcohol was inexpensive and easy
to obtain. There were few barriers to alcoholic consumption and little
condemnation of heavy social drinking. In 1722 Colin Maclaurin met, in
the suite of Lord Polwarth at the Congress of Cambrai, 'a young Gentleman
unhappily addicted to drinking to the highest degree; who was kept abroad
on purpose lest his grandfather should find out his follies and disinherit
him'. Eight years later a drunken brawl involving young Englishmen in
Paris was reported in the London press. The following March, Edward
Mellish reported from Blois: 'Sr. Thomas Twisden asked the Dr [King] to
drink a bottle of Extraordinary, upon which the Dr replyed if you insist
upon it, I shall make you repent of it upon which there was a trial of skill;
and Sr. Thomas was wursted, and was obliged to quit the field of battle
and retired to bed.' In August 1734 the Duke of Queensberry's party 'went
drunk to bed' at Brussels. Nine years later Horace Walpole directed his
acid at the pretensions of 'the Dilettanti, a club, for which the nominal
qualification is having been in Italy, and the real one, being drunk: the two
chiefs are Lord Middlesex and Sir Francis Dashwood, who were seldom
sober the whole time they were in Italy'. *The Gentleman's Guide* noted, 'There is
a famous tavern or wine-cellar, where all sorts of good wines may be had,
on the road to Sèvres. The English are so accustomed to resort thither, that it
will not be difficult for any stranger to find it out.' Walker spent a sleepless
night at Milan because of the antics of a group of drunken English: 'last
night a party of them, about a dozen, drank thirty-six bottles of burgundy,
claret, and champaign, (as our landlord showed us in his book) and made
such a noise till six in the morning we could not sleep'. In 1792, Brand
complained of the 'bad sort' of English at Vienna: 'They are of the two-idea
sort – The Bottle is one.' The same year Lord Auckland, the envoy in The
Hague, reported:

> Lord Galway has been here in a state of continued intoxication, which
> must soon put an end to him: his understanding (such as it was) is
> quite gone; he lives in the streets and is incessantly in quarrels with
> the lower people: He came to me at two o'clock in the morning to
> desire protection against a Jew whom he had taken by the beard, and

by whom in return he had been treated with an unChristian severity. His servants had requested me to have him by some means sent back to his friends in England; luckily the want of money (for he spent £150 here in two days) has forced him back.[43]

Robert, 4th Viscount Galway (1752–1810), privy councillor and a Knight of the Bath, was not in fact to die soon; indeed he was re-elected to the Commons in 1796.

Critics were correct in claiming that some tourists were more interested in sex, gambling and drink than improving themselves. However, many of them would probably have acted in the same fashion at home. The Grand Tour served the useful purpose of letting people sow their wild oats abroad. Some commentators suggested that many tourists were too young: 'Of old, not boys, but men, were sent to travel, for the views of men in leaving their own country was not to see fashions, to examine how periwigs or coats were made, but to inquire into the excellency of the laws of other nations, and, by comparing them with their own supply their defects . . .' Andrews was firm on the point:

Until we are five-and-twenty, little or no benefit results to the far greater part of those who make what is called the grand tour. Nature has given to few men such talents as will enable them to travel at an earlier period. A Bacon, a Wotton, and a few others, are exceptions which will not justify the sending abroad mere youths, unacquainted with their own country, and totally unfit therefore to draw those comparisons between it and others, which are the very intent of travelling . . . I remember to have heard a Swiss gentleman of excellent capacity remark, that most of our English travellers were sent abroad much too young and inexperienced in the affairs of their country. Without a competent knowledge of which, he was positive in his conviction, that travelling became no better than a mere amusement. No man, till he had attained his four or five-and-twentieth year, was fit to judge with solidity concerning the transactions and business of his own country, much less of another, to which he was an utter stranger. The only reasonable expectation to be formed in regard to a travelling youth, was the acquisition of foreign languages. Were it not to this intent, he would often say, that no people could betray more thoughtlessness and imprudence than the English, in suffering, or rather indeed encouraging their young gentlemen to make such long and expensive excursions.

Brand, who had considerable personal experience of the difficulties presented by young charges, wrote from Dresden in 1791

I am very much concerned at a practice which gains ground every day, that of sending, not young men, but *boys* to travel thro Europe when they ought to be learning logic and mathematics in some sound seminary at home. They are launched into vicious society before they know even any theory of virtue and morality and being too childish for the company they are introduced to they lose the consideration which an Englishman has hitherto had on the Continent and they become a more easy prey to the villainous and interested of both sexes.[44]

Possibly these commentators were correct. The most perceptive and best-informed accounts of Europe written by those who travelled for pleasure, tend to have been written by older travellers such as Gardenstone, Holroyd, Mitchell and Walker. The correspondence of young tourists, and of their bearleaders, was often about debts, gambling and the purchase of clothes. On the other hand some young tourists, such as William Bentinck and Thomas Pelham, sent informed and intelligent letters. Given the length of time that a major tour entailed it was understandable that most tourists were young. Older men had their careers to pursue, their estates to manage; not that either of these precluded many from foreign trips, albeit often short ones to Paris, such as those Lord Fife took in the 1760s or that Lord Cassillis made in 1788. Older men who travelled for a long time tended to have a specific reason: health and/or retirement as with Gardenstone, Sir Richard Lyttelton and Sir Humphrey Morice; the death of a spouse as with Mitchell and Lord Stormont; or a need, often fiscal or political, to be out of Britain.

Thomas Barrett-Lennard (1717–86) went to Italy in 1750 with his wife, Anne, following the death of their child. However, some older men did take long trips for pleasure. The very wealthy Joseph Leeson, later first Earl of Milltown (1701–83), visited Rome in 1744–5 and also 1750. Sir Matthew Fetherstonhaugh (1714?–74) travelled in France, Italy and Austria with his wife and several relations in 1749–52. James Alexander (1730–1802), a very wealthy Ulster landowner who had made a fortune in the East India Company, visited Rome with his wife in 1777.

These were exceptions however. Most older men could not spare several years for a foreign tour, and the Grand Tour in the strict sense, the protracted trip to France and Italy, tended to remain the prerogative of youth. As such it fulfilled a major social need, namely the necessity of finding for young men, who were not obliged to work and for whom work would often be a derogation, something to do between school and settling into matrimony. University could only be a temporary stopgap as few scions of the aristocracy stayed for three years or read for a degree. Foreign travel filled the gap. It was expensive, but less expensive than many parliamentary contests. It allowed the young to sow their wild oats abroad and it kept them out of trouble, including disputes with their family, at home. A certain amount of drinking, gaming and wenching was an acceptable cost of the system.

NOTES

1. Bod. Mss. Douce 67 pp. 74–6.
2. BL Add. 31192 f. 12.
3. A. Moore, *Norfolk and the Grand Tour* (Norwich, 1985), pp. 17, 147–8; Francis, BL Add. 40759 f. 20; Stanford and Finopoulos (eds), *Charlemont* p. 5; Tavistock to Upper Ossory, 29 July 1764, Russell; Journal possibly by Marmaduke William Constable-Maxwell, Hull UL DDEV 61/1; Sackville, Hull UL, DDHo/4/23; Beinecke, Osborn Shelves c 200.
4. *Craftsmen* 21 July (os) (1739); *Gentleman's Guide* pp. 124–5.
5. Rockingham to Essex, 2 Feb. 1734, BL Add. 27733; Hotham to Dear Cousin, 14 Sept. 1754, Buckinghamshire to Hotham, 14 June –, Hull UL DDHo/4/5, 6; Shaw, *Letters to a Nobleman* (1709), xx.
6. Beinecke, Osborn Shelves c 366 1 p. 91; HW vol. 52 f. 129, 145, 53, 86.
7. Black, 'Fit for a king', *History Today*, 37 (April 1987), p. 3.
8. HW vol. 51 f. 140.
9. Digby to Hanbury Williams, 4 Dec. 1751, HW vol. 54.
10. HW vol. 67 f. 203–9.
11. P. Langford, *A Polite and Commercial People, England 1727–1783* (Oxford, 1989) concentrates on middle-class gentility, pp. 59–121.
12. Black and J. Gregory (eds), *Culture, Politics and Society in Britain 1660–1800* (Manchester, 1991) pp. 3–9.
13. E.M. Bénabou, *La Prostitution et la Police des Moeurs au XVIIIe Siècle* (Paris, 1987); *General Evening Post* 12 Sept. (os) 1734; Thompson I, 31; Glenorchy to Duke of Kent, 13 Jan. 1721, Bedford CRO L30/8/10/8.
14. *London Evening Post* 27 Jan. (os), *Daily Advertiser* 27 Jan. (os) 1737; *St James's Chronicle* 12, 17 May 1764; Thicknesse 1768, pp. 169–70, 179–80; Hervey to Richmond, 27 Dec. (os) 1733, Bury St Edmunds CRO 941/47/25; *Owen's Weekly Chronicle* 1 Sept. 1764; *Newcastle Courant* 18 Dec. 1784; *Felix Farley's Bristol Journal* 5 Jan. 1788; Pottle (ed.), *Boswell* p. 250; Foote, *The Capuchin* (1776): Sir Harry Hamper and Mademoiselle Mouche.
15. Rolt, *Crawford* pp. 52, 55; PRO 78/201 f. 181; H. Duranton (ed.), *Journal de la Cour et de Paris* (St Etienne, 1981), 28 Nov. 1732, 1 June 1733; BL Add. 51345 f. 73; M. Vallet de la Touche to Hardwicke, 4 Jan. 1737, BL Add. 35586; J. Mackay to Charles Hotham, 8 Jan. 1752, Hull UL DDHo/4/5; Winchester CRO, Malmesbury vol. 159; S. Checkland, *The Elgins, 1766–1917* (Aberdeen, 1988), pp. 15–16; HL, Loudoun papers 11333; Aylesbury, Buckinghamshire RO D/LE 2/13.
16. Francis, BL Add. 40759 f. 20; Stevens p. 360; Pococke, BL Add. 22978 f. 84; HMC *Denbigh* V, 221; Horace Walpole, *Commonplace Book* p. 293; Tavistock to Upper Ossory, 12 Sept. 1763, Russell.

17. P. Jenkins, *The making of a ruling class. The Glamorgan gentry 1640–1790* (Cambridge, 1983) pp. 227–8; HW vol. 52 f. 115; Ms. Cardiff 4/7.

18. *Yale Edition of Horace Walpole's Correspondence* 30, 6.

19. Lincoln to Newcastle, – April 1741; BL Add. 33065 f. 406.

20. *Horace Walpole's Correspondence* 30, 43–6, 74, 1.

21. HW vol. 69 f. 80–1.

22. M. Wyndham, *Chronicle of the Eighteenth Century* I, 21; *Queen of the Blues* I, 121; HL Mo 1313, 1315; *Walpole Correspondence*, 21, 156, 162; Tavistock to Robinson, 10 April, 22 Dec. 1762, Russell vols 45, 46; Trevor to Keith, 15 Dec. 1785, BL Add. 35535; J.P. Shipley, *James Ralph: Pretender to Genius* (Columbia, PhD, 1963) p. 380; Mann–Walpole Correspondence IV, 284; *St James's Chronicle* 23 May, 8 Aug. 1765; *Westminster Journal* 9 Jan. 1773; *Welbeck Abbey* II, 37; NLS Ms. 5539 f. 74, 5541 f. 136.

23. HP II, 37; Murray to Keith, 11 Nov. 1785, BL Add. 35535.

24. *Harcourt Papers* III, 3; BL Add. 24157 f. 138; Craven, *Memoirs* I, 71; Knight, pp. 210–11; BL Add. 34444 f. 73; Petworth Archives 6320, 8 Mar. 1730; Nottingham UL NeC 2406; B. Fothergill, *Sir William Hamilton* (1969) pp. 163–6.

25. Swinton, 2 Nov. (os) 1730; Davenant to Stair, 8 Dec. 1716, SRO GD 135/141/6; Bod. Ms. Douce 67 p. 46; Fothergill, *Beckford of Fonthill* (1979) pp. 85, 182; NLS Ms. 5549 f. 59, 99–100; Buckinghamshire to Hotham, 12 July 1783, Hull UL DDHo/4/22.

26. *Auckland Correspondence* I, 399; Riddell to Keith, 6 July 1784, BL Add. 35532; Brand to Wharton, 3 Jan. 1791, Durham, Wharton; HW 67 f. 169.

27. Brand to Wharton, undated, Durham, Wharton; HW 67 f. 159; *Newcastle Journal* 29 Aug. 1752.

28. Brand to Wharton, 17 Nov. 1783, 26 Mar. 1793, Durham, Wharton.

29. BL Add. 69288 Nos 19–20, 69289 Nos 13–16; Wharton to his mother, 18 May, Wharton to Thomas Lloyd, 21 Sept., Wharton to Miss Raine, 7 Oct. 1775, Durham, Wharton; Chester CRO DBW/N/Bundle E, Packet A.

30. Memoir by Lady Louisa Stuart as introduction to *Letters and Journals of Lady Mary Coke* (1889–96) I, lii-liv; Horace Walpole *Correspondence* 30, 19.

31. Beinecke, Osborn Shelves c 331; Matlock CRO 239 M/.O 518; Constable–Maxwell?, Hull UL DDEV 61/1; *Harcourt Papers* III, 13; Bentinck, BL Eg. 1711 f. 610; Windham p. 4.

32. Mellish to father, 25 April 1731, Nottingham CRO, Mellish.

33. Fox to Lord Fitzwilliam, 27 Oct. 1767, BL Add. 47576; Earl of Ilchester (ed.), *Henry Fox, First Lord Holland* (2 vols, 1920) I, 170.

34. Thompson I, 32.

35. Mitchell, BL Add. 58314 f. 8, 27.

36. Sarah Marlborough to Fish, 12 Oct. (os) 1727, BL Add. 61444; Mellish to John Gore, 17 Nov. 1730, Mellish to father, 25 Feb., 18 April 1731, Nottingham CRO, Mellish; Wyndham, *Chronicles* I, 115–16.

37. Charles Stanhope to 3rd Duke of Marlborough, 30 Sept. 1729, BL Add. 61667; Wyndham, *Chronicles* I, 10, 16; Harry to Thomas Pelham, 6 Nov. 1776, BL Add. 33127; *Daily Universal Register* 5 Sept. 1786.

38. Montagu to Earl of Albemarle, Ambassador in Paris, 24 Dec. 1751, judgement of court, 21 Aug., J. Jeffreys to Hardwicke, 23 Aug., Albemarle to Newcastle,

31 Aug. 1752, BL Add. 32832, 35630 f. 49, 48, 32839; HP II, 461; Knight pp. 10, 31; *Deffand–Walpole correspondence* V, 6.

39. Walker p. 36; Thicknesse 1786, pp. 4, 102–10, 126–45.

40. Stanhope to 3rd Duke of Marlborough, undated, BL Add. 61667 f. 86; Horatio Walpole to Robert Trevor, 5 April (os), 3 May (os) 1737, Trevor Mss vols 7, 8; Balderston (ed.), *Goldsmith* p. 24; Pottle (ed.), *Boswell* pp. 176, 200, 238, 261.

41. *St James's Chronicle* 28 Dec. 1771; Brand to Wharton, 3 Jan. 1791, 26 Jan. 1793, Durham, Wharton; Knight pp. 176, 179; Tavistock to Robinson, 22 Dec. 1762, Russell vol. 46; Haggerston to Anderton, 20 Dec. 1717, Thornton to Anderton, 31 Sept. 1718, NRO Haggerston.

42. Bentinck to mother, 14 June 1727, BL Eg 1711.

43. Maclaurin f. 200, Aberdeen UL; *London Evening Post* 21 May (os) 1730; Edward Mellish to father, 12 Mar. 1731, Nottingham UL Mellish; Queensberry, BL Add. 22626 f. 69; *Walpole–Mann correspondence* II, 211; *Gentleman's Guide* p. 231; Walker p. 381; Brand to Wharton, 30 June 1792, Durham, Wharton; BL Add. 58920 f. 100.

44. *Mist's Weekly Journal* 18 Sept. (os) 1725; Andrews pp. 1–2, 18–19; Brand to Wharton, 20 Aug. 1791, Durham, Wharton.

10

SOCIAL AND POLITICAL REFLECTIONS

The road from Naples as far as Barletta is very good, for which the public is obliged to the King's liking the chase of Bovino; as it is obliged for the road from Naples to Rome, to His Majesty's being married; – Kings in these regions are not Kings of the people, but the People, People of the Kings.

William Young, 1772[1]

. . . there is a little policy working at such times as the Carnival, and it is actually a measure of Government, not merely to wink at excesses, but even to furnish the poorer sort with money to produce them; for the more debauched men are, the more abject and the more contented under their slavery they become, and, deluded by the false glare of riot and intemperance, the less likely are they to form reflections which in the end might be dangerous to their Tyrant! I know it is the fashion to say that the lower classes of people in France are happy and contented – I own I have my doubts about it. There is a sort of *rivalship* in gaiety, and probably the effect of habit; but they have many *actual* wants, and though they sing away their cares, it is like the moaning song, perhaps, of a poor weak child who puts himself to sleep that way.

Frances Crewe, Paris, 1786[2]

. . . the finest country in the world ruined by the badness of the government and people literally dying of hunger in the granary of Europe.

Sir James Hall, Sicily, 1785[3]

In an important recent article Heinz-Joachim Müllenbrock has suggested that a shift in the nature of English travel literature took place during the eighteenth century. He claimed that in the opening decades of the century it was characterized by a political fervour directed against arbitrary power, and that in the second half of the century a shift occurred towards a more tolerant stance: 'English writers slowly groped their way towards a more conciliatory treatment of other countries.' Müllenbrock suggested that the 1760s 'saw the beginning of a tentative emancipation from the conventional Whig attitude towards the outside world'. English travel literature became more sympathetic to countries hitherto grossly stereotyped and 'former ideological prejudices were shed'.[4]

Müllenbrock's thesis is an important one, particularly as it draws attention to the need for an analysis of how the ideology of the Grand Tour altered with time. Britain's political situation vis-à-vis the Continent changed dramatically in the eighteenth century. In the first years of the century, before Marlborough's victories, France under Louis XIV still represented a major threat to Britain and appeared capable of dominating Europe. However, Marlborough's victories, the peaceful accession of the Hanoverian dynasty (1714), the suppression of the 1715 Jacobite uprising, French weakness in the 1710s and early 1720s and the Anglo-French alliance of 1716–31 produced a period of relative self-confidence that reflected the diminution of the French threat.

In the 1730s and 1740s the situation changed again. The collapse of the Anglo-French alliance in 1731, French successes in the War of the Polish Succession (1733–5) and the growth of French naval and colonial power in the 1730s reawakened British fears of France, which had not been forgotten during the years of alliance. There was a marked increase in the expression of xenophobic sentiment in the press in the late 1730s. The War of the Austrian Succession (1740–8) was inconclusive politically, but it damaged British self-confidence. Britain failed to sweep Spain from the West Indies and British armies failed to repeat Marlborough's successes. Richard Hopkins was worried by what he saw of French strength in 1749. At Nantes he was

> much surprised and indeed sorry, to see so much appearance of wealth and commerce, the more so when from many hands I was assured there was not a merchant in the town who had not lost almost all their vessels in the war, and . . . that they had nevertheless lost nothing by it, for they were all insured in London . . . in every river, in every seaport town, nay in every ditch, they are building to restore, rather to increase their commerce above what it was at the beginning of the last war.

It was not until the Seven Years War (1756–63) that Britain defeated France in the struggle for colonial hegemony. These victories and a growing economic strength led to a sense of national complacency that was tempered, but not obscured, by fears concerning domestic and European developments. Subsequently defeat and national isolation during the American Rebellion led again to uncertainty and pessimism that did not lift until 1787, when growing signs of French internal difficulties and British success in the Dutch crisis, led to a revival in optimism. Britain's international status experienced, therefore, considerable change and this was related closely to shifts in national self-confidence. The optimism of the early 1760s had been replaced by pessimism twenty years later. Any European commentator asked in 1780 to predict which European country would experience revolution before the end of the decade would have selected Britain, not France.

The degree to which these shifts were reflected in the attitudes of tourists is not easy to interpret. With printed works there is the difficulty often of establishing the date of authorship. Did printed journal entries relate to the period of the tour, which is not always easy to determine, or were they altered or written later? In some cases there was a substantial gap of time. Sacheverell Stevens began his tour in September 1738. His *Miscellaneous Remarks made on the Spot* . . . did not have a publication date, but the dedication was dated 3 July 1756. When such comments in the book as these were written is unclear:

> I beg leave to conclude with the following short reflection, which is, that if, from the foregoing faithful account of the wretched and miserable state of slavery and subjection, both ecclesiastical and civil, both in body and soul, other nations are reduced to by their arbitrary tyrannical governors, one single reader should be made sensible of the inestimable blessings he enjoys, be upon his guard against any attempts that may be made to deprive him of them, either by wicked ministers at home, or by enemies from abroad, and become a better subject, or a sincerer Christian and Protestant, it will afford me the highest satisfaction, and I shall flatter myself, that I have not altogether laboured or lived in vain.[5]

Such a statement makes blatant the ideological intentions of the author, as indeed did Stevens's dedication to Augusta, the Princess Dowager of Wales:

> The following faithful Narrative will plainly show under what a dreadful yoke the wretched people of other nations groan, their more than Egyptian task-masters having impiously robbed them of the use of that glorious faculty, their reason, deprived them of their properties, and all this under the sacred sanction of religion; . . . they thus

miserably lie under the scourge of the tyrant's rod, and the merciless phangs of ecclesiastical power, . . .

However, despite these statements, Stevens's lengthy book is remarkably short of ideological comments and is largely devoted to the mechanics of tourism. It could be suggested that he added the conclusion, as he certainly added the dedication, at a later date, and that to concentrate upon them is to misunderstand the emphasis of the work. In some cases ideological comments should be treated as a convention that reflects what was expected in the genre rather than the opinions of the writers. There is often, with these comments, a sense of artificial interjection and conscious striving after effect. This is similar to some of the paeans to nature that occurred towards the end of the century, such as John Villiers's rhapsody on the sublime vastness of the Channel and the sense of grandeur that this awakened in his soul, when the reader would rather have expected vigorous puking.[6]

Given this convention in the printed sources, it is not surprising to find that the essentially private unprinted tourists' accounts are somewhat lacking in ideological content. In so far as tourists made ideological remarks they tended to concentrate upon religious factors. These factors were both far more overt and more obviously different from the situation in Britain. It was easier to note the plentiful presence of crucifixes and wayside shrines, the pomp, magnificence and alien quality of Catholic ceremonies and the large number of clerics than it was to perceive the role of the French *Parlements*, the nature of political power in German principalities or the fiscal system in their Italian counterparts. Furthermore, once a tourist had noted the more obvious political differences, such as the greater number of soldiers in Berlin, there was little variation about the political systems that he encountered in much of Europe that aroused notice and therefore comment.

Much comment centred upon states that were republics – the United Provinces, Switzerland, Genoa, Venice, Lucca and San Marino. Most remarks were, however, brief and impressionistic. This was only to be expected, given the difficulty of assessing a foreign political system when most of the attempt to do so had to be conducted in a foreign language. A further problem was that tourists tended to visit only the major cities of states and so could often only grasp a metropolitan perspective on political developments.[7] The theme that Paris was not France was repeated by several writers because they feared that the attractions of life in Paris would blind susceptible tourists to the realities of life elsewhere in the country. Tourists who visited Berlin and Vienna and stopped elsewhere in the Prussian and Austrian dominions merely to sleep (apart usually from a day in Prague) would only have a limited understanding of the political systems of these countries. The same was even more true for the small number of tourists who visited Denmark, Portugal, Russia and Sweden. Capitals displayed the power and prestige of monarchy and gave the impression of autocratic, often efficient, states. They were a poor guide to the compromise between monarchical centralization and aristocratic particularism that underlay so much of the so-called absolutisms of the period. This was true, for example, of France, where the authority, and still more, the power of the monarch were limited. If they realized this, few tourists troubled to record it. They were, however, correct in stressing the manner in which Catholicism aided state authority. States such as France, Austria and Spain owed their political stability not so much to coercion, as to the ideological consensus of obedience and community that stemmed largely from Catholicism, although in France this was compromised by the Gallican and Jansenist controversies. By drawing attention to the interrelationships of Catholicism and political power, tourists perceived the strength and stability of many states. However, their conclusions concerning the impact of this relationship, particularly its supposed deleterious effect upon the economy, society and morality, were often shallow and inaccurate, reflecting prejudice rather than perception.[8]

Tourists often had an opportunity to acquire a certain amount of political information. Well-connected tourists spent much of their time at courts or in court society. This was true of the German, Iberian and Scandinavian states, and of Russia, although it was not true of France, the Low Countries and Italy. The Brussels court of the Austrian governor and the Hague court of the Prince of Orange were visited, but were not centres of interest and activity for many tourists. British tourists in Italy were presented often to the Pope, the Kings of Naples and Sardinia, the Grand Duke of Tuscany, the Dukes of Parma and Modena and the Governor of Milan, but their courts did not dominate the pastimes of British tourists to the peninsula, with the exception of the King of Sardinia's court at Turin. Versailles was visited by many British tourists but few spent much time in court society. In Paris, however, there was no shortage of opportunities for acquiring information and opinion concerning political developments. Archibald Macdonald (1747–1826), later Attorney-General, wrote from Fontainebleau in 1764:

> A British subject ought of all others to be most curious to see a court so different from ours; and a king who is feasted every hour of the day with some fresh object of dissipation in order to distract his attention from those matters which he is supposed alone to direct and on which he alone ultimately decides: to see the different manners which are fallen upon of laying siege to this single man, who becomes at last a mere automate.

In court society well-connected tourists could expect to be favourably treated. They would be received by the monarch, would dine often at court, would be permitted to attend court functions, particularly balls and royal hunting parties, would mix in a society of ministers and diplomats and have their activities supervised and entrées arranged by British envoys. These activities were regarded as an essential part of the social education of tourists and they could also be very enjoyable. Lord Pelham wrote to his son, Thomas, in 1777: 'I wish much to have you introduced to all Courts, for though they are not always equally agreeable yet the best company at every place must resort to Court.' The Earl of Essex found his visit to Munich in 1751 boring because of the absence of the court. Edward Southwell the younger encountered the same problem at Turin in 1725.[9]

Court society continued to be reasonably open to tourists even if diplomatic relations with Britain were tense. Despite a press report in 1725 that poor Anglo-Austrian relations had led to a bad reputation for British tourists in Vienna, Edward Southwell the younger was well received the following year. The Duke of Richmond was extremely well received at Madrid in 1728, 'as no other stranger can boast of'. He was allowed to hunt with Philip V, a great honour.[10]

Southwell's good reception at Vienna reflected the strength and number of his letters of introduction: 'wherever he went, he found extraordinary reception being recommended with a portmantle full of letters to the greatest powers in every Court'. Indeed he took more than ten letters to Vienna. Letters of introduction were essential for a good reception in court society and they ensured the continued dominance by high-ranking tourists (with the addition of military men) of travel in Germany in the latter half of the century, at a time when increasing numbers of the 'middling orders' were visiting France, the Low Countries and Switzerland. A tourist recorded of his arrival in Lunéville in August 1720: 'gave our letter to Baron Sauter who received us very civilly carried us to the play and got us presented to both their Royal Highnesses. The Duke spoke to us in German very civilly.' In 1734, Richard Pococke had letters for the great Italian scholar, Muratori; Mitchell for the Sardinian foreign minister, Ormea. George, Viscount Mandeville's tour of Italy in 1758 was assisted by the British envoy in Naples, his bearleader writing from Milan that May, 'We are still sensible of Sir James Gray's obliging behaviour. His recommendation to Monsignore Picolomini at Rome introduced us to the nuncio at Venice, whose letter to the Duchess Serbelloni of the Case Ottobini, and one of the first rank, presented us to the chief of the nobility in this city.'

Thomas Pelham found his progress eased by numerous letters in 1776–7. He was taken to an assembly by the Governor of Cordoba, given dinner by the Captain General of Spain, who arranged transport for him to Cadiz, and was given nine letters alone for Naples by a leading Spanish courtier. In Turin, he found that 'Lord Grantham's letter to the Spanish Ambassador and Comte Massin's to a lady here has procured me the acquaintance of the first people in this Court . . .' In Rome he benefited from a letter to the Spanish nuncio and in Genoa 'in respect to Society my letters from Spain procured me that of the first people here'. Unsurprisingly he stressed the importance of such introductions:

> . . . with regard to Paris . . . I find that it is necessary to be furnished with the most particular recommendations to gain admission into the society of the people of fashion, and that without a residence of some time your acquaintance with people of merit and distinction will be much confined; for the generality, not to say all the English, who have been at Paris lately have conducted themselves in such a manner as to be shunned universally and consequently obliged to live at publick places and in such *company* as may be found more or less in every town.

Despite Anglo-French hostilities, a letter introduced Philip Yorke to the hospitality of the French Cardinal Bernis in 1778, while Charles Drake Garrard delayed his journey to Montpellier until he could receive the necessary letters. Brand, dissatisfied with the response to his letters in 1780, found them useful in Paris in 1781, Bologna in 1783 and The Hague in 1789–90, and suffered from the lack of them at Dijon in 1786 and Heidelberg in 1791. Aikin and Levett Hanson benefited from letters at Rotterdam and Milan respectively; Thicknesse and Townsend recommended them for Spain; and Andrews for France. The Earl of Radnor observed in 1783 'that there have been so many impositions at foreign courts, as to make a proper introduction extremely desirable'. Four years later, the Marquis of Lansdowne informed the Abbé André Morellet, one of the contributors to the *Encyclopédie*, that his heir, Earl Wycombe had set off for 'Dijon and Lyons in preference to Switzerland, which may be better as he cannot see too much of France, provided he keeps out of English company there. I hope you have given or procured him letters to the Church, so that he may go from one bishop to another.' Dalrymple sought a letter at Strasbourg in 1789 in order to refute a damaging 'report of my being a person of extreme low birth, who ought not to be taken notice of by anybody of rank and consequence in the town'.[11]

Thus, letters of introduction could serve to introduce tourists to the highest ranks of European society, and, as it was mainly from these ranks that the ministers of princes were drawn, they provided ample opportunity to broaden political understanding. Acquiring social skills, not political information, was the principal purpose of being at court, and the Earl of Huntingdon, who saw the Duchess of Parma perform in a palace production of an opera, or the numerous aristocrats who enjoyed hunting expeditions with the court, were 'typical' tourists.[12] However, attendance at court did provide opportunities to meet the powerful. Accepting the criticism of tourists as gleaning 'every vice and folly they meet with', *The Universal Spectator* of 3 April 1742 nevertheless declared:

> we have, however some exceptions, and some young noblemen who have done an honour to their country abroad; and by acquiring a knowledge of men, of commerce, of the interests and tempers of foreign courts, with the different policies of different nations, will be of service to their country at home. Lord Halifax, in the House of Peers, and Lord Quarendon, in the Commons, are illustrious examples for the young British gentry.

The *Public Advertiser* of 3 March 1792 stated: 'it must give great pleasure to the impartial observer, that the debate on Wednesday turned upon the great questions of the Laws of Nations, and of the interests of Europe, which were treated so ably by young travellers, who have acquired their information upon the large scale of the Continent of Europe'.

Lord Euston was received by Charles Emmanuel III of Sardinia in 1734 and the King discussed Anglo-Sardinian relations and the international situation with the young man, leading a British diplomat to send a report on the conversation. Doubtless this reflected the fact that Euston's father, the Duke of Grafton, George II's Lord Chamberlain, was a royal favourite. Though in Thomas Pelham's reception by the Austrian first minister, Count Kaunitz, 'all political questions are carefully avoided', when Pelham went to see the Portuguese first minister, Pombal, at his country house he was given an audience of four hours: Pombal 'talked a great deal of the expulsion of the Jesuits out of Portugal and the attempt against his own life in the execution of it with the firmness and composure of an Old Roman'. William Lee, son of the Lord Chief Justice of King's Bench, was received by Frederick the Great at Potsdam in July 1753

> with great politeness and affability. He not only asked us from whence we came and where we were going which are generally the royal questions to foreigners, but talked much to us about Italy and particularly about the state of Herculaneum . . . he asked many questions about England, joked upon the naturalization of the Jews . . . as they will have the power of purchasing lands they will likewise have a power of being members of Parliament says he unless you have restrictive clauses to prevent them. He talked to us I believe a quarter of an hour with the same ease and affability as men of equal

rank would converse together . . . he conversed with the same ease at dinner as he did before. Asked a thousand questions, enquired much after my Lord Chesterfield, Lord Granville . . . The English foxhunters he seemed not to hold in the highest veneration. They are a race of people says he who are obliged medicinally to use that hard exercise from the great quantity of beef and pudding that they eat and the punch which they drink.

Randle Wilbraham, however, wrote home from Vienna in 1794, 'Although we are as you justly observe in the centre of politics, yet they are seldom if ever the topic of conversation, as despotic governments are not favourable to free discussions upon these topics, we therefore only hear of facts without any comments.'

When Lord Hervey discussed the abilities of Charles Emmanuel III with George II and Queen Caroline in 1733, he was able to speak with authority on the basis of 'the short acquaintance he had with him five years ago at the Court of Turin'. In a parliamentary debate on Anglo-Prussian relations eight years later 'Ld. Baltimore said he knew the King of Prussia personally and he was sure that a precipitate resolution of this House at the end of the last session lost the King of Prussia to the Emperor'.[13] Whether or not tourists got the opportunity of discussing political issues with rulers and ministers, those who wished to could acquire the 'diplomatic habit', and for most this was the real political benefit of their court attendances.

Tourists who visited courts were not the only travellers who discussed politics. In 1714, James Hume had a long discussion with an Irish merchant at St Malo concerning Anglo-French commercial relations. In 1725 Edward Southwell discussed the international situation with members of the British diplomatic mission at the peace congress at Cambrai. In 1729 the British envoy in Brussels commented on awareness of desire for the return of Gibraltar to Spain: 'Travellers observe with amazement the general eagerness of the people, throughout these countries, for the said restitution, and the invidious eye with which they see Great Britain possessed of that place, as if their own welfare was at stake by it.' The following year the Duke of Norfolk, dining at the British envoy's in Paris, remarked 'upon the French hating of us'. In 1731, Thomas Robinson MP, who had dined recently with Cardinal Fleury, the leading French minister, also commented on French hostility to Britain.

Swinton's journal contained many remarks on the political situation in Italy. In June 1731, travelling to Paris, he was accompanied by a Castilian aristocrat, who discussed recent Italian history with him, and added: 'The English must never think of being friends with the Spaniards till Gibraltar and Minorca were restored, but withall added that the Spaniards could never take those places by force of arms as long as the English continued masters of the sea.' In 1740, Chesterfield referred in Parliament to the knowledge acquired by travellers: 'Do not our common news-papers, does not every traveller that comes from abroad, inform us, that our conduct in the war is ridiculed and hooted at in every court, and in every city in Europe?' In Italy in 1769 William Drake was often asked why the British ministry was not supporting the Corsicans against France. In 1785 a newspaper cited as its source for a report that France was likely to support the Dutch against Austria, a letter that a London politician (possibly Lansdowne) had received from his travelling son. The same year William Bennet dined at a table d'hôte in Lucerne and commented: 'there was a very large company, and a dispute about liberty begun by the French Marquis who did not know what liberty was, and asserted his own nation was freer than ours. I was glad to see all the Swiss present inclined to the English side . . .'[14]

As some tourists clearly did discuss politics, it is not surprising that criticism of travel was expressed on this account. On the grounds of politics, tourism could be attacked either because of specific views that a tourist might adopt, particularly Jacobite views, or because of the danger that he might sympathize with European political practices, particularly absolutism. One of the leading opposition London newspapers, the *Craftsman*, noted in 1728 of a tourist recently returned from Italy: 'I was extremely pleased to find, that notwithstanding his travels into countries of slavery and arbitrary power, he was still full of those noble and virtuous sentiments, which are so peculiar to us Englishmen and so much to our honour.' Nine years later a speaker in a fiscal debate in the Commons claimed:

. . . our travellers who make but very superficial enquiries into the manners or customs of any country they pass through, may perhaps imagine the people in France or Holland are more heavily, or more oppressively taxed, than the people of this Kingdom, because they hear the people complain there as well as they do here; but any gentleman who understands these things, and has made a proper enquiry, may soon be convinced of the contrary.

Later in the century, John Richard, writing at Bremen, suggested that northern Europe was of little interest to most tourists. His point was important, as it was in Austria, Prussia and Russia that the most significant political developments were taking place in the second half of the century – until the French Revolution changed almost everything. Richard claimed:

This part of the world would furnish no entertainment to a young traveller, who seeks no other end in his travels than amusement or gallantry, masquerades or operas; nor would he, in Westphalia or the neighbouring countries, be the admiration of the ladies, merely for being a coxcomb. Such persons do very wisely, in beginning their tour, by shutting their eyes till they arrive at Paris, and endeavouring to sleep between city and city till they arrive at Rome or Venice.

It was certainly true that comparatively few tourists, other than military men, visited Berlin and St Petersburg. However, it is by no means true that all those who visited France and Italy were motivated by hedonism, or that hedonistic interests were incompatible with perceptive observations.[15]

It is the duty every man owes his country, to observe the methods of government used in other states, and adopt that which is founded on wisdom and true policy into their own ... a strict regard is to be had to the particular turn of our own constitution; for what may be a necessary step in one state, may prove to be the destruction of another ...

Thomas Robinson, House of Commons, 1734

In 1738 the Oxford don, Joseph Spence (1699–1768), who successively accompanied Charles, Earl of Middlesex, John Trevor, later an MP and a Lord of the Admiralty, and Henry, 9th Earl of Lincoln as bearleader, wrote to William Burrell Massingberd, then in Paris:

I need not tell you that the chief thing for a gentleman to attend to anywhere abroad, is the laws and constitution, the polity and temper of the nation he is in; its good, and its bad institutions; its strengths, and its weaknesses. The chief point for a gentleman to drive in England, especially in our days, is to make some appearance in our Parliament: and all these things may be of use to him on some occasion or another there. All this sort of knowledge is better got from the conversation of knowing men, than from books.[16]

An assessment of the political reflections in accounts left by eighteenth-century British tourists suggests that Müllenbrock's concept of a stridently Whig travel literature becoming more conciliatory is not appropriate in the case of tourist accounts that were not designed for publication. Tourists were rarely as histrionic or rhetorical as travel literature in the early eighteenth century, but they manifested in general a tempered criticism of what they saw. This continued to be the case in the latter half of the century, although there are changes that can be discerned. First, whereas in the first half of the century most political reflections related to the situation in France, Italy, Switzerland and the Low Countries, in the second half there was increased interest in the Empire, and, in particular, in Austria and Prussia. The Emperor Joseph II's policies in the 1770s and 1780s attracted particular interest. His policies of secularism and 'Enlightened Despotism' came to the attention of many tourists in the Austrian Netherlands and Austria. Randle Wilbraham wrote from Vienna in 1794 about

> the court at Vienna. The fact is there is none, that ceremony having been broken through by Joseph the Second, both from hatred of form and from wish to lower the pride of the noblesse who during the reign of Maria Theresa were the only body of men considered. Joseph had sense enough to perceive that mercantile people were of more solid advantage to his country than counts and barons the whole merit of many of whom consisted in having 16 quarters on their coats of arms. He therefore endeavoured as much as possible to raise the former and mortify the latter, but proceeded like most reformers with unwarrantable violence, sanguinely expecting to realise, in the course of a few years, a plan which it was obvious to all but himself would require many ages thoroughly to accomplish.

Again, in the second half of the century, there was less stress on religious differences. The importance of confessional strife diminished markedly in Europe and the secular, often anti-clerical, policies of many Catholic rulers, symbolized by the expulsion of the Jesuits from the whole of Catholic Europe, rendered obsolete the picture of mutually reinforcing absolutism and Catholicism that was so strong an element in early eighteenth-century travel literature. In the case of this literature, it can be suggested that Müllenbrock over-emphasized the extent to which there was an ideological shift during the century. Although some works in the latter decades were relatively free from former ideological prejudices the majority were not, and the overwhelming assumption, stated frequently, was that Britain was the best country to live in. On the other hand, though the underlying assumptions remained, the stridency disappeared. This can be seen as an ideological shift, to which changing attitudes to religious differences and the improved relative position of Britain both contributed.

In the first half of the century tourists agreed that much about the political system of most Continental states was inequitable. Royal authority was held to be too great and this was believed to be against the interests of the people, whose wretched condition was held up as evidence of the drawbacks of absolutism. Tancred Robinson, who travelled on the Continent in 1683–4, observed, 'The inhabitants of cities, towns (the capital ones excepted) appear very miserable and poor, and the country naked of all gentry; the miserable effects of arbitrary governments. The people generally dispirited and desirous of liberty.' Richard Creed, who was in Rome in the winter of 1699–1700, wrote, 'The country or Campania of Rome turns to very little account; there not being people to manage it, it is naturally low, but for want of care is all boggy; and so produces a very ill unwholesome air; the Roman government depopulates and ruins all the country; here it ruins the soil as well as the body.'

In theory it could be expected that all systems of government were relative. An anonymous description of Germany stated 'no Country or People can be said to be great or small, good or bad, unless when compared to others'. Joseph Shaw wrote, 'where the People are most wisely and best taken care of, according to their Climate, Situation, Religion, Laws and Customs, that seems the best Government, at least for that people: And hence it is that almighty God, who with watchful eyes governs the world, had ordained so many different forms of government in it'.[17] Such moderate statements did not prevent slashing attacks upon European autocracies from being written. Shaw's vigorous denunciations of France and praise of Dutch social policy is understandable as Britain was then allied with the Dutch in a war against France. However, a similar stance, though less obsessively anti-French, was maintained during the years of the Anglo-French alliance. An anonymous tourist of 1720–1 wrote:

> Such a length is expiring liberty come to in France, [that] it would be well worth while for the noisy supporters of that destructive authority (as hereditary right not to be resisted gives to princes) in England, to spend a little time in France; and see the dismal effects of such principles as that a man can call nothing his own, neither life, nor fortune, nor are the affairs of the church in a much better condition.

In 1727 the ministerial *London Journal* printed a letter by Philopatris:

> All our travellers observe, that though France and Italy are incomparably more rich and better furnished with all the pleasures and conveniences of life, than Switzerland is, yet Italy is almost quite dispeopled, and the people in it are reduced to a misery that scarce can be imagined by those that have not seen it; and France is, in a great measure dispeopled, and the inhabitants are reduced to a poverty that appears in all the marks in which it can shew itself, both in their houses, furniture, cloaths and looks . . .[18]

This uncompromising stance was not universal. Some printed accounts praised specific details of European political organization, and others, such as the travels of Charles Thompson, were relatively free of xenophobic rhetoric. Thompson noted that in Genoa wines were not adulterated because culprits were sent to the galleys. He did not comment on this either to condemn the severity of the action or to praise the effect of strong government. John Macky wrote of the Flemings, 'They are an open, free-hearted people, like the English, and are great lovers of liberty; so that, though their religion is Roman-Catholick, they are not Priest-ridden' – a striking reversal of the usual association of absolutism and Catholicism. Another writer who printed the stock contrast of happy Switzerland and unhappy Italy, nevertheless added: 'The Peasantry of France are not rich, but free; and they have the Laws of the kingdom to protect them.' There were indeed few serfs in France. Liberty was the keynote and industry must be a sign of it, or so it was believed. Thus, John Mitford wrote in 1776:

> one cannot but admire the industry of the Savoyards throughout their country. Every spot which the art of man can render capable of producing anything, becomes fruitful under the hands of this laborious people . . . one must conceive a species of liberty is under this arbitrary government left to the peasant in a country so assiduously cultivated; the security of enjoying the property made purely his own as the sole offspring of his industry, could alone induce even the active spirit of the Savoyard to take such astonishing pains.[19]

The happiness of the French perplexed some tourists. Hume noted in 1714 that the French were happy, though oppressed. Twenty-five years later Stevens, travelling from Paris to Lyons, 'passed through several towns and villages, which had great appearance of poverty; but notwithstanding that the inhabitants were full of life and gaiety'. Such a contrast could be explained by reference to the strength and seductive appeal of Catholic indoctrination. Alternatively it could be suggested that absolutism was entirely appropriate for the French. Shaw wrote: 'the French Government, which is very severe, and as arbitrary as any under Heaven, yet best for the French, whose natures are too wicked, and too insolent to be trusted with liberty; . . . hence it is that they are so much at Union . . .' In 1729, George Lyttelton argued that: 'the French love that their monarch should be gallant, magnificent and ambitious, and do not care what price they pay for it, provided there be great news from Flanders and fine entertainments at Versailles'.[20]

Some tourists were interested in the political systems of the countries they visited. Several journals contain long, and somewhat boring, accounts of the constitutions and governmental systems encountered. These can be seen as a convention of the unpublished account, designed to show the parents at home, and possibly the writers, that the tourists were fulfilling the function of observer expected of them. On the other hand, the combination of the role of republicanism in the classical heritage and the recent experience of constitutional change in Britain made governmental systems a subject of attention. There was particular interest in those Italian states whose constitution included a republican component and comments were made about their effectiveness. Mitchell described the governments of Bologna and Venice, Parker those of Bologna and Lucca. In 1705 Metcalfe Robinson observed that Pisa 'which was so famous when a republic, is now almost dispeopled'. Edward Southwell the younger sent from Genoa some routine praise of republican liberty: 'Liberty makes even poverty tolerable, it makes a wilderness a standing water and water springs of a dry ground.' He was also capable, however, of sending from Turin brief comments on Victor Amadeus II, his policy, army, finances and government. Hervey, touring Italy with Stephen Fox, versified his comments in 1729:

> Throughout all Italy beside,
> What does one find, but Want and Pride?
> Farces of Superstitious folly,
> Decay, Distress, and Melancholy:
> The Havock of Despotick Power,
> A Country rich, its owners poor;
> Unpeopled towns, and Lands untilled,
> Bodys uncloathed, and mouths unfilled.
> The nobles miserably great,
> In painted Domes, and empty state,
> Too proud to work, too poor to eat,
> No arts the meaner sort employ,
> They nought improve, nor ought enjoy.
> Each blown from misery grows a Saint,
> He prays from Idleness, and fasts from Want.

In contrast, the more sober, and certainly less poetic, Robert Trevor and William Mildmay commented on the political situation in Lorraine in 1728 and Italy in 1730, while another tourist attributed the Regent's unpopularity in 1720 to his moves against French liberty. Hume claimed in 1714 that the French peasants were miserably oppressed by the Intendants and the tax-farmers, 'the meanest paying sometimes half their income to the Crown'. Perceval wrote from Amsterdam in 1718, 'having cursorily run over Flanders and Holland, and seen the advantages which liberty and freedom in the exercise of religion bring to mankind'. In 1732 Waldegrave wrote from Paris: 'I was surprised the other day with a visit from mylord Onslow, and you will be more surprised when I tell you his Lordship is already half a Frenchman . . . he says he never saw such a country in his life and cannot praise this, without reflecting on his own . . . he praises everything excepting some inscriptions in the Place des Victoires, which he wants to have altered.' Unfortunately there is no indication as to what led to Onslow's change of mind. Mitchell's portrayal of France was far from simplistic. He noted limits on royal absolutism and commented on the dispute between the *Parlement* of Paris and the Crown, which had been very bitter in 1730–2: 'It is true the laws concerning private property, which regulate the succession, and contacts among men are still preserved entire, . . . The Parliament seems to be the only body in the kingdom that strikes for its libertys and privileges. The King treats them as a Court of Justice but does not care they meddle in state affairs.' Commenting on the royal seizure of papers belonging to a Benedictine monastery, a prelude to attempted despoliation, Mitchell wrote: 'such proceedings occasioned very loud baulking even in France where property is not upon the surest footing'.

Some tourists did not, therefore, share the simplistic views of much travel literature. They appreciated the existence of political controversy within supposedly absolutist states, and realized that the impact of absolutism and Catholicism upon European societies was more complex than many claimed. A few praised aspects of state activity – Mildmay applauded the French roads in 1748 – and some were driven by visiting Genoa and Venice to question the received wisdom of the superiority of republics. Alan Brodrick (1702–47), later 2nd Viscount Midleton, was disabused of his notion 'of the grandeur of the noble Venetians' when he visited the Senate in September 1724.[21]

A variety of political reflections were expressed freely in the second half of the century. A good example of this was the continuing difference of opinion concerning the states where governmental authority was weak. Most could agree that Poland was not a praiseworthy state – Wraxall wrote of Cracow in 1778, six years after the First Partition of Poland by Austria, Prussia and Russia: 'It is half in ruins at this time; and the greatest happiness which can befall it would be that the Emperor would take it into his own hands.' He thought the court and kingdom 'devoid of every noble and honourable principle'. The United Provinces and Switzerland were viewed more favourably. George Keate, who spent 1756 in Geneva, published five years later his *A Short Account of the Ancient History, Present Government, and Laws of the Republic of Geneva*, which presented the republic as the temple of virtue and liberty. In 1759 Thomas Robinson, later 2nd Earl Grantham and Foreign Secretary, wrote of Berne: 'the great and laudable spirit of its citizens who in all public edifices, roads etc. spare no cost, which can make them magnificent . . . The great neatness of this town is also admirable and appeared so especially to me, as the towns of Piedmont are remarkable for their dirt.' In 1765 Thomas Pennant praised the Swiss custom of partible inheritance: 'which preserves an equality among these people'. Thicknesse claimed that the people of southern Europe were uglier than the British and the Swiss, and, attributing this to either climate or lack of liberty, he praised liberty enthusiastically. Bennet noted in Berne in 1785: 'There is a neatness and a care for the publick ease so conspicuous in all the works ordered by the Senate, the people seem so happy under their administration, that an aristocratic government begins to lose a great deal of the horror with which the dark and tyrannical councils of Venice and Genoa had inspired me.'

There was, however, less enthusiasm for republics than there had been at the beginning of the century, and this change, though not noted by Müllenbrock, would help to substantiate his claim of a move away from Whig ideology. This may have partly reflected changes in the fortunes of various European states. The United Provinces, whether it was in 'decline' or not, became relatively poorer, its one-time unique social and economic institutions were matched elsewhere, the state was affected by internal disorder, particularly in the 1750s and 1780s, and in 1780 it joined the Americans and French in the anti-British camp. The splendours of Venice and Genoa became increasingly tarnished, and Genoa was badly damaged during the siege of 1747–8. Within Italy, social, economic and political progress appeared to be most marked, not in the republics, but in the duchy of Milan and, in particular, Tuscany under Grand Duke Leopold, 1765–90. Tourists, such as Francis, making political points, contrasted Tuscany and the Papal States, rather than the republics and the non-republics. Increasing numbers of British tourists visited Switzerland, but the civil disorders in Geneva, an independent but allied state, confused the political response to Switzerland. A hint of ambivalence is present in both Bennet's and Brand's accounts. Bennet noted that the clocks in Basle were an hour fast, 'preserved unaltered' by an 'unwillingness to change' which he saw as a distinguishing feature of its government. Brand claimed that the Swiss treated Lugano, a subject district, very badly. Oliver Goldsmith wrote of the republics of Genoa, Switzerland and the United Provinces: 'the people are slaves to laws of their own making, little less than in unmixed monarchies where they are slaves to the will of one subject to frailities like themselves'. William, 2nd Earl Fitzwilliam (1748–1833) liked Geneva in 1765 and was struck by the 'order and tranquillity' with which political disputes were pursued. This rapidly ceased to be true. Visiting the city in 1782, Robert Ellison sent his British correspondents accounts of the political dissensions there.

Yet, it is important not to overemphasize any shift in attitudes towards republics. The attitude of Whig tourists towards the Italian republics at the beginning of the century was one of ambivalence. Some noted signs of corruption and oppression, while the Catholicism, however anti-clerical, of Venice, Genoa and Lucca, differentiated them from the United Provinces and the bulk of the Swiss cantons. William Mildmay, in 1730, condemned the distortion of the Genoese constitution by the nobles who sought to avoid burdens; he also thought that the frequent governmental changes in Lucca decreed by the constitution were bad for policy. Thus criticism of the Italian republics in the second half of the century was not new. It was rather the attitude to the Dutch that altered. One-time allies of Britain against Louis XIV, the Dutch were neutral in the Seven Years War and were then replaced as Britain's Protestant ally by Prussia. This was paralleled by an alteration in tourist routes. At the beginning of the century the United Provinces and Geneva were commonly the only Protestant territories visited by British tourists, so it was understandable that the contrast between Protestantism and Catholicism should be confused with that between republicanism and absolutism. By the second half of the century, it became increasingly common to visit other Protestant states, mostly in Germany, and this altered the ideological experience of tourists. Prussia was an autocratic militaristic Protestant state, a new experience that clashed with the conventions of Whig ideology. Robert Molesworth had written about a similar state in the 1690s – Denmark – but Prussia was the first such state many British tourists had encountered. One wrote of Stettin, 'as its a Prussian town, I need not mention anything about the government which you know is slavish.'

As the conflation of republicanism and virtue was increasingly ignored, criticism of the Italian republics increased. The Marquis of Tavistock advised the Earl of Upper Ossory in 1763, 'to study a little the constitution of the Republic of Venice, in order to inspire you with a proper dread of aristocracy – I am sure it is very useful for an Englishman'. In 1782, Andrew McDougall wrote from Venice, 'their government we could not possibly bear, sure there cannot be a greater shame for a free people (at least a people that call themselves so) than to suffer the first of their nation to be accused, without knowing by whom.' Walker launched a savage attack on the city five years later:

> On the whole, Venice is still a large and fine city, it is certainly not equal to what it had been; declination is visible in every feature of it; the people are too soft, luxurious, and indolent to cut any figure in trade; the pride of family is another bar against resurrection; and the great baits which make all gape, are the easy emoluments of office . . . Where the singularity of situation must necessarily beget an artificial and unnatural mode of life and living; it is no wonder that corruption and effeminacy originated here. To that place is Europe indebted for the refined system of rendering the multitude the slaves of the few, by the means of corruption, luxury, and effeminacy.

The more down-to-earth Pratt noted that living in the Prussian possession of Cleves was less expensive than in the United Provinces, and wrote: 'in this instance, at least, whatever may be your political principles, you would prefer the despotic states to the Republics'.[22]

Many tourists condemned absolutism in the second half of the century. John Northall, who visited Naples in 1753, wrote: 'the prerogatives of the Crown are of such a nature, the authority of the nobility over their vassals so exorbitant, and, above all, the power and property of the clergy so excessive, that there are hardly any countries where the generality of the people are more dissolute in their morals, or more wretched in their circumstances . . .' Nine years later Valltravers observed: 'We were greatly shocked at the scenes of Poverty, Distress, and Despondence, which offered themselves to our view in the Austrian Netherlands, and in France.' Smollett was no apologist for the French system: 'The interruption which is given, in arbitrary governments, to the administration of justice, by the interposition of the great, has always a bad effect upon the morals of the common people. The peasants too are often rendered desperate and savage, by the misery they suffer from the oppression and tyranny of their landlords.'

The same year, 1763, Elizabeth Montagu wrote from Düsseldorf: 'It grieves one to see Princes so magnificent and luxurious while their subjects are so poor and wretched.' Three years later the road from Calais to St Omer led to a fresh statement of the autocracy/Popery viewpoint: 'Great numbers of crosses and little images are stuck up everywhere along the side of the road, to which the people always pull off their hats, and in short you plainly discover everywhere under what an arbitrary Government they live, and how much they are bigotted to their religion.' In 1767 Charles James Fox wrote from Florence, 'there had been a woman of fashion put in prison lately for f———g (I suppose rather too publickly) a piece of unexampled tyranny – and such as could happen in no place but this', an appropriate contrast to Robert Gray's subsequent praise of Leopold's legislation and legal reforms in Tuscany. William Young attacked the situation in Sicily in 1772 in conventional terms, 'feudal and ecclesiastical tyranny . . . Industry sinking under united desolation, superstition and rapine? Francis in 1772 questioned whether the Venetian system of anonymous denunciations was actually in use, observing: 'In most of our political systems, the theory of the constitution points one way, the practise another. If we rely upon the direction of the needle, without calculation of the variations, we shall always be mistaken.' In Ghent he wrote: 'We have passed through a rich, open corn country, in which the peasants, who cultivate the soil have not bread to eat. There is something uncommonly ingenious in a system of government, under which the people starve in the midst of plenty.' At the Comédie in Paris, Francis witnessed a small riot when the pit called for the author of the play, who was in prison. Troops restored 'what these people call peace and good order. Yet they made more resistance than I expected.' A week later he encountered difficulties in obtaining a passport to leave the country: 'Everything in this country is calculated for check and control.' Jervis attacked 'the oppressive laws' under which the French peasant 'in general an inoffensive, peaceable, slave' lived. A visit to Lisbon in 1775 led Thomas Pelham to praise Britain:

> with what joy and gratitude must every Englishman reflect on the happiness of his own nation in comparison of any other; when he sees in a country like this, the nobles from their greatness and tyranny exposed every hour to attacks from the people and the people from their poverty rendered the most abject slaves . . . they are in general poor from the indolence that must necessarily follow so despotic a government . . .

The following year a tourist in France wrote:

> I am of opinion that the constitution of the government has more influence upon manners than is generally allowed to it, and that to this ought commonly to be referred what is attributed to climate and the natural character of nations. The distinction between noblesse and bourgeoisie in France, and the exclusion of the former from most means of acquiring wealth, have strong effects upon the national manners. They give the noblesse an exclusive right to pride with poverty: they give to the bourgeoisie an exclusive right to wealth with *grossièreté* [vulgarity].

Noting the effect of the limited governmental authority in the Comtat, the Papal enclave in southern France around Avignon, he observed: 'This freedom makes trade and agriculture flourish even under the government of the Pope, generally so notoriously blasting to both.' Mitford thought Piacenza 'miserably oppressed to support the grandeur of the little court of Parma', and wrote of

> the Duchy of Massa suffering under the iron rod of the Duke of Modena. It is miserable to be the slave of a rich and powerful monarch, but much more so to be the subject of a poor, petty, prince with difficulty supporting the state he assumes, and wringing from the hands of the peasantry every farthing they can scrape together. This disgusting reflection does not long dwell upon the mind. Three hours journey with miserable posthorses crosses the Duchy of Massa, and an hour more a little branch of the Tuscan dominions, and then liberty with the comfortable rewards of an honest industry give to

the inhabitants of the Lucchese territories far other looks than those of the emaciated peasantry of Massa. Viareggio, a flourishing little town, is the port of Lucca. Its buildings, its inhabitants, its crowded canal, its frequented streets all show the plenty arising from freedom. This prospect is soon clouded. The road again enters the Tuscan dominions and reaches the decayed town of Pisa . . . The buildings erected as receptacles for the victorious galleys of the republic, are now made the stables of the prince. The loss of liberty has reduced this once flourishing town from one hundred and sixty thousand inhabitants to about fifteen thousand . . . the present Grand Duke [Leopold] sometimes residing in the town gives it a sort of momentary life in the concourse of people which his presence occasions. He has likewise undertaken a princely work in draining some marshes north of the town, and digging for that purpose canals which serve at the same time the purposes of commerce.

In July 1783 Robert Ellison crossed Lake Geneva by boat from Lausanne with a party that included two British women travellers. They stayed at Evian, from which they visited a famous monastery, the Grande Chartreuse, where they 'saw no appearance of mortification and abstinence, but in a half starved shaking servant old, weak and withered – we saw two of the fathers – smooth, oily, and fat with contented countenances'. Ellison noted of Evian,

> little to be seen but the appearance of dirt and poverty – the people in its neighbourhood are like its inhabitants – effect of bad government and high taxes. It is said that the King of Sardinia draws annually £170,000 from his subjects in Savoy, which is supposed to be equal to ¾ of the product of their labour and property . . . The people do not seem sensible of the misery in which they live – the appearance of content is often here through dirt and poverty: and want has not made them dishonest . . . It is a mortifying sight to see such a country and such inhabitants, where nature seems to intend so many blessings, and tyranny does so much to prevent the enjoyment of others.

In 1784 George Norman, returning via Courland from his trip to St Petersburg, commented on the oppression of the tenantry. The following year Petty noted the contrast between the wealth of Galicia and the poverty of the people. Visiting Liège in 1785, Bennet condemned the idea of an ecclesiastical principality: 'the ill effects of the Government are very apparent: an ecclesiastic elected by a Chapter of strangers, without hereditary right, and invested with absolute authority, can have little regard for the people whom chance has made his subjects: and if there should be a Prince Bishop who preferred their interests to his own, his plans would perhaps all be overthrown by the different views or caprice of his successor.'

The majority of political reflections in tourist accounts written in the years immediately preceding the French Revolution, would not have been out of place at the beginning of the century. Space only permits a few examples. Lady Craven was very critical of Naples: 'At Naples, where the Government supplies nothing for the ease of its subjects, and where none are rich, because relative luxury conducts everyone to poverty; where public misery is concealed under national pomp; where indigence inhabits the palaces of the great as well as the cottages of the poor, – every one hurries after spectacles, diversions, and games . . .' Travelling from Paris to Strasbourg in early 1785, Robert Arbuthnot 'could not avoid being struck with the appearance of poverty and wretchedness which is observable among the peasants and common people, in the provinces through which we passed, particularly in Lorraine, where in every town where we stopped to change horses, half the inhabitants seemed to be beggars, who surrounded the carriage with the most rueful and meagre looks I ever saw.' In 1786, St John contrasted British freedom and degenerate French luxury, and condemned the opulence of the Orangery at Versailles, a 'shameful' luxury when many of the poor had 'not a place to lay their heads in'. The following year Arthur Young attacked the tyranny of French *lettres de cachet* and Walker commented on 'the baleful hand of power and priestcraft' in Italy. The situation in Sicily was attacked by Watkins in 1788 and Brand in 1792, while Watkins also attributed the prevalence of crime in Italy to 'bad government and superstition'.[23]

Continuity in the critique of Continental society was the dominant theme, but alongside it there were also signs of a more tolerant attitude. Some travellers drew attention to the various possible responses. Gardenstone's views on France changed in response to the excellent burgundy he had with his dinner at Breteuil in September 1786. Entering Spain from France in 1791, Townsend noted, 'the face of the country immediately before me appeared desolate and barren . . . I was at first to attribute this dismal aspect of their want of industry, to some vice in their government, or to some error in their political economy; but, upon examination, I soon discovered the real cause of this barrenness, in the hungry nature of the soil, and the want of those two inestimable feeders of vegetation, the limestone and the schist'.[24] Some tourists noted the happiness of those who were the victims of oppression. John Moore, Hester Piozzi and Lord Gardenstone noted it in the case of the French; and Hester Piozzi commented also on the happiness of the people of Milan.[25] A favourable response to specific aspects of absolutist rule was shown by several tourists. One wrote from Paris in 1764 to Sir John Cust, Speaker of the House of Commons: 'I find in general *here* that the free and independent persons in the kingdom begin to be weary of the extraordinary extension of the power usurped by Parliaments. The long and vexatious opposition they have given here to the Inoculation, and free exportation of grain has shown the majority to be no way qualified to conduct a great nation in its economical interests.' Five years later William Windham noted that in France, unlike Britain, the equivalent of the Vauxhall pleasure garden was taxed in order to support charitable purposes.

Wharton commented on the Parisian theatres in 1775: 'there is no mobbing they dare not be noisy for there are soldiers ready to arrest the troublesome person. This may appear a mark of despotism but it is yet comfortable to the peaceable spectators.' Three years later Philip Yorke wrote of Lucca, '. . . amongst these sumptuary regulations that of not wearing a sword is the most rational, and so convenient that I could wish it were adopted everwhere'. Bennet was clearly impressed by the energy and power of France: 'Strasburg when the French took possession of it [1681], was like most of the other towns of Germany, old, badly built, and ill fortified, but as soon as it fell into the hands of this active and intelligent people, it assumed a very different face.' John Richard praised the simplicity of the Prussian law code and claimed that there were too many laws in Britain. Gardenstone praised French road laws: 'In this country all kinds of vehicles on the high-roads must give way to post-carriages, by the king's ordinance, which is constantly observed. – Our commonality are apt to spurn at such useful regulations – If they had a proper sense of liberty, they would at least be as well disposed to obey the acts of our legislature, as the French are to revere the royal edicts.' In fact, the repeated reissue of the relevant edicts show how little they were observed. Brand clearly had a sympathy for Continental orderly behaviour. He wrote of the Château d'If near Marseilles: 'a sort of Bastile where are a few state prisoners and [obscured by tear] young men whose excesses have procured them lodgement there at the recommendation of their fathers. This violation of liberty is very revolting to an Englishman but I am inclined to think that many of its victims rejoice in maturer age that their fathers had such a power.' At Prague Brand attended a fête given by the Estates (Parliament) in honour of the Emperor: 'The wonderful order with which all this was conducted surprized and surprizes me still. I contrasted it with England and could not avoid some unpatriotic reflexions upon our want of police and our propensity to picking pockets and every species of theft. But, then say the Philosophers we have Liberty and you and your Bohemians are mechanical Slaves?'[26]

There is no firm conclusion to the question of whether tourism served as a political education. Much depended on the inclinations of the tourist and the people whom he met, but the openness of European society to aristocratic travellers provided many opportunities for the acquisition of information and opinion. Lord Mandeville discussed Anglo-Austrian relations at Milan in 1758; the extensive European tour that he took during the recess of 1781 convinced Gilbert Elliot MP that European opinion favoured American independence; and Early Wycombe wrote from Peterwardein in Austrian Serbia in 1786: 'It is . . . impossible for any man however incurious his disposition may be, to [gap in text] through this country the dissatisfaction which is everywhere produced by the new assessments that are about to be established. Whether this dissatisfaction results from real hardship or simply from the odium which constantly attends new calls for money' he did not know.[27]

Whether the disposition of others were similarly curious is unclear. Andrews thought it necessary to warn tourists against being dazzled by the glitter of Paris.[28] Wharton read Montesquieu's *L'Esprit des Lois* at Dijon because, 'I am going into different nations differently governed. That is the only book to enable me to judge of, and profit by seeing their governments.' There are few signs that others prepared themselves in the same fashion.[29] Peter Beckford stated that: 'It is not in looking at pictures and statues only, that travelling is of use, but in examining the laws, customs, and manners of other countries, and comparing them with our own.'[30] The examination, however detailed, led most tourists to praise their own country. John Richard claimed that '. . . from every nation, from even every circumstance, travellers will find many occasions to admire the constitution and comforts of their own country'. Pratt stated, '. . . in all which are justly called the comforts of life, Holland, Guelderland, Prussia, Germany, and other countries, are so many hundred years behind us, that we have just cause to be at once proud and grateful: proud of our happy island, and grateful for the benign government, under which it flourishes'.[31] Other factors, such as family, friends, language and the attraction of the familiar, made tourists glad to return home, but the claims above were broadly true, though they must be set alongside the pleasures of Continental life that many tourists clearly enjoyed and the willingness of many, particularly in the latter half of the century, to visit the Continent more than once. There are innumerable instances of the latter, including Sir Humphrey Morice, Stephen Fox, James Caulfeild, 4th Viscount Charlemont, Joseph Leeson, 1st Earl of Milltown, Henry Ellison of Hebburn, Lord Pomfret, Frances Crewe, Adam Walker, Lord Gardenstone, James, 2nd Earl of Fife, James, 6th Earl of Salisbury, David Garrick, Lord Perceval, Edward Southwell junior, Caroline, Lady Holland, James Bland Burges, Arthur Young, John Moore and William Mildmay. There were also some prominent individuals who stayed abroad for many years, including John, 2nd Earl Tylney (1712–84), who died in Naples where he had lived for many years and the 3rd Earl Cowper (1738–89), a patron of the arts, who lived in Florence from 1759.

Comments on the political situation in Europe were often related closely to reflections on social customs. As in the case of political reflections, there was a general sense that the British social order was better, accompanied by support for specific foreign social customs. Lord Charles Somerset (1689–1710), grandson of the 1st Duke of Beaufort, visited Amsterdam in 1708 and praised the 'Rasphouse' where 'fellows that are above measure idle and debauched were forced to work'. He reflected: 'If we had this excellent way of managing idle vagabonds at their first beginning in wickedness, we should save ourselves frequently from losing our money and now and then our lives with it, and those miserable wretches from losing theirs on the Gallows, and with it a great venture of their afterbeing.' Having visited the workhouse in Lille in 1764, Thomas Greene observed that the British should adopt the regulation that 'the overseers set out so much work as would be a pretty good days work and for their encouragement all that they do more they are paid for'. William Drake praised the Amsterdam prisons in 1769; Edmund Dewes, a servant, commended in 1776 the Berne system by which criminals were chained to wagons and made to clean the streets: 'I think such punishment in every country town, where prisoners are convicted, would have better effect than to send them all to the Thames in England', a reference to the prison ships; Richard Garmston commented on the Berne system in 1787; and Thicknesse urged that Britain copy the prison system of the Austrian Netherlands.[32] Peckham praised the policing and firewatching of Amsterdam and Lady Craven the caution shown in dispensing drugs in Venice: 'You cannot buy a drug at the apothecaries here, without an order from a Physician. A very prudent caution against the madness of those who choose to finish their existence with a dose of laudanum, or their neighbours with one of arsenic.'[33]

Robert Wharton was amenable to many French customs, or at least found them ridiculous rather than threatening. In Paris he parted from a Frenchman of his acquaintance: 'I had the honour to kiss him on each cheek, a ceremony that we should think rather ridiculous in England; but I have mentioned before, that it is quite the Ton here.' The previous day he had attended the *Concert Spirituel* and noted, as many tourists did in Paris, that 'the attention and silence of the audience was astonishing . . . . I thought of the English audience and felt for my Countrymen'. From Dijon he reported: 'Gentlemen go out of a room full of company as quietly as possible without saying a word to anybody. This seems to be a good custom as it does not set all the company in a bustle as is the case often with us.' At Lyons he discovered, to his surprise, that women bathed in the Saône, and wrote home suggesting that British women acquire the habit of summer bathing and that the British adopt the French habit of a separate glass for each person at meals. Frances Crewe noted in Paris, 'much more attention and greater respect is paid to old age here than in London', and that old women were treated at suppers with good humour and cheerfulness by their juniors.[34]

Many Continental customs were attacked. British tourists claimed frequently that not only were people less clean in their personal habits, but also that they were indelicate. The general practice, particularly in France, of urinating in public caused widespread comment and complaint. There was great surprise that the practice also extended to women. Frankness also caused comment. Wharton wrote from Dijon: 'the people make not the least scruple of using the words, pisser, etc.... I had a long dispute with an Abbé about delicacy in these affairs, which he said was highly ridiculous. "Every one", says he, "knows that these things are natural and necessary, and it is therefore absurd to think of concealing them ...".' Robert Gray noted of his visit to the Instituto in Bologna:

> We were disposed to make some comparison in favour of English ladies, when we observed with what sang-froid some Italian women, who accompanied us in the rooms of the Instituto, examined the monsters and nudities exposed to view. How offensive it is to see the female character devoid of delicacy, that timid and engaging charm which shrinks with sensibility from every object that might excite a blush, which is the peculiar grace of English women, and the great and fascinating ornament which secures those lasting attachments that we form in our country.[35]

The swaddling of Italian infants, the nursing of their French counterparts, and the custom in both countries and in the United Provinces of dressing children like adults were attacked.[36] Gray claimed that Italian institutions for the relief of those incapable of working supported the indolent; Peter Wauchop in Lille in 1775 found 'their wooden shoes and dogs drawing carts are laughable enough'; and Lady Craven was scandalized by a 'very abominable' custom at St Petersburg: 'noblemen, who are engaged to marry young ladies ... embrace them in the midst of a large company at a ball'. William Young wrote:

> I am strange enough to imagine that the one and the other extreme, the French Court and Calabrian Wood, may be regions equally barbarous; that happy medium alone, which teaches the genuine social duties of hospitality, unadulterated by new fangled ceremonies, and influences to mutual assistance and services, untainted by false and barbarous distinctions, and interests; that happy medium alone, is the true, best state of humanity civilized.

Mitford drew a distinction between honest provincials and dissolute Parisians. On a less elevated plane, Frances Crewe attacked the formality of Parisian etiquette in matters such as visiting and balls.[37]

Aside from specific issues, the general view was that British society was more free, less constrained by social distinctions and the privileges of rank. George Lyttelton wrote from Lyons of French social restrictions, the 'chimerical distinction between a gentleman and a marchand', while George Norman suggested that a major difference between Britain and the Continent was the stress on rank in the latter.[38] There is little suggestion that these views changed during the century. Possibly the Anglomania that affected large areas of Continental aristocratic and intellectual society in the latter half of the century, particularly in France and Germany, encouraged British tourists in a feeling of national self-confidence. Visiting Paris in the aftermath of the Seven Years War, the 2nd Viscount Palmerston commented, 'The King's palaces and some of the public buildings in Paris are fine but in general the town appears to me much inferior to London and the country as far as I have seen infinitely to England in point of improvement populousness or beauty.'[39]

There are no signs that tourists responded to visiting countries ruled by the so-called Enlightened Despots by wishing to create one in Britain. Neither are there as many signs as might be expected that political reflections varied in response to Britain's international position. There were, it is true, some shifts in emphasis. It is difficult to imagine many tourists in the 1780s reiterating George Carpenter's statement of 1717 that he agreed with Addison that it was best to live under small commonwealths, although the virtues of enlightened government in states such as Baden and Tuscany were possibly not known to enough tourists to make them dissent from the second half of the maxim, that it was worse to live under rulers of small territories.[40] It is also difficult to imagine many bearleaders of the 1710s sharing Brand's reflection of 1790 on Lord Bruce's opinions during his Swiss tour: 'he is convinced that a peasant may be happy and will I hope benefit by the train of reflections which this expedition had at different times suggested'.[41]

Whatever the shifts, most tourists remained convinced that Britain was the best country in Europe. Despite the hospitality they received and the access they were granted to continental society at its highest reaches, it would not be unfair to claim that many returned to Britain as better-informed xenophobes. Andrew Stewart suggested in 1789 that travel encouraged sympathy for foreigners: 'I have often thought that in our island too little attention is paid to the consequences of well judged acts of generosity, humanity or attention from one country to another. Those who remain generally on the same spot are not so sensible of it, as those travellers who in visiting different countries in Europe happen to mix with the societies there.'[42]

Though true on the personal level, Stewart's observation failed to give due weight to the conviction that Britain, or, for English tourists more clearly, England, was best. This conviction was differently expressed and had various and varying bases. The religious aspect, which had played such a major role in the first half of the century, was less prominent by the 1780s. Nevertheless, the conviction was a strong one. Continental regimes were denounced on the evidence of poverty and hardship that travellers saw, but there was a strong tendency to assume that things were better in England. Visiting the National Assembly while in Paris in 1790, Charles Sloane was convinced 'that there is no country like old England – for ever!'[43] In October 1787 John Mitford returned to Dover and wrote:

the traveller bids adieu to all his sufferings, to the wretchedness of sea sickness, the jolting of a *pavé*, and the filth of the French. He sees a cleanly country before him, and on all sides as he advances; he hugs himself in the thought that he is again in England, and if he draws comparisons his country does not suffer. Such are the reflections of an English traveller. What may be those of a Frenchman, or a man of other countries, it is difficult for an Englishman to guess. But a man used to England, and to all its comforts, cannot but feel pleasure that he has them within his reach, and thinks with perfect indifference of all the magnificence he has left behind him. Of the dirt he has escaped from he cannot think with equal indifference, it will excite in his mind disgust when considered singly, and pleasure the moment he draws a comparison. He flies for English travelling compared with French is flying, to the busy smoaky town of London, and finds it, with all its faults, less offensive than Paris . . . A footpath, raised above the road, runs along the whole way, from Dover to London for the accommodation of the lowest ranks of travellers. It immediately occurs that the new *streets* of Paris have no such conveniency, nay, that on expressing [surprise] at the omission of the French noblesse, the answer is, 'that the people ought not to be too much at their ease; that therefore the new streets in Paris have no *trottoir*, and many of them are too narrow to admit of the convenience'. The recollection also occurs that the French noblesse, indignant that the people should be accommodated with seats in the parterre at the new Comedie Francoise, have nearly deserted that entertainment. When these, and many similar reflections, occur to an English traveller quitting France, he cannot refrain from crying out with the Brussels patriots, *Vivat aurea libertas*.[44]

NOTES

1. BL Stowe 791, p. 15.
2. BL Add. 37926, f. 112.
3. Hall to Keith, 5 July 1785, BL Add. 35534.
4. H.J. Müllenbrock, 'The political implications of the Grand Tour: Aspects of a specifically English contribution to the European travel literature of the age of Enlightenment', *Trema*, 9 (1984), pp. 7–21.
5. Hopkins to Pryse Cambell, 29 Aug. 1749, Carmarthen CRO Cawdor Muniments Box 138; Stevens, p. 391.
6. [Villiers], *A Tour through part of France* (1789), p. 7.
7. John Mitford, travelling through France in 1776 wrote of 'the cursory view of a posting traveller'. Gloucester RO D2002 F1.
8. [Lady Miller], *Letters from Italy in the Years 1770 and 1771* (3 vols, 1776), I, 14.
9. Macdonald, BL Add. 34412 f. 80; Pelham to Thomas, 5 Oct. 1777, BL Add. 33127; Count Preysing, Bavarian foreign minister, to Count Haslang, Bavarian envoy in London, [5] July 1751, Munich, Bayr. Ges. London; Edward Southwell to Perceval, 2 Nov. 1725, BL Add. 47031.
10. *Mist's Weekly Journal*, 25 Sept. (os) 1725; Southwell to Perceval, 27 July 1726, BL Add. 47031; Keene to Delafaye, 13 Dec. 1728, PRO 94/99.
11. Perceval to brother, 21 Nov. (os) 1726, Southwell to Perceval, 27 July 1726, BL Add. 47031; Anon., BL Add. 60522; Mandeville, Huntingdon CRO DD M49/7; Pelham to Lord Pelham, 3, 15 Oct. 1776, 8 Feb., 1 April, 26 July 1777, to Lady Pelham, 16 Sept. 1776, 15 Mar. 1777, BL Add. 33127; Yorke to Keith, 15 Dec. 1778, BL Add. 35515; Garrard to Drake, 19 Oct. 1778, Aylesbury CRO D/DR/8/10/6; Brand to Wharton [Nov.–Dec. 1780], 10 May 1781, 17 Nov. 1783, 14 Mar. 1786, 15 Dec. 1789, 15 Feb. 1790, 26 Aug. 1791, Durham, Wharton; Aikin, I, 84; Hanson to Keith, 10 Jan. 1788, BL Add. 35540; Thicknesse, 1777, I, 136–42; J. Townsend, *A Journey through Spain* (3 vols, 1791), I, i; Andrews, 1785, p. 44; Matlock CRO 239 M/O 538; Beinecke, Osborn Files, Lansdowne; Dalrymple to Keith; 19 Oct. 1789, BL Add. 35541.
12. Lady Mary Coke to Keith, 23 Nov. 1773, BL Add. 35006; Southwell, BL Add. 34753, f. 6.
13. Villettes to Newcastle, 25 Dec. 1734, PRO 92/37; Pelham to Lord Pelham, 19 Dec. 1777, 30 Oct. 1775, BL Add. 33127, 33126; Beinecke, Lee corresp. Box 3; Chester CRO DBW/N/Bundle E, Packet A; R.R. Sedgwick (ed.), *Some Materials towards Memoirs of the Reign of King George II, by John, Lord Hervey* (3 vols, 1931), I, 220; Ryder diary, 18 Dec. 1741.
14. Hume, BL Add. 29477, f. 18; Paris, Bibliothèque Nationale, Ms. Ang. 194 f. 11–12; Daniel to Tilson, 20 April 1729, PRO 77/76; Waldergrave jnl, 1 Sept. 1730, Chewton; HMC, *Carlisle* pp. 89–90; Swinton, 7, 12, 15, 16, 29 Jan. (os), 21 Feb. (os), 21 Mar. (os), 31 May (os), 7 June (os) 1731; Cobbett, 11, 822; *Daily Universal Register*, 5 Jan. 1785; Bennet, 31 Aug. 1785.
15. *Craftsman*, 6 July (os) 1728; Cobbett, 10, 173; Richard, *A Tour from London to Petersburg* (1780), pp. 198–9.
16. Cobbett, 9, 300; Beinecke, Osborn Shelves c 455 1/66.

17. Chester CRO DBW/N/Bundle E, Packet A; Leeds AO NH 2911; *Present State of Germany*, I, xix; J. Shaw, p. xvi.
18. Shaw, xiii–xiv, 38; BL Stowe 790 f. 10; *London Journal*, 4 Nov. (os) 1727; *Weekly Journal or Saturday's Post*, 15 Dec. (os) 1722.
19. Carleton, pp. 249, 311; Thompson, I, 72; Macky, *A Journey Through the Austrian Netherlands* (1725), xxviii; *Present State of Germany*, II, 432; Gloucester CRO D 2002 F1.
20. Hume, BL Add. 29477, f. 23; Stevens, p. 67; Shaw, p. 150; M. Wyndham, I, 23; Mildmay jnl, Chelmsford, 15 M50/1302, p. 60.
21. BL Add. 53816, f. 61–4, 53815, f. 25–41; BL Stowe 750, f. 356; Southwell to Perceval, 27, 2 Nov. 1725, Hervey to Lady Hervey, Trevor to Thomas Trevor, 27 Aug. 1728, BL Add. 47031, 51345, f. 18–19, 61684; Robinson, Leeds AO Vyner Mss. 6005; Mildmay jnl., Chelmsford, 15M50/1303, pp. 15–18, 53–5; anon., BL Stowe 790, f. 9; Hume, Perceval to Chamberlayne, 9 July 1718, BL Add. 29477, f. 18, 47028; Waldegrave to Delafaye, 9 Aug., Waldegrave to Tilson, 15 Aug. (quote), Waldegrave to Essex, 12 Aug. 1732, PRO 78/200–1, BL Add. 27732; Mitchell jnl, BL Add. 58314, f. 8, 24, 48; Guildford CRO Brodrick Mss. 1248/6.
22. Wraxall to Keith, 8 June, 10 Aug. 1778, BL Add. 35514; Leeds AO Vyner Mss. 6032 No. 12299; G.R. de Beer (ed.), *Tour on the Continent 1765 by Thomas Pennant* (1948), p. 107; Thicknesse, 1777, I, 125–6; Bennet, 2 Sept., 12 Aug. 1785; Brand to Wharton, 21 July 1791, Durham, Wharton; Fitzwilliam, WW R1–541; Ellison, Gateshead, Public Library, E1/3, 17 Sept., 3 Oct. 1782; *Public Ledger*, 19 June 1760; Mildmay jnl, 15M50/1303, pp. 15, 32; Beinecke, Osborn Shelves f c 52 p. 9; Tavistock to Upper Ossory, 12 Sept. 1763, Russell; McDougall to Keith, 27 Jan. 1782, BL Add. 35515; Walker, pp. 173–4; Pratt, III, 80.
23. J. Northall, *Travels through Italy* (1766), p. 183; Smollett, p. 25; Montagu, I, 57; Tracy and Dettand, Bod. Mss. Add. A 366, f. 4; Fox to Lord Fitzwilliam, 27 Oct. 1767, BL Add. 47576; Gray, pp. 306–11; Thicknesse, 1768, pp. 43–4; Young, BL Stowe, 791, pp. 116, 119; *Tour*, pp. 229–30; Francis, BL Add. 40759, f. 9, 2, 23–4; Jervis, BL Add. 31192, f. 36; Pelham to Lord Pelham, 30 Oct., 3 Nov. 1775, BL Add. 33126; Anon., BL Add. 12130, f. 49–50, 158; Mitford, Gloucester CRO D 2002 F1 pp. 5, 93–6; Moore, *A view of Society and Manners in France, Switzerland, and Germany* (2 vols, 1779), I, 32; Ellison, Gateshead Public Library, E1/6 pp. 1, 3, 5–6; Norman to his stepmother, 10 Sept. 1784, Kent CRO, U310, C3; Bennet, 6 July 1785; Craven, I, 306–7; Arbuthnot, BL Add. 35533 f. 256; St John, pp. 127–8, 96, 36–7; Young, I, 55; Walker, pp. 330, 353; Watkins, II, 6, 358; Brand to Wharton, 3 April 1792, Durham, Wharton.
24. Gardenstone, I, 13–15; Townsend, I, 89.
25. R. Anderson (ed.), *The Works of John Moore* (7 vols, Edinburgh, 1820), III, I; Gardenstone, p. 13; Piozzi, *Observations and Reflections made in a Journey through France, Italy, and Germany*, pp. 9, 56.
26. W.R. to Cust, L. Cust, *Records of the Cust Family*, III (1927), p. 242; Windham, Wigan, D/DZ EHC 20; Wharton to Miss Lloyd, 29 Feb. 1775, Durham, Wharton; Yorke to Keith, 28 Sept. 1778, BL Add. 35515; Bennet, Bod. Ms.

Eng. Misc. f. 54 f. 70; Richard, pp. 152–3; Gardenstone, I, 18; Brand to Wharton, late Aug. 1783, 14 Aug. 1792.

27. Otway, Mandeville's tutor, to the latter's father, the Duke of Manchester, 30 May 1758, Huntingdon, CRO dd M49 A and B, bundle 7; HP, II, 395; Wycombe to Keith, 12 April 1786, BL Add. 35535.
28. Andrews, 1785, pp. 41–2.
29. Wharton to Thomas Wharton, 13 June 1775, Durham, Wharton.
30. Beckford, *Familiar Letters from Italy, to a friend in England* (2 vols, Salisbury, 1805), I, 9.
31. Richard, p. 221; Pratt, II, 527.
32. Badminton, 'An account of my Travels', pp. 14–15; Greene, Preston CRO DD Gr F/3 f. 12; Drake, Aylesbury, D/DR/8/20; Dewes, Bod., Mss. Eng. Misc. d 213, pp. 84–5; Garmston, BL Add. 30271, f 14; Thicknesse, 1786, p. 51.
33. *Tour of Holland*, pp. 73–4; Craven, 1789, I, 151–2.
34. Wharton to mother, 10, 9 April, 29 May, to Miss Raine, 31 Aug. 1775, Durham, Wharton; Crewe, BL Add. 37926, f. 60.
35. Wharton to mother, 18 May 1775, Durham, Wharton; Gray, p. 302.
36. Wharton to mother, 18 July 1775; Walker, p. 415; Thicknesse, 1768, p. 53; Brand to Wharton, 30 July 1779.
37. Gray, p. 255; Wauchop to Keith, 4 Nov. 1775, BL Add. 35509; Craven, p. 183; Young, BL Stowe 791, pp. 40–1; Mitford, Gloucester CRO D 2002 F1 pp. 67–70; Crewe, BL Add. 37926, f. 34–5, 44, 59, 67.
38. M. Wyndham, I, 25; Norman, 22 Sept. 1784, Kent CRO U310 C3.
39. Beinecke, Osborn Gift 29, 222.
40. Carpenter, Bod. Ms. Douce 67, pp. 248–9.
41. Brand to Wharton, 25 Aug. 1790.
42. Cambridge UL Add. 6958 No. 695.
43. House of Lords RO CAD/4/29.
44. Gloucester CRO D 2002 F1.

11

RELIGION

I have found . . . the Church of England very much esteemed by all the
men of learning I met with abroad.

Dr James Walker, Lille, 1722[1]

Last week I went to see the treasure of Saint Denis . . . while I was
observing these curiosities with much attention; a Priest told me seriously
that if I would but touch those Holy Relicks, it might convert me, upon
which I replied, that if by touch I could but convert those precious stones
into gold and silver for my own use, I should make a better use of them,
upon which he laughed, and so ended our dispute upon Religion; upon
which subject the women of this country as well as all other countries
often dispute about, for they generally think that their own religion is
the best and in France I have been often obliged to defend my religion
against the Ladys, whose arguments and persons may be very powerful
and persuasive in all cases except that of religion.

Edward Mellish, Paris, 1731[2]

Anti-Catholicism was the prime ideological stance in eighteenth-
century Britain. The methods, practices and aspirations of
the Catholic Church appear to have genuinely appalled many
Englishmen of the period. Newspapers, sermons, processions,
demonstrations and much correspondence reveal a response to
Catholicism that was based not simply upon the repetition of trite anti-
Catholic maxims but also upon a deep-felt repulsion. Catholicism was
equated with autocracy; it drew on credulity and superstition and led to
misery, poverty, clerical rule and oppression. The perceived danger from
Catholicism was increased by historical factors, by the close association
of Catholicism and Jacobitism and by the fact that Britain's principal
enemies, France and Spain, were Catholic powers. That Britain also allied
with Catholic powers – Austria (1702–11, 1731–3, 1741–56), France

(1716–31), Portugal and Savoy-Piedmont – did not shake this perception, Catholicism therefore excited fear or unease. It also aroused interest and, at times, humour or ridicule. The last were most conspicuously aroused by relics. Relics symbolized the inversion of reason that was held to characterize Catholicism. Credulity and superstition were seen both as the essential supports of a Catholic ascendancy and as the products of it. By means of a tight control over education and the propagation of religious practices that ensnared reason and deluded the senses, the Catholic Church wove a poisonous web that entrapped the people of Catholic Europe. This was seen most clearly in the widespread respect for relics, which was regarded by most tourists as relic-worship.

James Hume, an Anglican clergyman, was told in Paris in 1714 that the relics of James II of England that were kept there could cure; a neat portrayal of the threatening combination of Catholicism and Jacobitism. An anonymous tourist, who saw an annual miracle in Douai in 1721 in which an image produced two drops of blood and the figure of a child appeared, was very sceptical, adding: 'had I not been an eye witness I could never have believed so much ignorance was in practice'. Colin Maclaurin (1698–1746), Professor of Mathematics in the Marischal College of Aberdeen, and bearleader to the eldest son of Lord Polwarth, was very sceptical about the relics he encountered at Auxerre and Dijon in 1722. Edward Mellish saw a relic in procession in Mons in 1731 and commented, 'we never pay so much honour to inanimate beings, neither would we be guilty of so much idolatry and superstition'. Two years earlier an Anglican cleric, Dr Joseph Atwell, bearleader to the 2nd Earl Cowper, scorned the relics of the eleven thousand virgins at Cologne and mocked those at Aachen. He wrote that the latter included 'Some of the Virgin Mary's shifts (which by the way were not very clean) some of the Jesus' swadling clothes . . . some of the Manna that fell in the wilderness and such trompery as would not be worth seeing, if it was not for the silver and jewels with which they are adorn'd.' Walker was similarly sceptical about the Aachen relics in 1787.

The zealous Tory and prominent Jacobite, Lord Quarendon, was sufficiently moved by the miracle of the liquefaction of the blood of St Januarius at Naples, a ceremony many British tourists mocked, to compose a blasphemous and witty poem. He recorded of his visit to Saumur in June 1739: 'Nothing worth observation except a Chapell to the Virgin which does great miracles, the walls are all surrounded with the *Tabulae Votivae* of persons sav'd from eminent dangers . . . the whole quarter of the town consists of people whose only trade is to make chaplets, these when rubb'd over the Virgins lap are greatly efficacious, the *Pères de l'Oratorie* are the actors of this comedy which indeed they perform as if they themselves believe it.' Walter Stanhope mocked French relics in 1769.[3]

Nunneries were another great source of interest. It was very common for tourists to visit them, particularly convents of British nuns, of which there were several in northern France and the Austrian Netherlands. Several tourists attended ceremonies in which women renounced the world to enter nunneries. James Hume visited the Dieppe convent of the Ursulines and talked with two English nuns in Dunkirk, staying for two hours. Wharton and Lady Knight were both interested in nuns. Mrs Montagu, in the Earl of Bath's party to Spa in 1763, wrote: 'We visited the Nunnerys in every town; Mrs. Carter constantly expressing the greatest abhorrence of their strict vows, and sequestered life . . .' The fascination that nunneries excited was speedily quenched. Those who visited nunneries discovered that most nuns were not beautiful, sensual women held against their will, and many were disappointed by their looks. Joseph Atwell thought the ceremony of the taking of the veil that he saw at Florence in 1730 'the most melancholy sight which I have seen'. A tourist who in 1751 saw a convert from Lutheranism take the veil at Duderstadt was much moved by what he called 'the sacrifice . . . the tragical scene' and he wrote: 'God forgive her, poor unhappy creature, and all those who are led astray by the craft and vilany . . . thank God it is my happy lot to be of a nation a long time since by the protection of heaven delivered from such pernicious bigotted and mistaken zeal.'[4]

In both guidebooks and private journals the general response to the Catholic Church was abhorrence coupled with respect for particular customs. Charles Hotham visited Rome in 1712

in time to see all the functions and ceremonies of the Holy Week. Without having been in Rome one can't imagine the Pageantry and outward show of religion one sees here at the same time that in reality there is nowhere less. They carry things here to so great a height that I have seen Roman Catholics themselves ashamed of them; and of all the places I have seen I know none so fit to convince a man of the absurdity of Popery as Rome itself.

James Hume was generally critical. He was unimpressed by the monastery he visited; by the lack of Sabbath observance; and by the appearance of Jesus on signs, pointing the way, for instance to taverns. He debated religion with a monk at Caen and witnessed the celebration of Mass at Guingamp: 'I stood behind a pillar and observed the old man's antick postures and grimaces, but could not hear what he mumbled, with his back turned to the people, who behaved themselves very devoutly though they understood not one word of what was said.' His reflections on French Catholicism were, however, mixed. After Ascension Day mass in Paris he wrote, 'he that sees and considers what the Roman Catholics call the service of God cannot choose but love the Church of England the better for it'. He was also, however, very impressed by the manner in which Catholics prayed at their bedside in inns and at home and thought this was 'extremely fit to be imitated by Protestants'. Thomas Pelham was as usual priggish; and Philip Francis facetious. The former wrote of 'the Roman Catholics, whose behaviour and manners may be made useful to a Protestant who compares them with his own', the latter, in Tuscany, 'after dinner discussed a few points of controversy, with a friar of the order of redemption. I thought he seemed edified with some inward workings of Grace which he discovered in my Signoria . . .' Martin Folkes (1690–1750), Vice-President of the Royal Society, who travelled with his family to Venice via Germany and the Tyrol in 1733, wrote to the 2nd Duke of Richmond, praising Bavarian architecture and painting, but attacking the superstition, ignorance and superficial devotion of Catholics. Messrs Tracy and Dentand, travelling from Calais to St Omer in 1766, noted, 'Great numbers of crosses and little images are stuck up everywhere along the side of the road, to which the people always pull off their hats, and in short you plainly discover everywhere under what an arbitrary government they live, and how much they are bigoted to their religion.'

There was considerable ambiguity about religious art. Andrew Mitchell admired the paintings he saw in Italy, but nevertheless noted:

One cannot help regretting (after seeing the vast profusion of paintings in these churches, by the ablest masters), the bestowing so much industry and art upon so silly subjects as the life and actions of one enthusiast and the fabulous martyrdom of a bigot. Corporal and ridiculous representation of the Deity serve to corrupt and debauch our ideas of him . . .

In 1764 Thomas Greene visited France with his friend George Romney. In Dunkirk he commented on 'a large picture by Rubens of Heaven, Hell and Purgatory. What a pity it is such a genius should have been wasted upon such a ridiculous subject.'[5]

The sensual and physical appeal of Catholicism to tourists, who believed the religion to be irrational, evil and spiritually corrupt, posed a difficult problem of balance for them: many specific aspects of Catholic religion were commented upon unfavourably: pilgrimages, mariolatry[6] and scourging: 'One sees such processions, such penitents, and such nonsense, as is enough to give one ye gripes.'[7] Monasticism was also attacked. Monks were widely held to be idle in all but their greed.[8] Catholic religious observances were usually treated either as credulous superstition or as empty and formal. Tourists did not agree as to the extent of Catholic observance. Most thought the Catholics were religious, by their standards. Swinton wrote of 'the superstition and bigotry of the Ligornese'. Stanhope wrote from Paris, in 1769, that 'ye common people are ye most superstitious in ye world'.[9] And yet Garrick commented, in 1751, that the post-boys near Paris did not take off their hats to the roadside crucifixes as those in Picardy had done; and Wharton on the same journey twenty-four years later noted that the peasants and a *curé* ignored these crucifixes. He presented the French as essentially hedonistic, eating meat during Lent: 'in short the study of this people seems to tend to this one point, the comfort and present happiness of themselves and all around them. As for care, of what kind so ever, they seem utter enemies to it.' A Capuchin friar from Parma assured Norton Nicholls in 1772 that he

> should meet with very unprejudiced people at Rome, he said the Romans are like the sacristan of a church who when there are spectators bows and makes a genuflexion every time he passes before the image of the Virgin or the altar, but when the doors are shut continues to sweep and walks by a thousand times without showing any mark of respect.[10]

Some, but not all, tourists encountered hostility to Protestantism. Swinton was particularly conscious of religious struggle. In Genoa, where, according to him, the population was controlled by Jesuits, he met Count Fiesco who 'complained much of the taxes and impositions yt were laid upon the Roman Catholics in England'. The following month he noted in Livorno: 'The natives of ys place are very insolent, and bear an implacable hatred to the English upon account of their religion, (not with standing they are the main support of ys place) in which, as in other Popish countries, they are spirited up by their ignorant and furiously zealous priests; which they frequently show by placing horns of a large size upon the most remarkable of the English monuments, and defiling them with odure and all manner of filth.' Swinton was in no doubt of the threat posed by Catholicism. In Genoa he noted in his journal:

> What perfect pleasure it affords the Papists abroad to see the Protestant interest in England so weaken'd by our factions and intestine divisions at home – would all true Protestants consider ys, and could they but see the true proper genius of Popery, as 'tis exercised abroad, and observe how the Papists abroad are always on the watch to lay hold of and improve every opportunity yt offers itself of reestablishing their power and authority in England, I am persuaded, they would be more heartily disposed to a union amongst themselves.

In 1739, Sacheverell Stevens found himself one Sunday in an inn at Ponte Cento. He was told that he ought to go and hear Mass: 'I heard them say that I was an Englishman, and consequently no Christian.' In 1740 two Englishmen in Calais 'were very much abused by the mob there, for not paying a proper respect to the host', which was being carried in the street to the house of a sick person. Visiting a church in Rheims in 1767, Countess Spencer 'was for the first time it ever happened to me mobbed for being in my riding habit which was a mighty unpleasant operation'.[11]

The conduct of some British travellers was such as not to help matters. In May 1726, the Presbyterian clergyman, Robert Wodrow, librarian of Glasgow University, noted:

Provost Drummond tells me that he had the following account from one of the gentlemen, which happened some years ago in Spain or Italy . . . Two Scots gentlemen were travelling in one of these places where Popery is in very great bigotry; and when they were coming to a famous church, the one of them would lay a wager with the other that he would ease nature on the steps of the altar, in a publick meeting, [when] some extraordinary relict or the hosty was exhibited. The other diswaded him but he insisted on it; and said he would venture, and the other should see his excrements should be honoured as relicts, and the effect of a miracle. He prepared himself by taking somewhat laxative, and came in on a solemn day, thrumbled in to the very altar, and there voided himself. Very soon, we may be sure, a cry arose; and he only desired liberty to tell the occasion. He had his story ready for delivering, that for many days he had been under a violent consumption; that he believed nothing would relieve him but this; that as soon as he came to the relict or hostee, by faith in it, this cure was wrought. And, upon this, the priests presently took it as a miracle, and published it to the people, and he was the happiest that could get some of the excrements. This is another instance of the stupid bigotry and superstition of the Papists.

The accuracy of this account may be doubted but it is an interesting indication of what could be believed. Stevens, when he witnessed the miracle of St Januarius in Naples, found several English captains of merchantmen swearing in English 'at the folly and superstition of the populace; they being my countrymen, in a very friendly manner I cautioned them against the risk they run, if they should happen to be understood . . . all the return I had for my friendly, salutary advice, was to be damned for a Papist'. Stevens himself was the innocent cause of disorder in a Paduan church for his dog leapt upon the back of a priest celebrating Mass and attempted, unsuccessfully, to seize the host.[12]

Some tourists were clearly not too bothered by religious differences or treated them as curiosities, no more serious than the difference in food or language. Waldegrave's chaplain, Anthony Thompson, told Poole in Paris 'that the people who come here, generally leave their religion at London'. It is not clear how many tourists attended the Ambassadors' Chapels; very few left any account of doing so. Edward Mellish at Angers had to make do with his own copy of the Book of Common Prayer, but was not sure whether other Britons there had copies. The Duchess of Ancaster organized English prayers at Spa in 1785, and William Drake had a service in his Parisian hotel. Some tourists, such as James Essex, described Catholic ceremonies and processions without any criticism and others, such as Wharton, encountered hospitality and politeness from Catholic clerics.[13] The French Revolution led to an increased tolerance of Catholicism. Having visited Loreto with Lord Bruce in 1792, Brand wrote to Wharton from Pesaro:

> Ld. B. has a sort of *awe* in seeing these kind of scenes which I never dare to touch upon but leave just as it is. I think it necessary only to drop a slight remark on the credulity of the Romish Church without exposing it too much. Our friend *Jack* you know in tearing off the fringe in his rage made a terrible *Rent* in the paternal coat and in these times of turbulence and *Philosophy* everything that throws contempt even on the Catholic Church is as well avoided.

The following year, visiting Vallombrosa, he joined with the monks in denouncing the Revolution. Pratt, who deplored the number of saints' days, was moved by his abhorrence of the atheism of the Revolution and the havoc it had wreaked in the Rhineland, to praise some aspects of Catholicism. Attending a Catholic service near Cleves, he was very impressed by Catholic piety. He claimed that 'the influence of the Catholic faith on the subordinate ranks is, almost without an exception, a sober and sincere attention to the duties it enjoins'.[14]

Catholicism was not, of course, the only alien church that tourists encountered. Compared, however, to the wealth of comment on the Catholic Church, the other Protestant churches attracted much less attention. James Porter visited Count Zinzendorff's Moravian settlement, and it was common for tourists in Amsterdam to sample the rich variety of church services on offer. Attending services in three different churches was one way to pass an Amsterdam Sunday. Few devoted as much attention to other Protestant churches as Anglican clerics did. Brand was particularly wide-ranging. In 1779 he visited a Dutch Moravian settlement and in 1787 delivered his opinion on the Lutheran clergy of Saxony: 'They are queer fellows are *Martin*'s black servants. I think they have more pedantic stupidity in their looks than either Jack's or Peter's . . . I peeped into a church where one of them was catechizing some children and I never saw anything so outré as his manner and gesture'. Alan Brodrick was surprised by the numerous crucifixes he saw in Lutheran churches in Nuremberg in September 1724 and viewed them as a sign of Catholic tendencies.[15]

Brand disliked the Netherlands – 'this vile country of Canals and Calvinism'.[16] Other Protestant travellers found more to praise in the Netherlands and in the Empire, particularly if they had just arrived from a Catholic country. It was common to contrast the Austrian Netherlands and the United Provinces (modern-day Netherlands). Perceval did so; while another tourist noted at Breda, 'were not a little rejoiced at our entering a Protestant country for several reasons'. Shaw claimed that an observant traveller could not help but notice the effect of Catholicism: 'as soon as he has left the Dutch Government, and comes into a Popish country by a looser freer air and weakness of manners, running through all sorts of people you meet, who are strangers to the wise and strict morality of the Dutch, and which contributes so much to their power and riches'. John Richard contrasted the United Provinces and the Bishopric of Münster.[17]

Many were impressed by the Calvinism of Geneva, an important factor in leading to so many being educated there. Caroline, Lady Holland, wrote in 1767: 'At Geneva there appears to me to be affluence without luxury, piety without superstition, great industry and great cleanliness.'[18] Sacheverell Stevens was impressed by the churches in Nuremberg, which were not excessively ornamented and seemed 'more adapted to the plain, decent, and solemn worship of the Protestants . . . than to the glaring ridiculous fopperies of Popery'. John Richard was struck by the devotion of the carriers on the road from Gdansk to Berlin and wrote: 'it is usual, in this part of the world, to join in prayer and other devotion, in the morning, on the road, and often at other times; religion does not seem here the effect of hypocrisy or enthusiasm, but the natural consequence of an early endeavour in parents to instil religious motives in their children'.[19]

Some travellers, particularly clergymen, were concerned by the plight of Protestant minorities in Europe. One tourist noted at Nîmes, in 1776: 'Parties of soldiers are constantly sent to apprehend the priests and disperse the congregations; but always with private orders not to find them.' Robert Wharton was interested in the fate of the Protestants in southern France; and another tourist visited a Protestant assembly in a valley near Nîmes in 1785, writing: 'This scene recalled the idea of those times when the primitive converts to our religion performed the duties in defiance of severe persecution.' Bennet discussed the situation with the minister of the Bordeaux Protestant congregation. He had earlier visited

Toulouse, 'remarkable for its gloomy bigotry and stained with the blood of the unfortunate Calas', and Montauban, an old Protestant city, where he thought the people looked more active.[20]

Most tourists did not, however, mention the fate of Protestant minorities abroad, and in most cases an awareness of religious conflict stemmed either from personal experience or from the prevalent ideology in Britain. Many tourists were, of course, treated well by Catholics, and noted this in the case of Catholic clergy. In the 1770s, it became relatively common for Protestant tourists to be received by the Pope. Philip Francis was most impressed by his reception by Clement XIV in 1772. The Pope told him that he would have supported Henry VIII, and Francis noted that he 'converses freely and amicably with heretics, and has no idea of converting them . . . Though not a convert to the doctrines of this Church, I am a Proselite to the Pope. Whoever has the honour of conversing with him will see, that it is possible to be a Papist without being a Roman Catholic.' Philip Yorke was presented to Pius VI with six other British tourists in 1778: 'he was civil and polite and thanked Lord Lucan for the favours that had been lately shown to the Roman Catholics in Ireland. The only ceremony to which we were obliged to conform was that of taking off our swords and arms and hats and making genuflexion to his holiness on entering and going out of the room.'[21] Charles, Lord Lucan (1735–99), was a champion of more rights for Ireland. Other Catholic clerics were also hospitable as, earlier in the century, Cardinal Albani had been in Rome. Thomas Greene found the Jesuit Church in Lille shut in 1764, 'but a good looking old Jesuit . . . with very great civility opened up the door and showed us the place', refusing to take any money. Andew McDougall was entertained in Bologna in 1782 by the Cardinal-Governor: 'he speaks very good English and seems to be much interested for the *Welldoing* of the nation'.[22]

Certain tourists stressed confessional tension, often inadvertent, but sometimes dangerous. Parker, visiting the Vatican in July 1721, noted the wall painting of the murder of Admiral Coligny, the sixteenth-century Huguenot leader. If Sacheverell Stevens is to be believed, he was nearly mobbed in Montreuil, for a lack of respect displayed while visiting a church during Mass, and in Rome for laughing at popular belief in a miracle. He was obliged also to conceal roast meat during Lent, and commented on the lack of respect shown to Protestant graves in Rome. An anonymous tourist in Béziers in 1754 had a 'dispute with an officer and some others at the ordinary upon religion'. The same year Lord Nuneham witnessed a Mass in Rheims, and wrote to his sister: 'the ceremony is to me a most delightful amusement, I was again at sermon . . . in the evening . . . I just entered time enough to hear half the Discourse, which ended with an account of the heresies of Great Britain, in which we poor wretches were miserably clawed and abused. Was not I in luck? I assure you I thought myself so, for I love to hear arguments as well against as for.' Nuneham's mother, Lady Harcourt, was concerned about whether he would seek an audience with the Pope:

> I am glad to find you have no thoughts of kissing the holy toe. Those that have done it, I can't help saying, have acted with the greatest impropriety; for his power has never been acknowledged by the English Protestants since the reformation. Sir J. Dashwood acted in character when he did it, for a great Jacobite is not far from being a very good catholic, but as there is not many, I hope, of our nobility and gentry of that way of thinking, one can't help wondering they should take pains to make the world believe that they are so.

There were attempts to convert some visitors, such as Boswell, to Catholicism, and several tourists, particularly those who travelled by public transport, engaged in discussions on religious topics. One tourist recorded an interesting conversation between his servant and a Rhône boatman in 1776, in which the latter complained about the abolition of the boatmens' patron saint. Samuel Smith visited the cathedral in Arras in 1752 and noted: 'I turned aside from the altar without bowing which greatly offended an old woman and made her complaints to the priest who was wiser than to take any notice.' John Villiers toured Cherbourg in 1788 with an Englishman whom he met there and wrote: 'a farce in the church . . . Having never before been spectators at the ceremony of mass, I was at once entertained and astonished. We waited till the host was exposed, during the service; when being pointedly called upon, by two very zealous young priests, to kneel, my companion objected to it, and we retired.'23

Seeking to avoid difficulties, some writers urged tourists to adopt a tolerant stance towards Catholicism and an accommodating attitude towards its practices. Philip Thicknesse suggested that Protestants visiting Catholic churches should dip their fingers into the holy water and make the necessary sign of the cross. He also defended the principles of Catholicism: 'there is nothing so very alarming in the Roman Catholic religion to one who is a good Christian, when we hear their articles of faith expounded by men of sense and candour.' These points were not accepted by all. Robert Gray wrote: 'The volcanic nature of the country about Rome tends to confirm the opinion of those who, from the language of St. John recollect that Rome, like Sodom, shall "be utterly burnt with fire" . . . Rome should be visited with the lantern of Christianity, that we may justly discriminate between the parade of religion and the real impiety of this dark, gloomy, and superstitious city.'24

There are some signs that religious antagonism became less of a theme in the accounts of many tourists in the second half of the century, but it is important not to exaggerate the scale of any change that took place. Jacobitism became a curiosity rather than an issue, and religious tension in Europe, which had been so important in the first half of the century, with prominent events, such as the 'Thorn massacre' of 1724 and the emigration from Salzburg of 1731–2, reported fully in the British press, became less significant after the Seven Years War. Many travellers, however, continued to stress the pernicious consequences of Catholicism. This was particularly marked in the case of southern Italy and Sicily, an area not much visited by British tourists before this period. Tourists, such as Watkins and William Young, wrote of the dire consequences of feudal and ecclesiastical tyranny. Thomas Pelham, who praised the devotion of the Portuguese, nevertheless wrote to his father, 'with what joy and gratitude must every Englishman reflect on the happiness of his own nation in comparison of any other; when he sees in a country like this . . . Religion which should be the basis of all kingdoms made their ruin'. Bennet compared Zurich and Lucerne, writing of the latter, 'Within there is less industry and less riches. For Lucerne is Catholic, and I must say without partiality, that the different spirit of the two religions is very apparent in the two towns, as well as in almost all I have seen: Protestantism has every advantage by the comparison.' An anonymous visitor wrote in 1782: 'One quarter of the inhabitants of Bologna seem to be beggars – the streets are crowded with them, and one quarter priests, friars etc. – there is no effect without a cause.'[25] Baltimore drew attention to a more mundane problem in 1764: 'Triers . . . It is a melancholy old city, crowded with churches and convents; so that as soon as I laid down to rest I was immediately waked by the tolling of a dozen belfries: a circumstance as contrary to sleep as would have been a battery of cannon: the same disturbance happened at Namur and in many other Roman Catholic cities.'[26]

Apart from the small number of tourists who visited the Turkish empire, and came away in general with a somewhat unsympathetic view of Islam, the only non-Christian religion witnessed by tourists was Judaism. There were large Jewish communities in Dutch cities, such as Amsterdam, Italian cities, such as Venice and Rome, German cities, such as Frankfurt, and in Avignon. Visitors to Amsterdam, the city in Europe with the greatest variety of religious services, often visited the synagogue. One in 1758 heard 'three remarkable fine voices there', before spending a Sunday attending 'Persian worship, the Russian worship – mass – Quakers' meeting'. Given the presence of a sizeable Jewish community in London, Jewish practices should not have been strange to British tourists, but it is apparent from their accounts that, for many, the Jewish ceremonies they witnessed abroad were few. Pococke saw a circumcision at Rome, 'a most terrible execution'. Sacheverell Stevens wrote in Rome:

> I saw one day an odd kind of ceremony performed with great pomp and solemnity; they carried about their Synagogue, a thing drest like a baby, with a rich embroidered cloak upon it, and a silver crown on the head, to which were affixed two scepters and silver bells hanging down them; the people, as it passed along, went up and kissed the cloak, and some rubbed their eyes with it; being carried to a kind of pulpit, they began to undress it, when it appeared to be only a large roll of parchment, filled with writing in a large Hebrew character; they all sat their hats on, and some with a piece of flannel over their shoulders . . .

Tourists sometimes made critical remarks. One wrote of the Frankfurt Jews in 1743:

> . . . they have a particular quarter of the town assigned them, which is remarkable for nothing but filth and nastiness, and in which they are locked up every night. They are a crafty set of people. They crowd the inns in quest of strangers and travellers, to whom they are very troublesome.[27]

A certain number of British tourists were Catholics. They followed the same routes as Protestant tourists, though fewer appear to have visited the United Provinces. For many a visit to the Continent was linked to the education of children in schools and convents, particularly in the Austrian Netherlands and northern France where there were many that catered for British Catholics. Nicholas Blundell visited his daughters in their French school in 1723. On his return to Britain his 'luggage was searched and some spiritual books and pictures taken from me to be burned'. The scholar and botanist Thomas Clifford, later Sir Thomas Constable (1762–1823), was educated in the academy opened at Liège by the English ex-Jesuits after their expulsion from Bruges. He continued his studies at the College of Navarre in Paris, and then travelled through Switzerland.

Not all Catholics travelled for educational reasons. Henry, Lord Arundell, purchased a number of religious paintings in Italy. William Constable visited Italy, where he had relations, on several occasions; Henry Swinburne published important accounts of his travels in Spain, France and southern Italy; and Sir Carnaby Haggerston arranged at Loreto the saying of Masses that his mother desired. An anonymous Catholic defended the shrine there but noted that he could not 'give into all those spiritual fopperies, and out of the way devotions, that some of our own communion unthinkingly run into'.[28] Some Catholic tourists displayed overt sympathy for the Jacobite cause, but so did Protestant tourists, such as the Duke of Beaufort in 1726. The British envoy in Naples reported of the Earl of Stafford in 1740 that he 'shews a disposition very different from most I have met with of the same persuasion, and is not byassed in his principles, as to government, by the usual prejudices, which the religion he professes, carrys with it'. Increasingly, Catholics could rely on the hospitality of British envoys.[29] Often educated abroad, and many with relatives abroad, Catholic tourists tended to be less critical of Continental society. Aside from their religious devotions and their visits to foreign relatives – Sir John Swinburne's brother and successor Edward was a Bordeaux merchant, his sister Anne a nun, and he visited both of them – Catholic tourists did the same on the whole as their Protestant compatriots.

There is little information concerning Jewish tourists, though William Lee wrote from Mannheim in August 1753: 'Mr. Potter has been here with Mr. Franks the Jew. They both dined with the Elector. It was not known that Mr. Franks was a Jew till after dinner. The courtiers are much offended that a Jew should presume to offer himself to be presented at court. They are not naturalized in this country nor upon the same footing as in England.'[30] Thomas Potter (c. 1718–59) MP, was a son of the previous Archbishop of Canterbury. Later that year he was to oppose the repeal of the Jewish Nationalization Act.

Religion, as much as language, food and currency, helped to make the Continent foreign. It was one of the major changes that tourists commented on as soon as they arrived in France. Religious symbols, such as crucifixes and shrines, were everywhere; as were members of the regular and secular clergy; processions were encountered frequently in the streets; religious buildings dominated towns. That tourists commented so often upon religious matters did not, therefore, reflect an obsession, but a response to the situation they encountered. Many were very hostile to Catholicism, many simply critical. Most discussed Catholicism without mentioning the situation in Britain, though Gardenstone commented in 1786: 'The Capuchins are respectful, generally modest in their applications, and very piously thankful, returning prayers as value for our charity; and what better pennyworths have we from our own established clergy?'[31] Possibly the lack of sympathy with and understanding for Catholicism led to an inadequate appreciation of many aspects of Continental society and culture. This was not a feature of tourism that contemporary critics condemned; rather they drew attention to what they regarded as the ideological and religious dangers presented by travel to Catholic countries. Given the nature of British religious education and ideology, it is not surprising that tourists were hostile to Continental Catholicism.

Attitudes changed, however, during the century, although this should not be exaggerated. Arriving in France in 1785, Thomas, 7th Earl of Elgin, was shocked by outdoor shrines and crucifixes, images in cathedrals, the use of the name of God in conversation and the opening of shops and theatres on Sundays.[32] Nevertheless, the defeat of Jacobitism played a crucial role, but other factors were also important. Eighteenth-century 'rationalism' emphasized the unity and, generally, the soundness of Christian tenets, while deriding the non-rational elements in both Catholic and Protestant observances. A stronger distinction began to be drawn between religious observance and the clergy. As more tourists met priests, monks, cardinals and other Catholic clerics they discovered that the clergy were actually human and usually educated, sensible people, rather than 'whores of Babylon'. *The Daily Universal Register* reported on 17 January 1785:

> When the present Pope passed through Munich . . . the English Minister was introduced to his Holiness, who received him in a manner peculiarly affectionate and condescending. He assured him, that he had a partiality for the English nation, which he would be happy to have frequent opportunities of showing. He desired the Minister would send letters directed to himself (the Pope) with such English gentlemen, or students in painting or architecture, as he might wish to recommend to him: and he promised he would feel a pleasure in taking them under his own immediate protection.

In addition, the power of the clergy in most of Catholic Europe was increasingly restricted, especially in the 1760s, 1770s and 1780s. Mitford claimed in 1776 that the French were 'aiming at a reformation in their religion'.[33] Familiarity bred a measure of tolerance, and eventually positive sympathy towards Catholicism when the whole Christian value system appeared to be threatened by the violence and atheism of the French Revolution.

NOTES

1. Walker to Archbishop Wake, 2 July 1722, Christ Church, Wake Mss.
2. Mellish to mother, 12 May 1731, Nottingham UL, Mellish.
3. Journal of Sir William Mildmay, Chelmsford CRO 15M50/1303, p. 57; Drake, 10 April, 3 May 1769, Aylesbury CRO, D/DR/8/2/11, 13; Thomas Pelham to mother, 19 Dec. 1776, BL Add. 33127; James Fortrey to Perceval, 20 Nov. 1725, BL Add. 47031; Black, 'The Catholic Threat and the British Press in the 1720s and 1730s', *Journal of Religious History*, 12 (1983); Hume, 28 April 1714, BL Add. 29477; BL Stowe 790 f. 53–5; Maclaurin, Aberdeen UL f. 191–2, 194; Edward to Joseph Mellish, 25 May 1731; Atwell to Lady Cowper,

28 Oct. 1729, Herts, D/EP F 234; Walker, pp. 41, 410; Quarendon jnl, Oxford CRO, Dillon papers, xx/a/7a; Walter Stanhope to mother, 11 July 1769, Bradford; Andrews, *Letters to a Young Gentleman*, pp. 282–3; Brand to Wharton, 11 Sept. 1790; Garmston, 23 Oct. 1787, BL Add. 30271; Montagu, I, 55; Moore, II, 252; Thomas Wagstaffe to Lord Craven, 15 Oct. 1765, Aylesbury, D/6R/6.

4. Hume, 30 Mar. 1714, BL Add. 29477; Pococke, 13, 19 June 1734, BL Add. 22978; Leven, I, 354; Wharton to Thomas Lloyd, 4 April 1775; Knight, pp. 17, 28–9; Montagu I, 49; Carleton, *History*, pp. 245–8; *Gray Correspondence*, 30 Mar. 1739; Swinton, 11 Mar. (os) 1731; Hertford CRO D/EP F234, p. 106; Beinecke, Osborn Shelves c 53 f 67, 70, 75.

5. Hotham to father Sir Charles, 2 April 1712, Hull UL DDHo/13/4; Pelham to mother, 23 Nov. 1775, 19 Dec. 1776, Francis, 25 Oct. 1772, BL Add. 33126–7, 40759; Swinton, 1 June (os) 1731; Tracy and Dettand, Bod. Ms. Add. A 366 f. 4; Mitchell, BL Add. 58316, f. 14, 40; Greene, Preston CRO DDGr F/3 f. 9; Aikin, I, 89–90; Chelmsford, 15M50/1302, p. 7; Mildmay jnl; Gray, p. 347; Perceval to Charles Dering, 25 June (os) 1718, BL Add. 47028; Shaw, pp. 60, 74.

6. Garmston, 23 Oct. 1787, BL Add. 30271; *Tour of Holland*, p. 230.

7. Earl of March, *A Duke and his friends: The life and letters of the second Duke of Richmond* (2 vols, 1911), I, 175–6; Swinton, 12 Mar. (os) 1731; Stevens, pp. 200–1, 209–10.

8. Wyndham, *Chronicles*, 125; *Tour of Holland*, pp. 106, 231; Northall, p. 118; Young, BL Stowe, 791, p. 117; anon, 28 Dec. 1726, Bedford CRO, L30/8/1; Mildmay jnl, 15M50/1302, p. 21, Young I, 36; Stevens, p. 52.

9. Swinton, 1 May (os) 1731; Stanhope, 21 June 1769, Bradford; Mitchell, BL Add. 58314, f. 47; Brand to Wharton, 14 Mar. 1786; John Russell, *Letters from a Young Painter* (1748), p. 8; Stevens, p. 293; Smith jnl, CUL Add. 7621, 9 July 1752.

10. Garrick, 1751, p. 5; Wharton to mother, 26 Feb., 5 Mar. 1775; Beinecke, Osborn Shelves c 467 II no. 5; Andrews, *Letters to a Young Gentleman*, p. 84; Orrery, p. 113; Jervis, BL Add. 31192, f. 38.

11. Swinton, 5 Feb. (os), 23 Jan. (os), 18 Jan (os) 1731; Stevens, p. 157; *Newcastle Journal*, 28 June (os) 1740; BL Althorp F60.

12. R. Wodrow, *Analecta, or Materials for a History of Remarkable Providences Mostly relating to Scotch Ministers and Christians*, III (Edinburgh, 1842), 305–6; Stevens, pp. 298, 340.

13. Poole, I, 50; Mellish to mother, 19 Feb. 1731, Nottingham UL Mellish; Essex, pp. 51–4; Wharton to mother, 1 May 1775; Bennet, 10 July 1785; Townson to Drake, 12 Oct. 1768, Aylesbury, D/DR/8/31.

14. Brand to Wharton, 20 May 1792, 3 Aug. 1793; Pratt, pp. 101–7, 231.

15. Brand to Wharton, 27 Aug. 1779, 10 Sept. 1787, 4 June 1780; Guildford CRO Brodrick Mss. 1248/6.

16. Brand to Wharton, 15 Dec. 1789.

17. Anon., BL Stowe, 790, f. 158; Shaw, p. 72; Perceval to Chamberlayne, 9 July 1718, Perceval to Daniel Dering, 5 June (os) 1726, BL Add. 47028, 47031; Richard, p. 202.

18. Holland, BL Add. 51445 B, f. 10.

19. Stevens, p. 375; Richard p. 143.

20. Anon., BL Add. 12130, f. 81; Wharton to Brand, 5 May, Brand to Wharton, 27 May, 16 July 1783; anon., 20 Mar. 1785, Bod. Mss. Eng. Misc. f 55; Bennet, 3, 5 Oct. 1785; J.E. Smith, I, 140.

21. Francis, BL Add. 40759, f. 16–17, 25–7; Yorke to Keith, 15 Dec. 1778, BL Add. 35515; *Daily Universal Register*, 17 Jan. 1785.

22. Greene, Preston CRO DDGr F/3 f.13; McDougall to Keith, 27 Jan. 1782, BL Add. 35515; Shaw, p. 92; Stevens, p. 52.

23. Stevens, pp. 6, 221–2, 163, 187; Beinecke, Osborn Shelves c 200, 5 June 1754; Nuneham to sister, D/LE E2 No. 5; *Harcourt*, III, 82–3; anon., BL Add. 12130, f. 66; Smith, 22 July 1752, CUL Add. Mss. 7621; Villiers, p. 31–2; Thicknesse, 1768, p. 73.

24. Thicknesse, 1786, p. 182; Andrews, 1784, p. 243; Smith, I, xxv–xxviii; Gray, pp. 380, 425, 385, 402–3.

25. Pelham, BL Add. 33126, f. 178–9; Bennet, 29, 30 Aug. 1785; Beinecke, Osborn Shelves c 289.

26. *A Tour to the East* (1767), p. 165.

27. Beinecke, Osborn Shelves c 469 p. 77; Pococke, BL Add. 22978, f. 75; Stevens, pp. 192–3; Anon. 1743, CUL Add. 8789; Mitchell, BL Add. 58319, f. 60; Aikin, I, 80, 82.

28. T.E. Gibson (ed.), *Blundell's Diary* (Liverpool, 1895), p. 196; J.D. Alsop, 'John Macky's 1707 Account of the English Seminaries in Flanders', *Recusant History*, 15 (1981), pp. 337–41; Black and A. Bellenger, 'The foreign education of British Catholics in the eighteenth century', *Downside Review*, 105 (1987), pp. 310–16; Beinecke, Osborn Shelves c 366 2, p. 293.

29. Allen to Newcastle, 22 Mar., 22 May 1740, PRO 93/10.

30. Beinecke, Lee Box 3, 28 Aug. 1758.

31. Gardenstone, I, 15.

32. Checkland, *Elgins*, p. 11.

33. Gloucester CRO D 2002 F1 p. 22.

12

THE ARTS

. . . notwithstanding all I had seen in Italy and came almost surfeited with Paintings, the Pictures at the Palais Royal, the Luxembourg Galleries, and in many private collections could not but charm me; yet I do not profess myself a General Admirer either of French Painting or Statues.

Henry Ellison, 1781[1]

There was a dead Christ over a door most horridly natural the gaping wounds, the blood settling in the extremities, all quite shocking. Painters had not yet learnt to improve and soften nature.

Bennet, Basle public library, 11 August 1785

MUSIC

. . . à quoy aboutit pour les Anglois tous ces voyages en Italie, qu' à y prendre le gout de la peinture, des statues, et de la musique, toutes choses qui n'engagent qu'à des depenses.

St Saphorin, envoy in Vienna, 1722[2]

The most fashionable music in eighteenth-century Britain was foreign, principally Italian opera and German orchestral music. British tourists expected to attend musical performances while abroad, and to enjoy the music that they heard. Music played a large part for many tourists and it is clear that many were observant and sensitive critics of what they heard.

Opera

> The opera with the old style of French music than which, nothing in nature can be more disagreeable; For my part I could not help asking the Gentleman who sat next me whether they were singing an air or a Recitative it mattered not which for both are equally detestable . . . the eye is the only organ to be pleased at the French opera . . .
>
> Wharton (Paris) to Miss Lloyd, 29 February 1775

Alongside Italian painting, the opera dominated the cultural consciousness of British tourists. There are far more references to it than to other forms of music, and, in so far as comparisons are possible, it aroused more interest than architecture in most tourists. Opera was a sensitive political and cultural issue in Britain. The preference of aristocratic society for this expensive foreign art form led to widespread condemnation, particularly in the second quarter of the century. Opera was held to be an unnatural art, an attitude expressed most strongly in press criticism of the popularity of Italian castrati. Aristocratic preference for opera led to attacks on the supposed abandonment of British culture in favour of a pernicious, effeminate import. Two different, though interrelated, disputes, opposed British and foreign culture, vernacular works, such as Gay's *Beggar's Opera*, and Italian opera. Little of this criticism was voiced by aristocratic British tourists, though the 2nd Earl Cowper's response to the opera in Rome in 1730 was that it was very disagreeable to see men 'drest in women's cloaths'. The majority of the attacks made by tourists on opera, as opposed to criticism of specific performances, came from those who were not members of the British élite. The Anglican clergyman, Robert Gray, while visiting Rome criticized the idea of men dancing dressed as women. Walker, touring Italy in 1787, launched savage attacks on opera:

> . . . of all the seminaries appropriated to the wise purpose of propagating folly, none ever equalled the Italian Opera: Here, indeed, the god Fashion displays his mental triumph! Reason is led into captivity by the ears! Virtue and public spirit take opiates from the hands of Circe! – and effeminacy, lewdness, and perverted ideas gambol in the train! Let the monarch who wishes to render himself despotic over tame and unreflecting slaves, give countenance to this school of softness and debility . . . though the sneers of wit stigmatize the absurdity of whimpering in Recitativo – the accompanying groan uttered as echo from the mechanic Orchestra – Caesar degraded by tall plumes, an hoop-petticoat, or by uttering artificial love like a snivelling schoolboy – more ridiculous and absurd the better – it will

dispose the mind to that finical trifling, that simpering vacuity of
conversation – that yielding softness, and tender compliance to every
proposition not understood – that makes men – like Venetians.[3]

Such sentiments were voiced by few, and Walker's attack was made late
in the century when new vernacular forms were rising at the expense
of older ones. Most tourists sought to attend the opera in all the towns
that they visited, and many altered their route in order to attend specific
performances and hear famous singers perform. It was the singers that
commanded attention rather than performances of specific operas.
Opera played a large role in tourism in Italy – it was one of the principal
attractions of the peninsula, the prime glory of modern, as opposed to
ancient, Italy. Particular towns that attracted tourists as a result of their
operas were Bologna, Reggio, Milan and Naples. Allen noted in 1729 'a
good many English Gentlemen at Milan in order to take the diversion
of the opera'. The Earl of Essex went to Bologna in 1733 to hear 'the
finest opera that ever was heard, and a vast deal of company, there was
32 English'. Earlier that year Earl Stanhope wrote from Milan: 'The opera
is the chief entertainment of all the strangers here.' The following year
Stanhope's brother George referred to British tourists travelling in order
to hear the celebrated castrato Carlo Broschi, better known as Farinelli.[4]

In Paris, at the beginning of the century, Joseph Shaw attended
'several Operas, whose musick pleased not my ears, and is much
inferior to the English and Italian, but their Dancing superior'. In 1709,
Lord Charles Somerset visited the opera in Bologna 'which appeared
to me extraordinarily delicate and fine; but was esteemed by them but
as one of the middle rank, so much does the excellent musick of this
country excell any that we can pretend to, that I am sure 'twould be the
highest vanity for us in England to compare the best of any of our new
Operas to that which was counted but indifferent among the Italians'.
Anthony Grey attended a very expensive opera in Vienna in 1716; and the
following year George Carpenter found in Bologna 'a very fine opera. I
went to it every night: the singing and music was incomparable.' Viscount
Parker visited Reggio in July 1720 in order to attend the opera; and
another tourist was very impressed that year by the chief dancer at the
opera in Valenciennes. Lord Boyle complained about the noisy audience
at the Paris opera in 1725. In 1726, Lord Perceval was upset that the Lille
opera was not performing: 'These amusements which perhaps I should
not mind if I were settled at home, have their value with strangers being
a refreshment from their fatigue of travelling.' Swinton was delighted by
the opera at Genoa which he attended on several occasions. Earl Stanhope
found the audience very noisy, the orchestra very good and the dancers
poor at Milan, where he also attended rehearsals.

In 1734 Richard Pococke attended the opera at Rome (where the Pretender was a member of the audience), was disappointed by the opera at Venice, and travelled to Vicenza (as did Sir Henry Liddell and Sir Hugh Smithson) 'to hear the opera of the famous Farinelli'. Mitchell attended the opera at Paris: 'the most frequented of all the spectacles, the connoisseurs in music cannot bear it, the lovers of dancing admire it . . . The scenes and decorations are very beautiful and the dresses of the actors very rich. The house is large and very well contrived . . . The French are very bigotted to their own music, I have seen the musicians hissed for playing one Italian air.' Sacheverell Stevens was pleased by the Siena opera: 'the singing is extremely fine, the performance noble, and the scenery magnificent'. David Garrick thought the singing in Paris very bad in 1751.

The following year Samuel Smith visited the Paris opera, sharing a box with four British friends. They thought the performance and opera house worse than those in London. Nevertheless they made themselves 'very merry . . . a Courtisan came into our box with whom I had some conversation and invited her to our hotel'. Two years later he heard an 'Italian opera tolerably well performed' at Frankfurt. Orrery preferred British to Italian Opera, and complained, in 1754, that the audience at the Florence opera was too noisy for him to hear the production. In 1760 Thomas Robinson went to the opera in Parma, writing, 'The magnificence of the Italians and the taste of the French contribute unitedly to render it so agreable as it is.' Joshua Pickersgill complained, in 1761, that the tragic opera was only changed once during the Turin carnival and he ascribed audience noise to their consequent boredom with the repetition; he was, however, pleased by the low price of admission. William Wyndham was pleased by the decoration of the opera house and the quality of the dancing in Paris in 1769. Francis attended several opera houses in Italy: at Naples he 'saw a miserable thing they called an opera buffa'; he was pleased by the opera house at Lucca; but at Turin he 'killed the evening at a comic opera', though he enjoyed the same production when he saw it the following evening.

British tourists in general had a poor opinion of French opera, apart from the dancing and scenery. Wharton was not very impressed by the Parisian opera in 1775: 'The music at the Opera when it is true French music is detestable. The Dances are very "superbes et magnifiques".' This preference for the visual rather than the musical aspects of Parisian opera was expressed widely, one anonymous tourist writing:

> If I could leave my ears at home, and wished to give my eyes, the first amusement, this world can afford them, I would certainly betake myself to the French opera. The house is indeed magnificent, and the scenes and decorations, I am persuaded, are as perfect, as the art of man can

produce; whilst the dancing is somewhat more than human . . . it is rather allied to the arts of sculpture, and of painting, and in the most lively manner, presents to you the effects which the varied passions and emotions of the soul, produce upon the human frame – love and hatred, pity and resentment, hope and despair, are finely pictured and sculptured, in the features, the attitudes, and graceful movements of the French dancers. They can inculcate virtue or instruct in vice.

Thomas Pelham attended the opera at Florence in 1777: 'it is tolerable and by far the best I have heard in Italy for that at Naples the great school for music was abominable; the management of the theatre being in the hands of people whose only interest is to get money; and who consequently are satisfied provided that their house be full.' At Bologna he visited the elderly Farinelli. The following year Philip Yorke 'heard the Gabrielli sing in the opera of Armida' at Lucca and found that the opera at Venice was 'the only place where one sees the society of the place'. Charles Drake Garrard compared the London and Paris opera in 1779, to the advantage of the former – while Henry Ellison suggested that the sets of the Paris opera were better than the music. Brand was critical of the quality of the Parisian singing he heard in 1781 and 1783, though reasonably pleased with the operas he attended at Turin and Alessandria in the latter year. In 1784 he was shocked by the representation of God on stage at Bologna and went en route from Venice to Geneva with Sir James Graham and Sir James Hall 'by Mantua on purpose to hear [Luigi] Marchesi in the opera of the Fair . . . all fell asleep during the performance! The heat was intense and we were fatigued beyond all conception.' In 1787, Brand attended a performance of an Italian opera at Brunswick; and, in 1790, 'had an excellent opera' at Florence and went to Bologna partly to hear the famous Italian tenor, Giacomo Davide, perform. The following year he heard a good German opera in Frankfurt – 'now and then a harsh German word did violence to the melody but less frequently than you would imagine', and attacked the excessive flourishes of Italian opera singing: 'This is the degenerate taste of Italy, where methinks everything else is equally degenerate.' However, in 1792 he praised an oratorio he heard in Palermo and a burletta in Milan. In May 1793 Brand heard Davide sing at Florence and wrote, 'I think him too French in his manner of passing from the extreme of sweetness to that coarse bellowing which he calls expression and force.' Later in the year, at Milan, he 'feasted on a charming Burletta of more sense as well as humour than the general run of those great products of whim and caprice'. Bennet and the Rolles, visiting Paris in 1785, went

. . . to the Opera of the Danaides. The music loud and noisy in the French taste, and the singers screamed past all power of simile to represent. The scenery was very good, no people understanding the *jeu de theatre* or tricks of the stage, so well as the French. We had in the ark scenes not above one light, and in the bright ones above twenty large chandeliers, so as to make a wonderful contrast, nor was there the least error or blunder in changing the scenes, except once when a candle pulled up too hastily, was very near to setting fire to a whole grove of trees. The stage being deeper than ours, was filled sometimes with fifty persons, a great advantage to the Chorus's and bustling parts; but not equal to the theatre at Turin, where they can (by throwing back partitions) open a large field behind the playhouse, and introduce upon occasion a body of Cavalry. Our Opera ended with a representation of Hell, in which the fifty Danaides were hauled and pulled about as if the Devils had been going to ravish them. Several of them in the violence of the French action being literally thrown flat upon their backs; and they were all at last buried in such a shower of fire, that I wonder the Playhouse was not burned to the ground. We paid somewhat more than 6 shillings each for our places, and were on the whole well entertained.

That spring, James Dawkins wrote from Dresden: 'after having left Vienna, it is not an easy matter to be pleased with an opera'.

The appeal of opera was widespread though for a variety of reasons. Lord Dalrymple was not the only tourist who chased the 'filles de l'*opéra*'. Bennet wrote in Paris in October 1785, of 'Madame de Gazon, a lively little opera singer well known to many young Englishmen who have shared her favours, and as *Gazon* signifies turf, are said by the wits of Paris to have been on the turf. Mr L: lately a fellow commoner of Trinity, and heir to one of the first fortunes in Durham is the reigning favourite at present', a reference to William Lambton (1764–97), who was to be MP for Durham and to die of consumption at Pisa. Boswell had a similar conquest in Naples. The social nature of the opera was commented on by an anonymous visitor to Turin in 1782: 'the music is never attended to by the people of the country unless a new opera and the first representation perhaps – or a favourite air by a favourite singer – it appears to be rather a general conversazione, and that on a high key'. Robert Gray heard the great castrato Girolamo Crescentini, at Bologna, and had his pocket picked; Robert Arbuthnot complained about 'the vile screaming of the French singers' at Brussels; James Robson praised the performance of a comic opera he saw in Geneva; and Richard Garmston deplored the dancers showing their legs in France and Turin, and the 'very tiresome' five-hour-long performance of a serious opera in Naples, where the female dancers displayed their behinds. He did, however, applaud the scenery and the dancing at the Rome opera. Frances Crewe left a fascinating account of the Parisian opera in the mid-1780s, which reflected the controversy in France over the merits of French and foreign operas and the success of the latter:

> Gluck and Piccinni are now the favourite Composers here. Their taste in Music is, I think, much improved within these ten or twelve years, and their Theatres on that account much worth going to. I still think, however, one may trace a great deal of the abominable French stile of composition: but this is more, perhaps, in the manner of expression: than in the composition itself. The Dancing is very fine . . .

> . . . been at the great Opera last night – a more striking entertainment, take it for all in all, I never saw. It is certain our stage almost every year affords one or two singers, which connoisseurs may think compensate for all droning recitative, and insipid Dancers, Gestures and Scenery, but indeed, since Sachini and Gluck are the composers of their Opera here, and since the performers have left off the strange and disgusting French manner of singing, it is impossible not to be often delighted with the great Opera at Paris. That which I saw last night is called Dordanus; a piece tho not remarkably well written, yet full of Interest – and here I must venture to observe that, in my opinion, the Greek Model, which has had so much said for and against it, seems to be quite calculated for an opera – The Strophes and Antistrophes last night had a remarkable effect upon all the Audience – and as no opera can ever produce that sort of sympathy, which regulated Tragedies, and other dramatic Representations, being more like reality, are formed to excite, what can be wished for, than to be quite overwhelmed with sounds of harmony and influenced by a system, as it were formed 'to elevate and surprise'. They have a very full Orchestra here, and a new Instrument in it which, I think, is called un Trombeau – It has a mixed sound of Drum and Trumpet and produced great effect. The scenery of this Theatre is remarkably magnificent and the Machinery is managed with infinite Dexterity. As to Dancing, that has always been in the greatest Perfection here, and one is not shocked, as with us, at an immense distance between the leaders and Figurantes. I cannot quit this subject without expressing a wish that something of this kind of opera was attempted in our language.
> . . . Surely people would be more affected by Distress conveyed in a language they understood than by mere sounds which are all our fine operas have to bestow upon the generality of Auditors . . . Here indeed the audience, even to the lowest of them, by the shouts which they frequently send forth, and the many inconveniences which they contentedly suffer on crowded nights, sufficiently prove how capable they are of tasting this species of entertainment.[5]

It is clear that tourists expected a high standard of performance, and were a critical and appreciative audience. In no sense can they be described as provincial or as praising whatever they saw. This stemmed from the high level of musical culture in London and the well-developed awareness of operatic technique. In opera, as in much else, British tourists were part of an international society in which cultural forms were common even if cultural suppositions, particularly in the case of religion, were very different.

Other Musical Forms

Much to my surprise, I hear little or no music; there is ten times more in London all the year round, than in any city in Italy, except perhaps during the Carnival. Neither do the Italians appear to me half so fond of music as the English though I believe they understand it better. They have no such thing as Ballad-singing; except upon a few particular days; nor an opera but at particular seasons, and then they never listen to it. I fancy we import all the music from Italy, as we do all the claret from France. These commodities are not to be found upon the spot where they grow, but among the people who can purchase them. I say this upon my own experience only, which I admit is not very great.

Philip Francis, 'Hints to Travellers', 1772[6]

The musical experiences of British tourists were dominated by opera, but many enjoyed other aspects of the Continent's varied musical life. Some of this can best be described as exotic. Thomas Pelham, on his way from Madrid to Cadiz saw the gypsies who visited the inns of southern Spain 'and entertain Travellers with Fandangos, Sequidillas etc.'[7] Lady Craven heard the Prince of Wallachia's orchestra in 1786; and was much struck at St Petersburg by the extraordinary sounds produced by horns. Most tourists, however, heard music similar to that which they could hear in Britain – for, as a character in a London play of 1737 complained: 'The reigning Taste's all Italian. Music has engrossed the attention of the whole people: The Duchess and her woman, the Duke and his postilion, are equally infected – The contagion first took root in the shallow noddles of such of our itinerant coxcombs as were incapable of more virtuous impressions.'[8] It was certainly true that some tourists helped to spread interest in foreign music. John, Earl of Orrery, wrote from Cork in 1737:

We have a Bishop, who, as He has travelled beyond the Alps, has brought home with him, to the amusement of our mercantile fraternity, the arts and sciences that are the ornament of Italy and the admiration of the European world. He eats, drinks and sleeps in taste. He has pictures by Carlo Morat [Maratti], music by Corelli, castles in the air by Vitruvius; and on high-days and holidays we have the honour of catching cold at a Venetian door . . . Under the reign of Dr [Robert] Clayton we sing catches, read *Pastor Fido*, and talk of love.[9]

As a Tory, Orrery was sceptical about the value of such foreign cultural importations. Such scepticism was shared by others. Sarah Marlborough was opposed to her younger grandsons being taught architecture and music 'which are all things proper for people that have time upon their hands and like passing it in idleness rather than in what will be profitable'.[10] Despite these criticisms, tourists attended concerts abroad and took music lessons. Interest in the musical life on the Continent was strengthened by the very successful publication of Charles Burney's *Present State of Music in France and Italy* (1771) and his *Present State of Music in Germany, the Netherlands, and the United Provinces* (1773). They were based on his two tours in 1770–2.

Many tourists were impressed by what they heard. Walker, whose critical comments upon opera have already been quoted, heard a concert in the Louvre in November 1787, and his response was very positive: 'Am just returned in great rapture. I fear the French outdo us in music!' Paris was a major centre of music and many tourists attended concerts there. Perceval and his wife were frequent attenders in 1725–6, and enjoyed the concerts. They also hired a music master, presumably for their sons. Mitchell was very impressed by the *Concert Spirituel*, though Frances Crewe was less so by the sacred music she heard: 'I went to the Kings Chapel to hear a high mass yesterday morning – The music was fine, but the drums and fiddles in my opinion spoiled the effect which good choirs ought to have – It was indeed far from "Dissolving the Soul in Ecstacies" or bringing "all Heaven before our Eyes". However it was harmony for all that, and good in its Gothic way.' At a concert in the Louvre in 1781, Robert Ellison found 'beaucoup de bruit; peu de musique'.[11]

Italy, 'this country of Musick' as Francis Head described it in 1724, offered many opportunities for the music lover. Richard, 3rd Earl of Burlington, who returned to Britain in 1715 with 878 trunks, crates and other items of baggage, as well as the sculptor Giovanni Battista Guelfi and the violinist Pietro Castrucci, had ordered harpsichords in Florence and Venice. Swinton, who attended a concert in Paris, was delighted by the musical lovers he heard in Livorno and found the voices of Genoese castrati 'exceeding sweet and melodious'. In 1775 Wharton heard in Rome some apprentice barbers give a very good vocal serenade for a few women. He also attended some small private concerts where Boccherini quintets were played. Nine years later Brand complained from the same city: 'there is nothing to be heard but now and then an Oratorio with a wretched band and worse voices', but he added three weeks later: 'The holy week is at last over that season of wonder and enjoyment for all that are not blind or deaf. The first verse of the Miserere frightened me it so far exceeded all ideas I formed of it.' In 1791 Brand rushed to Venice, travelling, against his custom, by night, to hear an oratorio, Ninive conversa, by Anfossi. He was delighted with the performance: 'I never expect so long as I live to hear such music and such execution. The accompanied recitatives especially were beyond all conception expressive. I assure you such a Jonas as Bianca Sacchetti might turn more to repentance than the preaching of ten metropolitans or twenty archdeacons.' Four years earlier James Robson had been pleased by the oratorio he heard in Venice.[12]

Germany and Austria had a rich musical life, though not all tourists appreciated it. Harry Digby attended a concert at Vienna in 1751 'of which I shall say nothing as in musick I have no opinion'. In 1787 Brand attended concerts and purchased music in the same city: 'heard some excellent fiddling and harpsichord playing at Mainz', and wrote, 'in this country every human being is musical.[13] He attended concerts at Geneva in 1780 and was amazed by a solo on the double bass which he heard at an excellent concert at The Hague in 1790. In his letters Brand also described the musical life of the Germans and a concert he heard in Salzburg. Not all music was orchestral. Richard Garmston's supper at Mâcon was accompanied by a band, and many tourists left accounts of the rich and varied musical life of the Continent. Most enjoyed the music that they heard, though, like so many of the tourist pastimes, it was confined largely to the major cities.[14]

This was also true of the theatre. Tourists tended to be more critical of Continental theatre than opera. The British believed the Garrick school of acting to be superior to Continental acting styles, and this opinion was echoed by foreign visitors to London who were particularly impressed with English comedy. In 1755 Lord Nuneham, accompanied by George Viscount Villiers, later 4th Earl of Jersey (1735–1805), and their bearleader, the poet William Whitehead, visited Leipzig for the fair. He thought the acting company

> execrable, they never seem to feel in the least their character, and are always looking about without meaning. In tragedy they have not any action and in comedy are so dressed and place themselves in such horrid attitudes with such awkward strange gestures that it is impossible to forbear laughing . . . I wish you were to see a Ballet *à la française* as they call it, with a Polish tune, by eight or ten people who never learnt one step, which you may imagine has an excellent effect . . . the ladies who attempt to be fine and cut entre shats (which

by the by I do not know how to spell) [entrechats] have one petticoat which reaches not farther than their knees which when they jump high discovers to the spectators a large pair of black plush breeches.[15]

PAINTING

I am in high spirits at the thought of seeing Italy in so short a time, ever since I can remember I have been wishing to go into a country, where my fondness for painting and antiquities will be so indulged, I expect every day a letter from Mr. [George] Knapton with a catalogue of all the finest galleries and his remarks on them, for I intend not only to improve my taste, but my judgement, by the fine originals I expect to see there, I have attempted all sorts of painting since I left England.

Lord Nuneham to his sister, 1755

I went last week with my Spanish master to see pictures in the palace which are exceedingly fine and very valuable from having the works of some masters who are almost unknown in any other collection; I intend visiting them often not only with a view of learning their different perfections or faults, but of talking Spanish on subjects different from what I should meet with at home.

Thomas Pelham, Madrid, 1776[16]

Renaissance and later Italian paintings were valued greatly in Britain, where they were regarded as the best example of their art. For many tourists seeing these paintings was a major motive for their trip to Italy. Whereas French cooking and Italian opera could be sampled in London, it was necessary to visit Italy in order to appreciate, to any degree, Italian art and architecture. This was despite the increasing number of Italian paintings that were imported into Britain in the eighteenth century. Many tourists purchased paintings and they were willing to buy paintings on most topics, including religious ones. Furthermore, tourists were willing to commission paintings by Italian artists, such as Batoni, and by British artists resident abroad.

Many British artists travelled in Europe. Most, such as James Barry, Alexander Cozens and his son John Robert, Nathaniel Dance, Gavin Hamilton, William Hoare (Hoare of Bath), Thomas Jones, William Kent, William Marlow, John Parker, Allan Ramsay, Joshua Reynolds, George Romney, Jonathan Skelton, Francis Towne, Richard Wilson, Wright of Derby, and the sculptors Joseph Nollekens and Joseph Wilton, visited Italy but some travelled further afield. Gavin Hamilton painted portraits of tourists such as the 8th Duke of Hamilton. The duke also commissioned him to paint *Hector's Farewell Andromache*. Willey Reveley accompanied Sir Richard Worsley as 'architect and draftsman' to Italy, Greece, Constantinople and Egypt in 1784–9. His drawings of the pyramids were based on measurements. Lady Craven noted that Worsley 'had a person with him to take views'. Revett and James Stuart travelled to Greece in 1751–4 drawing and measuring most of the antiquities in and near Athens. After the foundation of the Royal Academy in 1768, artists increasingly took on the role of Grand Tourists, but their motivations and approaches were different, while Picturesque Tourism played a role for some. Just as artists like James Barry went to Italy to look at ancient sculpture, in his case in 1766, so J.F. Cozens went there to look for beautiful scenery. Market forces directed the actions of some artists and even required them to have spent a period in Italy. Joseph Wright of Derby went there in 1773 in the hope of fanning his reputation, and he abandoned his 'Flemish' style upon his return, in favour of the then popular classical manner of Joshua Reynolds. The Italian school of painting was considered superior to the Dutch school.

Some painters went to Italy and stayed there. The Scot Jacob More (1740–93), worked in Rome from around 1777 until his death, while James Durno (c. 1745–95) worked there from 1774 until he died. Like other artist-residents, Durno also engaged in art dealing for British patrons. Purchases, engravings and the dispatch of paintings for exhibition at the Royal Academy ensured that painters who settled in Italy were not lost to British view. More sent five works to be exhibited at the Society of Artists in 1775–7 and eleven to the Royal Academy in 1783–9. Travel to Italy gave some painters the opportunity to meet British patrons. Studying painting in Rome, William Kent met Richard, 3rd Earl of Burlington, and he brought Kent back to England in 1719 to complete the painted decorations of Burlington House. William Hoare of Bath (1707–92) spent nine years (1729–c. 38) in Rome, improving his technique, which was influenced by antique sculptures, and copying paintings for tourists. It was probably through Joseph Spence, whom he met in Rome in 1732, that Hoare made the contacts that were to lead to numerous commissions from the Pelham family. The impact of their travels on British artists varied greatly, which was not surprising as some went to Italy when young and in order to be educated, while others, such as Joseph Wright of Derby in 1773–5, travelled when already established.[17]

British tourists employed painters for a variety of reasons. Many wanted their portraits painted often in elevating poses in classical surroundings. These portraits were usually painted in Italy, often in Rome, by artists such as Batoni, Carriera, David, Nazari, Dupra, Masucci, Mengs and Trevisani.

Masucci and Trevisani were most popular earlier in the century, Batoni and Mengs later. It is known that Batoni painted 154 British tourists.[18] Drouais, Greuze, La Tour, Roslin and Van Loo all painted portraits of British tourists in Paris. British painters, such as Dance, also painted the portraits of tourists. The British were not unique in this: at Vienna there is a splendid portrait of the future Joseph II and his brother Leopold, painted by Batoni while on their Grand Tour. Many of the portraits were extremely good, and William Bentinck wrote to his mother: 'I have also sent you my picture done by Rosalba Carriera and which will always be worth something for the painting.' Lady Coningsby, however, was unwilling to pay the price Hyacinthe Rigaud expected for a portrait in Paris in 1738.[19]

Others commissioned paintings of places that they had seen. Christopher Crowe commissioned a painting of the Piazzetta in Venice from Luca Carlevaris. Many tourists purchased views of Venice. Canaletto painted several hundred, virtually all of which were sold to British buyers, many of them while in Venice. The Canalettos now at Woburn were doubtless ordered by Lord John Russell, later 4th Duke of Bedford (1710–71), when he was in Venice in 1731 with the Earl of Essex and the Duke of Leeds. Lewis Goupy, a French painter resident in London, accompanied the 3rd Earl of Burlington to the Continent and painted many scenes for him. The painter George Robertson (c. 1748–88) accompanied the Duke of Dorset and William Beckford and painted various scenes, and John Robert Cozens (1752–99) painted at least ninety-six watercolours for Beckford, with whom he travelled extensively in Italy. Cozens had earlier been to Switzerland with Richard Payne Knight, and produced fifty-four watercolours for him. Richard Wilson developed his Italianate and classical style as a landscape-painter while in Italy in the 1750s. He travelled from Rome to Naples with the Earl of Dartmouth, for whom he drew several landscapes. William Pars (1742–82) accompanied Henry, 2nd Viscount Palmerston, to the Continent producing drawings and watercolours. Those shown at the Royal Academy in 1771 were some of the first Alpine views to be exhibited in England. Pars died in Rome.

Some tourists commissioned reproductions of paintings that they liked. Henry Hoare had Batoni and Jeremiah Davison paint copies of four Renis and one each of Veronese, Guercino, Bourdon and Van Dyck for Stourhead. Batoni, Mengs, Masucci and Costanzi collaborated on copies for Northumberland House, Batoni copied a Subleyras portrait for Burton Constable and Reni's *Aurora* was copied for Buckland, Castletown, Fonthill, Hovingham, Northumberland House, Rievaulx, Shugborough, Wardour and West Wycombe. Sir Richard Hoare had copies made of many of the Raphael frescoes in the Vatican in 1793, and Brand commissioned a copy of a 'head of Rossi in the gallery of Florence, an angel playing the guitar, the sweetest thing I ever beheld, more than Correggesque'. Franciszek Smuglewicz, a Polish artist in Rome between 1763 and 1784 painted large copies of Guercino's *Death of Dido* and Reni's *Rape of Helen* for Sir John Goodricke.[20]

The purchase of paintings was mainly concentrated in Italy, though it was not only British dealers, in the growing secondary art market in London, who bought some of the vast numbers of Dutch pictures that came to this country in the eighteenth century. Tourists preferred Italian to French art, and contemporary Italian art was less popular than the painters of the previous two centuries, though certain modern Italian painters, such as Canaletto, were viewed with favour. Coke, Burlington and William Windham built up impressive collections. Thomas Coke, later 1st Earl of Leicester (1697–1759), was abroad from 1712 till 1718, mostly in Italy. He prided himself on becoming 'a perfect virtuoso', was acquainted with many contemporary painters, purchased many paintings, some of which he had specially commissioned, and had his portrait painted by Francesco Trevisani in 1717. Later tourists tended to collect less because of the increasingly active art market in London, export controls in Italy and the drying up of supply, which in itself created a more efficient agent network. In 1785 James Byres had to resort to subterfuge in order to purchase Poussin's *Seven Sacraments* from the Bonapaduli family of Rome. In order to evade strict export regulations, copies were secretly produced and hung in their place. Bought for £2,000, the paintings were sold to the Duke of Rutland. At the end of the century revolutionary disturbances led to fresh sales, William Beckford purchasing the Altieri Claudes for £6,825. Aside from purchases, foreign artists were brought to England by travellers to Italy and elsewhere.

Some tourists, such as Lord Camelford in 1788, admired but did not buy,[21] but others such as the 2nd Marquis of Rockingham, Henry Arundell and Henry Blundell bought many. The antiquarian and collector Sir Andrew Fountaine (1676–1753) visited Italy in 1702 and the mid-1710s, collecting coins. A bronze portrait-medal of him was made at Florence in 1715 by antonio Selvi. George, Viscount Parker, in Padua in September 1720, 'bought some pictures amongst which there is a very fine deluge of Giulio Romano which everybody here thinks cheap at the price I gave for it viz: a hundred pistoles'. The 3rd Duke of Beaufort, visiting Italy in the late 1720s, purchased paintings by or attributed to Raphael, Veronese, Palma Vecchio, Caravaggio, Domenichino, Rosa and Reni, many of whose works were also acquired by other British tourists. Beaufort also commissioned the elaborately inlaid cabinet later to become celebrated as the 'Badminton Cabinet'. When sold in 1990 it became the most expensive piece of furniture in the world. Robert Jones of Fonmon Castle, Glamorgan (1706–42) went on a Grand Tour in 1731 and appears to have spent about £700 on paintings while in Italy, where he also had his portrait painted by Francesco Solimena. In

1730 Jones had been advised that a young gentleman should see his own country before travelling abroad, lest foreigners regard him as ignorant. John Bouverie (1722–50), who made several trips to Italy, brought back the first large collection of Guercino drawings to enter England. He also collected medals and cameos. Bouverie died at Magnesia on the way to Palmyra with Robert Wood. George Viscount Mandeville, later 4th Duke of Manchester, bought a Tintoretto in Italy in 1758. Charles Townley (1737–1805) purchased copies of three paintings, including a Titian, at Florence in August 1786; James Robson bought some old drawings and some Piranesi prints in Rome in 1787. Paintings could be expensive. In October 1778 an anonymous tourist found Batoni asking £700 for his latest Holy Family, the colours of which the tourist thought 'too glaring'. Many tourists purchased not only when abroad, but also after their return to Britain. Having returned from his Grand Tour in 1769, Frederick, 5th Earl of Carlisle (1748–1825), spent heavily to build up a major collection of old master paintings at Castle Howard. Philip Yorke (1757–1834), later 3rd Earl of Hardwicke, visited Italy in 1778–9. Because of the War of American Independence the shipping of his artistic purchases back to England was delayed. Yorke subsequently commissioned James Byres to obtain a set of busts for his library, and ordered two paintings from Jacob More.[22]

Agents, often ciceroni (guides), such as John Parker, Colin Morison and James Byres in Rome and Owen McSwiney in Venice, assisted in arranging purchases. McSwiney introduced Canaletto to the British and really began his career as a popular view painter. However, it was not long before Joseph Smith took over, thus beginning an association that lasted throughout the artist's life. Lady Pomfret wrote from Rome, 1741: 'Mr Parker is a Gentleman who goes about with the English to show them what is most remarkable assisting them also in buying what picture paintings and other curiosities that they fancy most.' Parker, a painter himself, was secretary to the Society of Artists in Rome. Thomas Jenkins in Rome and Consul Joseph Smith in Venice acted as bankers as well as helping to arrange purchases. In Florence, Ignazio Hugford, a painter of British parentage who was Secretary of the Academy from 1762 until 1772, arranged art deals for tourists. Jacob More acted as an agent for the Earl-Bishop of Derry.[23]

Some of the paintings purchased, as with some of the medals and some of the supposedly antique statues, were fakes. They were manufactured in considerable quantities in Italy and purchased by gullible tourists misled by dishonest guides. Northall wrote, in 1753, of young British aristocrats deceived in Rome by antiquarian guides into purchasing copies, rather than originals, of works by Raphael, Titian and Michelangelo. The engraver, Robert Strange, was sceptical about the originality of some of the pictures purchased by George, Viscount Fordwich, later 3rd Earl Cowper, from Thomas Jenkins in Florence. More warned the Earl-Bishop of Derry about the many forgeries of Raphael, Reni and Titian. In his 'Hints to a Traveller', Francis claimed:

> We English, before we see Italy, are apt to think that we can purchase the best works of the great masters, and that many of them have actually been brought away within these few years. There cannot be a grosser mistake. The Italians are too cunning to suffer the market to be removed out of Italy. As for parting with a valuable antique statue, they would much sooner give up their seven sacraments. Pope could make his people Protestants much more easily, than persuade them to let the Apollo out of Rome . . . The best pieces we have in England are I believe only good copies.[24]

Francis's suggestion, which was inaccurate, was linked to a feeling that many tourists did not truly appreciate art, and that their pretensions to culture were superficial and dangerous, dangerous in that they left tourists open to the possibility of being tricked into purchasing fakes and also to neglect British in favour of foreign culture. Thus, the terms cognoscente and connoisseur became terms of abuse. Francis wrote: 'To a man really curious in the polite arts, Rome alone must be an inexhaustible fund of entertainment; but what can be more disgustful, than to see our young people give themselves the airs of cognoscenti.' Cultural pretentiousness and praise of foreignness for its own sake, were mocked in the *Connoisseur*, a London weekly of 1754–6, and by Hogarth. This criticism must be set alongside the often exaggerated praise of the cultural sensitivity of British tourists. John, 3rd Earl of Bute (1713–92), formerly First Lord of the Treasury, was very scathing in 1770:

> . . . how often have I heard very ignorant people decide in the most peremptory manner, on very doubtful paintings, fall into ecstasies on the names of Raphael, Titian or Correggio, who never thought of a picture till they crossed the Alps, and acquired their enthusiastic erudition in the course of a few months. How shall we account for this? Is the climate of Rome infectious? I do believe it.

An example of the nature of the aritistic criticism written by a young tourist is provided by a letter from Bologna, sent by Alan Brodrick on 8 November 1724:

> I have endeavoured to get what information I could from the greatest virtuosi I could find; and am apt to think, that (generally speaking) their judgments are more to be relied on with relation to the ancient painters than the modern; for I have often thought that people's prejudices

for or against particular persons have made them praise or dispraise unreasonably . . . though [Veronese] was certainly an excellent painter, yet he had several faults. None of that school [Venetian] were ever counted accurate drawers, nor indeed have his figures that turn of shape, which one meets with in the Bologna School. Their colouring is admirable, but what Paulo seems to me to have excelled most in, is the disposition and dress of his figures; yet he is sometimes faulty even in that; and does not sufficiently distinguish his principal figures. The strongest instance . . . is in his famous picture of the Martyrdom of St George, where the figure of the saint is undoubtedly the weakest part of the piece. Titian's excellence lies, I think, mostly in his colouring, and in pictures of two, or three figures at most; for he does not always succeed in great undertakings. His portraits are inimitably fine, and prodigiously esteemed . . . I immediately grew an admirer of the Carraccis, and indeed of the Bologna school far preferably to the Venetian . . . they have an accuracy and correctness in drawing which distinguishes them sufficiently from anything I ever yet saw.

Brodrick found a painting that he wished to purchase and revealed his judgment in his comments on it:

The story is Sophonisba receiving the poison, done by Carlo Maratti; the figure of Sophonisba is extremely good, in an admirable attitude, finely painted and coloured, and the drapery mighty well done. The soldier that brings the poison is a fine figure and expresses a great deal of concern at being charged with such a commission . . . Two or three more figures of servants very well done, and the grief finely expressed, make a great harmony in the whole picture . . . The price of it is . . . about £50, but my objection to it is that the figures are not quite so big as the life.

Brodrick noted the general opinion that Italian sculpture, painting and architecture 'are much on the decline', but saw this from the perspective of a Whiggish conviction that culture flourished most in a free, i.e. Whiggish, society:

it is much more wonderful to me how they stand their ground so well, in spite of the disadvantages they labour under in an absolute government . . . It is certain however, (and I think not at all to be wondered at) that learning of all kinds decays extremely; and it is certain that the most knowing men here look on England as the most learned country in the world . . . Nothing that I see abroad gives me so sensible a pleasure as the consideration of the happyness we enjoy more than all the world.

At Rome the following spring Alan Brodrick, who had been commissioned to spend up to £300, purchased two paintings for his uncle: Benedetto Luti's story of *Rebecca at the Well* and Poussin's *Tincture of Coral*. He had little to say about the Luti, beyond an account of its size, provenance and cost, £31 50, but he wrote at greater length about his second purchase:

> the other by N: Poussin is the story of Ovid's Metamorphoses of Perseus, who after having freed Andromeda conducts her to the island; the painter has introduced several figures, representing fountains and sea nymphs, who supply Perseus with water to wash his hands; he has given the Medusa's head to be washed by others of them, in whose hands the blood of it turns into coral. There is a figure of Fame gathering Palms to make a chapelet for Perseus, and a Pegasus in the air, which figure was accounted for to me, by saying it denoted it to be a subject of poetry. The figures are about nine inches long, and there are twenty of them in a cloth of two foot six inches length, and one foot ten depth. This is not the only piece which Poussin has done on this subject, but is certainly the first of them. It is not altogether in his last manner, but this is so far from being an objection to me, that I protest I should for myself prefer it on that account. Everybody knows that his pieces in his last manner are not so finished as those in his first; on the contrary it is as certain that those in the last exceed the others in the graces of the heads, and ease of the draperies. Now this picture is a mixture of both, and is universally allowed to be done when he was changing his manner. Tis higher finished than almost anything I ever saw of him; nor can one find more grace in any figures than several of those. The landscape and perspective are extremely well done, and the distances finely observed. It cost . . . £60 7s 6d . . . had I not waited till the strangers had pretty well left Rome before I dealt for it, I must have paid more, or not have had it. I would not be understood to mean that I should prefer a piece of his wholly in his first manner to one entirely in his second; but that a picture, where the force of both is united, and that with all imaginable harmony, seems to me preferable to either.

In his last letter from Italy, written in Parma on 1 June 1725, Alan complained, 'pictures of all kinds (I mean good ones) are very rare; for the prodigious demand there has been for them of late years, and the great decay of painting here, makes them extremely rare and highly prized'. Five years later Sir Robert Walpole's second son Edward (1706–84), then on a tour with Lord Boyne, found it impossible to purchase antique sculptures in Rome: 'those that are valuable and most entire are either entailed or in the hands of people that won't part with them'. Sir Robert, however, was able to buy many paintings through agents. Italian marbles and pictures were among the cargo of a ship wrecked on the South Devon coast in 1757. Visiting Parma in 1777, John Mitford found only two paintings 'of distinguished merit' in the ducal gallery: Correggio's *Virgin with St Jerome*, and Bartolommeo Schedoni's *Entombment* of which he wrote: 'The colouring and effect are very fine. The St. John is a beautiful figure; the Joseph of Arimathea has a dignity of age which well suits his character. The Magdalen is well painted but has a very mean countenance.' Mitford also described and commented on Correggio's *Madonna della Scodella*, now in the National Gallery in Parma, but then in a church: ' . . . The mildness of rustic simplicity, and the almost folly of maternal tenderness are fully expressed in the countenance of the Virgin. The Jesus is a delicate pleasing figure. The Joseph is aged, but is a reverend old man. The beauty and justness of the character, and the elegance, truth, and harmony of the colouring is admirable.'[25]

Art interest and purchases were not confined to Italy. Robert Trevor, who purchased prints and books in Paris in 1728, had more ambitious plans on a trip to Lorraine that August:

In passing through Nancy . . . I took some pains to hunt after Callot's engravings, thinking it probable I might find some very fair originals of that master in a city, where he generally lived . . . but I found but few and they happening to be in the hands of persons, that knew the value of their countrymens pieces, were very dear. Among others there were his three great sieges complete, but as they were pasted upon cloth, and framed, they were too great an embarras for a traveller to carry about with him in posting; but it was a great mortification to me to leave them.

Bennet and the Rolles, visiting Berne in 1785, 'called on Aberli the Painter of the coloured views of Swisserland . . . and all of us laid out some money with him'.[26] Outside Italy, British tourists were most interested in the art of the Austrian Netherlands, where the themes of the paintings, principally religious, were similar. The paintings of Rubens, in particular those in Antwerp cathedral, were praised greatly. Peckham wrote of Rubens' *Descent from the Cross*: 'the varied expressions of the same passions in the different countenances of the weeping matrons surpass our imagination'. John Aiken observed of the Rubens in the cathedral: 'It is impossible to conceive painting to go beyond this; but the solemnity of the effect is somewhat diminished by being shown the portraits of Rubens' three wives among the figures . . . The Madonna of Rubens must excite emotions in the most insensible.' Brand was similarly struck in 1779: 'The instant I got into the Cathedral of Antwerp I lost my breath and stood still with wonder. The superb altars, the colossal statues the pictures, the solemnity of the people and all together deprived me of all my faculties; I gaped and stared . . . The descent of the Cross in the Cathedral by Rubens and the Christ in the Church of the Beguinage by Vandyke and either of them worth a journey from England.'

Tourists also praised paintings in other towns, such as Bruges, Brussels and Ghent. Walker liked the paintings in the cathedral at Ghent, including Rubens' *St Sebastian*: 'the anxiety of an old woman looking on, exhibits an expression such as I never saw before on canvas!' William Drummond noted: 'Here is also a fine picture of St. Sebastian painted by Girard Honthorst stuck with arrows, and two women attending him. The sedate countenance of the woman pulling them out, is a fine piece of art.'[27] Walker, however, also drew attention to a major problem in appreciating the art of this region: the prominence of Catholic themes. He wrote of the church of St Pierre in Ghent: 'The tapistry and Paintings in the Church, denoting the triumph of Popery over Luther and Calvin makes one forget the absurdity of the subject in the excellence of the pieces,' Perceval enjoyed visiting the churches of the Austrian Netherlands, 'where the paintings, sculpture, and other ornaments surpass imagination; but the bigotry of the people is so great that what we admire we cannot like'. Brand, as an Anglican clergyman, was forced to defend his views on Antwerp paintings:

> . . . the letter in which you abuse my affection for the Antwerp churches: but you cannot think me so absurd as to have the least affection for the Roman Catholic religion. There is surely a wide difference between the admiration of fine painting, sculpture and music and the adoration of a full dressed Virgin, be she wax, Ivory or even Ebony (for such I have seen) or the silver lillies of St. John or golden rule and compasses of St. Joseph. Though we pitied the people who could submit to the absurdities we saw every day and had a hearty contempt for the fat, bloated, heavy-eyed monks and shuddered at passing a confessing chair yet we had the greatest pleasure imaginable in viewing the ecstasies of St. Augustine, St. Francis and St. Theresa. And I assure you that I lament very much the necessity under which the reformers were under of banishing pictures from their churches.[28]

Few French paintings outside Paris were mentioned, though the *Death of St George* by the Antwerp painter Pourbus in Dunkirk was praised in 1720, and James Hume in 1714 attacked the representation of God in a painting in Nantes.[29] In Paris there were many paintings to be seen: a large number were in churches, but it was also possible for well-dressed tourists, often without any letter of introduction, to gain access to private houses where paintings could be viewed. The Luxembourg palace was open to visitors twice weekly. Andrews wrote in the early 1780s: 'no people display more willingness to exhibit their stores of this kind than the French, especially to foreigners. They consider themselves as bound in a particular manner to satisfy the curiosity of such as visit France – looking upon these exhibitions of their artists, as proofs of the superior ingenuity of the natives, they are desirous you should carry away with you an ocular conviction how much they excel all other people.'[30] In 1726 Perceval was affected by Le Brun's *Mary Magdalen* in the Carmelite church. Two years later Robert Trevor was impressed by the Duke of Orléans' collection at the Palais Royal, 'a cabinet of the finest pictures I ever yet saw'. It was the most frequented of all the Parisian collections. Nixon found there in 1750 'an epitome of all that's most valuable in painting, at least on this side of the Alps'. Garrick showed less enthusiasm in 1751: 'No Hotel has so good a collection of pictures as there is at Chiswick. In general rubbish to 'em.' William Drake was impressed by Guido Reni's *Salutation* and Le Brun's *Magdalen* in 1768, and also praised Charles Van Loo's *St Charles Borromeo taking the Sacrament to the Plague Sufferers*, which he saw at Notre Dame: 'the zeal and sympathy of the good man, the extreme sickliness of the patient, who is brought out in her bed to receive the sacrament, the languishing of several other persons visited by this terrible calamity, are most naturally and inimitably expressed'. Wharton was told, in 1775, to look out for 'the Vision of Ezechiel in the Palais Royal Collection (which is said to be the second in Europe,)' and he commented on the prevalence of religious themes. Six years later Brand attacked 'the studied attitudes' of French paintings.[31]

The two principal German galleries that attracted tourists were both at Catholic courts: Düsseldorf and Dresden. In the first half of the century Düsseldorf was the most visited, as a trip to Düsseldorf, Cologne and Aachen was a convenient appendage to a tour in the Low Countries. It was, however, off the route from Amsterdam to Hanover, which became increasingly important. This deterred the Earl of Essex from visiting the gallery in 1752. Late in the century Dresden became more important. The Wittelsbachs largely abandoned their palace at Düsseldorf, while Augustus III of Saxony (1733–63) created a superb collection at Dresden, mostly by purchasing paintings from Italians such as the Duke of Modena. Lord Charles Somerset found in Düsseldorf, in 1708, 'three or four large chambers filled with the most curious collection of original pictures by the hands of the best and most famous masters in all parts of Europe'.[32] Sir James Hall visited Dresden in 1783:

I stopt above a week at Dresden to see the pictures and went no less than eight times to the cabinet where I found full employment for my time – there is a very fine collection of the best masters of both schools – I made it my business to study the Italians – I believe I have picked up some knowledge – but what I value more I have learnt a good deal of diffidence in judging of pictures as I saw many that were certainly very fine that I should have thought nothing of if I had seen them in another place.

Brand wrote four years later:

The Gallery of Pictures you know is one of the first in Europe. The great Raphael of the Virgin, St. Sixtus and St. Barbe, the famous *Notte* of Corregio and other spoils of the Modena collection are very fine. I spent four mornings there deliciously. Of the Flemish school too there are some very fine things. You have no doubt heard of the famous Rembrandt of the Rape of Ganymede. The poor boys fright is wonderfully expressed in his face but that was not enough for a Dutch painter! But let us not be too partial. There is a young Bacchus by Guido as indelicate as this Ganymede.[33]

The frightened boy is shown as urinating. Brand was contrasting northern realism and southern classicism.

Few tourists visited Spain, but Thomas Pelham benefited in his artistic appreciation from his meeting with Mengs, with whom he went to see the paintings in the royal palace at Madrid.[34] Just as most tourists ignored German Renaissance paintings, so the Dutch school found far less favour than Italianate paintings. Visiting The Hague in 1779, Brand regretted the small number of Italian masters, and his response to 'the burlesque Flemish painting' he described there was mixed: 'Boors dancing, cattle, cocks and hens inside of churches and a variety of subjects are so highly finished that it really looks like enchantment. But one can't help pitying the dull patience of the artist.'[35]

Those who travelled to the United Provinces tended to visit the major accessible collections, such as that of the Prince of Orange at The Hague. Henry Ellison found that gaining access to private collections in Rotterdam was not without its problems. He wrote of one owner, 'the Gentleman being strongly prejudiced in favour of a bad Painter, to recommend ourselves to him we were obliged to commend at the expense of truth by which means we ingratiated ourselves with him so much, that he gave us an invitation to make a second visit to his Pictures etc., a favour he does not often grant.' Hugh Dunthorne has drawn attention to greater interest in Dutch art than in the seventeenth century, but a comparison of tourist comments with those made in Italy and the Austrian Netherlands suggests that the appeal of Dutch art was not as great for most tourists.

Italy was, therefore, the centre of attraction for those interested in paintings. As in the Austrian Netherlands, difficulties were created for some by the prevalence of religious themes, though many of those who complained were Anglican clergymen. Catholic art was believed by many to represent a threat. Even Samuel Davies, an American non-conformist clergyman touring Britain on a fundraising mission, was affected. At the University of Glasgow he saw 'a collection of pictures lately imported from France. One was the picture of the dead body of Christ taken off the Cross and carrying [sic] to the Sepulchre. The prints of the nails in his hands and feet, the stab of the spear in his side, the effusion of the blood, etc. were so lively that they unavoidably excited a sort of popish devotion in me.'[36]

Swinton condemned some pictures and statues that he found in Italian churches as obscene. Sacheverell Stevens's response to the statue of God at the altar of Florence cathedral was a mixed one:

prodigiously fine; the statue of the first, on reflection somewhat shocks a Protestant, to see the infinite, invisible, and ineffable Deity, represented in stone! Whether this be consistent with Christianity, of which the members of the Parish Church pretend to be the only true professors, might safely enough be left to the determination even of the most bigotted papist, if he would only give himself time to reflect a little seriously, what an offence and stumbling-block these kind of representations are, and eternally will be, to Jews and Mahometans.

Gray attacked the Catholic priesthood for teaching 'their wealthy followers to display their idle vanity in costly . . . representations of the circumstances of Christ's nativity'. Most tourists did not share these views; few were Anglican divines. Mitford, however, commented on St Peter's in Rome in 1776:

The amazing length of the vestibule, and the elegance of its terminations adorned in a most picturesque manner by equestrian statues of Constantine and Charlemagne, will always charm a person seeking only to be pleased; but if reflection is permitted to step in, and to suggest that this is the entrance to St. Peter's church, the approbation of the architecture, and the pleasure derived from it, will suffer a little allay. Perhaps it is better to enjoy the delusion, to approve, and be pleased.[37]

Italian art was accessible. Much of it was in religious establishments which were, bar a few nunneries, open, while access was freely given to ducal collections, such as the Uffizi, or private collections such as those in the palaces of Genoa and Venice. Walker noted in 1787, 'we found the palaces of the noble Venetians very open to our curiosity, and their pride no way hurt by the presents their domestics exacted from us.'[38]

Judging from their correspondence and journals, many tourists were or sought to be discerning critics. Criticism can be just as frequently a sign of ignorance or prejudice as of discernment; political and religious biases could colour responses and it is interesting to note the way descriptions of works of art often avoided sensitive religious issues. And yet, it is striking how far British tourists sought to counter such prejudices and to respond to paintings as works of art. Mitchell, revisiting Bologna in 1734, criticized the lighting and hanging of the paintings (as Thomas Pelham was to do in Madrid), and noted that he was no longer so impressed by paintings that he had once admired. Mitchell was unable to decide whether he had been 'satiated by the vast variety of paintings in these churches and palaces of Rome, or the taste refined by frequent looking upon the works of the best masters'. Lord Nuneham, who had executed a landscape in crayon in the Rhineland, went repeatedly to the Uffizi in 1756. Caroline, Lady Holland, praised Correggio's *Marriage of St Catherine at Parma*, while William Drake wrote from Bologna in 1769, 'We have found here good amusement in the picture-way, having seen the principal works of the great masters of the Lombard school.' Francis observed in Rome three years later, 'As for Pictures and Statues, I have really seen so many that I remember nothing. In a very large mixed company, one seldom contracts a lasting acquaintance.' Thomas Pelham was impressed by the paintings in Genoa and Parma and benefited from Mengs's advice in touring Rome. Philip Yorke spent over a week examining the paintings at Bologna; and Andrew McDougall stayed over ten days in Florence in 1783:

> I by no means pretend to be a *connoisseur*, either in painting or sculpture, but at the same time, they give me great pleasure; I believe some of my countrymen pretend to receive a great deal more pleasure, than what is real, and wish to have the name of *connoisseurs*, by praising the noted pictures, but before they begin, they have the good sense, (in general) to enquire the name of the painter.

Five years later James Robson was impressed by the paintings in Mantua, but condemned Giulio Romano's *Fall of the Giants* in the Palazzo del Tè 'which though esteemed an inestimable composition amongst the connoisseurs, I think loses all its grandeur and majesty in so small a room, by bringing such monstrous figures of human form, down to a level with the eye, nay even to the floor you walk upon. For want of height and distance they lose much of their dignity of character, and so does the scenery that accompanys them.' He thus missed the point of the frescoes, designed to make the spectator find himself involved in the giants' fate. Lady Craven regretted that she could not spend three months in Genoa examining the paintings in the palaces at her leisure and copying a few of them.

Neglecting the appeals of antiquity and pleasure, James Smith, President of the Linnaean Society, wrote, 'The fine arts must always make a principal feature in an Italian tour, indeed that country itself would hardly be amusing, nor would an account of it be interesting, to those who are quite devoid of taste and curiosity on this subject.' Many tourists, including Robert Gray and Philip Francis, compared the Medici Venus and Titian's Venus in the Uffizi. Walker left an interesting account of his response to Raphael's curtain-draped St Cecilia, which hung in Bologna:

> The curtain drawing, I must confess I expected to have fell on my knees with admiration! – but I find it is an education of some time and application to learn to see – I stood a quarter of an hour between doubt of my own, or other peoples tastes. My own is certainly defective; for I must honestly confess, at the end of the said quarter of an hour, I found my refractory opinion as obstinate as at first. Can that have no excellence which all the world admires, and has admired for this 250 years?
>
> For the future I shall be doubtful what I say of pictures when in this I can find nothing but a vulgar Wench looking as if she was selling the organ she holds in her hand, to three insipid bystanders, and was abusing them for not bidding her enough for it. St. Peter looks as if he was considering whether the instrument was worth the money.
>
> St. John, like an ignorant boy, who liked a tune, but knew nothing about the value of an organ. St. Mary and her companion seeming to wait for another tune before they quitted the sale, etc.

Brand's responses varied. In 1790 he wrote from Pisa:

> From Milan we went by Placentia Parma Modena and Bologna to Florence. I suppose that in those days of rapture when I first set foot on Italian ground I rav'd much about Corregio and Caracci and Guido and Guercino. If I am more moderate now it is not that I have felt less pleasure in seeing these wonderful works a second time but from the conviction that words can very ill express the impressions which they make and that there are few things more ridiculous than an affected description of a picture.

The following year he added, 'The Italian painters the Italian sculptures the Italian poets are all so many idolaters of affectation. With such divine models before their eyes they only worship extravagance and the

Raphaels and Michaelangelos serve only to lead them still further from nature.'[39]

Clearly responses to painting, as to other arts, could be very different. If only for this reason, the excessively stereotyped nature of the contemporary debate on the virtues of travel and on the nature of Britain's cultural relationship with the Continent must be questioned. Whatever the supposed cultural threat, money and patronage were clearly critical issues. 'There is no being a virtuoso, or gratifying that itch in building, medals, statuary, or painting, upon the foot of moderate estate', warned the Bishop of Chichester in 1739.[40] Aside from the cost to the individual patron there was also the cost to the community. This was particularly an issue in the case of paintings and of opera. Most famous opera singers were foreigners and there was criticism of the substantial sums that they were paid. Architecture was a less contentious issue, largely because the money was spent on buildings in Britain, and because the leading architects of the century patronized by the British élite were British.

ARCHITECTURE AND OTHER ARTS

All the fine houses are shacked in the English manner, and not that odious one of Paris, where using no putty, they fit their panes with paper and paste, which with the soil of flies and dust of the streets takes off the beauty of their built palaces, and has indeed a beggarly look.

Lord Perceval, Ghent, 1726[41]

Many of our modern houses have been built from Italian models, without the least reference or conformity to the change of country. On account of heat in Italy, it is necessary to have but few windows. This must ever make a building not only appear heavy, but of course produce a contrary effect to that which ought to be sought for in a northern clime; besides, windows in England are of themselves a great ornament, where they are always glazed, and not infrequently with the finest plate glass.

Joseph Cradock[42]

A lively interest in architecture was one of the attributes of gentility in eighteenth-century Britain, and many members of the élite were knowledgeable enough to play a role in the construction or alteration of stately houses. British architecture, in the design both of houses and of interior layouts, was heavily influenced by Continental models, first those of Palladio and subsequently of a wider variety of sources including ancient Roman and eventually, in the 'Greek Revival', Greek. Tourists paid great attention to Palladian buildings and, particularly in the first half of the century, a visit to Vicenza was considered an essential part of the Italian section of the Grand Tour. William Lee was there in 1753: 'I saw the Rotunda from whence Lord Westmorland's house in Kent [Mereworth] is taken, and the hint of Lord Burlington's at Chiswick. The copies are different from the original and in external beauty exceed it.'[43] Interior decorating was greatly influenced by Italian artists who came over to work in Britain at houses such as Burghley, as well as by the light, elegant style introduced by Robert Adam. This included ornamental motifs from classical antiquity, especially after the discoveries at Pompeii. Paris was an important source of furniture and furniture designs. Some tourists sought the advice of foreign architects. Sir Carnaby Haggerston planned, in 1718, to discuss possible changes to his seat and gardens at Haggerston with Italian architects. In 1734, Andrew Mitchell described the lazaretto being built in Ancona, noting: 'the architect Luigi Vanvitelli is a civil sensible man, he shewed me the plan and elevation of it'. The Earl-Bishop of Derry planned the rebuilding of Ickworth while in Italy, and the principal architect was an Italian, Mario Asprucci the Younger.[44] Many clearly appreciated the buildings that they saw on the Continent. Brand was very impressed by the new church of Ste Geneviève in Paris, later the Panthéon: 'It is very fine – the Corinthian order shines in all its purity and just proportions – There are no buildings near it. It is seen to great advantage and does infinite honour to the taste of the architect.'[45] Mist's Weekly Journal condemned the ignorant and uncritical nature of British tourists in Paris: 'they commonly take a turn to Versailles, Marli etc. and gaze at the fine Buildings and Statues of these places, with the same wonder that a country fellow does at some strange sight, without considering, or acquiring the least knowledge into the design of the architect, or skill of the statuary.'[46]

The validity of this comment is dubious, while, far from being uncritical, some tourists condemned the buildings that they saw. William Young wrote of the provincial Baroque he found in Gallipoli in southern Italy, 'The churches in the town are of a bad taste of architecture, as are all public buildings in this part of Italy, heavy charged with profusion of minute work; in short the very reverse of that simplicity which characterized the Greek orders in their ancient pure taste.' Peter Wauchop, visiting Lille, claimed that 'the nasty small windows disfigure all the houses'. Bennet thought that French architecture was too heavy, that their cathedrals and monasteries were worse than their British counterparts. He wrote, '. . . the cathedrals of Viviers, Valence, Avignon, Limoges, Cahors, Vienne, Toulouse, and even Lyons itself, would hardly be esteemed an ornament in any of our principal market towns'. He objected to the addition of classical parts to Gothic cathedrals, as in Orleans, to 'those clumsy awkward domes, with which so many of the French buildings . . . are spoiled'. Many other tourists objected to the characteristic French mansard roofs; one wrote of 'that most deforming protuberance of summit with which the northern parts of France abound'.[47]

Italian buildings were also criticized. Walker thought Milan 'not a beautiful city; it is built of brick, and plastered smooth over like most towns in Italy'. Robson thought Verona cathedral 'a heavy lumpish building' and wrote of its Paduan counterpart, 'the cathedral is but a heavy dull building much in want of cleanliness and repair'. Both were 'Gothic' buildings and therefore open to criticism. Brand wrote of Turin: 'if the houses in general are well built, in the churches and palaces there is a wonderful deficiencey of good taste. The materials the marbles especially are costly and rich but everything is cut into angles and broken curves sometimes concave sometimes convex but always deviating from elegance and simplicity.'[48]

Tastes varied, but there was a marked preference for the classical over the Gothic that led most tourists to ignore or dislike the architecture of Germany, most of provincial France, and some of northern Italy. Old towns were disliked; the preference was for wide, straight streets, as in Turin or the newer sections of Marseilles. George Berkeley praised the regularity of Catania in Sicily, rebuilt in Baroque style after the devastating earthquake of 1693. Narrow, twisting streets were associated with dirt, disease and poverty. Wharton disliked Mâcon, and Maclaurin disliked Sens for that reason. Tancred Robinson, who travelled on the Continent in 1683–4, wrote, 'Our great cathedrals in England do far exceed the Italian churches for height and bulk; but then they are inferior as to finesse of architecture; they being generally Gothic, but the Italian of the Greek and Roman architecture, which is the most accurate, and polite besides their fine sculptures, paintings, mosaic work, gildings, marble etc.'

Charles Drake Garrard wrote of Toulouse and Montauban, in 1779: 'they are both of ancient structure and consequently have nothing strikingly beautiful'. Arthur Young shared these prejudices, which were understandable given eighteenth-century problems with cleanliness and fire. Of Abbeville he wrote: 'it is old and disagreeably built; many of the houses of wood, with a greater air of antiquity than I remember to have seen, their brethren in England have been long ago demolished'. In the Dordogne, he noted: 'The view of Brive, from the hill, is so fine, that it gives the expectation of a beautiful little town, and the gaiety of the environs encourages the idea; but, on entering, such a contrast is found as disgusts completely. Close, ill built, crooked, dirty, stinking streets exclude the sun, and almost the air, from every habitation, except a few tolerable ones in the promenade.' Cahors was 'bad; the streets neither wide nor straight . . . Lodeve, a dirty, ugly, ill built town, with crooked close streets'. Pamiers and Poitiers were also condemned. Wilbraham criticized Vienna in 1794: 'The town itself is old and dirty. The streets are extremely narrow and the houses high, nor is there any appearance of magnificence in the palace or public buildings.' This sensibility was related to one that had long found flat country preferable to mountains. This could be true as late as 1794 for, though Wilbraham found the journey across the Slovakian Carpathians to Upper Silesia 'extremely romantic', he added that countries 'where the striking features are rocks and torrents' did not 'admit of that diversity which our extended landscape presents to the eye. About Teschen we left Hungary and entered Silesia where we were delighted to find a tolerably level country, civilised inhabitants and good accommodation.' On the other hand, William Beckford was already enthusing about wild, primitive scenery, while in 1784 the new sensibility made northern Spain attractive to Henry Read: 'the journey proved more agreeable than I expected. The country and mountains in Biscay are very romantic and the variety of views must ever be pleasing to a traveller'. Two years later, Joseph Townsend rode on horseback in Spain from Leon to Oviedo 'through the wildest and most romantic country which can be imagined, rendered tremendous by the rocks and beautiful by the wood and water . . . I have taken some views'.[49]

Many of the buildings that tourists admired were relatively modern, classical or baroque in style – St Paul's in London, the Invalides in Paris, palaces such as Versailles and the Upper and Lower Belvederes in Vienna. The response to older buildings was generally unfavourable, unless they dated from classical times, though in the second half of the eighteenth century an appreciation of Gothic emerged. The strong influence of a classical education and of a public ideology that drew strongly on classical images and themes can be seen in the accounts of many tourists. It played an important role in every Italian trip and represented a significant aspect of the appeal of Italy, counteracting the pernicious consequences of Italy being the seat of Roman Catholicism.

Outside Italy there were few classical remains that were visited regularly other than those in the south of France: Nîmes, Orange and the Pont du Gard. St John visited a Roman camp in eastern France, while the 6th Earl of Salisbury visited Roman sites near Besançon and in Savoy. At Aix-les-Bains he found the remains of a Roman temple dedicated to Diana, and at Avanche 'a very high marble pillar, which seems to me to have belonged to a gate of some fine temple'. James Hume was very impressed by the statues on classical themes in the garden at Versailles: 'to carry a young scholar thither would be an excellent introduction to Ovid's Metamorphoses'. Thomas Pelham was keen to see the Roman remains of Andalusia. Having discussed with Lord Grantham the route he should take in Spain, he wrote: 'we have agreed that I shall see the south of Spain, which is not only a very interesting tour from its' having been the scene of so many transactions in the Roman History and consequently retaining many curious antiquities but likewise as being the most fruitful and commercial part of modern Spain.'⁵⁰ The Italian classical remains and sites that most tourists saw were Roman. The large number of sites near Naples was the furthest south that most travelled, though many went from Naples to Paestum on the Gulf of Salerno. The Greek temples there played a major role in the controversy of the late 1760s over the respective merits of Greek and Roman styles. In 1777 Thomas Pelham visited Paestum with Sir James Long MP (c. 1737–94) and the latter's wife Harriet. The trip was not without its problems, an anonymous tourist recording in January 1779: 'as there is no house to sleep in at Paestum we were obliged to set off early . . . As we were on the road upwards of 3 hours before sunrise we suffered extremely from the cold notwithstanding we were tolerably provided with great costs and pelisses and were happy to warm ourselves by a fire in a miserable hut while our carriages were passing a ferry.'

It was only a small number of tourists, and those mostly later in the century, that visited the Greek sites in Sicily, and only a few, among whom were Berkeley and William Young, visited those in Apulia and Calabria. Giving the reasons he liked travelling in Italy, George Carpenter wrote,

> above all the ancient inscriptions: ruins: and antiquities: which are very curious and instructive to one that takes delight in such things: Most of the places have been famous for some notable action: they are easily found out by one that travels for his instruction: and will take a little pains and be curious . . . I took a great deal of pleasure in comparing the descriptions that are given us by the ancient authors of particular places as rivers mountains etc. with what they are at present. I found that time had made such vast alterations in landscapes that it was not easy to know them by the descriptions.

Addison had been the pioneer popularizer of this approach. Francis Head noted of Italy: 'one meets almost everywhere with some marks of the old Roman greatness'. In Rome in 1726 Edward Southwell junior made some remarks that prefigured the response of Gibbon:

> I have spent 3 months with great pleasure and some profit among the ancient and modern curiosities of this famous city, which have cost me daily reading and application and filled 140 pages in my journal

and I must own these heaps of magnificent ruins, and the view of so many places not only renowned for the actions and fate of so many heroes, but by the pens of so famous writers do fill the mind with great ideas of the Roman grandeur as also with various reflections upon the vicissitudes of all human things.

By the remains of above 40 temples one sees how devout and magnificent the Romans were in their religion, but their palaces, circus's amphitheaters and baths, testify that they were no less luxurious in their diversions. Their aqueducts which convey water 10, 17, 22, 35 and 45 miles, and their paved causeways which reached 30, 40 and even 180 miles to Capua, and some of which were the expence of one private man, are noble monuments of a publick spirit and disinterested regard to the good of ones country, and the triumphal-arches pillars and statues which were erected to the Patriots at home and the avengers abroad, are instances of the gratitude and honour the Romans paid those benefactors by whose means they reaped the advantages of war and the blessings of peace. There is a sensible pleasure in viewing the place where Marius Curtius leaped into the Gulph, and devoted himself to the safety of his country.

He was also moved by visiting other similar sites. Addison consulted Horace and Virgil when travelling between Rome and Naples in 1701 and Juvenal, Manilius, Ovid and Seneca on Rome. Andrew Mitchell verified Virgil's description of the falls of Terni in 1734, but found it 'difficult to trace the situation of Marseilles as described by Caesar'. Sacheverell Stevens described Virgil's alleged tomb near Naples and the Sybil's grotto at Cuma. Frederick, 6th Lord Baltimore, matched his predecessor's Baltic cruise by a tour to Greece, Constantinople and the Balkans and wrote: 'what I saw in my travels recalled strongly to my remembrance the classical erudition I was so happy as to receive at Eton College'. William Drake and James Robson had very differing responses to Mantua, Virgil's birthplace. The first noted in 1769 that it 'afforded us no small pleasure, as one naturally interests oneself in the most minute things that regard famous persons'. The second was less satisfied by his visit to classic ground in 1787: 'but now alas! not a stone nor monument to stamp it sterling; a mere hovel adjoining to a cottage. How frequently the traveller and antiquarian are disappointed in their pursuits and expectations. We expected to feel as it were an electrical shock on approaching the sacred turf once pressed by the favourite poet of antiquity.'

Roman works were purchased, Byres acquiring the glass vase later known as the Portland Vase in about 1780. In 1785, on his third trip to Italy, Richard Payne Knight bought 'Diomede', an antique head, from Thomas Jenkins, the dealer at Rome, beginning his large collection of classical sculpture. Francis wrote a Latin epigram on an antique stone lion he saw in Florence. Wraxall found that the Neapolitan sites still resembled closely the descriptions in Pliny, Strabo and Virgil and wrote of 'the celebrity of the surrounding country in Roman fable and history. All these circumstances conspire to charm the mind and warm the imagination.' Sir James Hall was delighted by Agrigento: 'he talks in raptures of the gigantic antiquities of Agrigentum and Selinunte and laying very comfortably to sleep in the flute of a broken column'.

Richard Garmston and Lord Belgrave viewed Virgilian sights; and Thomas Watkins referred continually to the classics in his description of Sicilian towns such as Syracuse. His party 'arrived at the banks of the Rubicon, with Lucan in our hands'. Sir Richard Colt Hoare repeated Horace's journey from Rome to Taranto; and Brand was very impressed by the classical sites in Sicily. Charles Sloane, who in 1785 had been impressed by the 'magnificent remains of antiquity' at Agrigento, wrote from Rome in 1789: 'I have been for a good while past the constant companion of Livy, Virgil, Horace etc.' Several of his letters from Italy were written in Latin.[51]

Given this strong grounding in the classics, the appeal of Italy and of the remains of ancient buildings is not surprising, though some tourists had different views. In 1770 Bute criticized the role of the classics, adding:

. . . had it pleased Providence to destroy the works, the writings, the very memory of the Greeks and Romans with their Empires, we now should brag of poets, architects, sculptors etc. as we do of Newtons, Raphaels and other superior beings, whose vast inventive geniuses have soared to science and arts, that scarce were known before, Milton would have wrote a divine poem, though he had never known Homer; Adam would have erected buildings worthy of the British nation, in a British taste, and instead of wandering to Spalato [Split], for the remains of Diocletian's palace . . .[52]

Classical sculptures were of great interest to many tourists. Famous examples were described frequently, and many sculptures, including a few fakes, were purchased. The Marquis of Tavistock noted in 1762 that seeing classical sculptures in Italy 'had at once opened my eyes to the beauties of this branch'. Twenty-six years later Samuel Nott visited Florence, 'where I first began to have some just idea of Grecian sculpture: Before that, animated stone was to me nothing more than a strong figure of expression; I never expected to see the Passions chiselled into actual life; But how was I entranced, when I beheld the Venus de Medicis, the Wrestlers . . .'[53] In 1749 the 1st Marquis of Rockingham instructed his eldest son Charles, Lord Malton (1730–82), later 2nd Marquis and head of ministries in 1765–6 and 1782, to obtain in Rome statues for his rebuilt seat of Wentworth Woodhouse. Malton purchased four copies of antique sculptures, and a marble group of Samson slaying the Philistines by Vincenzo Foggini. William Locke (1732–1810) assembled a collection of antique sculptures in Rome in mid-century, as well as purchasing Claude's *St Ursula*. William Weddell (1736–92), a leading member of the Society of Dilettanti, went to Italy in 1765 and sent nineteen cases of classical statuary back to Britain. Interest in acquiring paintings declined after about 1750, but the discovery of Pompeii and Gavin Hamilton's excavations around Rome (1769–92) stimulated great interest in sculpture. The seeds of full-blown Neo-Classicism, as against the earlier Greek v. Roman debate, were sown by this interest. While Malton and his generation were satisfied with copies, Weddell, whose collection is still complete at his seat of Newby Hall, Yorkshire, was not. Hamilton acted as agent for a number of major British collectors, including Charles Townley and William, 2nd Earl of Shelburne. Townley established one of the leading collections of the period. A Catholic Lancashire landowner, educated at Douai, he spent 1765–72 in Italy, mostly in Rome, though also visiting southern Italy and Sicily, and thereafter he revisited Rome on a number of occasions. While in Italy, Townley purchased a number of antique sculptures, cooperating with Hamilton in his excavations. Thomas Jenkins was another of his agents. In addition to sculptures, Townley also acquired a collection of Roman coins and terracotta reliefs. After Townley's death his collection was acquired by the British Museum, a new gallery being built for the marbles and terracottas. The new Neo-Classicism was of growing interest to tourists, one writing from Rome in the mid-1780s: 'Canova is one of the most excellent sculptors since the revival of the arts, his Theseus and the Minotaur is equal in my opinion to almost any antique.'[54]

The scale of the importation of sculptures was such as to be quite as significant as that of paintings, and arguably more so. Few were outright 'fakes', though they were often heavily restored and occasionally so retouched as to make them unrecognizable. There was also an interest in ancient coins, many of which were purchased in Italy. Collecting was a major activity of tourists, an important aspect of the cultural influence of tourism, and a major theme in the public debate over the Grand Tour.

Acquiring knowledge of the arts was a reason advanced to justify tourism,[55] though some tourists displayed little interest. Lord Warkworth wrote of Florence: 'There are a great many curiosities at this place in the Grand Duke's Gallery and also in several private houses' and nothing more; of Rome: 'During my stay here went to see the antiquities and palaces as *vide Roma antique and moderna*'.[56] Judging from surviving letters and journals many tourists were not uncritical purchasers and praisers of Continental art. Thomas Robinson sent his sister from Turin in 1759 a critical commentary on the Italian theatre:

> Their tragedies are execrable, no probability in the plot, no dignity in the diction . . . As to the action of the Italian actors, it is very bad, in high parts; and where any delicacy of sentiment or stroke of passion is required to be well expressed, they know nothing of the matter, but for the common scenes of life, I cannot help thinking they execute them more naturally and with less stiffness than we do.[57]

The length of foreign tours, the guidance available, both from experienced bearleaders, such as Brand, Patrick Brydone, John Clephane,[58] William Coxe, Jonathan Lippyeatt, Robert Livingstone, Henry Lyte, William Rouet, Adam Smith, Joseph Spence, Thomas Townson, William Whitehead and Robert Wood, and from local guides, such as Byres and Parker in Rome, and the interest of most tourists, helped to ensure that many acquired considerable experience in assessing operas, paintings and buildings. Some were more critical than others, but standards were high in general and tourism served to enrich the British élite culturally. Whether that was in the interest of British culture is a different question and one that aroused heated debate at the time.

NOTES

I owe an especial debt to Edward Chaney, Francis Haskell, J.G. Links, Peter McKay and Shearer West for their comments on earlier drafts of this chapter.

1.   Ellison to brother George, 13 June 1781, Gateshead, Ellison, A 11 No. 2.
2.   St Saphorin to Townshend, 28 Nov. 1722, PRO 80/47.
3.   Cowper to sister, 10 March 1730, Herts., D/EP 234; Gray, p. 424; Walker, pp. 178–9, 378.
4.   Allen to Newcastle, 3 Sept. 1729, PRO 92/33; Essex to his agent Thomas Bowen, 30 June 1733, Stanhope to Essex, 6 Jan. 1733, BL Add. 60387, 27732; Stanhope to Earl Stanhope, 25 Oct. 1734, Kent, U1590 C708/2.
5.   Shaw, *Letters to a Nobleman*, p. 105; Somerset to Lady Coventry, 21 July 1709, Badminton; Carpenter, Bod. Mss. Douce 67, p. 145; anon, BL Add. 60522; Southwell, BL Add. 34753, f. 14; Cork and Orrery I, 43; Perceval to Daniel Dering, 22 May (os) 1726, BL Add. 47031; Swinton, 24, 26, 27 May (os) 1731; Mitchell, BL Add. 58314, f. 29–30; Stevens, p. 99; Garrick, p. 8; Smith, CUL Add. Mss. 7621, 14 July 1752, 23 Sept. 1754; Orrery, 11, 57, 140; Leeds AO Vyner 6032 No. 12328; Pickersgill to sister, April 1761, Oct. 1768, Aylesbury, Saunders; Francis, BL Add. 40759, f. 15 19, 21; Wharton to Brand,

17 Mar., Wharton to his uncle, Thomas Lloyd (quote), 24 Mar. 1775; SRO GD 267/7/20 vol. 2; Pelham to mother, 8 Sept., 2 Oct. 1777, BL Add. 33127; Yorke to Keith, 28 Sept., 27 May 1778, BL Add. 35514–5; Drake, Aylesbury, D/DR/8/10/11–12; Gateshead, Ellison, A 11, No. 2; Brand to Wharton, 10 May 1781; Wharton to Brand, 4 June 1781; Brand to Wharton, 2 Feb., 24 Oct., 17 Nov. 1783, 16 May, June 1784, 18 Oct. 1787, 6 Dec. 1790, 26 Aug. 1791, 3 April, 5 Oct, 1792, 25 May, 24 Sept. 1793; Brand to sister Susan, 2 Dec. 1790, CUL Add. 8670/35; Bennet, 14 Oct. 1785; Dawkins to Keith, 5 April 1785, BL Add. 35534; Bennet, 15 Oct. 1785; Beinecke, Osborn Shelves c 289; Gray, pp. 298–9; Arbuthnot to Keith, 6 May 1787, Robson, 30 July 1787, Garmston, 6 Oct., 4 Nov. 1787, 28 Jan. 1788, Crewe, BL Add. 35538, 38837, 30271, 37926, f. 43, 51–3.

6. BL Add. 40759, f. 31.

7. Pelham to mother, 28 Sept. 1776, BL Add. 33127.

8. Lynth, *The Independent Patriot*, p. 2.

9. Cork and Orrery, I, 206–7.

10. Marlborough to Fish, 12 Oct. (os) 1727, BL Add. 61444.

11. Walker, p. 432; Perceval to Edward Southwell, 30 Oct. 1725, Perceval to Daniel Dering, 16, 23 April, 4 May 1726, BL Add. 47031; Mitchell, BL Add. 58314, f. 29; Crewe, BL Add. 37926, f. 84; Ellison, 19 June 1781, Gateshead, Public Library E/E1.

12. Swinton, 10 Mar. (os). 9 May (os) 1731; Wharton to Brand, 15 Nov. 1775; Brand to Wharton, 26 Mar., 17 April 1784, 14 Oct. 1791; Robson, 24 Aug. 1787, BL Add. 38837; Knight, p. 176.

13. Digby to Hanbury-Williams, 25 Dec. 1751, BL Add. 51393; Brand to Wharton, 27 June, 4, 26 Aug. 1787.

14. Brand to Wharton, 10, 20 Jan. 1780, 9 April 1790, 26 Aug., 22 Sept. 1791; Garmston, 4 July 1787, BL Add. 30271.

15. Aylesbury CRO D/LE E2/12.

16. Aylesbury, D/LE E2/16; Pelham to his mother, 26 Feb. 1776, BL Add. 33126.

17. Craven, I, 170; Ainslie to Keith, 3 Dec. 1785, BL Add. 35535; Patricia R. Andrew, 'Rival Portraiture: Jacob More, the Roman Academician', *Apollo*, 130 (Nov. 1989), pp. 304–7; *William Hoare of Bath* catalogue by E. Newby (Bath, 1990) pp. 9–10; *Wright in Italy* catalogue by D. Fraser (Sudbury, 1987); D. Bull, 'Sudbury and London, England and Italy', *The Burlington Magazine*, 129 No. 1016 (Nov. 1987), pp. 761–2; *British Artists in Rome 1700–1800*, Kenwood exhibition catalogue by L. Stainton (1974); D. and F. Irwin, *Scottish painters at home and abroad 1700–1900* (1975); Stainton, '"Classic Ground": British artists in Naples in the eighteenth and nineteenth centuries', in *In the Shadow of Vesuvius.Views of Naples from Baroque to Romanticism 1631–1830* (Naples, 1990), pp. 23–9.

18. *Pompeo Batoni and his British Patrons* (1982), catalogue of Kenwood exhibition; *Souvenirs of the Grand Tour* (1982), Wildenstein catalogue; A.M. Clark, *Pompeo Batoni* (Oxford, 1985).

19. Bentinck to mother, 28 April 1727, BL Eg. 1711; HW 71 f. 13.

20. *Richard Wilson*, Tate exhibition catalogue by D.H. Solkin (1982); F. Russell, 'The Stourhead Batoni and other copies after Reni', *National Trust Year Book 1975–76* (1976), pp. 109–11; Brand to Wharton, 23 Nov. 1793.

21. F. Haskell, 'Eighteenth-Century Art', in A. Burgess, *The Age of the Grand Tour* (1967), pp. 33–4; J. Lees-Milne, *Earls of Creation* (1986), pp. 109–11; Camelford to William Pitt, 10 Feb. 1788, PRO 30/8/120 f. 5.

22. T. Clifford, 'Sebastiano Conca at Holkham: a Neapolitan painter and a Norfolk patron', *Connoisseur*, (1977) pp. 93, 99; Bod. Mss. Add. D71, f. 45; O. Sitwell, *Sing High! Sing Low!* (1944); inventory of paintings at Fonmon Castle, 1743, Cardiff, Glamorgan CRO D/D F F/190; Jenkins, *Ruling Class* p. 228; Huntingdon CRO DDM 49/7, 30 May 1758; Robson, 7 Sept. 1787, BL Add. 38837; Anon., 28 Oct. 1778, Beinecke, Osborn Shelves c 332; Black and N. Penny, 'Letters from Reynolds to Lord Grantham', *Burlington Magazine*, 129 No. 1016 (Nov. 1987), pp. 731–2; Belfast PRO, Northern Ireland, Caledon papers, D 2433/D/5/21, 27.

23. J. Fleming, 'The Hugfords of Florence', *The Connoisseur*, 36 (1955), pp. 197–206; Pomfret, Leics. CRO DG7, Finch D5; McSwiney correspondence with 2nd Duke of Richmond, Goodwood Mss. 105, vol. I; Pears, 'Patronage and learning in the Virtuoso Republic; John Talman in Italy, 1709–1712', *Oxford Art Journal*, 5 (1982), pp. 27–9; Patricia R. Andrew, 'Jacob More and the Earl-Bishop of Derry', *Apollo*, 124 No. 294 (Aug. 1986), pp. 91–2.

24. Northall, p. 127; Andrew, 'More and . . . Derry', p. 92; Newcastle, Northumberland CRO Z SW/554 17–18; Francis, BL Add. 40759, f. 30.

25. Francis, BL Add. 40759, f. 30; L. Bertelsen, 'Have at you all: or, Bonnell Thornton's journalism', *Huntingdon Library Quarterly*, 44 (1981), pp. 269–72; R. Paulson, *Hogarth: His Life, Art and Times* (2 vols, New Haven, 1971), II, 153–87; Bute to John Symonds, CUL Add. 8826; Guildford CRO Brodrick Mss. 1248/6 f. 88–9, 219–20, 245–6; J.H. Plumb, *Sir Robert Walpole. The King's Minister* (1960) p. 86 fn. 2; Wreck, Exeter CRO 1508 M/Devon/Harbours 23; Gloucester CRO D 2002 F1 pp. 87–9.

26. Trevor to half-brother Thomas, 27 Aug., 3 July 1728, BL Add. 61684; Bennet, 3 Sept. 1785.

27. *Tour of Holland*, pp. 98–9; Aikin, I, 89–90; Brand to Wharton, 12 Sept. 1779; anon., BL Add. 60522; Bennet, 24 June 1785; Walker, p. 17; Beinecke, Osborn Shelves c 331; HW 67 f. 169.

28. Walker, p. 19; Perceval to Charles Dering, 25 June (os) 1718, BL Add. 47028; Brand to Wharton, 16 Oct. 1779.

29. Anon., BL Add. 60522; Hume, BL Add. 29477 f. 14.

30. *Tour of Holland*, p. 143; Andrews, 1784, pp. 204–5.

31. Perceval to Daniel Dering, 9 April 1726, Trevor to Thomas Trevor, 3 July 1728, BL Add. 47031, 61684; Nixon, BL Add. 39225 f. 93; Garrick, p. 33; Drake, Aylesbury CRO D/DR/8/2; Wharton to Thomas Wharton, 19 April 1775; Brand to Wharton, 10 May 1781.

32. HW 67 f. 169; Somerset to Lady Coventry, 24 Nov. 1708, Badminton; Daniel Dering to Perceval, 20 Aug. 1723, BL Add. 47030; anon., BL Stowe, 790, f. 111.

33. Hall to Wharton, 6 Oct. 1783; Brand to Wharton, 10 Sept. 1787, 11 Sept. 1792.

34. Pelham to mother, 26 Feb., 28 July, to father, 29 Feb., 1776, BL Add. 33126–7.

35. Brand to Wharton, 30 July 1779.

36. H. Dunthorne, 'British travellers in eighteenth-century Holland; tourism and

the appreciation of Dutch Culture', British Journal for Eighteenth-century Studies, 5 (1982), pp. 80–1; Henry Ellison junior to Henry Ellison senior, Gateshead, Ellison, A15, No. 22; G.W. Pilcher (ed.), The Reverend Samuel Davies Abroad. The Diary of a Journey to England and Scotland, 1735–55 (Urbana, 1967), p. 102.

37. Swinton, 1 June (os) 1731; Stevens, pp. 111–12; Gray, p. 402; Gloucester CRO D 2002 F1 pp. 9–10.

38. Walker, p. 169; Orrery, p. 90.

39. Parker, BL Stowe, 750, f. 378; Swinton, 3 Mar. (os) 1731; Mitchell, BL Add. 58319, f. 33; Nuneham, Aylesbury, D/LE E2/16, 20; Holland, BL Add. 51445 B, f. 8; Drake, Aylesbury, D/DR/8/2/16; Francis to Dr Campbell, 17 Oct. 1772, Pelham to mother, 15 Mar., to father, 1 April 1777, Yorke to Keith, 12 May 1779, McDougall to Keith, 27 Jan. 1782, Robson, 19 Aug. 1787, BL Add. 40759, 33127, 35516, 35525, 38837; Craven, p. 88; J.E. Smith, A Sketch of a Tour on the Continent in the years 1786 and 1787 (3 vols., 1793), I, xix; Gray, p. 312; Walker, pp. 188–9; Brand to Wharton, 6 Dec. 1790, undated [1791]; Camelford to Pitt, 10 Feb. 1788, PRO 30/8/120.

40. HMC Hare, p. 249.

41. Perceval to Daniel Dering, 22 May (os) 1726, BL Add. 47031.

42. Cradock, Literary and Miscellaneous Memoirs (1826), II, 57–8.

43. Lee, 26 April, 1743, Beinecke, Lee corresp. Box 3; Stevens, pp. 360–1; Francis, 8, 9 Aug. 1772, Robson, 31 Aug. 1787, BL Add. 38837; Walker, pp. 134–6.

44. Haggerston, 26 Nov. 1718; Mitchell, BL Add. 58319, f. 23; P. Tudor-Craig, 'The Evolution of Ickworth', Country Life, 153 (1973) p. 1363; Andrew, 'More and . . . Derry', pp. 93–4.

45. Brand to Wharton, 10 May 1781.

46. Mist's Weekly Journal, 18 Sept. (os) 1725.

47. BL Stowe, 791, pp. 27–8; Wauchop to Keith, 4 Nov. 1775, BL Add. 35509; Bennet, 16 Sept., 8, 11, 17 Oct. 1785; anon., BL Add. 12130, f. 183.

48. Walker, p. 379; Robson, 19, 22 Aug. 1787, BL Add. 38837; Brand to Wharton, 31 Mar. 1787.

49. Wharton to Thomas Lloyd, 14 Aug. 1775; Brand to Wharton, 31 Mar. 1787; Thompson, 1, 45–6, 55, 90; Maclaurin, f. 189; Leeds AO NH 2911; Drake, Aylesbury, D/DR/8/10/10; Young, I, 5, 17, 19, 51, 53, 63; Chester CRO DBW/N/Bundle E, Packet A; NLS Ms. 5541 f. 136, 5545 f. 9.

50. Salisbury, Hatfield, Cecil Papers, Mss. 340; Hume, BL Add. 29477, f. 27; Pelham to father, 11 Mar. 1776, BL Add. 33126.

51. Anon., 28 Jan. 1779, Beinecke, Osborn Shelves c 332; Carpenter, Bod. Mss. Douce, 67, p. 153; Christ Church, Head to Wake, 9 Mar. 1725; Southwell to Perceval, 9 April 1726, BL Add. 47031; Mitchell, BL Add. 58319, f. 7, 78; Stevens, pp. 313, 319–20; Baltimore, A Tour to the East, in the years 1763 and 1764 with Remarks on the City of Constantinople and the Turks (1767), ii–iii; Drake, Aylesbury, D/DR/8/2/17; Robson, 19 Aug. 1787, BL Add. 38837; Francis, BL Add. 40759, f. 28; Wraxall to Keith, 22 June 1779, BL Add. 35516; Hall to Wharton, 2 Aug. 1785; Brand to Wharton, undated; Garmston, 16 Nov. 1787, Belgrave to Keith, 19 May 1787, BL Add. 30271, 35538; Watkins, Travels through Swisserland, II (1792), 97; Hoare, CUL Add. Mss. 3549; Brand to Wharton, 3, 22 April 1792; House of Lords RO CAD/4/6, 22–4, 27.

52. Bute to Symonds, 1770, CUL Add. Mss. 8826.

53. Nott to Hotham, 2 April 1788, Hull UL DDHo/4/23; Tavistock to Robinson, 2 Feb. 1762, Russell Manuscript Letters vol. 45.

54. Hull, University Library, journal of a tour possibly by Marmaduke William Constable-Maxwell.

55. [Hurd], *Dialogues on the uses of Foreign Travel; Considered as a part of An English Gentleman's Education* . . . (1764), p. 57.

56. Alnwick, Alnwick Castle Ms. 146.

57. Leeds AO Vyner 6032 No. 12304.

58. P. Jenkins, 'John Clephane: A New Welsh Source for the History of Enlightenment', *National Library of Wales Journal*, 22 (1982), pp. 416–27.

13

THE DEBATE OVER THE GRAND TOUR; CONCLUSIONS

There are indeed some that go abroad merely to eat and sleep: and think if they have been at the places it is enough for them: of this number are generally those that travel young with governors: who sometimes come home as knowing as they went out.

George Carpenter, 1717[1]

The misfortune is, that young men who want experience; and have not the happiness to be under the influence of somebody, who should have an authority over them, they are guided by their own humours and make themselves appear in the world to great disadvantage, and commit many follies, which they may possible live long enough to repent of, but can never retrieve.

Edward Carteret on Lord Dysart, 1728

. . . those are the best of our countrymen that are not much altered by their continental peregrinations.

John Boyd on Wraxall, 1787[2]

Tourism was attacked on many grounds, ranging from cost to culture, the dangers from Catholicism to the dangers from venereal disease. Much criticism was expressed in public: in print, in the theatre and even in Parliament. Others expressed their criticisms privately: guardians, parents, diplomats and tourists themselves. In turn, tourism was defended, both in print and privately, though this defence was never as vigorous nor as bitter as much of the printed assault. Most of the criticism related to a more general attack on Hanoverian society and culture and, in particular, on foreign influences, such as French food and Italian opera, and their supposed pernicious effects. Very little criticism referred solely to tourism. It is difficult to assess changes in the content or quality of the criticism. Most of the themes remained remarkably constant. This was due partly to constant features of tourism, such as its cost and the loss of wealth to the country, and partly to the character of xenophobia, a fusion of conservatism and vigour. Strong criticism contined to be expressed in the second half of the century, but it appears to have been less constant a theme than in the 1720s and 1730s. In that period London opposition newspapers, such as the *Craftsman* and *Mist's Weekly Journal*, attacked tourism on many occasions. Some critics had themselves spent time abroad. John Wilkes, a prominent opponent of George III who had been a contemporary of Alexander Carlyle, William Dowdeswell and Charles Townshend at Leyden University, wrote from Parisian exile in 1766 to the Marquis of Rockingham about

> . . . that mistake we too often run into, of sending our young nobility and young gentlemen upon their travels . . . before they know enough of the constitution of their own country to give a just or even tolerable account of it; and consequently before they are qualified to gain any real improvement (*as candidates for the Legislature*) from what they meet with in foreign nations; and their tutors, generally taken out of the inclosures of our universities, are too often but ill qualified to assist them in this material point. This makes them very apt, from what they see abroad, to imbibe false or inadequate ideas of the true foundation and end of government. The consequence of which is that when, by inheritance or election, they are admitted to a share in the legislative authority of their own country, they are in great danger of espousing, perhaps honestly, the wrong side of the question . . . If they were never sent upon their travels until they were masters of what is to be learnt here, they would not want a tutor to attend them, and might escape much of that ridicule abroad which is bestowed upon them by foreigners of sense and learning; and probably would return home with benefit to themselves and their country, or at least with wisdom enough to leave behind them all principles inconsistent with the constitution of this kingdom, and all manufactures prejudicial to its trade.[3]

THE BENEFITS OF TOURISM

Our joyous situation . . . you see two of the happiest fellows in life having left every care behind them in their native land, in high spirits, breathing the most delicious air in the world, in a fine summer-morning, rolling along on a broad smooth causeway considerably elevated above the plain, as it were on purpose to show us the adjacent country to the greatest advantage.

Reverend John Nixon, near Paris, 1750[4]

From both trouble and pleasure I assuredly derived instruction; and on many occasions I have essentially profited from this my first entrance into the world. To many perhaps the experiment might have been dangerous: to me fortunately it proved of the most real and lasting advantage.

As I now attained the age of 21, my good father, who was earnest to qualify me in every respect for my approaching entrance into the active world, proposed to me a second tour . . . The variety of scenes through which I had lately passed, the society into which I had been introduced, and the manners and information which I had acquired, made me on my return extremely acceptable to all my old friends, and procured me the acquaintance of many, to whom I otherwise had small pretensions to be known . . .

James Bland Burges, 'Memoirs'[5]

Those who defended tourism rarely stressed the pleasures of foreign travel. Such a stress would have appeared trivial, and to defend the heavy cost of tourism it was necessary to advance reasons more consequential than those of enjoyment. It was not a motive that could be proposed usually to parents or guardians, nor one that could be advanced by moralists. A certain amount of (self-)deception without doubt played a role in the discussion of motives for travel. As with travel to Bath, many tourists who sought cures for their health were also influenced by the desire to travel, and, particularly in the case of Aachen and Spa, to socialize. The relationship between the debate over travel and the actual views of tourists is a complex one, and the latter are often difficult to elucidate. Many journals that were not published in the eighteenth century were nevertheless written for others to read. Jervis's is a good example. Maclaurin hoped that his account would be of interest to friends and relations. Perceval congratulated Edward Southwell junior on his description of Geneva and wrote of the 'pattern it gives my son how to write when it becomes his turn to voyage as you do'.[6] Unpublished defences of tourism tend to advance reasons similar to those in contemporary printed material.

The principal arguments advanced in favour of foreign travel were that it equipped the traveller socially and provided him with useful knowledge and attainments. It was partly for this reason that many had part of their formal education, at school, academy or university, abroad, though other factors played an important role, such as the traditional preference of the Scots for Dutch universities, which led Andrew Mitchell after his studies at Edinburgh University to Leyden, and the wish of Catholics to educate their children abroad.[7] Education had been a central theme in British travel abroad from the outset. The demands were often onerous. In 1639 Roger Boyle, later 1st Earl of Orrery (1621–79), who had gone to Paris after Oxford, complained to his father Richard, 1st Earl of Cork, 'We do follow the exercises so hard that we have not one spare hour in the day, for in the morning from six till ten we ride the great horse and run at the ring, from 10 to 12 we fence, from 1 to 3 we dance, and the rest of the day we spend in reading either some geography book, or history or Italian.'[8]

Foreign education was not free from hazard. There was a risk of conversion to Catholicism, as happened to George, 3rd Earl of Cardigan, in 1703–4, though he came of a Catholic family and anyway rejoined the Church of England in 1708.[9] Stevens was particularly worried about the dangers posed by foreign education: 'I cannot help thinking it worthy the consideration of the legislature, to prevent, as much as possible, the sending our young people, of both sexes, into foreign parts to receive their education: they imbibe such principles, both religious and political, that, on their return, make them enemies to the mild religion and government of their native country.'[10]

Despite these dangers, many were partly educated abroad. One tourist found six British students at the Academy in Lunéville in 1720. In May 1725 seven out of forty-four were British.[11] Academies at Angers, Besançon, Blois, Brunswick, Caen, Colmar, Hamburg, Lunéville, Paris, Tours, Turin and Vaudeuil received British students; so also did universities such as Göttingen, Leipzig, Leyden, Utrecht and Wittenberg. The quality of the education varied. Brand criticized the Academy at Brunswick, but Philip Yorke praised the lectures he attended at Leyden, and the 2nd Earl of Dartmouth was impressed by those he heard at Leipzig. Educated privately at Berne in 1750, the 4th Earl of Essex had 'a professor for arithmetic, geometry and natural law for four days in the week, and another for geography and history who attends me three times a week, for two hours each lesson'. The following year the 3rd Duke of Richmond studied 'belles lettres' and mathematics assiduously in Geneva. Many hired language teachers. Haggerston did so at Rome. The Earl of Harold and John Clavering studied French in 1715 in Geneva and Hanover respectively.[12] An anonymous tourist visiting Florence in 1778 recorded: 'The Abbé Pelori who comes to me every day for two hours is the best Italian master I ever met with and the circumstance of having so good an interpreter of this difficulty has made me undertake to read the *Inferno* of Dante. There are many fine passages in it and a great deal of fire and imagination.' Sir John Blair was boarded in a French house in Paris in 1787 in order to hear 'no other language spoken at Table'. His guardians wished him to be educated 'in such a manner as to fit him for availing himself' of prospects of employment but 'at the same time that due attention is to be had to procure him every accomplishment otherwise suitable for his fortune and expectations'. Robert Arbuthnot, Blair's tutor, did not think it sufficient for him to be trained as a man of business, 'to those qualities should I think be added an acquaintance with human affairs in general, and with the polite arts, which may place him above professional peculiarities of manner, or professional littleness of character'.[13] Such an ambiguity existed generally. Tourists were expected to improve themselves and to behave like gentlemen. The two were believed to be compatible and mutually supporting, but there was often a tension between them, particularly in the matter of expenditure. Sarah Marlborough was sceptical of the value of tourism. She wrote to her grandsons' bearleader, Fish:

> I never thought travelling was of much use but to teach them perfectly the language and to keep them out of harms way, while they are so young that they cannot keep the best company in England, and to make them see that nothing is so agreeable as England take it alltogether, but what I value more than anything you will see abroad is the constant application to what Mr Chais will read and teach them.

Charles, 2nd Viscount Fane, urged the Spencers, then at The Hague, to accompany him to Paris. Fish reported that Fane.

> . . . reckoned up several advantages we should find there, such as . . . better opportunities of growing perfect in the French, better masters for mathematics (which he has a mind to apply himself to for some time) and for any exercise of accomplishment that any of us might have a mind to advance or perfect ourselves in such as dancing, fencing, drawing, architecture, fortification, music, the knowledge of medals, painting, sculpture, antiquity, or whatever we would . . . Mr. Charles [Spencer] gave his voice strongly for Paris as well as for the reasons Mr. Fane gave as because he thought there would be a great many agreeable entertainments . . . which would keep us in better humour and better spirits for the mornings' application.

Sarah Marlborough was not so sure:

> Useful learning is what I have always earnestly recommended, and
> next to that . . . good company is the most desirable thing. But I should
> naturally have thought, that the worse the company is at any place,
> and the duller, the more likely it would be for young men to apply
> themselves . . . The mathematics I have always thought was the most
> desirable knowledge . . . To speak the French language perfectly well is
> certainly very agreeable and upon many occasions will be more useful
> even than Latin . . . Dancing gives 'em a good air; and fencing should
> be learnt, because it is possible that it may be of use . . . I give you full
> power to go where you will, since I believe, that wherever the children
> are they will be very idle, and notwithstanding all the pains that I have
> taken, they will never know anything that is of any more consequence
> than a Toupee, a laced coat, or a puppet-show.[14]

Sarah Marlborough's harsh words may have been justified for her
grandsons, all of whom proved disappointments, and two of whom
gambled heavily while abroad.

Other tourists achieved a better balance in acquiring what
one bearleader writing of his charge termed in 1685 'all those
improvements that befit his quality'. William Blathwayt was willing to
have his sons stay two months in Turin, 'provided they pass the best
part of that time in riding the great horse, fencing and dancing and
visiting the court'. In 1717, the Duke of Kent ordered his heir the Earl
of Harold, then in Paris, to hire a fencing and dancing master, both
teaching skills necessary 'for the port and carriage of the body'. Mellish
engaged dancing and fencing masters in Paris, but he also worked hard
to improve his knowledge of French, Alan Brodrick hoped that his
father would:

> have no reason to be discontented with . . . my travels, since I have
> used my utmost endeavours to improve myself in whatever the place I
> was in, could inform me of.
>
> I have done what has been in my power towards perfecting
> myself in French, and have learnt as much Italian as the small share
> of conversation, which strangers can have with the people of the
> country would admit of. As for the German language it is so extremely
> difficult, my stay has been so short in any one place, and the accents
> and manner of speaking so different all over Germany, that I could not
> propose to myself to make any progress in it; so that I have entirely let
> alone, what I could not hope to arrive at.

Robert Wharton, who translated 'Montesquieu's Lettres Familieres and Persanes . . . backwards and forwards', informed his uncle that he did not 'think a lesson in the art of walking, bowing, giving, receiving, standing etc. *avec bonne grace*, too ridiculous to receive'. He took lessons in riding '*à la Françoise*' in response to his uncle's wishes. The scholarly Thomas Pelham had lessons in dancing and perspective in Turin.[15] He was convinced of the value of travel. From Spain he informed his father:

> I think it very necessary and right that every young man should know that there are other countries than those he lives in; that there are rational creatures out of his island and though men are very different in themselves they live all under the same heavens and are governed by the same all seeing Providence; – the seeing those countries which are famous as scenes of so many actions in History are highly conducive to the enlarging and opening of the understanding – the total change in the face of those countries is the most convincing proofs of the uncertainty of things in this world; the flourishing state of some and the miseries and wretchedness of others is the best cure for a mind prejudiced with an idea that no country is equal to his own, and shew in the strongest light that happiness is not confined to one quarter of the globe, and that a Spaniard may be as easy in servitude as an Englishman in liberty. In short visiting other countrys is the best indeed the only way of learning how to weigh the perfections and imperfections of our own. In respect to societies, few I fear are open to a young traveller that he can gain any improvement from; In Italy I believe none; and should only be *visited* as a country of fame without any regard to its inhabitants; and I much doubt whether in any nation a young man who comes there only for a few weeks or months will gain much from the company he will live with . . .[16]

Others disagreed and felt that young tourists could benefit greatly from the social life that they might enjoy. Edward Carteret hoped in the case of Lord Dysart 'that affability, and good breeding will introduce him into the best of company which is the greatest advantage that can be acquired by travelling into foreign countries'. Sholto Douglas wrote from Turin: 'the principal advantage I shall reap here is I fancy an *easier air* in company, as I am to be introduced to the king and the principal nobility at the return of the court'. Thomas Worsley was regarded as greatly 'improved by going to Paris' in 1739: 'talks more, very cheerful and gay, makes very good remarks and quite agreable . . . will make a great figure in whatever situation he is in'. Beaumont Hotham wrote in 1749 to his son Charles, then in Paris:

I am glad of the opportunities you have of mixing with people, who must give you by observation such an insight into the manners of men, as may be of great use for your future conduct, since it is to be hoped you will thereby see the advantage, as well as have the satisfaction which doing right always gives to one's own mind, of imitating what is commendable, and shunning what is wrong or disgusting in human nature.

In 1778, the Earl of Pembroke thanked Keith for looking after his son in Vienna: 'The good company, to which you have introduced him, must be of the greatest consequence to him at his period of life.'[17] Aside from mixing in society, tourism could also be of use in acquiring information. Martin Sherlock, in his *New Letters from an English Traveller*, claimed:

Nothing is so useful as travelling to those who know how to profit by it. Nature is seen in all her shades, and in all her extremes. If the mind of the traveller be virtuous, it will be confirmed in the love of virtue, and in the abhorrence of vice; because he will everywhere see that virtue is esteemed by the persons who practice it the least. If the traveller has the seeds of one or of several talents, he will find men of the first merit in every line, who will think it a pleasure to encourage and unfold those seeds, and to communicate knowledge . . . The traveller has, besides, the advantage of making continual comparisons, which strengthen his judgment extremely . . . it is more than probable that every man who goes to exhibit his insignificancy in foreign countries, without parts, and without an object, will collect there only vice, follies, and absurdities.

Commentators differed on what was held to be useful information. In 1747 John Quicke, then in Geneva, received advice from William Graves:

You seem to be sensible of one advantage acquirable by travel, which I entirely neglected and which perhaps is the most essential of any: I mean the attending to the government and policy of the several states through which you pass. Switzerland affords the best plans of a true republican constitution, and therefore what are mostly to the purpose of an Englishman; whilst other countries where arbitrary power is lodged in the hands of the King, only show us the inconveniences of such a government and what we ought to avoid and abhor. It is very certain that though a man reads of the different effects produced by free and despotic constitutions, attended with the truest reflections and reasonings of sensible writers; yet these by no means affect the mind of the reader or imprint the ideas so strongly in the imagination as the actual view of the consequences themselves. And without doubt these are the things most worthy the consideration of gentlemen; along with the knowledge of the several branches of trade, and the reasons of their establishment, increase and decrease . . . Unquestionably every gentleman should likewise acquaint himself with things of virtuoso-kind, though not strictly reducible to any use in society, yet as the marks of gentility and a polite education: besides, some knowledge of buildings, paintings, statues, and medals creates a very fine amusement, and communicates a wonderful air of elegance to the sensible connoisseur . . . As to my own countrymen I would always avoid them, unless they were men of figure and fortune or very ingenious and could serve some of the purposes I wanted, and whose acquaintance might afterwards do me honour and perhaps service in life.

William Lee wrote in 1749 from Paris to his father: 'the small experience I have had at present has given me no insight into the police, the manners and customs and other such like laudable ends of a traveller's enquiry'. Peter Beckford stated:

It is not in looking at pictures and statues only, that travelling is of use, but in examining the laws, customs, and manners of other countries, and comparing them with our own. Agriculture, Natural History, Trade, Commerce, Arts, and Sciences, all present themselves under various forms to improve and enlarge the understanding; while a continual habit of receiving favours will put us in good humour with the rest of the world, remove our prejudices, increase our sensibility, and inspire in us that general benevolence which renders mankind so serviceable to one another.

George Carpenter and Thomas Pelham both stressed the classical heritage of Italy. The former wrote in 1717:

There is certainly more pleasure and advantages in travelling in Italy than in any other country whatsoever: you see greater varietys in nature than anywhere else: besides the prodigious diversity of Governments: the fine paintings and sculptures: but above all the ancient inscriptions: ruins: and antiquitys: which are very curious and instructive to one that takes delight in such things . . .

Sixty years later, Pelham wrote to his mother from Rome: 'the great use I found is the obtaining clearer ideas of the Roman magnificence than history conveys, and the reflections that must necessarily arise on the comparing our situation with theirs, with the melancholy thoughts of the imperfection and instability of every work of man', a reference to the War of American Independence.[18]

Comparisons of the situation in Britain and other countries were held to be an important aspect of foreign travel. Robert Poole discovered in 1741 that the Sabbath was profaned a lot in Paris. He had hitherto thought the situation in London bad, but he found that it was worse in Paris:

> Hence travelling is of use to enable a person to form juster notions of things, and to see in what respect his own country exceeds, or is exceeded by others, whereby the better to value what is valuable, and disregard what is not so. And hence I am enabled to have juster notions from experience, by comparison, concerning religion, in regard to the exterior part of it, now, than before I could . . .

Thomas Pelham also found travel useful in comparing Protestantism and Catholicism – a comparison many critics of tourism feared. He wrote to his mother: 'I think that the comparing them together and weighing the perfections and imperfections of Romish and Protestant tenets may enable a private man to arrive at a nearer pitch of Christianity – let a Protestant engraft the zeal of a Roman on the sincerity of his own faith and in my opinion he can not be a very bad Christian.' John Richard claimed that

> The pleasures of travelling are certainly beyond common conception; from every nation, from even every circumstance, travellers will find many occasions to admire the constitution and comforts of their own country. To a traveller of observation many things appear of consequence which others esteem as trifles. Happy will he be on his return, if he can retain and follow good examples he has met with, and forget the bad ones.

Arthur Young's first foreign trip confirmed him in 'the idea, that to know our own country well, we must see something of others. Nations figure by comparison.' The ever-hyperbolic John Villiers noted in Cherbourg in 1788: 'we know not the value of our privileges . . . till we have felt the loss of them; and every young man ought to go abroad, to make him the more attached to his own country. I find everything here so extremely inferior, that I glow with pride and rapture, when I think I am an Englishman.'[19]

There were social benefits in Britain for those who returned having been polished by Continental society. Lady Mary Wortley Montagu wrote of how lords newly arrived from abroad won the admiration of women at court. Many agreed with Mr Classic, a character in Samuel Foote's *The Englishman at Paris*, in praising the advantages of a visit to Paris: 'I think a short residence here a very necessary part in every man of fashion's education.' Frances Crewe drew attention to the powerful appeal of snobbery, the manner in which the returned tourist appeared part of a charmed exotic world. Bored at a Versailles ceremony, she wrote:

> It will, at all events, serve to vapour about when I get to England – Oh! how shall I show off amongst you all with 'my Alps, my Appenines, and River Po'! or, at least, My Spa, my Brussells, and the River Seine! Not one of which, however, between you and me, is worth an evenings walk over poor Philip's Hill, when one makes some new remark upon Beeston Castle, and find out that the Welsh Hills are pretty objects from that spot.

The countryside near Crewe Hall clearly appealed to her, but when she contemplated her return to it she wrote: 'I shall show off with my Paris fashions, and make you believe anything I please!' A sense that Britain was less interesting was expressed by Lady Anson, who wrote to her brother-in-law Thomas Anson MP, who visited France in 1748: 'What a poor figure must any intelligence from hence make in comparison with the history of your travels. As for instance, if I should tell you, that we have walked round Mr Southcote's Ferme ornée, and seen Lord Lincoln's Terrass, how trifling must that sound, to one who has spent four days at the Magnifique Palais de Versailles.' The following year Thomas Gage noted how arrivals from Paris in Dublin were 'greatly admired by all the women and fops'. In 1750 Gage planned to spend a month in Paris, 'which I imagine will be long enough to get a right cock to my hat, and a suit or two of clothes *à la mode*; which will serve to inform the world at my return that I have been travelling; and as I have been so long out of England, many will believe that I have done the Grand Tour.'[20]

Not all sought or acquired such polish. In 1786 Charles Sackville of Stoneland noted of his more distinguished relative, Lord Sackville, that he was 'very averse to the idea of going abroad, and giving up spurs and leather breeches'. Four years later Brand wrote from Lausanne: 'We have a prodigious medley of society here. French Dukes in great abundance, Russian and Polish princes, Barons and Comtes of all countries and Yorkshire squires. These last would be vastly more in their element at home.'

The benefits of travel and the processes by which these benefits were to be acquired were not often explained. Edward Southwell junior returned from his travels 'very much improved'; John Rogerson hoped that by travelling his nephew's 'mind may be opened and his acquaintance with the world enlarged'; John Moore argued that 'one end of travelling is to free the mind from vulgar prejudices'.[21] There was little agreement as to how best to achieve these noble aims, and it was accepted that much depended on the abilities of the individual tourist. Richard Dreyer began his account in 1791 by relating how he was 'impelled by that desire of seeing, which has led wiser men abroad for improvement and which has tempted those of weaker understanding to exchange the follies of their own country for the absurdities of another'. It was agreed in general that it was best to avoid the company of other tourists, but comments varied on the dangers of mixing in local society. Bolingbroke wrote to Sir William Wyndham in 1736 from his seat in the Loire valley:

> I agree that Mr Leveson must know the language so as to speak it with ease, before he can mix in the good company of this country with pleasure and profit. I agree likewise that it will be necessary he should wear off that awkward shy habit, which our young fellows contract, and which his natural temper fortifies perhaps, before he can make such a figure in this company as it becomes him to make, and as it will be expected he should make, even at his first appearance. If he was at Paris therefore I should not advise producing him yet a while in much company . . . the objections against his being at Paris, drawn from the danger of falling into the habits of his kinsman, and the other English are strong.

Thirteen years later Hanbury Williams advised Essex to

> avoid as much as possible the company of your own countrymen for by experience I know that there are no people on earth who for the generality travel to so little purpose as the English, which I attribute entirely to their always keeping company with one another and by that are hindered from making any observations upon the manners, customs and government of the countries through which they travel. In short if a man is resolved to keep none but English company, it would be more advantageous to him to stay in England, where he will be able to find much better English company than he possibly can abroad.

In 1777 Lord Pelham wrote to his son Thomas: 'I am afraid you will have a great many English at Vienna this winter, and should think your friends in Spain might get you recommendations to some of the Spanish houses that would take you a little from the company of your own men who are of all others the most to be avoided in a foreign country.'

There were also differences of opinion concerning how long tourists should spend in particular towns. Perceval, an experienced tourist, argued that 'to travel to purpose men should fix at Courts, and not lose their time in lesser towns where nothing but the outside of houses and inside of churches is to be seen'.[22] Most could agree that tourists should seek to acquire political information, but the means by which they were to do this were unclear. *Mist's Weekly Journal* claimed that tourists simply wenched and drank: 'If you ask them questions concerning the laws or governments of the countries they have visited, you will find they know no more of those matters than they do of *Terra Australis incognita* . . .'[23] The *Craftsman* of 7 July 1739 declared:

> If this travelling education had any real advantage, we might suppose that it would qualify our young noblemen and gentlemen of rank for foreign employments; but if we look abroad, we shall find that there is, at this time, but one English nobleman in any public character, and one of a noble extraction; the last of a family very much distinguished for having educated not only the youngest, but likewise the eldest branches in learning and the knowledge of our laws.

Mist's criticism was valid for many tourists, but others acquired a lot of information, often through the hospitality of British envoys. The Earl of Morton wrote from Warsaw, in 1782: 'I shall certainly use my utmost endeavours to form a proper notion of the state and constitution of this country.' In 1785 Bennet determined to read a history of European treaties as soon as he returned home: 'It is astonishing how interested one becomes in the fate of a country, when one has travelled through it. All the books in the world will never inspire the warmth, or give the information and I have learned more in a three month tour, than I could by silent meditation for half a century.' The same year the Marquis of Lansdowne outlined his wish that his heir, John, Earl Wycombe, should be

> a loyal subject, a good citizen, and a happy man, which he cannot be in his situation without instruction. With this view I would . . . that he was put in the way of observing the effect of the Emperor's civil regulations, and to hear them fairly discussed . . . and . . . to see the different manners and state of society in the several parts of the Emperor's German dominions, Hungary etc. I likewise wish him to pass as little time as may be among his own countrymen, as I do not desire his stay out of this kingdom may be longer, than is necessary to the attainment of what he cannot find in it.

Despite his father's continual fussing, Wycombe did indeed become well informed.[24] Difficult as it was to explain the exact benefits of travel, many were agreed, nevertheless, that not to travel was bad, and that it led to boorishness and narrow-mindedness. Baltimore wrote of the Turks: 'They are enthusiasts in their religion, they look on those who differ from them as despicable as dogs, hogs, and devils. This is from want of travelling; for they are in the most deplorable ignorance of other nations . . .' Thomson observed of the Danes: 'They are much addicted to intemperance in drinking, and convivial entertainments; but their nobility, who now begin to visit the other courts of Europe, are gradually refining from the vulgar habits of their ancestors.'[25]

The defence of tourism was conducted therefore on a variety of fronts. Its principal characteristic was an idealistic one. Few advanced pragmatic defences, such as that tourism enabled young men to sow their wild oats abroad or kept heirs from seeking to influence the management of parental estates. Instead the defence of tourism, unlike much of the attack upon it, was conducted on an elevated and often abstract plane. Lynch's *Independent Patriot*, which satirized the cultural gullibility of many tourists, was dedicated nevertheless to Burlington, for whom travel served only 'to improve his mind for the embellishment of his country'. The variety of benefits that were assumed to derive from tourism stemmed largely from the differing assumptions and interests of tourists. It was hoped that Henry Nassau, Viscount Boston, would acquire social knowledge and manners that would be useful to him for the rest of his life. Perceval was pleased that his eldest son gained in Paris an interest in seals and 'virtuosoship'. Robson noted: 'I hope this tour into foreign parts will have its uses upon conduct in life in future, and teach me humiliation and submission to the will of heaven.' The Reverend William Cole acquired from his visit to Paris the habit of burning the incense used in French churches in his house after dinner to remove the smell of cooking.[26] Whatever the benefits were believed to be they were rarely stated as vigorously as the ciriticisms.

CRITICISM

Travelling has for some time I think been much in fashion with our Gentry; I doubt whether they improve much by it, but this I am sure of, that it must carry a good deal of money abroad.

Charles Delafaye, 1732[27]

I suppose a little tour of Italy, will be the next excursion; it furnishes rather an additional fund for elegant amusements in private life than anything useful.

Lord Findlater to James Oswald re latter's son, 1768[28]

The British gentlemen, who have more British wealth than British virtue, sense or honour, listless of their mother country's bleeding distress, are at present (when they might be most useful at home) very numerous in this city [Rome]: to their eternal infamy be it remembered. Lately, after kissing, as I presume, the Pope's toe, and receiving his absolution for the parricide waste of Britannia's portion on foreign wines and foreign whores, they came to a unanimous resolution, of piously performing the penance His Holiness enjoined them, neither to drink French wine whilst here, so long as the Holy Father's vineyards, and their injured Mother's cornfields, afford them the means of drowning their sins in sweet potions of Italian Lachryma Christi; nor to drink at home on their return (which must be expected, until they have no more pence than grace or sense) any but the most German wines: which indeed, by racking their tenants, and gloriously forming a Gallican conspiracy against English partridge and hare-killers, they may purchase, as I am credibly informed, at the cheap price of an equal quantity of those bitter draughts, called Lachrymae Posterorum et Patriae.

London Evening Post, 12 May 1757

Much of the printed criticism of tourism was xenophobic in content and intention. It was often witty and interesting, but related only tangentially to tourism, which Owen's Weekly Chronicle of 26 February 1763 regretted was not prohibited by law. Tourism was treated as but one example of a generalized failure to defend the integrity of British life and society in the face of all things foreign. The London paper that complained in 1757 of travel to France struck the usual tone: 'the egress of our fools thither, to glean up their vices, fashions and frippery manufactures, to the discouragement of our own arts at home, and the disgracing of them in the eyes of all Europe'. Tourism was a good instance of this failure, in the eyes of the critics, though it was less striking and possibly less immediately apparent to a metropolitan audience, than opera. Though urban British society was, in some measure, increasingly orientated towards oceanic trade and colonies, the Continental emphasis of the Grand Tour was not usually attacked on that basis. In 1780, however, during a period of growing despair about Britain's failure to defeat her rebellious American colonists and their Bourbon allies, the Scottish philosopher Adam Ferguson wrote:

If ever we are set down again in peace with anything like our old connection with America, I should certainly venture a crusade to obtain an association of some leading and fashionable people to send their sons on the tour of America and the West Indies instead of France and Italy, and to visit [military] camps instead of conversatziones and operas.

Ferguson's hope of making 'our statesmen warriors' was not to be realized, and the only prominent aristocrat who travelled to America was not to be one. John, Earl Wycombe MP (1765–1809), later 2nd Marquis of Lansdowne, visited the United States on the extended foreign tour from 1788 to 1792 that also took him to Canada, western Europe and Russia, but he was not a typical tourist. He was abroad for an unusually long period, having already travelled in Europe for most of 1784–7.[29]

Specific discussion of the merits of particular routes or particular activities while abroad was less common than criticism of the general practice of tourism. Tourists were aware of the generalized debate within Britain, though it is difficult to ascertain how far this influenced them. Wharton wrote from Dijon that he did not wish to act in a manner similar to that which was attacked in print.[30] However, in general, tourists were influenced not so much by printed criticism, as by the advice or entreaties of parents, guardians and bearleaders. These individuals were themselves aware of printed criticism. In 1753 Colonel John Lee wrote to his brother, Sir William, about the latter's son, then touring: 'What a different use does he make of travelling from the young man that the last *World*, but one, makes mention of.' Many were disenchanted with tourism, not so much for xenophobic reasons as for others linked to cost. Edward Mellish's father and uncle were clearly sceptical about the value of travel:

I do not apprehend real advantages from seeing fine paintings and buildings, can yet be of any real advantage to you in the life you are like to lead hereafter and may . . . give you a taste of living beyond your circumstances . . . a habit of negligence in your own affairs, which is but too often seen amongst very agreeable Gentlemen which have spent a great deal of time in travelling, and have by it improved themselves in every valuable qualification, but that one the most essential, which is, solid good Judgement.[31]

Possibly there is a social bias in the evidence. Most of the criticism of tourists comes from those who could not be described as being at the highest reaches of society: diplomats such as Robert Murray Keith, and travellers such as Robert Wharton, Philip Francis, Arthur Young, John Macky, Thomas Watkins and Thomas Pennant. Andrews attacked 'the frivolous pursuits of the plurality of our travellers'; and Pennant attacked those educated at the Academy of Geneva:

. . . it is folly to send here the grown up youth of our country as many parents have done. They come here corrupted by the dissipation of our island, spurn at all discipline, and either give themselves up to the rural sports of the country or abandon their studies for the enervating pleasures of the South of France, unknown to their friends who are regretting the unaccountable expenses of an education they were taught to believe was as reasonable as it was good.[32]

Whether these views were shared by those at the top of the social pyramid, the parents of Keith's 'brawny beef-eating barons' without any 'notion of taste or elegance', or of Wharton's 'Jolly-boys', is unclear. Judging from the attitudes of parents such as Sarah Marlborough, the 1st Lord Grantham, the 1st Earl of Macclesfield, the 4th Earl of Northampton and Thomas, Lord Pelham, many were prudent and not prepared to see their heirs waste their estate in folly and dissipation. There were other tourists whose parents or guardians could not control them or did not seek to do so. Possibly the extent of tourist 'vice' was exaggerated, and many tourists should have been castigated rather for sloth and a failure to consider seriously what they saw, than for wenching, drinking and gambling. The 4th Earl of Essex was criticized in 1752 for being very given to 'loitring away his time'. The following year, William Bentinck was surprised that an Austrian visitor to England 'for his amusement . . . wishes of all things to see the Newmarket Races to their best advantage'. Garrick recorded of one of his days in Paris, 'did very little this day but idle and eat and drink'.[33] These appear to have been more common than the 'vices' castigated by many, but, because they were less provocative, they received less attention. Many critics could not accept that tourism, despite the ideology of education and improvement, was primarily a holiday. Francis noted at Florence in 1772: 'Travelling perhaps may polish the manners of our youth: but quaere whether Italian polish be worth the price we pay for it.' Brand complained in 1790, 'Shall we be driving post from place to place, living in noisy dirty Inns, grumbling (perchance swearing) at postboys and visiting vast snowy mountains . . . And all this to acquire what? At best a little knowledge of Geography – Alas Alas! How strange a system of Education have I engaged in.' Lady Knight wrote from Rome three years later: 'I am very apt to think that the present mode of travelling is turned rather to amusement than to improvement.'[34]

Because tourism was debated largely as a means of education and not as a leisure pursuit the debate on its merits appears often to be remote from the activities of many tourists and to be somewhat artificial. Furthermore, the debate became increasingly irrelevant as the nature of tourism altered during the century. In the first half of the century the perception of tourism was dominated by the classical Grand Tour – young men travelling with tutors for several years to Paris and Italy in order to finish their education. In the second half of the century, many still travelled in this manner, but there were also larger numbers of other tourists: travellers not on their first trip, women, older tourists, families, those of the 'middling sort' who tended to make short visits. These groups, usually unaccompanied by any guide, except in major cities where they might hire a *laquais de place*, did not stress education as the prime motive for travel. Instead enjoyment and amusement came increasingly to the fore. Possibly this was linked to a discernible shift in guidebooks towards a less didactic and more practical pattern that devoted more attention to information such as prices, transport and conversion rates. Arthur Young was naive in attacking 'those whose political reveries are . . . caught flying as they are whirled through Europe in post-chaises'. According to him they failed to tackle questions concerning the bases of French power.[35]

Young and many other critics failed to appreciate the shift in social values that underlaid changes in attitudes towards travel. There was a growing acceptance by tourists that the purposes of travel were not primarily educational. It was quite acceptable for William Drake to inform his father, a former tourist, in 1769 that he stayed in Florence longer than anticipated 'in order to see a little the humours of a masque Ball'.[36] Such actions had always been common; but in the second half of the century tourists appear to have regarded them as appropriate activities that did not need defending.

CONCLUSIONS

Travellers always buy experience which no books can give.

Bennet, 9 August 1785

Foreign travel is knowledge to a wise man, and foppery to a fool.

Cradock, *Memoirs* II, 67

For a historian trained in diplomatic archives, tourism is an intriguing topic largely because the accounts left by tourists are so disparate. Despite contemporary criticisms that they stayed together too much and were insufficiently perceptive, there is an astonishing variety in the written records left behind. If John Stoye could characterize English travellers of the previous century as 'receiving the same memories or images, learning to share the same stock of historical commonplaces', the same is demonstrably untrue of eighteenth-century travellers such as Holroyd, Mitchell, Parker, Perceval, Quarendon and Southwell.[37] Many tourists were intelligent and perceptive and left informed accounts of what interested them: agricultural methods, a popular topic,[38] or opera, court society or religious ceremonies. These accounts were often prefaced or concluded by statements that the situation in Britain was better, but such remarks do not vitiate the interesting accounts that accompany them. Some tourists developed and pursued cultural and scientific interests abroad. Sir George Shuckburgh (1751–1804) spent three years in France and Italy after leaving Oxford in 1772. He devoted himself to scientific investigations for which he was elected a Fellow of the Royal Society in 1774 and a member of the Lyons Academic Society in 1775. His investigations with William Roy of the Royal Engineers were published as *Observations made in Savoy to ascertain the Height of Mountains by the Barometer* (1777).

Given the extraordinary variety of tourists and their writings it is difficult to summarize the evidence on such questions as how far they were affected by the experience of travel. It is reasonable to suggest that the consequences of having a large number of the men of the upper orders abroad during their formative years must have been considerable. Clearly exposure to foreign influences was lessened by the employment of bearleaders, the majority of whom were British, the preference for the company of other British tourists, the tendency to visit towns where there were reasonable numbers of such tourists, the habit of attending educational establishments patronized by compatriots, and the important entertainment role of British diplomats in courts such as Dresden and Vienna. Nevertheless, a large number of tourists met and conversed with foreigners as social equals and attended ceremonies or visited institutions which it was more difficult to attend and visit in Britain – such as Italian operas and Catholic ceremonies.

The cultural influence of this appears to have been considerable. Predisposed by an education in the classics to take an interest in the past achievements of Italian society, the upper orders, through tourism, became aware of the current achievements of Continental society and culture. Some of this awareness was faddish: the large numbers of tourists who visited Voltaire at Ferney, and who made a pilgrimage to Rousseau's tomb at Ermenonville, the somewhat uncritical praise that some lavished on the domestic and religious policies of Joseph III. Spectacular landscape became a subject of growing interest in the second half of the century. More tourists commented on the impact of light and on the appeal of wild and impressive scenery, especially mountains. In August 1782 Robert Ellison took evening walks in the countryside near Geneva. On the 23rd he 'stayed till after the sun was set behind the Jura mountains – The shades on these hills, and the lights in the Alps opposite them, and the calmness of the lake between them, very striking.' The following evening he took the same walk, 'sat down by the side of the lake before sun-set . . . saw the sun go down behind those mountains [Jura] – The shadow on the hills gradually changing from light and misty grey to darker, till they became of a deep and glossy blue in some parts verging to purple. Above them a clear and bright sky, without a cloud excepting a few that attended the sun at his setting and were beautifully illuminated by him, some of them fringing the blue tops of the hills.'[39]

British tourists had sufficient self-confidence and national pride not to praise things simply because they were foreign; despite the claims of contemporary critics, there was relatively little unthinking assumption of foreign customs, manners and mores. Rather the upper orders were open to continental influences and willing to consider foreign habits. There was less insulation from local society than in the Victorian and Edwardian periods.[40] It is important not to exaggerate the openness of British society at the highest ranks and to contrast it too sharply with a supposedly more xenophobic and less open climate of opinion among the lower orders. The position varied by individual; for as long as the history of eighteenth-century xenophobia remains unwritten, it is difficult to assess the attitudes of particular groups in society. Nevertheless, the upper orders do appear to have been relatively open to foreign influences and it could be suggested that tourism played a significant part in this process.

'As to travelling, it is only eligible from the difficulty of finding employing for a young man not yet of age', Lady Polwarth argued in 1778.[41] The importance of this aspect of the Grand Tour has often been overlooked. Tourism clearly served an important social purpose for the sons of the landed property owners, a purpose and a social group not always appreciated by the urban 'middling orders'; it was the latter which left many of the surviving accounts of tourism. However, it would be a mistake to present the Grand Tour as a simple response to this important social problem. Evidence of a major demographic crisis in the upper orders in the early eighteenth century, of many landed families finding it difficult to ensure direct male descent,[42] would suggest that there were signficant social reasons why sons should not be sent abroad on a lengthy and often hazardous Grand Tour, which sometimes, as with the Duchy of Somerset, led to deaths that produced a breach in the direct line of succession. There is insufficient evidence surviving to permit any conclusive general explanation as to why sons were nevertheless sent abroad, but it could be suggested that social emulation and a belief in foreign travel as a means of education and, particularly, of social finishing, were the key factors. This conflation of social and educational aspects was possibly crucial in the development of the concept of the Grand Tour in its classic mould – education for aristocratic youth – but during the course of the eighteenth century the stress on educational aspects declined. Finishing remained important. Having described the circles into which he had been introduced in Paris in 1775, George, Viscount Lewisham (1755–1810), wrote to his father, the 2nd Earl of Dartmouth, who had himself gone on the Grand Tour: 'From this account you will certainly be very much surprised if you find me in the spring as unlicked a cub as when I left England'.[43] Historians have pointed to the increasing importance of leisure activities in eighteenth-century British society. Leisure clearly became more of an accepted aspect of foreign travel. This was not acceptable to many contemporary critics, but their views had little apparent effect on the activities of tourists. In 1786 the Foreign Secretary referred to 'Lord Robert Fitzgerald, who is travelling for his amusement and improvement'. It was clear by the second half of the century that tourists travelled not only 'to see and hear everything that is to be seen and heard',[44] but also to enjoy themselves.

NOTES

1. Bod. Mss. Douce, 67, pp. 153–4.
2. Carteret to Wetstein, 8 Aug. (os) 1728, Boyd to Keith, 17 July 1787, BL Add. 32415, 35538.
3. WW R1–606.
4. Nixon, BL Add. 39225, f. 87.
5. Burges, Bod. Dep. Bland Burges, vol. 75, f. 105, 107, 165.
6. Aberdeen UL Maclaurin, f. 187; Perceval to Southwell, 1 Dec. (os) 1725, BL Add. 47031.
7. Haggerston, Northumberland CRO; Bennet, 7 July 1785.
8. Beinecke, Osborn 86.11.1.
9. *North Country Journal*, 10 Sept. (os) 1737; Smollett, p. 16; Mrs Montagu, II, 127.
10. Stevens, p. 6; St Saphorin to Townshend, 28 Nov. 1722, PRO 80/47; B. Skerrett to Mrs James Wallace, 17 Oct. 1776, Northumberland CRO ZHW/2/3.
11. Anon, BL Add. 60522; Southwell, Paris, Bibliothèque Nationale, Ms. Ang. 194 f. 28–9, BL Add. 34753, f. 7; Fish to Marlborough, 11 Nov. 1726, BL Add. 61444.
12. HW 51 f. 154–8; Trembley to Mylord, 29 Jan. 1751, BL Add. 32724 f. 77; Haggerston, Northumberland, 24 May 1718; Clavering to Lady Cowper, Herts., Panshanger, D/EP F196.
13. Beinecke, Osborn Shelves c 332, 9 Oct.; Arbuthnot to Keith, 10 Nov. 1787, BL Add. 35539.
14. Marlborough to Fish, 26 June (os), Fish to Marlborough, 12 Oct., Marlborough to Fish, 12 Oct (os) 1727, BL Add. 61444.
15. Gloucester CRO D 340a C 18/8, D 2659/4; Bedford CRO L 30/8/33/31; Mellish to father, 25 April 1731; Guildford CRO Brodrick Mss. 1248/6 f. 303; Wharton to Thomas Wharton, 19 May; Wharton to mother, 29 May 1775; Pelham to father, 15 Feb. 1777, BL Add. 33127.
16. Pelham to father, 2 June 1776, to mother, 27 May 1777, BL Add. 33126.

17. Carteret to Wetstein, 27 June (os) 1728, Douglas to Keith, 23 Sept. 1775, Pembroke to Keith, 1778, BL Add. 32145, 35509, 35515; Elizabeth Worsley to Frances Robinson, 16 Jan. 1739, Leeds AO NH 2825; Hotham, Hull UL DDHo 4/3.

18. Sherlock, *New Letters* (1781), pp. 147–9, 152; Devon CRO 64/12/29/1/24; Lee, 18 May 1749; Beinecke, Lee corresp. Box 3; Beckford, I, 9; Carpenter, Bod. Mss. Douce 67, pp. 152–3; Pelham, 23 April 1777, BL Add. 33127; Sherlock, *Letters from an English Traveller* (1780), p. 173.

19. Poole, I, 50; Pelham, 4 Dec. 1775, BL Add. 33126; Richard, p. 221; Young, I, 99; Villiers, p. 33; Wharton to Miss Raine, 7 Oct. 1775.

20. R. Halsband (ed.), *Montagu correspondence* (3 vols, Oxford, 1966), II, 100; Foote, I, i; Crewe, BL Add. 37926, f. 71, 104; Lynch, *Independent Patriot* (1737), pp. 44, 50; Stafford CRO D615/P (S)/1/3/8; Gage to Hotham, 20 Nov. 1749, 4 May 1750, Hull UL DDHo4/3; 4; *Adams's Weekly Courant* 28 April 1752; *Owens's Weekly Chronicle* 11 Aug. 1764.

21. Sackville to Sir Charles Hotham, 9 Oct. 1786, Hull UL DDHo/4/22; Brand to sister, 25 Sept. 1790, CUL Add. 8670/34; Perceval to brother, 21 Nov. (os) 1726, Rogerson to Keith, 27 May 1788; BL Add. 47031, 35540; Moore, *Collected Works*, I, 358.

22. Beinecke, Osborn Shelves f c 11 p. 1; Bolingbroke to Wyndham, 12 Jan. 1736, Petworth House Archives 23 pp. 53–4; HW 81 f. 37; Pelham to son, 10 Aug. 1777, BL Add. 33127 f. 293; Perceval to Southwell senior, 22 Jan. 1726, BL Add. 47031.

23. *Mist's Weekly Journal*, 18 Sept. (os) 1725.

24. Morton to Keith, 28 Aug. 1782, Hanbury-Williams to Lord Holland, 23 Mar. 1752, BL Add. 35526, 51393; Bennet, 4 Aug. 1785; Lansdowne to Keith, 4 Feb. 1785, Sir James Harris to Carmarthen, 19 Dec. 1786, BL Add. 35533 f. 208–9, Eg. 3500 f. 37.

25. Baltimore, *Tour to the East*, p. 76; Thomson, p. 27; Hurd, pp. 41–2.

26. De la Harp, Boston's tutor, to Earl of Grantham, 24 June, 3 Nov. 1716, Herts., D/E Na F8; Perceval to Edward Southwell, senior, 7 May (os) 1726, Robson, 1 Sept. 1787, BL Add. 47031, 38837; F.G. Stokes, *The Bletcheley Diary of the Rev. William Cole* (1931), p. 23; Hurd, pp. 51–5; Andrews, 1784, pp. 4–5, 16–17.

27. Delafaye to Waldegrave, 30 Nov. (os) 1732, Chewton.

28. *Memorials of . . . James Oswald* (Edinburgh, 1825), p. 206.

29. *Herald* 8 October 1757; *Mist's Weekly Journal*, 14 Aug. (os), 18 Sept. (os) 1725, 8 July (os) 1727; *Craftsman*, 6 July (os) 1728, 7 July (os) 1739, 12 July (os) 1740; *London Journal*, 7 Aug. (os) 1731; Rolt, *John Lindesay, Earl of Crawford*, p. 96; Lynch, *Independent Patriot*, p. 27; J.M. Smythe, *The Rival Modes* (1727); Ferguson, BL Add. 34417 f. 8.

30. Wharton to Dr Baker, 20 May 1775, Durham, Wharton.

31. John to Sir William Lee, 29 July 1753, Beinecke, Osborn Shelves, Lee papers vol. 2. Lee was presumably referring to the issue of 3 May, No. 18, written by Chesterfield. J. to E. Mellish, 15 April, John Gore to E. Mellish, 10 Dec. 1730, Nottingham UL Mellish.

32. Keith to Bradshaw, 13 Oct. 1773, G. Smyth (ed.), *Memoirs*, I, 446; E. Carteret to Wetstein, 27 Sept. (os) 1728, BL Add. 32145; Knight, p. 179; Watkins, 22

April 1788; J. Macky, *A Journey through England* (5th edn, 1732), iv; Andrews, 1784, pp. 16, 5; Pennant, pp. 69, 84; Wharton to Dr Baker, 12 Mar., Wharton to Thomas Wharton, 13 June, Wharton to Thomas Lloyd, 30 June 1775, Durham, Wharton; Dundas to his son, G. Omond, *Arniston Memoirs* (Edinburgh, 1887), p. 80.

33. Hanbury-Williams to Lord Holland, 11 June 1752, BL Add. 51393; BL Eg. 3481 f. 55; Garrick, 1751, p. 34.

34. Francis, 2 Nov. 1772, BL Add. 40759; Brand to Wharton, 9 April 1790, Durham, Wharton; Knight, p. 179.

35. Young, I, iii.

36. Aylesbury CRO D/DR/8/26.

37. Stoye, *English Travellers Abroad, 1604–1667* (1952), p. 18.

38. Robert to Thomas Trevor, 28 Sept. 1728, Pococke, Mitchell, Jervis, Robson, BL Add. 61684, 22978, f. 76, 58319, f. 12, 31192, f. 3, 22, 38837, f. 49; Bennet, 27 Oct. 1785.

39. Gateshead, Public Library, Ellison Mss. E 1/3.

40. J. Pemble, *The Mediterranean Passion: Victorians and Edwardians in the South* (Oxford, 1987); J. Towner, 'Tourism and Cultural Exchange: An Historical Perspective', *Visions in Leisure and Business*, 9 (1990), p. 29.

41. Polwarth, 27 March 1778, Cambridge CRO 408.

42. T. Hollingsworth, *The Demography of the British Peerage*, supplement to *Population Studies*, 18 (1964); Hollingsworth, 'Mortality among Peerage Families since 1600', *Population Studies*, 32 (1977); L. and J.C. Stone, *An Open Elite? England 1540–1880* (1984), pp. 96–104.

43. Lewisham to Dartmouth, 22 Dec. 1775, HMC *Dartmouth* III, p. 223. The original correspondence has not survived.

44. NLS Ms. 5544 f. 116; Lady Margaret Fordyce to Keith, 27 July 1783, BL Add. 35529.

EPILOGUE

THE COMING OF REVOLUTION

The French Revolution was to wreck the Grand Tour, but initially it was more a cause of surprise, wonder and enthusiasm than of concern about the consequences for France, Britain and Europe. A young Catholic Londoner, then being educated in Paris, who had recently been following the customary tourist trail, visiting Versailles and the Italian playhouse, seeing the machine at Marly and a rhinoceros at the menagerie and purchasing caged birds, was affected on 27 April 1789 by a shutting up of shops caused by riots in the Faubourg Saint-Antoine. He recorded the next day: 'After dinner took a walk in the King's Gardens. Saw clouds of smoke occasioned by the guns in the Faubourg St. Antoine.' The Réveillon riots were suppressed by the Guards, and the anonymous Londoner was soon able to record signs of normality: 'took a walk . . . to see the Dauphin lie in state at Meudon. Dined upon the road upon an omelete and some cold pork. Walked about the gardens at Meudon. An immense crowd to get in, but we being English they let us in.' On 25 June, however, he noted signs of discontent: 'saw some Guards at Palais Royal who had deserted. They were much applauded'; on 12 July, 'the revolt began. Burnt down the Barriers'; next day, 'The rebellion still increasing shops were everywhere shut up'; and on the 14th, 'Could not stir out the revolt continued . . . We were obliged to have cockades.'

The next day, the anonymous Londoner wrote: 'We were very much alarmed in the night by the firing of cannons just by us and by crys of "to arms to arms".' A week later, on his way back from a play, he 'met the body of M. Foulon who had his head cut off for having said he would make the people of Paris live upon grass and they were dragging his bloody body naked through the streets.' The following month a scarcity of bread was noted, but the Londoner was still in Paris during the October Days. On 5 October 1789 he wrote, 'The revolt began again. We took a walk in the Tuilleries and in the Chams Elisees we were stopped by the women who took away our cockades. About 3 or 400 women were putting themselves in order to go to Versailles with cannons to ask the King to come to Paris.' On the next day, 'We took a walk in the Tuilleries. Saw two of the heads of the Garde de Corps whom they were carrying about Paris upon spikes.'

Commonplace tourist activities continued. On 27 October the Londoner walked round Paris, a journey of twenty-eight miles: 'breakfasted upon the road upon *boeuf à la mode'*. The following February he saw a bullbaiting. There were also new sights, the ruins of the stormed Bastille in August 1789, the National Assembly in Versailles in October, the taking of an 'oath of fidelity to the nation' in February 1790. The situation was not unbearable, although a new order was clearly being imposed. It was impossible to get into the Tuileries without a cockade. By March it was thought appropriate to leave. A passport from the British envoy, endorsed by the French authorities, allowed the young Londoner to leave and on 16 March 1790 he crossed from Boulogne to Dover.[1]

Samuel Boddington (1766–1843) was more enthusiastic about what he saw. A curious and intelligent young man, he was the son of a distinguished city merchant, who was a leading dissenter, sympathetic to radical political circles, and who had been one of the dissenters responsible for lobbying Parliament to secure the repeal of the Test and Corporation Acts. Samuel crossed from Dover to Calais on 3 July 1789 and travelled straight to Paris.[2] He wrote thence to his father on 13 July, capturing well the excitement and uncertainty of developments:

I imagine you have seen frequent accounts of the unsettled disposition of the inhabitants of this City in the public prints. They have been so irritated by a circumstance which occurred yesterday that there is no saying to what lengths their passions may hurry them. It was at the French Theatre that our party was first informed of it. We had returned from Versailles to a late dinner with a Mr. Dallas a friend of Mr. Rigby's and afterwards adjourned to the Theatre where instead of the gaiety which usually is displayed on the drawing up of the curtain one of the principal actors came forward in deep mourning and told us that there would be no play. The audience immediately demanded the cause. '*Le peuple ne le veut pas*' said he. We soon learned that this prohibition (which has been general against all amusements whatever) was on account of the dismission of Monsr. Neckar the Prime Minister who by command of the King set off on Saturday night at 9 o'clock with the greatest secrecy in a cabriolet without any attendants to quit the Kingdom. Madam Neckar and his suite followed him yesterday morning. I suppose you saw some account in the newspapers of his being ordered to deliver up his office the week before last and of the King's receiving him into favour again through the interposition of his Citizens of Paris who repaired to Versailles in large bodies to express their disapprobation of His Majesty's conduct. The soldiers were ordered to fire among and disperse them but absolutely refused saying that they would on no account kill any of their fellow-citizens. The army which is assembled in the neighbourhood appears equally friendly. Large bodies of them have marched from their camp last week and voluntarily taken an oath of the people not to take up arms against them. But to return to my narration. From the theatre we went to the Palais Royal a large square inclosed with the Palais and the houses belonging to the Duc D'Orleans who is at this time one of the most popular characters in France – here it is that the politics of the times are discussed and since we have been here it has been one continued scene of bustle. Scarcely a moment in the day without half a dozen parties of twenty and thirty each with the utmost eagerness delivering their opinions and making their comments on the measures of the National Assembly. We did not find this place more crowded than it usually is of an evening but two or three of their orators were haranguing the people with uncommon earnestness when about 7 o'clock a fellow came running in and said he had just been wounded by a hussar. It is inconceivable the ferment the people were thrown into and a dirty fellow having put an old military cap on his stick cried out to arms, to arms, there is nothing left but for each man to defend himself. The whole assembly as if they had been animated with one soul immediately rushed out of the gates and spread the tumult everywhere. We thought it most prudent to retire to our Hotel which is just by. In a short time the whole City appeared to be collected together by far the greatest part armed with muskets the rest with cutlasses, bludgeons etc. We saw them as they passed by the end of our street into the Palais Royal a most terrible sight. It was not so much in itself as in the consequences to be apprehended. We saw large bodies of the military who appeared to have joined with them. We heard the report of a considerable number of muskets as it appeared to us at that time. Scheilds has just informed me that it was the fire of two regiments who attempted to disperse the mob. He hears that many were killed on each side. He says that everything appears quiet at present. The noise has ceased since about 5 o'clock, but such a night I never passed before. We did not go to bed till morning when the firing appeared to have abated but it was impossible to sleep. Every now and then the report of a cannon then a volley of musket. Carriages going past into the country. Men hallowing and women screaming. In short it was one continued scene of alarm and confusion. From what I saw in the morning and have since heard

I imagine the firing has been more from the desire of showing their power and their numbers than directed to any object. I saw many of them fire into the air evidently from no other view but to make a noise and the [torn away] of time and irregularity of the firing evidently proves that it could not [tear] any attack. What will be the consequence of this confusion it is hardly possible to conjecture especially as we are not yet certain of what part the army took last night. Their numbers amount to about 35,000 encamped within a quarter of a mile of the city composed of Swiss, German and provincial troops but as both officers and men are in general favourably disposed to the cause of liberty I do not see how contention can last for a long time between people who appear to be of the same mind and I will hope that the tumult of last night will only occasion a little humiliation on the part of the Court. For ourselves we propose to leave them to their own devises in the course of the day if possible. For however we rejoice in the glorious revolution which has imparted the blessings of liberty to four and twenty millions of people we rather prefer to leave the reestablishment of this happy event to their own exertions and shall be contented to hear of their proceedings instead of being in the midst of them . . . PS My hairdresser informs me that there have been only 20 slain and those of the people who were obnoxious to the mob. The military he says did not fire. If this be true they certainly have wasted an immense quantity of powder and shot.

The enthusiast for liberty sent his next letter to his father from Paris on 14 July:

I embrace the opportunity of Mr. Erskins going to England to send you a few lines in addition to what I wrote yesterday. I find that the attack was begun on the Saturday night by the hussars[3] and that in a most wanton manner but they were driven off by the populace and three or four of them left dead on the spot. The whole body of French Guards consisting of 1200 men joined the People and those it was which we saw marching with them Sunday night. During the course of yesterday the mob assumed a very different appearance. All the principal inhabitants who before stood aloof now came forward and declared themselves. They assembled in the different churches and there determined to put themselves under the tuition of the Guards and form into a regular militia. They afterwards went to the different monasteries to search for ammunition of which they found a large quantity. They also found flour which they secured for the public use. They have bound themselves to secure peace and order. Through the City all the rabble are now driven away and none but the most respectable bourgeois suffered to carry arms. Every measure is adopted with the utmost unanimity. A whole regiment from the camp joined them last night. I mentioned in my letter of yesterday that there was 35,000 men in the camp by the Gates. I should have said in the neighbourhood that is within a day's march. The camp does not consist of more than 5 or 6,000. I do not hear of any blood being shed last night but a whole regiment joined them from the camp.

The period was so interesting and Mr. Jefferson the American Ambassador assured Mr. Morgan that our situation and our character as Englishmen secured us from any danger that we determined to stay till this day. We set off for Dijon at 10 o'clock.

The King and Queen have not been seen since Sunday. No one is suffered to enter their apartments and it is imagined they are gone to one of their Palais's at a distance from the capital.

Boddington's next letter, sent to his mother on 19 July, still found him at Paris, for, as Andrew Stewart wrote from the city that day, British tourists had been affected by a ban on strangers leaving:

. . . Monday last [14th]. Our curiosity led us to stay that day hoping we should find no more difficulty in proceeding the day following than there was then but during the course of it the face of affairs took a surprising change. What in the morning was a lawless rabble in the space of a few hours became a respectable army of Bourgeois. The arms were taken out of the hands of the mob and the City with one accord rose up to defend themselves. Everything was conducted with wonderful regularity and it was astonishing with what prudence everything was conducted to guard against disorder and with what spirit and activity every measure was taken for the defence of the City. All Tuesday morning we saw nothing but loads of provisions which had either been procured from the country or from the different monasteries in the City every one [of] which were obliged to deliver up the stores for the public service by noon this day. It was computed there were 80,000 citizens in arms and a very considerable part armed with muskets. At our return from a walk in the afternoon we heard the joyful though hardly to be credited news of the Bastile being taken, not many minutes after hearing a great shouting we ran out of our Hotel into the Palais Royal (a large square where everything new is generally known). There I first beheld the horrid effects of war. The heads of the Governor and Commandant of the Bastile just cut off from their bodies carrying in triumph . . . there were only 8 prisoners found in it, one of them a Count D'Auche had been confined two and forty years in one of the dark dungeons. I never beheld so affecting a spectacle. His beard was of a great length and his hair which appeared never to have been combed was entangled in large nets as if it had been wove. It was parted into two long parts and coming over his shoulder reached below his knees. His face was [obscured] but quite pale and he looked about him as one should conceive a man to do whom for the first time had the use of his eyes. In the evening it was rumoured about the City that the Duc D'Artois the Queens Brother[4] was within a few miles of the City with 30,000 men and [tear] to make an assault upon it that night. Although this appeared [tear] hazardous a scheme that no man in his senses would attempt — yet the possibility of its being true from the violent character of the Duke — the sound of all the bells of the City calling to arms, drums beating and cannon drawing about — the pavement before our hotel taking up and carried to the top of the opposite house to throw upon the soldiers in case of an assault, together with the impression made on our minds by the sights we had just seen, all tended to have an effect upon us which was not of the most agreeable kind. The morning however came to destroy these phantoms. Good news was said to have been received from Versailles and everything wore a better appearance. Wednesday a deputation came from the National Assembly to ensure the people of the King's readiness to comply with their requests. And yesterday he came to fulfil his promise. I never saw a sight which could bear the shadow of a comparison to it. No less than 200,000 men in arms [tear: escorted him?] along to the Town Hall. There he sanctioned what had been done. The King came without any of his usual pomp guarded only by the Citizens of Paris. The troops near the City are to be withdrawn immediately but the citizens are too wise to lay down their arms. They intend to form themselves into a militia to the amount of 30,000 ready to act at any emergency. I spent half an hour with great pleasure in surveying the exterior of the Bastile. There are about 300 men employed in pulling it down in a fortnight. They hope that horrid evidence of evil will be no more. They propose to erect a temple to Liberty in its stead.

We hope to set off tormorrow. As everything is now quiet we go to Dijon and to Lyons.

As is clear from Boddington's journal, the outbreak of violence had disrupted the usual tourist round. On 8 July he had visited St Sulpice, the Carmelite church, the Invalides church and the Italian theatre; on the 9th Notre Dame and a glass factory; on the 10th the King's Library, the Duke of Orleans' picture collection and 'the Opera which I thought much more absurd than our own'; on the 11th and 12th Versailles, where he saw the King and Queen at Mass, the royal picture collection and the opera house,[5] a court on the eve of collapse.

Boddington left Paris on 20 July and travelled through Fontainebleau and Auxerre to Dijon, whence he wrote to his father on the 22nd:

> I arrived at this place last night after being detained at Paris many days contrary to our inclinations. I assure you myself and party were happy to hear the last centinel at the Barrier order the post boy to drive on . . . It is wonderful how much the love of liberty has diffused itself all over this kingdom. Every town and village we have passed through have cried out *Tiers Etat pour toujours* and when we showed them our cockades we have always been applauded by them. They are Englishmen say they, our friends. We also shall be free now. Even the people we have met on the road have always asked if we were for the *Tiers Etat*.

On the journey from Dijon to Lyons:

> we met about 120 of the inhabitants some on horseback others on foot with cockades for the *Tiers Etat*. Our Post Boys in the true spirit of servants of Le grand Monark hallowed to this band of Patriots (who were returning in triumph to their several villages from whence on the news of the troubles in Paris they had marched to the protection of Dijon) to make way and rudely drove on amongst them which insult they reproved by cutting the hempen traces of the horses. We had not time to feel any anxiety concerning the event of this little obstruction as the leaders of the party immediately came to the windows of our carriage and with all the politeness of the French nation begged we would not be under any alarm as the reprimand was only intended to chastise the insolence of the Post Boys. Our traces were repaired immediately and we proceeded amidst the huzzas of the party whom we soon convinced of our hearty interest in their cause and attachment to liberty. Our cockades on this and many other occasions procured us every respect and made way for us with the greatest facility.[6]

On 24 July Boddington wrote to his father from Lyons, presenting the Revolution as a liberation of national energies and making his own sentiments clear, as a Whig opposed to George III:

> . . . to have a true idea of the riches and population of this kingdom is only to be obtained by travelling through it. I have not seen one heath or common throughout the whole journey. The soil in general fertile but such is the temperature of the climate that the most barren parts are productive in a surprising degree . . . If such has been the situation of a country under the iron hand of despotism what may not be expected from it now the shackles of industry are broken and

a free government is about to be established. The clergy and nobility of this kingdom are computed to amount to 300,000. What an idea does it give one of the oppression the common people have laboured under to consider that almost all the wealth of a kingdom containing four and twenty million of inhabitants has flowed into their hands. They who could best afford it have paid no taxes but have rioted in abundance obtained from the industry of the honest peasant. Their day is now over. The eyes of the kingdom are now opened and they have those ideas of their own consequence and the rights and privileges they are entitled to that I trust will effectually humble that superiority which the nobles have so long unjustly arrogated to themselves. When the King came to Paris it was not as formerly *Vive le Roi* but *Vive la Nation*. I hope Englishmen will have the good sense to take a hint and not let their late loyalty carry them too far.

This was a reference to the celebrations that had greeted George III's recovery earlier in the year after a serious illness, and the consequent ending of the Regency Crisis. At dinner at a table d'hôte in Marseilles, Boddington found 'the conversation was entirely political', and when on 1 August 1789 the travellers entered the county of Nice, part of the dominions of the Kingdom of Sardinia, they were obliged to show their 'passport which on account of the late troubles at Paris was not in the usual form', and therefore led to some difficulties.

Boddington left France convinced of the value of the Revolution and the merits of France:

The industry of the French is astonishing. This added to their happy climate and fruitful soil and enjoying as they soon will do the blessings of Liberty must make them a very happy and glorious people. I wish the English would take a lesson from the French mode of living. I think it would go a great way to rid us of our gloom and formality.

Boddington's letters capture the exhilaration and confusion of the overthrow of royal power. The Revolution had two apparently contradictory consequences for tourists. On the one hand it made tourism more difficult, if not, really or apparently, hazardous. On the other it made France, in particular Paris, more exciting to visit. As many tourists were young men it is not surprising that the increased difficulties did not outweigh the excitement, but often increased it.

In literary terms the most prominent of these young men was William Wordsworth, only recently turned nineteen when the Bastille was stormed. Wordsworth was already a modest traveller at that point, having journeyed widely in his native Lake District, but he had never been abroad. In 1790 he decided to make such a trip with his Welsh friend, Robert Jones. Both were comparatively poor and their travels were to be on foot. Sailing from Dover on 13 July, they found France 'standing on the top of golden hours', the people 'mad with joy' at the early stages of the Revolution. Travelling through Paris and Lyons they went on to Switzerland, northern Italy and the Rhineland. Wordsworth's second foreign tour began in November 1791 when, as beneficiary of a legacy, he decided to travel and learn French. Passing through Paris in December, he visited the recently famous Champ-de-Mars and both 'clamorous Halls', the Assembly and the Jacobins, and acquired a relic of the Bastille, before passing on to Blois where he spent much of 1792 in revolutionary company. He returned to Paris in October 1792, by which time Pitt's government had broken off diplomatic relations with an increasingly violent and volatile French government which was experiencing the cathartic effects of first invasion and fear and then conquest and exultation. In late 1792 the varied hopes of British supporters of the Revolution and expatriates living in France were thwarted. It became apparent that although the Pitt ministry had not joined in the coalition against France, relations between Britain and France were deteriorating and war seemed increasingly likely. Secondly, though more slowly, expectations of the strength of British radicalism and the likelihood of revolution in Britain were disappointed. Whatever the basis, good relations between the two governments and two peoples appeared increasingly remote. As they drifted apart, Wordsworth returned to Britain in December 1792.

Wordsworth was not a typical tourist, though it is unclear that such an individual existed in this period. The conventional image of the tourist – an aristocratic youth in search of easy enlightenment and the enlightenment of ease in Paris and Italy – had fragmented as a consequence of the increasing variety in British tourism, a variety in personnel, intentions, routes and activities. The increasingly complex pattern of experiences and responses that characterized British tourism in the closing years of the European *ancien régime*, and indeed in the closing decades of what is now increasingly termed the British *ancien régime*, has received insufficient attention.

Nine years before Wordsworth set foot in France, Brand drew attention to what was to be one of the principal themes of travellers' comments in the years before the Revolution, namely the contrast between their expectations of the French population and the 'freedom' with which the latter conducted themselves. The emotional response in Wordsworth and others, who flocked to Paris from 1789 onwards, to the Revolution as a sudden and savage ignition and inspirer of popular freedom was somewhat misplaced. Other tourists had already noted an air of freedom in France that they had not anticipated. In an undated letter sent in the summer of 1781 Brand informed the Reverend Robert Wharton, who had himself visited Paris in 1775, about the Parisian response to the royal dismissal of the popular leading minister Necker:

> It is amazing how they talk of their monarch with as little ceremony as the English talk of Buttonmakers. Mr. Necker's dismission was on the Saturday. On the Sunday they played the Partie de Chasse de Henry IV at the Comedie Francoise. Everything respecting Sully that could possibly apply to the actual circumstances was applauded in a most astonishing manner and the passages that were usually applauded were passed over in an obstinate . . . silence. When Henry says *on m'a trompe et* goes off the stage . . . *parterre* reechoed *oui, on a trompe le Roi* . . . people talk and act as if they lived in a free country – In my next letter I will give a proof of the contrary in the persecution of my old friend the Abbe Raynal.[7]

Brand's comment on the theatre is a valuable reminder of the role of cultural agencies in pre-revolutionary France in providing a focus and occasion for the expression of political opinions. There was no sense that culture was separated from political debate. The political commitment that so many artistic and literary figures, both French and foreign, were to display during the revolutionary period represented a continuation of the pre-revolutionary situation when the artistic public, whether in the theatre or the salon, expected the arts to display commitment. The pre-Romantic period was heavily influenced by cultural patterns and beliefs that have been described as Neo-Classical, and in this cultural milieu the arts were driven by a moral imperative and were expected to be didactic. As political criticism was commonly moral in intention and tone, an affirmation of dedication, such as David's picture *Le serment des Horaces* (Oath of the Horatii), exhibited at the Salon of 1785, could not but point a contrast to the corrupt and opportunist ethos of court culture that was revealed in the Diamond Necklace affair, even if it was subsequently bought by Louis XVI.

The British response to France had been made more complex in 1778–83 by French participation on the American side in a war with Britain that aroused a distinctly ambivalent response in the latter. In place of the clear antagonism towards France displayed by all strands of British opinion during the Seven Years War (1756–63), in both the American and French revolutionary wars there was a degree of ambivalence that affected attitudes not only among those sympathetic to the cause endorsed by France, but also among others, as easy stereotypes were challenged.

The Peace of Versailles, signed in September 1783, was followed by an explosion of British tourism in France. The war had not precluded it for all, but it had prevented it for many. By January 1785 one bearleader could write from Angers: 'All this country is overrun with English, it seems a *maladie* which gains ground every day.'[8] They found a society that was less oppressed than anticipated, though not without its disadvantages. William Bennet, then a tutor of Emmanuel College, Cambridge and later Bishop of Cloyne, enjoyed the company of one potentially dissident group, the French Protestants, being, for example, shown round Bordeaux in 1785 by the Protestant minister there. Bennet noted: 'The Protestants are still numerous in the Southern Provinces, and Government connives at without tolerating them, only now and then hanging an old Priest by way of checking their progress and of late has omitted even this too sanguinary method of pleasing the bigotted Catholics.'

Bennet himself displayed a characteristic feature of British tourists in contrasting and comparing aspects of the two countries. The idea that developments during the Revolution should act as an inspiration or warning for Britain was anticipated by the widespread habit, among tourists and commentators, of comparing and contrasting the two countries. Much of this process was completely unrelated to political reflections. Landscape or the details of life tended to be more important. Bennet commented on the view from Montpellier:

> An English eye will survey it with impartiality, will allow its extent, and admire its magnificence, but accustomed to the charming landscapes of Devonshire and Yorkshire, will look in vain for the richness of our forests, and the verdure of our fields. Indeed the want of shade and the brown barren tinge of the country, is the great defect of all the views in the South of France. The soil is a light sand, or a barren rock, the olive though a rich is not a pleasing tree, his leaves being a dull green, in the shape and colour of the willow; hence almost all the prospects in this part of the world have disappointed me, they possess grandeur but they want beauty.[9]

In political matters many tourists were more willing to present a favourable or less unfavourable portrayal of France than their predecessors earlier in the century. Though 1784–7 were years of diplomatic rivalry and tension, culminating in a major confrontation during the Dutch crisis of 1787, there was a noticeable relaxation of xenophobic fervour among British tourists compared to the accounts of some, though by no means all, of their predecessors earlier in the century. Much may have been due to general relaxation in religious antagonism among the European upper orders and to a greater willingness to differentiate between the French government and the French people, both cause and consequence of a more discriminating and less deterministic assessment of their characters and interrelationship. In 1786 Francis Lord Gardenstone, who had earlier been to France to act as a lawyer during the Douglas case, went again for reasons of health. His journal, published during the Revolution, is of considerable interest. As a young man he had volunteered to fight the '45, a Jacobite rising eventually supported by France, and had nearly been killed as a result. In 1786 in Paris, where he did not like the 'almost suffocating' smell of cooking, he wrote,

> The inferior ranks of mankind, down to the lowest commonalty in Britain, certainly enjoy more effectually an equal and impartial administration of law and justice in all points, either civil or criminal. They are much more secure from the haughty insults or cruel oppressions of the great, the powerful and the nobles, than in France – This is very obvious even on a transient comparison of the condition and manners of the people in London and Paris. Our people in general are also less involved in the miserable delusions of superstition and priestcraft. These are glorious advantages for us; but sensible and considerable men will not vainly boast of and overvalue those benefits. Trace out history fairly, and it will be found evident that we owe them more to accidental and fortunate circumstances, than to superior virtue or exertions. We owe the reformation of religion to the brutal passions of one tyrant, and of government, to the extraordinary folly and ignorance of another. In point of abject credulity, we are a match for the French. Not to mention any absurdities in the common tenets of our established faith . . . in divinity, physic, law, and politicks, quacks thrive among us, and no people on earth are more egregiously duped. The Catholic belief of miracles and cures performed by relics of saints, is not a greater proof of weakness in the human understanding, than our prevailing credulity in the advertised puffs of infallible remedies, for every distemper. We are, almost in a constant succession, misled by pretenders to Patriotism. In politics, those who are not the interested creatures of faction and party, form their opinions from the superficial information of feeble news-mongers, and declamatory pamphleteers.[10]

Gardenstone's acceptance that Britain was not unique, that British developments were the result of contingencies and not of innate national characteristics, was common to many tourists, insofar as their attitudes can be gauged. Such an attitude discounted the differences between Britain and France, directed attention to political events and suggested that the context within which France and French developments should be regarded was not one of inherent British superiority. By demoting national characteristics as the explanatory model, writers such as Gardenstone introduced a note of volatility into the perception of both Britain and France.

In 1787 the rule of contingency noted by some writers and the increasing freedom of French public debate commented upon by tourists were combined in the assessment of the French political crisis of that year. Tourists became increasingly convinced with reason that France was approaching a politicial crisis. In that year Mitford visited France. His comments are worth quoting at length, because he was a perceptive commentator and his account is not referred to in John Lough's recent work on British travellers in this period.[11] Mitford was convinced both that the political atmosphere in France had changed and that politics had become more important:

> the Parisians are already as grave as if they really governed the country: and the *Palais Royal*, no longer the patient sufferer of continual repetition of frivolous *entretiens* on love, or dress, or *spectacles*, or dancing etc. etc. now resounds from morning till night with the loud whispers of important politicians, who decide daily the fate of their country.

Visiting Lille, Mitford wrote:

> Lille gives an instance of the economy practising with respect to the army which must reduce the influence of the crown over that body. The citadel of Lille had always a governor distinct from the town. The governor died, he is not replaced, and it is intended not to fill the vacancy. This reform is to prevail in all places where there are double garrisons for citadels and towns. For the nation the reform perhaps is good, though these appointments were the principal objects for officers to look to whilst struggling with difficulties from the smallness of their pay. But in consequence, the crown having fewer benefits to bestow must have less influence. In fine matters in France seem drawing to that conclusion to which they will probably arrive e'er long all over Europe; for nations will not use their reason freely, and remain slaves. The crown must economise or raise more money. Either will be accomplished with difficulty, and the accomplishment of either seems necessarily to lead to an alteration in the government. Temporising can only increase the embarrassment, which must in the end have the same effect . . . the people feel that the time is not fully come. But they think it will come; that the event is unavoidable; and they wait patiently for its arrival, keeping a steadfast eye on the circumstances which may lead to it. In such a state their minds cannot

be perfectly easy, and they have therefore lost much of their gaiety. The same eagerness of the French in everything they do is nowhere more remarkable than on their stage. The lover, in a *petite piece* of one act, telling his passion to his mistress, works himself into a violent perspiration; and *les pleurs et sanglots* of a comedie *larmoyante* are always accompanied with so much agitation as to produce most profuse symptoms of exertion on all the performers. If singing is added, the violence used in producing the shrieks necessary to give it effect with a French audience puts the poor wretch in such a state that nothing but habit could prevent their catching violent colds in bad weather. The French probably like to see the effects of these exertions apparent on the bodies of the performers; for neither actor nor actress takes any pains to prevent the external appearance on cloathes or face. Yet it may be suspected whether all this noise and violence is so much the real taste, as it is the habitual taste of the nation. When Mademoiselle Renaud sings in a more gentle and elegant stile she is highly applauded, and the French can listen with attention to the music of the Italian opera.

Returning to England on 13 October 1787, Mitford was in a reflective mood:

Leaving France on the eve, possibly, of a war between the two countries, an English traveller will reflect a little on what he has seen and heard in France. He has seen a great, rich, and powerful country, ill governed. He has heard that the country is distressed, is oppressed by taxes – But if he compares the two countries in point of extent, produce, and number of inhabitants, he finds England much more heavily burthened. It therefore appears indisputable that bad government is the cause of the distress in France, and that well governed it is in much better condition than England.

Mitford thought that an Estates General would be called, leading to reforms in French government: 'Upon the whole there seems a strong probability that France will soon be free.' The following month, Robert Arbuthnot wrote from Paris: 'Among the persons of inferior rank there seems to reign almost universally, a seditious and discontented spirit.'[12]

Thus, prior to the disturbances in the summer of 1789, there was already a sense that the situation was volatile, major change possible. It would be misleading, however, to suggest that most tourists in this period commented solely or even greatly on political matters. For many tourists the differences between Britain and France that were most apparent and interesting continued to relate to social matters and the details of life. John Villiers, later 3rd Earl of Clarendon, commented:

Nothing can be more ridiculous to an English eye; nor, one would think, to the eye of common sense, than the dress of this people. Every rank, age, and sex, with their hair dressed, powdered, and toupee'd from a child of six to a man or woman of sixty. Sailors, friseurs [hairdressers], and gentlemen, all dressed without distinction. The habits of the women are still more curious, and disgusting than those of the men; they go without hats; the lappets of their ugly caps flying about their ears, and their petticoats scarcely reaching their knees: – indeed their ideas of delicacy must be totally different from those of their sex on our side of the water; it is very common to see a woman, or half a dozen together standing in the open streets; and without a blush, or the least consciousness of impropriety, performing the offices of nature.[13]

Scenes of a different interest were soon to be offered. In 1789 came the Estates General, the Great Fear, the breakdown of order and the realization that it would be reimposed only with difficulty. A fortnight after the storming of the Bastille, the ambassador, the Duke of Dorset, reported to the Foreign Secretary, the Duke of Leeds, that

the lawless set of people whom the late tumults have set to work, make it very unsafe travelling at present, especially by night, and I really think it necessary that some public caution be given to put those upon their guard who may propose to visit this part of the Continent.

Three days later, Leeds wrote:

In the present distracted state of France, it is much to be wished, that His Majesty's subjects should abstain from visiting that country as much as possible, and that they should not sacrifice to curiosity, either their own individual safety or the attention due to their character as British subjects. As however it is almost impossible, that a considerable number of the King's subjects should not be at Paris, as well as in other parts of France . . . earnestly . . . represent to them the necessity of the most cautious behaviour during the present disturbances, and that they must be particularly careful, both in word and action, to avoid giving any reasonable ground of offence to any of the different parties, into which that kingdom is at present divided.

In its early stages the response of tourists to the Revolution varied. For some it inspired the desire to travel to Paris. In general eighteenth-century British tourism was not characterized by a wish to witness particular political events, though coronations were an obvious exception. Paris in 1789–90, before violence dulled its appeal and the appeal of the revolutionary message, was the most obvious instance of the attraction of a place in a particular political conjuncture.

At the same time that Wordsworth arrived in France, Lord Henry Fitzroy wrote to his father the Duke of Grafton, a former Prime Minister, to describe the celebrations at the Champ de Mars for the first anniversary of the fall of the Bastille:

I am so tired that I can scarce hold the pen in my hand, notwithstanding I must write you these few lines to give you a description of this day, which has already attracted the attention of the whole world and will hereafter be the subject of much conversation. No description can give a just idea of the thing, therefore don't expect much. History never did before nor probably never will again give a description of so many people assembled together; my opinion is that there were about 400,000 tho' I make no doubt it will be reported that there were 5 million. The Champ of Mars about 2 miles round was like a large amphitheatre with benches of about 50 rows in breadth all round, besides a great space behind them; the ground, on which these benches were, was raised to a descent. These seats were all full, tho' the spaces behind, where I fixed myself by choice, were but thinly occupied. In the centre was an altar of a considerable height; at the top the throne for the King, and seats for the royal family and national assembly. At the bottom 3 triumphal arches, at which all the guards, deputies, etc. entered about 1 o'clock; the middle space was crowded with these and the national guards. As soon as all the people had entered, high mass was said upon the altar, after which the standards of the different provinces were carried up to it, and their deputies took the oath, immediately after La Fayette, as representative of the whole people ascended aloft upon the altar, and there took the oath in the name of the people amidst the hues and cries of the whole mob and uplifting of the swords of the deputies and guards. Innumerable canons were fired close to the place during the whole fete, but I cannot say that the applauses of all the throng of people equalled the [word obscured by tear] of God save the King in London last year. The King was expected to have descended from his throne and taken the oath at the altar, but did not, which seems to have given great offence to many people, and I dread the consequences. The day stormy to a degree, and of course about 5000 people will have violent colds. By good management I did not get wet. I can assure you that the whole was managed with as much order and regularity as a dinner of 10 people could have been at your house: at last the people grew rather intoxicated and seemed inclined to riot; tho' at present I have heard of none. There is a pitiful illumination at present, which does not light so much as London is in general. I would upon no account have missed the sight, yet to see it again, would not give sixpence.[14]

At this stage the Revolution did not appear too threatening and Wordsworth, having left France for Switzerland, could write to his sister Dorothy, on 6 September 1790, contrasting the French favourably with the Swiss, a dramatic reversal of the common pre-revolutionary praise for the latter:[15]

We not only found the French a much less imposing people, but that politeness diffused through the lowest ranks had an air so engaging, that you could scarce attribute it to any other cause then real benevolence. During the time which was near a month which we were in France, we had not once to complain of the smallest deficiency in civility in any person, much less of any positive rudeness. We had also perpetual occasion to observe that cheerfulness and sprightliness for which the French have always been remarkable. But I must remind you that we crossed it at the time when the whole nation was mad with joy, in consequence of the revolution. It was a most interesting period to be in France, and we had many delightful scenes where the interest of the picture was owing solely to this cause.[16]

The enthusiasm of youth, and possibly a lack of interest in political detail, led Wordsworth to ignore the state of Anglo-French relations in 1790. This was certainly apparent in the 'Prelude', which was understandably more appropriate as a coherent account of the poet's personal development than as a decription of bitty, unfocused and elusive reality. It was also neither contemporary nor spontaneous:

> . . . 'twas a time when Europe was rejoiced,
> France standing on the top of golden hours,
> And human nature seeming born again.
> How bright a face is worn when joy of one
> Is joy of tens of millions.
>
> . . . we bore a name
> Honour'd in France, the name of Englishmen.[17]

On the other hand, on 16 June 1790 France's ally Spain made a formal request for French assistance in her escalating dispute with Britain over Pacific trade arising from the Nookta Sound incident. This request was presented to the National Assembly on 2 August, and on

26 August the Assembly decided to increase the fleet in order to enable the government to help Spain. Furthermore, rumours circulated about Britain's intentions towards France. The refusal in July 1789 to heed French requests to permit the export of flour to France had increased animosity, and rumours about 'Pitt's gold', alleged secret intrigues of the British ministry, did not help matters. The sympathy of Dorset for the émigré Artois played a role in Dorset's departure in 1789. In 1789 the atmosphere in Paris was recorded by Mrs Martha Swinburne:

> its being reported that England was going to declare war and had already distributed 20 French millions in Paris – such nonsense could only have gained credit with the mob, but then it is King Mob that governs . . . The merest trifle is enough to inflame the populace who never consider but take fire at the first word.[18]

This volatile atmosphere of fear, bred of ancient animosities and present suspicions, appears to have left little mark on Wordsworth. This lack of perception was possibly as serious as that which led him to underrate the spiral of violence in which the Revolution and the revolutionaries were already trapped. Wordsworth himself admitted the unfocused nature of his political interests in the section of the 'Prelude' describing his second visit to France:

> Amused and satisfied, I scarcely felt
> The shock of these concussions, unconcerned,
> Tranquil, almost, and careless as a flower
> Glassed in a Green-house, or a Parlour shrub
> While every bush and tree, the country through,
> Is shaking to the roots;[19]

With no clear understanding of French developments, Wordsworth's response in 1792 was greatly affected by his relationship with his lover, Annette Vallon, and with the charismatic officer Michel Beaupuy. Isolated in Blois and finding his studies 'tedious'[20] Wordsworth was susceptible both politically and emotionally. He became 'a Patriot'.[21] When at Blois he wrote the *Descriptive Sketches in verse taken during a pedestrian tour in the Italian, Grison, Swiss, and Savoyard Alps* and referred to the Swiss routing superior Austrian forces in the Middle Ages,[22] he was probably also thinking of the Austrian preparations for an invasion of France. Wordsworth's displays of optimism may well have been in part a response to and escape from a bleak pessimism that gripped him at times when he thought seriously about French developments. In May 1792 he wrote from Blois to William Matthews, expressing moral repugnance about the conduct of the French army – flight, murder of General Dillon and the killing of prisoners –-'events which would have arrested the attention of the reader of the annals of Morocco, or of the most barbarous of savages'. Wordsworth was pessimistic about the prospects for France:

> The approaching summer will undoubtedly decide the fate of France. It is almost evident that the patriot army, however numerous, will be unable [to] withstand the superior discipline of their enemies. But suppose that the German army is at the gates of Paris, what will be the consequence? It will be impossible to make any material alteration in the constitution, impossible to reinstate the clergy in its ancient guilty splendour, impossible to give an existence to the *noblesse* similar to that it before enjoyed, impossible to add much to the authority of the King.[23]

Revolutionary France offered Wordsworth both a political and a sentimental education. In each case he discovered in 1792 that the responses of others could be unpredictable and unreasonable. His liaison with Annette Vallon could certainly be seen in this light, though it has been suggested that the importance of the affair might have been over-emphasized.[24] Possibly more significant was the obvious fracturing of revolutionary enthusiasm in France, the sense of disillusion that resulted from a realization both that hopes were not shared and that, not least for this reason, they were unrealistic. As important for an Englishman in France may have been a corrosive doubt about the future, a sense that the unfolding of liberty so apparent in 1790 was no longer clear, that unpredictability shrouded the future of the Revolution in France, its success in fending off enemies already declared and the development of Anglo-French relations.

Doubts on each of these scores affected British tourists in 1792, and Wordsworth's revolutionary enthusiasm, however affected and confused by an affair of the heart, did not free him from concern. British tourism became a victim of revolutionary change: diminished in scale, altered in character, forced to follow different routes, and uncertain. An apparent marked increase in crime in France led Edward Ramage, in Paris in March 1792, to conclude that it was not safe to travel. In March 1793 the Duke of Leeds wrote that his son George, later 6th Duke (1775–1838), 'is just gone abroad. He is now in Holland on his way to Lausanne where I proposed he should pursue his studies for some time. I hope there at least he may be quiet, though the present state of Europe is such, as to render, a situation of perfect tranquillity very difficult to be found.'

British newspapers warned of an upsurge in crime in France. Fearing the French advance, the Earl of Findlater fled Frankfurt in late 1792. In the preface to his *Letters during the Course of a Tour through Germany, Switzerland and*

Italy, in the years 1791 and 1792, published in 1794, the clergyman Robert Gray (1762–1834), later Bishop of Bristol, noted:

> the Author, on his return from the Continent, had no intention of presenting his Journal in any form to the public . . . it occurred to him [later] that his descriptions and remarks might, perhaps, interest attention at a time in which an intercourse with the continent, for excursions of pleasure, is almost cut off: when some of the scenes which the author visited, are disfigured by recent devastation, or clouded by the terrors of approaching storms; when he who forsakes England must mark, wherever he may travel, the track of armies, and behold suspicion and distrust, and the influence of evil principles in societies, where confidence and chearfulness formerly prevailed.

Gray's remarks are interesting not least because another writer hoping to pursue a career in the church in 1792 was Wordsworth. Though Wordsworth shared Gray's admiration for the Swiss terrain, it is difficult to see him echoing Gray's remark: 'The author has been careful that they who travel with him should find him at least harmless; picking up no scraps of infidelity, collecting no trash of foreign politics.' Gray's *Letters* revealed the impact of the Revolution on neighbouring countries. His last, sent from Brussels on 23 March 1792, recorded finding Oppenheim 'full of Frenchmen, exiles from a once happy and flourishing country. What scenes of private distress has this mad and ill-conducted Revolution occasioned.' At Luxemburg 'on application to the commandant to see the fortifications, we were told not only that we must not see them, but that we must immediately leave the town, unless we were detained by necessity. Such being the jealousy at this critical period, when all Europe seems prepared to arm, that no stranger is allowed to stay above twenty-four hours in the town.' A commission established later that year at Munich to question foreign visitors, led to complaints from the British envoy who argued that his compatriots should be exempted from all other enquiry as soon as they declared their national identity.[25]

If the Revolution affected tourism outside France, it and the subsequent Napoleonic period also altered France, Britain and the rest of Europe. Tourists who visited France both before 1793 and after 1814 commented on these differences. Edward Nares, later Regius Professor of History in Oxford, made a brief foreign tour in 1785 which he subsequently described in his autobiography:

> I know not whether these differences will ever again be so marked and striking. The suppression of monasteries and nunnerys, and the

changes of dress, which have since taken place, must tend exceedingly to alter the appearance of all French towns.[26]

The impression that the destruction of the *ancien régime* had brought fundamental cultural and social changes that could not be reversed with the restoration of the Bourbons in 1814 was general. It was a theme in *Two sketches of France, Belgium, and Spa, in Two Tours, during the summers of 1771 and 1816* (1817) by the much-travelled man of letters, Stephen Weston (1749–1830). Weston had already published in 1792, 1793 and 1803 his separate impressions of Paris in the previous years. In 1821 James Mure made a long comparison between France then and the country in the early 1770s, when he had been educated there. His comparison was generally hostile. If Mure's complaints about the decline in French bread and cookery may appear inconsequential, his comments on the Jardin des Plantes are of considerable interest:

> The collection is said to be a fine one and well arranged: the rooms, too, are large; but were soon so crowded with dirty people, common soldiers, beggars, labourers just off their work, that you could neither examine any of the curiosities, nor feel comfortable as to the contact you of necessity came into at every step with filth and dirt. I cannot conceive the propriety of opening collections connected with taste and science to the daily inspection of persons nine-tenths of whom can neither write nor read. It encourages idleness . . .[27]

This was the authentic note of the British *ancien régime*, one that was not swept aside in the early 1790s. As so often, however, variety was the keynote of the British response. In early 1791 Samuel Rogers, a banker and poet from a dissenting background, who was sympathetic to the cause of reform in Britain, visited Paris. He sent his sister an account of his activities, which included dining with such liberal figures as Lafayette and La Rochefoucauld. Rogers complained about nothing, and presented a society in lively ferment:

> On Monday morning we went to the National Assembly which sits in the riding school of the Thuilleries a very long narrow building . . . We heard a very violent debate on the subject of the Hospitals, in which 3 or 4 often spoke at once and the bell which the President rings to impose silence, was as often rung in vain . . . saw a piece which is now acting in every theatre in France, which is a simple representation of the taking of the Bastille. Between the acts 'Ça Ira' was played by the orchestra and the audience clapped in time with the music, with an enthusiasm that would have animated a stone. An English nobleman is

introduced who utters the noblest sentiments and, assures the people, that the English are not their enemies, but their rivals in glory and draws his sword in their cause. He concludes the piece with these words, *Francais, vous avez conquis la Liberté, tachez de la conserver* . . . made a second pilgrimage to the Champ de Mars, the scaffolding still stands, and conveys the clearest idea possible of what was exhibited on the 14th July.[28] The grandeur of the scene in its present state, was far, very far beyond my expectation . . . In the evening (for everybody goes to one of the theatres and there are 12 open every night) we saw a new piece – A nobleman just released from a long confinement by illness and ignorant of the Revolution, is shocked to find that his servants are out of livery, and to hear himself addressed without a title. His daughter whom he had destined to a convent is in love with a bourgeois and he writes for a *lettre de cachet* to confine him. To crown all, his creditors have the insolence to demand the payment of his debts – but after much point and equivoque he is at last brought to reason. It was received with the most rapturous applause.[29]

That July, George Koehler, a German in British service, who had fought for the Belgian 'Patriots' against the Austrians in 1790 and was sympathetic to the cause of revolution, travelled through France to Turin

without the least unpleasant accident of any kind . . . I saw in my tour through France more order more arrangement, and law, than I by any means *supposed* possible, they seem very diffident of the English, and appear preparing for war[30] every village has political clubs; and newspapers without end, but all seem to adore their Assembly National, and their decrees, as to the rest of their rural occupation, commerce, entertainments etc seem to go on as smooth as ever, their Guards National make a good appearance, and the military seem every day to settle as to subordination and discipline, there are no doubt many dissatisfied and affected to the old government but by everything which I could perceive they appear to be extremely outnumbered by the friends to the present constitution.

Francis Moore was also struck by the order and quiet of Paris that July. The Earl of Pembroke observed in January 1791, 'I am sorry for the Revolution in France, because I am afraid of being lanterned. I never loved London, and I do not think I ever shall. Paris was a pleasant capital; but *selon moi, il n'en reste plus à present.*' And yet, five months later, Thomas Pelham, now an MP, 'found everything as quiet as it had been while I was here last year', and thought the response to Louis XVI's flight to Varennes moderate rather than violent.[31]

A more detailed response had been provided by Thomas Brand in 1790, Brand, acting as bearleader for Lord Bruce, the eldest son of the Earl of Ailesbury, had visited France on several occasions and his comments are thus of particular interest as he was best placed to note changes. Brand emphasized popular support for the monarchy, which was now identified with liberty, and hostility towards monks and nuns. He seems to have as much trouble with 'bourgeois' as modern historians, and uses the word in three different ways: first to indicate a civilian, then in the general sense of someone conscious of his inferior station, then of the 'exertion of Bourgeois authority', where the word suggests people proud of their active participation in the Revolution. The three meanings are not entirely contradictory, but they at least imply different points of view and none of them carries any specifically economic connotation. Brand's prediction 'the word Bourgeois will be no more heard of' is a good example of the prophecies that the Revolution inspired. He wrote to Wharton from Paris on 17 July,

> . . . the grand day of the Federation which passed off with the utmost order and propriety . . . The nation, my dear friend, is changed beyond every idea I could have formed. The nobility have fled and the people have assumed a manly look. The master of my hotel and his son are changed from simple Bourgeois to a Captain and Lieutenant of the national guard. Mr Perregaux the Banker is the only man I have seen who seems ashamed of his commission.[32] To be sure a spontoon is an awkward thing for a hand which never flourished but with a quill. The word Bourgeois will be no more heard of: it might even be the death of Monsieur Jourdain, if the wit of Moliere was mortal.
>
> A beggar addressed me yesterday not by the title of Excellence or Monseigneur, but *mon bon Citoyen* . . . Were you to see the national guard, you would be amazed: our militia even at their best, did not make so good an appearance and I suspect that their courage is very different from that of the old mercenary army that the common soldier now will have all the resolution of the *ci-devant* officer.
>
> The smart pert abbé is seen no longer. His crest is fallen never to rise again . . . one of my new caricatures is a soldier shaving a monk and a milliner bringing a new cap to a nun and the title is *on me raze ce matin et je me marie le soir*. But to return to the Federation . . . the day as you know was wet beyond example: of 300,000 men I was one of the few hundreds who were under cover; but not a soul stirred and the circumstances showed the only remains of the old national character which I could remark. During the greatest violence of the storm which English troops would have turned their backs to and born with stoical fortitude or in sullen silence, the soldiers who occupied the

Arena formed thousands of circles and danced to the sound of the drums. Sometimes they united, sometimes they separated. One single circle spread itself entirely across the field and must have consisted of some hundred of these Pyrrhic Figurants. A procession of unfortunate priests had just reached the altar when the deluge poured down. At the beginning of their march, a flight of doves were let off, some say they were Emblems of the St. Esprit, others that they were typical of the demolition of the seigneurial rights of Pigeon-houses, others that they were mere signals. So do they fly from Tiburn.[33] [Part of next section torn off, but some phrases visible] Much as I detest . . . the national assembly . . . I could not help feeling a sort of enthusiasm . . . believe me the cry *Le Roi* on that occasion was neither mockery nor flattery it was certainly the voice of gratitude to the assertors of their liberty and of attachment to the house of Bourbon.

Poor Henry IV on the Pont-neuf is so be-ribban'd and be-bouqueted and fêted that there is hardly a bit of bronze to be seen. I think all idea of a contro-revolution must be given up. The King and the noblesse (Ah! cowards to forsake their cause and country!) must wait till the fury of rival demagogues give them an opportunity of recovering their influence which I think must happen sooner or later in this vast single assembly which has no constitutional check.

I don't imagine that in the whole history of mankind there ever was a more magnificent sight than the Champ de Mars on that day. It has given me infinite satisfaction that we came this way. But what an awful sight for an hereditary branch of the English parliament!!

Having 'left that seat of crazy Liberty' on 18 July, Brand's enthusiasm had cooled by the time he next wrote to Wharton, from Geneva on 27 July 1790:

. . . We slept the first night at Sens and found the accommodations good and the roads clear for we set off before those swarms of national deputies had finished their business at Paris. To say the truth I doubt whether it will be as easy to rid the capital of them as it was to assemble them. They began to be very riotous at all the public places and if the *Aristocrates* had plied them well with money and mistresses Messieurs le Assemblé Nationale might have cursed the day that they took it into their heads to blow up so solemn a feast in the new moon.

I had taken care to get passports both from Lord Gower and from Monsr. de Montmorin[34] which was fortunate as they were demanded at Montbard, at Dijon, at Auxonne and at Dole. Our adventure at the first of those places was excellent. The postillion ignorant of the order to stop at the corps de garde drove furiously by and provoked the indignation of two fierce national centinels who ran after us, caught us at the hill, presented their muskets to the drivers and demanded our passports. We had unluckily shifted them from one pocket of the carriage to another and could not immediately find them. I was therefore ordered to go before the Commandant. Figure to yourself my surprise when instead of the imposing figure of the Commandant of former times I was carried to an unwieldy animal in a linen waistcoat a white drill jacket and a nightcap who looked as if he had just killed a calf and expected a customer to buy the veal. He was civil as to say (passing his hand between his bare scull and the nightcap) that perceiving by my accent that I was not a Frenchman he would venture to let me pass. I made my bow and was retreating when Lord Bruce came up with the passports . . . In my hurry to convince my good friend that he had done right I gave him — not either of the passports but the printed order which we had to the Poste at Paris for horses which having sagely examined through a small pair of spectacles he declared to be a passport in due form! The centinels returned their firelocks to their shoulder, the postilions flourished their whips and off we went cracking, through a vast crowd who had assembled at this edifying exertion of Bourgeois authority! So much for Montbard where I suppose there has been no guard since the old civil wars with the Barons.

How great was my surprise at Besançon (formerly a most jealously garrisoned frontier) to be simply interrogated who we were, whence we came and whither we were going by . . . an Old Woman! who could scarce totter up to the carriage. *C'est le siecle des Revolutions.*[35]

Eighteen months later the situation was less humorous, and one tourist was mistaken for Louis XVI, who had already tried once to escape from Paris:

About ten days ago, as the Earl of Grandison, was on his tour through France, he was stopped by the populace at Macon; they took him for the king. The embarras was not little, while it lasted; but, by showing, among other vouchers, the circular letters of Lockhart and Sir Robert Herries with their notes, it appeared who he was; and he was dismissed by their Highnesses the Mob.[36]

British tourists were affected when Nice was overrun by French troops in late 1792. Their homes did not escape pillage.[37] Brand's scorn would have seemed very dated to Randle Wilbraham, who had left England in 1793, to visit much of Europe, Turkey and the Middle East. He returned in 1798 and found it necessary to obtain from the French *chargé d'affaires* a passport from Naples to Florence. It was dated in the new calendar of the new French republic.[38] A different world had indeed come to much of western Europe. The persecution of the Church and the break with the Holy See affected life throughout French-dominated Europe. Italy was especially changed by French dominance. Venice lost its independence under the Treaty of Campoformio (1797), becoming first Austrian and then in 1805 part of the French kingdom of Italy. For many, the fall of Venice was as powerful a symbol as that of Constantinople to the Turks in 1453. The artist's colony in Rome, already badly hit by the expulsion of the French students at the academy, disintegrated; Gavin Hamilton died in Rome in 1798; the Earl-Bishop of Derry, arrested by the French in Italy in 1798, died in Albano in 1803; Byres, Jenkins and Sir William Hamilton managed to return home; and architectural links with Italy were severed, helping to swing taste in favour of Greece.[39]

Having conquered Italy and rearranged it politically, a process that was to reach its apogee with the annexation of Etruria (former Tuscany) in 1807 and the Papal States in 1809, the French then embarked on their artistic rape. The Treaty of Tolentino was only the best known of their confiscation treaties. Derry's valuable collection of antiquities was seized in 1798. Such confiscations were to help make Paris the art capital of the world, and, furthermore, in terms of the art theory of the time, the moral capital. The Italy that eighteenth-century tourists had known was partly swept away, and this was to condition nineteenth-century tourism to the peninsula. The Italian states were not alone in being swept away or dramatically altered in the Revolutionary and Napoleonic period. Alongside the cleaving to Church and Crown that characterized so much of Europe in that period in reaction to the new order being created by France, there was change and disruption, new artistic styles and novel ideas. The Continent changed and British tourists who visited it after the defeat of Napoleon and the restoration of the Bourbons were conscious that they were seeing a different world to that toured by their pre-Revolutionary predecessors.

NOTES

1. Beinecke, Osborn Shelves c 393 pp. 8, 13, 16–20, 23, 29–31, 34–5, 39, 46, 49, 51, 57.
2. Guildhall Library, London, Boddington papers. There is a manuscript diary of Samuel's, Ms. 10823/5A and fifteen letters from him to his family 5B. He was a companion of Edward Rigby, on whom see Lady Eastlake (ed.), *Letters from France etc.* in 1789 (1880).
3. German cavalry in service of Louis XVI.

4. The Comte d'Artois (1757–1836) was the brother of Louis XVI and not of Marie Antoinette.

5. Ms. 10823/5A f. 5–6.

6. Ms. 10823/5A f. 6–7; Cambridge UL Add. 6958, No. 695; BL Add. 33121 f. 12.

7. Brand to Wharton, [summer 1781], Durham, Wharton. Sully was Henry IV's reforming minister.

8. Livingston to Keith, 5 Jan. 1785, BL Add. 35533 f. 152.

9. Bod. Ms. Eng. Misc. f. 54. fos. 161, 154.

10. Gardenstone, I, 31, 34–6.

11. J. Lough, *France on the Eve of Revolution. British Travellers' Observations 1763–1788* (1987).

12. Mitford Journal, Gloucester CRO D 2002 F1; BL Add. 35539 f. 244.

13. Villiers, *A Tour through part of France* (1789), pp. 12–13.

14. PRO FO. 27/32 f. 403, 27/33A f. 3–4; Fitzroy to Grafton, 14 July 1790, Bury St Edmunds, West Suffolk RO Grafton papers 423/422.

15. G. Keate, *A Short Account of the Ancient History, Present Government, and Laws of the Republic of Geneva* (1761); W. Coxe, *Travels in Switzerland* (1789).

16. A.G. Hill, (ed.) *Letters of William Wordsworth* I (Oxford, 1984), p. 5.

17. Wordsworth, *The Prelude or Growth of a Poet's Mind* 1805 text, ed. Ernest de Selincourt (Oxford, 1933), VI, 352–4, 359–60, 409–10.

18. Political Extracts from Mrs Swinburne's letters, 28 July 1789, BL Add. 33121 f. 15.

19. *Prelude* IX, 85–90.

20. *Prelude* IX, 122.

21. *Prelude* IX, 124.

22. Wordsworth, *Descriptive Sketches* 1793 text, ed. Eric Birdsall (Ithaca, 1984), p. 90; C.N. Coe, *Wordsworth and the Literature of Travel* (New York, 1953), p. 55.

23. Hill (ed.), *Letters*, p. 11.

24. F.M. Todd, *Politics and the Poet, A Study of Wordsworth* (1957), p. 41.

25. Ramage, NLS Ms. 5568 f. 63, 80; Leeds to George Hammond, 1 Mar. 1793, New York, Public Library, Montague collection, vol. 7; *Public Advertiser*, 6 Jan. 1792; Gray, Letters (1794), iii-iv, vii, vi, 464, 466; 2 Dec. 1792, Munich, Bayerisches Haupstaatsarchiv, Abteilung II, Gesandtschaften London 262.

26. Nares autobiography, Merton College, Oxford, E. 2.42, 91–2.

27. Mure to George Jardine, 8 April 1821, *Selections from the Papers Preserved at Caldwell* (Glasgow, 1854), II, ii, 380–96, quote 385–6.

28. The Fête de le Fédération on 14 July 1790.

29. Beinecke, Osborn Files, Samuel Rogers, 4 Feb, 1790 (for 1791).

30. In support of Spain in her confrontation with Britain over Nootka Sound, and trade on the western coast of North America.

31. Bod. Bland Burges 36 f. 93, 45 f. 67, 71; Winchester CRO, Malmesbury vol. 163.

32. The Swiss banker Perregaux who lived in Paris. During the Terror he not merely helped counter-revolutionaries, but was the agent through whom the British government trasmitted funds to agents in the Jacobin Club who posed as extremists. It is interesting to find him cited as early as 1790, as singling himself out by his dislike to the Revolution.

33. Where hangings took place in London.
34. British envoy and French foreign minister.
35. Durham, Wharton.
36. St James's Chronicle, 21 Jan. 1792.
37. John Trevor, envoy in Turin, to Earl of Elgin, 8 Oct. 1792, Broomhall, Elgin papers 60/1/182; AE CP Ang. 583 f. 47.
38. Chester CRO DBW/N/E packet G1.
39. F. Salmon, 'British Architects and the Florentine Academy, 1753–1794', Mitteilungen des Kunsthistorischen Institutes in Florenz, 34 (1990), p. 208.

BIBLIOGRAPHY

For reasons of space only some of the primary and secondary material used has been mentioned. There are no references to newspaper, pamphlet, parliamentary and theatrical material, nor to material in the Public Record Office (in which State Papers Foreign was consulted extensively), and in foreign diplomatic archives. Unless otherwise stated, the place of publication is London.

MANUSCRIPT SOURCES

Aberdeen, University Library: Duff of Braco, Maclaurin, Ogilvie papers.
Aberystwyth, National Library of Wales: Penrice and Margam papers.
Alnwick, Alnwick Castle: vols 113 (Beauchamp), 146 (Warkworth).
Aylesbury, Buckinghamshire Record Office: Craven, Drake, Lee, Saunders, Trevor, Wagstaffe papers.
Badminton, Badminton House: Beaufort papers.
Bangor, University Library: Penrhos letters.
Bedford, Bedfordshire Record Office: Lucas papers.
Birmingham, Central Library: Malies diary.
Bradford, Public Library: Spencer Stanhope, Tong papers.
Bristol, Avon Record Office: Harford journal.
Broomhall, Fife: Elgin papers.
Bury St Edmunds, West Suffolk County Record Office: Grafton, Hervey papers, Mason journal.
Cambridge, Cambridgeshire Record Office: Chapman diary, Green diary, Townley journal, Polwarth letters.
    Fitzwilliam Museum: William Fitzwilliam journal.
    University Library: Anon. (Add. 8789), Brand (Add. 8670), Bute (Add. 8826), Hoare, Pitt, Ratcliffe, Smith papers.
Carlisle, Cumbria Record Office: Pennington papers (journal of William Weddell).
Carmarthen, Dyfed Record Office: Cawdor Muniments, Box 138.
Chelmsford, Essex Record Office: Barrett, Braybooke, DuCane papers.
Chester, Cheshire Record Office: Leicester, Stanley, Wilbraham papers.
Chewton Mendip, Chewton House: papers of James, 1st Earl Waldegrave.
Chichester, West Sussex Record Office: Goodwood papers; anon (add. mss 7236–7).
Durham, University Library: Wharton papers.
Edinburgh, National Library of Scotland: Elliot, Liston, Tweeddale papers.
    Scottish Record Office: anon. (GD26/6/233; 38/1/1253/14; 267/7/20), Barclay, Clark, Clerk, Coke, Dalhousie, Dalrymple, Deskford, Grant, Morton, Oliphant, Stair papers.
Exeter, Devon Record Office: Addington, Hatsell, Quicke papers.

Farmington, Connecticut, Lewis Walpole Library: Hanbury Williams, Horace Walpole, Weston papers.

Gateshead, Public Library: Ellison papers.

Gloucester, Gloucestershire Record Office: anon. (D1799/A325, C7), Anstruther, Blathwayt, Freeman, Milles, Mitford, Ducie-Morton, Player, Sutton, Wetenhall papers.

Guildford, Surrey Record Office: Brodrick papers.

Hatfield, Hatfield House: Cecil papers.

Hawarden, Clwyd Record Office: Lowther papers.

Hertford, Hertfordshire Record Office: Leake, Panshanger papers.

Hull, University Library: Constable-Maxwell, Hotham papers.

Huntingdon, Huntingdonshire Record Office: Manchester papers.

Ipswich, East Suffolk Record Office: Leathes, Straton papers.

Kidderminster, Public Library: Knight notebooks.

Leeds, District Archives: Newby Hall, Vyner papers.

Leicester, Leicestershire Record Office: anon. diary (DG7/4/12), Finch papers.

Lincoln, Lincolnshire Record Office: Massingberd papers.

London, Bedford Estate Office, Russell Letters.

  British Library – Additional manuscripts: anon. (12130, 60522), Althorp, Auckland, Blakeney, Blenheim, Burnet, Caryll, Compton, Crewe, Dropmore, Dysart, Egmont, Essex, Finch-Hatton, Flaxman, Fox, Francis, Garmston, Grant, Grantham, Grey, Hardwicke, Holland House, Hume, Keith, Macclesfield, Milles, Mitchell, Mountstuart, Newcastle, Nixon, Pelham, Spark Molesworth, Pococke, Rainsford, Robson, St Vincent, Southwell, Suffolk, Swinburne, Ward, Weston, Wetstein, Whitworth, Wodehouse papers.

  - Egerton manuscripts: Bentinck, Holdernesse, Southwell papers.

  - Sloan manuscripts: vol. 4045.

  - Stowe manuscripts: anon. journal (790), Macclesfield.

  Guildhall: Boddington papers.

  House of Lords Record Office: Cadogan papers.

  Public Record Office: Gower, Pitt papers.

  University Library: anon. journal (Ms. 491).

Longford Castle, Wiltshire: Radnor papers.

Maidstone, Kent Archive Office: Norman, Polhill, Sackville, Stanhope, Twisden papers.

Manchester, John Rylands Library: Stanley, Walsh papers.

Matlock, Derbyshire Record Office: anon. journal (D2375M/76/186), Fitzherbert, Perrin papers.

Mount Stuart: papers of the 3rd Earl of Bute.

Newcastle, Northumberland Record Office: Blackett, Haggerston, St Paul papers.

New Haven, Beinecke Library: Osborn Collection, Shelves: b 266; c 23–4, 49, 53, 114, 200, 289, 319, 331–2, 365–6, 393, 396, 455–6, 467, 469; f b 90, 201; f c 11, 16, 52, 97; Blathwayt boxes; Files: Clayton, Dorset, Hutton, Lansdowne, Palmerston, Samuel Rogers, Temple, Thomas, 8.77, 19.252; uncatalogued: Boyle, Courtown, Young; Lee, Manchester papers.

New York, Public Library: Montague collection.

Northampton, County Record Office: Isham papers.

Norwich, Norfolk Record Office: Gurney, Ketton-Cremer, Lothian papers.
Nottingham, Nottinghamshire Record Office: Rolleston papers.
    University Library: anon. journal (Me/2L/2a), Clumber papers, Mellish letters.
Oxford, Bodleian Library: anon. (Ms. Eng. Misc. d. 213), Bennet, Bland Burges, Butler, Carpenter, Dashwood, Folkes, Milles, North, Rawlinson, Tracy, Tucker, Wilberforce papers.
    Christ Church Library: Wake papers.
    County Record Office: Dillon papers.
    Merton College Library: Nares autobiography.
    Wadham College Library: Swinton papers.
Paris, Bibliothèque Nationale: Southwell papers, Journal du voyage de la Porte du Theil.
Petworth, Petworth House Archives: Letters of Sir William Wyndham.
Preston, Lancashire Record Office: Farrington, Greene papers.
Providence, Rhode Island, John Carter Brown Library: Codex Eng. 74, Thomas Hulton autobiography.
Reading, Berkshire Record Office: Aldworth-Neville, Barrett papers.
San Marino, California, Huntingdon Library: Ellesmere, Loudoun, Montagu, Pulteney, Stowe papers, HM 18940, 41763.
Sheffield, City Archives: Wentworth Woodhouse papers.
Stafford, Staffordshire Record office: anon. journal CDD/SH 67/19 C/2480, Anson, Congreve papers.
Taunton, Somerset Record Office: Harbin-Bamfyld, Kemys-Tynte, Wadham, Wyndham papers.
Trowbridge, Wiltshire Record Office: Willes papers.
Warwick, Warwickshire Record Office: Newdigate papers.
Wigan, Town Hall: anon. (D/DZ), Leigh, Windham papers.
Winchester, Hampshire Record Office: Malmesbury, Mildmay papers.
Worcester, Worcestershire Record Office: Rushout papers.

GUIDEBOOKS, PUBLISHED TRAVEL ACCOUNTS AND CORRESPONDENCE

Addison, J., *Letters from Italy to the Right Hon. Charles Lord Halifax, in the Year 1701* (1703).
Addison, J., *Remarks on Several Parts of Italy, 1701–1703* (1705).
Aikin, L., (ed.), *Memoir of John Aikin M.D.* (2 vols, 1823), I, 69–95.
Andrews, J., *Letters to a Young Gentleman on his setting out for France* (1784).
    A Comparative View of the French and English Nations in their manners, politics and literature (1785).
Anon., 'Sketch of a Fortnight's Excursion to Paris in 1788', *Gentleman's Magazine* 67 (1797), pp. 723–35, 908–9.
    Travels though Holland 1768–70 (1773).
    A Descriptive Journey through the interior parts of Germany and France (1786).
    'Letters From France, 1788–89', J. Lough (ed.), *Durham University Journal* 54 (1961).
A.R., *The Curiosities of Paris* (1758, 1760).

Armstrong, J., ('Lancelot Temple'), *A Short Ramble through some parts of France and Italy* (1771).

Ayscough, G.L., *Letters from an Officer in the Guards to a Friend in England, containing some accounts of France and Italy* (1778).

Lord Baltimore, *A Tour to the East* (1767).

Beckford, P., *Letters and Observations written in a short Tour through France and Italy* (1786).
   Familiar Letters from Italy to a Friend in England (Salisbury, 1805).

Beckford, W., *Italy, with Sketches of Spain and Portugal* (1834).
   The Travel Diaries of William Beckford, ed. G. Chapman (1928).
   The Grand Tour of William Beckford, ed. E. Mavor (1986).

Bentley, T., *Journal of a Visit to Paris 1776*, ed. P. France (Brighton, 1977).

Berkeley, G., *The Works*, ed. A.A. Luce and T.E. Jessop (1955–6).
   Viaggio in Italia, ed. T.E. Jessop and F. Fimiani (Naples, 1979).

Berry, M., *Extracts of the Journals and Correspondence*, ed. T. Lewis (1865).

Blaikie, T., *Diary of a Scotch Gardener at the French Court at the end of the Eighteenth Century*, ed. F. Birrell (1931).

Boswell, J., in F.A. Pottle (ed.), *Boswell on the Grand Tour* (1952).

Breval, J., *Remarks on several parts of Europe* (1726).

Bromley, W., *Remarks on the Grand Tour* (1692).

Brydone, P., *A Tour through Sicily and Malta* (1775).

Burney, C., *The Present State of Music in France and Italy* (1771).

Calderwood in A. Ferguson (ed.), *Letters and Journals of Mrs Calderwood* (Edinburgh, 1884).

Cayley, C., *A tour through Holland, Flanders and part of France* (Leeds, 1773).

Charlemont in W.B. Stanford and E.J. Finopoulos (eds), *The Travels of Lord Charlemont in Greece and Turkey 1749* (1984).

Clubbe, W., *The Omnium: containing the Journal of a late three days Tour into France* (1798).

Coke, in J.A. Home (ed.), *The Letters and Journals of Lady Mary Coke* (Edinburgh, 1889–96).

Cole, W., in F.G. Stokes (ed.), *A Journal of my journey to Paris in the Year 1765* (1931).

Collier, G., in C. Tennant (ed.), *France, Holland, and the Netherlands, A Century Ago* (1865).

Coxe, W., *Travels into Poland, Russia, Sweden, and Denmark* (1784–90).
   Travels in Switzerland (1789).

Cradock, A.F., in O. Balleyguier (ed.), *Journal inédit* (Paris, 1896).

Cradock, J., *Literary and Miscellaneous Memoirs* (1828).

Craven, E., *A Journey through the Crimea to Constantinople* (Dublin, 1789).
   Memoirs of the Margravine of Anspach (1826).

Crawford, in R. Rolt, *Memoirs of the Life of the Right Honourable John Lindesay, Earl of Crawford* (1753).
   The Curious Traveller Being a choice collection of very remarkable Histories, Voyages, Travels etc. (1792).

Cust, L., *Records of the Cust Family III* (1927).

Dalrymple, W., *Travels through Spain and Portugal in 1774* (1774).

Dick, A., 'A Journey from London to Paris in 1736', *Gentleman's Magazine* 39 (1853).

Douglas, J., *Travelling Anecdotes through several Parts of Europe* (1785).
   'Journal of a tour in Holland, Germany, France', in W. Macdonald (ed.), *Select Works* (Salisbury, 1820).

Drummond, A., *Travels through different cities of Germany, Italy, Greece* (1754).

Dryden, J., *A Voyage to Sicily and Malta* (1776).

Essex, J., in W. Fawcett (ed.), *Journal of a Tour through part of Flanders and France in August, 1773*, (Cambridge, 1888).

Este, C., *A Journey in the Year 1793 through Flanders, Brabant and Germany to Switzerland* (1795).

Fife in A. and H. Tayler (eds), *Lord Fife and his Factor* (1925).

Memorials of Lady Gambier (1861) I, 17–99.

Gardenstone, *Travelling Memorandums made in a tour upon the Continent of Europe in the years 1786, 1787 and 1788* (Edinburgh, 1791–5).

Garrick, D., *The Letters*, ed. D.M. Little and G.H. Kehol (1963).

Garrick, D., in R.C. Alexander (ed.), *The Diary of David Garrick being a record of his memorable trip to Paris in 1751* (New York, 1928).

Garrick, D., in G.W. Stone (ed.), *The Journal of David Garrick describing his visit to France and Italy in 1763* (New York, 1939).

Gibbon, E., *Letters*, ed. J.E. Norton, (1956).

    Memoirs of my Life, ed. G.A. Bonnard (1966).

Gibbon, E., in G.A. Bonnard (ed.), *Gibbon's Journey from Geneva to Rome* (1961).

Grafton in W.P. Anson (ed.), *Autobiography and Political Correspondence of Augustus Henry Third Duke of Grafton* (1898).

Gray, R., *Letters during the course of a Tour through Germany, Switzerland and Italy* (1794).

Gray, T., in P. Toynbee and L. Whibley (eds), *Correspondence of Thomas Gray* (Oxford, 1935).

Harcourt in E. Harcourt (ed.), *The Harcourt Papers* (Oxford, no date).

Herbert, Lord George (11th Earl of Pembroke) in Lord Herbert (ed.), *The Pembroke Papers (1734–1794). Letters and Diaries of Henry 10th Earl of Pembroke, and his Circle* (1942–50).

Hervey, C., *Letters from Portugal, Spain, Italy and Germany in the years 1759–61* (1785).

Hill, B., *Observations and Remarks in a Journey through Sicily and Calabria in the Year 1791* (1792).

Hoare, R., *Recollections Abroad: Journals of Tours on the Continent between 1785 and 1791* (Bath, 1817).

    A Classical Tour through Italy and Sicily (1819).

Hobhouse, B., *Remarks on several parts of France, Italy, etc. in the years 1783, 1784, and 1785* (Bath, 1796).

Hurd, E., *Dialogues on the Uses of Foreign Travel* (1764).

Ireland, S., *A Picturesque Tour through Holland, Brabant and part of France made in 1789* (1790).

Jardine, A., *Letters from Barbary, France, Spain, Portugal* (1788).

Johnson, S. in M. Tyson and H. Guppy (eds), *The French Journals of Mrs Thrale and Dr Johnson* (Manchester, 1932).

Jones, T., *Memoirs of Thomas Jones* (1951).

Jones, W., *Observations on a Journey to Paris in the month of August 1776* (1776).

P. Knight in E.F. Elliott-Drake (ed.), *Letters from France and Italy 1776–1795* (1905).

Knight, Lady R.P., *Expedition into Sicily*, ed. C. Stumpf (1986).

Leven in W. Fraser (ed.), *The Melvilles Earls of Melville and the Leslies Earls of Leven* (Edinburgh, 1890).

Lister, M., *A Journey to Paris in the Year 1698* (1699).

Lucas, W., *A Five Weeks Tour to Paris* (1750).

Lyttelton in R. Phillimore (ed.), *Memoirs and Correspondence of George, Lord Lyttelton* (1845).

Macdonald, J., *Travels in various parts of Europe, Asia and Africa* (1790).

Mckay, J., *A Journey through the Austrian Netherlands* (1725).

Martyn, T., *The Gentleman's Guide in his Tour through Italy* (1787).

   The Gentleman's Guide in his tour through France (1787).

   Sketch of a tour through Swisserland (1787).

Miller, Lady A., *Letters from Italy* (1776).

Moore, J., *A View of Society and Manners in France, Switzerland and Germany* (1779).

   A View of Society and Manners in Italy (1781).

Morritt, J., in G.E. Marindin (ed.), *A Grand Tour: Letters and Journeys 1794–96* (1914, reprinted 1985).

Muirhead, L., *Journals of Travels in parts of the late Austrian Low Countries, France, the Pays de Vaud and Tuscany, in 1787 and 1789* (1803).

Nares in G.C. White, *A Versatile Professor: Reminiscences of the Rev. Edward Nares* (1903).

Northall, J., *Travels through Italy* (1766).

Northumberland in J. Greig (ed.), *The Diaries of a Duchess* (1926.

Nugent, T., *The Grand Tour* (1749), second, much expanded, edition 1756.

   Travels through Germany (1768).

John, Earl of Corke and Orrery, *Letters from Italy* (1773).

Orrery in Countess of Corke and Orrery (ed.), *Orrery Papers* (1903).

Owen, J., *Travels into Different Parts of Europe in the Years 1791–1792* (1796).

Palmer, J., *A Four Months Tour through France* (1775).

Parminter, J., in C.J. Reichel (ed.), 'Extracts from a Devonshire Lady's Notes of Travel in France 1784', *Transactions of the Devonshire Association for the Advancement of Science, Literature and Art* 34 (1902).

Peckham, H., *A Tour through Holland, Dutch Brabant, the Austrian Netherlands, and part of France* (1772).

Pennant, T., *Tour on the Continent 1765*, ed. G. de Beer (1948).

Pennington, T., *Continental Excursions, or Tours into France, Switzerland and Germany in 1782, 1787 and 1789* (1809).

Piozzi, H.L., *Observations and Reflections made in the course of a Journey through France, Italy and Germany* (1789).

The Piozzi Letters, ed. E.A. and L.D. Bloom (1989).

Playstowe, P.?, *The Gentleman's Guide in his Tour through France* (1770). For attrib. Factotum 19 (1984), p. 13.

Pococke, R., *A Description of the East and some other Countries* (1743–5).

Poole, R., *A Journey from London to France and Holland* (1746–50).

Pomfret in W. Bingley (ed.), *Correspondence between Frances, Countess of Hartford and Henrietta Louisa, Countess of Pomfret* (1805).

Pratt, S.J., *Travels for the Heart* (1777).

   Gleanings through Wales, Holland and Westphalia (1795).

   Present State of Germany (1738).

Radcliffe, A., *A Journey made in the Summer of 1794, through Holland and the Western Frontier of Germany* (1796).

Ray. J., *Travels through the Low Countries* (1738).

Richard, J., *A Tour from London to Petersburg* (1780).

Richmond in Earl of March, *A Duke and his Friends. The Life and Letters of the second Duke of Richmond* (1911).

Rigby, E., in Lady Eastlake (ed.), *Letters from France in 1789* (1880).

Russell, F., *A Descriptive Journey Through the Interior Parts of Germany and France* (1786).

Russell, J., *Letters from a Young Painter Abroad to his Friends in England* (1748).

John, 4th Earl of Sandwich, *A Voyage performed by the late Earl of Sandwich round the Mediterranean in the years 1738 and 1739* (1799).

St. John, J., *Letters from France to a Gentleman in the South of Ireland, written in 1787* (Dublin, 1788).

Sharp, S., *Letters from Italy* (1766).

Shaw, J., *Letters to a Nobleman* (1709).

Sherlock, M., *Letters from an English Traveller* (1780).

　New Letters from an English Traveller (1781).

Sinclair, J., *Correspondence* (1832).

Skelton, J., in *The Letters of Jonathan Skelton* (ed.), B. Ford (1959).

Smith, J.E., *A Sketch of a Tour on the Continent in the years 1786 and 1787* (1793).

Smollett, T., *Travels through France and Italy* (1766).

Soyer, D., (ed.), *Travels through Holland, Germany, Switzerland, and other parts of Europe* (1943–5).

Spence, J., in S. Klima (ed.), *Joseph Spence: Letters from the Grand Tour* (Montreal 1975).

Spencer, H., in Earl of Bessborough (ed.), *Lady Bessborough and her Family Circle* (1940).

Starke, M., *Letters from Italy* (1800).

Sterne, L., *A Sentimental Journey through France and Italy* (1768).

　Letters, ed. L.P. Curtis (Oxford, 1935).

Stevens, S., *Miscellaneous Remarks made on the spot in a late Seven Years Tour through France, Italy, Germany and Holland* (no date, 1756?).

Sutherland, D., *A Tour up the Straits, from Gibraltar to Constantinople* (1790).

Swinburne, H., *Travels through Spain in the years 1775 and 1776* (1779). 1787 ed. includes an account of his 'Journey from Bayonne to Marseilles'.

　Travels in the Two Sicilies, 1777–1780 (1783–5).

　The Courts of Europe at the Close of the Last Century, ed. C. White (1841).

Taylor, J., *The History of the Travels and Adventures of the Chevalier John Taylor* (1761–2).

Taylor, T., *The Gentleman's Pocket Companion for Travelling into Foreign Parts* (1722).

Thicknesse, P., *Observations on the Customs and Manners of the French Nation* (1766).

　Useful Hints to those who make the Tour of France (1768).

　A Year's Journey through France and part of Spain (Bath, 1777).

　A Year's Journey through the Pais Bas and Austrian Netherlands (1784).

Thompson, C., *The Travels of the late Charles Thompson* (Reading, 1744).

Thomson, A., *Letters of a Traveller* (1798).

Toland, J., *An Account of the Courts of Prussia and Hanover* (1705).

Townsend, J., *A Journey through Spain in the years 1786 and 1787, and remarks in passing through a part of France* (1791).

Veryard, E., *An Account of Divers Choice Remarks* (1701).

Villiers, J.C., *A Tour through part of France* (1789).

Walker, A., *Ideas suggested on the spot in a late Excursion* (1790).

　'A Sketch of the police, religion, arts and agriculture of France, made in an excursion to Paris in 1785', in *Remarks made in a tour from London to the Lakes* (1792).

Walpole, H., *Correspondence*, ed. W.S. Lewis et al (New Haven, 1937–83).

Watkins, T., *Travels through Swisserland, Italy, Sicily, the Greek Islands, to Constantinople* (1792).

Weston, S., *Two Sketches of France, Belgium, and Spa, in Two Tours, during the summers of* 1771 *and* 1816 (1817).

Wharton in G. Rodmell, 'An Englishman's Impressions of France in 1775', *Durham University Journal* (1969).

Whately, S., *A Short Account of a late Journey to Tuscany, Rome, and other Parts of Italy* (1746).

Windham, W., *A Letter from an English Gentleman giving an Account of the Ice Alps in Savoy* (1744).

Wortley Montagu, Lady Mary, *The Complete Letters*, ed. R. Halsband (Oxford, 1965–7).

Wraxall, N., *Cursory Remarks made in a Tour through some of the Northern Parts of Europe, particularly Copenhagen, Stockholm, and Petersburgh* (1775).

    A Tour through the Western, Southern, and Interior Provinces of France (1784).

    Memoirs of the Courts of Berlin, Dresden, Warsaw, and Vienna in the years 1777, 1778, and 1779 (1799).

Wright, E., *Some Observations made in travelling through France, Italy etc.* (1730).

Young, A., *Travels during the years 1787, 1788 and 1789* (2nd ed. 1794).

SECONDARY LITERATURE

Acton, H. and Chaney, E. (eds.), *Florence: a Travellers' Companion* (1986).

Adams, P., *Travellers and Travel Liars 1660–1800* (Berkeley, 1962).

Andrew, P., 'Jacob More and the Earl-Bishop of Derry', *Apollo*, 124, No. 294 (Aug. 1986).

Andrew, P.R., 'Rival Portraiture. Jacob More, the Roman Academician', *Apollo*, 130, No. 333 (Nov. 1989).

Arbellot, G., 'Voyages et voyageurs au temps de la Révolution', *Annales recherches urbaines* 43 (1989).

Ashby, T., 'Thomas Jenkins in Rome', *Papers of the British School at Rome* 6 (1913).

Bacigalupo, M.F., 'An Ambiguous Image: English Travel Accounts of Spain, 1750–1787', *Dieciocho* 1 (1978).

    'A Modified Image: English Travel Accounts of Spain, 1788–1808', *Dieciocho* 2 (1979).

Baridon, M. and Chevignard, B., (eds), *Voyage et tourisme en Bourgogne à l'époque de Th. Jefferson* (Dijon, 1989).

Batten, C.L., *Pleasurable Instruction: Form and Convention in Eighteenth Century Travel Literature* (Berkeley, 1978).

Bausinger, H., Beyrer, K. and Korff, G. (eds.), *Reisekultur. Von der Pilgerfahrt zum modernen Tourismus* (Munich, 1991).

Beer, E.S. de, 'The Development of the Guide Book until the early nineteenth century', *Journal of the British Archaeological Society*, 3rd ser., 15 (1952).

Beer, Sir G. de and Rousseau, A.-M. (eds), *Voltaire's British visitors* (Geneva, 1967).

Black, J.M., 'An Englishman Abroad in the 1730s', *Postmaster* 6 (1980).

    'British Travellers in Europe in the Early Eighteenth Century', *Dalhousie Review* 61 (1981–2).

    'Sicily 1792: The account of a British traveller', *Archivo Storico per la Sicilia Orientale* 80 (1984).

    'The Grand Tour and Savoy Piedmont in the Eighteenth Century', *Studi Piemontesi* 13 (1984).

'France and the Grand Tour in the Early Eighteenth Century', Francia 11 (1984).

'Une visite à Cîteaux en 1775', Annales de Bourgogne (1984).

'An Unprinted Account of Savoy-Piedmont in 1734', Italian Quarterly 25 (1984).

'Southern France in 1783', Provence Historique 34 (1984).

The British and the Grand Tour (1985).

'Dijon en 1725', Annales de Bourgogne 57 (1985).

'An Unprinted Account of Savoy-Piedmont in 1734', 'Turin in 1783', Studi Piemontesi 34 (1985).

'Florence in 1731', Bollettino del Centro Interuniversitario di Ricerche sul Viaggio in Italia 14 (1986).

'La Normandie en 1750', Annales de Normandie 36 (1986).

'Savoy-Piedmont in 1699', Studi Piemontesi 15 (1986).

'A Visitor to Revolutionary France', French Studies Bulletin 19 (1986).

'On the Grand Tour in a Year of Revolution', Francia 13 (1986).

'Portugal in 1730', British Historical Society of Portugal. Annual Report and Review 13 (1986).

'Through Savoy Piedmont in 1726', Studi Piemontesi 16 (1987).

'The Eighteenth-Century Grand Tour: A New Account', Lamar Journal of the Humanities 13 (1987).

'Englishmen on the Italian Grand Tour in the 1700s', Italian Quarterly 28 (1987).

'Pisa in due inedite relazioni di Viaggiatori Inglesi della prima meta' del Settecento', Bollettino Storico Pisano 56 (1987).

'Through Savoy-Piedmont in 1726', Studi Piemontesi 16 (1987).

'On the Grand Tour in 1699–1700', The Seventeenth Century 2 (1987).

'Portugal on the Eve of the Methuen Treaties. Richard Creed's Journal of 1700', and 'Portugal in 1775. The Letters of Thomas Pelham', British Historical Society of Portugal. Annual Report and Review 14 (1987).

'Viscount Beauchamp on the Grand Tour', North Dakota Quarterly 56 (1988).

'Portugal in 1760: the Journal of a British Tourist', British Historical Society of Portugal. Annual Report and Review 15 (1988).

'Savoy-Piedmont in 1701', Studi Piemontesi 17 (1988).

'France in 1730: A Tourist's Account', Francia 16 (1989).

'The Grand Tour in 1723–5', Bollettino del Cirvi 19 (1989).

'Tourism and Cultural Challenge: The Changing Scene of the Eighteenth Century', in J. McVeagh (ed.), English Literature and the Wider World. Volume I 1660–1780. All Before Them (1990).

'Fragments from the Grand Tour', Huntingdon Library Quarterly 53 (1990).

'Turin in 1737', Studi Piemontesi 19 (1990).

'Ideology, history, xenophobia and the world of print in eighteenth-century England', in J. Black and J. Gregory (eds), Culture, Politics and Society in Britain 1660–1800 (Manchester, 1991).

'A Stereotyped Response? The Grand Tour and Continental Cuisine', Durham University Journal 83 (1991).

'On the Grand Tour in 1771–3', Yale University Library Gazette 66 (1991).

'Archival Sources for the Grand Tour', Archives 20 (1992).

'Farmington: Diplomacy and the Doings of Golly Hogs' and 'Meeting Voltaire', Yale University Library Gazette 66 and 67 (1992).

'The Grand Tour' in S. Cavaciocchi (ed.), *Il Tempo Libero Economia e Società* (Florence, 1995).

'Italy and the Grand Tour: The British Experience in the Eighteenth Century', *Annali d'Italianistisa* (1996).

'English Views of France and Italy 1660–1800' in A. Montandon (ed.), *Le Même et L'Autre. Regards européens* (Clermont-Ferrand, 1997).

'The Grand Tour' in R. Myers and M. Harris (eds), *Journeys Through the Market, Travel, Travellers and the Book Trade* (Folkestone, 1999).

Eighteenth Century Europe (2nd edn, 1999).

Blondel, M., 'Le Récit de Voyage Féminin au XVIIIe siècle', *Bulletin de la Société d'Etudes Anglo-Americaines des XVIIe et XVIIIe siècles*, 17–18 (1983–4).

Bonnerot, J., *Les Routes de France* (Paris, 1921).

Bradshaw, A., 'William Van Mildert's visit to the Netherlands', *Durham University Journal* 71 (1978).

Braeur, G.C., *The Education of a Gentleman: Theories of Gentlemanly Education in England, 1660–1775* (New York, 1959).

Brown, H.F., *Inglesi e Scozzesi all'Università di Padova dall'anno 1618 sino al 1765* (Venice, 1921–2).

Burgess, A., *The Age of the Grand Tour* (1967).

Burke, J., 'The Grand Tour and the Rule of Taste', in R.F. Brissenden (ed.), *Studies in the Eighteenth Century* (Canberra, 1968) pp. 231–50.

Candaux, J.D., 'Du Mont-Cenis à Herculaneum en 1752–53 ou les Débuts du "Tourisme" Genevois en Italie', in L. Mornier (ed.), *Genève et l'Italie* (Geneva, 1969).

Répertoire chronologique des relations de voyage intéressant Genève, 1550–1800 (Geneva, 1975).

Chaloner, W.H., 'The Egertons in Italy and the Netherlands, 1729–34', *Bulletin of the John Rylands Library* 32 (1949–50).

Chaney, E., 'George Berkeley in the Veneto', *Bollettino del CIRVI* 1 (1980).

'"Philanthropy in Italy", English Observations on Italian Hospitals: 1549–1789', in J. Riis (ed.), *Aspects of Poverty in Early Modern Europe* (Florence, 1981).

'The Grand Tour and Beyond: British and American Travellers in Southern Italy 1745–1960', in E. Chaney and N. Ritchie (eds), *Oxford, China and Italy: Writings in honour of Sir Harold Acton* (1984).

The Grand Tour and the Great Rebellion: Richard Lassels and 'The Voyage of Italy' in the Seventeenth Century (Geneva, 1985).

'British and American Travellers in Sicily', in A. Macadam (ed.), *Blue Guide Sicily* (1988).

'Quo vadis? Travel as Education and the Impact of Italy in the Sixteenth Century', in P. Cunningham and C. Brook (eds), *International Currents in Educational Ideas and Practices* (1988).

'Architectural Taste and the Grand Tour: George Berkeley's Evolving Canon', *Journal of Anglo-Italian Studies* 1 (1991).

The Evolution of the Grand Tour (1998).

The Grand Tour. Travel writing and imaginative geography 1600–1830 (Manchester 1999).

Chard, C. and Langdon, H. (eds), *Transport, Travel, Pleasure and Imaginative Geography, 1600–1830* (New Haven, 1996).

Checkland, S., *The Elgins 1766–1917* (Aberdeen, 1988).

Clark, A.M., *Pompeo Batoni. Complete Catalogue* (Oxford, 1985).

Clarke, M. and Penny, N. (eds), *The Arrogant Connoisseur: Richard Payne Knight 1751–1824* (Manchester, 1982).

Clifford, T., 'Sebastiano Conca at Holkham: a Neapolitan painter and a Norfolk patron', *Connoisseur* 196 (1977).

Colyer, R.J., 'A Breconshire Gentleman in Europe, 1737–38', *National Library of Wales Journal* 21 (1980).

Connell, B., *Portrait of a Whig Peer* (1957).

Cook, B.F., *The Townley Marbles* (1985).

Coulson, M., *Southwards to Geneva: 200 Years of English Travellers* (Gloucester, 1988).

Cross, A.G., 'British Residents and Visitors in Russia during the Reign of Catherine the Great', in J.M. Hartley (ed.), *The study of Russian history from British archival sources* (1986).

Cusatelli, G. (ed.), *Viaggi e viaggiatori del Settecento in Emilia e in Romagna* (Bologna, 1986).

Dent, K.S., 'Travel as Education: The English Landed Classes in the Eighteenth Century', *Educational Studies* 1 (1975).

Diezinger, S., 'Paris in deutschen Reisebeschreibungen des 18. Jahrhunderts', *Francia* 14 (1986).

Duloum, J., *Les Anglais dans les Pyrénées et les débuts du tourisme Pyrénéen 1739–1896* (Lourdes, 1970).

Dunthorne, H.L.A., 'British travellers in eighteenth-century Holland', *British Journal for Eighteenth-Century Studies* 5 (1982).

Edwards, A.C., *The Account Books of Benjamin Mildmay, Earl Fitzwalter* (1977).

Egerton, J., *Wright of Derby* (1990).

Féliciangeli, D., 'Le développement de Nice au cours de la second moietié du XVIIIe siècle. Les Anglais à Nice', *Annales de la Faculté des Lettres et Sciences humaines de Nice* 19 (1973).

Fleming, J., *Robert Adam and his Circle in Edinburgh and Rome* (1962).

'Lord Brudenell and his Bear-Leader', *English Miscellany* (1958).

Fleming, J. and Honour, H., 'Francis Harwood – an English Sculptor in eighteenth century Florence', in *Festschrift Ulrich Middeldorf* (Berlin, 1968).

Florange, C., *Etude sur les Messageries et les Postes* (Paris, 1925).

Ford, B., 'Six Notable English Patrons in Rome, 1750–1800', *Apollo* 99 (1974), pp. 408–61.

'The Blathwayt Brothers of Dyrham in Italy on the Grand Tour', *The National Trust Year Book 1975–76* (1975), pp. 19–31.

'The Grand Tour', *Apollo* 114 (1981), pp. 390–400.

'The Englishman in Italy in G. Jackson-Stops (ed.), *The Treasure Houses of Britain: Five Hundred Years of Private Patronage and Art Collecting* (New Haven, 1985), pp. 40–9.

'The Byres Family by Franciszek Smuglewicz', *National Art Collections Fund* (1984).

Fordham, H.G., *Catalogue des Guides-Routiers et des Itinéraires Français, 1552–1850* (Paris, 1920).

Les Guides-Routiers, Itinéraires et Cartes Routières de l'Europe, 1500–1850 (Lille, 1926).

Fothergill, B., *Sir William Hamilton* (1969).

The Mitred Earl (1974).

Beckford of Fonthill (1979).

Frantz, R.W., *The English Travellers and the Movement of Ideas 1660–1732* (New York, 1968).

Friedman, T.F., 'Sir Thomas Gascoigne and his Friends in Italy', *Leeds Art Calendar* 78 (1976).

Fussell, P., 'Patrick Brydone: The Eighteenth-Century Traveller as Representative Man', *Bulletin of the New York Public Library* (1962).

Golden, M., 'Travel Writing in the Monthly Review and Critical Review, 1756–1775', *Papers on Language and Literature* 13 (1977).

Gooder, E., *The Squire of Arbury. Sir Richard Newdigate, second baronet (1644–1710) and his Family (1644–1710)* (Coventry, 1990).

Gosse, P., *Dr Viper: the querulous life of Philip Thicknesse* (1952).

Gotch, C., 'The missing years of Robert Mylne', *Architectural Review* 110 (1951).

Grosser, T., 'Reisen und Kulturtransfer. Deutsche Frankreichreisende 1650–1850', in M. Espagne and M. Werner (eds), *Transferts. Les Relations Interculturelles dans L'Espace Franco-Allemand* (Paris, 1988).

Grosser, T., *Reiseziel Frankreich. Deutsche Reiseliteratur vom Barock bis zur Französischen Revolution* (Opladen, 1989).

Halsband, R., *The Life of Lady Mary Wortley Montagu* (Oxford, 1956).
Lord Hervey (Oxford, 1973).

Harcourt-Smith, C., *The Society of Dilettanti: its Regalia and Pictures* (1932).

Hardwick, N., (ed.), *The Grand Tour: William and John Blathwayt of Dyrham Park 1705–1708* (Bristol, 1985).

Haskell, F., 'Norfolk and the Grand Tour', *Burlington Magazine* 128 (1986).

Haskell, F. and Penny, N., *Taste and the Antique. The Lure of Classical Sculpture 1500–1900* (1981).

Hautecoeur, L., *Rome et la Renaissance de l'Antiquité à la fin du XVIIIe siècle* (Paris, 1912).

Hawcroft, F.W., 'Grand Tour Sketchbooks of John Robert Cozens, 1782–1783', *Gazette des Beaux Arts* (1976).

Hayward's List – British visitors to Rome 1753–1775, *Walpole Society* 49 (1983).

Hibbert, C., *The Grand Tour* (1987).

Honour, H., 'Talman and Kent in Italy', *The Connoisseur* 134 (1954).

Ingamells, J., *A Dictionary of British and Irish Travellers in Italy 1710l–1800* (New Haven, 1997).

Irwin, D., 'Gavin Hamilton: Archaeologist, Painter and Dealer', *Art Bulletin* 44 (1962).
Scottish Painters at home and abroad 1700–1900 (1975).

Jenkins, P., 'John Clephane: A New Welsh Source for the History of the Enlightenment', *National Library of Wales Journal* 22 (1982).

Jones, W.P., 'The William Robinsons in Italy', *Huntington Library Quarterly* 4 (1941).

Kenwood, *British Arists in Rome 1700–1800* (1974), exhibition catalogue by L. Stainton.

Krasnobaev B.I., (ed.), *Reisen und Reisebeschreibungen im 18. und 19. Jahrhundert als Quellen der Kulturbeziehungsforchung* (Berlin, 1980).

Laubriet, P., 'Les guides de voyages au début du XVIIIe siècle', *Studies on Voltaire and the Eighteenth Century* 32 (1965).

Lees-Milne, J., *The Earls of Creation* (1962).

Lewis, L., *Connoisseurs and Secret Agents in eighteenth-century Rome* (1961).

Links, J.G., *Canaletto and his Patrons* (1977).

Lough, J., 'Letters from France, 1788–89', *Durham University Journal* 54 (1961).

France Observed in the Seventeenth Century by British Travellers (Stocksfield, 1985).

France on the Eve of Revolution. British Travellers' Observations 1763–1788 (1987).

'Regency France seen by British travellers', in G. Barber (ed.), *Enlightenment Essays in Memory of Robert Shackleton* (Oxford, 1988).

'France in the 1780s seen by Joseph and Anna Francesca Cradock', *Studies on Voltaire and the Eighteenth Century* 267 (1989).

McKay, P., 'The Grand Tour of the Hon. Charles Compton', *Northamptonshire Past and Present* 7 (1986).

McVeagh, J., (ed.), *English Literature and the Wider World. Volume 1 1660–1780. All Before Them* (1990).

Mainwaring, E.W., *Italian Landscape in Eighteenth Century England* (1925).

Maxwell, C., *The English Traveller in France, 1698–1815* (1932).

Mead, W.E., *The Grand Tour in the Eighteenth Century* (New York, 1914).

Michaelis, A., *Ancient Marbles in Great Britain* (Cambridge, 1882).

Mildmay, H.A., *A Brief Account of the Mildmay Family* (1913).

Millar, O., *Zoffany and his Tribuna* (1967).

Moore, A., *Norfolk and the Grand Tour* (Norwich, 1985).

Müllenbrock, H.J., 'The Political Implications of the Grand Tour', *Tema* 9 (1984).

Mullett, C.F., 'The Education of a Duke', *Midwest Journal*, 7 (1955).

Nash, D., 'The Rise and Fall of an Aristocratic Tourist Culture, Nice: 1763–1936', *Annals of Tourism Research* 6 (1979).

Nicholson, B., *Joseph Wright of Derby* (1968).

Oresko, R., 'The British Abroad', *Durham University Journal* 79 (1987).

Parks, G.B., 'The turn to the romantic in the travel literature of the eighteenth century', *Modern Language Quarterly* 25 (1964).

Pears, I., 'Patronage and Learning in the Virtuoso Republic: John Talman in Italy', *Oxford Art Journal* 5 (1982).

The Discovery of Painting. The Growth of Interest in the Arts in England, 1680–1768 (New Haven, 1988).

Pemble, J., *The Mediterranean Passion: Victorians and Edwardians in the South* (Oxford, 1987).

Pietrangeli, C., 'The discovery of Classical art in eighteenth-century Rome', *Apollo* (1983).

Pine-Coffin, R.S., *Bibliography of British and American Travel in Italy to 1860* (Florence, 1974).

Pitte, J.R., *Gastronomie Française: Histoire et géographie d'une passion* (Paris, 1991).

Possin, H.J., *Reisen und Literatur* (Tübingen, 1972).

'Englische Reiseliteratur des 18. Jahrhunderts. Ein Forschungsbericht', *Anglia* 102 (1984).

Redford, B., *Venice and the Grand Tour* (New Haven, 1996).

Richardson, A.E., *Robert Mylne* (1955).

Rodmell, G., 'An Englishman's Impressions of France in 1775', *Durham University Journal*, new ser. 30 (1969).

Roebuck, P., 'An English Catholic on tour in Europe. 1701–03', *Recusant History* 11 (1971–2).

Roget, S.R., (ed.), *Travel in the two last Centuries by three Generations* (1921).

Russell, F., 'The British Portraits of Anton Raphael Mengs', *National Trust Studies 1979* (1978).

Sacquin, M., 'Les Voyageurs Français en Angleterre et les Voyageurs Anglais en France de 1750 à 1789', École Nationale des Chartes, *Positions des Thèses* (Paris, 1977), pp. 137–42.

'Les Anglais à Montpellier et à Nice pendant la seconde moitié du siècle', *Dix-Huitème siècle* 13 (1981).

Salmon, F., 'British Architects and the Florentine Academy, 1753–1794', *Mitteilungen des Kunsthistorischen Institutes in Florenz* 34 (1990).

Schudt, L., *Italienreisen im 17. und 18. Jahrhunderts* (Vienna, 1959).

H. Schwarzwalder, 'Reisebeschreibungen des 18. Jahrhunderts über Norddeutschland', in W. Griep and H. Jager (eds), *Reise und Soziale Realität am Ende des 18. Jahrhunderts* (Heidelberg, 1983).

Sells, A.L., *The Paradise of Travellers. The Italian Influence on Englishmen in the Seventeenth Century* (1964).

Shackleton, R., 'The Grand Tour in the Eighteenth Century', in L.T. Milic (ed.), *Studies in Eighteenth-Century Culture* (1971).

Sitwell, O., *Sing High! Sing Low!* (1944).

Skinner, B., 'Some aspects of the work of Nathaniel Dance in Rome', *Connoisseur* (1951).

Scots in Italy in the Eighteenth Century (Edinburgh, 1966).

Sloan, K., *Alexander and John Robert Cozens* (1986).

Smith, E.A., 'Lord Fitzwilliam's "grand tour"', *History Today* 17 (1967).

Smout, C., 'Tours in the Scottish Highlands from the Eighteenth to the Twentieth Centuries', *Northern Studies* 5 (1983).

Solkin, D.H., *Richard Wilson*, Tate Exhibition catalogue (1982).

Stainton, L., *British Artists in Rome 1700–1800*, Kenwood catalogue (1974).

Stanhope, G., *The Life of Charles Third Earl Stanhope* (1914).

Stirling, A.M., *Annals of a Yorkshire House* (1911).

Stoye, J., *English Travellers abroad 1604–1667* (1952, revised ed. New Haven, 1989).

'Reisende Engländer im Europa des 17. Jahrhunderts und ihre Reisemotive', *Wolfenbütteler Forschungen* 21 (1982).

'The Grand Tour in the Seventeenth Century', *Journal of Anglo-Italian Studies* I (1991), pp. 62–73.

Strien, C.D., van, *British Travellers in Holland during the Stuart Period* (Leyden, 1991).

Stroud, D., *George Dance, Architect 1741–1825* (1971).

Sturdy, D.J., 'English Travellers in France, 1660–1715' (Dublin PhD, 1969).

'Images of France and Germany: The Accounts of English Travellers in the Seventeenth Century', in H. Duchhardt and E. Schmitt (eds), *Deutschland und Frankreich in der frühen Neuzeit* (Munich, 1987).

Sutton, D., *Souvenirs of the Grand Tour* (1982).

Thompson, J.M., (ed.), *English Witnesses of the French Revolution* (Oxford, 1938).

Towner, J., 'The European Grand Tour, c. 1550–1840: A Study of its Role in the History of Tourism' (Birmingham PhD, 1984).

'The Grand Tour: Sources and a Methodology for an Historical Study of Tourism', *Tourism Management* 5 (1984).

'The Grand Tour. A Key Phase in the History of Tourism', *Annals of Tourism Research* 12 (1985).

'Approaches to Tourism History', *Annals of Tourism Research* 15 (1988).

'Tourism and Cultural Exchange: An Historical Perspective', *Visions in Leisure and Business* 9 (1990).

'History and Tourism', *Annals of Tourism Research* 18 (1991).

Trease, G., *The Grand Tour* (1967).

Tuzet, H., *La Sicile au XVIIIe siècle vue par les voyageurs étrangers* (Strasbourg, 1955).

Viola, G.E., (ed.), *Viaggiatori del Grand Tour in Italia* (Milan, 1987).

Vivian, F., *Il Console Smith, mercante e collezionista* (Vicenza, 1971).

Watkin, D., *Thomas Hope and the Neo-Classical Idea* (1968).

Watson, F.J.B., *Thomas Patch (1725–82). Notes on his life together with a catalogue of his known works* (Walpole Scoiety vol. 27, 1938–9).

Wawn, A., 'John Thomas Stanley and Iceland: The Sense and Sensibility of an Eighteenth-Century Explorer', *Scandinavian Studies* 53 (1981).

West, J.F., (ed.), *The Journals of the Stanley Expedition to the Faroe Islands and Iceland in 1789* (Tórshavn, 1970–6).

Wiggin, L.M., *The Faction of Cousins* (New Haven, 1958).

Wittkower, R., *Art and Architecture in Italy 1600–1750* (3rd ed., 1973).

Palladio and English Palladianism (1974).

Woodhouse, A.F., 'English Travellers in Paris 1600–1789: A Study of their Diaries' (Stanford PhD, 1976).

'Eighteenth Century English Visitors to France in Fiction and Fact', *Modern Language Studies* (1976).

'A Visit to Paris, 1726', *Bodleian Library Record* 10 (1981).

Wyndham, M., *Chronicles of the Eighteenth Century: Founded on the Correspondence of Sir Thomas Lyttelton and his Family* (1924).

Zmijewska, H., 'Le Voyage de Stanislas Potocki en France et en Angleterre en 1787', *Kwartalnik Neofilologiczny* 29 (1982).

INDEX

Note: bold page numbers refer to major entries.